D1710070

This Great Nation

A History of the United States

This great nation will endure as it has endured. . . .
President Franklin D. Roosevelt
March 4, 1933

This great nation of ours is a caring, loving land.
Its people have a zest for life and laughter. . . .
President Ronald W. Reagan
January 28, 1982

Consultants

Thomas R. Brown
Social Studies Team Leader
Arbor Heights Junior High School
Westside Community Schools
Omaha, Nebraska

Dominick J. DeCecco
District Social Studies Supervisor
Bethlehem Central School District
Delmar, New York

Mary E. Keenan
Teacher
Jonas Clarke Junior High School
Lexington, Massachusetts

Dr. Jeanette Kirby
Consultant, Secondary Social Studies
Muscogee County School District
Columbus, Georgia

Michael S. Froman
Constitutional Consultant
Member, American Bar Association's
Youth Education for Citizenship
Committee
Skokie, Illinois

This Great Nation

A History of the United States

Henry F. Graff
Professor of History
Columbia University

THE RIVERSIDE PUBLISHING COMPANY
Chicago, Illinois

About Henry F. Graff . . .

Dr. Henry F. Graff is Professor of History at Columbia University where he serves as a member of the faculties of Columbia College, the Graduate School of Arts and Sciences, and the School of International Affairs. He received his education at City College of New York (B.S.S.) and at Columbia University (M.A. and Ph.D.).

After a five-year stint in the United States Army during World War II as a Japanese language officer in the Army Security Agency, Dr. Graff returned to civilian life as a teacher in the History Department of City College of New York. Shortly thereafter, he took a position at Columbia University. From 1961 to 1964, Dr. Graff served as Chairman of the Department of History at the university. He has also been a visiting professor at Vassar College. Over the years, Dr. Graff has lectured on college campuses throughout the United States.

The presidency and the foreign relations of the United States have been Dr. Graff's areas of special interest. His writings include such works as *Bluejackets with Perry in Japan* (1952) and *The Tuesday Cabinet: Deliberation and Decision on Peace and War Under Lyndon B. Johnson* (1970).

Dr. Graff's interests extend beyond the confines of the presidency and foreign relations. He served as historical consultant to Time, Incorporated and was Consulting Editor on *Life's History of the United States*. One of Dr. Graff's proudest collaborations was with Jacques Barzun as they wrote *The Modern Researcher*, now in its third edition.

The education of America's youth has been the drawstring that has held Dr. Graff's career snugly in place. In fact in 1981, the students of Columbia College gave him the Mark Van Doren Award for distinguished teaching and scholarship. Then in 1982 Columbia College's Society for Older Graduates honored Dr. Graff with their Great Teacher Award.

Dr. Graff has further demonstrated his commitment to the education of America's youth by coauthoring *The Adventure of the American People* (with John A. Krout) and *The Grand Experiment* (two volumes with Paul Bohannan). Dr. Graff's previous American history textbook for junior high school students was the widely used *The Free and the Brave*.

Printed in the U.S.A. ISBN 0-829-21501-8 Student's Edition
ISBN 0-829-21502-6 Teacher's Edition

CONTENTS

In This Teacher's Annotated Edition . . .

On the pages that follow, you will find a variety of teaching aids. Here is a list of those aids and a brief description of each one:

- **Unit opening statement:** At the beginning of every unit there appears a paragraph which serves as a succinct overview of the material that follows.
- **Chapter opening statement:** At the beginning of every chapter there appears a paragraph which serves as a succinct overview of the material that follows.
- **Lesson content objectives:** Near each lesson title there appears a list of the major topics students should know about after completing the lesson. This list of topics is introduced by the words "After completing the lesson, students will know. . . ."
- **Vocabulary:** Every lesson in the Student's Edition has a list of Special Vocabulary words. The same list appears among the annotations in the Teacher's Edition. This time, however, the words appear with their contextual definitions.
- **Group activity:** Every lesson contains a group activity among the annotations. The activity may be used as a whole class or small group activity for average students. Every group activity is accompanied by a clearly stated objective.

- **Discussion:** In every lesson there appears a discussion of a topic related to nearby material. The discussion could be used as a whole class or small group activity.
- **Answer to question in map caption:** Every map except those appearing in "Working with Skills: Map Skills" has a caption in which a skill-related question calls for students to study the map closely. Among the annotations are answers to each of these questions.
- **Answers to lesson-end review questions:** Every lesson ends with a review entitled "Answer These Questions." In the margin near this review, annotations appear which provide answers to these questions.
- **Working with Skills:** On each page containing a skill development lesson, there appear answers to all questions asked on the page, a group activity that provides further drill of the highlighted skill, and a list of related materials found in auxiliary components of *This Great Nation.*
- **Answers to items in each Chapter Test**
- **Answers to items in each Unit Test**
- **Related materials:** At appropriate places, annotations refer the teacher to materials in *This Great Nation*'s workbook, Duplicator/Copy Masters—Activities, and Duplicator/Copy Masters—Tests related to the chapter or unit.

AND

THE BANK OF UNITED STATES
BANK CLOSE
The Bank

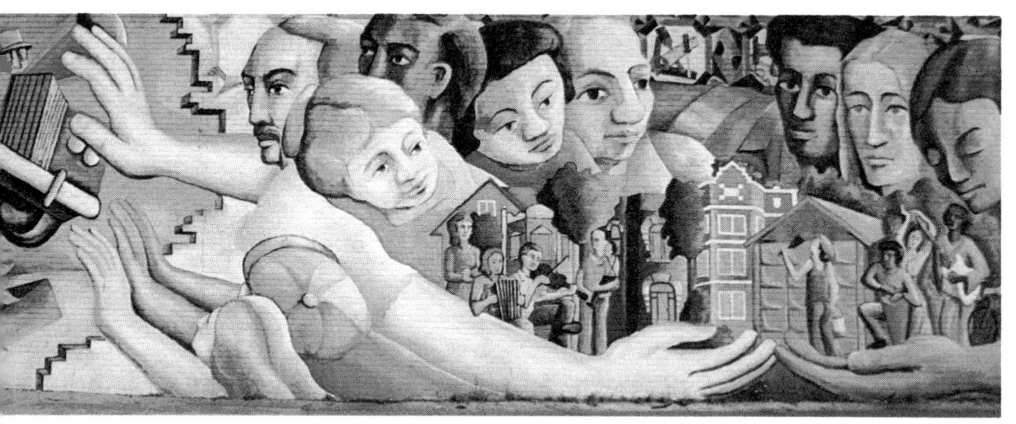

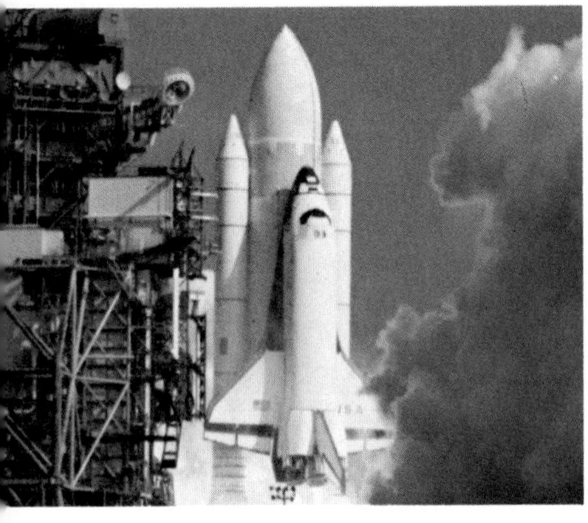

Map List

Study Aids

Introduction

ACTIVITY

Objective: To know the parts of a book

After the students have read this Introduction, they will know what *This Great Nation*'s features are. Then have the students locate the half-title page (p. i) and read the quotations there. Ask them: What do you think Presidents Roosevelt's and Reagan's attitudes were toward the United States? Why might the author have chosen the title *This Great Nation* for this book? Have students locate the title pages (pp. ii-iii). Have them locate the list of reader/consultants. Ask the students: Why might it be important for a book like this to have been read by experts before young people read it? Have the students look at the page containing information about the author (p. iv). Ask them: What has Henry F. Graff, the author of *This Great Nation,* done to merit the attention of young people? Have the students read the Contents of *This Great Nation* (pp. v-xiii). Have them locate the beginning pages of each unit of the book as listed in the Contents; then have them locate a few "Working with Skills" lessons and at least one "Law and the Citizen" and one "People in America" page. Have the students turn to the Appendices at the end of the book (beginning on p. 750). Ask them to identify the various appendices. Discuss the uses of the world map, the tables of useful information, the glossary, and the index.

All good books talk to their readers. A good American history book is no exception. It talks to you about important things, who did them, how they did them, where they did them, and why they did them.

An American history textbook must be all this—and more. A textbook must help you understand the information it contains. Here are a few ways *This Great Nation* helps you understand the information in it:

- It breaks up information into easy-to-understand chunks.
- It gives you clues to what is coming up in the next few pages so that you know what to expect.
- It provides help in reading and understanding difficult words and phrases.
- It teaches you the skills you need to read and understand the material in the book.
- It introduces you to the people in history.
- It highlights information about American law and citizenship.
- It provides frequent reviews and tests of your understanding and skills.

Examine the pages that follow. They show you the ways *This Great Nation* will help you read about and understand American history.

Perhaps you recognize the design of the pinwheels in this quilt. The design inspired part of the cover of *This Great Nation.* Patchwork quilting is one of America's oldest and most popular crafts. This quilt was sewn together around the year 1855.

*. . . is organized in **units, chapters,** and **lessons** and shows you clearly where each of these sections begins.*

Unit 2

ENGLISH AMERICA

Chapter 4 The Thirteen Colonies

Chapter 5 The Anglo-French Wars for Empire

Chapter 6 A New People

Chapter 1

THE BEGINNINGS

1-1 The First Americans

As you read, think about these questi
How long ago did the first Americans

This Great Nation

2-1 Early Explorers

. . . gives clues about upcoming information.

As you read, think about these questions:

What evidence is there that the Vikings established settlements in North America?

Why was an all-water route to the East important to the Europeans?

What contributions did Prince Henry make to the Age of Exploration?

*. . . includes **Special Vocabulary lists** of the important new words in each lesson.*

Special Vocabulary	saga	monopoly	compass
	colony	navigation	astrolabe

*. . . shows **Special Vocabulary words** in italics in the text and gives their meanings nearby.*

The Vinland Sagas. Among the Norse stories passed down from one generation to the next were the *Vinland Sagas*. A *saga* is a tale of heroic or brave deeds. The *Vinland Sagas* tell of a Viking named Gunbiorn being blown off course during

*. . . provides a **glossary** of the Special Vocabulary words at the end of the book, which includes pronunciation aids and meanings.*

sacred (**sā**′krĭd) holy
saga (**sä**′gə) a tale of heroic or brave deeds
secede (sĭ **sēd**′) withdraw
section (**sĕk**′shən) one square mile (division

. . . teaches you the skills you need to understand American history. In each unit, you will see pages like these:

Working with Skills

MAP SKILLS

Reading a Relief Map

A relief map is a map that s[...] region. These features may i[...] plains. To show something "i[...] out from its surroundings, as[...] a landscape.

Relief maps generally use[...] show physical features. On th[...] page, the mapmaker actually[...] realistic impression of their [...]

• *a lesson teaching an important* ***map reading skill***

Working with Skills

STUDY SKILLS

Research Papers

In a research paper, the wr[...] information from many sourc[...] depth. To prepare and write a[...] to use many of the study sk[...] earlier units.

The first—and perhaps mo[...] research paper is choosing a t[...] enough to be interesting, but[...]

• *a lesson teaching an important* ***study skill***

Working with Skills

READING SKILLS

Paraphrasing a Document

You will recall learning abou[...] Take some time now to review[...]

In 1977 the United States an[...] concerning the Panama Canal[...] belonged to Panama and that [...] control of the canal in 1999. [...]

• *a lesson teaching an important* ***reading skill***

This Great Nation

. . . *introduces you to the* ***people in history.*** *In each unit you will see a page like this.*

PEOPLE IN AMERICA

first major discoveries in the
ious figure to us. Information
tizenship, home, and family
Some historians have tried to
making many links between

rom Genoa, Italy. Columbus
wo men were about the same
n born in that year. Some have
ay have grown up together.
ot ever have met as adults?
dence that a man matching

. . . *highlights information on* ***American law and citizenship.*** *In each unit you will see a page like this.*

LAW AND THE CITIZEN

n Europe were governed by
ad few limits on their power.
epresentatives of the people.
called an absolute monarchy.
eens get so much power? The
than just having thousands of
ials to force people to follow
question is this: For a long
pted the idea that God chose

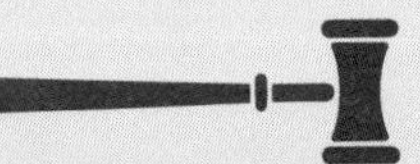

The American eagle has long stood for the strength and majesty of the United States. This eagle appears along with a shield that bears the red, white, and blue colors of the United States flag. The stars and stripes stand for the first thirteen states. The eagle and shield were part of a quilt made in 1853.

. . . provides frequent ***summaries*** *and* ***tests***

Chapter 1 SUMMARY

Most scientists believe that people probably first came to the Americas sometime between 25,000 B.C. and 10,000 B.C. They probably crossed into North America from Asia by means of a land bridge called Beringia. During this period, giant glaciers covered most of North America. To reach the area we know as the United States, the first Americans may have passed through a narrow corridor that appeared between

Chapter 1 TEST

WORDS TO REMEMBER

Choose the correct word from the special vo-cabulary to complete each sentence.

1. Stories handed down from parents to chil-dren over a long period of time are ________.
2. Scientists have discovered new ________, facts that seem to prove the theory of Beringia.
3. The ________ of North America—its cli-

Unit 1 TEST

WORDS TO REMEMBER

Write a definition for the word in italics in each of the following sentences.

1. Scientists and historians have a *theory* about the arrival of people in North America.
2. During the Ice Age, *glaciers* covered much of North America.
3. The *environment* of North America influenced the lifestyles of the early Americans.

8. The Aztecs
9. La Salle cla France.

THINK THIN

1. Did the Azt divine right in such an swers by ex

Now you have an idea of what to expect from your American history textbook. With this information in mind, you are ready to begin your study of *This Great Nation.*

Unit 1

THE MEETING OF CULTURES

Unit One examines the history of the Americas from the first arrival of people to the Age of European Exploration and the beginnings of colonization. A brief description of the subject matter of this unit includes the following topics: an overview of the culture groups who lived in North America before the arrival of Europeans; a description of the North American environment; an introduction to the causes of European exploration in the New World; an outlining of the Age of European Exploration and subsequent colonization; an overview of the interaction between American culture groups and European colonists.

Gold Inca mummy mask

World map by Sebastian Cabot, 1544

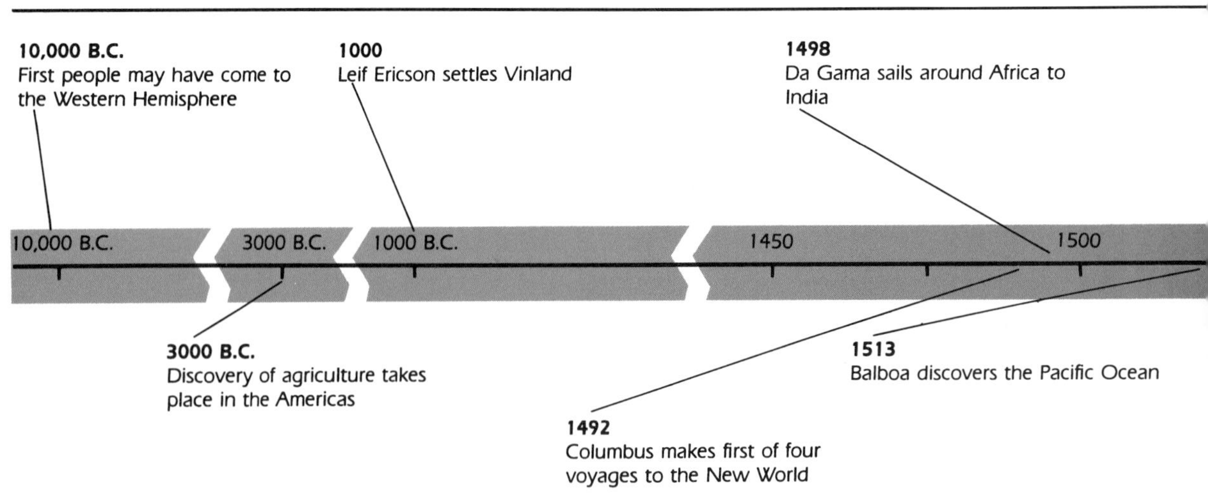
10,000 B.C.
First people may have come to the Western Hemisphere
1000
Leif Ericson settles Vinland
1498
Da Gama sails around Africa to India
10,000 B.C.
3000 B.C.
1000 B.C.
1450
1500
3000 B.C.
Discovery of agriculture takes place in the Americas
1513
Balboa discovers the Pacific Ocean
1492
Columbus makes first of four voyages to the New World

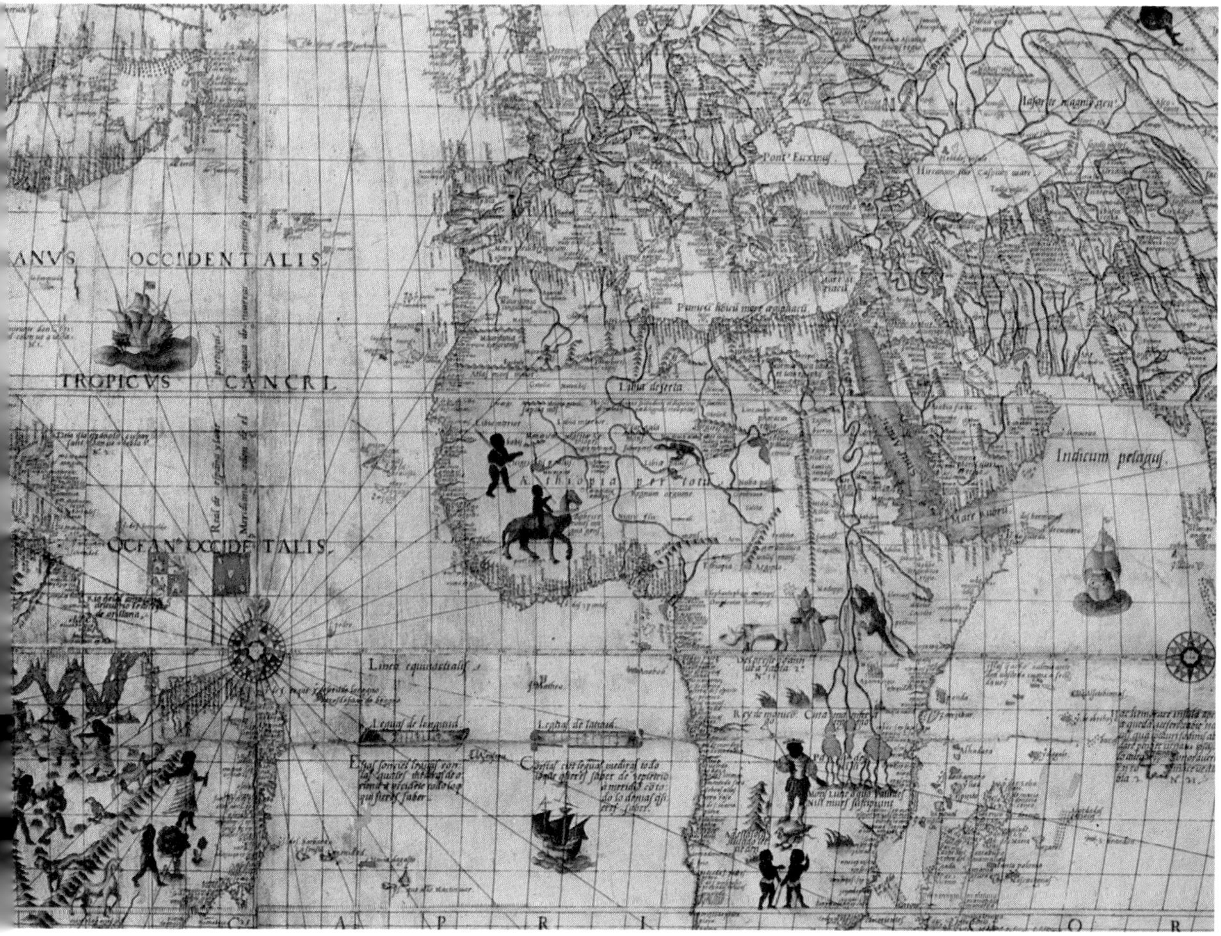

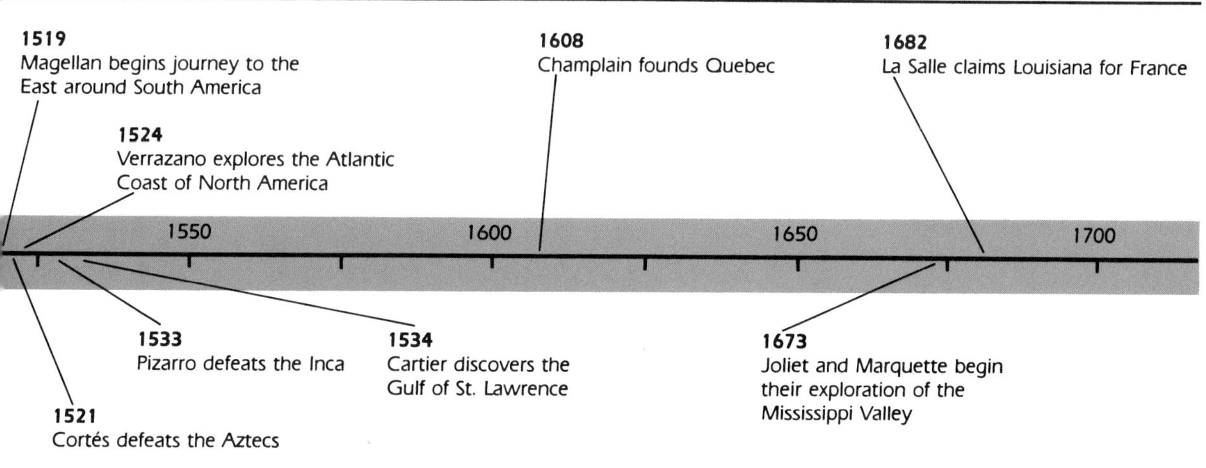
1519
Magellan begins journey to the East around South America
1524
Verrazano explores the Atlantic Coast of North America
1521
Cortés defeats the Aztecs
1533
Pizarro defeats the Inca
1534
Cartier discovers the Gulf of St. Lawrence
1550
1600
1608
Champlain founds Quebec
1650
1673
Joliet and Marquette begin their exploration of the Mississippi Valley
1682
La Salle claims Louisiana for France
1700

Chapter 1
THE BEGINNINGS

Chapter 1 introduces students to the geography of the North American continent and to the history of its earliest inhabitants. Lesson 1-1 outlines the theory of Beringia and the possible lifestyle of the big-game hunter. Lesson 1-2 discusses the natural history of North America with special emphasis on the development of regions in the United States. Lesson 1-3 focuses on the diverse Native American cultures, such as the Anasazi, which developed in North America.

CONTENT OBJECTIVES

After completing the lesson, students will know:

- the difference between a legend and a theory
- changes that occurred in North America as a result of the Ice Age
- the significance of archaeological discoveries such as those at Folsom and Clovis, New Mexico
- about the lifestyle of the big-game hunters

VOCABULARY

legend: a story handed down from parents to children over a long period of time

theory: a thoughtful guess by scientists to explain how and why something happens

evidence: facts that seem to prove a theory

archaeologist: a scientist who studies the things left behind by people who lived long ago

geologist: a scientist who studies the history of the earth and its life, especially as it can be known from rocks

glacier: a huge sheet of ice that covered the earth

1-1 The First Americans

As you read, think about these questions:

How long ago did the first Americans arrive in North America and how did they reach there?

What food did they eat and how did they get it?

What evidence is there that huge animals roamed North America?

What effects did the Ice Age have on the life of the first Americans?

Special Vocabulary	legend	evidence	geologist
	theory	archaeologist	glacier

The Keresans, a group of American Indians living in New Mexico, tell the following story about how people first came to North America:

In the beginning, people lived in a dark world beneath the earth. Of course, the people wanted light, so they began a long journey looking for the world of light.

They passed through four underground worlds, each of them a different color: white, red, blue, and yellow. Finally the people came to a tall spruce tree that reached all the way to the outer crust of the earth. A woodpecker poked a small hole through to the outside world. A badger enlarged the hole until the people could climb the spruce tree. Then they passed from the underworld to the outer world where people live today.

Many Indian groups tell *legends* like this one. Legends are stories handed down from parents to children over a long period of time.

Those who study science and history tell a different story about the arrival of people in North America. They do not call their story a legend; they call it a *theory*, which is a thoughtful guess by scientists to explain how and why something happens. Such an explanation is based on a collection of facts. The theory is accepted if it seems to fit the facts. The theory continues to be accepted until a new theory comes along that fits the facts better than the old one did.

ACTIVITY

Objective: To synthesize information and ideas

Review the definition of *legend* with the class. Tell them that together they are going to make up a legend to explain how the big-game hunters came to hunt bison. Have the students sit in a circle. Start by saying, "Once our people ate only those things which fell to the ground, like nuts and fruit. Then something terrible happened." Ask the student on your right to continue and then go around the circle.

The first people to cross Beringia may have looked like this. The spears these hunters are carrying have points shaped like the ones found in the southwestern part of the United States.

The Theory of "Beringia"

Until the early 1900s, most people believed that the first Americans arrived in North America about one thousand years before the birth of Christ. In the early 1900s, however, a new theory began. This theory has come to be called the theory of "Beringia." Year after year, historians and scientists have added new *evidence*, or facts that seem to prove the theory. The following paragraphs describe the gathering of some of these facts.

Folsom and Clovis Points. Around the year 1900, a cowhand named George McJunkin was riding through a dried out streambed near the town of Folsom, New Mexico. McJunkin was looking for a lost cow. By chance he found something that in time would change the way people thought about the first people who lived in North America. McJunkin found a bone sticking out of the bank of the streambed. The bone

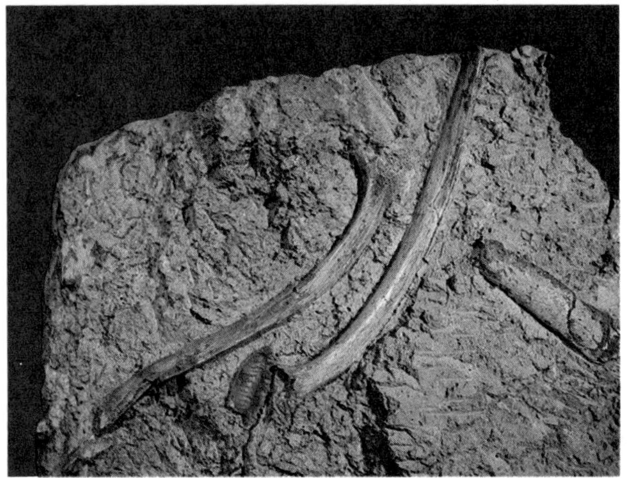

When mounted on shafts, Folsom points, like the one shown here among prehistoric bones, were capable of bringing down a giant bison.

looked like a cow's bone, yet it was bigger than any the cowhand had ever seen before.

Word of the bone McJunkin had discovered spread slowly. By 1926 Jesse D. Figgins, an *archaeologist,* was in Folsom digging up bones from the spot where McJunkin had made his discovery. An archaeologist is a scientist who studies the things left behind by people who lived long ago, things like bones, pottery, and tools. Figgins studied the bones and decided that they were not like those of any cattle alive at the time. They were the bones of a type of giant bison, or buffalo, that scientists believed had not lived anywhere on earth for about ten thousand years.

From this point on in this book, dates before the birth of Christ will be shown as B.C.—before Christ; dates after Christ's birth will be shown A.D., that is, *anno Domini*—"in the year of our Lord." If no letters appear, you will understand that the date is A.D.

DISCUSSION

Have the students discuss the differences between historical facts and historical theories. Have them also include in the discussion the roles that myths, legends, and traditions might play in finding historical truth. Use the Background Information essay "What is History?" (in the Teacher's Resource Book) as part of your own preparation to lead this discussion.

Other bones like these had been discovered before, but among the Folsom bones was something very startling. Between the ribs of the bison a spear point was stuck! Figgins had to come up with a theory to explain the presence of that spear point in the side of an animal that had not existed in North America for such a long time. His theory was this: The spear point had been used to kill the animal. Clearly, people must have lived in North America since at least 8000 B.C. Figgins's theory upset the accepted way of thinking about how long people had lived in the Americas.

The discovery of the bones and spear point at Folsom encouraged archaeologists all over North America and South America to track down more such bones and spear points. They looked for evidence that would support or dispute the theory of Jesse Figgins. Soon after the discovery at Folsom, archaeologists discovered other spear points. Many of them looked exactly like the point found at Folsom.

During the search, however, archaeologists found another kind of spear point at a place near Clovis, New Mexico, almost 200 miles (320 kilometers) south of Folsom. The Clovis point differed from the Folsom point. It seemed simpler, made by less skillful people. Archaeologists guessed that the Clovis point was about one thousand years older than the Folsom point. This theory argued that people had been in America even earlier than Figgins had thought. It also meant that early Americans had continually developed new and better tools to serve their needs.

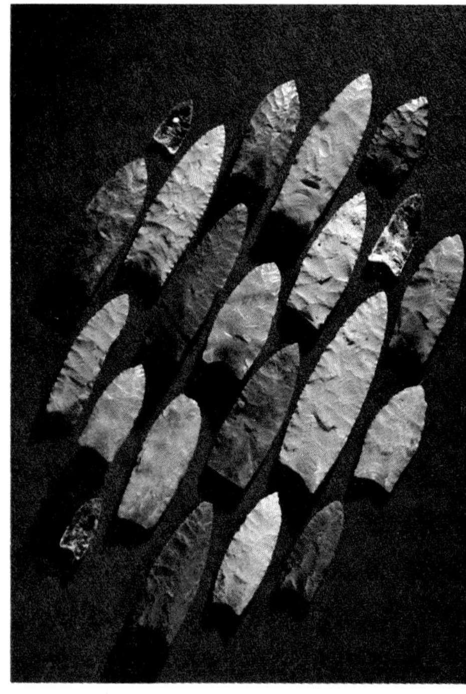
Careful chipping was needed to produce the particular shape and sharpness of these Clovis points. For this reason, scientists realized that no animal could accidentally have made them. Only humans are such precise workers.

Beringia. Other scientists, called *geologists*, also were interested in finding out about the early Americans. Geologists are scientists who study the history of the earth and its life, especially as it can be known from rocks. They stated a theory that the earth had undergone a long period when *glaciers*, or huge sheets of ice, had covered much of North America. This Ice Age, as the period is known, may explain how and when people came to North America. Scientists think during the Ice Age much of the water from the oceans became part of the glaciers. As a result, the level of the oceans dropped. The low level of the oceans' water caused land that ordinarily would be underwater to become dry. One such spot is located where North America and Asia nearly touch. Today this spot is beneath the waters of the Bering Strait. Scientists believe, however, during the Ice Age the spot was a bridge of dry land. No one knows what it was called. The scientists gave it the name Beringia.

Into the Heart of America. At some time between about 25,000 B.C. and 10,000 B.C., the glaciers melted enough to allow a narrow passage of land to appear between two walls of ice. The scientists believe such a passage developed between the eastern slope of the Rocky Mountains and the Great Plains. (See the globe showing routes of the first Americans on page 8.) At about that time, the first Americans probably followed the tracks of animals that crossed from Asia into North America by means of the bridge of land called Beringia. These people passed through the corridor and into the wide grasslands of the Great Plains.

Once on the Great Plains, these first Americans probably followed the same lifestyle they had always followed. They got their food, clothing, shelter, and tools by hunting mammoths and mastodons (both elephant-like animals), North

American camels, huge ground sloths, and giant bison. None of these kinds of animals live anywhere on earth today, but during the Ice Age they were plentiful.

We know very little about these big-game hunting first Americans. Only a few of their tools—made of bone, flint, and stone—have turned up. A few skeletons of these big-game hunting early Americans have been found, but scientists still argue about the dates during which these people actually lived. We do know, however, that archaeologists have discovered hundreds of Folsom and Clovis spear points all over North America and South America. Groups of big-game hunters must have ranged throughout the Americas in search of animals to kill.

Because of the huge size of these animals, the Ice Age hunters have been called big-game hunters. Scientists believe that the big-game hunters used every part of the animals they killed. The meat could be eaten. The fur and skin could be made into clothing and tents. The bones could be broken into pieces useful as weapons, scrapers, and fish hooks.

Routes of the First Americans

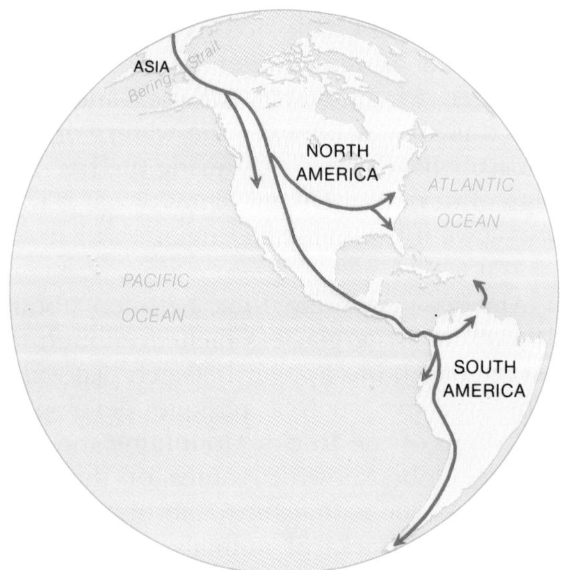

This global perspective illustrates the route most people believe the first Americans took into North America. Name the continent from which they began their journey and the strait that they had to cross.

Asia, Bering Strait

The End of the Ice Age. In time the Ice Age big game disappeared from the earth, never to be seen alive again. You will read why this probably happened in the next section. Today only the bones of a few of the animals remain. The period of big-game hunting that called for the Folsom and

These animals are probably very similar to those that roamed North America some 10,000 to 25,000 years ago. They include relatives of today's elephant, camel, horse, leopard, and tortoise. Farthest right is the bison.

Clovis spear points ended. The lifestyle of the big-game hunters also passed from the scene.

As the years passed, the people developed new ways of making a living. They still hunted, but now only small game. They also gathered roots, berries, nuts, and wild grains to eat. They fished when they were near the water. Some of them stopped their wandering ways and spent long periods of time in one area. Others, though, continued to move about, making their homes wherever they could get food.

Meanwhile, far to the North, the glaciers slowly melted to a size close to that of today. The resulting water created streams and rivers that ran into the oceans. The water level of the oceans rose, and Beringia disappeared under the waters of the Bering Strait. Without the land bridge to Asia, the people of the Americas were cut off from the people of every other part of the world.

ANSWER THESE QUESTIONS

1. Where was Beringia?
2. How did Beringia appear and disappear?
3. What discoveries were made at Folsom and Clovis, New Mexico?
4. Suppose Figgins's theory was incorrect. What are some other ways that the spear point could have gotten where it did?
5. How did the lifestyle of the first Americans change when the Ice Age ended?

ANSWER THESE QUESTIONS

1. at the spot where North America and Asia nearly touch
2. The level of the oceans changed with the freezing and melting of the glaciers.
3. spear points indicating that people had lived in North America since at least 8000 B.C.
4. Answers will vary; spear points could have been placed with the bones at a later time.
5. People hunted small game, gathered their food, and fished; some settled in one area.

1-2 The American Environment

CONTENT OBJECTIVES

After completing the lesson, students will know:

- the relationship between the warming trend in the earth's atmosphere and changes in the North American environment
- some of the changes that occurred in North America as a result of the comings and goings of the glaciers
- one theory scientists have to explain the disappearance of Ice Age big game
- several major geographic features of the regions of the United States

VOCABULARY

environment: a place's climate, land, water sources, and plant life
climate: a place's usual weather
atmosphere: the air that surrounds the earth
region: an area characterized by the look of the land, the climate, and the plants
intermontane: "between the mountains"
plateau: an area that is high, often higher than the surrounding regions

ACTIVITY

Objective: To provide information to complete a chart

Review the definition of *environment* and then have students describe their environment: its climate, land, water sources, and plant life. Write their answers on the chalkboard. When the class members agree on a response for each category, have them make up a chart using that information.

As you read, think about these questions:
What causes changes in the environment?
What effect did the glaciers have on North America?
What features do all regions have in common?

Special Vocabulary	environment	atmosphere	intermontane
	climate	region	plateau

The *environment* of a place is everything about it: its *climate*, or usual weather; its land; its water sources; and its plant life. The environment of most of North America changed after the Ice Age.

A Changing Environment

How did environmental changes come about? The disappearing of the glaciers of the Ice Age happened because the earth's *atmosphere*, or the air that surrounds the earth, began to warm. With the warming of the earth's atmosphere, the climate of North America changed drastically. Some places, including the areas around Folsom and Clovis, New Mexico, had once been cool and wet. Now they became hot and dry. Other places had once been covered with snow and ice all year round. Now they had seasons ranging from cold and snowy in the winter to very hot in the summer. The area around the Great Lakes is an example of this kind of change.

Changes Caused by Climate. In certain places, the changes in climate caused changes in the look of the land and in the kinds of plants and animals that lived there. For example, scientists think the areas around Folsom and Clovis were covered with thick grasses during the Ice Age. These plants were perfect for Ice Age animals that grazed, like mammoths and giant bison. The climate changed, however, and the land became very dry, much like a desert. To survive, the remaining scrubby bushes and scarce grasses needed every drop of water their roots could find. The Ice Age animals could not live on the meager supply of food in such places. Many

The Regions of North America

Imagine now that all the major changes in the North American environment caused by the Ice Age have taken place. The early Americans have developed lifestyles that depend on hunting, fishing, and the gathering of food. Their environment is much like today's. What would a map of North America look like?

Map makers divide the land areas of North America into *regions*. These are areas that have many things in common, such as the look of the land, the climate, and the plants. Very often the places within a region also share a common geographical history. This means that all the places in a certain region may have experienced many earthquakes and volcanos. Another region's places may be on the floor of an inland sea that has long since dried up and disappeared.

There are three main regions in western North America: the Pacific Coast, the *Intermontane Plateaus* (these words mean "the high lands between mountains"), and the Rocky Mountains. East of the Rocky Mountains, in what is today called the United States, there are four North American regions: the Interior Plains, the Ozark Plateau, the Gulf-Atlantic Coastal Plains, and the Appalachian Highlands.

Study the charts and maps on pages 12, 15, 16, and 17. They summarize the natural environments of the regions of North America, especially the regions within the United States.

ANSWER THESE QUESTIONS

of climate in North America at the

ANSWER THESE QUESTIONS

1. Areas once covered with thick grasses became deserts.
2. Illinois, Indiana, Ohio, and Pennsylvania
3. Thousands of lakes were formed; some major rivers arose in glacial areas.
4. They share common features, such as the look of the land, the climate, the plants, and geographical history.
5. Answers will vary; the climate would probably force people to move to other areas.

Objective: After completing these pages, the students should be able to read a chart.

Working with Skills

STUDY SKILLS

ACTIVITY

Objective: To make comparisons based on information in a chart

Ask the science teacher to help students identify each of the following: needle-leaved evergreen, broad-leaved evergreen, deciduous broad-leaved trees, broad-leaved bushes, cactus plants, and tall grasses. Take a walk around your school grounds or in a nearby park and make a list of the types of leaves you find. Review the chart on pages 15-17. Do the leaf types found in your area agree with the chart?

ANSWERS

1. "The Regions of Western North America" and "The Regions of Eastern North America"
2. Regions and States, General Look and History of the Land, Climate, and Plants
3. a. Climate b. Plants c. Regions and States d. General Look and History of the Land
4. water
5. tall grasses in the west; broad-leaved trees in the east
6. wet with warm summers and mild winters
7. low mountain ranges, a huge central valley; high, rugged mountain ranges
8. Interior Plains, Ozark Plateau, Appalachian Highlands, Gulf-Atlantic Coastal Plains, Pacific Coast, and Rocky Mountains

Reading Charts

Charts are a good way to organize information so that it can be quickly read and easily understood. All charts should have a title and headings to let the reader know what kind of information is in each of the columns.

Use the charts on pages 15–17 to answer these questions:

1. What are the titles of the charts?

2. What are the headings of the columns?

3. Under what heading would you look to find the following information:
- **a.** what the usual weather in a region is like
- **b.** whether an area does or does not have broad-leaved trees whose leaves fall off in the fall of the year
- **c.** what parts of the United States are included in a region
- **d.** what kinds of geographic features an area has

Use the information under the headings to answer the following questions:

4. What once covered the Intermontane Plateaus?

5. What kinds of plants grow on the plains?

6. What is the weather usually like on the Ozark Plateau?

7. What are three parts of the Pacific Coast region?

8. What six regions have broad-leaved trees whose leaves fall off in the fall of the year?

THE REGIONS OF WESTERN NORTH AMERICA

Regions and States	General Look and History of the Land	Climate	Plants
Pacific Coast (parts of Washington, Oregon, and California)	This region consists of three parts: low mountain ranges on the coast; a huge inland central valley; to the east, high, rugged mountain ranges, including the Sierra Nevada Range in the south and the Cascade Range in the north; this region experiences many earthquakes in the south and volcanic eruptions in the north.	In the northern part of the region, near the coast, the weather is usually wet with mild winters and cool summers; in the southern part, winters are mild and summers are hot and dry; high up in the inland mountains, temperatures range from cool during summer days to cold at night; during winter, much snow falls and mountain tops have year-round glaciers.	In the north there are many needle-leaved evergreen trees; the same is true in the high inland mountains in both the north and the south; in the lower parts of the south the common plants are evergreen shrubs that have broad leaves; between the north and south trees and shrubs have broad leaves, some evergreen, some with leaves that fall off in the fall of the year.
Intermontane Plateaus: the Columbia and the Colorado Plateaus; the Great Basin (parts of Washington, Oregon, California, Idaho, Utah, Colorado, and New Mexico; all of Nevada and Arizona)	These plateaus are sometimes mountainous, sometimes flat; in the southern parts of the region, there are deserts; the soft rocks of the Colorado Plateau and the Great Basin are easily worn away by the work of wind and water; much of the Intermontane Plateau area probably once lay at the bottom of a large inland sea.	The plateaus are generally dry; in the northern part of the region, the weather is always dry and hot in summer and cool in winter; the southern parts of the region are dry and very hot in summer.	Most North American deserts are in this region; needle-leaved evergreen trees grow in high places; in lower areas, evergreen shrubs, broad-leaved bushes, and cactus plants grow.
Rocky Mountains (parts of New Mexico, Colorado, Utah, Wyoming, Idaho, Montana, Oregon, Washington, and Alaska)	The Rockies extend all the way from New Mexico in the south, north through Canada, into Alaska; ranges include the Sangre de Cristo, the Big Horn, and the Wasatch; they stretch north to Alaska where they divide into the Alaska and Brooks Ranges; the Rockies are called a "young" mountain system because they are rugged; wind and water have not yet gotten a chance to wear them down and round off their tops.	The Rockies are generally cold and snow-covered in winter; they are so cool, even in summer, that snow remains on many of the Rockies all year round.	Most trees and shrubs in the Rockies are needle-leaved evergreens; in a few places there are broad-leaved trees whose leaves fall off in the fall of the year; at the very tops of the highest mountains there are almost no plants.

RELATED MATERIAL
Duplicator/Copy Master Activity 2

THE REGIONS OF EASTERN NORTH AMERICA

Regions and States	General Look and History of the Land	Climate	Plants
Interior Plains (parts of Montana, Wyoming, Colorado, New Mexico, Texas, Oklahoma, Missouri, Illinois, Minnesota, Wisconsin, Michigan, Ohio, Tennessee, and Kentucky; all of North and South Dakota, Nebraska, Kansas, Iowa, and Indiana.)	These plains stretch north from west central Texas to the Arctic Ocean; they reach from the eastern slope of the Rockies to eastern Ohio; near the Rockies, the land is high; it slopes to a lower level near the Mississippi River; from the Mississippi eastward, the land rises, except for spots near the Great Lakes; the Interior Plains may once have been covered with water; later, glaciers covered the northern part, pushing much earth ahead of them and creating the hilly parts of the north central states; glaciers also carved out the Great Lakes and thousands of small lakes nearby.	In the western high plains, the climate is very dry; there the winters can be cold and snowy and the summers dry and hot; the lower plains have hot, wet summers with mild winters in the south; warm, wet summers with cold, snowy winters in the middle part; and cool, wet summers with very cold, snowy winters in the north.	The most common plants in the western part of the plains region are short and tall grasses; another term for the plains with tall grasses is prairie; the most common plants of the plains east of the Mississippi are broad-leaved trees whose leaves fall off in the fall of the year.
Ozark Plateau (parts of Illinois, Missouri, Oklahoma, and Arkansas)	This plateau sticks out of the surrounding plains; it has low, rounded hills that probably were formed long before the Rocky Mountains; long periods of time have given wind and water a chance to wear away the tops of the Ozarks.	The climate of the Ozark Plateau is much like the plains that surround it, wet with warm summers and mild winters.	The most common plants are broad-leaved trees whose leaves fall off in the fall of the year.
Appalachian Highlands (parts of Alabama, Georgia, South and North Carolina, Kentucky, Tennessee, Virginia, Ohio, Maryland, Delaware, Pennsylvania, New Jersey, New York; all of West Virginia, Connecticut, Rhode Island, Massachusetts, New Hampshire, Vermont, and Maine)	The Appalachians are higher than the Ozarks; west of the Appalachians are a series of plateaus (such as the Cumberland Plateau) that serve as a system of foothills; the ranges of the Appalachians include the Great Smoky Mountains, the Alleghenies, the Blue Ridge Mountains, the White and Green Mountains; east of the southern Appalachians sloping toward the Atlantic is a wide band of foothills called the Piedmont; the Appalachians are older mountains than the Rockies; wind and water have worn them down and rounded them off.	The climate of the Appalachians ranges from wet and hot during the summer in the south to wet and cool during the summer in the north; winters in the north are wet and cold; in the south, they are wet and mild.	Most of the Appalachians are covered with a mixed variety of trees; evergreen needle-leaved trees and broad-leaved trees whose leaves fall off in the fall of the year.

The largest of the Anasazi dwellings, Cliff Palace, can still be seen by visitors to Mesa Verde National Park in Colorado.

Knowledge of agriculture spread from its probable place of discovery in northeastern Mexico to people living in the Southwest Culture Area. By about A.D. 1, people in the Southwest began their first experiments with growing corn.

Two major culture groups lived in the Southwest at the same time. One group is called the Hohokam (a Pima word meaning "the vanished ones"). A second group is known as the Anasazi (a Navajo word meaning "the ancient ones").

same information about how to hunt, grow plants, cook food, or make pottery. The legends and beliefs of such groups were also very much alike. (See the map of Native American culture areas on this page.)

East[illegible] Hohokam used grinding stones

The Northwest Coast Culture Area. The smallest of all the major Native American culture areas was on the Northwest Coast. There the Kwakiutl, the Nootka, the Chinook, and the Tillamook lived. These culture groups enjoyed the richest Native American lifestyles. Their dinners literally jumped into fishing nets when each fall millions of salmon swam upstream from the Pacific Ocean. These salmon came to have their offspring at the same spot where they themselves had been hatched. The Native Americans of the Northwest Coast eagerly awaited the arrival of this important part of their food supply. The ocean also brought huge whales and large ocean fish close to the shores.

THE ANASAZI OF MESA VERDE

Period	Years	Description
Basketmaker I	A.D. 1 to 450	At first, the Anasazi were a wandering people who depended on hunting and gathering food.They hunted with spears. The Anasazi lived in caves in the cliffs of a mesa on the Colorado Plateau. Later their home was called Mesa Verde by Spanish explorers. The name means "green tableland." The early Mesa Verde Anasazi did not yet know how to make pottery. Instead, they carried things in finely woven baskets. This is why anthropologists call the early Anasazi "Basketmakers."
Basketmaker II	A.D. 450 to 750	At about A.D. 450, the Basketmaker Anasazi learned about agriculture. They began to grow corn, beans, and squash on the top of the mesa. This discovery allowed the Anasazi to live in one place for a long time. In their caves, they built houses whose floors were a few feet below ground level. The walls were built up from there above ground. The people entered their houses from a hole in the ceiling by climbing down a ladder. This kind of house is known as a pit house. The Anasazi first began making pottery during this time, but they still depended on baskets. They also learned how to raise tame turkeys. They used the feathers of turkeys to make robes and blankets. The Anasazi of this time gave up the spear as their main hunting weapon. They began to use a new invention that came to them from other Indians, the bow and arrow. Their jewelry was made from shells and turquoise. The presence of shells shows that the Anasazi somehow traded with other culture groups. Some of these groups lived as far away as the Pacific Coast or the Gulf of Mexico.
Pueblo I	A.D. 750 to 1100	After the year 750, the people of Mesa Verde left their pit houses in the caves. They built apartment-like houses in rows on top of the mesa. This way they could be near their crops. These kind of row houses got the name *pueblo* from Spanish explorers. The word means "village" in Spanish. The houses had flat roofs. The Anasazi, however, did not forget the pit houses. The pit house, with a few changes, became a room known as the "kiva." The kiva was built underground. Kivas were used as a place of worship and by the men as a kind of clubhouse. The women owned the houses of the Anasazi. In addition, the family lines of the Anasazi were traced through the mother's side. The Anasazi women had a great amount of power. Basketmaking gave way to pottery making. Cotton was brought to Mesa Verde from other places. Anasazi men wove cloth well. As time passed, the Anasazi built their pueblos stronger than they had in earlier times.
Pueblo II	A.D. 1100 to 1300	The people of many small villages on the top of Mesa Verde got together and built large pueblos. Then, about the year 1200, the people left these villages. They built new ones in the caves on the sides of the cliffs. These steps may have been taken because the people of Mesa Verde feared some enemy, perhaps the Navajo and the Apache. During this time, the people of Mesa Verde developed beautiful pottery and jewelry. Then in 1276, a long dry spell began. It lasted for 24 years. By the year 1300, the Anasazi had left their Mesa Verde pueblos. Some anthropologists believe that they became part of other Pueblo-type groups in the Southwest.

Before the Great Plains Indians had horses, they hunted buffalo on foot, disguising themselves with animal skins to stalk the large herds. Artist George Catlin used the same trick to get close enough to paint this scene. Catlin and an Indian hunter are the figures at the far right.

The Eastern Culture Area. The Eastern Culture Area consisted of groups living in three main areas: the Great Plains, the Northeast (the Great Lakes and New England), and the Southeast. The Native American culture groups of the Great Plains to the west of the Mississippi River depended on the buffalo for almost everything they needed to live. They ate buffalo meat; they lived in shelters made of buffalo hide; they used buffalo horns for weapons and tools. Because they depended on the buffalo, many culture groups of the Great Plains tended to follow the herds as they *migrated*, or moved with the seasons.

When on the move, some Great Plains culture groups, like the Sioux and Cheyenne, lived in easy-to-move teepees. When staying put for a while, some groups, like the Pawnee and Mandan, built permanent houses of earth.

The millions of buffaloes on the plains seemed like a limitless resource. Native Americans of the plains saw no reason for seeking any other major source of food and shelter. They never felt a need to develop agriculture. Instead they hunted buffaloes, deer, and rabbits. Sometimes they fished in the streams and rivers of the region.

In the Northeast and Southeast, the culture groups took to agriculture well. Because of this, they tended to live in one spot for longer periods of time than the plains culture groups did. The Chippewa and Menominee of Minnesota and Wisconsin combined farming, hunting, and gathering to

ACTIVITY

Objective: To synthesize information and ideas in a graphic

Have students work in small groups to complete a chart like the one suggested in "Working with Skills" (p. 27). Students should include information about their own culture. They should use the same headings: Environment, Source of Food, Houses, and Customs.

DISCUSSION

Have the students discuss the causes of cultural differences. Use material from this lesson as data, but also include generally accepted data about other cultures from various periods and places.

make a living. The Algonkians and Huron north of the Great Lakes farmed, fished, and hunted.

South of Lake Ontario, a mighty culture group called the Iroquois developed. The Iroquois hunted, gathered, fished, and farmed. Groups of them lived in dwellings called longhouses. Iroquois women held a great deal of power. This was because the Iroquois traced their family line through the mother's side. Women showed their power in another way, too. They could approve or disapprove of the choice of male chiefs for the group.

In the Southeast, five culture groups stood out: the Choctaw, Chickasaw, Creek, Seminole, and Cherokee. These people lived in long-lasting towns. The towns were surrounded by *stockades*, or walls of tree trunks. Inside, the Southeastern culture groups had their homes, fields, and places of worship. They depended on agriculture for their living. They grew corn, beans, and squash to eat, and they grew cotton to make their clothes. They made their soil rich from the ashes of trees they cut down and burned. When the

A French writer illustrated his account of the Iroquois Confederacy in council about 1570. The wampum belt, shown in the foreground of the upper picture, was a woven fabric of beads and shells. The pattern of each belt represented a specific event. The belts were exchanged as a pledge of friendship.

The longhouse served as a dwelling for several Iroquois families. The building was divided into sections for each family, and clan symbols were placed above the entrance to represent the families.

soil no longer could grow enough food, they moved on and built another town.

Many groups throughout the Eastern Culture Area joined in *confederacies*. A confederacy is a number of groups that band together, pledging support to each other, usually in time of war. For example, in the area we call Virginia, several culture groups joined a confederacy during the late 1500s under a chief called Powhatan. At about the same time, a similar confederacy was created when the five Iroquois groups banded together. Those groups were the Mohawk, the Oneida, the Onondaga, the Cayuga, and the Seneca.

Other groups avoided confederacies. They simply occupied their own customary areas, growing crops, hunting, and fishing. The Wampanoag, Narraganset, and Pequot of the New England coast were such groups.

By the year 1450, Native Americans had rich and varied social customs, political lives, and economic ways. The time would arrive, however, when powerful newcomers to the hemisphere would put all these accomplishments to the test.

ANSWER THESE QUESTIONS

1. What is an anthropologist?
2. What made the lifestyle of the Northwest Coast peoples the richest of all Native American lifestyles?
3. What major change in lifestyle among Native American groups was made possible by the discovery of agriculture?
4. Why didn't Native Americans of the Great Plains develop an agricultural way of life?
5. How was the lifestyle of Native American groups in the Northeast and Southeast different from that of the Native Americans of the plains?

ANSWER THESE QUESTIONS

1. a scientist who studies groups of people
2. abundant resources, such as whales, fish, forest, wildlife, and plants
3. Wandering groups changed from hunting and gathering to farming and staying in one location.
4. They depended on the buffalo for almost everything they needed to live.
5. Native Americans in the Northeast and Southeast generally depended on agriculture and thus stayed in one place.

THINKING THINGS THROUGH

1. A spearpoint was found between the ribs of an animal that had not lived anywhere on the earth for 10,000 years. **2.** Climate and glaciers can cause change in environments. **3.** All Native Americans depended on their environment. **4.** An archaeologist studies things left behind by people who lived long ago. An anthropologist studies groups of people. **5.** At first, the

Chapter 1 SUMMARY

Most scientists believe that people probably first came to the Americas sometime between 25,000 B.C. and 10,000 B.C. They probably crossed into North America from Asia by means of a land bridge called Beringia. During this period, giant glaciers covered most of North America. To reach the area we know as the United States, the first Americans may have passed through a narrow corridor that appeared between two melting glaciers.

The first Americans were big-game hunters who killed giant animals that no longer exist. These people used spear points of the type first discovered near Folsom and Clovis, New Mexico.

After the Ice Age, the North American environment developed into the one we know today. North America has a variety of regions, each with its own landforms, history, climate, and plant life.

As time passed, different Native American cultures developed. Most North American culture groups hunted, gathered, and fished. Later, agriculture developed in Mexico and spread into almost every culture area. Each North American culture underwent various kinds of change; the Anasazi of the Southwest serve as an example of how cultural development might have taken place.

Chapter 1 TEST

WORDS TO REMEMBER

Choose the correct word from the special vocabulary to complete each sentence.

1. Stories handed down from parents to children over a long period of time are legends.
2. Scientists have discovered new evidence, or facts that seem to prove the theory of Beringia.
3. The environment of North America—its climate, land, water, and plants—changed after the Ice Age.
4. There are three main regions, or areas with common features, in western North America.
5. The culture, or way people live, of the Southwest was different from that of the Northwest.
6. The planting, caring for, and harvesting of crops is called agriculture.

THINKING THINGS THROUGH

Answer each of the following questions in a complete sentence.

1. What evidence have scientists found that supports the theory that people were living in America by 8000 B.C.?
2. Name two possible causes of change in environments.
3. In what ways were the Native American cultures of North America alike?
4. What is the difference between an archaeologist and an anthropologist?
5. Using the Anasazi group, explain how the practice of agriculture can lead to a great change in a people's culture.

RELATED MATERIALS

Duplicator/Copy Masters: Activities 1, 2; Quiz 1
Workbook pages 1-3

Anasazi were a wandering people who depended on hunting and gathering food. The discovery of agriculture allowed the Anasazi to stay in one place for a long time.

WORKING WITH SKILLS

Complete the following chart comparing the cultures of the Northwest Coast peoples, the Anasazi (last stage), and the Great Plains peoples. The information is in Chapter 1.

	Environment	Sources of Food	Houses	Customs
Northwest Coast Peoples	rainy climate; Pacific coast and rivers; softwood evergreen trees	fish, deer, moose, nuts, berries	built of wood planks	class rules; potlatches; family line traced through mother
Anasazi (last stage)	desert and dry land; oasis; few plants	agriculture: corn, beans, squash	in caves on sides of cliffs	kivas; family line traced through mother
Great Plains Peoples	tall grasses; generally cold, snowy winters and warm, wet summers	buffalo, deer, rabbits, fish	buffalo-skin tepees; earth homes	migrated with the seasons

ON YOUR OWN

1. Use the information from the map on page 12 to complete the following on an outline map of the United States:
   a. Use a color key to draw in the seven regions of North America.
   b. Add and label the major rivers.
   c. Label your state and city or town.
   d. Identify the region in which your city or town is located.
2. The Iroquois traced their family lines through their mothers. Trace your family line in the same manner. Write your name at the top of a sheet of paper, draw an arrow down from your name and then write in your mother's name; draw another arrow and then write her mother's name, etc. Go back as far as you can.

3. Study the above picture, which shows the ruins of Anasazi apartment-like houses in Chaco Canyon, New Mexico. Use the chart on page 22 to determine during which Anasazi period the Chaco Canyon site was constructed.

Chapter 2 introduces students to the Age of European Exploration and Colonization. Lesson 2-1 outlines the advance of the Vikings and their probable colonization in North America.

Chapter 2
THE AGE OF EXPLORATION

It also discusses the riches of the East and the European desire to share in that wealth. Lesson 2-2 details Columbus's theories and his discoveries in the New World. Lesson 2-3 examines Spanish and French efforts to find a western route to Asia.

CONTENT OBJECTIVES

After completing the lesson, students will know:

- the extent of Viking exploration and colonization in Iceland, Greenland, and "Vinland"
- why the period from 1450 to 1850 was called the Age of European Exploration and Colonization
- why Europeans sought an all-water route to Asia
- the contributions that Prince Henry made to the science of navigation

VOCABULARY

saga: a tale of heroic or brave deeds
colony: one or more settlements
monopoly: complete control
navigation: the science of determining a ship's position and course
compass: an instrument used in sailing that tells direction
astrolabe: a sailing tool that shows a ship's position in relation to the sun and other stars

2-1 Early Explorers

As you read, think about these questions:

What evidence is there that the Vikings established settlements in North America?

Why was an all-water route to the East important to the Europeans?

What contributions did Prince Henry make to the Age of Exploration?

Special Vocabulary	saga	monopoly	compass
	colony	navigation	astrolabe

The people of Europe could not imagine that a place like the Western Hemisphere even existed. They had a few clues, however. For example, some Norse people—people from Norway—paid a brief visit to North America in about the year 1000.

The Vikings

The Norse, or Vikings, as they are often called, were seagoing, fighting men and women. They ranged all over the North Atlantic area in their long boats in search of people to conquer. At a time when many peoples of the world were afraid to sail beyond the sight of land, the Vikings bravely set out upon the open seas. They made many discoveries on these trips. One of the most important occurred in A.D. 870 when they discovered Iceland, a large island in the North Atlantic Ocean.

Viking adventurers such as Leif Ericson explored the seas in ships like the one shown. Viking ships were long, slender, and flexible. Combining wind and human power, they were fast as well as seaworthy.

The Vinland Sagas. Among the Norse stories passed down from one generation to the next were the *Vinland Sagas*. A *saga* is a tale of heroic or brave deeds. The *Vinland Sagas* tell of a Viking named Gunbjorn being blown off course during a storm as he traveled to Iceland in about the year 970. When calm came again, he saw the island we know as Greenland. In 985 Eric the Red, a Viking who had been run out of Norway and Iccland for murdering people, led a group of people who set up a *colony* on Greenland. A colony is one or more settlements.

Soon other Vikings from both Iceland and Norway began to sail to Greenland. On one such trip, the Vikings made another accidental discovery. Under the leadership of Bjarni Herjulfson, a Viking crew battled a raging storm in the North Atlantic. The boat was driven far off its course and when the storm cleared, the Vikings saw a land of flat coasts and dense forests. It looked nothing like Greenland with its mountains of ice. The Vikings turned their boat around and put it on the correct course for Greenland.

Leif Ericson. The *Vinland Sagas* go on to tell that fifteen years later, Leif Ericson, a son of Eric the Red, heard stories about the mysterious land to the west. He set out to retrace Herjulfson's voyage. With a crew of thirty-five members,

Ericson eventually came upon land at about the place Herjulfson had described.

After Leif Ericson and the other Vikings explored the land, they decided to spend the winter there. When winter ended, Ericson returned to Greenland with stories of the land he had visited. Because Leif Ericson had seen so many grapevines there, he called his discovery Vinland.

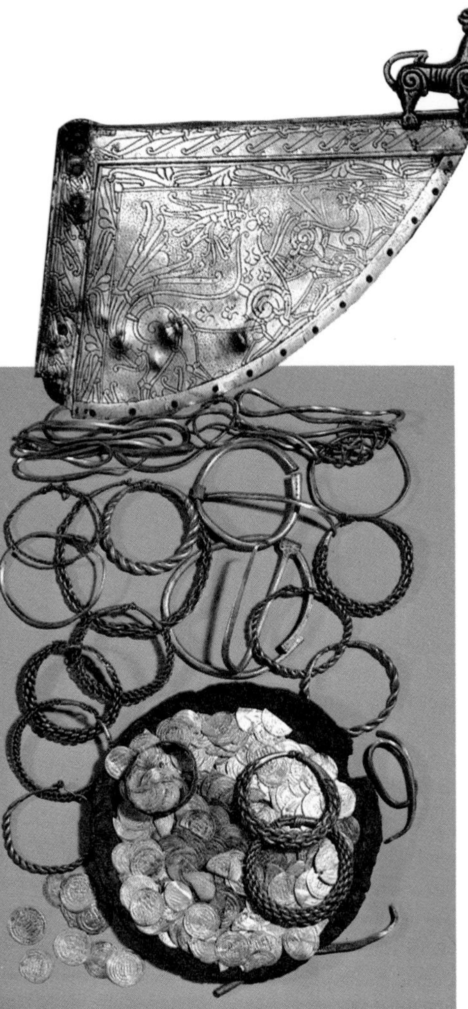

The Vikings traveled widely in their sturdy boats. The wind vane pictured at the top adorned the mast of a Viking ship. The silver treasure was taken from many parts of Europe by Viking explorers. It was buried in Sweden around A.D. 975.

Skrellings. The *Vinland Sagas* tell of another Viking crew led by Leif's brother, Thorvald. This crew also made a journey to Vinland. While exploring what was for them a new land, they were attacked by people who came out of the forests screaming and shouting, shooting at the Vikings with arrows from their bows. The Vikings called these people Skrellings, which means "screeching people." Thorvald was killed during the attack, but this did not stop other Vikings from trying to establish a colony in Vinland.

At first, the Vikings and Skrellings lived side by side peacefully. As time passed, however, the two groups began to fight. The Europeans found themselves outnumbered, and they returned to Greenland discouraged after only about ten years in Vinland.

A New Theory. Until the twentieth century, historians were not sure whether the stories found in the *Vinland Sagas* were true or made up. Then in 1960, a Norwegian archaeologist named Helge Ingstad started digging at a place on the coast of Newfoundland, an island off the coast of North America. The place is called L'Anse aux Meadows. There Ingstad found the ruins of houses that were much like the ones built by the Vikings of Norway, Iceland, and Greenland.

Ingstad also found the remains of iron tools nearby. The American people who might have lived near L'Anse aux Meadows, Indians or Eskimos, were never known to have made iron tools. The Vikings did! Ingstad used these facts to develop a theory that the ruins at L'Anse aux Meadows were in fact the remains of Leif and Thorvald Ericson's Vinland settlements.

Other Europeans Take to the Open Seas

As the age of Viking exploration ended, other western Europeans were beginning to travel farther and farther from their own lands. Starting in the mid-1400s, many countries in Europe competed with each other to explore and settle new lands. In fact, so many new lands were discovered and settled by Europeans that the period from the 1450s through the 1850s has been called the Age of European Exploration and Colonization.

What caused this burst of exploration and settlement? First, explorers and their rulers had a thirst for riches. They believed that these riches could be obtained in far-off lands. Second, Europeans had a strong wish to spread their Christian religion to all parts of the world. Third, both the explorers and the rulers who supported them wanted fame and glory.

The Riches of the East. As far back as the time of ancient Rome, the Europeans thought of the East as the wealthiest part of the world. From Persia, India, China, and a tiny island chain in the South Pacific called the Moluccas came gold, silver, ivory, silk, and spices. The Moluccas produced so many spices that they became known as the Spice Islands. Spices were valuable to Europeans in the 1400s because people had no way of refrigerating food. Meat spoiled quickly, but the spices could cover up the bad taste.

Few Europeans had ever visited the East, but one who actually did was Marco Polo. He was an Italian from the city of Venice. In 1271, when he was about seventeen years old, he left home to accompany his merchant father and uncle on a trip to Asia. After years of fascinating travel, most of which were spent in China, Marco Polo finally came home to Venice in 1295.

Once safely at home, Polo dictated an account of his experiences. Here is what he said about the island of Java, today part of Indonesia. (He visited Java on his way home.)

> The country abounds with rich commodities. Pepper, nutmegs, spikenard . . . cubebs [a kind of pepper], cloves and all other valuable spices and drugs, and the produce of the island which occasion it to be visited by many ships laden with merchandise, that yields to the owner considerable profit.
>
> The quantity of gold collected there exceeds all calculation and belief. From thence . . . is obtained the greatest part of the spices that are distributed throughout the world.

Excited by words like these, is it any wonder that wealthy Europeans wanted the goods of the East? No one in Europe

Marco Polo's stories of cities with a million people were met with disbelief. No European city of the time was that large.

ACTIVITY

Objective: To recall information

Prepare ten questions that reflect the important concepts of Lesson 2-1. Divide the class into two groups. Call a student from each group to the chalkboard and ask one of the questions. The first student to write down the correct answer receives one point for his or her team. Call on different students and ask the next question. Use this as a review for a quiz or test.

DISCUSSION

In a discussion, have the students compare the explosion of enthusiasm for European exploration in the fifteenth and sixteenth centuries with the space race of the late 1950s and the 1960s, culminating in the moon walk of 1969. Include a discussion of motives, events, and effects. Make sure to end the discussion with the question: Were the effects of these two movements worth it?

could have been happier about all this excitement than the Italian merchants living in Venice and Genoa. These merchants had worked out agreements with Asian traders who brought goods from Asia overland to Constantinople. Italian ships sailed to Constantinople to pick up these goods. The Italians then sold them to other merchants from all over Europe and the Mediterranean world. In this way they made good profits for themselves.

The merchants, rulers, and ship captains from other countries in Europe were very eager to break the Italian *monopoly*, or complete control, of the overland trade from Asia. The only way they could do this would be by sailing an all-water route to the lands of the East. If they could find such a route, they would be able to buy goods directly from the Asian merchants.

Henry the Navigator. The Portuguese began to search for an all-water route in the 1400s. Prince Henry, one of the Portuguese leaders, paid for trips of exploration. He also encouraged exploration by establishing a school of *navigation*. Navigation is the science of determining a ship's position and course. At this school, geographers, mathematicians, and other learned people from many countries came together to pool their knowledge of sailing. They developed faster ships by making them lighter. They also discovered a new sail design. Before this time, ships could only sail with the wind at their back. The new kind of sail was movable. Now, regardless of the direction the wind came from, the ship could continue on course. The ships with these sails were called caravels.

The astrolabe allowed sailors to plot location at sea by measuring angles between stars and the horizon. It was useful only in clear weather.

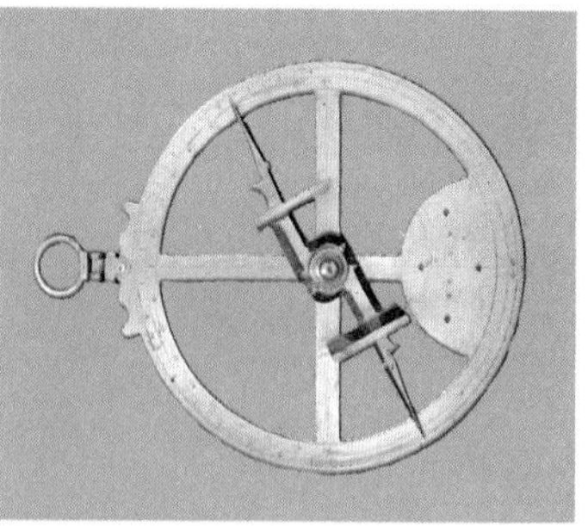

The Portuguese also improved two old inventions, the *compass* and the *astrolabe*. A compass is an instrument used in sailing that tells direction. An astrolabe is one that shows position in relation to the sun and other stars.

Because of the school, Prince Henry became known as "Henry the Navigator." He encouraged Portuguese sailors to set out and explore, promising them prizes if they found new lands. Soon, the Portuguese had taken the lead in the search for a new route to Asia.

Around the Cape. The Portuguese began sailing south along the western coast of Africa in hopes of trading for ivory and gold. They knew that Asia and all its riches lay on the other side of this continent. In 1488 the Portuguese sailor Bartolomeu Dias sailed around the Cape of Good Hope. The Cape of Good Hope is located at the southern tip of Africa. Dias

These Portuguese caravels illustrate the new "movable" sail design. Preparing the ships for sailing required hard work by the crew.

ANSWER THESE QUESTIONS

1. Ruins of houses and remains of iron tools in Newfoundland were like the houses and tools of the Vikings.
2. the age of European Exploration and Colonization
3. desire for riches, desire to spread Christianity, desire for fame and glory
4. Meat spoiled quickly without refrigeration, and spices covered up the bad taste.
5. Other Europeans wanted to break the Italian monopoly of overland trade from Asia so they could trade directly with Asians.

had to turn around and return to Portugal because his crew grew fearful of the unknown waters that lay ahead.

Ten years later, a ship captained by Vasco da Gama took up where Dias had left off. Gama actually reached Asia. He sailed from the Portuguese city of Lisbon to Calicut on the west coast of India. The Portuguese had at last made direct contact with the Asian traders and their precious goods.

ANSWER THESE QUESTIONS

1. What evidence suggests that the Vikings may have been the first Europeans to visit the Americas?
2. What is the period from 1450 to 1850 called?
3. What caused European interest in exploration?
4. Why were spices important to Europeans?
5. Why did Europeans seek an all-water route to Asia?

CONTENT OBJECTIVES

After completing the lesson, students will know:

- the theory Columbus believed in and whether or not it was valid
- about the main details of Columbus's four voyages
- the significance of the achievements of Columbus

VOCABULARY

mutiny: open rebellion

2-2 Christopher Columbus

As you read, think about these questions:

What was Columbus's theory about an all-water route to Asia?

What difficulties did Columbus have trying to prove his theory?

How did Columbus's later discoveries differ from his theory?

What were Columbus's achievements and what effect did they have on the world?

Special Vocabulary mutiny

The Westward Theory

Other Europeans besides the Portuguese dreamed of discovering an all-water route to Asia. For example, Christopher Columbus had dreams that seemed next to impossible to almost everyone in Europe. He wanted to sail west from Europe across the Atlantic Ocean to reach Asia. According to Columbus, such a trip would take only two months of sailing.

Columbus and his crew bid farewell to King Ferdinand and Queen Isabella. The queen had offered to sell the crown jewels in order to pay for Columbus's ships (pictured upper right), but this proved unnecessary.

Paying for the Voyage. A trip like the one Columbus had in mind would cost a lot of money. Columbus, an Italian from the city of Genoa, lived for a time in Portugal. He first approached King João II of Portugal with his scheme to sail west. The Portuguese king turned down the idea. João was putting his money into the search for an all-water route around Africa.

Columbus then traveled to Spain where after many years he convinced King Ferdinand and Queen Isabella to pay for a westward trip across the Atlantic. They gave Columbus the title of Admiral of the Ocean Sea and made him governor of all the lands he might discover on his trip.

Sailing Westward. Columbus could afford to obtain and outfit three small caravels with the money he received. The ships were named *Niña*, *Pinta*, and *Santa Maria*. To sail them,

King Ferdinand and Queen Isabella gave this coat of arms to Columbus after his first voyage. The lion and castle are symbols of nobility. The anchors represent mastery of the sea.

ACTIVITY

Objective: To collect information from a map

Organize the class into several groups of two to four students. Have each group turn to the map "The Four Voyages of Columbus." Using this map, have each group do the following: (1) Name each place Columbus explored on his first three voyages. (2) Give the dates for Columbus's fourth voyage.

DISCUSSION

Have the students answer this question: If you had been alive in 1492 and had had a chance to join Columbus on his trip (knowing nothing more about the trip's outcome than any other sailor then), would you have joined him? Make sure to have the students explain their answers.

Columbus signed up ninety people. The expedition set sail on August 3, 1492, from Palos, Spain.

At first, the ships moved along quickly. On the open sea, however, the wind changed directions often. Sometimes it even died altogether. As the days passed, the crew lost faith in Columbus and his plan. The crew members began to speak among themselves of *mutiny*, or open rebellion. They wanted Columbus to return to Spain.

The New World

On October 11, however, the sailors began seeing signs that land must lie ahead. Branches of trees and bushes could be seen floating in the water. On the morning of October 12, from aboard *Pinta* came the joyous shout: "Land! Land!" A member of the crew had glimpsed an island in the distance.

The People of Guanahani. The three ships came close enough to the island to drop anchor. Columbus took a handful of crew members from the ships to the beach in small boats. He was the first ashore. Ignoring the people there, he claimed the island for the king and queen of Spain. Later, he named it San Salvador, "Holy Savior." Of course, the people of San Salvador had not been waiting for visitors to give their island a name. They had always called it Guanahani.

Columbus believed that he had arrived in the Indies, islands lying off the coast of Asia, so he called the people of the island "Indians." Columbus was disappointed that nothing he saw matched the descriptions of China or India that he had heard. Among the Indians, however, Columbus noticed a few who wore golden jewelry. He wasted no time in inquiring where the gold had come from. Columbus reported what the Indians told him:

> By signs I was able to understand that, to the south . . . there was a king who had great cups full of gold and possessed a large amount of it . . . So I resolved to go to the southwest, to seek the gold and precious stones . . . I wish to go and see if I can find the island of Cipangu (Japan).

But Columbus never reached Japan. When he left San Salvador he sailed south, reaching the island now called Cuba. Still he found no fine cloth, no golden rooftops, no decorations of pearl, no precious jewels. In short, nothing looked like the lands Marco Polo had visited. Columbus continued to believe he had discovered unmapped islands off the coast of Asia, and he searched for three months for the mainland. He finally decided to go back to Spain.

The First Spanish Colony. Before setting sail for home, though, *Santa Maria* was wrecked on the northern coast of the island the Spanish called Hispaniola. *Niña* and *Pinta* were too small to take aboard all the crew members from the wrecked vessel. So Columbus decided to leave some people behind to set up a town on Hispaniola. Because the wreck had occurred on December 25, Columbus called the new town La Navidad, Spanish for Christmas.

In the following years, Columbus made three more trips to the New World. The second expedition included seventeen ships carrying more than one thousand people who wanted to settle at La Navidad. When the fleet arrived at Hispaniola, Columbus found the town had been destroyed.

Columbus built another town called Isabella, after the queen. This town also failed. In 1496 Columbus moved the settlers to another spot on the island and built a community, which he named Santo Domingo. This became the first lasting Spanish settlement in the New World.

No one knows for sure what Columbus looked like, since various artists have painted him differently. This artist shows Columbus as a stern and determined man dressed in Italian fashions of about 1500.

Columbus's Achievements. Think of Columbus's achievements. On his four voyages he had discovered Cuba, Hispaniola, Puerto Rico, Jamaica, and parts of what are now Venezuela, Honduras, and Panama. He had been the first European to set foot on the continent of South America. He had established the first European settlement in the Western Hemisphere since Leif Ericson's village on Newfoundland. His discoveries had set off a wave of excitement in Europe that caused an explosion of exploration. In spite of all these accomplishments, Columbus died in 1506 considering himself a failure. After all, his goal had been to discover an all-water route to Asia, and this he had not done.

ANSWER THESE QUESTIONS

1. What was Columbus's theory about an all-water route to Asia?
2. What caused Columbus's crew to consider mutiny?
3. What were Columbus's achievements?
4. What effect did Columbus's achievements have on the world?
5. Why did Columbus consider himself a failure?

ANSWER THESE QUESTIONS

1. Sailing west from Europe across the Atlantic Ocean to reach Asia would take only about two months.
2. The crew lost faith in Columbus's plan because the wind changed directions and sometimes died altogether.
3. Columbus discovered Cuba, Hispaniola, Puerto Rico, Jamaica, and parts of Venezuela, Honduras, and Panama.
4. They caused further interest in exploration.
5. He had failed to accomplish his goal of finding an all-water route to Asia.

Objective: After completing this activity, the students should be able to trace routes on a map.

Working with Skills

MAP SKILLS

ACTIVITY

Objective: To trace a route

If possible, obtain a copy of a map of your city. (Usually the local phone book has one.) Divide the class into small groups with each group having a copy of the map. Devise several imaginary trips from school—for instance, a field trip from school to City Hall. Try to devise a different trip for each group. On the maps, have members of each small group decide on a route to take on this trip. Make sure students name places along the route and indicate directions correctly on the map. If you have time, ask each group to switch trips with another group. Compare the routes taken by each group.

ANSWERS

Questions in Paragraph:

Venezuela
Hispaniola
Santo Domingo

Tracing Routes

Maps are a source of information, just like the other parts of your textbook. Maps give you important facts and dates, but in a visual manner. Together, maps and written explanations give you a fuller picture than you can get from just one or the other.

The map on the opposite page traces the routes of the four voyages made by Christopher Columbus in his search for Asia. It is one thing to read that "Columbus continued to believe he had discovered unmapped islands off the coast of Asia" and another to actually locate those islands on a map. The map allows you to see where the islands are in relation to one another. It also gives some hints about Columbus's thinking as he plotted each voyage along a different course, hoping finally to find the continent he believed lay beyond the islands. In this way, the map makes it easier to understand why Columbus continued to search the same area rather than giving up and trying a totally new place.

Notice that there are several colored arrows on the map. This is the method used by the mapmaker to show the different routes taken by Columbus. The dates of each voyage also appear on the map. By following each arrow all the way to the place where it ends, you can learn much about when and where Columbus traveled.

Trace the route taken by Columbus in 1498 by first finding the arrow representing that journey on the southeastern side of the map. (Remember that Columbus was sailing from Europe, which is not shown on this map.) Follow the arrow's westward course until you reach land. What region in South America did Columbus reach? Now continue to follow the same arrow northwest until you reach an island. What is it called? What city did Columbus visit?

Study this map to gain a clear picture of where Columbus went during the period 1492 to 1503. Then answer the following questions.

RELATED MATERIAL
Duplicator/Copy Master Activity 4

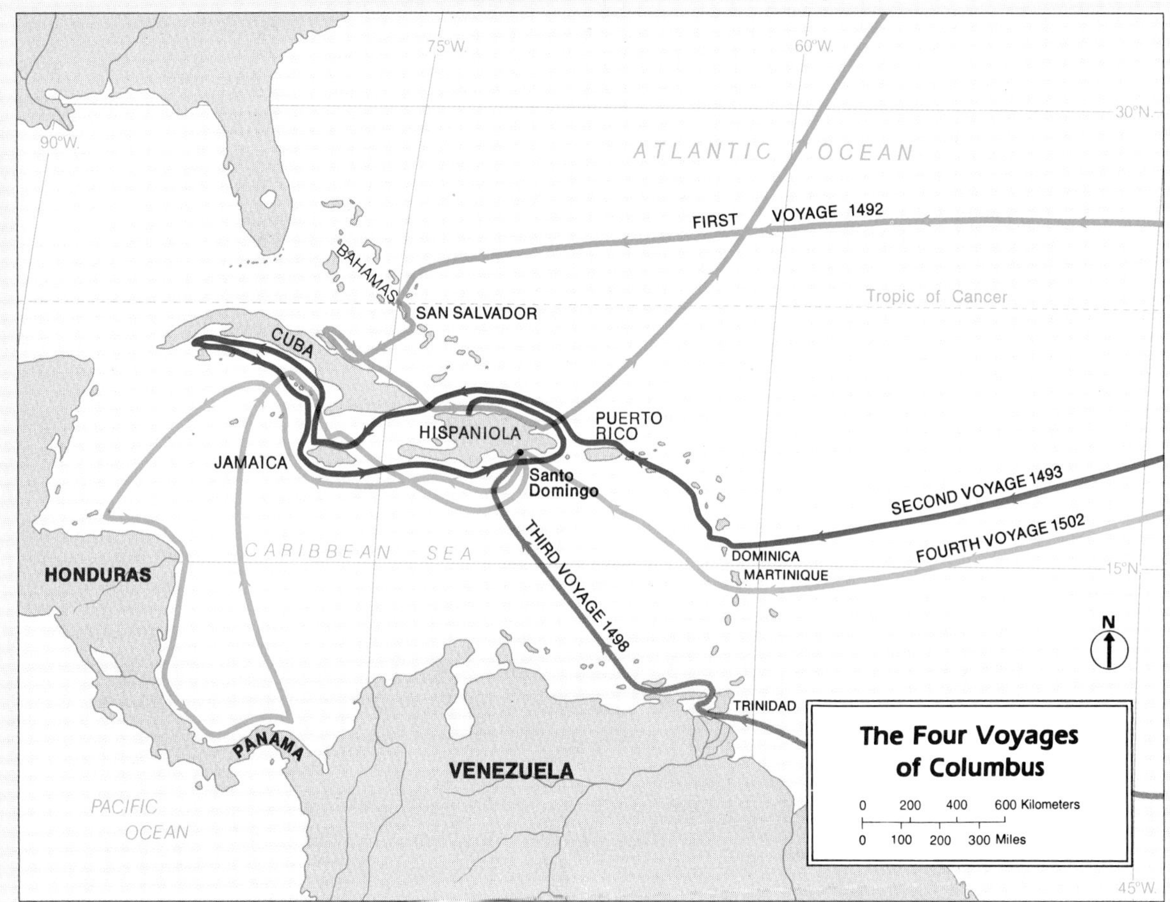

1. What date is shown for each voyage?
2. What is the color of the arrow for each voyage?
3. Where do you think each of these four voyages began? Where on the map might you find a hint of this information?
4. What ocean did Columbus cross on each of his four voyages?
5. On what sea did Columbus sail on his fourth voyage?

Numbered Questions:

1. (1) 1492 (2) 1493 (3) 1498 (4) 1502
2. (1) green; (2) red; (3) orange; (4) blue
3. Europe; arrows come from the east side of the map
4. Atlantic
5. Caribbean

CONTENT OBJECTIVES

After completing the lesson, students will know:

- the discoveries of the various explorers employed by Spain
- the significance of the Spanish voyages to the New World
- the discoveries made by French explorers Giovanni de Verrazano and Jacques Cartier
- the reasons the French explored where they did and the results of their expeditions

VOCABULARY

strait: a narrow channel

2-3 A New World to Explore

As you read, think about these questions:

What new theory did Amerigo Vespucci offer?

What were the two major accomplishments of Magellan's voyage?

Why did the French look for a strait to the north?

What did Cartier hope to find on each of his voyages to the New World?

Special Vocabulary strait

Spain Pushes Forward

The story of Columbus and his discoveries spread, creating excitement each time the tales of the voyages were told. Many people dreamed of someday making trips like these and becoming rich and famous.

Amerigo Vespucci. One such person was Amerigo Vespucci of Florence, Italy. Vespucci heard firsthand accounts of Columbus's adventures from several crew members who had sailed with him to the New World. At the first opportunity, Vespucci joined a Spanish expedition going to the New World. The ship carrying him explored along the coast of South America, possibly going as far south as Brazil.

The next year, 1501, Vespucci once again sailed to the New World, this time on a Portuguese ship. On this voyage, Vespucci decided that South America was much too large to be an island off the Asian coast.

Vespucci concluded that Columbus had in fact discovered a "New World" and not a part of Asia, after all. He wrote his theory in a letter in 1502. At about the same time, a geographer in Europe wrote a book discussing all known parts of the world. Since Amerigo was the first to recognize Columbus's discovery as a "New World," the geographer decided to name the continent "America" after Vespucci. The name stuck, and since that time the lands of the Western Hemisphere have been called the Americas.

Vasco de Balboa. Another person who dreamed of the excitement of exploration and discovery was Vasco de Balboa. He first failed as a farmer on the Spanish island of Hispaniola. He then gave up his farm on the island and hid aboard a slave ship bound for Colombia in South America. A few days after leaving the island, Balboa came out of hiding and announced himself to the captain. The captain nearly threw Balboa off the ship at the next island. He decided instead to allow Balboa to join the ship's crew.

Vasco Nuñez toma posesion de la Mar
del Sur

This unrealistic map shows Balboa at the Pacific. The castle-like building near the center is a product of the artist's imagination; no Indians would have built it.

On the return trip to Hispaniola, the captain stopped in Panama, where he wanted to establish a colony. At Darien, the site of the proposed settlement, Balboa turned on the captain, who was unfit, sent him back to Spain a prisoner, and took command of the expedition. He then began to question the local Indians about where gold might be found.

The Indians told Balboa that a fabulously wealthy kingdom existed somewhere to the south. Balboa and Francisco Pizarro, one of his crew members, listened closely as the Indians told this story. It included word of a great sea not far to the west.

Balboa and his people soon began the long 60-mile (96-kilometer) march that would take them to the cities of gold and the "great sea." They walked across Panama through mile after mile of almost impassable jungles and dangerous

Ferdinand Magellan served at the Portuguese royal court as a boy. There he learned about the voyages of Christopher Columbus and Vasco da Gama.

mountain passes. Many of the party became ill with fever along the way and died.

On September 25, 1513, Balboa, Pizarro, and the few others who survived slowly climbed the last hill. Before them lay the sea of which the Indians had spoken. Balboa named it the "South Sea" because it was south of where they stood. Later Balboa marched into the water in full armor, unfurled the Spanish flag, and claimed all the lands touching the "South Sea" for the king of Spain.

Ferdinand Magellan. News of the discoveries of Vespucci and Balboa soon reached Europe. Overnight, mapmakers drew maps explaining where these people had explored. Ferdinand Magellan, a Portuguese sailor, studied the maps carefully and developed a theory. He decided that he could reach the East by sailing down the eastern coast of Vespucci's new continent. There he might find a *strait*, or a narrow channel, through the land. Then he could sail into Balboa's sea. Surely Asia could not be far away once he was in the South Sea. From Asia, Magellan planned to sail west along Vasco da Gama's route around Africa to Europe. Magellan took his proposal to King Charles V of Spain, who agreed to pay for the trip. On September 20, 1519, a fleet of five ships and 239 people set sail from Spain under the command of Magellan.

The story of Magellan's trip is a thrilling one. It includes mutiny, hunger, sickness, and war. Magellan found the strait he was looking for at the tip of South America. Three of his ships sailed through it and entered Balboa's South Sea—

which Magellan renamed the Pacific Ocean ("the calm sea"). Finally in March 1521, the tiny fleet arrived in the Philippine Islands, where Magellan was killed during a local war. One ship, *Victoria*, made it to the Molucca Islands. Here the 18 people still alive out of the 239 who began loaded the ship with valuable spices. *Victoria* and its tiny crew struggled back to Spain, arriving in September 1522. (Find Magellan's route on the map on this page.)

Magellan's voyage had shown that a ship could sail west to reach Asia, just as Columbus had first said. In fact, *Victoria*

black arrows without dashes

This polar projection of the world shows the European search for an all-water route to Asia. Notice that explorers sailed toward both the east and the west in their attempts to find this route. What is the symbol for Magellan's voyage?

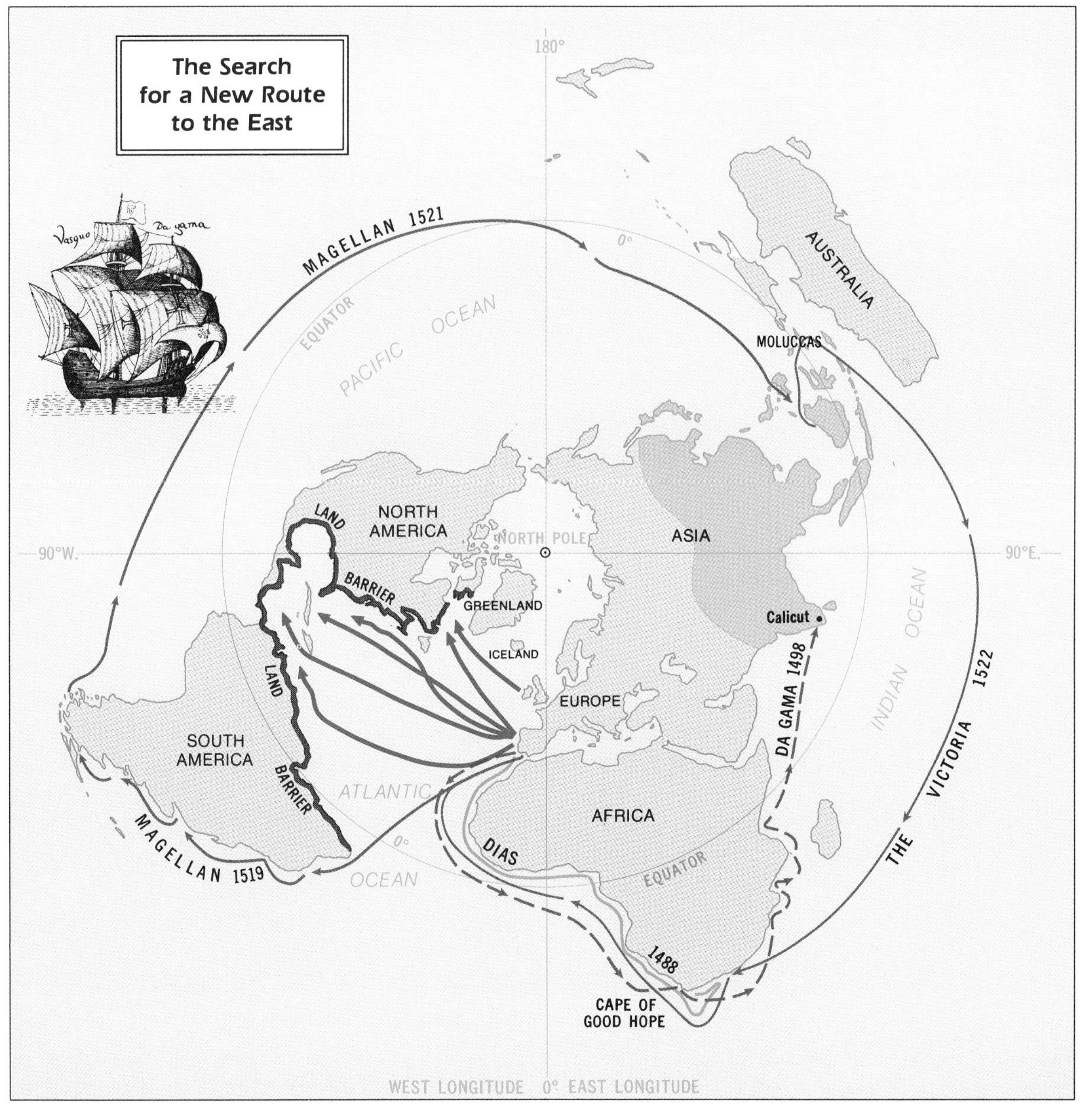

had sailed all the way around the world, the first ship ever to do this. As a result of the trip, the geographers of the day gained a truer idea of the size of the earth and of the Pacific Ocean than they ever had before. Magellan's accomplishment also gave Spain control of the Pacific Ocean for hundreds of years.

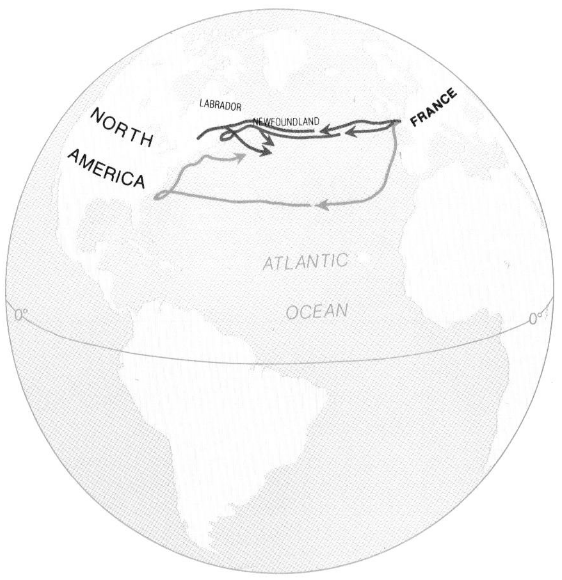

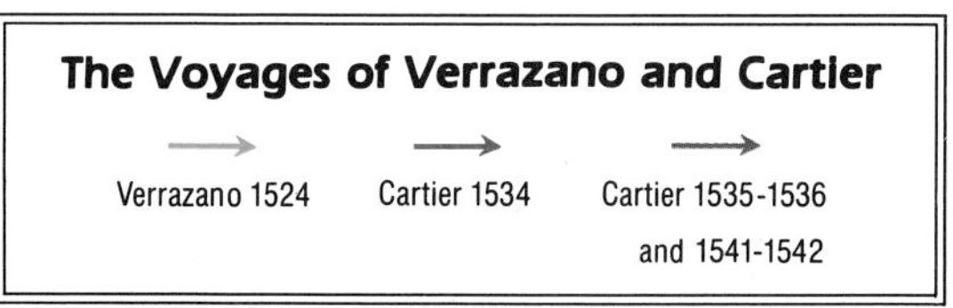

This globe shows the routes taken by Verrazano and Cartier and the dates of their expeditions. Which explorer took the southernmost route? Which explorer took the northernmost route?

Verrazano, Cartier

The French Experiment

By 1522, then, Spain and Portugal had found the only known water routes to Asia. Francis I, the king of France, hoped that there was still another route to Asia, one directly across the Atlantic Ocean from France. He decided to send his explorers in search of a strait that would take them to the riches of the East.

Giovanni da Verrazano. Francis I found just the person to lead his expedition. He was Giovanni da Verrazano, an Italian from Florence. On January 17, 1524, Verrazano, aboard *La Dauphine*, set out for Asia.

Verrazano's crossing of the Atlantic took seven weeks. Then his sailors began to sight the long, narrow islands off the coast of present-day North Carolina. These islands are so narrow that a person, even today, can see across them to the waters of Pamlico Sound. Verrazano believed that the waters of Pamlico Sound were those of a large ocean.

Sure that he had found the northern strait, Verrazano continued northward, sailing into the mouth of what is now known as the Hudson River. From there, he and his crew traveled north to Cape Cod, then along the New England coast to Newfoundland.

As time passed, Verrazano realized he had failed to find the strait after all. He recognized too that the land from Florida to Newfoundland was a different part of the New World from that discovered by Columbus.

The Gulf of the St. Lawrence. Francis I remained convinced that a strait must lead from the Atlantic Ocean to the Pacific. He therefore called on Jacques Cartier to continue the French exploration of the New World. On April 20, 1534, Cartier set sail.

Cartier reached the shores of Newfoundland and began exploring. He thought that he had at last found the northern strait when he sailed into the huge Gulf of St. Lawrence. For the next five months, Cartier and his crew searched diligently for the new route to China. The French explorers found no signs of Chinese culture, but they did meet hundreds of American Indians. Back in France, Cartier made a report to the king. The king was especially interested when Cartier told about the Gulf of St. Lawrence. Francis I was sure that this body of water must lead to Asia. He therefore ordered Cartier to prepare for a second voyage.

Jacques Cartier sought favor at the French court by exploring for gold in America. Cartier's clothing shows the lavish tastes of French nobles of that time.

Quebec and Montreal. On May 19, 1535, Cartier, in command of an expedition of three ships, departed from France. On the shores of the Gulf of St. Lawrence, Cartier made friends with a local chief who gave him the services of two Indian guides. These two young guides were the sons of a chief whose people, the Huron, lived many miles up the St. Lawrence River. The two Indians led Cartier into the heart of their country, which they called Canada.

Upriver, Cartier met the father of the two guides. His name was Donnaconna. Donnaconna showed his pleasure at seeing his two sons safely home by welcoming Cartier and his

ACTIVITY

Objective: To participate in a discussion

Use the guided reading questions, the lesson-end questions, and the chapter-end "Thinking Things Through" questions as a basis for a discussion of Spanish and French exploration. Point out to students that in a discussion, each person must be allowed to speak without interruption. Make clear that each person will be given the opportunity to answer a question or to offer an opinion. Try to involve as many students in the discussion as possible.

DISCUSSION

Have the students compare and contrast the experiences of the Spanish with those of the French as the two groups explored the New World.

ANSWER THESE QUESTIONS

1. Amerigo Vespucci—the first to recognize Columbus's discovery as a "New World"
2. It proved that a ship could sail west to reach Asia; it gave geographers a true idea of the size of the earth; it gave Spain control of the Pacific Ocean.
3. The land from Florida to Newfoundland was a different part of the New World from that discovered by Columbus.
4. Answers will vary; benefits might include adventure and discovery.
5. Answers will vary; drawbacks might include danger and sickness.

people to the island town called Stadacona. It was located at the place where Quebec now stands.

Cartier wanted to continue to explore for signs of China before the winter set in. He began the difficult voyage upstream. Three weeks later, Cartier and his group arrived in another Indian village called Hochelaga, the site of present-day Montreal.

Before Cartier returned to Stadacona, he heard of a great city to the west filled with gold, silver, and diamonds. The Indians called this city Saguenay. Cartier and his people quickly returned to Stadacona to discuss what they had heard with Donnaconna.

Saguenay. Donnaconna said he knew of Saguenay. In fact, he told Cartier that the place was filled with gold and jewels. Donnaconna was only telling the French what they wanted to hear. He did this too well. Cartier and his group kidnapped Donnaconna and took him back to France. They planned to make the Indian tell the king about Saguenay.

Donnaconna eagerly told the king of the treasures of the kingdom of Saguenay. His stories, along with a few "sparkling rocks" that Cartier brought back from Stadacona, persuaded the king to send Cartier back to Canada.

Cartier returned to the New World a few years later to continue his search for Saguenay but failed to find any such kingdom. The explorer finally returned to France with more barrels of sparkling rocks. The rocks turned out to be iron pyrite, sometimes called "fool's gold." Cartier and Saguenay became a laughing matter in the French Court.

Saguenay stands for much that has happened in American history. People have often come to America looking for one thing and found another. Whatever the dreams of newcomers, however, they have always found a land bountiful to hard workers. It has offered them a chance to start both their lives and their societies over again.

ANSWER THESE QUESTIONS

1. Who was America named after?
2. What were the results of Magellan's voyage?
3. What did Verrazano realize at the end of his voyage?
4. What, do you think, were some benefits of being an explorer in the fifteenth and sixteenth centuries?
5. What, do you think, were some drawbacks of being an explorer at that time?

PEOPLE IN AMERICA

John Cabot

John Cabot gave England its first major discoveries in the New World. Cabot is a mysterious figure to us. Information about his place of birth, citizenship, home, and family background remains unclear. Some historians have tried to piece together his life story, making many links between Cabot and Columbus.

Both men were probably from Genoa, Italy. Columbus was born in 1451. Since the two men were about the same age, Cabot also could have been born in that year. Some have even suggested that the two may have grown up together.

Could Columbus and Cabot ever have met as adults? There is some recorded evidence that a man matching Cabot's description with the name Johan Cabot Montecalunya visited Spain from 1491 to 1493. Columbus returned from his first voyage in March of 1493. The two may have seen each other then. Could Cabot have gotten his idea to sail to the New World after talking with Columbus? No one knows for sure.

Another link connects the lives of the two men. While awaiting word from the Spanish king and queen, Columbus had begged King Henry VII of England to pay for his westward voyage. Henry VII turned him down, passing up a chance, as it turned out, to be first in the New World. Columbus, we have seen, finally won the help of the Spanish and sailed to the New World in 1492. Cabot went to Henry VII in 1495 with the same request Columbus had made. This time Henry quickly granted it.

Cabot made two voyages for Henry VII. On the first, in 1497, he rediscovered Newfoundland and may even have reached the coast of Maine before sailing home. On the second voyage, Cabot explored the coast of North America, possibly as far south as the Chesapeake Bay near present-day Virginia. We will never know for sure because on this voyage, Cabot's ship disappeared at sea. Still, Cabot's voyages to North America later proved to be as important to England as Columbus's trips to the Caribbean were to Spain.

WORDS TO REMEMBER

1. The Vikings told sagas about their explorations. 2. C 3. C 4. Navigation is the science of determining a ship's position and course. 5. The compass is a tool that tells directions. 6. The astrolabe is a sailing tool that shows the position of the ship in relation to the sun and other stars. 7. C

THINKING THINGS THROUGH

1. The theory stated that the Vikings were the first Europeans to try to settle in North America. The ruins of houses and tools that Ingstad found on Newfoundland were like those of the Vikings. 2. European rulers and explorers had a thirst for riches. Europeans wanted to spread the Christian religion. Both the explorers and the rulers wanted fame and glory. 3. An

Chapter 2 SUMMARY

The earliest European exploration of the Americas took place around the year 1000. The Viking Leif Ericson visited Newfoundland and tried to set up a lasting colony there. This attempt failed, however.

In the late 1400s Europeans tried to open an all-water route to Asia. Such a route would help to make Asian goods more plentiful in Europe than ever before. The Portuguese used new knowledge and tools of navigation to become the first to find an all-water route to Asia. Through the efforts of Dias in 1488 and Da Gama in 1498, they discovered the route around the southern tip of Africa.

Then in 1492 Columbus attempted to find an all-water route to Asia by sailing west across the Atlantic. Instead of reaching Asia, Columbus discovered the Caribbean Islands and South America. By 1502 Amerigo Vespucci recognized that Columbus's discoveries were not part of Asia, but an entirely New World.

In 1519 a fleet under Magellan also attempted to find a westward passage to Asia. The trip was successful, but it cost Magellan and many others their lives. In 1522 one of Magellan's ships, *Victoria*, returned to Spain after having sailed all the way around the world.

The French searched for a westward passage to Asia by sailing north. Verrazano explored much of the coast of what is today called the United States. Later, Cartier sailed up the St. Lawrence River into Canada all the way to present-day Montreal.

Chapter 2 TEST

WORDS TO REMEMBER

The sentences below contain special vocabulary words used in this chapter. Each of these words is printed in italics. Read each sentence. If the vocabulary word is used correctly, put "C" next to the number on your paper. If it is used incorrectly, rewrite the sentence to make the usage correct.

1. The Vikings took long *sagas* to the New World.
2. The first *colony* Columbus established did not last.
3. The Italians had a *monopoly* on Eastern goods.
4. *Navigation* is the science of determining the height of waves while sailing.
5. The *compass* is a sailing tool that shows the position of the ship in relation to the sun and other stars.
6. The *astrolabe* is a tool that tells direction.
7. Columbus's crew members were ready to *mutiny* before they sighted land.

THINKING THINGS THROUGH

Answer each of the following questions in complete sentences.

1. In 1960 Helge Ingstad stated a theory about the Vikings. What was the theory and what evidence supports this position?
2. What are three reasons why Europeans began to explore and colonize new lands?
3. Why did the Europeans want to find an all-water route to Asia?

RELATED MATERIALS

Duplicator/Copy Masters: Activities 3, 4; Quiz 2
Workbook pages 4-6

all-water route to Asia would enable the Europeans to buy goods directly from Asia, thus breaking the Italian monopoly of overland trade from Asia. **4.** Both Cabot and Columbus were probably from Genoa, Italy. They may have met as adults. Henry VII granted Cabot's request for help, having turned down the same request from Columbus earlier. **5.** News of the discoveries of Vespucci and Balboa reached Europe. Magellan was able to study maps of these voyages and plan his route accordingly.

WORKING WITH SKILLS

1. The Search for a New Route to the East **2.** arrow; they are different colors **3.** Dias, DaGama, and Magellan **4.** DaGama; 1498; around the southern tip of Africa **5.** Magellan; 1519; 1522

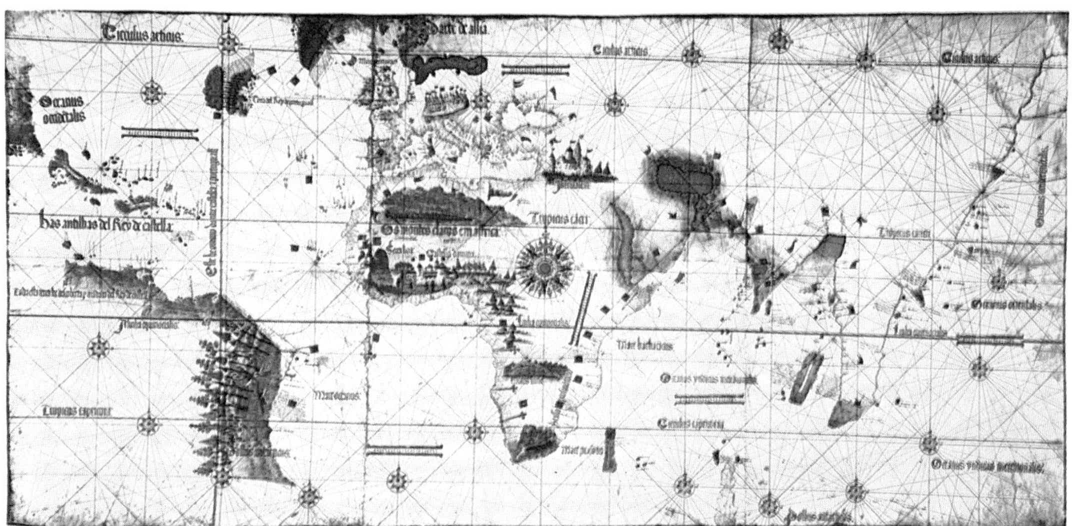

4. What evidence supports the theory that John Cabot could have gotten his idea to sail to the New World from Columbus?
5. How were the discoveries of Vespucci and Balboa important to Magellan's voyage?

WORKING WITH SKILLS

Look at the map on page 43 and answer these questions:

1. What is the title of the map?
2. What symbol stands for the route of an explorer?
3. Whose journeys are shown?
4. Who was the first European explorer to reach Asia by water? When did he sail? What was his route?
5. Who was the leader for most of the first voyage around the world? In what year did he set sail? When was the voyage finally completed?

ON YOUR OWN

1. Columbus had a difficult time convincing crew members to join his expedition because they were afraid to cross the Atlantic Ocean. Make a chart listing the advantages and disadvantages a crew member might face on such a voyage. Remember to give your chart a title and proper headings.
2. Look at the map on this page. It was drawn ten years after Columbus's first voyage to the New World. Compare this map to the world map on pages 750–751 of your book. Find the following places on the map above: Europe; Africa; India. Make a list of the places represented by the partly drawn lands at the far left.

Chapter 3 introduces students to the Spanish and French discoveries throughout the interior of North America and South America. Lesson 3-1 details the civilizations of the Aztecs and the Inca before their destruction by the Spanish conquistadores. It also describes the Spanish conquest of Mexico and Peru and their search for legendary cities and kingdoms. Lesson 3-2 describes the creation, exploration, settlement, and expansion of New France. It also outlines some features of Canadian society under French rule.

Chapter 3
THE CREATION OF NEW SPAIN AND NEW FRANCE

CONTENT OBJECTIVES

After completing the lesson, students will know:
- what a civilization is
- about the Aztec civilization and its conquest by Cortés
- about the Inca civilization and its conquest by Pizarro
- the results of the Spanish attempts to find Bimini, Cibola, Quivera, and California
- the governmental structure of New Spain under the viceroy
- the effects colonization had on the American Indians

VOCABULARY

conquistador: conqueror
civilization: a society in which people build cities and work at jobs other than farming
specialization of labor: a system in which each person has his or her own special job to do
terrace: a huge steplike piece of land with level surfaces
surplus: leftover portion
viceroy: a person chosen by the king of Spain to govern Spanish New World claims
presidio: a military base housing Spanish soldiers
mission: a religious center
land grant: the right to use a certain place
encomendero: a special friend of the Spanish king who received land grants
hacienda: large ranch house

3-1 New Spain

As you read, think about these questions:
What is a civilization?
What types of workers are needed in a civilization?
Why were the Aztec and Inca civilizations conquered by the Spanish?
What type of government was established in the Spanish New World?
How did New Spain get the workers it needed?

Special Vocabulary

conquistador	surplus	land grant
civilization	viceroy	*encomendero*
specialization of labor	*presidio*	*hacienda*
terrace	mission	

News that the Americas were not Asia but a land previously unknown to Europeans may have disappointed some explorers. Other adventurers were more hopeful. They believed that gold and glory awaited those Europeans strong and bold enough to force the American Indians to give up their land and wealth.

Cortés and the Fall of the Aztecs

The Spanish had a name for those bold, strong people who saw their chances for gold and glory in the New World. They called them *conquistadores,* conquerors. The most famous of the *conquistadores* was Hernando Cortés.

This painting shows Tenochtitlán, the huge capital of the Aztec nation, before it was destroyed by the Spanish. In the foreground, farmers, warriors, nobles, and shoppers mingle in a busy marketplace.

Hernando Cortés got his chance at gold and glory when, in the early 1500s, word came to the Spanish governor in Cuba of great discoveries in the West. Explorers had sailed westward and landed on the Yucatán Peninsula on the coast of what is now Mexico. There they saw that the Mayan people wore gold jewelry, drank from gold cups, and ate from gold dishes. This was the news the Spanish governor had been waiting to hear. In 1519 he gathered a force of Spanish soldiers and placed Cortés in command.

The Aztecs. The Mayas, whom the explorers met on the Yucatán Peninsula of Mexico, were not the rulers of Mexico. The rulers were the Aztecs. The Aztecs lived to the north and west of the Mayas in an area around their capital city, Tenochtitlán. Today, Mexico City stands on the site of Tenochtitlán.

The Aztecs were the largest Indian culture group in North America. By the early 1500s, more than one hundred thousand people lived in Tenochtitlán. Most Aztecs made a living by farming. They raised corn, beans, squash, cacao, tobacco, and cotton. The Aztec people grew so much food that some of them no longer needed to farm for a living. These people could build cities and do jobs other than farming. When the people of a society build cities and work at jobs other than farming, they are said to have created a *civilization*.

The Toltecs controlled central Mexico from their capital at Tula before the Aztecs came to power. Statues at Tula represent warriors of the Toltec people.

In a civilization, people have *specialization of labor*, that is, each person has his or her own special job to do. Other people depend on that person to do it. For example, a weaver may spend all day making blankets. The weaver depends on farmers to grow enough food to keep him or her alive. In turn, farmers do not have to spend time making blankets. Weavers can do this job.

Civilizations have people who specialize in running the government and representing others before their gods. These are the society's government officials and priests. Most governments also have soldiers. Soldiers keep order in the society and defend their society from outside attack. Sometimes they also attack other societies in hopes of spreading their own civilization.

The Aztec cities had government buildings and huge temples. Their pottery and cloth were among the most beautiful in the world. They used gold, silver, and turquoise to fashion handsome bracelets and necklaces worn by people as far away as the Yucatán Peninsula.

This portrait of Hernando Cortés was completed in 1530. At that time, Cortés was forty-five years old and, as conqueror of the Aztecs, was the richest man in Spanish America.

The Aztecs worshipped many gods. They had a Sun-Warrior God, a Rain God, a Wind God, and a God of Learning. According to legend, Quetzalcoatl—the God of Learning—was fair-skinned. He had sailed away from Mexico to the east, promising he would return one day.

By the 1500s the Aztec civilization had spread throughout most of what we today call Mexico. Aztec soldiers fought bravely with spears, bows and arrows, and swords. They took prisoners by the thousands and treated the peoples they defeated harshly.

The Arrival of Cortés. Cortés and his *conquistadores* landed in Mexico in 1519. The Spaniards' first problem was speaking to the American Indians they met. Cortés solved this problem when an Indian woman whom the Spanish called Marina joined his army. Marina hated the Aztecs for their harsh rule of her people. She spoke both Aztec and Mayan. Cortés, with the help of Marina, informed the Mexican Indians of his demands that the Aztecs surrender to him. Those who did not willingly join Cortés were defeated and forced to do as the Spanish wished.

Word of Cortés's approach to Tenochtitlán spread quickly. Montezuma II, the emperor of the Aztecs, was keeping in mind the legend of the fair-skinned Quetzalcoatl. The legend told of how Quetzalcoatl would return to Mexico one day, probably sailing there from the east. The fair-skinned leader Cortés had landed in the east and was proceeding west, conquering all peoples before him. Montezuma believed that Cortés was Quetzalcoatl.

Montezuma sent gifts of gold and precious stones to Cortés. This was a mistake. Instead of satisfying Cortés as a god might be satisfied, the gifts aroused Cortés's interest. He ordered his soldiers to speed up their trip to the Aztec capital, Tenochtitlán.

Montezuma II was emperor at the height of the Aztec Empire. At his coronation, shown here, Montezuma wore the garments of an Aztec noble—a colorful cape, leg ornaments, and a plume of green quetzal feathers (a symbol of the Aztec god of learning).

The Fall of Tenochtitlán. In time Cortés took Montezuma prisoner. Montezuma still thought that Cortés and his soldiers were gods, but other Aztecs believed differently. The Aztec warriors surrounded Cortés's army. To calm them, Cortés forced Montezuma to speak to them. Montezuma's own people began to think that their king was a coward, and they stoned him to death. Then they turned on the Spaniards and drove them off.

Cortés returned to the coast of the Gulf of Mexico, where he built a large and powerful army. This army included thousands of Indians from groups that hated the harsh Aztec rule. Ten months later, Cortés and his soldiers attacked Tenochtitlán again. This time Cortés defeated the Aztecs. By 1521 the Aztec Empire had been crushed. Cortés began sending shiploads of gold, silver, and jewels back to Spain.

Pizarro and the Fall of the Inca

The Aztec Empire was a rich prize. But 2500 miles (4000 kilometers) to the south lay the outposts of the Inca Empire, a kingdom even bigger and richer than that of the Aztecs. In 1521, however, knowledge of the existence of this far-off kingdom was only a rumor heard by a few Spaniards.

The Search for Peru. One of those Spaniards who heard the rumor was Francisco Pizarro. Pizarro had been a *conquistador* with Balboa on his journey of discovery in Pañama.

In 1524 Pizarro began his search for the rich kingdom. The first trip ended in failure. Then in 1526, the Spaniard and a few companions set out again. This two-year trip took Pizarro to Peru in South America. There he found sure evidence of the Indian civilization he was looking for.

Pizarro returned to Spain. He told the king of his find and of his plans. The king appointed him governor of all the

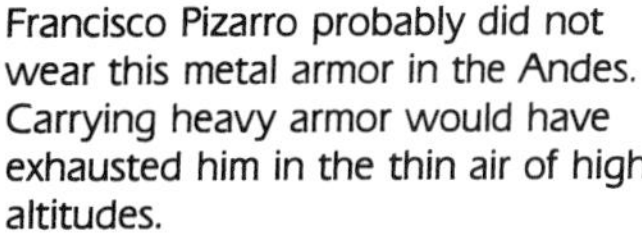

Francisco Pizarro probably did not wear this metal armor in the Andes. Carrying heavy armor would have exhausted him in the thin air of high altitudes.

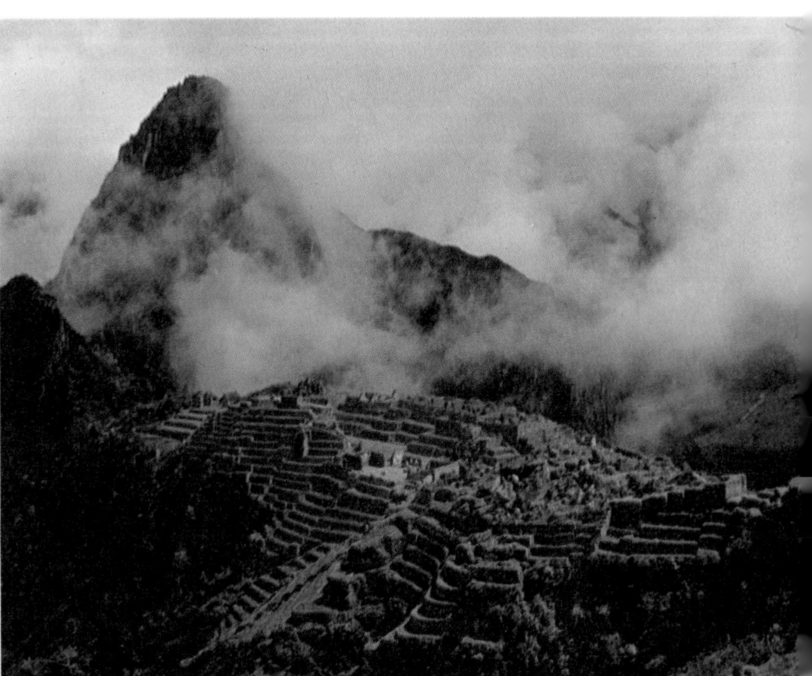

The Inca city of Machu Picchu was built on a mountain 8000 feet (2000 meters) high. Its terraced gardens were connected by more than 3000 steps.

lands he might discover. By 1531 Pizarro had returned to the New World and was ready to set forth for Peru with about one hundred eighty *conquistadores*. Reaching Peru in 1532, the expedition climbed high into the mountains to a city called Cajamarca. There Atahualpa, the ruler of this mysterious kingdom, had gathered a huge army. Atahualpa was called Inca, a term much like the English word "king." All of Atahualpa's people became known as the Inca.

The Inca Civilization. The Inca people had the largest and most prosperous kingdom in the New World. It stretched almost 3000 miles (4800 kilometers) along the mountainous western coast of South America.

The Inca had many rich, beautiful cities: Quito, Cajamarca, Machu Picchu, and the mountain capital Cuzco. Since many of these cities were perched high on mountaintops, the people had learned to farm on *terraces* built into the mountainsides. Terraces are step-like pieces of land with level surfaces. Farmers planted crops on these terraces and lived in the nearby towns and villages. The Inca farmers raised huge amounts of vegetables. They grew so much, in fact, they needed to store the *surplus*, or leftover portion, in huge warehouses throughout the empire.

The Inca built some of the finest roads ever made. These were needed because of the great distances and rough land between the cities. The Inca placed runners at regular spots along the roads to carry messages from city to city.

The Fall of the Inca. The Inca believed that their ruler Atahualpa was the son of the Sun God and a god himself. Therefore, when Pizarro and his *conquistadores* came to Cajamarca, the Inca had every reason to believe they would defeat the Spanish.

At Cajamarca, Atahualpa agreed to talk to Pizarro, and he was carried on a golden throne to the Spaniard. It seemed that only a Spanish priest and an Indian guide were there to greet the Inca emperor and the four thousand unarmed Inca who came with him. Hiding all around, however, were Pizarro and his soldiers. At a signal, cannons boomed, and the Spaniards charged. In a little while, thousands of Inca soldiers lay dead. Atahualpa was the prisoner of Pizarro.

Pizarro promised to release Atahualpa if the Inca would bring enough gold to fill a large room where the emperor was being held. Atahualpa's people wanted to help him, and

ACTIVITY

Objective: To classify information

Make a list that contains important information about the Aztecs and the Inca. The list should include such topics as Aztec and Incan agriculture, religion, housing, etc. Leave out all references to either group as you write the list on the chalkboard or give a copy to each student. Have the class decide which group the information is about. Put an A next to those items that refer to the Aztecs and an I next to those items that refer to the Inca.

DISCUSSION

In a discussion, have the students compare the general term civilized (i.e., at an advanced stage of development; progressed from a primitive society to a highly developed one) with the more specific, historical definition given the term in the text (i.e., characterized by cities and city life, with a specialized work force). Try to reach a class consensus about how to use the term so that each student knows what the others mean when they use words like civilized, civilization, and uncivilized.

so they brought great amounts of gold to the Spaniards. In a short time, the room was filled several times over with both gold and silver, but that did not satisfy the *conquistadores*. Pizarro falsely accused Atahualpa of trying to get the Inca to revolt. Finally, the Spanish leader put the king on trial for his life and had him killed.

In 1533 Pizarro and his soldiers marched from Cajamarca to Cuzco. As they traveled, they destroyed cities, farms, and thousands of people. In the end, the Inca suffered the same fate as the Aztecs had—the destruction of their civilization.

In Search of Lost Cities

In Mexico and Peru, the Spaniards had found riches beyond belief. In their dreams, they saw other such golden civilizations. Yet there were no more. Still, for years Spanish explorers continued to search. They searched for the legendary kingdoms of Bimini, Cibola, Quivera, and California. Many areas of the country we call the United States were explored by Spaniards searching for these wealthy kingdoms. Examine the chart on page 57 for details.

The Spanish Viceroyalties

San Jose Mission, near San Antonio, Texas, was built in 1720. It became one of the most successful missions in Texas. Its ornate carvings are typical of many Spanish churches of that time.

By the 1540s the Spanish claims in the Americas were vast. They extended from the southernmost point in South America to the northernmost point in New Mexico, about 7000 miles (11,200 kilometers). The Spanish king, therefore, decided he could not run his possessions well from his palace in Spain. He chose two people to go to the Americas to govern in his place. Such people are called *viceroys*. The Viceroy of New Spain put his capital in Mexico City. The other one, the Viceroy of Peru, set himself up in Lima, Peru. (See the map of Spanish lands in the Americas on page 58.)

From these capital cities, the viceroys sent out military governors to run the parts of their viceroyalties. These governors lived in capital cities such as Santa Fe in New Mexico and San Antonio in Texas. The military governors, in turn, sent soldiers to watch over even smaller towns. These soldiers lived on military bases called *presidios*.

At the same time that the king's viceroys set up their governmental organization, a different kind of community was also springing up. These communities began as religious centers and were called *missions*.

SPANISH EXPLORERS OF NORTH AMERICA

Explorer	Goal	Experiences
Ponce de León	Bimini	Ponce de León, governor of Puerto Rico, heard of an island called Bimini. Bimini was supposed to be a rich land with a wonderful spring of water. A person who drank from the spring would stay young forever. Ponce de León set out in 1513 to find Bimini and this "Fountain of Youth," but he had no luck. Instead he discovered the Florida Peninsula and claimed it for the Spanish king. Years later, in 1565, the Spanish built a town that is the oldest city in the United States, St. Augustine.
Narváez, Cabeza de Vaca, and Estevanico	Cibola	Narváez, another royal official, went to Tampa Bay in Florida in 1528 in search of gold. Finding none, Narváez and his group of four hundred settlers left for Mexico. A storm shipwrecked the group and only a few people survived. Cabeza de Vaca and Estevanico, a black servant, were among those who lived. The two wandered together for many years throughout the Southwest and finally reached Mexico City. In Mexico City, Cabeza de Vaca described an imaginary golden kingdom called the "Seven Cities of Cibola." Soon all the Spanish settlements in Mexico and the Caribbean were buzzing about the wealthy Seven Cities of Cibola to the north of Mexico.
De Soto	Cibola	De Soto heard the stories of Cibola and in 1539 went to Florida with six hundred *conquistadores* to search for it. From there, he traveled through what are now the states of Georgia, Alabama, Mississippi, Louisiana, Arkansas, and Oklahoma. Cibola was nowhere to be found. Weary and sick, De Soto died near the banks of the Mississippi River in 1542. His *conquistadores* finally reached Mexico in 1543. As a result of the exploration of western Florida, the Spanish set up a town called Pensacola in 1698.
Estevanico, Marcos de Niza	Cibola	Estevanico and Friar De Niza, a missionary explorer, went to New Mexico in1539 looking for Cibola. In western New Mexico, Friar De Niza, the leader of the group, sent Estevanico ahead. After a time, Estevanico saw the pueblos of the Zuñi Indians from a distance. They glistened in the sun and seemed covered with gold. Estevanico sent word to Friar De Niza that he had found Cibola. Shortly afterwards, the Zuñi killed Estevanico, but the false news of the discovery of Cibola was already out.
Coronado	Cibola, Quivera	Coronado led a huge army of *conquistadores* to New Mexico in search of Cibola. Coronado conquered many pueblos, and his soldiers discovered the Grand Canyon in northwestern Arizona. Still, Cibola was nowhere to be found. Instead, Coronado heard a new story of another fabulously rich kingdom called Quivera. Quivera was supposed to be located northeast of New Mexico in present-day Kansas. Quivera was just as hard to find as Cibola. In Kansas, Coronado found only a few huts of the Wichita Indians. In 1542, Coronado returned to Mexico City empty-handed.
Cabrillo	California	Cabrillo sailed up the California coast looking for a legendary island called California. The island, like Bimini, Cibola, and Quivera, was supposed to be filled with riches. Pearls were supposed to be lying in the streets ready for anyone to take. In 1542 Cabrillo sailed into San Diego Bay and claimed the area around it for Spain. Unfortunately, he did not find the rich island for which he searched. But he did discover part of present-day California.

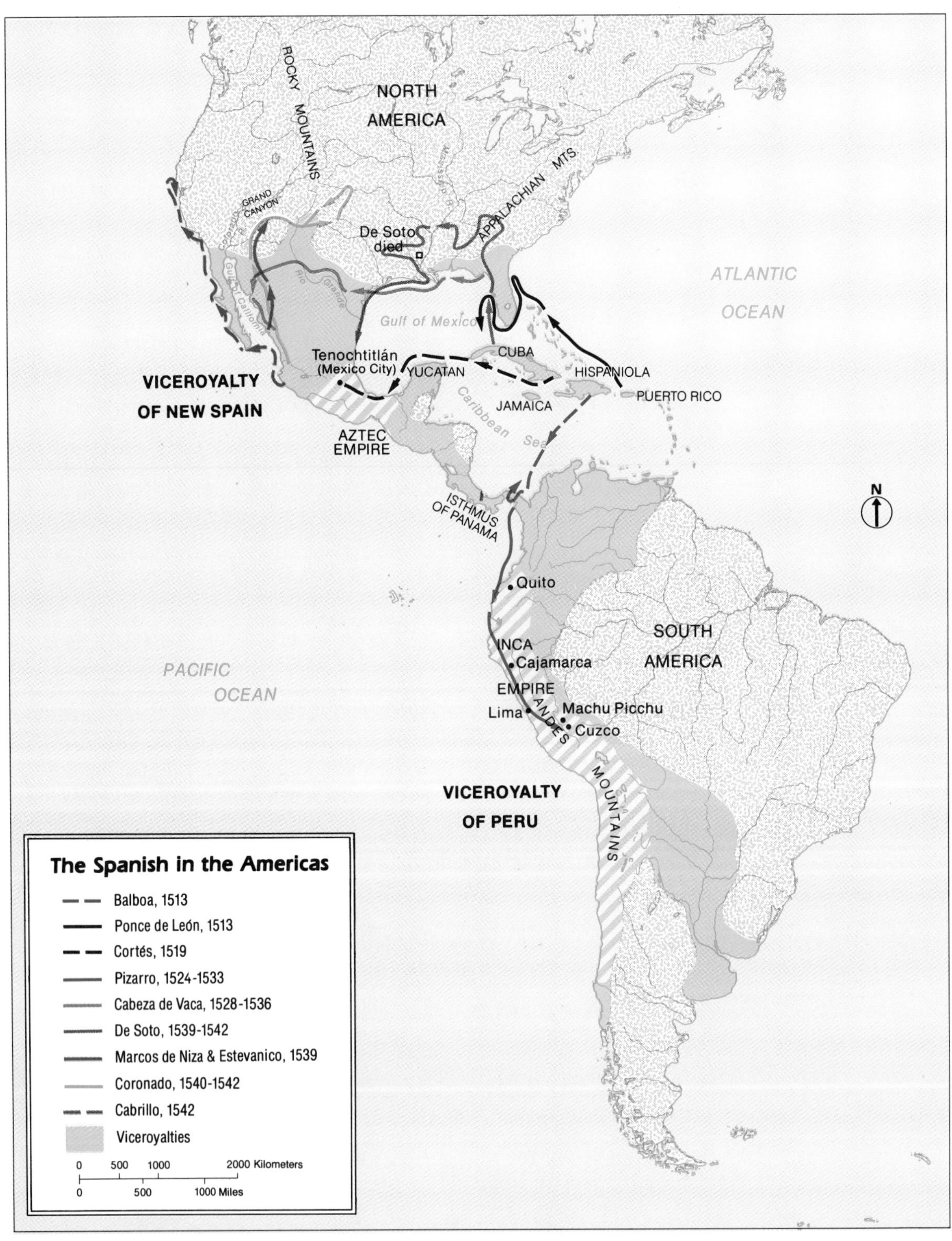

NORTH
AMERICA
ROCKY MOUNTAINS
APPALACHIAN MTS.
GRAND CANYON
De Soto died
ATLANTIC
OCEAN
Gulf of Mexico
Tenochtitlán
(Mexico City)
YUCATAN
CUBA
HISPANIOLA
PUERTO RICO
JAMAICA
Caribbean Sea
VICEROYALTY
OF NEW SPAIN
AZTEC
EMPIRE
ISTHMUS
OF PANAMA
N
Quito
SOUTH
AMERICA
INCA
Cajamarca
EMPIRE
Lima
Machu Picchu
Cuzco
ANDES
MOUNTAINS
PACIFIC
OCEAN
VICEROYALTY
OF PERU
The Spanish in the Americas
Balboa, 1513
Ponce de León, 1513
Cortés, 1519
Pizarro, 1524-1533
Cabeza de Vaca, 1528-1536
De Soto, 1539-1542
Marcos de Niza & Estevanico, 1539
Coronado, 1540-1542
Cabrillo, 1542
Viceroyalties
0 500 1000 2000 Kilometers
0 500 1000 Miles

Religious groups of the Roman Catholic Church sent missionaries out among the American Indians. Missionaries hoped to convert the Indians to Christianity. Missionaries built their churches, schools, hospitals, homes, and farms. Towns grew up around them. In the towns lived a few Spanish settlers and many American Indians who worked for the settlers and missionaries.

The presence of a mission and a town called for protection. So the viceroys set up a *presidio* nearby. Some of the towns built around a mission were San Antonio and El Paso in Texas, Santa Fe and Albuquerque in New Mexico, and San Diego and San Francisco in California.

Father Junípero Serra founded San Diego de Alcalá, the first Spanish mission in what is now California. By 1823 Franciscan missionaries had established a string of twenty-one missions, each a day's walk from the next along the coast of California.

Relationship with the Indians. Some of the settlers in New Spain were special friends of the Spanish king. These special friends received *land grants* in the New World. That is, they became owners of a certain place. They were also put in charge of the Indians living there. These people were called *encomenderos*. The *encomenderos* could put the Indians to work doing whatever the Spanish wished: clearing land, farming, mining, building roads.

The Indians did not live well under the *encomendero* system. They were, in fact, slaves. Indian men were away from home months at a time; many never saw their families again. Their traditional lifestyles, as a result, all but disappeared. Furthermore, diseases brought to the New World by the Spanish (such as smallpox and measles) killed many Indians because they had no natural immunity to them. So many Indians died from overwork and disease that whole culture groups came close to disappearing.

Attempts to Help the Indians. Some Spanish religious people tried to help the Indians. Bartolomé de Las Casas was one of them. Las Casas worked to get proper food, clothing, and shelter for the Indians of the *encomenderos*. He also urged that Indian children be educated in mission schools so that they would accept the Spanish way of living. Despite the help of Las Casas and others, the Indians continued to die at an alarming rate.

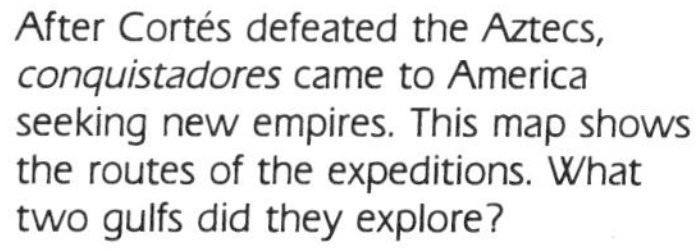

After Cortés defeated the Aztecs, *conquistadores* came to America seeking new empires. This map shows the routes of the expeditions. What two gulfs did they explore?

Gulf of Mexico and Gulf of California

Many slaves who worked on the sugar plantations lost their teeth early in life as a result of decay caused by chewing sugar cane.

The Spanish believed that they might relieve the Indians of their heavy labor by bringing black slaves to the New World to do it. As early as 1501, African blacks arrived to work in the Spanish mines. Later they were put to work on sugar plantations. Between 1550 and 1750, the Spanish brought at least three thousand slaves a year from Africa. Most of these slaves worked on Caribbean Islands, although some were brought to New Spain and Peru.

Black slaves in Spanish colonies could marry and buy their own freedom as well as the freedom of members of their families. They could go to court to protect the few rights they had. Still, their lives were very hard. They worked much, and they left their native cultures behind—forever.

Few Indians actually benefited from the arrival of black slaves. Many Indians had already died. The practice of forcing blacks to leave their homes in Africa simply caused the cruelty of slavery to be spread to another group.

Indian Rebellion in New Mexico. In New Mexico, the American Indians rebelled against the harsh treatment of the Spanish *encomendero* system. In 1675 Popé, an American Indian from the San Juan Pueblo, decided that the Indians had to force the Spanish to leave New Mexico. This was the only way he could see for the Indians to regain their old lifestyle. Popé moved from San Juan Pueblo to Taos Pueblo and began organizing the Indians against the Spanish. Finally, in 1680, the Indians attacked. When the assault was

The *conquistadores* put Indians to work constructing Spanish palaces and other buildings. Indian slaves were treated so harshly that many died.

over, more than four hundred Spaniards lay dead. The rest fled the Santa Fe area for El Paso.

For ten years, the Pueblo again lived in their old ways, without Spanish rule. Then in 1690, the Spanish returned. This time hundreds of Pueblo were killed. By 1692 the Europeans were in complete control again.

Peace allowed a particular New Spain lifestyle to develop. It included an easy, sociable life for the Spanish who enjoyed the land grants from the king. They built large ranch houses for themselves called *haciendas*.

The Spanish *encomenderos* were the richest, most powerful people in New Spain. Next to the *encomenderos* were the government officials, priests, and missionaries. The Indians and the blacks of the *encomenderos* were the poorest people in New Spain and had few real rights.

ANSWER THESE QUESTIONS

1. What were the names of the emperors of the Aztec and Inca empires?
2. Who were the Spanish leaders who conquered these empires?
3. Why did Montezuma think Cortés was Quetzalcoatl?
4. How were the civilizations of the Aztecs, the Inca, and New Spain alike?
5. How were the civilizations of these groups different?

ANSWER THESE QUESTIONS

1. Montezuma II was emperor of the Aztecs; Atahualpa was emperor of the Inca.
2. Hernando Cortés conquered the Aztecs; Francisco Pizarro conquered the Inca.
3. The legend of Quetzalcoatl told that the fair-skinned god would return from the east, which the fair-skinned Cortés did.
4. Answers will vary; each civilization had a government, religion, specialization of labor, and cities.
5. Answers will vary; each civilization had a different way of life.

Objective: After completing these pages, the students should be able to skim materials to collect information.

Working with Skills

READING SKILLS

ACTIVITY

Objective: To identify a primary source

Review with the class the definition of a primary source, the forms a primary source may take, and the usefulness of a primary source to historians. Ask students to think of primary sources that they come in contact with every day. List their suggestions on the chalkboard. Some suggestions may be: diaries, letters, newspapers, and notes from friends. Now ask students to list other documents that may be in their home. This may be difficult and may require your participation. List the following: birth certificate, rental contract, mortgage agreement, bank statement, stocks and bonds, deeds, tax forms, and report cards. Divide the class into small groups. Have each group decide on a primary source document to bring to class. Make sure students bring in a copy of the document, not the original. Also make sure that the group does not bring in a document that the family considers private. On the day when the documents arrive at school, divide the class into small groups. Then ask each group to answer the following questions about its document:

1. What is its title?
2. What information does the document contain? (who, what, where, when?)
3. Is this document a legal one? (That is, does it contain agreements that each party accepts?)
4. How can you tell?

Compare the answers arrived at by each group.

Skimming Materials to Collect Information

The paragraphs below were written by Cabeza de Vaca, who was shipwrecked in 1528 on an island off the coast of Texas. These paragraphs, describing the shipwreck, are an entry in Cabeza de Vaca's diary.

At the distance of two crossbow shots from shore we took in water over the side of our boat that completely soaked us. . . . The next blow the sea struck us capsized the boat. Three men held fast to her to save themselves. But the boat carried them over, and they were drowned.

As the surf near the shore was very high, a single roll of the sea threw the rest of our men half drowned upon the shore of the island. The survivors escaped as naked as they were born, losing everything they owned. Although their possessions were of little value, at that time they were worth much, because we were then in November and the cold was severe.

Looking like death itself we were so thin the bones of our bodies could be counted easily. For myself I can say that from the month of May on, I had eaten nothing other than corn, and sometimes I had to eat that uncooked. . . .

Thanks be to our Lord that, looking among the ashes we had left on shore, we found sparks from which we made great fires. And thus were we asking mercy of Him . . . shedding many tears. . . .

At sunset, the Indians came. . . . I gave them to understand by signs that our boat had sunk and three of our number had been drowned. . . .

At the sight of what had happened to us, and our state of suffering, the Indians sat down among us. From the sorrow and pity they felt, they all began to cry so earnestly that they might have been heard at a distance, and continued doing so more than half an hour. It was strange to see these men, wild and untaught, howling . . . over our misfortunes. It caused in me, as in others, an increase of feeling and a livelier sense of our great disaster.

This diary is called a primary source. A primary source is a first-hand account of some event. A primary source may be a

RELATED MATERIAL
Duplicator/Copy Master Activity 5

diary, letter, poem, song, or document. Historians use various primary sources to piece together an account of past events. In this way they attempt to learn what really happened in history.

In your first reading of the diary, you read each sentence carefully in order to understand exactly what happened. You can probably recall some specific details. If you were asked to answer questions about the entry, however, you would reread it more quickly. This quick second reading is called skimming. You skim a document in order to locate information quickly.

Skim the first paragraph. Look for the sentence that tells what happened to Cabeza de Vaca on that day. Did he shoot a crossbow twice? Was he soaked and did his boat capsize? Or did he save three men? Which is the correct answer?

Read the questions below. Then skim the last five paragraphs about Cabeza de Vaca's experiences to find the answers to the questions.

1. What did the survivors bring with them to the shore?
2. In what month did the accident occur?
3. What food did Cabeza de Vaca eat beginning in the month of May?
4. What did the Spaniards look like?
5. What did the explorers find on shore?
6. When did the Indians come to the island?
7. What was the Indians' reaction to this disaster?
8. What effect did the Indians' reaction have on the Spaniards?

ANSWERS

Questions in Paragraph:

no

he was soaked and his boat capsized

no

NUMBERED QUESTIONS:

1. nothing
2. November
3. corn
4. "like death itself"
5. sparks from which they made fires
6. at sunset
7. they cried
8. an increase in feeling and a livelier sense of disaster

CONTENT OBJECTIVES

After completing the lesson, students will know:

- the achievements of Samuel de Champlain
- the contributions of the *voyageurs* and *coureurs de bois* to New France
- the significance of the explorations along the Mississippi River by Joliet, Marquette, and LaSalle
- the fact that New France suffered from underpopulation
- the governmental structure of New France

VOCABULARY

alliance: an agreement between two or more groups to help each other in times of trouble

voyageur: a fur trader who traveled intc the wilderness of New France in search of furs

coureur de bois: a trapper who lived among the Indians of New France and often had a bad reputation

portage: a path between two rivers along which people must carry their boats

immigrant: a person who comes to live in one country after leaving his or her home country

seigneur: a French noble who was offered land cheaply to encourage immigration to New France

seigneuries: the land purchased by seigneurs

habitant: a simple person who worked the land of the wealthy and paid rent to the landowner

intendant: an official appointed by the king of France who held the real power in New France

ruling council: a group of officers that made the everyday decisions in New France, including writing the laws, seeing that they were obeyed, and judging those who disobeyed.

3-2 New France

As you read, think about these questions:

Why was Samuel de Champlain called the Father of New France?

Why were the *voyageurs* and *coureurs de bois* important to the success of New France?

How did the exploration of the Mississippi widen France's claim in North America?

What type of government was established in New France?

Special Vocabulary	alliance	immigrant	*habitant*
	voyageur	*seigneur*	*intendant*
	coureur de bois	*seigneuries*	ruling council
	portage		

Other nations besides Spain made claims in North America. Unlike Spain, however, these nations were slow to settle the areas they had discovered earlier. For example, France took more than sixty years before it set up a lasting colony in the place the Indians called Canada.

Champlain: The Father of New France

Without the work of one person, the settlement of New France might have been delayed longer than it was. That person was Samuel de Champlain, the Father of New France.

Champlain's life was filled with enough excitement and great discoveries to satisfy ten explorers. It was Champlain who set up the towns of Quebec and Montreal (in 1608 and 1611). He made *alliances* between the Algonkians and Huron and the French. An alliance is an agreement between groups to help each other in times of trouble. He discovered Lake Huron, fought against the Iroquois and the English, and became the governor of New France. The story of Champlain's life is a large part of the story of New France.

Fur Trading in New France. Another part of the story of early New France is about two kinds of adventurers. These adventurers lived lives just as exciting as Champlain's. However, no

In the painting above, Samuel de Champlain supervises the building of a wall in Montreal in about 1630. The bricks were probably ballast, heavy material used to steady ships on their voyages to New France.

individual among them became as famous as the Father of New France. These kinds of adventurers were called *voyageurs* and *coureurs de bois.*

The *voyageurs* were fur traders who traveled into the wilderness of New France in search of furs. Furs were valuable in Europe. During the 1600s, rich people in Europe wanted hats made of the soft fur from the undersides of beavers. *Voyageurs* traveled throughout New France bargaining with Indians for these furs. On such trips, the *voyageurs* claimed for the French king all the land watered by the rivers they found.

The *coureurs de bois* hunted and trapped in the woods and sold furs to the people of New France. They knew just as much about the wilderness as the *voyageurs* did. The *coureurs de bois,* however, had bad reputations in the colonial towns of New France. They had left the laws of France and New France behind and lived according to their own rules. This sometimes caused trouble. They therefore earned the name *coureurs de bois,* which means "runners of the woods."

Both the *voyageurs* and the *coureurs de bois* lived lives quite unlike anything ordinary French people could imagine. They made their homes among the American Indians. Some *voyageurs* and *coureurs de bois* married Indian women. Their children knew more about Indian lifestyles than about French customs. Étienne Brûle is an example of such a *coureur de bois.* At first, Brûle was Champlain's friend. He

Jean Nicolet's beautiful robe was made of Chinese cloth. Nicolet carried the robe to wear in case he reached China.

lived among the Huron and explored the Great Lakes region. Later, Brûle became an enemy of New France and sided with the British. In the end, Brûle was not welcome in the towns of New France. He lived the rest of his life among the Huron.

Searching for the Sea of the North. In time, the *voyageurs* and *coureurs de bois* pressed ever deeper into the North American wilderness. For example, by 1634, Jean Nicolet went west to Lake Michigan. He followed its western shore all the way to Green Bay in present-day Wisconsin and discovered the mouth of the Fox River. Nicolet hoped that the Fox River led to the "Sea of the North" and to far-off China. He was diasppointed, of course. Instead, he found that the river wound its way through present-day southern Wisconsin and northern Illinois. Nicolet was the first European to visit this part of North America.

Reaching Southward

The search for a river leading to the "Sea of the North" continued after the deaths of Champlain and Nicolet. In 1672 a trader named Louis Joliet planned a trip to the mouth of the Fox River. He wanted to take up the search for a passage to the Pacific Ocean where Nicolet had left off. Nicolet had heard of the Mississippi River, but he had known nothing of its course. Joliet hoped it ran westward into the Pacific Ocean.

Joliet had other goals as well. He hoped to make friends with the Indians along the way. He wanted to map the country. And most of all, Joliet wanted to claim all lands in

IN · HONOR · OF
LOUIS·JOLLIET·&·PÈRE·JACQUES·MARQUETTE
THE·FIRST
WHITE·MEN·TO
PASS·THROUGH
THE
CHICAGO·RIVER
SEPTEMBER
1673
THIS·TABLET·IS
PLACED·BY·THE
ILLINOIS·SOCIETY
OF·THE
COLONIAL·DAMES
OF
AMERICA
UNDER·THE·AUSPICES·OF·THE
CHICAGO·HISTORICAL·SOCIETY
1925

Father Jacques Marquette, seated in the front canoe, was important to Joliet's expedition because he could speak various Indian languages.

the Mississippi Valley for France as the king had instructed him to do. To help accomplish this goal, Joliet decided to take Father Jacques Marquette, a priest, along on the trip.

Exploring the Mississippi. In 1673 Joliet, Marquette, and their group paddled their canoes toward the mouth of the Fox River at Green Bay. They stopped there and gathered information from Indians. Then the French explorers went up the Fox River as far as they could. They found an Indian *portage* from the Fox to the Wisconsin River. A portage is a path between two rivers along which people must carry their boats. The group paddled down the Wisconsin to the place where it entered the Mississippi River.

The French were disappointed that the Mississippi flowed south instead of west toward the Pacific Ocean. But the goal of Joliet and Marquette was to find the mouth of the Mississippi, so they continued traveling down the river. In the place called Arkansas today, the group met Shawnee Indians who told the French that the Mississippi entered the Gulf of Mexico, not the Pacific Ocean.

La Salle and Louisiana. A second French voyage down the Mississippi began in January 1682. Robert Cavelier, Sieur de La Salle, set out with fifty-four people—twenty-three of them French, thirty-one Indians—to explore the Mississippi River. The trip was long and hard. Three months later, in April, La Salle and his people reached the mouth of the Mississippi and looked out on the Gulf of Mexico.

La Salle claimed all the lands watered by the Mississippi and the rivers that entered it. He named the claim Louisiana after Louis XIV, the king of France. (Examine the map on page 68 to get an idea of the size of the French claim.)

La Salle had dreams of setting up a French colony in the Mississippi River Valley. Back in France, he worked out a

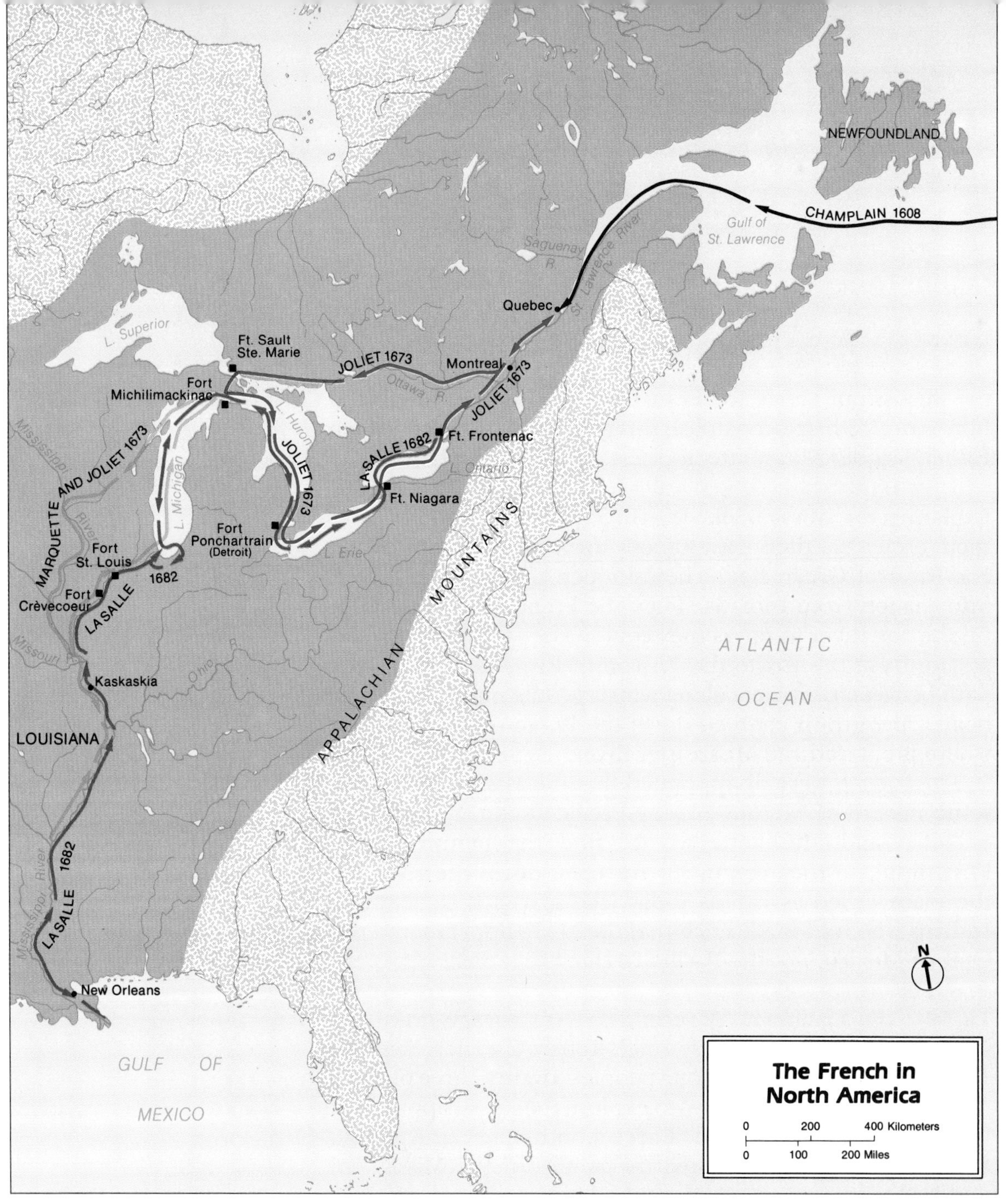

This map illustrates the expeditions of Champlain, Marquette, Joliet, and La Salle. What physical feature is common to all the forts and cities the French established?

They are all on rivers or lakes.

careful plan and sailed again in 1684 for the Gulf of Mexico. The mouth of the Mississippi River was his goal. There he hoped to set up a town to show the Spanish that other Europeans had claims in North America, too.

Unfortunately, La Salle's plan suffered some serious setbacks. Many of the people who intended to be settlers became sick on the trip across the Atlantic. Then La Salle was unable to find the mouth of the Mississippi and, instead, landed on the coast of Texas, part of New Spain. By this time, only a handful of his people remained alive. La Salle made two unsuccessful attempts to reach the Mississippi by traveling overland. On the third attempt, the people mutinied and killed La Salle. The people then tried on their own to set up a town in Texas. They failed. Several of them died of sickness and hunger. The Spanish captured the few survivors and sent them off to Mexico as prisoners.

Immigration to New France

Most French people saw little hope for a good life in New France. Because of this, Canada and Louisiana failed to lure large numbers of *immigrants* from France. An immigrant is a person who comes to live in one country after leaving his or her home country.

In 1627 the king allowed a company with a special new purpose to be formed in France. The company's goals were to build up the fur trading business of New France and to attract French immigrants to Canada. The company, called the One Hundred Associates, got its name from the number of people who gave money to start it in business.

In the 1630s Samuel de Champlain was the governor of New France, working for the One Hundred Associates and for the king. As governor, Champlain tried to encourage immigration by setting up towns such as Montreal. He sent missionaries into the wilderness to convert the Indians to

ACTIVITY

Objective: To skim material to collect information

List these dates on the chalkboard: 1617, 1627, 1630, 1660, 1663, 1665-1671, 1660-1700. Have students skim the section of Lesson 3-2 "Immigration to New France," pp. 69-72. The students should look for these dates and how they relate to attempts to encourage immigration to New France. Ask students to make their own chronological list of the dates and the information that goes with them.

DISCUSSION

Have the students discuss the following questions: By what right did the Europeans make claims to own areas in the New World? If they had a right, was that right moral? Did it depend solely on the doctrine "might makes right?" Then question the students as to whether present-day Americans have a responsibility to rectify immoral actions taken more than 400 years ago.

Montreal was first named *Ville-Marie* (Mary's City). The city later became well-known for its mountain *Mont Reál* (Royal Mountain). By the 1700s the city was called Montreal.

Christianity. He hoped this would make the countryside safe for Europeans. The measures he took did not work. Soon the king and the French company knew that greater attractions must be promised if many Europeans were to come to New France.

The One Hundred Associates decided to sell land cheaply to French nobles to get them to come to America. These nobles were called *seigneurs*. The land they bought got the name *seigneuries*. *Seigneuries* were cleared for farming and rented to simple people who worked the land and paid rent. These *habitants*, as the French called them, followed the same customs as they had back in Europe. Besides rent, they owed the *seigneurs* loyalty. They also were pledged to donate six days of work to their *seigneurs* each year.

The European Population of New France. The *seigneur* system also failed to lure large numbers of immigrants to New France. By 1660 all of New France had less than two thousand people.

The least promising fact about New France was that most of the two thousand or so French people who lived there were men. European women did not come to New France until 1617, when Louis Hebert arrived in Quebec with his wife and daughters. Just two years later, Hélène Champlain, the wife of Samuel de Champlain, joined her husband in Quebec. Hélène Champlain hated the lonely life of the Canadian wilderness and returned to France after four years in New France.

From 1665 to 1671, French officials organized a program for sending young, single women to live in Quebec. These women were most often orphans or the daughters of poor families. Their hopes for a good life in France were very dim. In New France, they would be a vital part of a growing, new society.

The *"filles du roi,"* or the "king's girls," as they were called, began arriving in Quebec in 1665. About 150 of them came to New France under the watchful eyes of Catholic nuns. For fifteen days, men from all over New France came to Quebec to try to arrange marriage agreements with the young women. This practice continued for only six years, but hundreds of young women came to New France in this way. Between the years 1660 and 1700, the European population of Canada increased about six times, from about 2,500 to about 15,300.

The beautifully dressed *"filles du roi"* were given a dowry by the king to make marriage attractive to the men. The dowry was usually an ox, a cow, two chickens, two pigs, two barrels of salted meat, and a few coins.

New France: The Royal Colony. By the mid-1600s, the French king decided that Canada needed a different kind of government. He declared that the company of One Hundred Associates should no longer run Canada. From this time on, New France became a royal colony, run by two officials appointed by the king himself. Under the new system, the colony still had a governor as it had had in the days of Champlain. Now, however, the governor was simply a soldier who saw to the safety of the colony.

Another official, called the *intendant*, held the real power in New France. He answered only to the king of France for his decisions. He had no responsibility to the business people, to the church, or even to the *seigneurs* of New France. The only person with more power over what happened in New France was the king himself.

The *intendant* of New France was the leading member of a *ruling council*. The ruling council was a group of officers that made the everyday decisions. Its members wrote laws, saw that they were obeyed, and judged people who did not follow them. In charge of all these activities was the *intendant*.

The first royal *intendant* was Jean Talon. Talon served twice, first from 1663 to 1668 and again from 1670 to 1672. On his arrival in 1663, Talon began working hard to build up the fur trade, encourage immigration, help the missionaries convert Indians to Christianity, and explore new lands.

The Comte de Frontenac sails in a birch bark canoe to Fort Cataraqui on Lake Ontario. Frontenac's hot temper often got him into trouble, but he was successful in governing New France.

The Defense of New France. The jobs of governor and *intendant* of New France grew more and more difficult as the years passed. Even as Quebec and Montreal grew stronger, the English colonies to the south were pressing westward. New Spain, near Louisiana, was jealously guarding its claims. The French believed that they had to build a strong system of forts with hundreds of soldiers ready, if needed, to fight against the English and Spanish.

The governor who served from 1672 to 1682 did much to protect Canada and Louisiana from the English and the Spanish. Louis de Baude, Comte de Frontenac, built a string of forts along the borders of New France. (Examine the map on page 68 to see where these forts were built.)

The French were wise to fear the English in America. In Europe the countries of England and France were long-time enemies who believed that the New World was just one more area in which they should fight against each other. Between 1629 and 1760, five wars took place between England and France in the New World. The last of these wars, beginning in 1754, resulted in the end of the French government's presence in Canada and the beginning of the English possession of the area. (See Chapter 5, pages 111–121 for a description of this war.)

ANSWER THESE QUESTIONS

1. Why was Champlain called the Father of New France?
2. What did the *habitants* owe the *seigneurs* for the privilege of farming the land?
3. Why was the fur trade an important business in New France?
4. Why was it so difficult to encourage people to come to New France?
5. Would you have gone to New France? Why or why not?

ANSWER THESE QUESTIONS

1. his work made possible the settlement of New France
2. rent, loyalty, and six days of work each year
3. Furs were very valuable in Europe.
4. Most French people saw little hope for a good life in New France.
5. Answers will vary; fur trade was profitable and the land was beautiful, but life in the wilderness was lonely.

LAW AND THE CITIZEN

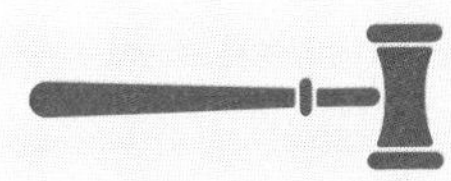

Monarchy

For many centuries, people in Europe were governed by strong kings and queens who had few limits on their power. Royalty had to answer to no representatives of the people. This kind of government was called an absolute monarchy.

How did these kings and queens get so much power? The answer to this question is more than just having thousands of soldiers and government officials to force people to follow orders. The real answer to the question is this: For a long time, the people themselves accepted the idea that God chose kings and queens. Whole nations, rulers and common people alike, believed that royal power came from heaven. Disobeying a royal law was the same thing as disobeying a law of God. This belief was known as the divine right of kings.

Two of the most powerful absolute monarchs in Europe during the period of exploration and colonization were Charles V of Spain and Louis XIV of France. Like all absolute monarchs, these two kings held all the power in their nations.

What kinds of power did these kings have? They had legislative power, that is, they made all the laws. They had executive power. This means that they saw to it that their laws were enforced, or carried out. They also had judicial power, which means that they judged those who did not follow their decisions or who broke their laws. Of course, these kings could not be everywhere. They had officials who also made decisions, carried them out, and judged lawbreakers. The officials were backed up by the king's army. These officials and soldiers answered to the king for their actions.

Both Charles V and Louis XIV realized that they would not be able to govern their New World claims from far away in Europe. Therefore, they appointed people to rule on their behalf, that is, in place of them. These were the viceroys of New Spain and Peru and the *intendant* of New France. They held legislative, executive, and judicial powers in the territories of the New World claimed by Spain and France.

The goals of the kings of Spain and France regarding the management of their claims in America were easy to understand. They wanted government and law in America to be a copy of government and law in Europe.

THINKING THINGS THROUGH

1. All were Spanish explorers who searched for legendary kingdoms. **2.** *Encomenderos* were wealthy settlers who were given land grants by the Spanish king. *Seigneurs* were French nobles who bought land in America. Both were wealthy landowners in America. **3.** Indian slaves did the work on Spanish farms. *Habitants* did the work on French farms. The *encomenderos* were

Chapter 3 SUMMARY

Both the Spanish and the French followed up their New World exploration by establishing colonies in the areas they claimed. Taking control of these lands was sometimes difficult for the Spanish. Only after bloody battles did Cortés and Pizarro gain New Spain and Peru.

The Spanish king ruled through viceroys he sent to the New World. Under these leaders the Spanish set up a New World society. They also sent out explorers to look for legendary American Indian kingdoms such as Bimini, Cibola, Quivera, and California. These kingdoms did not exist, but in searching for them, the Spanish explored and settled a large part of the Southeast and Southwest of the present-day United States.

In New France, the French created useful alliances with the American Indians. Champlain, the Father of New France, became friends with the Algonkians and with the Huron.

Some of the French in early Canada made remarkable journeys of exploration. *Voyageurs, coureurs de bois*, and missionary priests extended French claims in the New World to the Great Lakes, the Mississippi Valley, and finally to all of Louisiana.

The French set up fur trading as a business in Canada. They also hoped to turn the region into an area of small farms rented to common people by noble landowners. All attempts to greatly increase the population of New France failed.

Chapter 3 TEST

WORDS TO REMEMBER

Match each of the following words with the correct definition below.

e 1. *conquistadores*
f 2. civilization
m 3. specialization of labor
a 4. viceroy
b 5. *presidios*
i 6. *encomenderos*
c 7. alliances
d 8. *voyageurs*
l 9. *coureurs de bois*
g 10. immigrant
h 11. *seigneurs*
j 12. *habitants*
k 13. *intendant*

a. a Spanish governor
b. military bases
c. agreements between groups to help each other in times of trouble
d. fur traders
e. conquerors
f. a society in which people build cities and work at jobs other than farming
g. a person who comes to live in one country after leaving his or her home country
h. French nobles
i. wealthy settlers who were given land grants by the Spanish king
j. farmers who paid rent to a landowner
k. an official who held the power in New France
l. "runners of the woods"
m. a system in which each person has his or her own job to do

RELATED MATERIALS

Duplicator/Copy Masters: Activities 5, 6; Quiz 3
Workbook pages 7-9

put in charge of Indians who lived on their land, whereas the French had to try to lure immigrants to New France. **4.** Women who were orphans or poor were brought to Quebec by a program started by French officials. **5.** Viceroys were responsible to the king of Spain, and *intendants* were responsible to the king of France.

WORKING WITH SKILLS

Ponce de León, 1513, Florida; Narváez, 1528, Florida; De Soto, 1539, Georgia, Alabama, Mississippi, Louisiana, Arkansas, and Oklahoma; Estevanico and Marcos de Niza, 1539, New Mexico; Coronado, 1542, New Mexico, Arizona, and Kansas; Cabrillo, 1542, the California coast.

THINKING THINGS THROUGH

Answer the following questions in complete sentences.

1. What did the following men all have in common: Ponce de León, Narváez, Cabeza de Vaca, De Soto, De Niza, Coronado, Cabrillo?
2. What is the difference between the *encomenderos* and the *seigneurs*? How are they alike?
3. Who did the work on Spanish farms? On French farms? Why do you think these two nations did not solve the shortage of labor in the same way?
4. What steps were taken to encourage women to come to New France?
5. How was the Spanish government under the viceroy similar to the French government under the *intendant*?

WORKING WITH SKILLS

Skim the material in the chart entitled Spanish Explorers of North America. For each explorer listed, tell the date of the exploration and the parts of the present-day United States that were explored.

ON YOUR OWN

1. Imagine that you are Jean Talon writing a letter to the king of France. Outline for the king the problems facing New France and the solutions that you see for them. Be specific as to what you have done to solve these problems. Use the information in your book as a guide.
2. Using magazines, newspapers, and travel posters, find examples of Spanish and French culture in the United States today. Architecture, words, foods, and art are good examples to use. Cut out these examples and paste them on poster board for a bulletin-board display.
3. Look at the photograph on this page. It shows drawings made on stone cliffs by some of the Navajo people of the American Southwest. The artists drew scenes they had actually witnessed. Write a brief paragraph describing the scene from the Navajo's point of view.

WORDS TO REMEMBER

1. thoughtful guess based on a collection of facts to explain how and why something happens 2. huge sheets of ice 3. everything about a place—climate, land, water sources, and plant life 4. one or more settlements 5. the science of determining a ship's position and course 6. open rebellion 7. a society in which people build cities and work at jobs other than farming 8. people who come to live in one country after leaving their home country

THINK THINGS THROUGH

1. The Aztecs stoned Montezuma to death because they thought he was a coward. The Inca believed that Atahualpa was a god, and they brought great amounts of gold and silver to the Spaniards to save him. 2. Both the Anasazi and the Aztecs

Unit 1 TEST

WORDS TO REMEMBER

Write a definition for the word in italics in each of the following sentences.

1. Scientists and historians have a *theory* about the arrival of people in North America.
2. During the Ice Age, *glaciers* covered much of North America.
3. The *environment* of North America influenced the lifestyles of the early Americans.
4. The Vikings set up a *colony* on Iceland.
5. Prince Henry established a school of *navigation* to encourage exploration.
6. Columbus's crew began to speak of *mutiny* because they lost faith in their captain.
7. By the 1500s the Aztec *civilization* had spread throughout most of present-day Mexico.
8. New France failed to attract many *immigrants* from France.

QUESTIONS TO ANSWER

Indicate whether each of the following statements is true or false.

F 1. A legend is a statement of fact.

F 2. The first Americans came to North America from Europe.

F 3. The end of the Ice Age brought about no environmental changes.

F 4. Very few Native Americans were affected by the discovery of agriculture.

T 5. The *Vinland Sagas* are tales of Viking explorations.

T 6. For a long time, Italian merchants held a monopoly over the Asian trade.

F 7. Balboa discovered a strait which led to Asia.

T 8. The Aztecs were ruled by Montezuma.

T 9. La Salle claimed Louisiana for the king of France.

THINK THINGS THROUGH

1. Did the Aztecs believe in an idea like the divine right of kings? Did the Inca believe in such an idea? Give reasons for your answers by explaining how people treated Montezuma II and Atahualpa.
2. How were the societies of the Anasazi during their pueblo stage and of the Aztecs alike and how were they different?
3. How might the feelings of a *voyageur* or of a *coureur de bois* about the Indians be different from those of a newcomer to New France?
4. Explain how finding an all-water route to Asia would make Asian goods cheaper for Europeans.

An Aztec mural of 1541

RELATED MATERIALS
Duplicator/Copy Masters Test 4-6

were farmers, and both developed civilizations. The Anasazi disappeared, but the Aztecs were conquered by the Spanish. **3.** The *voyageurs* and the *coureurs de bois* lived among the Indians and understood Indian ways. A newcomer to New France might not have understood Indian lifestyles. **4.** Finding an all-water route to Asia would enable the Europeans to trade directly with the Asians, thus breaking the Italian monopoly of overland trade with Asia.

PRACTICE YOUR SKILLS

1. a. Quebec, Montreal
b. 1632
c. Cape Cod

PRACTICE YOUR SKILLS

1. Skim the following selection and answer the questions.

In 1601 the French king appointed Samuel de Champlain to go to New France. Champlain sailed up the St. Lawrence River as far as present-day Montreal. Three years later, with the help of Sieur de Mont, Champlain set up a colony in what is now Nova Scotia. Champlain sailed along the Atlantic Coast as far south as Cape Cod, Massachusetts, in 1605. The explorer obtained permission from the French king in 1607 to set up a colony along the St. Lawrence. A year later, Champlain set up the town of Quebec. Ten years after Champlain first sailed up the St. Lawrence, he set up the town of Montreal, and he became governor of New France. This was not the end of Champlain's accomplishments. In 1615 he discovered Lake Huron. In 1629 Champlain was captured by the British and taken to England. Three years later, however, he returned to Canada as its governor.

The pyramid at Santa Cecilia is near Mexico City.

a. What two towns did Champlain set up?
b. When did Champlain become governor of New France?
c. How far south did Champlain sail?

2. Use the information above to make a chart entitled "The Accomplishments of Samuel de Champlain." The chart should include the year of each major accomplishment listed.
3. On an outline map of North America, trace the routes of Champlain that are described in the selection above. Label the towns that Champlain set up.

Unit 2
ENGLISH AMERICA

Chapter 4 The Thirteen Colonies

Chapter 5 The Anglo-French Wars for Empire

Chapter 6 A New People

Unit Two examines the history of America from the first English settlers' attempts to tame the land to the growing friction between the colonists and the British. The unit covers the following topics: an overview of the various groups that landed in North America, intending to settle there; a description of the types of colonies that evolved; a review of the sources of conflict between the English and French settlers, and how the issues were resolved; an account of how relations between Great Britain and its colonists deteriorated to the point of open rebellion.

Colonial pewter pitcher

Pilgrims on their way to church

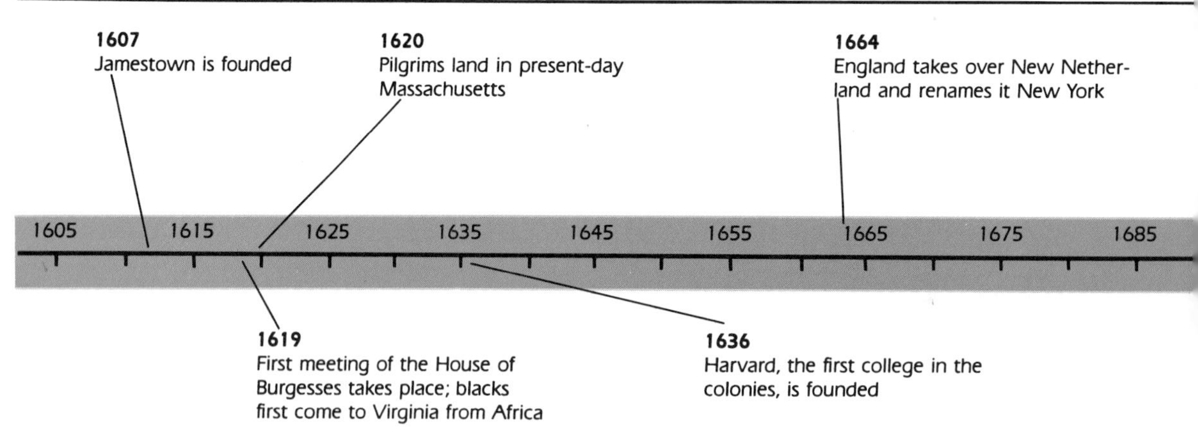

1607
Jamestown is founded
1620
Pilgrims land in present-day Massachusetts
1664
England takes over New Netherland and renames it New York
1605
1615
1625
1635
1645
1655
1665
1675
1685
1619
First meeting of the House of Burgesses takes place; blacks first come to Virginia from Africa
1636
Harvard, the first college in the colonies, is founded

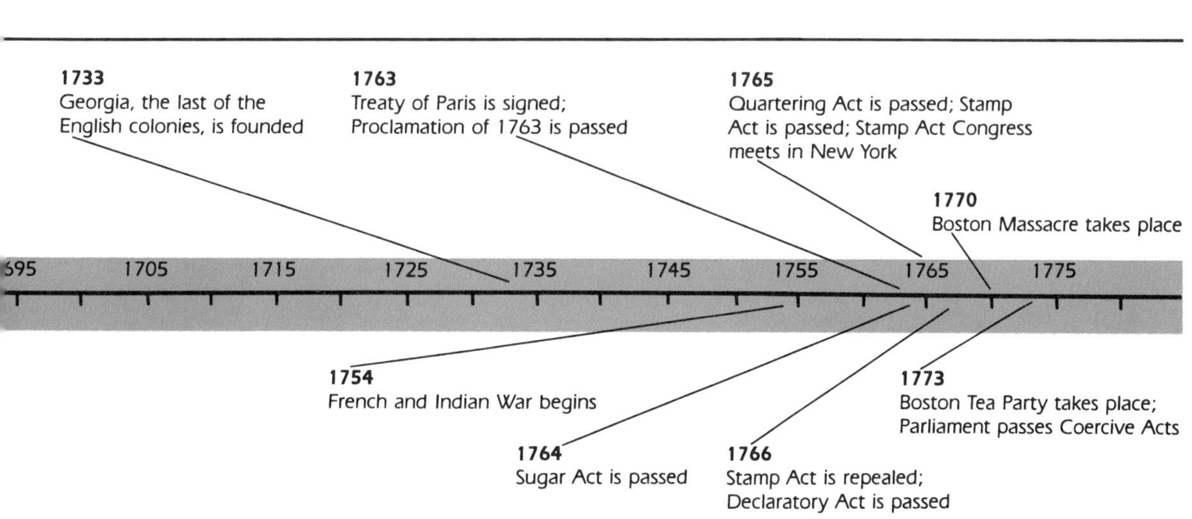
1733
Georgia, the last of the English colonies, is founded
1763
Treaty of Paris is signed; Proclamation of 1763 is passed
1765
Quartering Act is passed; Stamp Act is passed; Stamp Act Congress meets in New York
1770
Boston Massacre takes place
695
1705
1715
1725
1735
1745
1755
1765
1775
1754
French and Indian War begins
1764
Sugar Act is passed
1766
Stamp Act is repealed; Declaratory Act is passed
1773
Boston Tea Party takes place; Parliament passes Coercive Acts

Chapter 4
THE THIRTEEN COLONIES

Chapter 4 outlines the various groups that established colonies in the part of America claimed by the British; it describes from where they came and why. The chapter discusses the political and economic situations in each region in the British New World. Lesson 4-1 focuses on the southern colonies: Virginia, North Carolina, South Carolina, Maryland, and Georgia. Lesson 4-2 covers the New England colonies, and Lesson 4-3 tells about the middle colonies—New York, Pennsylvania, Delaware, and New Jersey.

CONTENT OBJECTIVES

After completing the lesson, students will know:

- how the first successful English settlements were established in the South
- that the southern colonies depended on farming as the basis of their economy
- the significance of the first meeting of the House of Burgesses

VOCABULARY

charter: license
economy: the way people produce, distribute, and use goods and services
legislature: a lawmaking body made up of representatives of the people
democratic: (the kind of government in which) the people, through their representatives, decide what to do in matters that concern everybody
indentured servant: man, woman or child who agreed to work for a master for a certain length of time in return for his or her passage

4-1 Virginia and the South

As you read, think about these questions:

Why was the winter of 1609–1610 known in Virginia as the "starving time?"

How was the economy of North Carolina different from that of South Carolina?

Why was the House of Burgesses important to the development of democratic government in America?

Special Vocabulary	charter	democratic
	economy	indentured servant
	legislature	

During the 1500s while England's rivals, Spain and France, were claiming land in America, great changes were taking place in England. English people were becoming manufacturers and traders seeking markets in many parts of the world. English people began to think that they would have to be as active as others in the New World. The stage was set for the establishment of English colonies in America.

The First Successful English Colony

In the early 1600s groups of English merchants had formed companies to set up trade with different parts of the world. One such company—the Virginia Company—obtained a *charter*, or license, from King James I to start settlements in North America.

The king divided the Virginia Company into two groups —the London Company and the Plymouth Company. He gave the London Company permission to settle between latitudes 34°N and 41°N. The Plymouth Company could settle between latitudes 38°N and 45°N. (Find these areas on the map on page 82.) These land grants made possible the first permanent English colonies in the New World.

In December 1606 the London Company sent out three ships under Captain Christopher Newport, which reached Virginia in April of 1607. They carried about one hundred people. The group sailed into Chesapeake Bay and up a river that they named the James River in honor of the king. At the end of May 1607, the English founded a settlement in a low, swampy place about 50 miles (80 kilometers) upriver. They called their settlement Jamestown.

Virginia was a beautiful place in the spring, and the English settlers misled themselves. They did not take steps to turn the place into home. Instead of building houses and putting in crops, many of them searched for gold. When winter came, they became sick and hungry. Many died.

Captain John Smith. The eventual success of Jamestown resulted from the strong leadership of Captain John Smith. By enforcing strict rules, Smith was able to get the settlers to clear the land, build houses, dig wells, and plant crops. Smith was a rough man, but he gained people's respect, including the Indians'. One story tells of Smith's capture by Chief Powhatan. The Indian wanted to kill Smith, but Pocahontas, the chief's daughter, saved Smith's life. For a while the relations between the English and the Indians improved.

John Smith, president of the Jamestown colony in 1608, was also an explorer and an author of many books. Pocahontas, who is said to have saved Smith's life, later married the English settler John Rolfe and converted to Christianity.

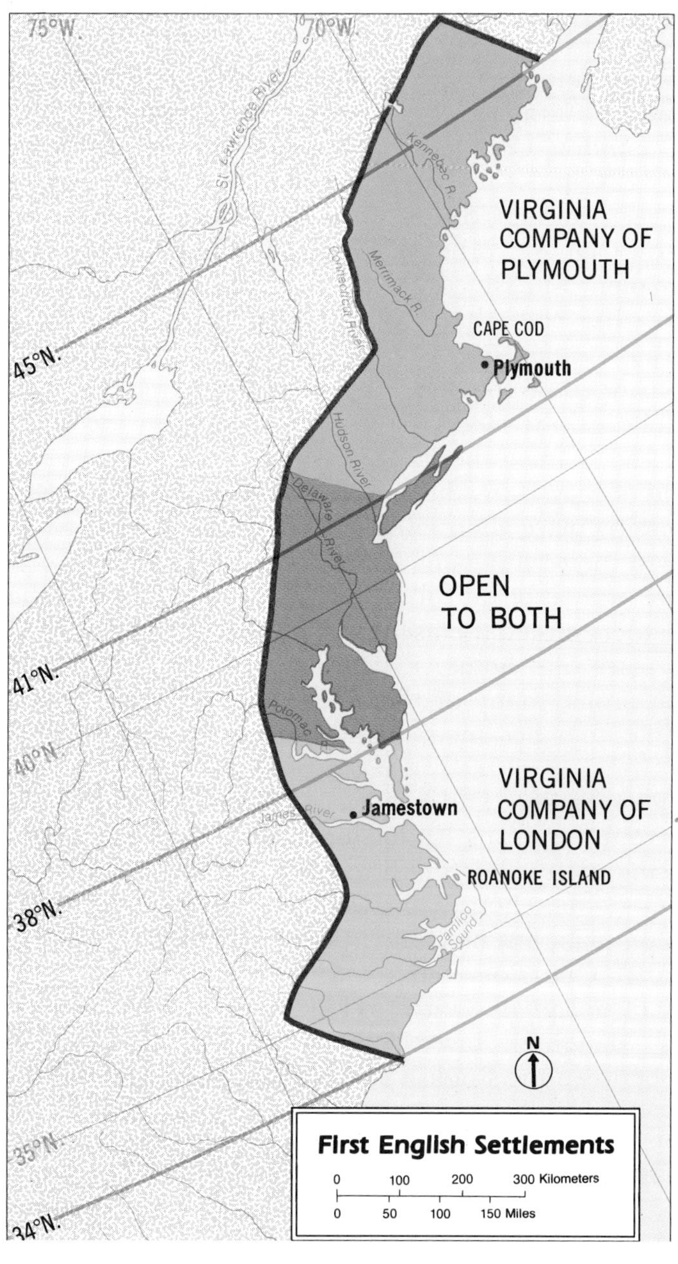

The first English settlements were made on the land grants shown here. Notice that the land grants of the Virginia Company and the Plymouth Company overlapped. The land between which latitudes was open to both?

41°N and 38°N

By the winter of 1609–1610, however, the colony was in trouble. More colonists had arrived from England, and there was not enough food for everyone. Captain Smith was badly hurt in a gunpowder accident and had to return to England. There was no leader to take Smith's place, and the colonists were afraid to go outside the stockade to look for food. That winter is known as the "starving time." By the spring only sixty colonists were alive.

One reason for the successful growth of Jamestown was that family life developed there after 1619. In that year, the London Company sent a number of single women to marry some of the discouraged settlers.

Change for the Better. The people of Jamestown were ready to give up and go home when ships arrived from England bringing Lord Delaware, Virginia's new governor, and fresh supplies. With hard work, the English were able to make their first colony a success. John Rolfe, who married Pocahontas, found a way to grow and prepare a plant from the West Indies called tobacco. He sent some of the tobacco to England where it was received with great enthusiasm.

Within a few years, tobacco had changed the *economy* of the Virginia colony. The economy is the way people produce, distribute, and use goods and services. Each settler was given land on which to grow crops. The tobacco crops were sold in England, enabling the colonists to buy goods they needed.

Other Colonies in the South

The growing of tobacco quickly wore out the soil. After farmers had grown tobacco on a piece of land for a few years, they had to move to fresh land. Slowly many of the Virginia colonists pushed inland. As a result, new communities came into being. The growth of Virginia paved the way for the settling of other colonies in the South.

The Carolinas. King Charles II gave eight of his friends a charter to settle the area known as Carolina. From the beginning of Carolina's settlement, the colony developed in two different ways, because two different groups of people settled it. In 1712 Carolina was divided into two separate colonies. The people of North Carolina raised tobacco, and they built ships using the lumber, tar, and pitch from their pine forests. The people of South Carolina made their living by growing rice as their main crop.

The first settlers who landed in Maryland erected a cross and gave thanks for their safe arrival. Other settlers, like those arriving in Savannah, Georgia, found disappointment rather than the attractive settlement shown in the advertisement above right.

Maryland. English settlers came to Chesapeake Bay in 1634. George Calvert, the first Lord Baltimore, had been promised a grant of land north of Virginia. Before he received the charter, however, he died. His son, the second Lord Baltimore, received the charter from the king, Charles I. The resulting colony, named Maryland, was started as a place that would allow Roman Catholics to follow their religious beliefs. In time Maryland passed a law that protected the rights of Christians to worship in their own way.

Georgia. The colony of Georgia had still another kind of beginning. It was established to block Spanish settlers who were trying to move into South Carolina from Florida. James Oglethorpe, the founder of Georgia, also had other reasons for starting this colony. Oglethorpe thought it wrong that people who could not pay their debts were put in prison where they could never earn money to pay them. Oglethorpe hoped that Georgia could be a place where people who had had trouble in Europe could get a fresh start. In 1732 Oglethorpe set sail with 120 settlers—poor people, people who had been in prison for debt, and people who were seeking religious freedom. They started the settlement of Savannah in 1733.

The South Prospers

By the mid-1700s, the southern colonies—Virginia, North Carolina, South Carolina, Maryland, and Georgia—were a prosperous part of the New World. (Find these colonies on the map of the southern colonies on page 85.) They had been settled by people from different backgrounds and different lifestyles, most of them seeking a new start in life.

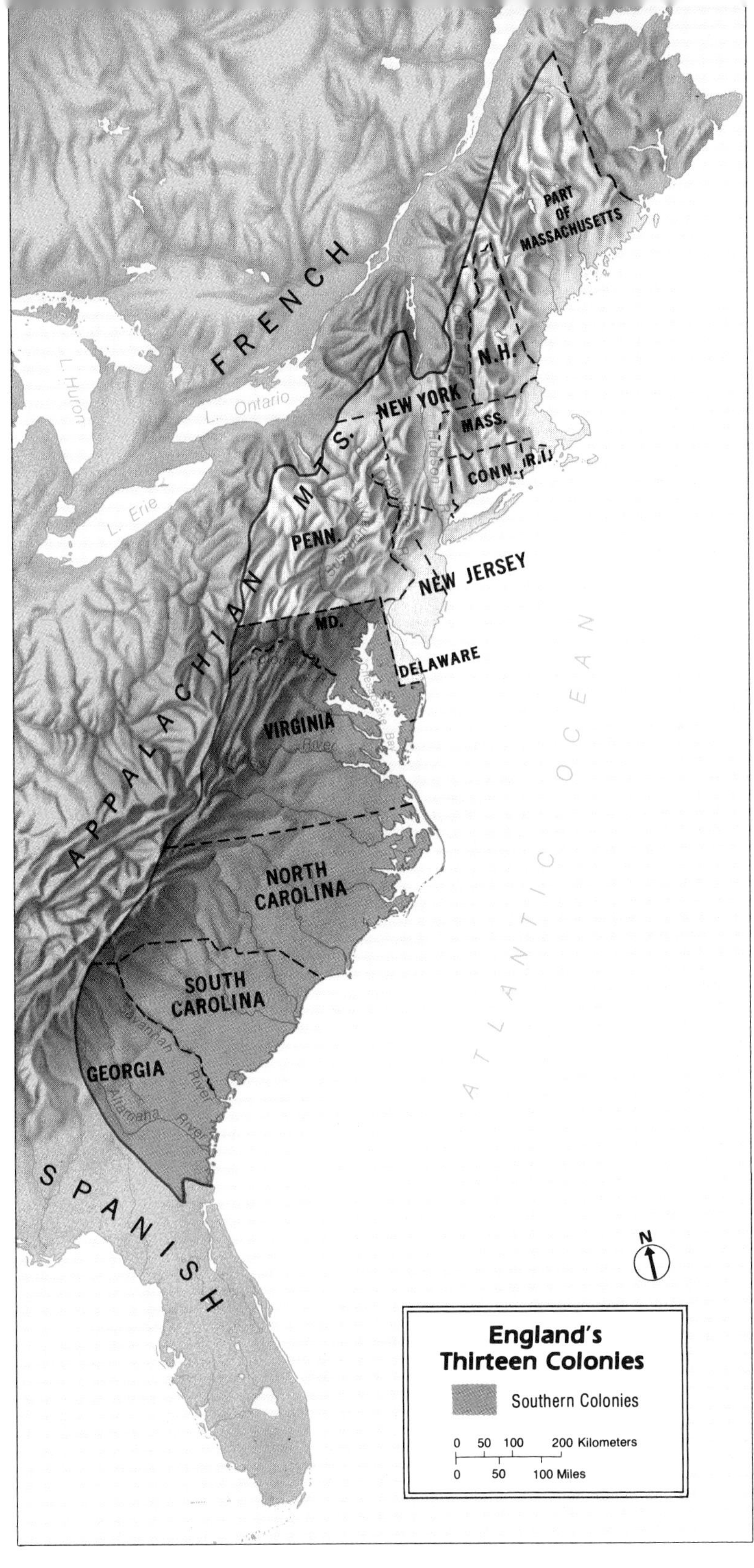

Georgia

The southern colonies differed from one another in population, in economy, and in purpose. Which southern colony was founded partly to keep Spanish settlers from moving north?

ACTIVITY

Objective: To classify information

Pose the question, "What was life like in the southern colonies in 1725?" Have students provide tentative answers as you list them. When speculation has ended, see if items can be grouped in categories such as jobs, recreation, food, and clothing.

DISCUSSION

Have the students discuss the advantages and disadvantages of being indentured servants. Find out whether they would have taken the opportunity to leave Europe to be indentured servants. What would have made them leave?

Government. The colonies based their government on that of England. One of the important features of English government was a *legislature,* a lawmaking body made up of representatives of the people. In time every colony set up a legislature. The first colonial legislature was in Virginia. Called the House of Burgesses, it met for the first time on July 30, 1619, in Jamestown. Later it moved to Williamsburg. The House of Burgesses was made up of a governor, appointed by the king, and members of the house, or burgesses. Two burgesses were elected by the people from each of the eleven divisions of Virginia. The burgesses could raise taxes and make laws. The governor, who was the leader of the House, had the power to approve or reject laws. The House of Burgesses may be thought of as the beginning of *democratic* government in America. In this kind of government the people, through their representatives, decide what to do in matters that concern everybody. This idea proved to be the basis of our country's government.

Economy. Farming was the basis of the economy of the southern colonies. People in Maryland, Virginia, and North Carolina grew large crops of tobacco. People in South Carolina and Georgia found the swampy land good for growing rice and indigo, a plant used in making blue dye.

These crops were raised on large plantations and sold in England. Many people in the South grew their own food on small farms. Some people worked in the pine forests, which provided materials for shipbuilding.

Slaves transported from Africa to the West Indies by the Spanish were treated like cargo aboard ship. This sketch was done on the spot by a British naval officer whose warship had just captured the Spanish vessel.

Way of Life. Most of the people who came to the South were *indentured servants,* men, women, and children who agreed to work for a master for a certain length of time in return for payment of their passage. Black people were first brought to Virginia from Africa in 1619. The first black child born in America was William Tucker, in 1624. Blacks first worked as indentured servants. In a few years they became slaves and were forced to work for their owners permanently.

A world separated the richest and the poorest people in the South. The rich were the plantation owners. They lived in large houses furnished with the finest goods. The poorest people were the slaves. They lived in separate quarters on plantations, and they had to depend on their masters for everything they needed. In between these two extremes were white people who lived on small farms.

Men usually handled the business of running a plantation. Women were in charge of running the house and caring for the sick. Some women, however, owned and ran plantations. The children of the plantation owners were taught by private teachers.

Some of the important cities in the English colonies were in the South. Charles Town (now Charleston), South Carolina, was the most important. It was a large and beautiful port that quickly became the social, cultural, and business center of the South.

ANSWER THESE QUESTIONS

1. What was the purpose of the charters granted to English companies in the 1600s?
2. How did John Smith help to make Jamestown a successful settlement?
3. What were the reasons for founding Maryland and Georgia?
4. What was the basis of the economy of the southern colonies?
5. How did the lifestyles of people in the South differ from one another?

ANSWER THESE QUESTIONS

1. to set up trade with different parts of the world
2. by enforcing strict rules and by improving relations between the English and the Indians
3. Roman Catholics settled Maryland to follow their religious beliefs; people settled Georgia to get a fresh start.
4. farming, with tobacco, rice, and indigo as the major crops; products from pine trees were used in shipbuilding.
5. Rich people owned plantations and lived in large houses; slaves depended on their masters for their needs; others were white people who lived on small farms.

4-2 Massachusetts and New England

As you read, think about these questions:
Who were the Pilgrims?
Who were the Puritans?
Why did each of these groups of people settle in America?
How did people in New England make a living?

Special Vocabulary	Pilgrim	import	artisan
	compact	export	apprentice
	Puritan		

A major change took place in England in the 1500s. In 1534 King Henry VIII broke away from the Roman Catholic Church and started the Church of England with himself as head. English people were required by law to belong to the Church of England. Not everyone agreed with the ideas of this church, however. Some people wanted change within the Church, while others wanted to break away from it. This desire for religious freedom was one of the reasons why people left England to settle in America.

CONTENT OBJECTIVES

After completing the lesson, students should know:

- where the Pilgrims came from, and why they settled in Massachusetts
- how the Puritans affected the laws of the New England colonies
- who Roger Williams was, and what types of people were attracted to his settlement in Providence

VOCABULARY

Pilgrim: person going on a journey for religious reasons
compact: agreement
Puritan: person who wanted to purify the Church of England
import: bring in from other places
export: send to other places to be sold
artisan: person who has been trained in a special skill
apprentice: person who works for a master artisan while being trained to become a skilled worker

The Pilgrims

One group of people who separated themselves from the Church of England became known as the Separatists. Unhappy in England, they moved to the Netherlands where they lived for twelve years. They had freedom of worship there, but their children were losing their English culture. Further, the Netherlands was at war with Spain, and the Separatists feared that they would be victims of it. As a result, they decided to move to America and resettle there. In this way, the Separatists became *Pilgrims*—people going on a journey for a religious purpose.

Voyage to America. The Pilgrims stopped off in England because the London Company was to pay for their trip to America. The plan was for the Pilgrims to travel to Virginia where they would work for the company for seven years. At the end of that time, they could take their share of the money the company made and start their own colony.

The Pilgrims—numbering about one hundred men, women, and children—sailed from Plymouth, England, on September 16, 1620. They had terrible weather crossing the Atlantic. When they finally landed in America, they realized that they had gone far off course. Instead of reaching Virginia, the Pilgrims had sailed to Cape Cod in present-day Massachusetts. (Find these places on the map on page 82.)

Miles Standish, one of the leaders of the Pilgrims, led a landing party ashore. They decided that the Pilgrims should settle there rather than sail south to Virginia. Many Pilgrims were upset with this decision. They had planned to make Virginia their home. Further, they had no right to the land to which they had come.

Still, a decision had been made. Being on their own, the Pilgrims saw that they would need a way to govern their colony. Before going ashore, forty-one Pilgrims signed a *compact*, or agreement, to form a government and make "just and equal laws." The Mayflower Compact was another step toward democratic government in America.

Help from the Indians. The Pilgrims named their settlement Plymouth, in honor of the city in England from which they had sailed. The area had a good harbor, and some of the land had been cleared by the Indians. Nevertheless the winter was harsh, and many Pilgrims died.

In spring, the Pilgrims were visited by Samoset and Squanto, two Indians who spoke English. Later Chief Massasoit came to the settlement and made a treaty with the colonists. Squanto stayed and helped the Pilgrims, teaching them how to plant corn and where to catch fish.

From the Indians, these Plymouth settlers learned many new words—including *squash, cigar, succotash,* and *hominy*—that became part of the English language.

The Puritans

Other people who were dissatisfied with the Church of England had not separated from it. They wanted, instead, to "purify" the church, or make it simpler. These people became known as *Puritans.*

Beginning a New Life. King Charles I did not like the Puritans. They decided to get away from England and make a new life for themselves in America. In 1629 the Massachusetts Bay Company was formed. It soon sent a small group of Puritans to set up a colony between the Merrimack and Charles rivers. Then in March of 1630, eleven ships set sail with more than one thousand people, the largest group of settlers that had ever left Europe. When these people arrived at Salem in June, they found that many of the first group of settlers had died during the winter. Almost immediately, two hundred of the new arrivals decided to return home. John Winthrop, the governor of the colony, sent a ship to England for supplies. Before the supplies arrived, however, two hundred more settlers had died.

Winthrop and the Puritans first settled at Charlestown. There they spent a very difficult winter. Winthrop realized that the water supply was too small for his large group. In the spring he moved his Puritan settlement to Boston, which became the main city of the Massachusetts Bay Colony.

Reliance on the Bible was as important a part of the Pilgrims' life as hard work, determination, and sincerity.

Different Ideas. Roger Williams was a young minister who came to the Massachusetts Bay Colony with the supply ship. His ideas were different from those of many of the other Puritans. Williams did not think the Church of England could be "purified." He urged the Puritans to separate themselves from the church.

Williams gained many followers, but others considered him dangerous. In 1635 he was ordered to leave the colony. Williams fled to Narragansett Bay, where he started a settlement called Providence on land bought from the Indians. In this settlement, all people were allowed to worship as they chose.

Anne Hutchinson's religious teachings split the Massachusetts colony. Although many people supported her, she was banished from Massachusetts and expelled from the church.

Anne Hutchinson came to the Massachusetts Bay Colony in 1634. She met weekly in her home with a small group of people. At first they talked about the minister's sermon of the Sunday before. Soon, however, Anne Hutchinson began to tell people her ideas about religion, which were different from those of the church leaders. In 1637 the leaders of the colony ordered Hutchinson to leave the settlement. Anne Hutchinson and her family moved near Providence.

Other New England Colonies. Several other settlements were started in the area near Providence. People in these settlements wanted to become part of a new colony. In 1643 Roger Williams went to England to obtain a charter, which he received in 1644. Settlements, including Providence and Portsmouth, banded together and later became the colony of Rhode Island.

Other people also left the Massachusetts Bay Colony. Some, looking for a better life, found rich land in the Connecticut River Valley. One group was led by Thomas Hooker, a church leader who had had trouble in the Massachusetts Bay Colony. This group settled in Hartford.

In 1637 people from some settlements in the Connecticut River Valley formed their own government. They set up a General Court that wrote a set of laws called the Fundamental Orders. In 1662 John Winthrop, Jr., son of the first governor of the Massachusetts Bay Colony, went to England. He persuaded the king to issue a grant for land between Long Island Sound and the southern border of Massachusetts. This land became the colony of Connecticut.

Still other people from the Massachusetts Bay Colony started settlements in what eventually became the colony of New Hampshire. These groups did not all have the same

Thomas Hooker, shown here with some followers approaching Hartford, Connecticut, was a founder of that colony. Hooker's ideas of popularly elected officials and independent churches were more readily accepted in Connecticut than in Massachusetts.

ideas about religion. Their disputes made it hard for them to set up a colony. They finally reached agreement, however, and in 1679 the king granted New Hampshire a charter.

New England Prospers

The New England colonies—Massachusetts, Rhode Island, Connecticut, and New Hampshire—were the most "English" of the colonies. This means that in New England most people had an English background and kept an English lifestyle, even though they lived far from England. (Find the New England colonies on the map on page 92.)

The New England colonies all had similar types of government. Each had a governor and an elected assembly, or legislature. Local leaders held town meetings at which people talked about matters that were of local concern. Anyone could speak at a town meeting, but only men who owned land could vote. In most of the colonies voters had to be members of a certain church, a membership not easy to get. During the early years in New England, therefore, many laws were based on Puritan beliefs.

Economy. The thin, rocky soil and short growing season in New England made farming difficult. Some food had to be *imported,* brought in from other places. Most New England settlements were near the ocean, so people who could not make a living by farming turned to fishing. The seacoast provided good harbors and large catches of fish. Salted and dried fish were *exported,* sent to other places to be sold. Some

ACTIVITY

Objective: To recognize a point of view

Ask students to pretend that they are sailing to the colonies and must decide what to bring. Each person is allowed three cubic feet of space. If students have no idea of the area of three cubic feet, demonstrate to them roughly what that means. You might ask students to play different members of a family: mother, father, teenage son or daughter, young child. Remind them that for survival, adaptation and sharing are necessary.

DISCUSSION

The town meeting, where people discussed local matters, was a very important part of New England social and political life. Discuss with students ways they could have a school town meeting. Have them choose a school problem. Discuss the problem, making sure that the students also include details about who would attend the meeting, who would lead the discussion, and how each person would have a chance to speak.

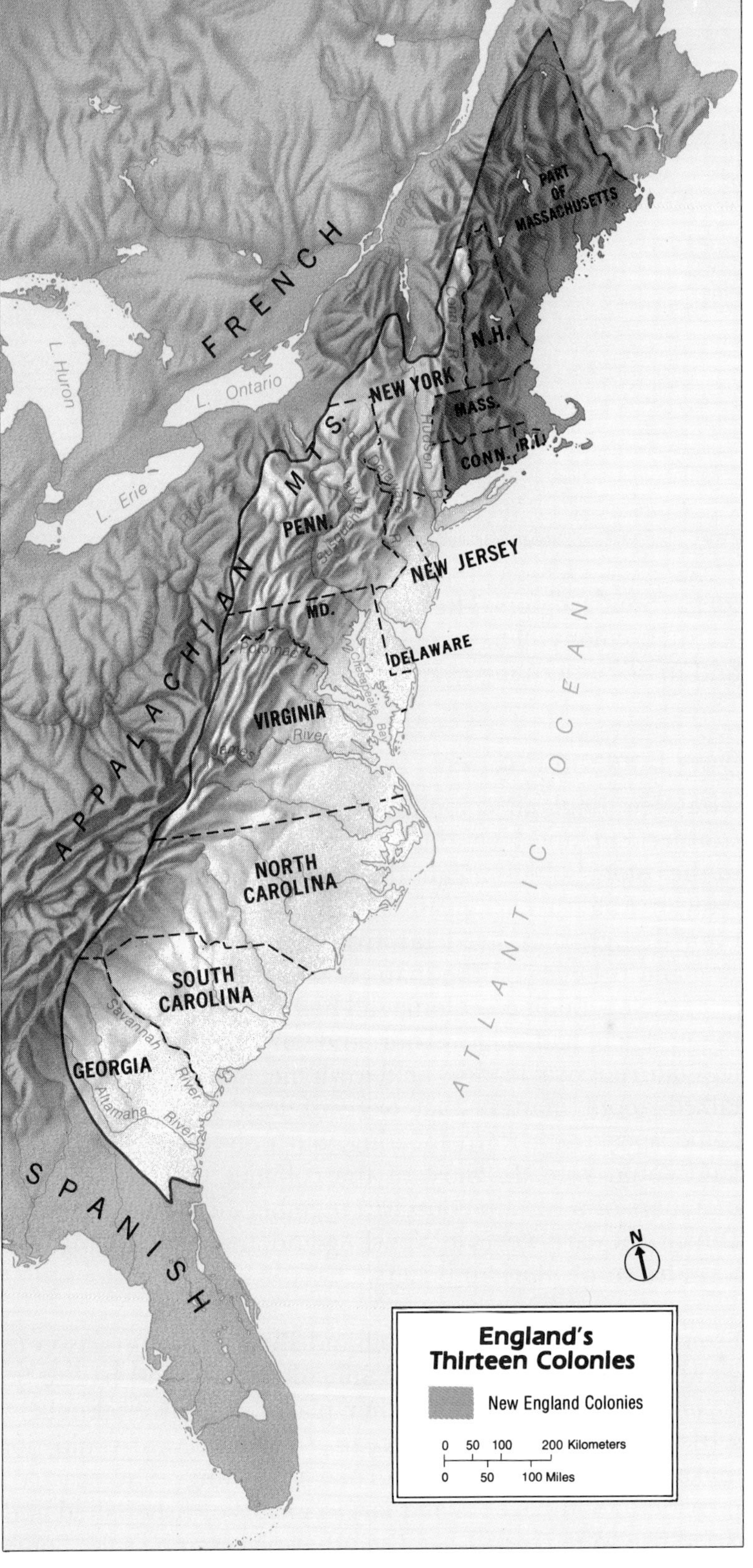

Maine is now where part of Massachusetts' territory was.

Compare this map of the New England colonies with a map of the present-day United States. How is this part of our country different from the way it was in colonial times?

New England colonists made a living by whaling. New England colonists made many products, including furniture, soap, candles, and cloth, mostly for local use. Other products, fish and lumber especially, were sold or traded.

Some *artisans*, people who have been trained in a special skill, worked in the towns and cities. Among them were carpenters, weavers, blacksmiths, silversmiths, barrelmakers, glassblowers, shoemakers, and printers. Young people learned these skills by becoming *apprentices*, people who work for a master artisan while being trained.

At Old Sturbridge Village, a restored Puritan settlement in Massachusetts, visitors may see craftworkers, such as this barrelmaker, working much as the colonists did in the seventeenth century.

Way of Life. A small number of non-English Europeans also came to New England. There were only a few black people, many of them employed as servants. Slaves remained few because the colonists did not believe they could be employed profitably during the winters.

The Puritans, the most influential group in New England, were hard-working, religious people who lived by strict rules. They wore simple clothing. Women wore long, dark dresses with white collars and cuffs. Men wore short jackets, long stockings, and loose-fitting pants that came just below their knees. Children dressed as the adults did.

The church was the center of social life in New England. People were required to attend Sunday services at the meetinghouse, which was generally near the center of town. Since church services often lasted many hours, people with long sticks walked through the meetinghouse to waken worshipers who fell asleep.

Schooling was very important to the people of New England. They passed laws that towns of a certain size had to have schools. The Puritans insisted that everyone be able to read the Bible. Children also learned writing and arithmetic, but they attended school for only a few years. Some girls did not go to school because schooling was considered necessary only for boys. Harvard, the first college in the colonies, was founded in Massachusetts in 1636 to train ministers.

ANSWER THESE QUESTIONS

1. Where in America did the Pilgrims settle?
2. How did the Indians help the Pilgrims?
3. What were some of Roger Williams's ideas about religion?
4. Why were many laws in early New England based on Puritan beliefs?
5. Why was the economy of New England based on the sea?

ANSWER THESE QUESTIONS

1. at Plymouth, at Cape Cod in present-day Massachusetts
2. by teaching them how to plant corn and where to catch fish
3. Williams did not believe the Church of England could be purified. He urged the Puritans to separate themselves from the church. He said that elected leaders had no right to make laws about religious beliefs.
4. Only members of the church could vote.
5. New England soil was not good for farming. The seacoast provided fish, whales, and good harbors.

PEOPLE IN AMERICA

Anne Bradstreet

Anne Dudley Bradstreet became America's first outstanding poet. She was born in England at a time when young women did not receive formal schooling. We know very little of her early life except that she read widely as a child. She married Simon Bradstreet when she was sixteen years old. In 1630 the Bradstreets left England to settle in Massachusetts.

The Bradstreets raised a large family—four sons and four daughters—and became involved in government in Massachusetts. Anne's father and her husband both served as governors of the colony.

In the evening when the children were in bed, Anne wrote poems. Much of her writing was about ordinary events in everyday life. By 1650 she had written enough poems to make a book. Unknown to Anne, one of her relatives took her poems to England, where they were published under the title *The Tenth Muse Lately sprung up in America.*

Anne Bradstreet had not intended for her poems to be published. She realized that her work was likely to be criticized because it was written by a woman. She expressed this feeling in the following poem:

I am obnoxious to each carping Tongue
Who says my hand a needle better fits,
A Poets pen all scorn I should thus wrong,
For such despite they cast on Female wits:
If what I do prove well, it won't advance,
They'l say it's stoln, or else it was by chance.

The book, however, was well received. It was the first book of poems written by an English colonist and the first major book of poems written by an English woman. The book was reprinted, with some changes, in Boston in 1678.

Through Anne Bradstreet's poems, we can gain some understanding of life in Puritan New England. Some of the feelings she expressed are common to people of all times and places. The lines that follow are about her children:

When each of you shall in your nest
Amoung your young ones take your rest,
In chirping language, oft them tell,
You had a Dam [e mother] that lov'd you well.

4-3 The Middle Colonies

As you read, think about these questions:
Where did the Dutch settle?
How did the owners of New Jersey encourage people to settle there?
What advantages did the middle colonies have?
What groups of people settled in the middle colonies?

Special Vocabulary cosmopolitan

CONTENT OBJECTIVES

After completing the lesson, students will know:

- how the middle colonies were originally settled
- that the relative mildness of the climate and the variety of people who settled there made these colonies very hospitable
- the many different lifestyles of the new settlers
- the story of William Penn, and how he created the largest city in the New World

VOCABULARY

cosmopolitan: the people taken together were a sample of those in various parts of the world

People who settled in the middle colonies came from many different countries. Each group brought its own language, foods, customs, and skills to America. The different backgrounds of these people helped to make the middle colonies hospitable and tolerant.

Dutch Beginnings in North America

In the 1600s England and the Netherlands both competed for world trade. Like other Europeans, the Dutch (people from the Netherlands) were interested in finding a route to Asia. The Dutch East India Company hired Henry Hudson, an English explorer, to find a northeast route.

Hudson set sail in 1609 on *Half Moon*. In September *Half Moon* entered what is now New York Harbor. Hudson sailed up the river that now bears his name.

The Dutch founded the colony of New Netherland and made their first settlement at Fort Orange in 1624. Peter Minuit, one of the Dutch leaders, bought Manhattan Island from the Indians. This land allowed the Dutch to control the Hudson River Valley.

The Dutch built a settlement at the south end of Manhattan Island. This settlement became New Amsterdam. (Find this place on the map of New Netherland on page 96.) Dutch settlement had a rather slow start because the Dutch did not come to America in large enough numbers. They were happy at home, and they did not have some of the problems that led other Europeans to seek a new start in the New World. By the early 1660s, however, New Amsterdam had become an important port, with a population of 2500.

Rivalry between the English and the Dutch in Europe was reflected in the New World. There were arguments over the boundary between New England and New Netherland. The English were moving into lands claimed by the Dutch. The English also passed laws that hurt Dutch trade in America.

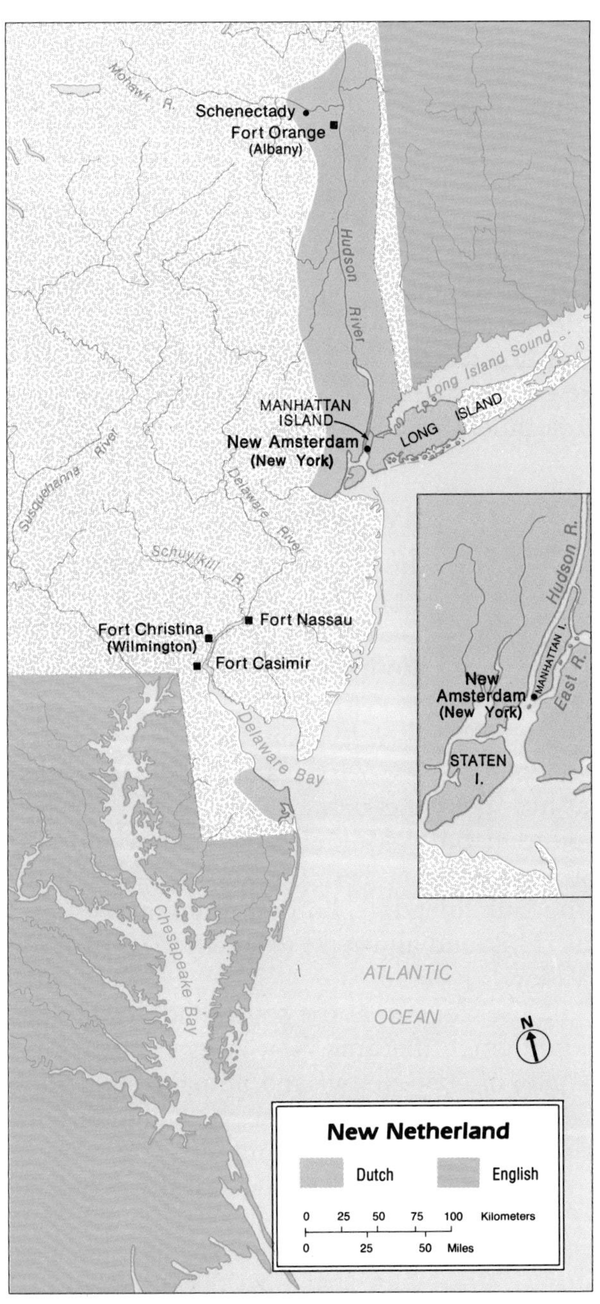

It controlled the Hudson River.

This map shows the areas settled by the Dutch. The inset map shows a more detailed view of New Amsterdam. Why was this a favorable location for a settlement?

The center square of Philadelphia, as drawn on this elegant colonial map of Pennsylvania, is today the site of City Hall. A bronze statue of William Penn atop the building makes it the tallest structure in the city.

Finally, in 1664, England sent four ships to take over New Netherland. At first Peter Stuyvesant, governor of New Netherland, refused to surrender. The Dutch, though, did not want to fight. Since they were almost out of gunpowder, they gave up their colony without firing a single shot. The English renamed the colony New York. Dutch people continued to live there peacefully under English rule.

Pennsylvania

The land that became known as Pennsylvania was settled by people seeking religious freedom. It became a "melting pot" of people from many different faiths and different countries. More than any other colony, Pennsylvania showed that free people could make a successful society. Pennsylvania rapidly became the leading colony in America. It grew out of the faith of William Penn, a leading member of a religious group called the Society of Friends, or Quakers.

William Penn. Many Quakers refused to support the Church of England and were sent to prison. Although William Penn was a Quaker, he remained on good terms with the king. Penn's father, an admiral, had died with the king owing him a large sum of money. In 1681 the king gave the son a grant of land in America as repayment of the debt. The huge area was named Pennsylvania in honor of the admiral. Penn decided to use it as a colony for Quakers.

Penn made detailed plans for the new colony. He carefully chose the site for the major settlement—at the place where the Delaware and Schuykill rivers joined. The city there would be called Philadelphia, meaning "brotherly love."

Penn also wrote what he called the Frame of Government for the colony, providing for a governor, a council of advisers, and a representative legislature. One of the first laws passed in Pennsylvania gave all Christians the freedom to worship as they pleased. Penn also established good relations with the Indians. Pennsylvania therefore became an attractive place for settlers. Philadelphia grew rapidly and was soon the largest city in the colonies.

Delaware and New Jersey. Although Pennsylvania was very large, it had no seaport. Penn asked for additional land and received a strip along the Atlantic coast. This land later became the colony of Delaware. (See the map of the middle colonies on page 99.)

In 1664 the Duke of York turned over some of his land in America to his old friends, John Lord Berkeley and Sir George Carteret. They shortly started the colony of New Jersey on their beautiful land between the Hudson and Delaware rivers. In order to encourage settlers to come to New Jersey, the owners promised freedom of religion, land on good terms, and the right to take part in the government.

ACTIVITY

Objective: To make comparisons

Discuss with students the government, economy, type of people, and the way of life in the middle colonies. On the chalkboard, put the four categories across the top and down the side list the three regions, the southern colonies, New England, and middle colonies. Have students fill in the chart. When the chart is complete, have the students compare the three regions in each category. In which categories are the regions similar? In which are the regions different?

DISCUSSION

Have the students review the characteristics of the two kinds of British colonies: royal, ruled by king; proprietary, ruled by a person or company with a charter. The royal colony governor was appointed directly by the king. Neither type of colonial government was controlled tightly by the king. Direct the students to Law and the Citizen at end of lesson 4-3. Ask them: "Why didn't the English king enforce strict control of the colonies? What do you think happened in America and in its government because of this loose control?"

The Middle Colonies Prosper

The middle colonies—New York, Pennsylvania, Delaware, and New Jersey—had many advantages. The climate was generally somewhat milder than that of New England. The middle colonies had wide river valleys, rich soil, a fairly long growing season, thick forests, and good harbors.

The governments of the middle colonies were set up much like those of New England. Most of the people who owned land had the right to vote. Some colonies, however, would not allow members of certain churches to vote.

Economy. Farming was the basis of the economy in the middle colonies. Farms were large, and the main crop was wheat. Other grains, vegetables, and fruits were also grown.

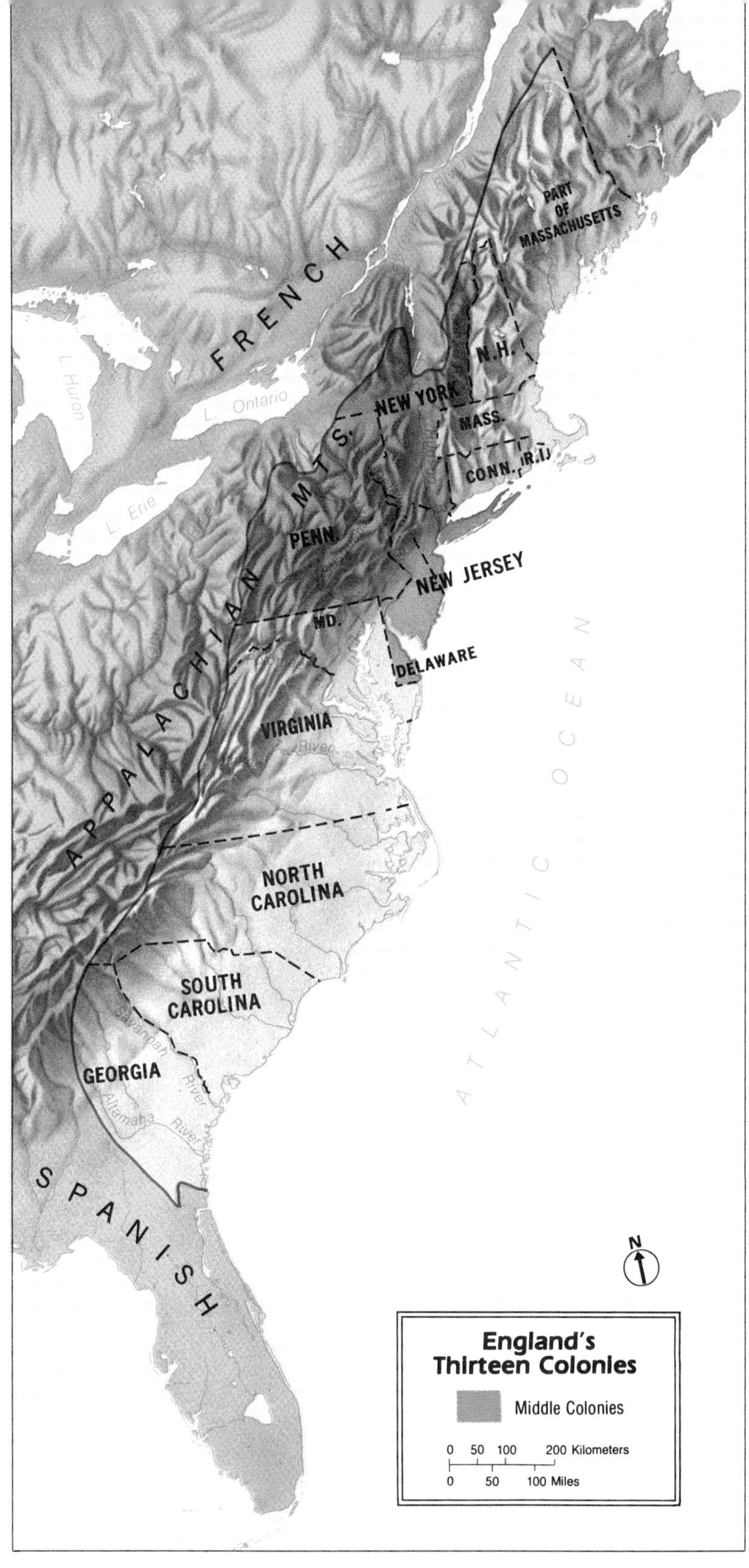

routes to the sea, good harbors

The middle colonies were sometimes called the "breadbasket" of the colonies. The favorable climate and rich soil made this area good for farming. Based on this map, what other advantages did the middle colonies have?

In 1754 Philadelphia, lying between two rivers, was the largest city and busiest port in the American colonies. Today it is only the fifth largest city in America, but it is one of the busiest ports in the entire world.

Hunting, trapping, fishing, and shipbuilding were among the other ways of earning a living in the middle colonies. People in the middle colonies, like people in New England, made many of their own goods. Artisans in cities such as New York and Philadelphia were well-known in the colonies. They made guns, iron, glass, wagons, furniture, fur hats, and leather goods that were even sold in other colonies.

Way of Life. Because the middle colonies were settled by people from many different backgrounds, these colonies were said to be more *cosmopolitan* than those of New England or the South. This means that the people taken together were a sample of those in various parts of the world. In addition to the English, there were Swedish, Finnish, Dutch, Welsh, Germans, and Scotch-Irish settlers. (The Scotch-Irish are people from Scotland who had lived in Ireland for many years.) Some blacks also lived here and there in the middle colonies. Most of them were slaves on large farms along the Hudson River. The first Jewish community in North America was started in New Amsterdam in 1654 by Jews fleeing from Brazil.

There were several kinds of communities in the middle colonies. Large ports, like New York and Philadelphia, were centers of activity. Their docks were often crowded with ships ready to take goods to England. The small towns in the middle colonies were the places where farmers sold their crops and bought supplies. Most of the people lived on farms.

Each group of people in the middle colonies brought its own customs to America. The Dutch used tile to decorate their houses, as they had done in the old country. The Swedes built log cabins. The Germans decorated their houses and barns with bright colors.

No one yet thought that the thirteen colonies would ever form one nation. Could the things they had in common bring them together? Or would their differences keep them permanently apart?

ANSWER THESE QUESTIONS

1. What result did the rivalry between the English and the Dutch in North America have?
2. Who were the Quakers?
3. What plans did William Penn make for his colony?
4. What was the basis of the economy of the middle colonies?
5. Why were the middle colonies considered cosmopolitan?

ANSWER THESE QUESTIONS

1. The English and the Dutch argued over boundary lines. The English moved into areas claimed by the Dutch and passed laws that hurt Dutch trade. In 1664 the English took over New Amsterdam.
2. The Quakers were a religious group persecuted in England.
3. Penn chose the site for Philadelphia, planned the city, and he also wrote a plan of government for the colony.
4. Farming was the basis of the economy, but hunting, fishing, trapping, and shipbuilding were other economic activities.
5. The middle colonies were settled by people from many different backgrounds.

Government in the English Colonies

The colonies were governed by the king of England, generally through agents he appointed. Each colony had a governor and a legislature. In *royal colonies*—those ruled by the king—the governor was appointed by the king. In *proprietary colonies*—those ruled by a person or company who received a charter from the king—the governor was appointed by the proprietor, or owner. Laws passed by colonial legislatures had to be approved in England. England, however, did not enforce strict control over the colonies. The colonists experimented with various forms of government. Some ideas they introduced later became important for our country's development. The greatest of these ideas was self-government.

The legislature, called the Assembly or General Court, in most colonies was made up of two houses, or parts. The one the people elected was called the lower house. It gave the people a voice in their government through the representatives they voted for. The upper house reflected the views of the governor. In most colonies the governor appointed the upper house. In Connecticut and Rhode Island the people elected the members of the upper house. In Massachusetts after 1691 the lower house elected the upper house.

Voting requirements varied among colonies and changed from time to time. No women, indentured servants, or slaves could vote in any colony. Some colonies required voters to be members of a certain church. Most colonies allowed men who owned land to vote. This was because the colonists believed that landowners had a strong interest in government. Since most free men were landowners, this requirement allowed nearly three fourths of them to vote.

The organization of local governments differed throughout the colonies. In New England the town was the basis of local government. Citizens voted on local laws and elected local leaders at town meetings. In the southern colonies the county was the basis of local government. This was because towns were farther apart in the South than in New England. The middle colonies had both counties and towns.

The ideas of self-government began to grow. English colonists enjoyed having a voice in government. As time went on, this led to problems between England and the colonies.

LAW AND THE CITIZEN

THINKING THINGS THROUGH

1. T Smith enforced strict rules to make the settlers build homes, dig wells, clear the land, and plant crops. 2. T Oglethorpe thought it unfair that people in England who could not pay their debts were put in prison. 3. F Most were from England, and many went to the same church. 4. T Land ownership and church membership were required for voting, and

Chapter 4 SUMMARY

Some changes that took place in England during the 1500s set the stage for the settlement of English colonies in America during the 1600s. People settled in America for different reasons. Some people left England to seek religious freedom. Others were seeking wealth. Still others wanted to make a new and better life. The first lasting English settlement began at Jamestown, Virginia, in 1607. By 1733 there were thirteen English colonies along the Atlantic coast from Massachusetts to Georgia.

The southern colonies were Virginia, North Carolina, South Carolina, Maryland, and Georgia. Farming became the basis of the economy, with tobacco and rice as the main crops. The people who settled the South came from different backgrounds. Plantation owners were the richest of these people, and slaves were the poorest.

The New England colonies were Massachusetts, Rhode Island, Connecticut, and New Hampshire. Since farming was difficult in New England, most people made their living from the sea. These colonies were settled by people who were seeking religious freedom.

The middle colonies were New York, Pennsylvania, Delaware, and New Jersey. Although farming was the basis of the economy, many people made their living by trapping, fishing, and building ships. The middle colonies were settled by people from many different backgrounds. Each group brought its own culture to America.

Chapter 4 TEST

WORDS TO REMEMBER

Choose the correct word from the special vocabulary to complete each sentence.

1. King James I granted a charter to the Virginia Company to start settlements in North America.
2. The way people produce, distribute, and use goods and services is their economy.
3. The House of Burgesses was the legislature of Virginia.
4. A democratic government is one in which the people, through their representatives, decide what to do in matters that concern everybody.
5. The Pilgrims on *Mayflower* signed a compact to form a government with just and equal laws.
6. The people in New England were able to export salted and dried fish.
7. Carpenters, weavers, and silversmiths were among the artisans who worked in cities.
8. Young people who were being trained as skilled workers were called apprentices.

THINKING THINGS THROUGH

Indicate whether each of the following statements is true or false. Then explain your answer in a complete sentence.

1. One of the reasons for the success of Jamestown was the strong leadership of John Smith.
2. James Oglethorpe started the colony of Georgia as a place where people who had had trouble in Europe could get a fresh start.
3. The New England colonies were settled by people from many different backgrounds.

RELATED MATERIALS

Duplicator/Copy Masters: Activity 7; Quiz 7

Workbook pages 10-13

only men could vote. **5.** F They were happy at home and did not have some of the problems that led other Europeans to settle in America. **6.** F They came from many different backgrounds and faiths.

WORKING WITH SKILLS

1. shipbuilding, whaling, ironworks, and fishing **2.** wheat
3. Maryland, Virginia, North Carolina, and South Carolina
4. North Carolina and South Carolina had needle-leaved forests that provided the naval stores. Wilmington and Charleston were on the coast. **5.** fishing; the symbol for fishing areas extends along the coast of all the colonies

4. In most of the New England colonies only men who owned land and belonged to the church could vote.
5. Many Dutch settlers came to America to escape problems in the Netherlands.
6. Most of the people in the middle colonies were Puritans.

WORKING WITH SKILLS

Use the map on this page to answer the questions that follow.

1. What were the sources of trade and wealth in Massachusetts?
2. What crop was grown in Pennsylvania?
3. In which colonies was tobacco grown?
4. Naval stores are forest products used in shipbuilding. Why do you think Wilmington, North Carolina, and Charleston, South Carolina, became shipbuilding centers?
5. What source of trade and wealth was common to all the colonies? How can you tell?

ON YOUR OWN

1. Make a list of what you consider to be the advantages and disadvantages of living in the southern colonies, in the New England colonies, and in the middle colonies. In which colonies would you like to have lived? Explain your answer.
2. You have read that many skilled workers in the colonies learned their jobs by becoming apprentices. A type of apprentice system is still used today. Interview someone who is a carpenter, a bricklayer, a printer, a construction worker, a plumber, or an electrician. Find out how that person learned his or her job. Did the person serve as an apprentice? If so, for how long?

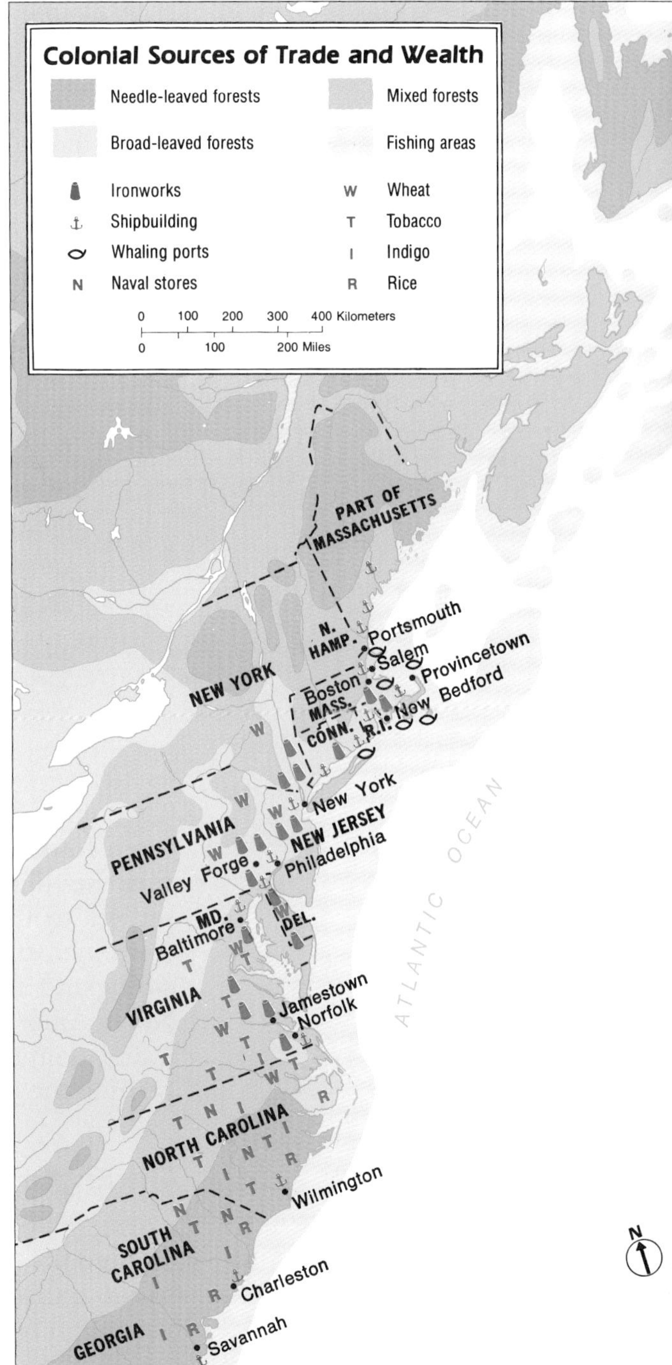

Chapter 5 introduces students to the conflicts that developed as England and France began to expand their territories, sometimes each claiming the same land as their own.

Chapter 5
THE ANGLO–FRENCH WARS FOR EMPIRE

Lesson 5-1 explains that their armies were organized differently, and that they had different attitudes toward the Indians. Lesson 5-2 focuses on the various battles that were turning points in the English army's eventual victory over the French.

CONTENT OBJECTIVES

After completing the lesson, students will know:

- why the French and the English were in constant conflict
- how events in Europe affected relationships in the New World
- how settlers differed in their relationships with the Indians

VOCABULARY

frontier: the edge of the settled area
land company: business (to) control the land
ally: a friend who helps another in time of trouble

5-1 Rivalry in North America

As you read, think about these questions:

How was the organization of the English colonies different from that of New France?

What were the causes of the English and French conflicts in North America?

How did the English relate to the Indians?

How did the French relate to the Indians?

What were the results of the early wars between the English colonies and New France?

Special Vocabulary frontier land company ally

Throughout their long history, the countries of Europe often found themselves angry with one another. It was no surprise that when these countries began sending their settlers to the New World, the troubles between countries continued there, too. Two longstanding enemies in Europe —England and France—constantly fought over their lands in North America. In fact, from the moment in 1497 when John Cabot claimed Newfoundland for England, North America became the prize in the contest between these enemies.

The English and French in North America

England and France knew that great fortune and power awaited the country that ruled North America. England tried to reach this goal by settling southward from Newfoundland

attacked the Pequots in their fort on the Mystic River. When the fierce battle was over, the Pequot tribe had been nearly wiped out.

Thirty-eight years later, the English settlers were once again faced with war. In 1675 the Wampanoag Indians, led by their chief Metacomet (called King Philip by the English), began attacking New England settlers who were moving into Wampanoag lands. As the fighting continued, four other tribes who also felt threatened—the Narragansett, Mohegan, Podunks, and Nipmucks—joined the struggle. The English fought back, punishing the Indians for their attacks against these villages.

Although the English did not have many trained generals or soldiers, there were four times as many settlers as there were Indians. The English also were better equipped. These English advantages finally wore the Indians down. In 1676 the colonists had won the war even though the fighting continued for awhile. The treaty ending King Philip's War was finally signed in 1678.

In spite of these two wars, a few English settlers were able to become the friends of the mighty Iroquois. Because the Iroquois hated the French, they became an ally of the English. The Iroquois helped the English attack French forts and settlements. Still, they never accepted the fact that their lands were being taken over by the same people they were helping. As a result, the Iroquois shrewdly played off the Europeans against each other.

The French and the Indians. The friendship between the French and the Indians in North America began with Samuel de Champlain in 1609. In that year, Champlain made an alliance with the Algonkian and Huron tribes. With that action, he set in motion Indian policies that would last for the next one hundred fifty years.

The French knew that the fur trade with the Indians was very important to New France. They developed friendships and agreements with the Indians that would protect the trade and the people who ran it. The friendship between the *coureurs de bois* and the Indians is one example.

Champlain's friendship with the Algonkian and Huron tribes helped the French many times. As more English settlers came to North America, the French found themselves in need of this friendship. The Algonkians, led by the French, made occasional raids into Iroquois and English

A party of *coureurs de bois* lands on the bank of the Mississippi River. Because they know the Indian language and customs, the French are greeted as friends.

territory, aiming to stop the flow of English settlers into French lands. The Algonkians also helped to guard the French forts in the Ohio River Valley.

Early Wars. The rivalry between England and France in Europe at times caused war between them. When this happened, there was war between the English and French in North America too. King William's War broke out in 1689. It gave the French a chance to strike at English settlements along Hudson Bay. Under the direction of Governor Frontenac, the French attacked these northern villages. Their Indian friends joined them in the battle. The treaty in 1697 ending the war returned all land captured to the country claiming it before the war had begun.

The European war in 1702, called Queen Anne's War, once again brought the English and French in North America into the struggle. The English destroyed French outposts to the north, while the Indian friends of the French attacked New England settlements. Newfoundland also became a battleground, with the French gaining control of the eastern borders. Under the treaty signed in 1713, England received Newfoundland, Acadia, and Hudson Bay. France kept its islands in the St. Lawrence River and in the Gulf of St. Lawrence.

Yet another war, King George's War of 1740, was fought in North America as well as in Europe. While there was some heavy fighting between the two countries, neither side was able to defeat the other. Like the treaty following King William's War, the treaty of 1748 returned all land won to the country that claimed it before the outbreak.

ANSWER THESE QUESTIONS

1. Where was the land claimed by both England and France located?
2. What steps did the French take to keep the English settlers out of their territory?
3. What three wars had been fought between England and France in North America by 1748?
4. What was the English relationship with the Indians?
5. Why do you think the French relationship with the Indians was more successful than that of the English?

ANSWER THESE QUESTIONS

1. Ohio River to the north, Gulf of Mexico to the south, Mississippi River to the west, Appalachians to the east
2. built more forts in the Ohio River Valley and called on Indians for help
3. King William's War, Queen Anne's War, King George's War
4. The English were frequently at war with the Indians; the Iroquois were the only major nation to become England's ally.
5. The French did not have many settlers and were less a threat to the Indians. The French *coureurs de bois* lived with the Indians. The French did not try to remove the Indians from their homes.

5-2 The French and Indian War

As you read, think about these questions:

What role did George Washington play in the French and Indian War?

Why did France seem to have the advantage in the war?

What was the Albany Plan of Union?

Why was William Pitt important to the English hopes for victory?

What was the English plan to take Canada?

What were the results of the French and Indian War?

Special Vocabulary	delegate	terrain	prime minister
	grievance	Parliament	strategic
	regiment		

The small wars fought between England and France in North America had not removed the causes of trouble between them. England remained determined to have part of the Ohio Valley for its fur trappers and settlers. France was just as determined that the English must be kept out of this land.

CONTENT OBJECTIVES

After completing the lesson, students will know:

- how small conflicts between the French and the English developed into a full-scale battle over possession of the Ohio River Valley
- the difficulties of unifying the English colonies
- how a lack of unity caused the English to suffer losses at the hands of the French
- how William Pitt convinced the English to cooperate with each other and thereby turned the tide of the war in favor of the English

VOCABULARY

delegate: person given power to act for others
grievance: reason for acting angry
regiment: military group organized to act as a unit
terrain: the physical features of a geographical area
Parliament: the lawmaking body of England
prime minister: leader of British Parliament
strategic: important for overall military success

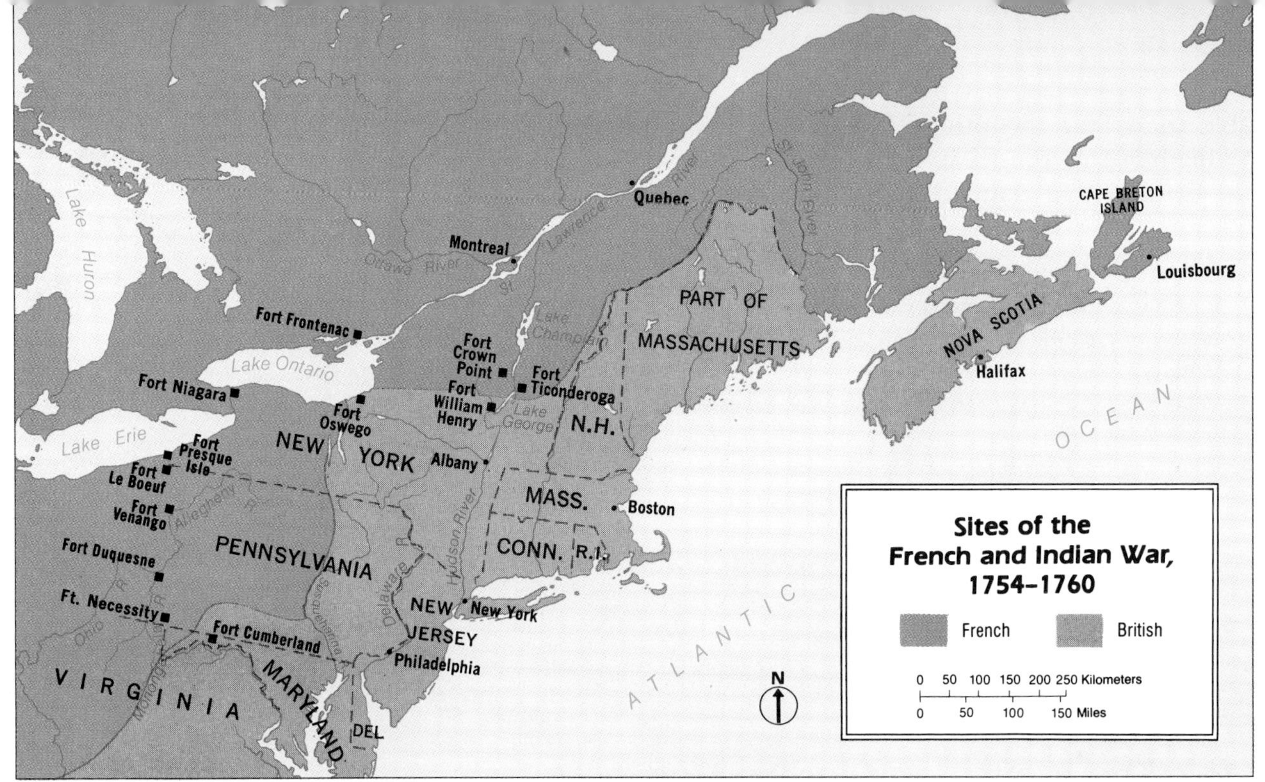

This map shows the forts built by both the English and the French in North America. Most of the fighting in the French and Indian War took place at these forts. Which country had the larger land area to protect?

France

The Fighting Begins

The truth was that the Ohio River Valley just west of the Appalachian Mountains held everything that England and France wanted in North America. It could be turned into plenty of rich farmland, and it contained many fur-bearing animals. Neither England nor France was willing to back off from its claims.

Getting Ready for War. In 1753 the French under the Marquis Duquesne decided to take the first step to secure the Ohio River Valley. They built two new forts—Presque Isle and Le Boeuf. The next year Duquesne ordered the building of Fort Venango on the Allegheny River. (See the map on this page for these sites.) The French then felt sure they could stop the English from entering their territory.

England knew that with these actions the French had challenged its power in North America. Robert Dinwiddie, lieutenant governor of Virginia, acting on orders from England, sent George Washington, a young Virginian just turned twenty-one, to warn the French that they had built their forts on English territory. Washington's orders were to find out how many French settlers had moved into the area. He was also to learn how the armies to the north in Canada

The French Fort Duquesne, site of two British defeats, actually was a poor stronghold. It flooded in heavy rains and could hold only two hundred soldiers during a siege.

would defend these French settlers if they were attacked by the English.

Major Washington visited two of the French forts, trying to learn the information wanted by his country. On January 16, 1754, Washington reported to Dinwiddie that the French planned to settle and arm the entire Ohio River Valley. In Washington's opinion, the only way to remove the French from the valley was by force.

Dinwiddie began to prepare for trouble by ordering that a fort be built where the Allegheny and Monongahela rivers join. While a group of forty English soldiers worked on the fort, five hundred French and Indians attacked them. The French finished the fort, calling it Fort Duquesne after their governor-general.

The English built a fort at a place called Great Meadows, naming it Fort Necessity. When Fort Necessity was finished, Washington pushed his soldiers toward Redstone Creek. Just as the English crossed the Appalachian Mountains, they received word that the French were advancing in large numbers. The English fell back to Fort Necessity and waited for the French to open fire. Washington's soldiers could not hold out for long. At the end of a battle on July 4, 1754, Fort Necessity surrendered. Washington and his soldiers were allowed to march away. He would never forget the humiliation of defeat that he felt. The war between the English and the French had started.

The Outlook for the War. At the beginning of the war, the French seemed to have the advantage. The English settlers far outnumbered the French settlers, but the French's Indian allies were very powerful. In fact, with the loss of Fort

ACTIVITY

Objective: Presenting different points of view

Divide the class into two groups of equal size. Group 1 represents British views and interests. Group 2 represents French views and interests. Direct the students to imagine they are living during the period just before the French and Indian War. Assign each student a role, such as a settler, a soldier, a New World government official, a European official faced with New World problems, a trapper, or a city dweller. Direct the groups to have each role player explain his or her country's views on the settlement and building of forts in the Ohio Valley, as well as its attitude toward Native Americans.

Necessity, some of the Iroquois who had been friends of the English began to join the French forces, as well. They thought that the French were unbeatable.

The English colonies, on the other hand, were not used to working and cooperating with one another. In fact, each of them acted like a separate country. Each had its own government, economy, and army. Each had its own frontier to protect. Rarely was it called upon to aid a neighboring colony. Unless the colonies learned to work together, the French did indeed have the advantage.

The Albany Plan of Union. The main concern of the English at home and in North America was to keep their Iroquois friends from joining France. The colonies needed to show the Iroquois they could win the war. On June 19, 1754, *delegates*—people given power to act for others—from eleven colonies met at Albany, New York, with the leaders of the Iroquois. The Iroquois listed their *grievances*, or reasons for being angry. On July 9 the English finally persuaded the Iroquois to rejoin them against their common enemies, the French and the Huron.

Benjamin Franklin drew this editorial cartoon in support of the Albany Plan of Union. He used the symbol of a snake in pieces to express his belief that the colonies would not survive unless they joined together.

A plan of union prepared by Benjamin Franklin was also considered at this meeting. This plan called for the election of a council by the colonial assemblies. The council could pass laws, collect taxes, handle Indian affairs, and raise armies. A president-general chosen by the king would be in charge of the council. This plan is known as the Albany Plan of Union. It was the first effort ever made to bring the English colonies together under single leadership.

The colonial legislatures rejected the plan. The colonies were not willing to give up any of their powers to a central government, though some things—like their defense against the French—could be better handled this way. When the colonies did not accept the plan, England let the matter die.

Braddock on the March. England sent two *regiments*, military units organized to act together, of soldiers to Virginia. Their general was Edward Braddock, a veteran of European wars. Braddock's first goal was to retake Fort Duquesne from the French. Braddock was not used to the *terrain*, the physical features of a geographical area, of North America. He began his march as if he were in England. He brought along pack animals, wagons, and heavy cannon, which he had to guide through thick forests and over unmarked trails. The animals and wagons had trouble keeping up. The march took so long that Braddock was afraid the French would have time to bring more troops to Fort Duquesne.

Braddock also thought that the Iroquois would send enough guides to lead the march. Instead only eight of them showed up. More time was lost as soldiers wandered off trails that were all but impossible to follow. To make the grim situation worse, supplies the colonies promised to provide never came. Many of Braddock's soldiers, including George Washington, became ill, delaying the march even more.

George Washington said about this battle, in which 900 French and Indians defeated General Braddock's 1440 soldiers, "You can see that life is unsure."

Braddock's Defeat. In July 1755 Braddock at last reached the Monongahela River at a point about 8 miles (12.8 kilometers) from Fort Duquesne. After crossing the river, Braddock sent four hundred fifty soldiers ahead to an area where he wanted to regroup before attacking the fort. Washington had had to be left behind because of his illness, so Braddock chose Thomas Gage to lead the troops. Before Gage could reach the planned place of battle, nine hundred French and Indians attacked his party. In panic Gage ordered a quick retreat. The French divided their forces and took positions in the nearby forest. From these hidden posts, the French easily spotted the English wearing bright red coats.

Braddock and his eight hundred soldiers swiftly moved up to join Gage, but the confusion was complete when the advancing force met Gage's in retreat. Braddock's linc of troops blocked any further escape. The English were trapped under the French and Indian fire. Braddock tried to rally his soldiers, but he was shot and died from his wounds a few days later. The English force was almost wiped out.

Other Losses. In the spring of 1756, England received another setback. The fine French commander Louis Joseph, Marquis de Montcalm, another veteran of wars in Europe, arrived in New France. He immediately prepared to attack the English in the Great Lakes area. Before long, Montcalm and France's Indian friends had taken Fort Oswego on Lake Ontario. The next year Fort William Henry fell. The English general, Lord Loudoun, could not break the string of French victories. He received little help from the colonies. He could not prevent his own Indian allies from joining the French. French control of the entire Great Lakes area stopped the flow of English settlers to the north.

DISCUSSION

Discuss with the students the differences between French settlers and English settlers. This discussion should include the differences in their governments, their economic systems, and their feelings about their new land. Ask students which settlers had more control over their lives. If the French had won the war, how might life be different in the United States today? Ask students about the language, the form of government, and the religion Americans might have.

The Tide Turns

Parliament, the lawmaking body of England, knew that the country needed a change in leadership. In 1757 Parliament took the important step of choosing a new *prime minister*, or leader. He was William Pitt. Pitt had boasted, "I believe that I can save this country and that no one else can." He set out to make good on that boast.

William Pitt. Pitt quickly sought the help of the best generals and military people he could find. He sent a large force of soldiers, well armed and well supplied, to the colonies to wait for orders. He also warned the colonies that he expected them to supply more soldiers and raise more money.

The first test for Pitt came at Louisbourg, a French stronghold on Cape Breton Island. Seizing this location at the mouth of the Gulf of St. Lawrence was *strategic*, important for overall military success, to Pitt's plan to defeat the French forces in Canada. Major General Jeffery Amherst, one of Pitt's appointees, commanded forty ships and nine thousand English regulars, in addition to five hundred colonists—the largest force the English had ever put together against the French.

The colonists kept track of the course of the war in prints like this one, called "Britain's Glory," circulated after the siege of Louisbourg.

The English surrounded Louisbourg both on land and on sea. For many weeks they fired at the French fort. Finally, on July 26, 1758, the French surrendered. The victory lifted English spirits and gave the English control of the entrance to the St. Lawrence River.

More English victories followed. A month after the capture of Louisbourg, Colonel John Bradstreet took Fort Frontenac. This victory allowed the English to close off the western end of the St. Lawrence River. The English now could move to retake the Ohio River Valley from the French. Under Brigadier General John Forbes, the English marched once again on Fort Duquesne. This time the battle favored the English. The attack on the fort proved so successful that the French quickly left, blowing up the fort behind them. The English army rebuilt it, naming it Fort Pitt in honor of the prime minister. (Today the site is called Pittsburgh, a major city in the state of Pennsylvania.)

A Plan for Victory. In 1759 the French no longer held the Ohio River Valley. Their last remaining stronghold was Canada. Pitt and his generals made plans to push the French out of there, too.

The English decided that three forts—Niagara, Crown Point, and Ticonderoga—had to be taken before a full attack on the principal cities of Quebec and Montreal could begin. (See the map on page 112.)

On July 25 Fort Niagara fell to two thousand English and one hundred Iroquois under the direction of Brigadier General John Prideaux. Amherst then marched on Fort Ticonderoga on July 26 and on Crown Point on July 31. He took both fortresses in short order. The English prepared to take Canada.

Quebec and Montreal. Quebec and Montreal stood as the last two symbols of the French empire in North America. Complete victory demanded that they must fall. The job of taking Quebec rested with General James Wolfe, Amherst's second in command at the battle of Louisbourg. Chosen by Pitt, Wolfe understood the difficulty of taking Quebec.

In this view of Fort Ticonderoga following its capture by the British, General Amherst's troops are seen spread out in front of the fort.

Quebec sat on top of high, steep cliffs far above the waters of the St. Lawrence River. Wolfe knew that it was impossible to attack the city from the river. With French guns trained on the attackers, the battle would be over before it began. The French general was Montcalm. Montcalm had defeated the English before. His soldiers knew that he could win again.

Wolfe had nine thousand troops at his command. Sailing up the St. Lawrence River to a place near Quebec, Wolfe ordered his soldiers to take all the lands surrounding the city. Montcalm tried to stop this operation by setting the English ships afire, but he failed.

Montcalm carefully watched the military moves of his enemy and decided that the English were planning to attack from the river. The general reinforced that side of the city to repel the English attack. Wolfe, however, had something else in mind.

On the night of September 12, Wolfe moved his troops upstream in small boats. Before dawn, the soldiers had marched west of Quebec to a place called the Plains of Abraham. Montcalm, dumbfounded, called his soldiers into battle without waiting for reinforcements. The French line

In this British view of the taking of Quebec, British soldiers appear almost half as tall as the cliffs that protected the city.

British boats, each armed with a single cannon, defeat a ten-gun French ship at Fort La Galette, allowing the British to advance down the St. Lawrence River.

quickly gave way. The English pushed forward into the city. Wolfe himself and sixty of his soldiers died in the tremendous English victory. Montcalm also gave his life—along with the lives of two hundred of his soldiers. Quebec surrendered September 18, 1759.

With Amherst in charge, Montreal did not hold out very long. He planned a three-way attack on the city. He moved up from Lake Ontario, William Haviland marched north from Crown Point, and Governor James Murray pushed down from Quebec. On September 8, 1760, this last French stronghold fell. England had finally won the French and Indian War.

Spain Joins France. Spain, the colonial power to the south of English America, feared an English victory over the French in the war. Spain figured that if France was driven out of North America, England would then be able to turn its attention to the lands to the south. For this reason, Spain prepared to enter the war against England. Before Spain could act, however, England declared war on Spain. England won a series of quick victories in the Caribbean Sea and on the Pacific Ocean.

Treaty of Paris, 1763. The treaty ending the French and Indian War was signed on February 10, 1763. The Treaty of Paris called for England to receive Canada and all French land in North America east of the Mississippi River. This did not include the city of New Orleans, which was instead given to Spain.

England returned the island of Cuba and the Philippines to Spain in exchange for Florida. France was allowed to keep its islands in the Caribbean Sea. To make up for the Spanish loss of Florida, France—in a separate treaty—gave Spain the area known as Louisiana. This was a vast area between the Rocky Mountains and the Mississippi River.

Results of the War. Now that France no longer held the Ohio River Valley, the barrier to the westward advance of the English colonists had been lifted. The land companies made ready to sell their acres at a good profit. The war also made England aware that the colonies needed to be watched more closely. The war, too, had been very expensive. Many in England believed that the colonies were easily able to bear some of the huge debt the war had produced for the home country.

Britain was now solely in control of much of North America. What would it do with its great opportunity? How would the colonies respond?

ANSWER THESE QUESTIONS

1. What was the reason both England and France wanted the Ohio River Valley?
2. How did the English try to keep their Iroquois allies?
3. What did the Albany Plan of Union try to establish?
4. Why do you think the colonies were unwilling to give up some of their powers to a central government like that outlined in the Albany Plan of Union?
5. Why do you think that the election of William Pitt as prime minister was so important to the English hopes for victory?

ANSWER THESE QUESTIONS

1. It held everything they wanted: rich farmland, furbearing animals, and room for settlers to build their homes.
2. In an effort to regain Iroquois support, delegates from eleven colonies met in Albany, New York, to meet the leaders and listen to the grievances of the Iroquois.
3. a president-general appointed by the king and a council elected by the colonial legislatures
4. The colonies had their own forms of government for a long time and were used to making all their own decisions about their colony. The people helped to make laws through colonial legislatures and a central government would take away that right.
5. Pitt would not accept defeat. His choice of generals gave the soldiers confidence. He made sure that there were enough soldiers to fight and that they had enough supplies. Pitt made the colonies take part in the waging of the war. They had to provide money, soldiers, and supplies. When Pitt's generals began to win, the English gained more confidence.

Working with Skills

READING SKILLS

ACTIVITY

Objective: To make comparisons

Divide the class into two groups. Assign one group to research the Albany Plan of Union. The other should investigate the Iroquois Nation (see Lesson 1-3). The students should find out the following: how each group planned to choose its leaders, how each would maintain control over its different divisions, and why each plan of government was important in the development of government in the United States. Have each group report to the class. Discuss the differences and similarities between the two plans of government.

Making Comparisons

The Albany Plan of Union prepared by Benjamin Franklin in 1754 was the first attempt to unite the colonies under one central government. Under this plan, each colony would keep its own government, but it would have to give up some of its powers. Below are several provisions—statements of conditions in a document—of the Albany Plan of Union.

1. The government under this plan will be run by a President-General, to be appointed and paid by the crown, and a Grand Council to be chosen by the representatives of the people in their colonial assemblies.
2. The Grand Council will meet in Philadelphia. The meeting will be called by the President-General soon after his appointment.
3. There will be a new election of the members of the Grand Council every three years.
4. The Grand Council will meet once in every year, and more often if it is required. In an emergency, the President-General can call a meeting if seven members agree.
5. The President-General must approve all laws of the Grand Council, and it is the duty of that officer to execute those laws.
6. The President-General with the advice of the Grand Council will make treaties with the Indians and if necessary, declare war against them. The council will regulate all Indian affairs.
7. The Grand Council will enlist soldiers and pay them, build forts for the defense of the colonies, and equip ships to guard the coasts.
8. For these purposes, the Grand Council can make laws and collect taxes as they feel necessary.
9. These laws will not be harmful and will be given to the king for his approval.

This plan contained many new ideas that the colonies did not agree with. They were afraid that this type of government would take away too much of their power. Read the

RELATED MATERIAL
Duplicator/Copy Master Activity 8

nine provisions of the Albany Plan of Union again. This time when you read, think about these questions: How would these provisions change what the colonial governments could and could not do? What powers would be taken away from the colonial governments and given to the Grand Council?

When you think about these questions, you are *making comparisons* between the Albany Plan of Union and the governments of the colonies. You are deciding how the Albany Plan of Union and the colonial governments were alike and how they were different. The words *alike* and *different* tell you that a comparison is being made.

Reread the paragraph entitled "Government" on page 86. Look for information about the House of Burgesses. How are that arrangement and the one proposed by the Albany Plan of Union *alike* and how are they *different*? Complete the following comparison chart on your own paper.

	House of Burgesses	**Albany Plan of Union**
When was each established or proposed?	1619	1754
Who was the leader (title)?	Governor	President-General
Who appointed the leader?	the king	the king
How were members chosen?	elected by the people	elected by the colonial assembly
Could the council or House make laws?	yes	yes
Who approved laws?	Governor	President-General
Could the council or House raise taxes?	yes	yes

ANSWERS

Questions in Paragraph:
They would take powers away from colonial governments.
power to make treaties with Indians, to declare war, to handle defense of colonies, and to pass laws and collect taxes for these purposes.

THINKING THINGS THROUGH

1. Both wanted to expand the empires; both came for business reasons—British to make a profit for companies, French to trade. 2. England would make money from its settlement. 3. Both wanted the land west of the Appalachians, were long-time enemies in Europe 4. The English were taking over Iroquois

Chapter 5 SUMMARY

England and France began to send their settlers to North America in an attempt to rule this land. These two countries organized their settlements differently.

The lands claimed by the two were very close together. Both countries wanted the lands west of the Appalachian Mountains.

The rivalry between England and France often caused war in Europe and in North America, too. These countries began to prepare for a war that would decide who would rule North America.

At the start of the final war between them, the French seemed to have the advantage owing to their friendship with the Indians. The English seemed weaker because the colonies could not work together.

The Albany Plan of Union aimed to solve the problem by setting up a government that would have a president-general and an elected council tying the colonies together. The plan was rejected by the colonies.

England tried to retake the Ohio River Valley and failed. Parliament elected William Pitt prime minister to turn these defeats around. The generals chosen by Pitt led England to victory in the Ohio River Valley and the Great Lakes area. Quebec and Montreal fell next.

The war was over. The Treaty of Paris was signed on February 10, 1763. With the French defeated, the English people could move westward. England realized that the colonies had to be watched more closely.

Chapter 5 TEST

WORDS TO REMEMBER

Select the best definition for each of the following vocabulary words.

1. *frontier:* border area
   border area small town fort
2. *ally:* friend
   friend neighbor enemy
3. *delegate:* representative
   voter soldier representative
4. *grievance:* complaint
   letter complaint agreement
5. *regiment:* military unit
   law-making body enemy military unit
6. *terrain:* land
   land moisture farm
7. *prime minister:* leader
   missionary leader teacher

THINKING THINGS THROUGH

Answer these questions in complete sentences.

1. How were the English reasons for settlement like those of the French?
2. Why was the land west of the Appalachian Mountains so important to the English?
3. What were the reasons the English and French had conflicts in North America?
4. Why were the Iroquois wary allies of the English?
5. Was the economy of the English colonies or of New France better able to support lasting colonies? Why?

RELATED MATERIALS
Duplicator/Copy Masters: Activities 8, 9; Quiz 8
Workbook pages 14-16

lands **5.** English colonies had more variety. If one part of the economy failed, another could succeed. In New France, if the fur trade failed, the claim was finished.

WORKING WITH SKILLS

Use your textbook to help you complete the following chart, which compares the battles of the French and Indian War.

Battle	Date (If Given)	Generals (If Given) English/French	Winning Side
Necessity	July 4, 1754	Washington	French
Duquesne	July 1755	Gage & Braddock	French
Oswego	———	Loudoun / Montcalm	French
William Henry	———	Loudoun / Montcalm	French
Louisbourg	July 26, 1758	Amherst	English
Frontenac	August 1758	Bradstreet	English
Niagara	July 25, 1759	Prideaux	English
Ticonderoga	July 26, 1759	Amherst	English
Crown Point	July 31, 1759	Amherst	English
Quebec	Sept 18, 1759	Wolfe / Montcalm	English
Montreal	Sept. 8, 1760	Amherst	English

ON YOUR OWN

1. Pretend that you are a colonist assigned to George Washington from 1753 to July 4, 1754. Write an entry into a journal for each event during that time described in your textbook. Be sure to use complete sentences.

2. Make up a word search or a crossword puzzle using the names of the battles and generals in the French and Indian War. Use clues to help your classmates remember these names.

Chapter 6
A NEW PEOPLE

Chapter 6 introduces students to the British colonies in the 1700s as established and relatively stable societies. As the colonies became more economically independent, the British tried to exert more control, and conflicts arose. Lesson 6-1 discusses the Navigation Acts and their effects. Lesson 6-2 mentions the colonists' growing dissatisfaction with British intervention. Lesson 6-3 outlines the events surrounding the Townshend Acts, the Boston Massacre, the Boston Tea Party and the Intolerable Acts.

CONTENT OBJECTIVES

After completing the chapter, students will know:

- that the colonists had an independent spirit in the early 1700s
- why the English felt it necessary to control trade in the colonies
- the economic and symbolic impact of the Navigation Acts

VOCABULARY

occupation: a job
tract: a stretch of land
commerce: the buying and selling of goods from different places
manufacturing: the making of large amounts of goods by hand or machine
foundry: a place where ore and metal are melted and molded
depression: a reduction or slowing of business activity
mercantilism: a theory stating that the country that had the most wealth had the most power
enumerated: listed
favorable balance of trade: when one country sells more goods to another country than it buys from it
smuggle: carrying goods to another country illegally
reservation: land set aside for a special purpose

6-1 The Colonial Economy

As you read, think about these questions:
What jobs were available in the colonies in 1760?
What was the population of the colonies in 1760?
What were the results of the Navigation Acts?
What was the Proclamation of 1763?

Special Vocabulary		
	occupation	mercantilism
	tract	enumerated
	commerce	favorable balance of trade
	manufacturing	smuggle
	foundry	reservation
	depression	

By the middle of the 1700s, Great Britain had been in America for about one hundred fifty years. By this time, some families had lived in the New World for four generations. This means, for example, that a young woman could have had a mother, a grandmother, and a great grandmother—all born in America. Families that had lived in the colonies for such a long time often felt they had little in common with their fellow British subjects back in England. The people in the colonies had their own ideas about how to make a living and to run a government.

The leaders in Great Britain, however, thought of the colonists as British subjects who should be willing to work at keeping Great Britain wealthy and powerful. Parliament and the king saw no difference between what was expected of people in Great Britain and those in the colonies.

Making a Living

If you were a visitor traveling to the colonies from England in 1760, a whole new experience would await you when you got off the ship in any of the large American ports. No longer would you find settlements surrounded by stockades and wilderness. Instead, in a few busy cities you would see a society bustling with business, trade, and government work.

Outside the cities, more than a million and a half other colonial people were engaged in raising agricultural products, trapping fur-bearing animals, and fishing. The thirteen colonies you would visit in 1760 were no longer struggling for survival. They had an air of prosperity and promise.

Boston was among the largest and most prosperous colonial cities in 1764. Even so, the harbor was probably not as busy as this watercolor indicates. Many cities of that time advertised themselves with prints of this type, often exaggerating their good points.

Opportunity in America. By 1760 an estimated 1,695,000 people lived in the thirteen colonies. The largest cities—Philadelphia, 23,750; New York, 18,000; Boston, 15,600; Charleston, 8,000; and Newport, 7,500—were ports through which colonial goods reached other parts of the world.

The colonies in 1760 provided many opportunities for people who were ambitious. A hard-working colonist could make a lot of money in America more easily than in any other place in the world. Many *occupations*, or kinds of jobs, were available.

For farmers, acres of rich land lay ready for the plow and seed. Almost any white male who wished to could own land. It was cheap and available. Many people made their fortunes by buying a large *tract*, or stretch of land, and selling it in smaller pieces. These landowners held much power and were respected in the colonies.

ACTIVITY

Objective: To make comparisons

Have students prepare two lists of common occupations, one titled: colonial times, the other: present day. Under colonial times students might have trapper, farmer, and artisan. Under present day, they might have secretary, computer programmer, and salesperson. Have students compare the two lists. Discuss those jobs, such as farmer, which have the same title but have changed significantly. Have the students explain why this change occurred. Some jobs are the same, but less important. Discuss with students why this happened. Have them explain why some jobs in the present-day list do not appear in the colonial times list.

A worker in a restored colonial village displays wool fibers that have been carded, or untangled and pulled into long strands. Colonists used carding machines like those pictured to prepare the wool to be spun into yarn.

Merchants, too, found America the place to be. Nowhere else in the world was *commerce*, the buying and selling of goods from different places, growing as quickly. Merchants, selling a wide range of goods, played the chief part in giving the colonists the hope that they could live better each year. The merchants depended heavily on the special goods that each group of colonies produced. From New England and the Middle colonies, the West Indies eagerly bought fish, lumber, corn, wheat, and livestock. From the Southern colonies, tobacco filled the ships that sailed for Great Britain. American merchants and English merchants knew that in America they could make a large profit.

Manufacturing, or the making of large amounts of goods by hand or machine, was also profitable. From the beginning of English settlement, colonists were turning out furniture, barrels, bottles, and spinning wheels. The raw materials for such manufactured goods were very plentiful and available. The growing population provided a ready market for them, and a good profit could be made.

Ironworks, too, began to dot the countryside. Hundreds of *foundries*, places where ore and metal are melted and molded, operated in the colonies. Because of its fine quality ore and abundant oak forests, used to fire the furnaces that melted the ore, Pennsylvania had most of the ironworks.

Fishing, although it was dangerous, was another attractive occupation offering profits. The Grand Banks of Newfoundland were often covered by fog and dotted with icebergs. Still, they yielded many kinds of fish wanted in the West Indies and southern Europe.

Paying for the French and Indian War

At the end of the French and Indian War, Great Britain faced a large war debt. In order to pay this debt, the government placed high taxes on the people of Great Britain. An army, moreover, was being kept in America to protect the colonists from Indian attacks. The cost of these troops added to the huge debt.

In the eyes of the British, the colonies had benefited from the protection provided by British soldiers during the war. King George III and his advisers believed that Americans should help pay for the services of the British army. Parliament, therefore, decided to tax the colonists just as it taxed British subjects at home.

The taxes came at a bad time for the colonists. After the French and Indian War, the colonies slipped into an economic *depression*, a reduction of business activity. Most of the British soldiers had returned home. Many of the goods and services they required were no longer needed. The colonists insisted they were unable to pay the taxes.

Mercantilism. A new theory and system called *mercantilism* had begun to be accepted by European nations during the 1500s. This theory said that the country that had the most wealth—measured in land, gold, and silver—had the most power. The chief way for a nation to grow rich was to have colonies. When Great Britain set up its colonies all over the world, it was following the ideas of the mercantile system. The leaders of Great Britain came to regard the thirteen colonies in North America as the greatest source of national wealth.

The colonists could manufacture goods, set up businesses, and carry on trade. However, the most important goal of the colonists—according to the mercantile theory—was to make Great Britain rich. This meant that the home country must control the economic activity of the colonists.

Navigation Acts. Parliament from the 1600s on carried out the ideas of mercantilism by passing a set of laws called the Navigation Acts. One of these laws said that the colonies had to sell the home country the sugar, tobacco, indigo, cotton, and wool they produced. These raw materials which *had* to be sent to Great Britain were called *enumerated*, or listed, articles. Great Britain would manufacture products from these materials and sell them back to the colonies for a profit.

Great Britain also tried to make it difficult, if not impossible, for foreign countries to trade with the colonies. Look at the chart on page 130. It shows the provisions of each of the Navigation Acts.

Results of the Navigation Acts. The goal of the Navigation Acts was to give Great Britain a *favorable balance of trade* with the colonies. This kind of trade exists when one country sells more goods to another country than it buys from it. The colonies imported from Great Britain most of the supplies necessary for living, including paper, tea, paint, nails, tools, farm equipment. On the other hand, the colonies sold Great Britain a few raw materials and tobacco. Great Britain, therefore, had a favorable balance of trade with the colonies.

Ships from Great Britain's eastern and western colonies unloaded their cargoes at the Custom House Quay, shown below. The quay was located on the Thames River in London.

THE NAVIGATION ACTS		
Year	**Provisions**	**Effects in the colonies**
1650	1) Ships from foreign countries could not trade in colonies without a special license. 2) No goods brought from Africa, Asia, or America could be traded into England or the colonies except in ships of which the owner, captain, and most of the crew members were English. 3) No European goods could be brought to England or the colonies except on English ships or ships from the country the goods came from.	Virginia refused to obey the laws. Massachusetts, Rhode Island, and Connecticut continued to trade with the Dutch—the nation this law was aimed at.
1660	1) No goods could be imported into or exported out of any English colony except on English built or owned ships. 2) Three fourths of the crew had to be English. 3) Sugar, tobacco, indigo, wool, and cotton could be shipped only to England.	The colonies did not like the fact that Great Britain would profit from selling their goods to other nations at higher prices than it paid to the colonies.
1663	European goods to be shipped to the colonies first had to stop in England. The goods then had to be transferred onto English ships.	This made the goods the colonies imported from Europe scarce. The goods that did come over were more costly.
1673	A fee was placed on enumerated articles shipped from one colony to another.	This made the price of these materials go up.
1696	1) All goods brought to the colonies had to be on English ships. 2) Custom officials were allowed to take stolen goods and to break into buildings to look for these goods. 3) Colonial laws that did not agree with the Navigation Acts were removed.	This now forced the colonies to begin an illegal trade with foreign countries.

Before the French and Indian War, Great Britain did not try to enforce the Navigation Acts. Afterwards, however, it decided to make the colonies obey the laws.

DISCUSSION

Discuss with the students the reasons why the colonists smuggled goods. Using the triangular trade map (p. 131), have the students name the different kinds of goods smuggled and trace the paths followed by these goods between the West Indies and the colonies. Be sure to ask the students if they think the colonists were right or wrong in carrying out these smuggling activities.

Triangular Trade. In order to keep buying the goods they needed from Great Britain, the colonies had felt forced to *smuggle*, or sell their goods to another country illegally. This way Americans could make enough money to pay for British products. Smuggling was a clear violation of the Navigation Acts, but the colonists believed they had no other choice.

New England colonists suffered most from the Navigation Acts. They had an illegal but profitable trade with Africa and the West Indies known as the "Triangular Trade." (See the globe of the triangular trade route on page 131.) New

A Triangular Trade Route

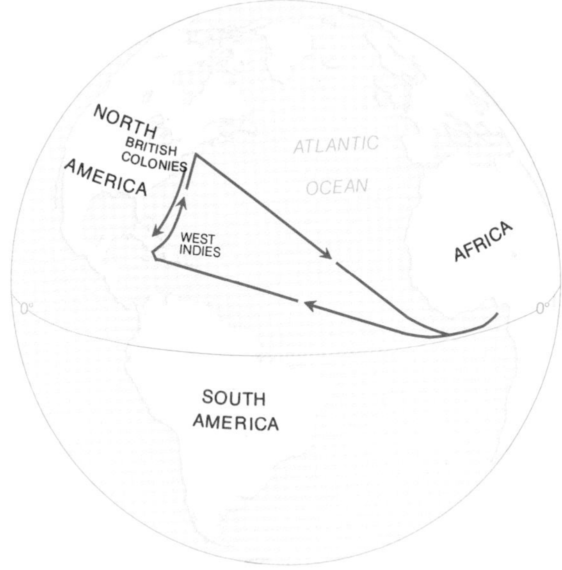

British Colonies, West Indies, Africa

This globe shows the route of New England traders. What three places made up the "triangle" of illegal trade?

England traders loaded their ships with fish and lumber and sailed to the West Indies. There they picked up sugar, molasses, and money in exchange for the fish and lumber. The ships then returned to New England, where the molasses was made into rum. The rum was then shipped across the Atlantic to Africa and traded there for slaves. The slaves were loaded on ships and taken to the West Indies and the southern colonies. There the slaves were traded for sugar, molasses, or tobacco. Then the trade began again. The greatest victims were the Africans.

This etching from the late 1600s shows the West Indian slaves carrying sugar cane to presses where the cane is squeezed to produce juice. The juice is piped to the stove in the center where the sweet liquid is boiled to form sugar.

Slavery in the Colonies. The use of slaves in the colonies was accepted by many. A few of the colonists, however, were calling for its end. Benjamin Rush, who was a well-known doctor in Pennsylvania, gave his opinion:

> The first step to put a stop to slavery in this country, is to leave off importing slaves. For this purpose, let our assemblies unite in petitioning the king and Parliament. . . . Let such of our countrymen as engage in the slave trade, be shunned as the greatest enemies to our country and let the vessels that bring the slaves to us be avoided. . . . The plant of liberty is of so tender a nature, that it cannot long thrive in the neighborhood of slavery. . . .

Many were influenced by these writings, but the southern colonies continued to import slaves. The demand for labor in these colonies was great. Southern tobacco growers believed they needed many people to work in the fields.

Proclamation of 1763. The middle and southern colonies were also hurt by a new policy. At the end of the French and Indian War, Great Britain owned most of the land between the Appalachian Mountains and the Mississippi River. (See the map of North America in 1763 on page 133.) This large area of land was the home of many Indian groups. Some of these groups understandably became very upset when English settlers moved into these lands. The Indians felt that the English fur trappers and land companies were stealing their lands. Great Britain, however, was slow to understand the problem.

The Ottawa chief, Pontiac, encouraged other Indians to join him in fighting the British. The resulting struggle that raged on the western frontier for months in 1763 is known as Pontiac's War. Pontiac and his warriors were able to capture every fort in the west except Detroit.

In order to stop the war, Parliament passed the Proclamation of 1763. The proclamation made the lands west of the Appalachian Mountains a large Indian *reservation*, land set aside for a special purpose.

The proclamation angered two groups of colonists. First were the English settlers of middle and southern colonies who were going to be kept from moving into this area. Second were the colonial land companies, which would be prevented from buying and selling land in the area. Great

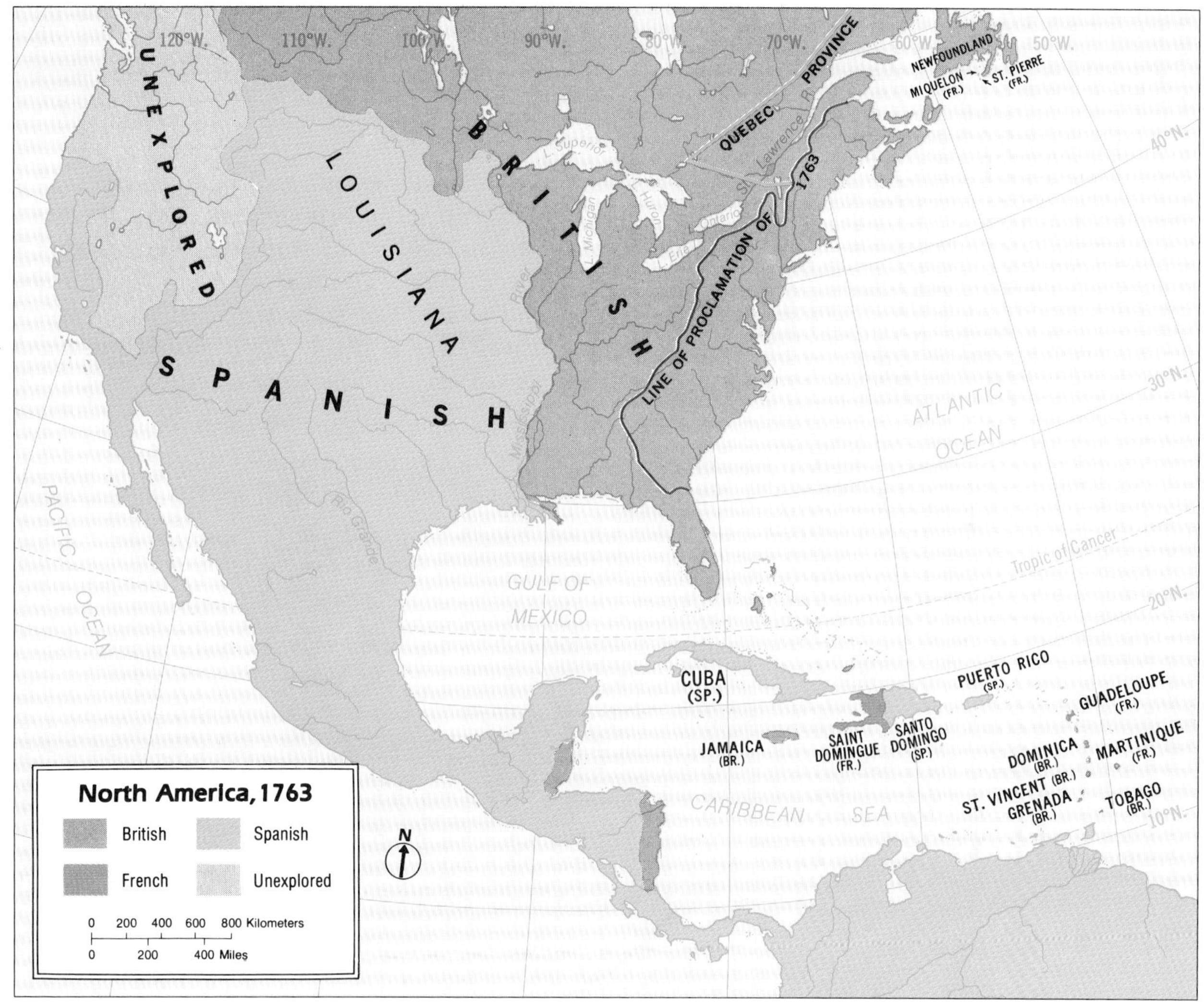

Britain did not make a reservation out of the lands west of the Appalachians only for the purpose of helping the Indians. After a short while, Great Britain hoped to set up its own land companies to make money that the colonists were no longer able to make.

In 1763 North America was controlled by only two countries—England and Spain. What was the dividing line between the English and Spanish claims?

The Mississippi River

ANSWER THESE QUESTIONS

1. farming, trading, manufacturing, fishing
2. Philadelphia
3. the theory that the nation with the most wealth has the most power
4. that a nation sells more goods to a nation than it buys from it
5. forced the colonies to sell products for less and buy for more; could only trade with Great Britain, making more money for Great Britain

ANSWER THESE QUESTIONS

1. What jobs were available in the colonies in 1760?
2. What was the largest colonial city in 1760?
3. What is mercantilism?
4. What is meant by a favorable balance of trade?
5. How did the Navigation Acts prove that Great Britain believed that the colonies were in North America only to help it make money?

Objective: After completing these pages, students should be able to locate places using latitude and longitude

Working with Skills

MAP SKILLS

ANSWERS

1. prime meridian 2. Greenwich 3. North Pole and South Pole 4. 20° west longitude; 20° east longitude

Using Longitude and Latitude

You have heard the terms longitude and latitude when you studied maps before. You should remember that these lines are important to the navigators of ships or to anyone who wants to read a map of the large areas on earth. Longitude lines run north and south, but they are used to measure distances east and west. Look at the globe showing lines of longitude and then answer the following questions.

1. The line marked 0° has another name. What is it?
2. What is the name of the city through which the 0° line runs?
3. All longitude lines meet at what two points?
4. What do you call the 20° line to the left of the 0° line? What do you call the 20° line to the right of the 0° line?

1. equator 2. no 3. 60° north latitude; 60° south latitude 4. North Pole and South Pole

Look at the globe showing lines of latitude. Latitude lines run east and west, but they are used to measure distances north and south. Answer these questions:

1. What is the 0° line called?
2. Do latitude lines ever meet?
3. What do you call the 60° line above the 0° line? What do you call the 60° line below the 0° line?
4. What two places are both 90°?

Lines of Longitude

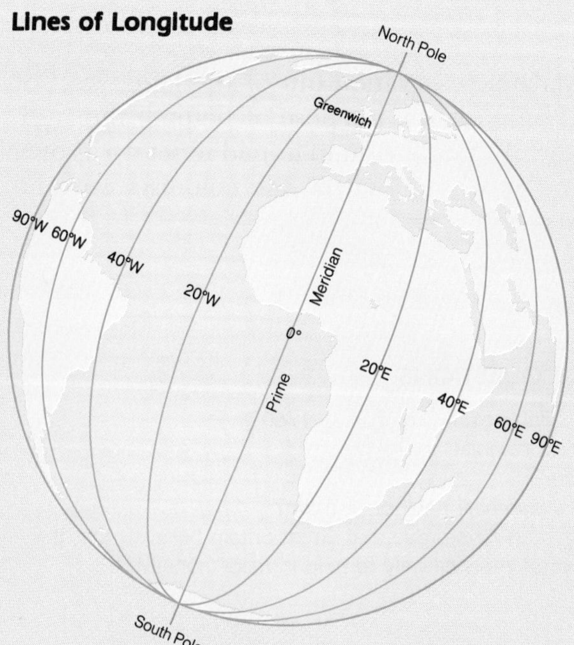

Lines of Latitude

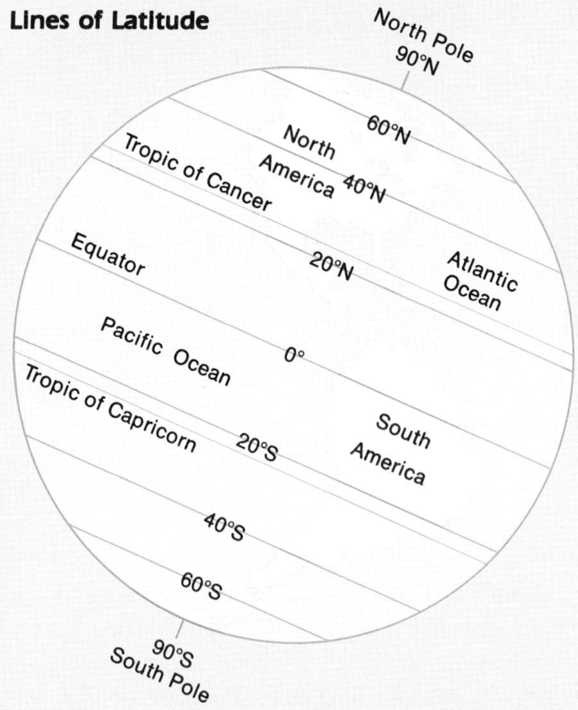

ACTIVITY

Objective: To use latitude and longitude

Have each student look at a map of the United States that shows latitude and longitude and shows the locations of cities. Call out the names of three or four cities and have students name the latitude and longitude of each. Then state the latitude and longitude of several cities. Have students find the location and name each city.

When mapmakers combine lines of longitude and latitude, the globe becomes a huge grid, as shown on the map on pages 750–751.

Turn to the map of North America in 1763 on page 133. Notice that this map contains longitude and latitude lines. These lines were important to the countries of Europe because the lines made it easier to decide where the borders of each claim were. Study this map carefully and then answer the following questions:

1. What large island in the Atlantic is located between 50° and 60° west longitude?
2. What Spanish island is located near the intersection of 20° north latitude and 80° west longitude?
3. What river empties into the Gulf of Mexico at the intersection of 30° north latitude and 90° west longitude?
4. Which country claimed most of the land between 70° and 90° west longitude?
5. What country claimed most of the land between 90° and 110° west longitude?

1. Newfoundland **2.** Cuba **3.** Mississippi **4.** Great Britain **5.** Spain

RELATED MATERIALS

Duplicator/Copy Master: Activity 10

CONTENT OBJECTIVES

After completing the lesson, students will know:

- the significance of the Sugar Act and other new regulations that indicated a shift in Great Britain's attitude toward the colonies
- how the issue of "taxation without representation" united the colonies against England
- why Parliament repealed the Stamp Act

VOCABULARY

quarter: provide living space for soldiers
indirect tax: a charge placed on goods when the customer buys them
direct tax: charge a customer must pay in addition to the price of the goods
resolution: formal expression of opinion
boycott: refusal to buy or use a product
repeal: withdraw
petition: make a formal request

DISCUSSION

Discuss with the students the way British taxation policy for the colonies was decided in the mid-1700s. Discuss the ways present-day American taxation policies are decided. Why did the colonists object to the British taxation? Ask the students whether they think representation in government might make a difference in the way people feel about taxation. How are Americans represented when tax laws are discussed and passed in government today?

6-2 Colonial Policies of Great Britain

As you read, think about these questions:

Why did the colonists object to the Sugar Act?

What is the difference between an indirect tax and a direct tax?

What did the colonies do to show their anger over the Stamp Act?

Why did Parliament repeal the Stamp Act?

Special Vocabulary	quarter	resolution	repeal
	indirect tax	boycott	petition
	direct tax		

By making sure the colonies obeyed the old Navigation Acts and the Proclamation of 1763, Great Britain changed its method of governing the thirteen colonies. For many years, the colonies had been left to themselves. Now they had to live under tighter control than they had ever known.

Colonists Battle Grenville

At the end of the French and Indian War, George Grenville, a new prime minister of Great Britain, had taken office. He soon went beyond merely enforcing the Navigation Acts and the Proclamation of 1763. He asked for new laws taxing the colonies. Parliament quickly passed them.

Sugar Act. Never before in colonial history had the government of Great Britain tried to raise money *in* the colonies. In 1764 with the passage of the Sugar Act, George Grenville changed that policy. The Sugar Act lowered the tax on molasses but made the cost of sugar higher. It put new products on the enumerated list and placed a higher tax than before on foreign goods being shipped from Great Britain into the colonies.

Grenville also took steps to make sure this law was obeyed. Colonists accused of disobeying it would have to go to Nova Scotia to stand trial. Colonial courts would not be allowed to hear the cases. In these trials the person would be guilty unless proven innocent. No jury would be allowed to judge

the case. The law and these new rules to carry it out caused an uproar in the colonies.

Parliament ruled that colonial merchants who violated the Sugar Act could not be tried at home. Instead, their trials would take place at the Admiralty Courts in distant Halifax, Nova Scotia, shown above.

Quartering Act. Parliament further angered the colonists by passing the Quartering Act in 1765. This law said that the colonial legislatures had to pay to *quarter* the British army in America. This meant the colonists had to give the British soldiers places to live while stationed in the colonies. The colonies also had to furnish the soldiers with all their supplies. The colonists protested that they were being asked to pay for something they had not voted for.

Stamp Act. Prime Minister Grenville and Parliament saw that the colonies would not accept the *indirect tax* that the Sugar Act placed on them. An indirect tax is a charge placed on goods before the customer buys them. This charge is included in the price of the goods when they are sold. If the colonies would not accept an indirect tax, Parliament said they would have to pay a *direct tax*. This tax is a charge a

According to the Stamp Act, colonists had to buy stamps like these for deeds, bills of sale, and other documents. The Stamp Act met with great opposition because it angered the most vocal colonists—among them, writers, ministers, and lawyers.

customer must pay in addition to the price of the goods. Therefore, in March of 1765, Parliament passed the Stamp Act. The Stamp Act put a tax on almost every kind of document used in the colonies. Marriage licenses, birth certificates, newspapers, decks of cards, and pamphlets all had to have a special stamp on them—paid for by the colonists. The money raised from this tax was to be used by Great Britain to pay the British soldiers protecting the colonies.

Most people in Great Britain thought that the Stamp Act was an acceptable way to raise money for the defense of the colonies. After all, British citizens had had their own stamp tax for a number of years. Grenville tried to make sure the colonies would not object to the tax by appointing Americans as the tax collectors. When word of this new tax reached the colonists, however, their reaction was swift.

Colonial Fears

The anger in the colonies quickly rose to fever pitch. The Stamp Act raised a number of fears in the colonies. If Parliament could directly tax the colonies this one time, it could do it again and again—anytime.

Further, because only certain courts could try people who did not obey the law, the right to a trial by jury might be taken away. The placing of this tax on the colonies when they were fighting the effects of a depression convinced many Americans that the home country was out to ruin the American colonies. These fears helped to unite the colonies in their feelings against Great Britain. The cry "no taxation without representation" rang throughout the colonies.

Colonies Acting Together. Throughout the colonies, legislatures raised their voices to protest the Stamp Act. The colony of Virginia passed a set of *resolutions*, or formal expressions of opinion. These stated the Virginians' view of the Stamp Act. Patrick Henry, a representative in the Virginia legislature, spoke in favor of these resolutions. He stated that only the Virginia legislature had the right to tax Virginians.

Various voices spoke out against the Stamp Act. Secret groups, made up of both wealthy and poor people, were formed in the summer of 1765. The purpose of these groups, known as the Sons of Liberty, was to organize the people against the Stamp Act. The Sons of Liberty rapidly grew in numbers. They succeeded in making every stamp tax collector in America quit before November 1, when the law was to go into effect. The Sons of Liberty also started a *boycott*, or a refusal to buy or use a product, of British goods. This boycott hurt the business of British merchants. The Sons of Liberty also used violence to make sure Great Britain knew how angry the colonies were about the Stamp Act.

Patrick Henry, a leading opponent of the Stamp Act, warned King George III that some kings had lost their lives for actions against their people.

Stamp Act Congress. The Massachusetts assembly, on a proposal of James Otis, voted to ask for a meeting of all the colonies in October of 1765. This meeting, called the Stamp Act Congress, met in New York City. Representatives from nine colonies attended. The Congress drew up a Declaration of Rights and Grievances which was sent to the king.

This declaration stated that the people in the colonies had the same rights as the people in Great Britain. One right was that people could not be taxed unless their representatives voted for those taxes. The colonists pointed out that they did not have a voice in Parliament. They declared, therefore,

This British etching from 1774 reveals the colonists' anger at British taxation. A reference to the Stamp Act appears on the tree. In the foreground, colonists force a tarred and feathered tax collector to drink tea, a protest against a tax on tea and other products.

ACTIVITY

Objective: To identify cause and effect relationships

Divide the class into two groups: Group 1 is the Stamp Act Congress, with colonial representatives, and Benjamin Franklin as one of the leaders. Group 2 is the British Parliament, with Pitt and Grenville as leaders. One student from Group 2 should introduce to the class the provisions of the Stamp Act. Direct Group 1 to present the reasons why they object to the act by presenting a formal written request to Group 2 urging repeal of the act. Group 2 should study the petition and decide what to do about the Stamp Act. After the students have done this, ask them to trace the chain of cause and effect that led to their decisions. Also discuss what they think might happen next. Use the actual events described in section 6-2 as a basis for the discussion.

ANSWER THESE QUESTIONS

1. George Grenville
2. marriage licenses, birth certificates, calendars, newspapers, decks of cards, and pamphlets
3. people in the colonies had the same rights as the people in Great Britain
4. An indirect tax is a fee placed on goods before a customer buys them. A direct tax is a fee added to the cost of the products when the customer buys them.
5. The colonists felt that only their own legislatures should be able to tax them. That way, they would have control over the taxes because they had elected the representatives. In Parliament, where they had no representative, they had no control over taxes passed.

that Parliament should not be allowed to tax the colonies. Only the colonial legislatures should have this right, the colonists insisted.

The colonists also stated that all British citizens had a right to a trial by jury. The courts hearing Stamp Act cases took away this right. The colonists objected very strongly to this part of the law. Finally, the colonists of the Stamp Act Congress demanded that the Stamp Act be *repealed*, or withdrawn.

Repeal of the Stamp Act. The colonies were united in their refusal to buy the special stamps required by law and in their boycott of British goods. Business almost stopped. Several companies in Great Britain had to close down because of the boycott. Soon the merchants in Great Britain *petitioned*, or made a formal request to, Parliament to repeal the law.

Parliament met to discuss the Stamp Act. Prime Minister Grenville asked Parliament to use the army to make the colonies obey the law. William Pitt, the prime minister during the French and Indian War, spoke for repeal. Many people were called on to speak. Benjamin Franklin argued that the colonies did not have the money to pay the tax. He warned Parliament that if soldiers were used to make the colonies obey this law, a revolt was possible. He, too, asked Parliament to repeal the Stamp Act.

On April 26, 1766, the news reached America that Parliament had repealed the Stamp Act. The colonies felt they had won a great battle. Parliament had granted the request of the colonies and the British merchants in repealing the Stamp Act. The very day of repeal, however, it passed another law which received little attention in the colonies. Under this law, called the Declaratory Act, Parliament said that it had the right to make all laws affecting the colonies in America. Parliament had not given away this right when it repealed the Stamp Act. Unfortunately, many colonists were left with the mistaken belief that it had.

ANSWER THESE QUESTIONS

1. Who was the prime minister when the Sugar Act was passed?
2. What documents were taxed by the Stamp Act?
3. What did the Declaration of Rights and Grievances state?
4. What is the difference between an indirect tax and a direct tax?
5. Why were the words "taxation without representation" so important to the colonists?

6-3 Opposing Views

As you read, think about these questions:
What were the provisions of the Townshend Acts?
What was the Boston Massacre?
What was the purpose of the Committees of Correspondence?
Why did Parliament pass the Tea Act?
What was the result of the Boston Tea Party?

Special Vocabulary writs of assistance, patriot, sentry, intolerable, tyrant

CONTENT OBJECTIVES

After completing the lesson, students will know:

- how the Townshend Acts created further strife in the colonies, to the point of open rebellion
- the significance of Samuel Adams' Committee of Correspondence
- the events leading to the Boston Massacre and the Boston Tea Party
- how the British punished the citizens of Massachusetts for their resistance

VOCABULARY

writs of assistance: legal papers allowing British soldiers to enter any home or store in search of smuggled goods
patriot: person who agreed with the colonists' side
sentry: a soldier stationed at a post to keep watch
intolerable: unbearable
tyrant: unjust ruler

The colonists hoped that trouble between themselves and Great Britain had now ended. They believed that Great Britain had acted fairly. It had repealed a law the colonies hated. This action by Parliament gave many colonists the idea that complaints and boycotts would cause the king and Parliament to back down. These colonists could not have been more wrong. In fact, Parliament was ready to begin a new round of taxes.

Charles Townshend

Grenville had left office after Parliament repealed the Stamp Act. William Pitt took his place. The colonists felt very lucky. They regarded Pitt as a friend. Pitt had taken their side in the repeal of the Stamp Act. However, after only a short while in office, he fell ill. Charles Townshend replaced him as prime minister.

Townshend believed that the colonies in North America existed to help the home country. He also felt that the French and Indian War had made the taxes on the people of Great Britain too high. He figured that taxing the colonies would help lower the taxes at home.

Charles Townshend's acts of taxation were so harsh that some critics predicted—correctly—that Great Britain would lose the colonies because of them.

The Townshend Acts. In 1767 Parliament passed a new set of laws known as the Townshend Acts. The Townshend Acts put a tax on all paint, glass, lead, paper, and tea imported by the colonies. The money raised by these taxes would be used partly to pay for the defense of the colonies. Part would also be used to pay the salaries of colonial governors and judges. In the past, colonial legislatures had always voted on these salaries, so the governors and judges had tried not to anger the colonists. The Townshend Acts took the vote on salaries away from the colonists. Now the officials did not have to worry about angering the colonists.

Under the Townshend Acts, the courts could give out *writs of assistance*. These were legal papers allowing British soldiers to enter any home or store in search of smuggled goods. Anger greeted the news of these latest laws passed by Parliament. Once again Americans began a boycott. Colonists everywhere pledged not to buy British goods. The Townshend Acts had helped bring the colonies together again.

Boston Massacre. Conditions in the colonies worsened. Some *patriots*, people who agreed with the colonists' side, even turned violent. Great Britain sent more soldiers to America to keep order. Most of them were stationed in Boston. There the patriots were strongest.

Pictures like this engraving by Paul Revere helped spread the word about the Boston Massacre. Such pictures were published quickly, much as paperback books about important events are today.

On March 5, 1770, a *sentry*—a soldier stationed at a post to keep watch—shouted for help. A noisy crowd of colonists had gathered. They were pelting the guard with snowballs. Captain Thomas Preston and six British soldiers came to see what the trouble was. They became the target of sticks, stones, and clubs, as well as snowballs. Preston could not get the crowd to stop its mischief. It closed in on the soldiers. Suddenly, the word "Fire!" was shouted—no one knows by whom. The soldiers fired into the crowd. Three colonists lay dead, and two others died later from their wounds. Crispus Attucks, an escaped slave who led the charge, was among those who died. He became a hero to many of the colonists.

The soldiers and Captain Preston stood trial for the death of the five colonists. Defended by colonial lawyers John Adams and Josiah Quincy, the seven soldiers were found not guilty. Yet word spread of "the Boston Massacre."

The Tension Continues

By 1770 Great Britain had lost much of its control over the colonies. Some Americans were talking openly of rebellion. Most people, though, were still loyal to the king. The patriots knew that to win more support for their side, things would have to be kept stirred up. Without widespread backing, any rebellion would fail.

Repeal of the Townshend Acts. The colonial boycott of British goods brought results. Lord North, yet another new prime minister, got Parliament to repeal some of the Townshend Acts. He did not want all the taxes removed. He was sure the colonists would see a total repeal as a sign of weakness on the part of Parliament. The tax on tea remained. Most people began to buy British goods after Parliament did as North asked. The anger in the colonies began to disappear. Trade and business returned to normal.

Violence at Sea. In spite of better enforcement of the Navigation Acts, the smuggling of foreign goods still went on. The British were determined to end it. They placed *Gaspee*, an armed ship, off the coast of Rhode Island. In June 1772, *Gaspee*, chasing a smuggler ship near Providence, Rhode Island, ran aground on a sandbar. That night, colonists from Providence went aboard the ship. They wounded the captain, captured the crew, and set the ship on fire.

ACTIVITY

Objective: To classify information

Certain Parliamentary actions passed in the mid-1700s caused unrest in the colonies. Put on the chalkboard two columns, one labeled Political Causes and the other labeled Economic Causes. Have students choose the acts of Parliament that involved restrictions on colonial voting, rights of assembly, control of colonial government and jury trials. Place these acts in the Political Causes column. Have the students explain why they caused tension. In the Economic Causes list, put those acts involved with the levy of taxes. Discuss with the class how these acts led to increased tension.

After the *Gaspee* was burned, a commission was appointed to bring the guilty colonists to trial. The people of Rhode Island would not cooperate with the commission, so it never found evidence to name the individuals involved.

The British were furious. They pledged that the guilty colonists—including some leading citizens of Providence—would be found. When caught, they would be sent to Great Britain for trial. The event stirred up the colonists again.

Sam Adams, a leader of the Boston patriots, saw the *Gaspee* incident as one more reason to push for the separation of the colonies from Great Britain. He organized a Committee of Correspondence. The purpose of this committee was to send people and letters from town to town throughout Massachusetts to let the colonists know of Great Britain's latest plans.

Virginia's House of Burgesses set up its own Committee of Correspondence. Four more colonies followed Virginia's lead. For the first time, important leaders in the colonies were working together.

Tea Act. One of the favorite drinks in the colonies was tea. Tea sold very well when its price was low. The cheapest tea had always been that which was smuggled into the colonies by Dutch traders. This smuggling hurt the British East India Company, which sold tea legally in the colonies. The company asked Parliament for help.

Not all the colonists shared the same ideas about the Boston Tea Party. Some of the people in the engraving above did not want the tea brought ashore, but they were upset about the destruction of private property.

Parliament passed a law called the Tea Act. This law allowed the East India Company to send its tea to America without having to pay the import tax required by Great Britain. Even with the Townshend tax on the tea, the tea would be cheaper than that smuggled into the colonies.

Parliament also said the East India Company could only sell tea to a few selected merchants. Parliament was trying to give the East India Company a monopoly on the sale of tea to the colonists. Moreover, if the colonists bought the tea, they would be agreeing to pay the Townshend tax.

Boston Tea Party. The East India Company sent its tea to Boston, New York, Philadelphia, and Charleston. All the tea sent to New York and Philadelphia was returned to Great Britain. Charleston accepted the tea but put it in a warehouse before it could be sold. Only in Boston did the tea force a showdown between the colonists and the British officials.

Governor Thomas Hutchinson was determined that the tea aboard *Dartmouth* and two other ships be unloaded from Boston Harbor. The colonists insisted that the tea be sent back to Great Britain with no tax being collected. Sam Adams, through the Committees of Correspondence, set up

DISCUSSION

Discuss with the students the reasons why colonies sometimes want to become independent. Have them imagine that they were colonists and ask them to describe the ways they would have chosen to oppose the actions of the British government. Try to arrive at a consensus of opinion about the best method of opposition—passive resistance, for example, boycotting of goods, or active resistance, such as throwing tea into Boston Harbor.

a meeting in South Church to talk about this situation. Over eight thousand people listened as the leaders from Boston and the surrounding towns made their decision. The tea would not be unloaded from Boston Harbor.

On December 16, 1773, a group of fifty colonists dressed as Mohawks marched to Griffin's Wharf. Working through the night, these "Indians" dumped all 342 cases of tea into the harbor.

The Intolerable Acts. Many Americans cheered the violent act. They made fun of the British by calling the event the "Boston Tea Party." News of it reached Great Britain in January. An angry King George III asked Parliament to punish the citizens of Massachusetts for this spiteful destruction of private property. Parliament acted quickly, for its members agreed with the king. The punishment of Boston would be an example to the rest of the colonies.

In March, Parliament passed three laws called the Coercive Acts. The colonists called them the *Intolerable*, or unbearable, Acts. The first law ordered that Boston Harbor be closed. No goods could be shipped in or out of the harbor until the colonists paid for the tea. The second law allowed British officers accused of crimes in Massachusetts to have their trials moved to Great Britain. This was to protect them from the anger of the colonists. The third law suspended the Massachusetts charter. The citizens of Massachusetts could no longer choose members of their legislatures. These would now be chosen by the king. The colonists would not be able to choose juries to hear trials either. These would now be chosen by the British sheriff. All town meetings in Massachusetts were forbidden.

By passing these laws, Great Britain had become the enemy in the minds of many Americans. The colonists came to regard King George III as a *tyrant*, an unjust ruler. The king was determined to stand up to them. He declared, "The New England governments are in a state of rebellion."

ANSWER THESE QUESTIONS

1. What products were taxed by the Townshend Acts?
2. What were the writs of assistance?
3. Who organized the first Committee of Correspondence?
4. What effect did the tax on tea have on colonists?
5. Why did the colonies call the Coercive Acts the Intolerable Acts?

ANSWER THESE QUESTIONS

1. paint, glass, lead, paper, and tea
2. legal papers allowing the British to enter homes, stores, warehouses in search of smuggled goods
3. Sam Adams
4. It reminded the colonists that Parliament believed it had the right to tax them—even without representation.
5. The colonies believed the laws eliminated all their freedom. They could not elect their leaders or their juries. They could not hold meetings. They could not get food in or out of their colony. Their courts could not hear cases against people who committed crimes in their colony. The colonies considered this limit to their freedom unacceptable.

Locating Information in a Library

Your textbook gives you information about many interesting people, places, and events in history. Sometimes you may want to find out more about one of these subjects. The library in your school or in your community has many books, but you need to know how to locate those you want.

The library card catalog lists all the books and other materials in the library. There are three kinds of cards in the catalog—author cards, title cards, and subject cards. These cards list the same basic information about a book, but you do not need to know all the information in order to find the book. You can locate the book by looking up the author's last name, the title, or the subject.

Look at the sample subject card below. It contains the following information: (1) call number, which tells you where to find the book in the library; (2) subject; (3) author or authors; (4) title; (5) city where the book was published; (6) publisher, or company that produced the book; (7) copyright date, or date when the book was published. Some cards may contain additional information, such as the name of the illustrator, or artist, if there is one; the number of pages in the book; or a brief summary of the book.

973.3 P — UNITED STATES—HISTORY—COLONIAL PERIOD

Phelan, Mary Kay

Story of the Boston Tea Party.

New York, T.Y. Crowell.

(c. 1973)

Refer to the sample subject card to help you answer the following questions:

1. Under what letter in the card catalog would you look to find this card?

2. Who was the author of the book?

3. Who published the book?

4. When was the book published?

Working with Skills

STUDY SKILLS

ACTIVITY

Objective: To use the card catalog to locate information

Prepare a list of topics from Chapter 6. Some examples might be: mercantilism, Navigation Acts, slavery, patriotism, and search warrants. Take the class to the library and hand out the list of topics. Each student should choose at least two topics. Have students use the card catalog to find the title of two books on each of their topics. They should write down the call number, the name of the book, and the author. If time allows, have students locate the books themselves.

ANSWERS

1. U **2.** Mary Kay Phelan **3.** T.Y. Crowell **4.** 1973

RELATED MATERIAL

Duplicator/Copy Master Activity 11

THINKING THINGS THROUGH

1. The more wealth Great Britain had, the more power it would have. North America had many resources that could be brought to Great Britain and be sold to others. **2.** British leaders thought colonists should support British government; Americans wanted to have local control. **3.** The Navigation Acts did not allow New England to trade with other countries, so these

Chapter 6 SUMMARY

In 1763 the colonies were prosperous. Great Britain, however, found itself in debt because of the French and Indian War.

Parliament had renewed the Navigation Acts to help it raise money. The British lawmakers thus unknowingly encouraged the colonists to smuggle.

Parliament passed new tax laws. One of these laws, the Stamp Act, directly taxed the colonists. The act made them buy stamps to put on the documents they used. The Sons of Liberty were formed to fight this law. Boycotts of British goods began. The Stamp Act Congress sent a petition to the king to ask for repeal of the tax. Finally, Parliament withdrew the hated law.

Parliament continued to tax the Americans. It passed the Townshend Acts, and violence swept the colonies. Soldiers were sent to the colonies to keep order. In Boston, though, British soldiers opened fire on a mob and killed five colonists. This was called the Boston Massacre.

Parliament let merchants ship cheap tea to the colonies. Sam Adams and the other leaders in Boston refused to allow the tea to be unloaded. On December 16, 1773, the Boston Tea Party took place. Colonists dressed as Indians dumped the tea into the harbor.

The king and Parliament acted quickly. The "Intolerable Acts" were passed. Boston Harbor was closed. The Massachusetts charter was suspended. Town meetings were forbidden. Great Britain was now the enemy to many Americans.

Chapter 6 TEST

WORDS TO REMEMBER

From the list on the right, choose the word, phrase, or name that best fits the special vocabulary word on the left.

c 1. mercantilism
g 2. enumerated goods
e 3. smuggle
a 4. quarter
h 5. indirect tax
i 6. direct tax
b 7. boycott
d 8. patriot
f 9. tyrant

a. providing a place to live
b. Sons of Liberty
c. gold or silver
d. Sam Adams
e. trade illegally
f. King George III
g. sugar, cotton, tobacco
h. Sugar Act
i. Stamp Act

THINKING THINGS THROUGH

Answer the following questions.

1. How would ruling North America help to make Great Britain a world power?
2. How did the Americans' ideas differ from those of the leaders of Great Britain with regard to government in the colonies?
3. Why were the colonists forced to smuggle?
4. Why were the Sugar Act and the Stamp Act so important?
5. Why did the colonists object to taxes imposed by Great Britain?
6. What did the Declaration of Rights and Grievances state to the king?
7. How did the Townshend Acts make the governors and judges depend less on the colonies?

RELATED MATERIALS

Duplicator/Copy Masters: Activities 10, 11, 12; Quiz 9
Workbook pages 17-19

colonies could not make the money to buy British goods. They were forced to smuggle to make money. **4.** The Sugar Act was the first time Great Britain tried to raise money for the government in the colonies. Stamp Act was first direct tax placed on colonies. **5.** colonists resented taxation without representation **6.** that the colonists had the same rights as citizens in Great Britain—like the right to be able to tax themselves and to have a trial by jury, asked king to repeal Stamp Act **7.** no longer allowed the colonies to pay the salaries of governors and judges. These officials did not have to try and please the colonists as much.

WORKING WITH SKILLS

1. author **2.** Robert N. Webb **3.** book **4.** *The Colony of Rhode Island* **5.** 89 **6.** No **7.** 1972 **8.** Franklin Watts **9.** New York

---

917.45 Webb, Robert N.
W

The Colony of Rhode Island
New York, Franklin Watts.
(c. 1972)

89 p.

This book traces the history of the smallest of the thirteen colonies from its founding in 1636 to statehood in 1790.

WORKING WITH SKILLS

Study the sample card from a card catalog. Then answer the following questions.

1. Is this card an author card, a title card, or a subject card?
2. What is the author's name?
3. Is this card for a book or a magazine?
4. What is the title of the material?
5. How many pages does it have?
6. Does the card tell you whether or not the material is illustrated?
7. When was the material copyrighted?
8. Who published the material?
9. In what city is the publisher located?

ON YOUR OWN

1. Go to the library and use the card catalog to find as many cards as you can that refer to the Boston Tea Party. Make a list of the authors, titles, dates, and the number of pages for each book. Then alphabetize the list according to authors' last names.
2. Using your list of references for the Boston Tea Party, choose one of the books you find interesting. Locate the book, read it, and write a brief summary of it. Include the main characters, the problems they have, and the solutions they find. Include your reactions, too. Use complete sentences.
3. Benjamin Franklin, as deputy general of the United States, traveled widely among the colonies. In the picture below, he is shown visiting with a colonist in front of his horse-drawn carriage. Beside him is a covered wagon. Read about methods of colonial transportation in the encyclopedia and list the number of ways Franklin could have traveled.

WORDS TO REMEMBER

1. legislature 2. compact 3. artisans 4. frontier
5. terrain 6. enumerated 7. repealed 8. sentry 9. intolerable

THINK THINGS THROUGH

1. for religious freedom, to escape overcrowded conditions, to start a new life; disease, lack of food, fear of Indians

2. southern—farming on large plantations; people lived far apart, some were rich, others were poor. New England—fishing, whaling, industry. middle—farming, trapping, fishing, shipbuilding; many kinds of communities, varied lifestyles
3. long-standing enemies in Europe, both wanted same lands in America 4. Great Britain tightened control over the colonies. Americans felt they had little in common with British, resented being taxed without their consent. Leaders thought Americans should pay taxes in the same way as other British citizens did

Unit 2 TEST

WORDS TO REMEMBER

Replace the word or term in italics in each sentence below with a word or term from this unit that has the same meaning.

1. The House of Burgesses was the first *law-making body* in the colonies made up of representatives chosen by the people.
2. The *agreement* signed by the Pilgrims to make just and equal laws was a step toward democratic government.
3. *Skilled workers*, such as silversmiths and carpenters, worked in colonial cities.
4. Merchants, bankers, and manufacturers in England hoped to encourage colonists to go past the *edge of the settled area.*
5. The English soldiers were at a disadvantage because they were not used to the *land features* of North America.
6. Sugar, indigo, cotton, and wool were *listed* articles which could be sold only to Great Britain.
7. The colonists demanded that the Stamp Act be *withdrawn.*
8. A noisy crowd of colonists in Boston were pelting an English *guard* with snowballs.
9. The colonists thought the Coercive Acts were *unbearable.*

QUESTIONS TO ANSWER

Choose the answer that best completes each of the following statements.

b 1. The success of Jamestown was due to
   a. the religious beliefs of Roger Williams
   b. the leadership of John Smith
   c. the surplus of food in the colony

a 2. The Pilgrims landed in present-day Massachusetts because
   a. they had sailed off course
   b. they had a charter to start a colony in Massachusetts
   c. they did not want to be part of Virginia

c 3. The colonial legislatures rejected the Albany Plan of Union because
   a. they did not have confidence in Ben Franklin's ideas
   b. they wanted the king to appoint their councils
   c. they did not want to give up their power to a central government

a 4. As a result of the French and Indian War,
   a. England received Canada and all French lands east of the Mississippi River
   b. France received Cuba
   c. Spain lost all land in North America

b 5. Great Britain passed the Navigation Acts
   a. to punish the colonies for the French and Indian War
   b. to set up a favorable balance of trade with the colonies
   c. to set up trade with foreign countries

THINK THINGS THROUGH

1. What were some reasons why people settled in the English colonies? What hardships did these early settlers face?
2. Briefly explain how the economy was different in the southern colonies, the New England colonies, and the middle colonies. How was the way of life affected by the economy in each of these places?
3. What were some reasons for the rivalry between the English and French in North America?

RELATED MATERIAL
Duplicator/Copy Masters Test 10-12

and felt Americans should help make Great Britain a powerful country. **5.** Colonists resented British soldiers; merchants faced ruin because of the East India Company's monopoly on tea. As punishment, Great Britain passed the Coercive Acts and became the enemy to many Americans.

PRACTICE YOUR SKILLS

1. Savannah: large population, all white; regularly laid out with straight streets and public squares; hard-working, law-abiding people. Williamsburg: small population, white and black; unpaved, dusty streets; lazy, easygoing people **2.** a. Maryland b. 36°N; 31°N c. 80°W d. Savannah; Williamsburg (or Jamestown)

4. How did the relationship between Great Britain and the colonies change after the French and Indian War?
5. Describe the tension in the colonies that led to the Boston Tea Party. How did this event mark a turning point in relations between Great Britain and the colonies?

PRACTICE YOUR SKILLS

1. Use the following quotes to compare two colonial cities. The first quote is about Savannah in 1734. The second is about Williamsburg in 1760. Compare the populations, the layouts, and the ways of life.

> The Towne is regularly laid out, divided into four Wards, in each of which is left a spacious Square for holding of Markets. . . .The Streets are all straight, and the Houses are all of the same Model and Dimensions. . . . For the time it has been built it is very populous, and its Inhabitants are all White People. . . . here we see Industry honored and Justice strictly executed, and Luxury and Idleness banished from this happy Place. . . .
>
> Williamsburg is the capital of Virginia. It consists of about 200 houses and does not contain more than 1000 souls, white and Negroes, and is far from being a place of importance. . . . The streets are not paved and are very dusty. The climate and appearance of the country make the inhabitants lazy, easy going, and good natured. . . .

2. Use the map below to practice your skills of using longitude and latitude. Answer the questions that follow.
   a. Which colony had a northern boundary of 40° north latitude in 1632?
   b. Which line of latitude was the northern boundary of Carolina in 1663? The southern boundary?
   c. What is the longitude of Charleston?
   d. Which city is located at about 32°N, 81°W? At about 37°N, 77°W?

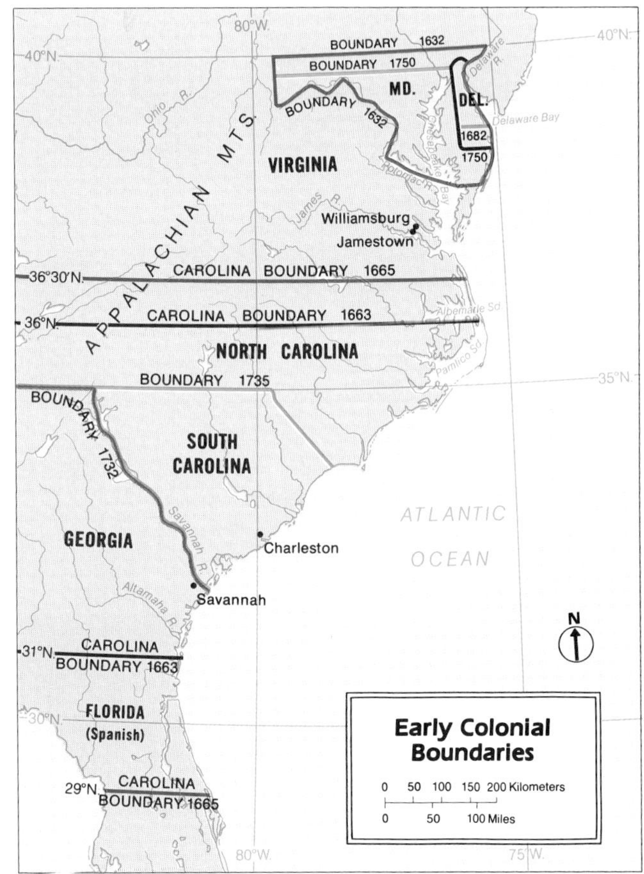

Unit 3

THE AMERICAN REVOLUTION

Unit Three presents the history of America from the first meeting of the Continental Congress through the emergence of the United States as a truly independent country. The unit covers the following topics: the Revolutionary War and how it was won; the struggle by the individual states to retain some autonomy; how a central government evolved that was flexible enough to meet the states' needs, but strong enough to hold the new nation together; the Constitution.

A North Carolina soldier's drum

The Battle of Princeton, January 3, 1777

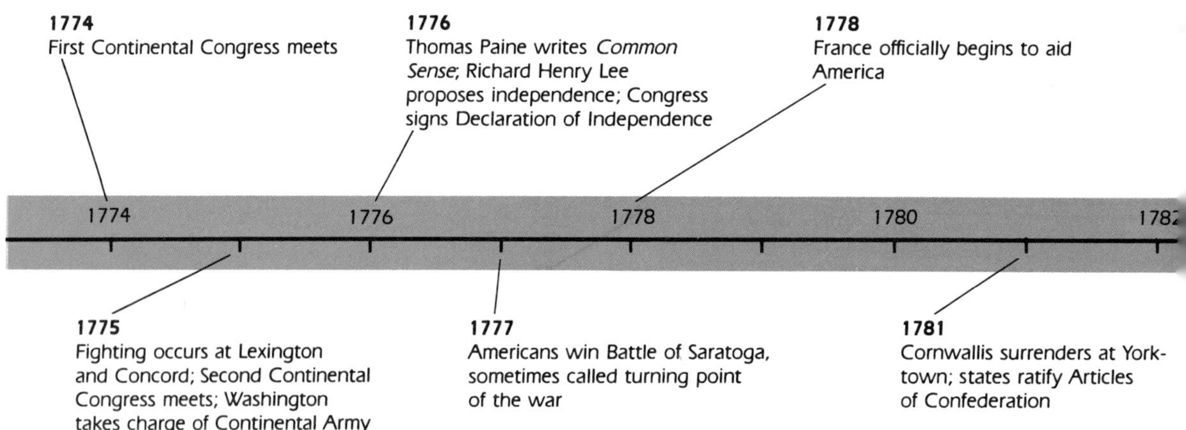

1774
First Continental Congress meets
1776
Thomas Paine writes *Common Sense*; Richard Henry Lee proposes independence; Congress signs Declaration of Independence
1778
France officially begins to aid America
1774
1776
1778
1780
1782
1775
Fighting occurs at Lexington and Concord; Second Continental Congress meets; Washington takes charge of Continental Army
1777
Americans win Battle of Saratoga, sometimes called turning point of the war
1781
Cornwallis surrenders at Yorktown; states ratify Articles of Confederation

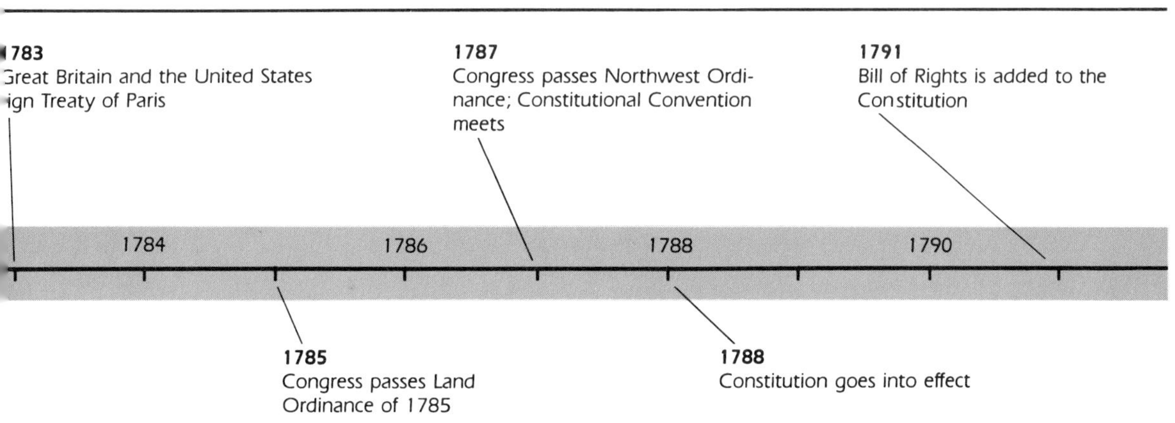
1783
Great Britain and the United States sign Treaty of Paris
1787
Congress passes Northwest Ordinance; Constitutional Convention meets
1791
Bill of Rights is added to the Constitution
1784
1786
1788
1790
1785
Congress passes Land Ordinance of 1785
1788
Constitution goes into effect

Chapter 7
THE REVOLUTIONARY WAR

Chapter 7 introduces students to the events surrounding the Revolutionary War and gives details of the significant battles leading to the defeat of the British. Lesson 7-1 discusses how Americans gradually became committed to achieving independence. Lesson 7-2 outlines the first battles of the war and the steps taken by Congress to formally declare independence. Lesson 7-3 reviews the major remaining battles.

CONTENT OBJECTIVES

After completing the lesson, students will know:

- that a sense of unity was achieved at the First Continental Congress in Philadelphia in 1774
- the events that led to the firing of "the shot heard round the world"
- why some Americans called for immediate independence, while others made one last effort at reconciliation with the Olive Branch Petition

VOCABULARY

unity: oneness
loyalist: American faithful to the king
minuteman: American volunteer soldier who had promised to answer without delay any call to fight

7-1 The Colonists Unite

As you read, think about these questions:
Why did the First Continental Congress meet?
What did the First Continental Congress actually do?
When and how did fighting between the colonists and the British begin?

Special Vocabulary unity loyalist minuteman

In the late summer of 1774, fifty-six colonists made their way by horse, carriage, or foot to the city founded by William Penn. With a population of almost 40,000, Philadelphia was the second largest English-speaking city in the world. London, with 750,000 people, was the largest.

The First Continental Congress

Thoughtful Americans saw danger ahead. All the colonies, except Georgia, agreed to send delegates to a September meeting. This was the meeting in Philadelphia to which the fifty-six Americans were heading in 1774.

The Philadelphia gathering is known today as the First Continental Congress. At the meeting the Americans hoped to decide what to do and say about the new British laws.

The Delegates. Many leaders who gathered in Philadelphia on September 5, 1774, met each other for the first time. Patrick Henry, a delegate from Virginia, described the group when he said, "There are no differences between Virginians, Pennsylvanians, New Yorkers, and New Englanders. I am not a Virginian but an American."

Patrick Henry's words described a spirit of *unity,* or oneness, that was increasing throughout the colonies even before the Philadelphia meeting. That feeling of unity had been created because Americans thought the British were conspiring against their liberties.

DISCUSSION

Have the students discuss what they think might have been the reaction in Great Britain to the Suffolk Resolves. For example, how would the British react to the refusal of the colonists to pay taxes, the establishment of a colonial government in Massachusetts, and the call for colonists to arm themselves? Were the colonists trying to start a fight with Great Britain by passing the Resolves?

The Suffolk Resolves. While the delegates were meeting, the tense situation in Massachusetts grew worse. A Boston doctor and patriot named Joseph Warren introduced certain proposals at a meeting in Suffolk County. These "Suffolk Resolves" declared that nobody should pay taxes to Great Britain until

The corner of Second and Market Streets in Philadelphia was a familiar one to members of the First Continental Congress, who met a block away in Carpenters Hall.

the rights of Massachusetts had been returned. The Resolves said that Massachusetts should set up its own government and collect its own taxes. The Resolves also said that colonists should prepare for trouble by arming themselves. Finally, the colonists should refuse to do any business at all with Great Britain. The Resolves were quickly accepted by the Continental Congress.

Many of the leading figures of Colonial America, including John Hancock, president of the Second Continental Congress, sat for portraits by John Singleton Copley. Copley was considered the greatest portrait painter of his time.

ACTIVITY

Objective: To compare and summarize information

"Paul Revere's Ride," from *Tales of A Wayside Inn,* by Henry Wadsworth Longfellow, is a well-known American poem. Read it to the class. Then have them read the text paragraphs describing the beginning of the fighting at Concord and Lexington. Have students write summarized versions of these two descriptions of the same event. Discuss how a poem, a textbook account, and a summary differ in purpose. Which version do the students enjoy most?

Another Boycott. Not all the delegates were ready for such a strong stand. The representatives at the Congress agreed, however, that the colonies should refuse to buy goods from Great Britain. Finally, they decided to meet again in spring 1775, should the need arise.

This boycott caused the British to pass a law controlling Massachusetts's trade. According to the law, Massachusetts colonists could trade only with Britain and its colonies in the West Indies. Parliament would eventually make this trade law apply to all the other colonies. The British government also wanted Sam Adams and John Hancock arrested for the parts they played in the Boston Tea Party and in stirring up rebellion in Massachusetts.

The Fighting Begins

Spies working on the colonists' side watched every move the British made. In the same way, the British and the *loyalists,* Americans faithful to the king, kept track of the patriots. Through spies, General Thomas Gage, the British commander-in-chief in the colonies, knew that Sam Adams and John Hancock could be found outside Boston in a little town called Lexington. He also knew that the patriots were storing guns and ammunition there and in the nearby town of Concord. Gage made plans to seize the arms as well as Adams and Hancock.

The Minutemen. The patriots learned of Gage's plan. They found out the date the British planned to swoop down on Lexington. They arranged to have someone signal as soon as the British left Boston. Paul Revere was to carry a message that would tell of the coming of the British troops to Lexington and Concord. Revere and the patriot spy agreed, "If the British went by water, we would show two lanterns in the North church steeple; and if by land, we would show one lantern as a signal."

Shortly before midnight on a chilly April 18, 1775, Gage sent his soldiers toward Lexington. Within a short time, two lanterns were hung in the church tower. The British were coming by water. Revere and William Dawes, a Boston leatherworker, left to tell the *minutemen,* a special group of American volunteer soldiers who had promised to answer without delay any call to fight. Near Lexington, Revere found Adams and Hancock and helped them escape.

"Disperse Ye Rebels." Just before daybreak, the sound of drums brought seventy minutemen to the Lexington village green. The redcoats were not far away. Captain John Parker, one of the minutemen, shouted: "Don't fire unless fired upon, but if they mean to have a war, let it begin here."

One of the redcoats yelled the order, "Disperse, ye rebels!" Shots were fired on both sides. When the fighting ended, eight colonists were dead and ten wounded.

Then the British soldiers headed west for Concord. Minutemen from every nearby town and village poured into Concord. The patriots made their stand against the British at the North Bridge.

As in Lexington, shots were fired. This time a few British soldiers lay dead. The British officer in charge ordered his

One of the most popular American poems, "Paul Revere's Ride" by Henry Wadsworth Longfellow, was inspired by Revere's daring dash to Lexington. Responding to the message Revere brought, colonists by the hundreds left their homes to meet the enemy at Concord.

soldiers to begin their return march to Boston. As the British marched, the minutemen fired at them from behind trees and rocks.

As a result of the fighting on that mid-April day in 1775, forty-nine Americans were killed and another forty were wounded. Two hundred seventy British soldiers were killed or wounded. Americans have come to call the first shot fired at Lexington the "shot heard round the world." The American Revolution had begun. Many people would recognize it also as the War for Independence.

Samuel Adams was constantly active in America's cause—from 1764, when he helped organize opposition to the Sugar Act, to 1794, when he served as governor of Massachusetts.

The Second Continental Congress

After the events at Lexington and Concord, the delegates of the Continental Congress knew another meeting had to be held. On May 10, 1775, the Second Continental Congress began in Philadelphia.

Some of the delegates like Sam Adams and Patrick Henry wanted to declare independence immediately. John Adams, Sam's cousin from Massachusetts, wanted to take all British officers prisoner. Others disagreed. John Dickinson of Pennsylvania wanted one last chance to make peace with the king. He had many supporters in the Congress.

The delegates decided to try making peace while at the same time preparing for war. They established a Continental Army to fight the British and appointed George Washington commander-in-chief.

Dickinson and his supporters took their chance to avoid war. They sent George III a paper now called the Olive Branch Petition (an olive branch is a symbol of peace). The petition sought a peaceful end to the conflict. The petition also warned the king that Americans would use force if necessary to resist any abuse of power by his government.

ANSWER THESE QUESTIONS

1. Who were four delegates to the First and Second Continental Congress?
2. What political idea did Patrick Henry present during the First Continental Congress?
3. Where was the "shot heard around the world" fired?
4. Do you think John Dickinson of Pennsylvania had any hope of ending the troubles with the Olive Branch Petition? Why or why not?
5. How were the actions of the Second Continental Congress like and how were they different from the actions of the First Continental Congress?

ANSWER THESE QUESTIONS

1. Patrick Henry, Virginia; Sam Adams, Massachusetts; John Dickinson, Pennsylvania; John Adams, Massachusetts.
2. the rising sense of unity among Americans
3. Lexington, Massachusetts
4. Answers will vary. Dickinson's petition, however, had little chance with the king since it warned him against abusing his power.
5. The first congress met to discuss British abuses and to call for restraint; the second met after war had broken out and supported the actions of the patriot soldiers.

7-2 From Rebellion to Independence

As you read, think about these questions:

How did the early battles of the Revolution turn out?

What was Washington's army like when he took charge in July 1775?

What did the Declaration of Independence gain for the Americans?

Special Vocabulary	artillery	tory
	campaign	civil war

CONTENT OBJECTIVES

After completing the lesson, students will know:

- that the Continental Army either defeated or did much damage to the British in the first battles of the war
- the make up of the patriot army, including the role of women and blacks in the war
- why the British campaign in the South was a failure
- the steps taken by Congress to declare independence from England

VOCABULARY

artillery: cannon and other large guns
campaign: series of planned battles
tory: loyalist
civil war: a war between citizens of the same country

The battles at Lexington and Concord had shocked everyone on both sides of the Atlantic. The British must have asked why the Americans would want to risk their lives, homes, and fortunes by refusing to obey the law. The patriots must have surprised even themselves by their bold behavior. They had met British soldiers in battle and defeated them.

Early Battles

The Olive Branch Petition came to nothing in England. Meanwhile important developments were taking place in New England during May and June 1775. There the second major battle of the American Revolution took place.

The Green Mountain Boys. With cooperation from Massachusetts and Connecticut, Ethan Allen and the Green Mountain Boys, a group of patriots in present-day Vermont, made a surprise attack on the British. They captured the British outposts on Lake Champlain called Fort Ticonderoga and Fort Crown Point.

The capture of Fort Ticonderoga gave the patriot cause a second victory against the British. It also gave them more than fifty pieces of *artillery*, or cannon and other large guns, that guarded the fort. These weapons would come in handy in later battles.

The Battle of Bunker Hill. The victory at Concord on April 19, 1775, had caused thousands of colonists to flock to New England. The patriots wanted to move the British out of

Boston. In hopes of carrying out this plan, on the night of June 16, 1775, the patriot army took up positions on Breed's Hill. It planned to take nearby Bunker Hill as well. The next morning, before the Americans could complete their plans, the British attacked. The fight was actually *for* Bunker Hill, but it took place *on* Breed's Hill. The name of the battle has come down to us as the Battle of Bunker Hill.

Three major generals—William Howe, Henry Clinton, and John Burgoyne—were sent to assist General Thomas Gage. At Gage's order, the British marched up Breed's Hill. The Americans held their fire until the enemy was about 40 yards (36 meters) away from them. Then they opened fire. Hundreds of redcoats fell dead or wounded. The rest fled in panic. In another attack, the British gained the top of the hill and drove off the Americans.

Washington Takes Control

George Washington arrived in Massachusetts July 3, 1775, to take control of the Continental Army. In a short time the army had accomplished much. It had defeated the British at Concord, Fort Ticonderoga, and Crown Point. It had harmed the enemy severely at Breed's Hill, even though the battle had been lost. The British soldiers were still penned up in Boston.

The Patriot Army. The army over which Washington took control in July 1775 was made up mainly of white men who worked as farmers or at some trade. A few volunteers brought slaves with them. Many of these slaves fought in the major battles of 1775. Some blacks, like Prince Easterbrooks, fought at Concord. Some, like Peter Salem and Salem Poor, fought at Breed's Hill. Eventually over five thousand black troops served in the American forces. They fought in almost every major battle. Native Americans also played a role in the early battles of the Revolution. A group of Stockbridge Indians volunteered as minutemen.

In the 1700s women usually traveled with the army, serving as cooks, cleaners, water carriers, and nurses. They were often in the thick of the battles facing as much danger as the soldiers. In times of need, women even took the part of soldiers, as did Margaret Corbin, who took her husband's place in the ranks when he was killed in battle. Deborah Sampson actually disguised herself as a soldier and joined the army. Later, however, she was discovered and made to leave the service.

The Invasion of Canada. In September 1775, the patriots decided to attack the British army in nearby Canada. This was the first real *campaign*, or series of planned battles, begun by the Americans. Two groups took different routes to Quebec, Canada. One was led by Philip Schuyler (later replaced by Richard Montgomery), and the other was led by Benedict Arnold, a soldier from Massachusetts who had been with Ethan Allen at Fort Ticonderoga. (See the map on page 162.)

Mary Ludwig earned the nickname Molly Pitcher by carrying water to thirsty troops during the Battle of Monmouth. When her husband fell, she took his place and fought the rest of the battle.

By the middle of November, the two groups met outside Quebec. Several weeks later, Montgomery and Arnold led an attack against Quebec. The patriot effort failed, and Montgomery was killed in the battle. Arnold stayed outside Quebec until spring when the British forced the patriots away from the city.

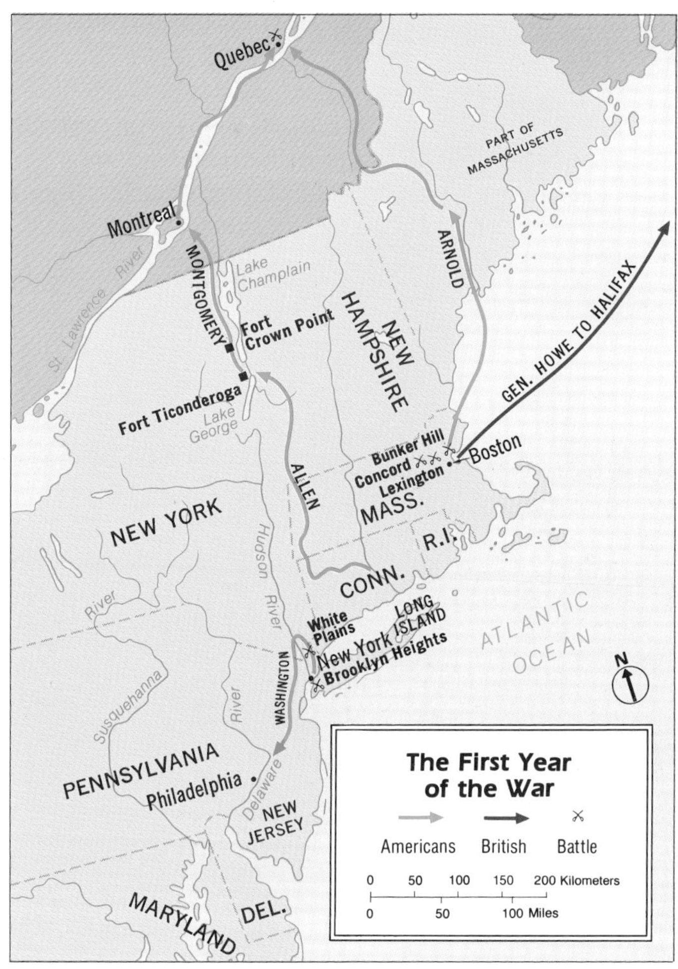

Maps of military campaigns show the routes of the troops led by each general in a battle. Trace the routes of Arnold and Washington.

Early British Campaigns

The British were not discouraged by the early defeats in the war. They did, however, decide to change their commanders. In October 1775, General William Howe took the place of Thomas Gage as leader of the British army in America. General Howe had for a long time been a hero to the British people. His latest victory was the costly attack on Breed's Hill in Boston.

The British Campaign in the South. Howe hoped the *tories*, or loyalists, in the South could convince other Americans to support the king. Howe believed he could send warships and a small army to North Carolina as a show of strength. He thought this military presence would give the loyalists there enough confidence to keep the southern colonies on Britain's side.

The British plan fell apart when, in February 1776, a group of southern patriots beat the tories in a battle at Moore's Creek Bridge near Wilmington, North Carolina.

The American victory at Charleston left two hundred British soldiers dead or wounded and every enemy ship damaged. This victory ended British attacks in the South for two years.

The patriots captured over 850 loyalists. By the time the British ships and army arrived, the British had lost their best chance to win the South for the king.

The ships then sailed south to Charleston, South Carolina, in hopes of capturing the town. In June 1776, they attacked Charleston. Colonel William Moultrie and his six hundred soldiers were waiting for the British. The patriots fired on the British ships. The badly damaged ships left and finally sailed toward New York. The British had suffered yet another defeat.

COMMON SENSE;

ADDRESSED TO THE

INHABITANTS

OF

AMERICA,

On the following intereſting

SUBJECTS.

I. Of the Origin and Deſign of Government in general, with conciſe Remarks on the Engliſh Conſtitution.

II. Of Monarchy and Hereditary Succeſſion.

III. Thoughts on the preſent State of American Affairs.

IV. Of the preſent Ability of America, with ſome miſcellaneous Reflections.

Man knows no Maſter ſave creating HEAVEN,
Or thoſe whom choice and common good ordain.

THOMSON.

PHILADELPHIA;
Printed, and Sold, by R. BELL, in Third-Street.
MDCCLXXVI.

Thomas Paine had only been in America two years when he wrote *Common Sense.* Later, his *Crisis* papers, which began "These are the times that try men's souls," were read to patriot soldiers to inspire them.

The British Leave Boston. General Howe's bad luck continued in New England. The cannon taken from the British at Fort Ticonderoga finally reached the patriot army outside Boston. Howe felt forced to move his troops out of Boston, leaving the city in the hands of the patriots. On March 26, 1776, the British and about one thousand New England loyalists sailed to Halifax, Nova Scotia.

The Great Declaration

When the Americans began fighting, most hoped only to win back their rights as British subjects. Only a few Americans had pushed for independence from Great Britain. As time passed, however, the idea of independence became more and more popular. One of the most important reasons for the growing popularity of independence was the writings of Thomas Paine.

Common Sense. Paine's pamphlet, called *Common Sense*, appeared early in 1776. Paine's arguments were powerful. They helped many Americans to accept happily the idea of breaking away from Great Britain and fighting for independence. Here are a few of his words:

> Every thing that is right shouts for separation from Britain. The Americans who have been killed seem to cry out "'TIS TIME TO PART." England and America are separated by a very great distance. That is itself strong and natural proof that God never expected one to rule over the other.

Lee's Proposal. Members of Congress also seemed to see that much could be gained by declaring independence. Foreign countries, for example, could send help. Up to now foreign countries had considered the battles taking place in the colonies part of a *civil war*, or a war between the citizens of the same country.

The chronological list on page 165 will help you understand some of the steps toward independence that took place in 1776. One member of Congress, Richard Henry Lee, took the first big step. He made a motion that Congress declare the colonies to be free and independent states. The members of Congress debated Lee's proposal for months. Meanwhile, they chose a group of people to prepare a statement. This statement would announce that the Americans declared themselves free of Great Britain. It would also present the reasons why the colonists had taken this daring step, so that everyone could understand them.

The people chosen to write the document were Thomas Jefferson of Virginia, Benjamin Franklin of Pennsylvania, John Adams of Massachusetts, Roger Sherman of Connecticut, and Robert Livingston of New York. They talked over the main ideas that should be in the paper. Then Jefferson wrote the document.

On July 2, 1776, members of Congress voted to accept the paper which they called the Declaration of Independence. On July 4, John Hancock, the president of the Congress, became the first to sign the Declaration. Other members followed his lead.

DISCUSSION

Have the students discuss the influence of Thomas Paine's pamphlet *Common Sense,* which said "England and America are separated by a very great distance." Do the students think that a pamphlet, such as *Common Sense,* could really make people decide to break with England? Have them give an example of how they have been influenced by something they have read or heard.

STEPS TOWARD INDEPENDENCE, 1776

June 7	Richard Henry Lee introduced a resolution: "That these United Colonies are, and of Right ought to be, free and independent states."
June 11	Thomas Jefferson, Benjamin Franklin, John Adams, Roger Sherman, and Robert Livingston were chosen to write the Declaration of Independence.
July 1	Congress debated Lee's resolution.
July 2	Twelve of the thirteen delegations voted to accept Lee's resolution. (New York did not vote.)
July 3	Congress read and debated the Declaration of Independence.
July 4	The Declaration of Independence was adopted by twelve of the thirteen colonies. (New York did not vote.) John Hancock signed the Declaration.
July 8	The Liberty Bell rang to announce the adoption of the Declaration.
July 15	New York voted to accept the Declaration of Independence.
August 2	Fifty members of the Congress signed the Declaration of Independence.

ACTIVITY

Objective: To synthesize information

Ask students to memorize the first two sentences of the second paragraph of the Declaration of Independence, which begin "We hold these truths to be self-evident . . ." Discuss with the students the significance of these words. How do they see the ideas having an effect on their everyday life?

Stephen Hopkins of Rhode Island, suffering from palsy, said as he added his unsteady signature to the Declaration of Independence, "My hand is shaky but my heart is not."

Some Immediate Effects. After the patriots had declared that the Americans were an independent people, they could set up state governments. They could also set up a government for the entire country, a national government. In addition, they could, and did, send people to represent them in foreign countries. The most important of these was Benjamin Franklin, who arrived in France in December 1776 and immediately tried to get the French to help the Americans in their war for independence.

ANSWER THESE QUESTIONS

1. Prince Easterbrooks, Concord; Ethan Allen, Fort Ticonderoga; Salem Poor, Peter Salem, Breed's Hill; Benedict Arnold, Fort Ticonderoga and Quebec; Richard Montgomery, Quebec; William Moultrie, Charleston, South Carolina.
2. Concord, Fort Ticonderoga, Crown Point, Moore's Creek Bridge, and Charleston.
3. North and South Carolina
4. Patriots used artillery captured at Fort Ticonderoga to drive the British from Boston and Boston Harbor.
5. It allowed Americans to set up new states and a central government as well as send people to represent them in foreign countries to ask for aid.

ANSWER THESE QUESTIONS

1. What were the names of some Americans who fought in some of the battles of the American Revolution in 1775 and 1776?
2. What were some names of places where Americans won victories in 1775 and 1776?
3. Where did General Howe believe he could win a big victory in 1776?
4. How did the capture of Fort Ticonderoga in 1775 affect the British in Boston in 1776?
5. Why was a Declaration of Independence important to Americans in 1776?

Paraphrasing a Document

Working with Skills

READING SKILLS

Documents are often difficult to read and understand. This is so for many reasons. Readers may never before have seen some of the words in a hard-to-read document. The author of the document may have meant it to be read by only a few people with special knowledge. The document may have been meant to be studied, not read quickly and forgotten. The author may have written the document so long ago that some of his or her words are no longer in common use. The topic of the document might be so difficult that anyone reading it would have trouble understanding its meaning. As is partly the case with the Declaration of Independence, some documents are difficult to understand for all of these reasons.

One way to understand a difficult-to-read document is to *paraphrase* it. A paraphrase is a sentence-by-sentence restatement, in simpler words, of a difficult-to-understand passage.

On the pages that follow, in the left-hand column, is one of the great documents of American history, the Declaration of Independence, written by Thomas Jefferson in June of 1776. First, read the document as Jefferson wrote it. Then, as you finish each paragraph, read its paraphrase in the right-hand column.

ACTIVITY

Objective: To paraphrase

Ask each student to write a brief account of a recent event in his or her life. Then ask students to work in small groups, taking turns reading aloud what they have written. The other students in the group should paraphrase what they have heard, either out loud or by writing it down.

THE DECLARATION OF INDEPENDENCE

When, in the course of human events, it becomes necessary for one people to dissolve the political bands which have connected them with another, and to assume, among the powers of the earth, the separate and equal station to which the laws of nature and of nature's God entitle them, a decent respect to the opinions of mankind requires that they should declare the causes which impel them to the separation.

At times, it is necessary for one group of people (the colonists) to break away from the country (England) that has been governing them, and to form their own country. When this happens, the world should be told why this action is being taken.

RELATED MATERIALS
Duplicator/Copy Master Activity 13

We hold these truths to be self-evident:—That all men are created equal; that they are endowed by their Creator with certain unalienable rights: that among these are life, liberty, and the pursuit of happiness. That, to secure these rights, governments are instituted among men, deriving their just powers from the consent of the governed; that, whenever any form of government becomes destructive of these ends, it is the right of the people to alter or to abolish it, and to institute a new government, laying its foundation on such principles, and organising its powers in such form, as to them shall seem most likely to effect their safety and happiness.

It is believed that all people have an equal right to life, liberty, and the chance to be happy. These rights are given to the people by God and cannot be taken or given away. Governments are set up by the people to protect these rights. When the government doesn't protect or defend these rights, but tries to take them away, it is the right of the people to do away with that government and set up another one that will protect their rights.

Prudence, indeed, will dictate that governments long established should not be changed for light and transient causes: and, accordingly, all experience hath shown that mankind are more disposed to suffer, while evils are sufferable, than to right themselves by abolishing the forms to which they are accustomed. But, when a long train of abuses and usurpations, pursuing invariably the same object, evinces a design to reduce them under absolute despotism, it is their right, it is their duty, to throw off such government, and to provide new guards for their future security.

Governments should only be changed when it is absolutely necessary. In fact, history shows that people are willing to suffer a long time before they take this drastic step. However, when the government continues to take away the rights of the people, it is their duty to change the government.

Such has been the patient sufferance of these colonies; and such is now the necessity that constrains them to alter their former systems of government. The history of the present King of Great Britain is a history of repeated injuries and usurpations, all having, in direct object, the establishment of an absolute tyranny over these States. To prove this, let facts be submitted to a candid world.

The colonies have been patient a long time, but the government must now be changed. The king of Great Britain and his government have tried to rule without the colonies' consent. The king has tried to take away the rights of the colonists in America. Here is a list of the king's actions against the colonies for the world to see:

He has refused his assent to laws the most wholesome and necessary for the public good.

The king has:
refused to pass laws the colonies need.

He has forbidden his Governors to pass laws of immediate and pressing importance, unless suspended in their operation till his assent should be obtained; and, when so suspended, he has utterly neglected to attend to them.

refused to allow his governors to pass the laws that the colonies need unless they wait for his approval. Then while the colonies wait for the laws to be approved, he won't even think them over.

He has refused to pass other laws for the accommodation of large districts of people, unless those people would relinquish the right of representation in the legislature—a right inestimable to them, and formidable to tyrants only.

refused to approve laws for the larger cities and districts unless these people give up their right to have representation in their colonial legislatures—a right that is of greatest importance to the people and one that only an unjust ruler would take away.

He has called together legislative bodies at places unusual, uncomfortable, and distant from the depository of their public records, for the sole purpose of fatiguing them into compliance with his measure.

called meetings of the colonial legislatures at far away places so that when the delegates arrive, they are too tired to argue with his policies.

He has dissolved representative houses repeatedly, for opposing, with manly firmness, his invasions on the rights of the people.

canceled meetings of the legislatures when the delegates refuse to agree with his laws and policies.

He has refused, for a long time after such dissolutions, to cause others to be elected; whereby the legislative powers, incapable of annihilation, have returned to the people at large for their exercise; the State remaining, in the meantime, exposed to all dangers of invasion from without, and convulsions within.

refused to allow for the election of new members to the legislatures—a right that never should be taken away—making the colony unable to defend itself from enemies and riots.

He has endeavored to prevent the population of these States; for that purpose obstructing the laws for the naturalization of foreigners; refusing to pass others to encourage their migration hither, and raising the conditions of new appropriations of lands.

tried to stop people from coming to the colonies by refusing to pass immigration and naturalization laws, and by raising the price of new lands.

He has obstructed the administration of justice, by refusing his assent to laws for establishing judiciary powers.

refused to pass laws creating a justice system in the colonies.

He has made judges dependent on his will alone for the tenure of their offices, and the amount and payment of their salaries.

kept the colonial judges under his authority by controlling how long they can remain in office and how much they will earn.

He has erected a multitude of new offices, and sent hither swarms of officers to harass our people and eat out their substance.

sent many new officers to the colonies to bother the people, live in their homes, and eat their food.

He has kept among us in times of peace, standing armies, without the consent of our legislatures.

sent soldiers to the colonies without the approval of the colonial legislatures.

He has affected to render the military independent of, and superior to, the civil power.

given the army a separate set of rules to live by and, in fact, given it authority over colonial legislatures.

He has combined with others to subject us to a jurisdiction foreign to our constitutions, and unacknowledged by our laws; giving his assent to their acts of pretended legislation:

He has made laws that go against our constitutions and present laws. He gives his consent to laws that:

For quartering large bodies of armed troops among us;

force us to house British soldiers.

For protecting them, by a mock trial, from punishment for any murders which they should commit on the inhabitants of these States;

protect soldiers who have committed crimes in the colonies from being punished by pretending to give them a trial.

For cutting off our trade with all parts of the world;

cut off our trade with the rest of the world.

For imposing taxes on us without our consent;

tax us without the approval of our colonial legislatures.

For depriving us, in many cases, of the benefits of trial by jury;

take away our right to a trial by jury.

For transporting us beyond the seas, to be tried for pretended offences;

force colonists to sail to England to stand trial for crimes they never committed.

For abolishing the free system of English laws in a neighboring province, establishing there an arbitrary government, and enlarging its boundaries, so as to render it at once an example and fit instrument for introducing the same absolute rule into these colonies;

take away the rights of people in neighboring areas to set an example of what could happen in the colonies.

For taking away our charters, abolishing our most valuable laws, and altering, fundamentally, the forms of our governments;

take away our form of government and replace it with one more suitable to himself.

For suspending our own legislatures, and declaring themselves invested with power to legislate for us in all cases whatsoever.

take away the right of the colonial legislatures to make laws and instead make the laws for the colonies himself.

He has abdicated government here, by declaring us out of his protection, and waging war against us.

He has:
declared war against his own colonies.

He has plundered our seas, ravaged our coasts, burnt our towns, and destroyed the lives of our people.

attacked us at sea and along our coasts, burned our towns and destroyed people's lives.

He is at this time transporting large armies of foreign mercenaries to complete the works of death, desolation, and tyranny, already begun with circumstances of cruelty and perfidy scarcely paralleled in the most barbarous ages, and totally unworthy the head a civilized nation.

hired foreign soldiers to come to America to carry out his orders of death and destruction such as the world has rarely seen before.

He has constrained our fellow-citizens, taken captive on the high seas, to bear arms against their country, to become the executioners of their friends and brethren, or to fall themselves by their hands.

captured American sailors at sea and forced them to fight against their country, friends, and families, or to die themselves at the hands of their fellow citizens.

He has excited domestic insurrection amongst us, and has endeavored to bring on the inhabitants of our frontiers the merciless Indian savages, whose known rule of warfare is an undistinguished destruction of all ages, sexes, and conditions.

caused riots in our cities and encouraged the Indians to attack us.

In every state of these oppressions we have petitioned for redress, in the most humble terms; our repeated petitions have been answered only by repeated injury. A prince whose character is thus marked by every act which may define a tyrant is unfit to be the ruler of a free people.

The colonists have tried repeatedly to make Great Britain see what effect these laws and policies are having in the colonies by writing petitions to the king. Each time our petitions are ignored and a new law is passed to punish us. A king who does such things to his people is unfit to rule them.

Nor have we been wanting in our attentions to our British brethren. We have warned them, from time to time, of attempts by their legislature to extend an unwarrantable jurisdiction over us. We have reminded them of the circumstances of our emigration and settlement here. We have appealed to their native justice and magnanimity; and we have conjured them, by the ties of our common kindred, to disavow these usurpations, which would inevitably interrupt our connections and correspondence. They, too, have been deaf to the voice of justice and of consanguinity. We must, therefore, acquiesce in the necessity which denounces our separation; and hold them, as we hold the rest of mankind, enemies in war, in peace friends.

We, the colonists, have appealed to the people of Great Britain. We have tried to tell them how we feel about the unfair laws and harsh actions by the king. We have reminded them why we came to America in the first place. We have asked them as fellow citizens to support us in the colonies by asking the king to stop these policies. The people, too, have not listened. We, the colonies, must separate ourselves from Great Britain, and think of the people of Great Britain as we would the people of any other nation.

You have read most of the Declaration of Independence as Jefferson wrote it and in paraphrased form. Now try your hand at paraphrasing the last paragraph of the Declaration. First, read the paragraph as Jefferson wrote it. Then, on a separate sheet of paper, write out your own paraphrase of the paragraph. Make sure to use a dictionary as you work.

Therefore, as representatives of a new nation, the United States of America, appealing to God who knows that our feelings are sincere, do as representatives of the people of these colonies, declare that these colonies are and have a right to be free and independent, no longer governed by the king of Great Britain. As an independent nation, we have the power to declare war, make peace, sign treaties, establish trade, and do everything an independent country has the right to do. Relying on the protection of God, we pledge our lives, our money and property, and our honor in support of this declaration of independence.

WE, THEREFORE, the REPRESENTATIVES of the UNITED STATES OF AMERICA, in General Congress assembled, appealing to the Supreme Judge of the world for the rectitude of our intentions, do, in the name and by the authority of the good people of these colonies, solemnly publish and declare, That these united Colonies are, and of right ought to be, FREE AND INDEPENDENT STATES; that they are absolved from all allegiance to the British crown, and that all political connection between them and the state of Great Britain is, and ought to be, totally dissolved; and that, as free and independent states, they have full power to levy war, conclude peace, contract alliances, establish commerce, and to do all other acts and things which independent states may of right do. And, for the support of this declaration, with a firm reliance on the protection of Divine Providence, we mutually pledge to each other our lives, our fortunes, and our sacred honor.

7-3 A Hard Road to Victory

As you read, think about these questions:

Which three military campaigns helped determine the outcome of the American Revolution?

How did George Washington and his soldiers help keep American spirits high during the winter of 1777?

What was the winter at Valley Forge like?

How did the French help the Americans?

Special Vocabulary patriotism stalemate

CONTENT OBJECTIVES

After completing the lesson, students will know:

- the significance of the American army victories in Trenton, Princeton, and Saratoga
- which European countries aided the Americans
- details of the major battles in the South between 1778 and 1781
- how Cornwallis's retreat to Yorktown caused the war to end

VOCABULARY

patriotism: a feeling of keen pride in one's nation

stalemate: a time when neither side is winning

After the signing of the Declaration of Independence, the fighting in the American Revolution continued. The outcome of the war was decided during three main campaigns:

- the battles for New York and New Jersey, August 1776 to January 1777
- the British Campaign to separate New England from the other colonies, July to October 1777
- the war in the South, December 1778 to October 1781

The Battles for New York and New Jersey

Let us study the New York campaign of 1776 through the story of a young soldier. He was Nathan Hale, whose name has become famous as the finest example of *patriotism* in American history. Patriotism is a feeling of keen pride in one's nation.

Many young Americans, including Nathan Hale, felt a burst of patriotism in 1775 when the exciting events at Lexington and Concord took place. They wanted to play a part in the drama that surely lay ahead. Hale was among the thousands of Americans who streamed into the area around Boston after the war began. Then, like many others, he joined the new Continental Army. It was soon evident that leadership was one of Hale's strengths. His promotions, therefore, came quickly. By January 1, 1776, he was made a captain in the Continental Army.

DISCUSSION

Discuss the word patriotism, which means keen pride in one's nation. A good example of this feeling was Nathan Hale's spy expedition behind British battle lines. Ask the students if they think their patriotism is as strong as Nathan Hale's. Would they volunteer for a dangerous assignment like spying? Have students discuss whether they would give up their life for their country. What reasons do they have for their choice?

Hale Goes to New York. Hale's commander-in-chief was George Washington. Only four days after the British left Boston, Washington made an important guess about what Howe's next move would be. The British, Washington figured, would try to capture the city of New York and move from there against Philadelphia. Washington's orders spread quickly among the soldiers around Boston. Within days, young Captain Hale and the soldiers under his command were on Long Island near New York City.

By August 1776, Howe had sent more than 20,000 troops to Long Island. In late August, Howe's soldiers met the Americans in battle at Brooklyn Heights and defeated them.

If the Continental Army fought on, the entire army could be lost and the war would end in terrible defeat for the Americans. Washington believed the risk was too great. He decided to leave Long Island with his army and go to Manhattan. Hale was among the soldiers who crossed the East River from Long Island to Manhattan.

In September 1776, Nathan Hale and a small group of his soldiers recrossed the East River and entered Long Island, which was held by the British. The brave young Americans wanted to learn the British plans for defeating Washington and the Continental Army. Hale disguised himself as a Dutch school teacher and carried out his assignment. On September 21, 1776, he was caught by the British, dragged before General Howe, and ordered to say what he had been doing behind the British lines. Hale would not give Howe the answer. The general ordered the young man hanged as a

Nathan Hale was only twenty-one when he was hanged by the British as an American spy. Many believe that a loyalist cousin of Hale's betrayed him.

Following the surrender at Trenton, some Hessians were won over to the American cause. Many of the 30,000 Germans who fought in the war stayed on in the United States.

spy. Early on the morning of September 22, Hale spoke his last words: "I only regret that I have but one life to lose for my country."

The Battle of White Plains. Howe caught Washington's army at White Plains, New York, on the mainland. There the British and Americans fought a costly battle in October 1776. Howe won, but Washington and his army slipped away once again. Almost a month later, the British captured Washington's fort on Manhattan Island. The British took the American defenders prisoner. Washington and his forces raced out of New York, into New Jersey, and then into Pennsylvania.

The Battles at Trenton and Princeton. The British had hired foreign soldiers to help them fight the Americans. Many of these soldiers came from the German state named Hesse-Kassel. Hessians was the name applied to all of them. The Hessians had fought well on Long Island and at White Plains. Now they were left to guard the tiny American army.

On the day after Christmas 1776, Washington and his soldiers secretly crossed the Delaware River from Pennsylvania to reach Trenton, New Jersey. The Hessians were taken by complete surprise. The Americans captured almost a thousand officers and soldiers. Washington's soldiers also captured the Germans' ammunition and gunpowder. The Americans badly needed supplies like these.

A few days later, on January 3, 1777, Washington and his soldiers won another surprise battle nearby at Princeton, New Jersey. The two surprise victories greatly helped the American cause.

The British Campaign of 1777

The British decided to cut off New England from the other colonies by taking over New York. This campaign would have three parts. First, from Canada, General John Burgoyne and his soldiers would march south to Lake Champlain. Second, Colonel Barry St. Leger would bring a second British force south from Canada. Third, General Howe would lead troops north from New York City to meet Burgoyne and St. Leger at Albany. (See the map of northern campaigns on page 177.)

Seven hundred Americans died or were wounded in the Battle of Germantown, which was shrouded in heavy fog much of the time.

Capturing Philadelphia. London ordered Howe to capture Philadelphia before marching north. Howe and his soldiers sailed from New York to Chesapeake Bay. They landed south of Philadelphia. Washington's troops met Howe's at Brandywine Creek in September 1777, and lost a big battle there. Fifteen days after their victory, the British marched into Philadelphia.

The Congress got out of the city safely, and Washington's army avoided final defeat. A few days later, Washington's army attacked the British at Germantown, Pennsylvania. The Americans again lost the battle but not their army. By now, time had run out for Howe to carry out his part of the plan to conquer upper New York.

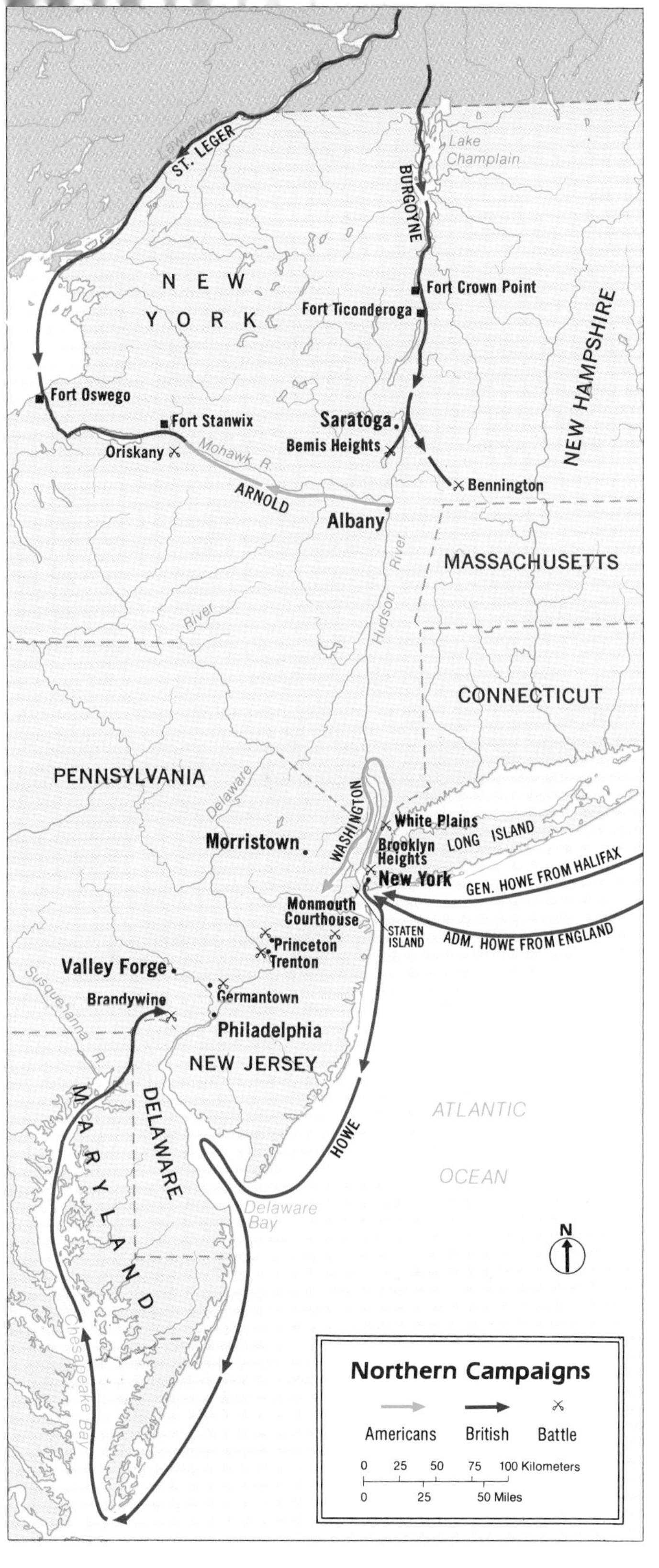

Howe and St. Leger failed; Burgoyne reached Albany, but without aid he had to surrender.

Read the plans for the British campaign of 1777 on page 176. Trace the proposed routes on this map. Which parts of the plan failed?

Two Armies Leave Canada. Meanwhile, Burgoyne and his soldiers came south and captured Fort Ticonderoga in July 1777. The British then marched confidently on, sure they would meet St. Leger at Albany.

St. Leger, however, had trouble with his part of the plan. He led a force of loyalists and Indians from Fort Oswego on Lake Ontario into the Mohawk River Valley. There in August 1777, at Oriskany, a patriot force under General Nicholas Herkimer stalled the British advance. Then one thousand volunteers under Benedict Arnold drove the British back to Fort Oswego. Meanwhile, John Burgoyne's British troops arrived outside of Albany, New York.

Burgoyne's early successes caused Washington to place a new general in charge of the American troops facing the British. He was General Horatio Gates, who took charge of the patriot armies in August 1777. In October, Burgoyne took his tired, hungry soldiers to the town of Saratoga where he hoped they could defend themselves.

The end of Burgoyne's part in the big plan was near. He had little food and ammunition left. Patriots were coming to Saratoga (near Albany) in large numbers to fight against him. No one could come to his aid. For these reasons, on October 17, 1777, Burgoyne surrendered his almost 5700 soldiers to the Americans.

Valley Forge. The Americans won other great victories in upper New York in late 1777. Discouragement among the Americans, however, was widespread because of the two big defeats at Brandywine Creek and at Germantown and the loss of Philadelphia to the British. Even more discouraging was the winter that Washington and his soldiers experienced at Valley Forge outside Philadelphia in early 1778.

On December 23, 1777, George Washington (here reviewing troops on a white horse) wrote from Valley Forge, "We have . . . no less than 2873 men . . . unfit for duty because they are barefooted and otherwise naked."

Baron von Steuben drilled Washington's troops at Valley Forge in a system of field formations that greatly improved their fighting ability.

Washington wrote to Congress from Valley Forge that about 2900 of his soldiers could not fight because they were "barefoot and otherwise naked." This complaint points out a sad truth about the American Revolution: the Americans at home had failed to back up the troops. First, the Congress had little money to spend on supplying the soldiers with food, clothing, shelter, and ammunition. Second, dishonest suppliers often took goods meant for the American army and sold them to the British.

Spring brought an end to the suffering of the Continental Army at Valley Forge. The troops could turn their attention to preparing for the battles ahead. The Baron Friedrich von Steuben, a military officer from Prussia, came to America to aid the patriots. Steuben knew a good army must be well-trained. In a short time, he greatly helped the Americans.

Help from Europe. In 1776 Congress sent Arthur Lee of Virginia, Silas Deane of Connecticut, and Benjamin Franklin to France. Their job was to win French support for the American Revolution. The three Americans finally succeeded. The French signed the Treaty of Alliance and Friendship at Paris in February of 1778. They vowed to help the Americans struggle for independence.

Actually, the French had been secretly helping the Americans since 1776. They were afraid to let the British know about the help, however, until they were sure the Americans could win. The news that Burgoyne had surrendered at Saratoga reached Paris in December 1777. This news spurred the French to give the Americans help openly.

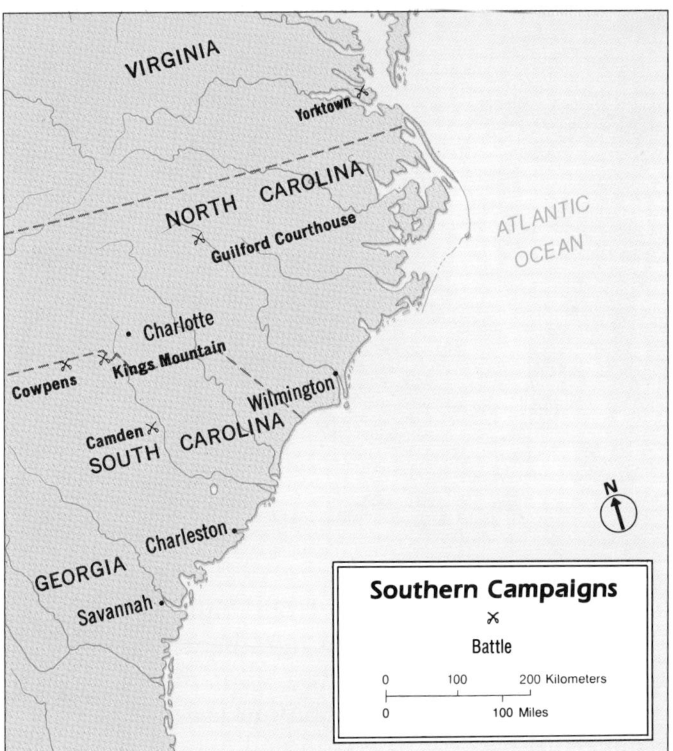

It does not show routes of generals.

This map shows the major places where fighting took place in the South during the Revolution. How is this map different from the map of Northern Campaigns on page 177?

Other enemies of Great Britain also helped the Americans. In 1779 the Spanish went to war against Great Britain. In the following year, the Dutch joined the fight.

The War in the South, 1778–1781

Early in the summer of 1778, the war had reached a *stalemate*, or a time when neither side was winning. Washington and his army had come out of winter camp at Valley Forge to win a major battle at Monmouth Courthouse in New Jersey. After the battle, however, the Americans were short of soldiers. As a result, they failed to follow up their advantage against the British.

A New British Campaign. Leaders in London replaced General Howe with Sir Henry Clinton. They also decided that perhaps the southern colonists would support the king better than those in the North. Sir Henry Clinton moved south from New York in June 1778. (See the map of Southern Campaigns on this page.) With him went his most trusted officer, Charles Cornwallis.

On December 29, 1778, Clinton's soldiers captured Savannah, Georgia. In May 1780 they also took the city of

Small bands of patriot raiders like these kept the enemy in South Carolina busy until General Gates was ready to attack in force at Camden.

Charleston, South Carolina. The American general, Benjamin Lincoln, surrendered more than five thousand soldiers to Charles Cornwallis. Lincoln also turned over supplies, weapons, and several ships. This was the biggest American loss of the war.

A Traitor and a New Leader. In August 1780, the Americans and the British battled at Camden, South Carolina. Hungry and tired, many of the Americans fled without firing a shot. The British had another victory.

Another event also distressed Americans. On September 25, 1780, Benedict Arnold, a hero at Fort Ticonderoga and Quebec, was discovered to be a traitor. He had sold information about the American army to the British. His treason was discovered, and Arnold had to flee for his life. He became a general in the British army and commanded troops in raids against Americans in Virginia until the end of the war.

Washington appointed a new general to lead the army in the South—Nathanael Greene. Even before Greene took over, the Americans' luck changed. In October 1780 patriot soldiers captured or killed 1100 loyalist troops at Kings Mountain, on the border of North and South Carolina.

At last, Washington added soldiers to Greene's army. In March 1781, the patriot army attacked the British at Guilford Courthouse, in North Carolina. Cornwallis and his troops pushed the Americans back, but over five hundred British soldiers were killed. The victory had cost Cornwallis his army's strength. He knew that he would lose if he fought again, so he led his army out of North Carolina into Virginia.

ACTIVITY

Objective: To locate information

Divide the class into small groups and ask them to prepare a short biography of one of the Europeans who helped the Americans during the Revolutionary War. Some of the names you might suggest are Rochambeau, Duportail, Pulaski, de Grasie, de Kalb, and von Steuben. Suggest that one of the reasons these Europeans offered their assistance was that they were frightened of Great Britain's power and were anxious to see the British defeated. Have several students read their biography to the class.

French and American troops witnessed the surrender of the British at Yorktown. Leading the defeated officers is General Benjamin Lincoln, on horseback.

The Battle of Yorktown and the End of the War. On August 1, 1781, Cornwallis made a serious mistake. He moved his army to Yorktown, Virginia. Yorktown is located on a narrow peninsula between the York and the James rivers.

The Americans saw their chance. Washington and the French General de Rochambeau marched their soldiers across New Jersey toward Yorktown. Admiral de Grasse sailed a French fleet into Chesapeake Bay off the shores near Yorktown. Cornwallis's army was soon blocked by land and by sea.

The Battle of Yorktown began near the end of September 1781. Cornwallis sent for additional troops and tried to hold out until they arrived. The help came too late. Cornwallis surrendered his army to the Americans and their French allies on October 19, 1781. The war was over.

At the surrender ceremony, the British band played the tune "The World Turned Upside Down." The world must have seemed that way to both sides. The humiliation of the British was complete when the French general Lafayette then ordered the band to play "Yankee Doodle Dandy."

ANSWER THESE QUESTIONS

1. George Washington, led the Continental Army to victory; Nathan Hale, killed behind enemy lines; Ethan Allen, captured Fort Ticonderoga.
2. Franklin won French support for the American cause.
3. Americans defeated the British and thwarted the plan to cut New England off from the other colonies; the victory convinced the French that the Americans could win their battle for independence.
4. Both fought bravely and were inspiring leaders; Nathan Hale died for his patriotism; Arnold became a traitor.
5. By keeping his army alive, Washington kept the Revolution alive; one victory or loss meant little compared with victory for the Revolution.

ANSWER THESE QUESTIONS

1. Who were three heroes of the American Revolution?
2. What part did Benjamin Franklin play in the American Revolution?
3. What happened at Saratoga in 1777? Why was the event important to the Americans?
4. How were Nathan Hale and Benedict Arnold alike and different?
5. Why were George Washington's decisions to keep his army alive, even at the cost of losing some battles, an important strategy in winning the war?

George Rogers Clark

PEOPLE IN AMERICA

We often think of the American Revolution as a war that happened in the Thirteen Colonies. The war, however, also spread into the Ohio River Valley. The person who led the fight for American rights against the British and their allies in the Ohio River Valley was George Rogers Clark.

Clark was born in 1752 only three years before Nathan Hale. While Hale stood for everything New Englanders could ask for in a hero, Clark represented a typical western frontier hero. Hale was highly educated. Clark had little schooling, but learned surveying from his grandfather. Hale was a teacher before the Revolution. Clark went west from his birthplace in Charlottesville, Virginia, and explored the Ohio and Kentucky rivers in 1772 and 1774.

The differences between Hale and Clark were many. Still, they both were patriots and leaders. In 1778 Clark and less than two hundred volunteers set out from Kentucky for southern Illinois. There the British and their Indian allies held forts at Kaskaskia, Cahokia (both in present-day Illinois), and Vincennes (in present-day Indiana.) On July 4, Clark captured Kaskaskia. One month later he had also captured Cahokia and Vincennes. (See the map on page 229.)

Word of these victories came to Colonel Henry Hamilton, the British commander of Fort Detroit. Hamilton had a terrible reputation among the American settlers in the Ohio River Valley. They called him "Hair Buyer" because he often paid the Indians for scalps they brought him in Detroit.

Hamilton and his British soldiers attacked Vincennes in December 1778, and took the fort back. They then settled down in a winter camp in Vincennes expecting that Clark would also wait for spring before attacking.

Hamilton was wrong. Clark and his soldiers marched through the severe cold weather for eighteen days on a trip to Vincennes. There they surprised "Hair Buyer" Hamilton, took the fort a second time, and took Hamilton prisoner.

Because of the farsighted bravery of George Rogers Clark, the Americans controlled the Ohio River Valley. When the war ended, and a treaty was signed, the Americans could claim all the territory south of the Great Lakes and north of the Ohio River, all the way west to the Mississippi River.

Chapter 7 SUMMARY

The Coercive Acts passed by Parliament after the Boston Tea Party caused people in the Thirteen Colonies to react against the British government in America. Concerned members of colonial assemblies sent delegates to attend a Continental Congress being held in Philadelphia in 1774. There they hoped to discuss ways of ending the dispute between the colonists and the British king and Parliament.

The Congress accepted the Suffolk Resolves, which challenged the Coercive Acts. Then they went home, ready to return to Philadelphia if necessary.

In 1775 the patriots and the British army met in battle at Lexington and Concord. The American Revolution had begun. A Second Continental Congress came together in 1775. The Congress appointed George Washington commander-in-chief of the American forces and made one last attempt at peace. Finally, in 1776, the Congress declared that the United States were independent of Great Britain.

The patriots and the British fought many battles during the war. Washington's strategy was to engage in battles, but never to risk losing his army. He and his generals carried out many successful surprise attacks during the war. The Continental Army also lost many battles and suffered a great deal. Because of Washington's strategy, many instances of individual bravery, help from other nations, and British mistakes, the patriots finally won their independence at Yorktown in 1781.

Chapter 7 TEST

WORDS TO REMEMBER

Match each of the following words with the correct definition below:

h	1. loyalists	c	5. campaign
d	2. unity	g	6. civil war
b	3. minutemen	e	7. patriotism
a	4. artillery	f	8. stalemate

a. cannon and other large guns
b. volunteer soldiers who answer the call to fight without delay
c. series of planned battles
d. feeling of oneness
e. feeling of national pride
f. neither side wins
g. battles between citizens of the same country
h. American supporters of the king

THINKING THINGS THROUGH

Choose the phrase that best describes a cause of each of the following:

c 1. The First Continental Congress
   a. the capture of Philadelphia
   b. the Battle of Bunker Hill
   c. the Coercive Acts.

a 2. The Second Continental Congress
   a. Lexington and Concord
   b. the Declaration of Independence
   c. the Olive Branch Petition

a 3. The British leave Boston
   a. artillery from Fort Ticonderoga
   b. the Battle of Bunker Hill
   c. the Battle of Quebec

RELATED MATERIALS
Duplicator/Copy Masters: Activities 13, 14; Quiz 13
Workbook pages 20-22

WORKING WITH SKILLS
Paraphrases will vary.

4. Opinion swings toward independence
   a. victory at Quebec
   b. *Common Sense*
   c. the Battle of Moore's Creek Bridge
5. The shame of Valley Forge
   a. American soldiers' heroism
   b. lack of support by Americans at home
   c. help from foreign countries
6. French aid
   a. victory at Saratoga
   b. victory at Yorktown
   c. Bunker Hill

WORKING WITH SKILLS

Below is a quotation of a famous statement made by the patriot Patrick Henry in Virginia only days before the events at Lexington and Concord. Sometimes the words are difficult to understand. Using a dictionary, write out a paraphrase of this selection.

> . . . Gentlemen may cry peace, peace, but there is no peace, the war is actually begun. The next gale that sweeps from the north will bring to our ears the clash of resounding arms. Our brethren are already in the field. Why stand we here idle? What is it that gentlemen wish? What would they have? Is life so dear, or peace so sweet, as to be purchased at the price of chains and slavery? Forbid it, Almighty God! I know not what course others may take, but as for me, give me liberty, or give me death!

ON YOUR OWN

1. Using an encyclopedia, learn about the following heroes of the American Revolution. Choose three of these people and write a paragraph describing the part they played in the war: Peter Salem, Salem Poor, Margaret Corbin, Thaddeus Kosciusko, Marquis de Lafayette, Kazimierz Pulaski, Betsy Ross, Sybil Ludington, John Paul Jones, Lydia Darragh, Mary Hays, John Muhlenberg, Catherine Schuyler.
2. The picture below shows the battle between the British ship *Serapis* (right) and the *Bonhomme Richard,* commanded by the American war hero John Paul Jones. Knowing that the British guns could not operate at close range, Jones tied the two ships together. The hand-to-hand battle went on for three and a half hours before the *Serapis* gave up. Imagine that you were one of the sailors on board Jones's ship and write a one-page letter home, describing the fierce fight.

Chapter 8 introduces students to the challenges faced by Americans after they achieved independence from Great Britain. Lesson 8-1 gives the details of the Treaty of Paris and discusses how the Articles of Confederation tried to give structure to the new nation. Lesson 8-2 outlines the consequences of having a central government too weak to deal effectively with national problems.

Chapter 8
A CONFEDERATION OF STATES

CONTENT OBJECTIVES

After completing the lesson, students will know:

- the details of the Treaty of Paris
- the new boundaries of the United States
- the good and the bad effects of the Revolutionary War on the lifestyle of the American people
- the origin of the Articles of Confederation

VOCABULARY

negotiate: work out terms
ratify: approve
constitution: a written plan of government

ACTIVITY

Objective: To write original statements

Review the definition of *negotiation.* Give examples of modern-day negotiations in labor disputes and government. Then divide the class into two groups, one representing the American delegation at Paris, the other, the British. Each should present to the other written requests that must be met before they will agree to settle the war. The British will strongly favor keeping lands in the West. The new nation would oppose this. Students should have at least two differences to negotiate. Have them write out the results of their negotiations in original statements. Then discuss why compromise was difficult.

8-1 Peace at Last

As you read, think about these questions:
What treaty ended the American Revolution?
What were the boundaries of the United States in 1783?
What were some changes that the American Revolution had brought about?
What were some problems that the new nation faced?
Who wrote the Articles of Confederation?

Special Vocabulary negotiate ratify constitution

The dramatic surrender of Cornwallis did not bring complete joy to Americans. True, the bloodshed had come to an end, and for that all the people could be grateful. The matter of a treaty of peace remained to be settled. What kind would it be? People were afraid that the British might force a settlement on the former colonies that would take from them territory which the redcoats had not been able to win on the battlefield. The new nation might even be hemmed in on its borders, unable to expand westward.

Treaty of Paris, 1783

At last, however, in January of 1783 good news arrived from Paris. The two sides had agreed to the terms of a treaty. The war would be officially over when the final treaty was signed the following September. The Americans had done a very good job of *negotiating*, or working out terms of, the treaty. Led by the famous and highly respected Benjamin Franklin, the American team also included John Jay, John Adams, and Henry Laurens. It had succeeded in making a treaty that was generally favorable to the Americans.

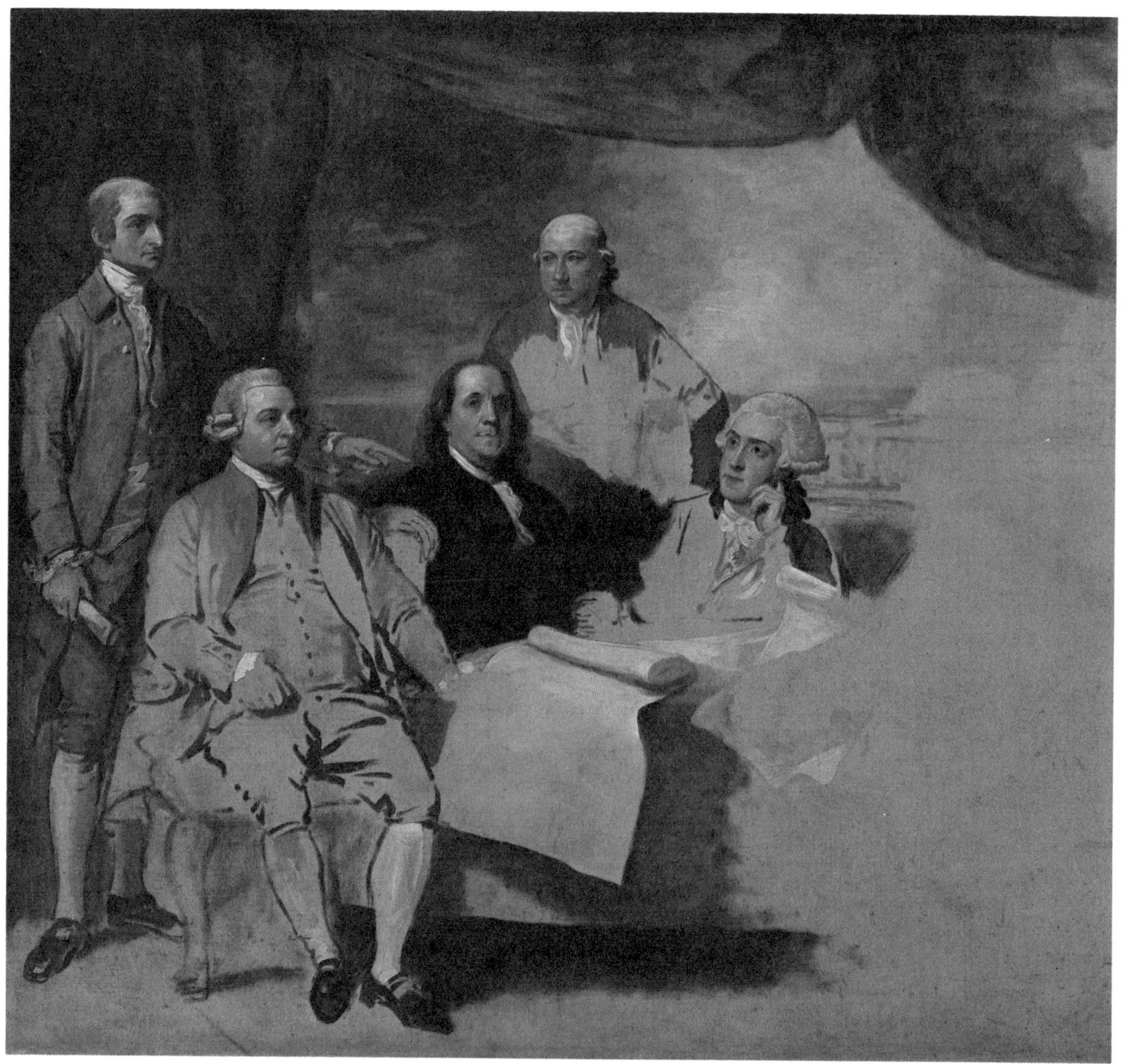

The American negotiators, pictured left to right, were John Jay, John Adams, Benjamin Franklin, Henry Laurens, and Franklin's grandson William. The painting is unfinished because the British delegate, who felt he was unattractive, refused to pose.

Terms of the Treaty. The British and Americans had agreed to the following terms:

1) Great Britain recognized the United States as a free and independent nation.

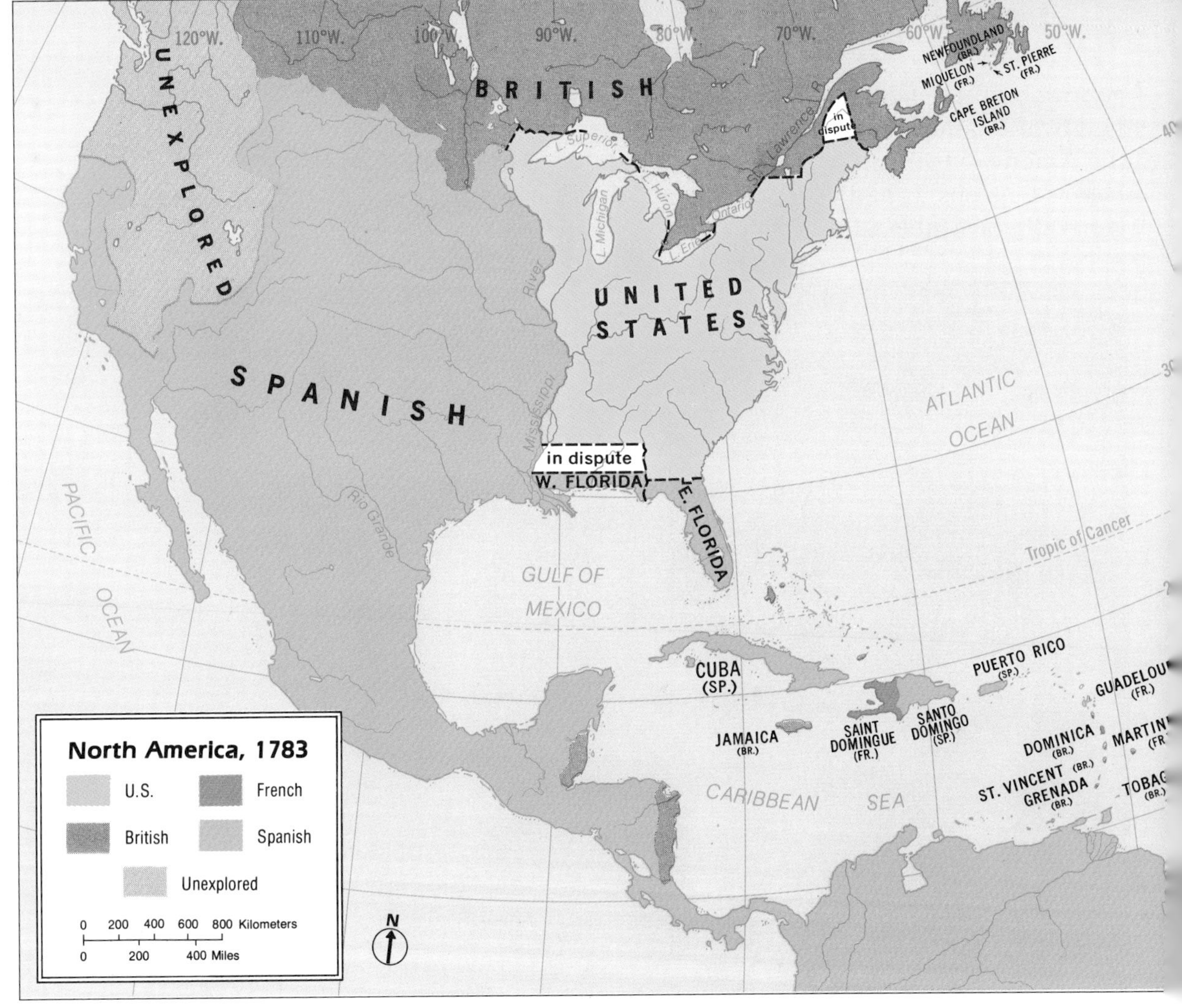

This map shows North America after the Treaty of Paris, 1783. Compare the boundaries on this map with the boundaries on the map of North America in 1763 on page 133. What changes have taken place?

The western boundary of the United States extends to the Mississippi River; Quebec has been eliminated; Spanish territory has grown.

2) The boundaries of the new nation were decided upon. They were roughly north to Canada, west to the Mississippi River, and south to East and West Florida, which Great Britain returned to Spain. (Find these boundaries on the map of North America in 1783 on this page.)
3) Americans had the right to fish off the coasts of Newfoundland and Nova Scotia (both of which were controlled by the British).
4) All debts on both sides were to be paid.
5) The United States Congress would recommend that property taken from Loyalists during the war be returned to them.
6) All fighting was to come to an end, and all British troops were to leave the United States "with all convenient speed."

Approval by Congress. Americans were generally pleased with the treaty of peace, which is known as the Treaty of Paris, 1783. They had not gotten everything they wanted. Some people had hoped that Canada would also become part of the new nation. Others had not wanted to agree to pay all debts. Nevertheless, the most important points had been worked out. The United States, with generous boundaries, was a free nation! Congress *ratified*, or approved, the treaty on January 14, 1784. The new nation could get on with the work of establishing itself.

DISCUSSION

Discuss with the students some groups that were not treated equally after the Revolution. For example, you might consider American Jews, blacks, Indians, and women. Then have the students discuss the progress American society has made in its treatment of these groups through the years. Try to make the point that American society has been in a constant state of change, with improvement of social relationships as its ongoing goal.

Life in the New Nation

The war had brought marked changes to the country—some, caused by the fighting itself, were bad. For instance, many people had been killed, and many had been severely wounded. Homes, farms, and businesses had been destroyed. Some changes—which could not be seen so easily—were good because they improved the way people lived and the way they felt about themselves.

New Respect for the Common Folk. The war had caused people to act in a more democratic way. For example, officers and their soldiers had sat together around the campfires at Valley Forge and other places. In trying to keep warm in the freezing cold, it had not mattered much who was an officer and who was not: all were equal.

During the war, few immigrants had come to America. As a result there was a labor shortage. So, many employers no longer were fussy about what religion a worker practiced or where he or she was born. They were glad simply that their employee had the necessary skills. Workers, therefore, had new opportunities to improve their positions.

The Exceptions. Of course many things remained as they had been before the war. People like Haym Salomon, who had given much of their own money to finance the American army, could not hold public office because they were Jews. In some states, a person still had to own property in order to vote. Women were not allowed to vote anywhere, and in some places they could not own property. Slavery continued to exist in many places. Some blacks who had fought with the patriots were set free after the war. Still, they were not accepted as equals in most places.

Haym Salomon, right, was an American patriot who raised money for the Revolutionary War effort. He is shown with George Washington and Robert Morris.

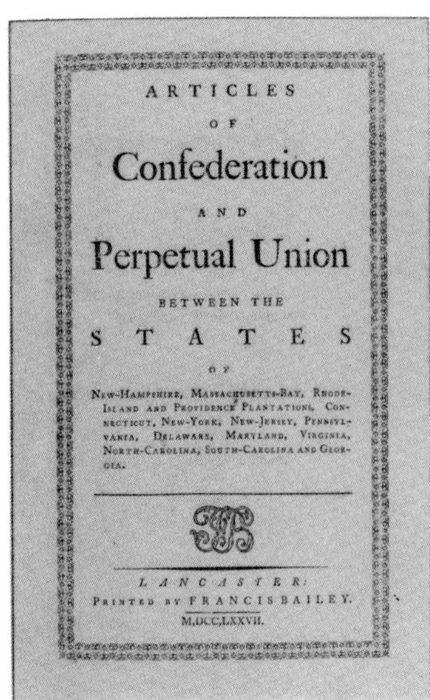

ARTICLES
OF
Confederation
AND
Perpetual Union
BETWEEN THE
STATES
OF
New-Hampshire, Massachusetts-Bay, Rhode-Island and Providence Plantations, Connecticut, New-York, New-Jersey, Pennsylvania, Delaware, Maryland, Virginia, North-Carolina, South-Carolina and Georgia.

LANCASTER:
Printed by FRANCIS BAILEY.
M,DCC,LXXVII.

This official copy of the Articles of Confederation reflected Congress's hope that the union of the colonies would be "perpetual." In fact, the Confederation lasted only eight years.

The American Indians who lived west of the Appalachian Mountains also gained little from the Revolution. They had fought in two wars trying to protect their lands, and they had lost them. Now, as the flood of settlers increased, the Indians were being pushed even farther west. In addition, Indians who lived in the states were often mistreated and denied their rights.

Governing the States

From the time the colonies had decided to declare their independence, they had recognized the need for a plan of government. During the Revolution most of the states drew up state *constitutions*. A constitution is a written plan of government. It tells how the government is to be set up.

The patriots realized, however, that if the states were to work together to fight against the British, a plan for a central government was also needed. John Dickinson of Pennsylvania was chosen to prepare the plan. His task was not an easy one. Dickinson hoped to write a set of rules that would create a strong central government. At the same time, he did not want to take too much power away from the states. After all, the states were breaking away from a British government they resented as being too strong. They did not want to replace it with another strong central government, even if it was their own.

Dickinson's plan, called the Articles of Confederation, set up something like an alliance of the states. The national government would have to depend on the states for money. This meant that they were, in fact, more powerful than the national government. Congress approved the Articles of Confederation in 1777. The Articles were then sent to each state to be ratified.

ANSWER THESE QUESTIONS

1. When did Great Britain officially recognize the United States as a free and independent nation?
2. In what ways was the Treaty of Paris, 1783, favorable to the United States?
3. How had the Revolution provided more opportunities for workers?
4. Why did the patriots feel that a plan for a central government was needed?
5. Why, do you think, did the Articles of Confederation make the states more powerful than the national government?

ANSWER THESE QUESTIONS

1. upon acceptance of the terms of the Treaty of Paris, 1783
2. The United States was a free and independent nation with generous boundaries.
3. Since few immigrants had come to America during the Revolution, employers were glad to hire any workers who had the necessary skills.
4. The states needed a central government to help them work together to fight the British.
5. The states were breaking away from a strong British government; they did not want to give up power to another strong central government.

8-2 Government under the Articles of Confederation

As you read, think about these questions:

What served as our country's plan of government from 1781 to 1789?

What caused the delay in approving the Articles of Confederation?

What were some powers of Congress under the Articles of Confederation?

How was the Northwest Territory divided under the Land Ordinance of 1785?

What were some weaknesses of government under the Articles of Confederation?

CONTENT OBJECTIVES

After completing the lesson, students will know:

- the extent of Congress's power under the Articles of Confederation
- the significance of the Northwest Ordinance in defining how new states would enter the Union
- about the development of land companies in the Northwest Territories
- trade and domestic problems caused by the weakness of the government
- how economic problems quickly developed into the violence displayed in Shays's Rebellion

Special Vocabulary	critical	section	adjourn
	ordinance	territory	arsenal
	township		

VOCABULARY

critical: testing
ordinance: law
township: square parts of the Northwest Territories, each 6 miles (9.6 kilometers) on a side
section: one square mile (2.6 square kilometers)
territory: a region with lawmakers and a delegate to Congress
adjourn: stop meeting
arsenal: a storehouse for weapons and ammunition

The Articles of Confederation could not go into effect until all the states had approved them. It took four years for this to happen. Finally, in March of 1781, the Articles went into operation. By then, of course, the war was nearly over.

The Articles never served their original purpose: to lead a united country in the struggle against Great Britain. Nevertheless, they served as the country's plan of government from 1781 to 1789. These years are sometimes called "the *critical* period," because it was the time which tested whether or not the United States could succeed as an independent nation.

Powers of the Government

One reason for the delay in approving the Articles of Confederation had been an argument among the states over the ownership of western lands. Some states, including Virginia, claimed lands west of the Appalachian Mountains because their charters had said that they owned them. Other states without land claims, including Maryland, demanded that the states with land claims give up their western lands.

These so-called "landless" states refused to accept the Articles until all western lands were given up. In 1781 Virginia promised to give up its western lands, opening the way for the other states to approve the Articles. This question of the western lands is but one example of how jealously the states guarded their authority.

Powers of the Congress. Under the Articles of Confederation, the central government was the Congress. The Articles gave the Congress some extremely important powers. Congress could:

1) make peace or war; raise an army or navy
2) make treaties and alliances; send representatives to other countries; receive representatives from other countries
3) manage affairs with the Indians
4) settle disputes between states; set up state boundaries; admit new states
5) borrow money to pay government expenses
6) set up post offices; arrange for mail service
7) coin money

Powers of the States. The states were afraid to give too much power to the central government. They kept all the powers that were not specifically given to the Congress. The states sent delegates to the Congress, and they could call their delegates home at any time. These delegates voted on the laws. Each state had one vote in Congress regardless of the number of its delegates. The Congress, therefore, represented the state governments rather than the people.

Strengths and Accomplishments

The Articles of Confederation may today be viewed as an experiment in government. As an experiment, it was only partly successful. The Confederation had many weaknesses. Still, those who served it successfully solved some of the most important problems of the times. Furthermore, some of the work of the Confederation had lasting effects.

Keeping the States Together. We must remember that the states were still not truly united. By ratifying the Articles of Confederation, they had only agreed to enter what John

Dickinson called "a firm league of friendship." Congress kept this league together by settling disputes.

One of the biggest conflicts facing the new government involved land. Several states, as we have seen, had agreed to give up their western lands to the central government. The government then had to come up with a plan for governing and settling this vast region.

A great number of people had moved from the thirteen states onto these lands before the war was over. Many families cleared land and farmed. A few people became famous for leading groups of settlers west. Among the best known of these leaders were Daniel Boone, James Robertson, and John Sevier. Boone blazed trails through the wilderness and then helped found a settlement in Kentucky in 1775. Robertson and Sevier settled the area near the Watauga River in what is now Tennessee.

Daniel Boone's party of Kentucky settlers followed the famous Wilderness Road that Boone himself had helped to cut through the Cumberland Gap in the Appalachian Mountains.

Would these new settlements become new states? If so, how large should they be? Would they have a place in the Confederation equal to that of the original thirteen states? How would their governments be formed? The Congress had to find answers to such questions as these.

Many pioneer families settled in "the tall timber country" of the Northwest Territory, believing that the thicker the trees were, the more fertile the soil would be.

ACTIVITY

Objective: To summarize information

The Articles of Confederation solved some important problems facing the new nation. For example, the Articles provided a means for settling boundary disputes between the states and established a method for new states to enter the Union. Direct the students to write several summaries of the solutions achieved through the Articles. Show them how to be brief but accurate. An example might be: "Passage of the Land Ordinance, 1785, gave farmers land in new territories, provided land companies a good profit, and prepared the settlement of the Northwest Territories." Have several students read aloud their summary sentences.

Dividing the Western Lands. Congress first concerned itself with the area known as the Old Northwest, or the Northwest Territory. It was made up of land north of the Ohio River that the states had turned over to the central government. In 1785 Congress passed a land *ordinance*, or law, that provided for the sale of this land. Before this time, land had been free or almost free to willing settlers. Congress now had decided to sell the land because it needed money.

The Land Ordinance of 1785 divided the Northwest Territory into square parts called *townships*. Each township was 6 miles (9.6 kilometers) long on each side, for a total of 36 square miles (93.6 square kilometers). Then each township was divided into thirty-six equal *sections*. Each section was 1 square mile, or 640 acres (2.6 square kilometers, or 260 hectares). Each section was given a number. Look at the map and diagram on page 201.

The smallest amount of land that could be bought was one section, costing $640. Four sections in each township were to be set aside for the use of the United States government. Money from the sale of Section 16 was always to be used for the public schools.

Governing the Western Lands. Not everyone who wanted to buy land had $640. Many would-be farmers did not want to buy an entire section of land. As a result, several land companies were formed. These companies bought large tracts of land, which they persuaded Congress to sell at a low price. The companies then sold small plots of land to farmers. The farmers got their land, and the land companies made a good profit.

Congress believed that the land companies would bring large numbers of people into the Northwest Territory. For that reason, Congress passed the Ordinance of 1787, or the Northwest Ordinance. This law, based on the ideas of Thomas Jefferson, set up the rules for government in the Northwest Territory. In so doing, the Northwest Ordinance provided a means for adding new states to the original thirteen.

Congress decided that the Northwest Territory would be divided into at least three but not more than five states. As soon as a *territory*—a region with lawmakers and a delegate to Congress—had 60,000 people, it could become a state. It would be admitted to the Union "on an equal footing with the original states in all respects whatever."

The Northwest Ordinance forbade slavery within the Northwest Territory. It also set up the beginning of free public education. The Northwest Ordinance is considered the most important law passed for the country under the Articles of Confederation. From that time on, all new states would enter the Union (the United States) according to the method set forth in the ordinance.

Weaknesses of the Articles of Confederation

The government had much to be proud of in producing the land ordinances. These ordinances provided for an orderly expansion of the United States. There were, however, many problems that the government under the Articles of Confederation could not solve.

Problems with Other Countries. Foreign countries had little respect for the United States government because it was so weak. Great Britain retained its forts in the Old Northwest, refusing to live up to the terms of the Treaty of Paris, 1783. As a result, Americans could not feel free to use the Great Lakes. Spain controlled New Orleans and began to tax American goods passing through that port. Most western farmers had no other way to get their goods to markets in the East. The United States government, however, was not

DISCUSSION

Have the students discuss the ways the Articles of Confederation allowed foreign countries to show disrespect for the United States. These include the inability to enforce the terms of the treaty, failure to raise an army, and problems with trade. Ask the students if they think citizens of the United States also lacked respect for the government. Why or why not? They should mention state boundary disputes and trouble with debts. Have students give examples of how they show respect for our government and examples of ways people show disrespect.

Great Britain maintained its control of Fort Detroit until 1794, thereby limiting American use of the Great Lakes.

strong enough to deal with Great Britain or with Spain on these important matters.

According to the Articles of Confederation, Congress could raise an army and a navy. It could do so, however, only by asking each state for troops. The states refused such requests. The United States government, therefore, had no armed forces to strengthen its position in dealing with other countries.

Many of the problems between the United States and other countries had to do with trade. Great Britain no longer relied on the United States for raw materials like timber and iron. Furthermore, the British government reduced the amount of trade it would permit the Americans to carry on with the British West Indies. Many New England merchants and southern farmers were hurt by this restriction on American trade.

Eager merchants looked for new places to sell their goods. In 1784 a business group sent a shipload of trade goods to China. The ship *Empress of China* returned with a rich cargo of silks, teas, and cheap cloth. When the merchants sold these goods, they were able to profit handsomely.

Trade with China helped the new nation, but it was not enough. The growth of trade with other countries would be slow though steady. Many Americans who depended on

The only Chinese city open for foreign trade before 1842, Canton welcomed traders from America and elsewhere. No women or firearms were allowed; American traders had to leave both behind in Macao.

trade for their livelihood became critical of the Confederation because it was weak.

Problems at Home. Some of the problems in the United States during the critical period were the result of a lack of money. Bad times made it hard for people to pay their debts. Many soldiers who had fought in the Revolution had not been paid for their services. The prices of farm goods dropped sharply after the war, so farmers especially felt squeezed. Many farmers were told that they must repay their loans or lose their land.

From place to place in the United States, the ways of dealing with money problems differed. In some states, people demanded that more paper money be printed. Paper money usually represents a certain amount of gold or silver which the government has in safekeeping. This paper money is regarded as "sound money." To make more money available, debtors wanted the state governments to print bills even though there was no gold or silver to back them up. When a large amount of paper money is printed without backing, the value of the money drops. It becomes "cheap money." That is, the paper money buys less goods or services than it should. Then more money is needed to pay for the usual goods and services.

In those states that issued money without backing, it was easier for people to pay their debts. This pleased debtors. Lenders, however, angrily opposed the practice of printing increasing amounts of paper money without proper gold or silver backing. They had lent sound money and now were being repaid with cheap money. The debtors sometimes came out better than the lenders.

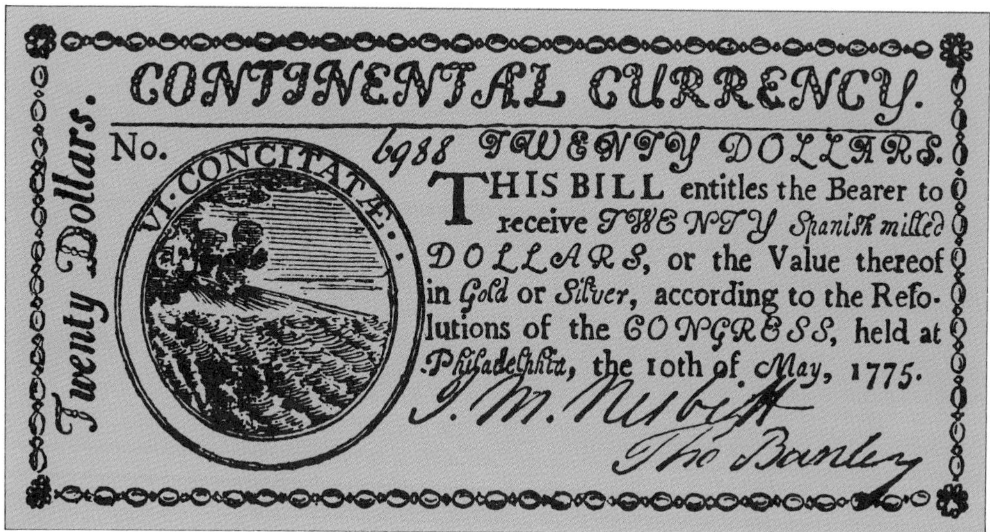

CONTINENTAL CURRENCY.
Twenty Dollars.
No. 6988 TWENTY DOLLARS.
VI CONCITATAE
THIS BILL entitles the Bearer to receive TWENTY Spanish milled DOLLARS, or the Value thereof in Gold or Silver, according to the Resolutions of the CONGRESS, held at Philadelphia, the 10th of May, 1775.

The phrase "not worth a Continental" reflects disrespect for the value of paper money issued by the Congress after the Revolutionary War.

Problems Lead to Violence. The state of Massachusetts refused to print paper money without backing. This meant that many farmers would lose their land because they could not pay their taxes. The farmers grew angry. At first they sent a petition to the Massachusetts legislature asking for relief. When this failed to bring results, the farmers decided to use force.

In 1786 Daniel Shays, a local hero of the Revolution, and about 500 followers forced the court at Springfield to *adjourn*, or stop meeting. Two months later, Shays and a force of 1200 attacked the federal *arsenal*, a storehouse for weapons and ammunition, in Springfield. Soldiers were sent to stop the uprising that became known as Shays' Rebellion.

Shays fled to Vermont, and the rebellion ended. The uprising, however, had an important effect on the nation. Leaders throughout the thirteen states began to think about the central government. Some realized that the Articles of

Confederation had set up a government that was too weak to deal with the serious problems that faced the United States. Many began to fear what the British and other Europeans were expecting and even hoping for—that the new nation would fail.

Shays' Rebellion failed to stop Massachusetts from imprisoning debtors. Shays—who was sentenced to die for his crimes—was later pardoned.

ANSWER THESE QUESTIONS

1. What powers did the states have under the Articles of Confederation?
2. What were some accomplishments of the government under the Articles of Confederation?
3. Why is the Northwest Ordinance considered the most important law passed under the Articles of Confederation?
4. Why did farmers and merchants face hard times after the Revolution?
5. What money problems led people to realize that the central government under the Articles of Confederation was weak?

ANSWER THESE QUESTIONS

1. all powers not specifically given to Congress
2. kept states together; provided for division of western lands
3. provided a means for adding new states to the Union
4. Spain's control of New Orleans made it difficult for western farmers to ship their products to market. Great Britain and France limited trade with the United States.
5. When some states printed paper money without backing and others did not, the central government was unable to handle this problem.

Objective: After completing these pages, the students should be able to understand a map scale.

Working with Skills

MAP SKILLS

ACTIVITY

Objective: To understand a map scale

Provide students with several differently scaled maps of their community. Have them use the distance scale to measure distances between several places they know. Contact the chamber of commerce, municipal offices, or local historical society for copies of local maps. Do all the maps show the same distances between places? If not, ask students which they think is more accurate?

Understanding Map Scale

All maps are drawn to *scale*. This means that a small measure on a map represents a larger measure on the earth. The same idea is used in making model airplanes and dollhouse furniture. Architects use scale when they draw up plans for a house or other building. In each of these cases, the model or drawing is a small, but accurate, version of the object it represents.

Mapmakers use scale to make sure that maps are an accurate representation of the area they show. A *small-scale* map is one that shows a large area of the earth without much detail. A *large-scale* map is one that shows a small area of the earth with much detail. For example, a small-scale map might show all of North America. It might include the countries and major bodies of water. A large-scale map, however, might show just one state of the United States. Such a map might include highways, cities, state parks, and many other features that could not be shown on a small-scale map.

There are different ways to express scale on a map. On some maps, the scale is expressed in words and figures. For example, 1 inch = 1000 miles (1609 kilometers). This means that each inch on the map stands for 1000 miles, or 1609 kilometers, on the surface of the earth.

Another way to express scale is by means of a representative fraction, for example, 1:63,360 or $\frac{1}{63,360}$. This means that one unit of measurement on the map represents 63,360 of the same units on the surface of the earth. Since the unit is the same, the scale may mean that 1 inch = 63,360 inches or that 1 centimeter = 63,360 centimeters. Both measurements would be correct.

Most of the maps in this book use a graphic scale. This is a straight line on which distances have been marked off. Each mark represents a certain number of miles or kilometers. Look at the graphic scale on the map on the next page. Use a ruler to determine how many miles or kilometers are represented by each inch on this map.

RELATED MATERIAL

Duplicator/Copy Master Activity 16

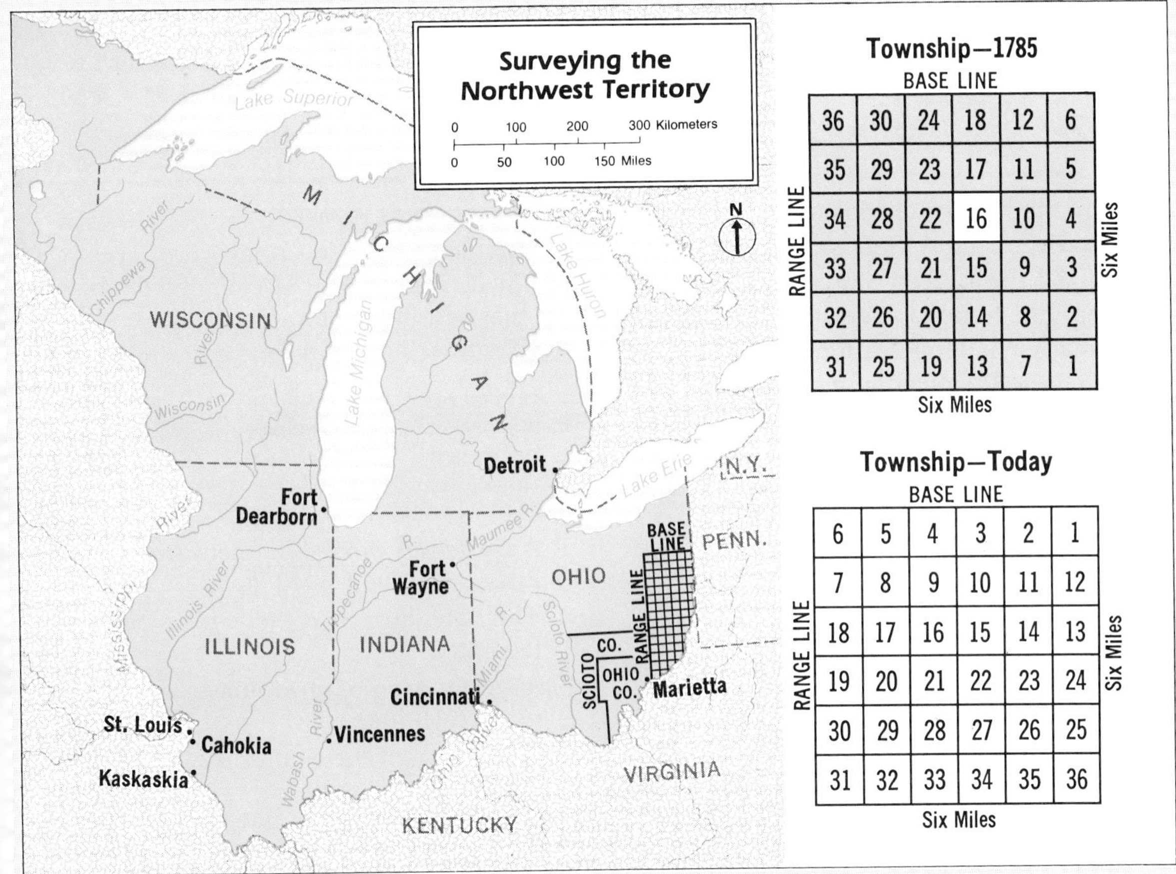

Now look at the map of North America, 1783, on page 188. Compare that map with the map of the Northwest Territory on this page. Then answer each of the questions.

1. In what ways are the two maps alike?
2. Does 1 inch represent more miles (kilometers) on the map of North America or on the map of the Northwest Territory?
3. Which map represents more of the earth?
4. Which map shows more detail?
5. Which map is drawn to the larger scale?

ANSWERS FOR MAP SKILLS

1. Both maps show the Northwest Territory
2. North America
3. North America
4. Northwest Territory
5. Northwest Territory

THINKING THINGS THROUGH

1. People had gone through a terrible war together. The need for workers made employers hire almost anyone who could work. Greater opportunities for improvement were available after the war. 2. Jews, women, blacks, and American Indians 3. to organize the states into an effective force against Great Britain 4. They had just broken away from the strong central govern-

Chapter 8 SUMMARY

The Treaty of Paris, 1783, was very favorable to the United States. Great Britain recognized the United States as a free and independent nation. Americans, however, faced many challenges after the war.

During the Revolution, most of the states had written state constitutions. A plan called the Articles of Confederation had provided for a national government, but the Articles were not approved by the states until 1781. The government under the Articles of Confederation kept the states together and passed laws for dividing and governing the western lands. The Northwest Ordinance set up a plan for adding new states to the Union.

The states had been afraid to grant too much power to the central government. As a result, the government under the Articles of Confederation was too weak to deal with the many problems that faced the new nation. Foreign countries had little respect for the United States government. Great Britain limited its trade with the United States. Spain hurt trade by taxing American goods passing through New Orleans.

American merchants, farmers, and many others faced large debts. People began to demand that the states print paper money that was not backed by gold or silver. When Massachusetts refused to do this, a large group of farmers, led by Daniel Shays, took part in a violent uprising. People realized that the central government was weak and that the new nation might fail.

Chapter 8 TEST

WORDS TO REMEMBER

In each sentence below some words are underlined. Select the word from the following list that best fits the meaning of the underlined words.

a. ratified	e. ordinance
b. arsenal	f. adjourn
c. negotiated	g. territory
d. constitution	

c 1. A treaty was worked out between Great Britain and the United States.

a 2. The states approved the Articles of Confederation.

d 3. A written plan of government was drawn up by each state.

e 4. A law allowed the land of the Northwest Territory to be sold.

g 5. A region with lawmakers and a delegate to Congress could become a state.

f 6. The courts were forced to stop meeting.

b 7. The place where weapons and ammunition were stored was surrounded.

THINKING THINGS THROUGH

Answer these questions.

1. How did the Revolution cause people to act in a more democratic way?
2. What groups of people were still not considered equal after the war?
3. Why was a central government needed after the colonies declared independence?
4. Why were the states afraid to give too much power to the central government?
5. What problems did the farmers of Massachusetts have?

RELATED MATERIALS

Duplicator/Copy Masters: Activities 15, 16; Quiz 14
Workbook pages 23-25

ment of Great Britain. **5.** They did not have enough money to pay the taxes on their land and the state of Massachusetts was slow to help them solve this problem.

WORKING WITH SKILLS

1. Surveying the Northwest Territory **2.** North America, 1783 **3.** Surveying the Northwest Territory **4.** Surveying the Northwest Territory—because the area is smaller and the map maker can put more detail on the map. **5.** North America, 1783

WORKING WITH SKILLS

Turn to the maps of North America, 1783, on page 188, and Surveying the Northwest Territory on page 201. Answer these questions.

1. On which map are the Great Lakes drawn to the larger scale?
2. On which map does three-quarters of an inch equal 800 kilometers?
3. On which map does one inch equal 300 kilometers?
4. On which map would you be more likely to find the name of a city or town? Why?
5. On which map can you find the entire length of the Mississippi River?

ON YOUR OWN

1. Turn to Chapter 4 (pages 80–103). Make a list of each of the maps in that chapter. Next to each map title, write down whether the map is drawn to a small or large scale.
2. Go to your school or community library and get a copy of the *Winter Hero* by James and Lincoln Collier. This is a book about Shays' Rebellion. Write a brief summary of the book. Include the names of the main characters, the problems they had, and how the problems were solved. Also include your favorite part of the book.
3. Make a chart to show some of the major weaknesses of the Articles of Confederation and the results of these weaknesses. The following is an example:

Weakness	Result
Congress had no power to tax the people.	The government had trouble paying its debts.

4. The pioneers pictured on this page are typical of those who settled the Northwest Territory. Facing a long trek on foot across the mountains, they took with them only what they would need to survive the trip, in this case from North Carolina to Ohio. Draw up a list of the items this family has taken and explain why they would have chosen each one.

Chapter 9 shows students how American leaders struggled to form a central government that was very strong but still allowed the states to maintain a powerful voice. Lesson 9-1

Chapter 9
A NEW CONSTITUTION

describes the unsuccessful meeting of state leaders at Annapolis in 1786 and the problems that threatened to disrupt the Constitutional Convention in Philadelphia. It also gives details of the New Jersey and Virginia Plans. Lesson 9-2 tells how the delegates resolved their many conflicting viewpoints and successfully developed the Constitution. The three branches of government are described and the concept of checks and balances is explained.

CONTENT OBJECTIVES

After completing the lesson, students will know:

- the difficulties the United States faced because of the lack of unity among the states
- the results of the convention in Annapolis in 1786
- the major disputes brought up in the Constitutional Convention
- the details of the New Jersey Plan and the Virginia Plan
- how the delegates compromised to form a House of Representatives and a Senate, and to have a President chosen by electors

VOCABULARY

convention: formal meeting
interstate: between the states
amendment: addition or change
bicameral: made up of two houses
veto: the power to refuse a law proposed by the legislative branch
unicameral: a legislature consisting of one house
compromise: an agreement in which each side gives up something it wants
elector: a person chosen by state officers for the specific purpose of electing the President and Vice President
candidate: a person who runs for political office

9-1 The Constitutional Convention

As you read, think about these questions:

What weakness of the Articles of Confederation did the states find most troublesome?

What was the result of the Annapolis Convention?

What were the provisions of the Virginia Plan?

What were the provisions of the New Jersey Plan?

What was the Great Compromise?

Who elects the President and Vice President of the United States?

What is the "Supreme Law of the Land?"

Special Vocabulary	convention	bicameral	compromise
	interstate	veto	elector
	amendment	unicameral	candidate

By the middle of the 1780s, the United States needed help badly. The states were quarreling constantly, and they were united in name only. The people rebelled against their government. The national government was not respected abroad. Many felt that if the Articles of Confederation were not changed soon, the United States would stop being a country. The leaders of Europe were sure that no country could succeed where the people ran the government.

Revising the Articles of Confederation

Both the states and the Congress of the Confederation were concerned with the direction the new country was taking.

The Articles of Confederation simply could not keep the thirteen states together as one strong country. Attempts to change the Articles began slowly. First a few of the states took some steps. Then the Congress tried to revise the Articles. Soon, all the states were involved in the great task.

The Annapolis State House, built in Maryland in 1772, served as a meeting place for the convention on interstate trade and later as the United States capitol from November 26, 1783, to June 3, 1784.

Problems of the States. One weakness of the Articles of Confederation that seemed more troublesome than others was that trade between the states was not under the control of Congress. Each state had its own rules for regulating trade. Virginia and Maryland, for example, fought over the right to navigate the Potomac River, the boundary between the two states. In an attempt to solve this particular problem, a meeting was held at Mount Vernon, George Washington's home. The meeting was a success. Both sides agreed to set up rules for traffic and trade on the river.

The Virginia legislature decided that all states should meet to talk about their trade problems. It invited the twelve other states to attend a *convention*, or formal meeting, at Annapolis, Maryland, in September of 1786. The purpose of this convention was to discuss *interstate* trade, that is, trade between the states.

Nine states accepted the invitation to attend the Annapolis Convention, although only five states had delegates there when the meetings began. Alexander Hamilton of New York, James Madison of Virginia, and John Dickinson of

Delaware led the convention. Because so few states were represented at the meeting, the convention quickly broke up. The twelve delegates decided that a discussion of the trade problems of the states was not possible.

Under the direction of Alexander Hamilton, however, a report was written and sent to the states. This report called on all states to send delegates to a new convention to be held in Philadelphia in May of 1787. This meeting would not only discuss trade problems, but also would decide what could be done to make the Articles of Confederation stronger.

Revisions by Congress. Congress, too, was concerned about the weaknesses of the Articles of Confederation. In 1786 Charles Pinckney of South Carolina asked that Congress consider changing the Articles. As a result, Congress set up a committee that suggested many *amendments*, additions or changes, to the Articles of Confederation. The purpose of these amendments was to solve some of the problems of the Confederation.

Like the Annapolis Convention, the work of the Congress came to nothing. The Congress, therefore, joined the delegates at Annapolis in calling for a meeting in Philadelphia to discuss the problems of the Articles of Confederation. On February 21, 1787, Congress asked the states to elect their delegates to the meeting.

The Philadelphia Convention. When the convention gathered in Philadelphia on May 14, 1787, eleven states had chosen delegates. Only New Hampshire and Rhode Island had not made a decision to attend. On May 25, delegates from seven states were present, and the convention began. Within a few weeks, every state except Rhode Island was represented.

All told, fifty-five delegates came together in Independence Hall, the site of the signing of the Declaration of Independence eleven years earlier. Eight of the delegates had been among the signers. Two others had signed the Articles of Confederation. Seven had been present at Annapolis. Three had served as president of the Congress of the Confederation.

Two of the greatest heroes of the country were also at this convention: George Washington and Benjamin Franklin. They had the respect of all the delegates. They could see that once again the country required their talent and service.

Thomas Jefferson, too, believed that the Philadelphia

Independence Hall was not the only site of discussion at the Constitutional Convention. Many conversations were held in the various Philadelphia rooming houses where the delegates stayed.

convention was very important. From France, where he was representing the United States he wrote, "I hope Good from their meeting. Indeed if it does not do good it must do harm, because it will show we are not wise enough to govern ourselves." Together these fifty-five delegates seemed determined to shape a government of the United States that would work well for its people.

The Work of the Convention

When the convention opened, the delegates set out to change the Articles of Confederation. They understood that

More than half the delegates to the Constitutional Convention, here being addressed by Washington, were lawyers. The rest were planters, merchants, physicians, and college professors.

many changes would have to be made to make the Articles a better plan of government. As the delegates began this work, many of them realized that changing the Articles might not be enough. They were ready to decide that a new *form* of government was needed.

The delegates felt this decision was so important that they decided to keep all their debates secret. No word of what went on in Independence Hall was to be made public. The delegates also showed their respect for George Washington by unanimously electing him chairman of the convention.

Disagreements. The delegates to the convention had various ideas about how a new government should work. The first major disagreement at the convention was between the large and small states. The large states of Virginia, Pennsylvania, New York, Massachusetts, and North Carolina wanted more power in the government than they had under the Articles of Confederation. The smaller states like Delaware, New Jersey, and New Hampshire were afraid that the larger states would have too much power in the new government. These differences of opinion threatened to break the convention apart.

The Virginia Plan. The dispute began on May 29, 1787, when Governor Edmund Randolph of Virginia presented a plan written by the Virginia delegates. This plan became known as the Virginia Plan or the large-state plan. It gave most of the power of the new government to the large states. The Virginia Plan called for:

1) A government with three branches or parts—a legislative branch to make the laws; an executive branch to enforce, or carry out, the laws; a judicial branch to interpret, or explain, the laws.
2) A *bicameral* legislature, or a legislature made up of two houses. The membership of the two houses would be based on population. The more people a state had, the more representatives it would have. The lower house would be elected by the people. The upper house would be elected by the lower house.
3) The executive branch would be elected by the legislative branch.
4) The judicial branch would be elected by the legislative branch.

5) A council would be formed from the executive and judicial branches. This council would have the *veto* power, or the power to refuse a law proposed by the legislative branch.

Leaders of the large states believed that this plan corrected many of the weaknesses of the Articles of Confederation. It also gave the large states more control over the government. Under the Articles, each state received only one vote, regardless of size. The Virginia Plan changed this arrangement. Randolph's resolutions were hotly debated by the delegates.

Edmund Randolph, left, presenter of the Virginia Plan, became Washington's secretary of state. William Paterson, right, who introduced the New Jersey Plan, later became a Supreme Court justice.

The New Jersey Plan. The smaller states realized that they needed a plan to put forth their own ideas about how the government should work. The New Jersey Plan, or the small-state plan, was introduced by William Paterson of New Jersey. This plan had the support of the delegates who did not want a strong central government. These delegates feared that in a government where population was so important, the small states would always have to give in to the larger states. The New Jersey Plan called for:

1) A government that had three branches—a legislative branch to make the laws; an executive branch to carry out the laws; a judicial branch to explain the laws.

ACTIVITY

Objective: To draw conclusions

Have students look up the term census. Then discuss the practice in the United States of taking a census. Then ask students to use almanacs to find the most recent census figures showing state populations. Have them find the populations of the thirteen original states. Which state had the most people in the 1780s? Which state has the highest population today? Discuss with students how the census is taken today. Have each student write a paragraph describing the census, why it is taken, and its importance in American political life today.

2) A *unicameral* legislature, that is, a legislature consisting of one house. In this house each state, regardless of size, would have only one vote. The legislature would have the power to tax the states and to control trade.
3) The executive branch would be run by more than one person. These people would be elected by the legislature. The executive branch would not have the veto power.
4) The judicial branch would be made up of one Supreme Court.

The delegates now had two very different plans to consider. Before either plan was voted on, however, the delegates decided that the convention again had to answer one important question: Should the convention try to amend the Articles of Confederation, or should it instead try to form a new government? After three days of debate, the delegates voted 7–3 to form a new government. The convention now became the Constitutional Convention. At that point, the argument over the provisions of the Virginia and New Jersey plans began.

DISCUSSION

Discuss with the students what they think the United States would be like if the New Jersey Plan had been accepted. What difference would a unicameral house have made in our history? An executive office with more than a single person?

The Great Compromise. For six weeks the debate went on in the convention over which plan was better. Neither side was willing to give up any of its demands. Finally, Roger Sherman and some of the other Connecticut delegates worked out a *compromise*. A compromise is an agreement in which each side gives up something it wants. In return for giving something up, each side receives something it wants. The agreement worked out by Roger Sherman took parts of both the Virginia and the New Jersey plans and made a new plan. This was called the Connecticut Compromise. It is also called the Great Compromise because it settled the argument that could well have torn the convention apart. The Great Compromise called for:

1) A legislature made up of two houses.
2) The lower house would be called the House of Representatives. Its members would be elected by the people for a two-year term, or length of time in office. This house would be based on population. The more people a state had, the more representatives it would have.

3) The upper house would be called the Senate. Its members would be elected by the state legislatures for a six-year term. The membership in this house would favor the small states. Each state, regardless of size, would have two senators.

Before the convention approved this compromise, another problem had to be solved. How was the population of a state to be counted? The answer was very important in determining how many representatives a state would have in the House of Representatives. The northern states wanted only the white population to be counted. The southern states wanted slaves to be included in the count as well. This would give the southern states more representatives in the new legislature. Again a compromise was worked out. It was decided that all whites and three fifths of the black population would be counted to determine the number of representatives a state could send to the House of Representatives.

Other Compromises. The work of the convention went on. More decisions had to be made concerning how much power this new government would have. Under the Articles of Confederation, trade between the states had caused many problems because nobody had authority to make rules about trade and see that they were carried out. The delegates tried to assure that these problems would not happen again.

The Arch Street ferry, which crossed the Delaware River from Philadelphia to New Jersey, was a busy one. By 1790 Philadelphia had about 28,500 residents.

The convention decided that the new Congress—the legislative branch of government—should control trade. Congress would do this by passing laws that all states would have to follow. These laws would have to be passed by a majority of the members of Congress. A majority is one more than half the members. The delegates tried to calm the fears of the southern states by making sure that Congress could not pass an export tax—the kind of tax that could be laid on southern products. In addition, Congress could not pass any law that would interfere with the slave trade for twenty years—or until 1808.

Another problem still facing the convention was the election of the executive. The convention decided that the executive branch would be headed by one person. However, the method by which that person was to be chosen caused some problems.

Many delegates felt that the President, the name given to the executive officer, should be chosen directly by the people. Others felt that the people might be too easily influenced by unimportant matters. The voters, some thought, were not intelligent enough to elect such an important officer.

There were also those who argued that Congress should choose the President. Others pointed out that this would give Congress too much control over the President.

Another compromise emerged. Neither the people nor Congress would elect the President. Instead, this decision would be left to a group of people called *electors*. Electors would be chosen by their state officers for the specific purpose of electing the President and Vice President. Each state could have as many electors as it had senators and representatives in Congress.

When the electors met, each one would vote for two *candidates* for President. A candidate is a person who runs for political office. Each elector would vote for at least one person not from that elector's state. The candidate that received the highest number of electoral votes would become the President. The person who received the second highest number of electoral votes would become the Vice President. If no candidate received a majority of the electoral votes, the House of Representatives would decide which candidate was to become the President. These electors that chose the President and Vice President would become known as the Electoral College.

This rare cartoon of 1787 indicates a troubled time when men like George Washington, Robert Morris, Benjamin Rush and Alexander Hamilton (represented in the cartoon) were building the structure of the Constitution (the fort on the right) and protecting it against those at work against its adoption.

The question of how much control the new government would have over the states also needed to be discussed. The New Jersey Plan suggested that the laws of Congress be called "The Supreme Law of the States." The delegates decided, however, that the Constitution, the laws passed by Congress, and the treaties agreed to by the government were more important than that. The delegates made these documents, therefore, "The Supreme Law of the Land." Every person and every state had to obey them. Now the work of the Convention was nearly completed.

ANSWER THESE QUESTIONS

1. Where was the conference between Virginia and Maryland held?
2. What was the result of the Annapolis Convention?
3. What plan called for two houses in the legislative branch of the new government?
4. What were the differences between the Virginia and New Jersey plans?
5. What parts of the Virginia Plan did the Great Compromise include? Of the New Jersey Plan?

ANSWER THESE QUESTIONS

1. Mount Vernon
2. A new convention was called for to look at the questions of trade and the revision of the Articles.
3. the Virginia Plan
4. Virginia Plan wanted two houses, New Jersey—one; Virginia Plan wanted both houses based on population, New Jersey wanted every state to have only one vote; Virginia wanted a council with a veto power, New Jersey did not. Virginia Plan tried to form a new government, New Jersey Plan tried to amend the Articles.
5. Great Compromise: Virginia: Two houses; One elected according to population. New Jersey: One house would favor small states—each state would have two senators.

Working with Skills

STUDY SKILLS

ACTIVITY

Objective: To use reference materials

Have the students look up information about the Electoral College. For example, explain that electors are pledged to vote for a specific candidate. Explain that the electors meet to vote for President in December, about a month after the general election. Have the students find out what happens if a candidate dies after the general election in November, but before the electors meet in December. Has this happened and when? What was the result? Have the students provide specific references as to where they obtained the information.

Using Reference Materials

You are often given assignments which require you to look up specific information which was not given in your textbook. The library in your school or community most likely has the materials you will need to find specific information. These materials are called *Reference Materials.* The most commonly used reference materials are *The Readers' Guide to Periodical Literature*, encyclopedias, and almanacs.

The Readers' Guide to Periodical Literature is an alphabetical listing of authors and/or subjects found in over one hundred magazines. It also gives the names of the magazines, the volume number, pages, and the date of each article. Look at the example of a *Readers' Guide* entry below.

UNITED STATES—Congress

House—Voting

June 26: a day in the life of Congress [House vote on budget] N. Amidel. Commonweal 108:427-9 Jl 31 '81

Liberal dupes [Democratic support of Reagan's tax cuts] Nation 233:102 Ag 8-15 '81

Rest in peace, New Deal [Reagan's tax triumph] P. Goldman and others. il pors Newsweek 98: 16-20 Ag 10'81

The subject area is the United States. The specific information is Congress—House—Voting. Articles about these subjects are listed next. The first article is called: "June 26: a day in the life of Congress (House vote on budget)." The author of the article is N. Amidel. The magazine is *Commonweal.* The volume of the magazine is 108. The article is found on pages 427–429. The date of the magazine is July 31, 1981.

Encyclopedias are resource books that cover almost every topic of importance or interest. The list of subjects covered by encyclopedias ranges very widely. Encyclopedias are used mostly to find a clear, overall summary of a topic. Encyclopedias generally have many volumes and are arranged alphabetically by topic. Here is an example of a paragraph about the Constitution from an encyclopedia.

United States Constitution

The Constitution is the supreme law of the land. It sets up a federal system of government by dividing powers between the central and state governments. The powers of the central government are separated among three branches—the executive, the legislative, and the judicial. The

RELATED MATERIAL
Duplicator/Copy Master Activity 18

executive branch, represented by the President, enforces the laws. The legislative branch, represented by the Congress, makes the laws. The judicial branch, represented by the Supreme Court, explains the laws.

An almanac is a one-volume book that is published once each year. The almanac contains up-to-date information about an immense variety of topics. It often lists famous people, awards and prizes given the previous year, statistics about births, deaths, crimes, and stories of importance that occurred in the previous year. Many times almanacs include copies of famous documents that are considered important. Here is part of a table of contents from an almanac.

Refer to the examples of the *Readers' Guide*, encyclopedia, and almanac to answer these questions.

1. What is the title of the article found in *Nation* magazine?
2. What volume of *Newsweek* is needed for the article called, "Rest in Peace, New Deal"?
3. Who is the author of "Rest in Peace, New Deal"?
4. What is the supreme law of the land?
5. What are the three branches of government?
6. The legislative branch is represented by what body?
7. What page in the almanac is the Constitution on?
8. What would you find on page 127 of the almanac?

ANSWERS
1. "Liberal Dupes"
2. vol. 98
3. P. Goldman and others
4. The Constitution
5. executive, legislative, and judicial
6. Congress
7. page 134
8. 1980 Election Results

CONTENT OBJECTIVES

After completing the lesson, students will know:

- the structure of the Constitution
- the three branches of government—legislative, executive, and judicial—and what their responsibilities are
- the importance of checks and balances to government stability
- the progress of the Federalists's fight for ratification of the Constitution
- how power was divided between the state and federal governments
- who the Antifederalists were and why they opposed the Constitution

VOCABULARY

preamble: introduction
bill: a written proposal for a new law
checks and balances: each branch of the government has some power over the other branches
federal: a system that divides the powers of government between the states and the central government
concurrent: shared
Federalist: in favor of the Constitution
Antifederalist: those opposed to the Constitution

9-2 A More Perfect Union

As you read, think about these questions:
Why are the powers of government separated into three branches of government?
What are the three branches of government?
What powers does each branch of government have?
Why was a court system included in the Constitution?
What are checks and balances?

Special Vocabulary

preamble, bill, checks and balances, federal, concurrent, Federalist, Antifederalist

The work of the convention drew to a close. On September 17, 1787, Benjamin Franklin made a final plea to the weary delegates. He wanted all of them to voice support for the document. He was sure that the new constitution was going to be a shining success. He said:

I am amazed to find this government being formed so well. I think that it will surprise our enemies. They are waiting to hear that our meeting produced only talk, that our states are ready to divide. They think that we plan to meet again only to cut each other's throats.

The Accomplishment

Indeed, the leaders of Europe were surprised by the results of this convention. Far from breaking apart, the states had formed a strong union. Some delegates were not totally in favor of this new Constitution they had written. Most felt, however, that the Constitution represented the only hope the United States had to survive as a country.

The delegates to the Constitutional Convention had put together a splendid frame of government. The Constitution begins with a *preamble,* or an introduction. The preamble lists the six purposes of the Constitution. Then the Constitution is divided into seven sections called articles. Each article deals with a different aspect of the new government.

CHECKS AND BALANCES IN THE FEDERAL GOVERNMENT

LEGISLATIVE		
• Congress checks and balances the power of the President and the Judiciary.	**Executive** • The Senate can approve or reject the President's appointments. • The Senate can approve or reject treaties recommended by the President. • Congress decides how much money the Executive Branch can spend. • The House of Representatives can impeach the President and Vice President. • The Senate can convict the President and Vice President in an impeachment trial.	**Judicial** • The House of Representatives can impeach or accuse judges of some misconduct or misuse of power. • The Senate can convict judges in an impeachment trial. • The Senate approves or rejects the President's choices for judges. • Congress creates lower courts. • Congress can propose amendments that overturn court decisions.
EXECUTIVE		
• The President checks and balances the power of the Congress and the Judiciary.	**Legislative** • The President can veto laws passed by Congress. • The President can propose laws.	**Judicial** • The President appoints all federal judges. • The President can pardon persons convicted of federal crimes.
JUDICIAL		
• The Supreme Court checks and balances the power of the President and the Congress.	**Executive** • Federal judges are not controlled by the President because they are appointed for life. • The Supreme Court can decide if actions taken by the President agree with the Constitution.	**Legislative** • The Supreme Court can decide the meaning of laws passed by Congress. • The Supreme Court can decide if laws passed by Congress agree with the Constitution.

Powers of the Government

The Constitution was written so that there was a balance between the powers of the central government and the powers of the state governments. It created a better *federal* system of government than the Articles of Confederation had. A federal system of government is one that divides the powers of government between the states and central government. The central government has the power to handle the problems that affect the entire country. The states, on the other hand, have the power to handle local problems directly affecting their people.

The powers given the central government were called federal powers. The delegates to the Philadelphia Convention gave the central government more power than it had had under the Articles of Confederation. The delegates also understood that the state governments needed to be able to handle their own problems, such as education and crime. Important powers were left in their hands. The convention realized, too, that certain powers were needed by both the states and central government, including judicial power and the power of taxation. These shared powers are called *concurrent* powers. See the chart below.

DIVISION OF POWER BETWEEN STATE AND CENTRAL GOVERNMENTS

Powers Given to Central Government	Powers Reserved for the State Governments	Concurrent Powers of State and Central Governments
• Coin money and regulate its value	• Provide systems of education	• Raise and collect taxes
• Establish post offices	• Regulate trade within state borders	• Borrow money
• Regulate interstate and foreign trade	• Construct roads, bridges, parks, and other public works within the state	• Establish courts
• Declare war	• Punish crimes committed in a state	
• Make treaties with foreign powers	• Make laws on marriage and divorce	
• Raise and maintain an army and navy	• Provide for local government	
• Make all laws which are necessary and proper to carry out the above duties	• Provide for the health, safety and welfare of the people	

The Ratification Fight

The writers of the Constitution made a plan to carry out the Constitution. After nine states had approved it, the new federal government would begin to operate. No one state could stand in the way. (Recall that the Articles of Confederation could not go into effect until *all* the states had approved them.)

The delegates arranged for special state conventions to be held to approve or disapprove the finished Constitution. This provided a way for the people to show their feelings about the new kind of government.

Working for Approval. People who were in favor of the Constitution were called *Federalists*. With great skill, they worked to get the Constitution approved. In December 1787 and January 1788, Delaware, Pennsylvania, New Jersey, Georgia, and Connecticut approved it. Other states did not accept it as quickly.

Virginians, for example, feared the Constitution for a number of reasons. First, they complained that the Constitution failed to state that various rights of individuals would be

THE

FEDERALIST:

A COLLECTION

OF

ESSAYS,

WRITTEN IN FAVOUR OF THE

NEW CONSTITUTION,

AS AGREED UPON BY THE FEDERAL CONVENTION, SEPTEMBER 17, 1787.

IN TWO VOLUMES.

VOL. I.

NEW-YORK:

PRINTED AND SOLD BY J. AND A. M'LEAN,
No. 41, HANOVER-SQUARE.
M, DCC, LXXXVIII.

The essays in *The Federalist* stressed the need for a strong federal government. These essays were the most influential of all the publications about the Constitution.

protected. Second, many Virginians were suspicious of a strong central government where the power of the executive branch was placed in the hands of one person. Soon, however, word spread that George Washington would be elected as the new President. Washington was himself a Virginian and respected by his fellow citizens. Few could imagine that he would abuse the powers of the President. On June 25, 1788, the Virginia convention voted in favor of the new Constitution. The delegates voted also to add a bill of rights to the Constitution.

Another key state in the battle to get the Constitution ratified was New York. The leader of the *Antifederalists*, or those opposed to the Constitution, in New York was the popular governor, George Clinton. Like many others who were against the Constitution, Clinton feared that he would be "left out" of the new government. He knew that he had power as chief executive of a large state. He was uncertain of what his part in the central government would be.

Working for the Constitution in New York were James Madison, Alexander Hamilton, and John Jay. They wrote more than seventy essays in support of the new government. These essays appeared in newspapers. Later the essays were published in a book called *The Federalist*. Many people came to support the Constitution because of these brilliant articles. While New Yorkers were arguing the advantages and disadvantages of the new Constitution, Maryland, South Carolina, and New Hampshire had voted to accept it.

The delegates to the Massachusetts convention were much like those in Virginia. They, too, were afraid of a strong central government. Before the Massachusetts convention voted to ratify the Constitution, those in favor of the new government promised to add a bill of rights to the document at the earliest possible date.

This bill of rights would list certain rights of the individual that the federal government could not take away. In 1791 just such a list of rights protecting individual freedoms was adopted. This was in the form of the first ten amendments to the Constitution.

Now nine states had voted to adopt the Constitution. The government could officially begin, but until the large state of New York approved the plan, the new government could not work very well.

On July 26, 1788, New York finally accepted the Constitution. The vote was a close one, 30 to 27. Even though North

Carolina and Rhode Island had still not accepted the Constitution, the Congress of the Confederation decided it would end its work. It set dates for the election of the President and for the first meeting of the new Congress. Nobody knew it yet, but a glorious new era was about to begin for Americans —and eventually for all peoples.

New York celebrated the ratification of the Constitution with a giant parade of five thousand people and many colorful floats like this one.

ANSWER THESE QUESTIONS

1. What is the reason the Constitution has a preamble?
2. What is the President's term in office?
3. What are concurrent powers?
4. Why do you think the leaders of Europe were so surprised by the work of the Constitutional Convention?
5. Why are the ideas of separation of powers and checks and balances important?

ANSWER THESE QUESTIONS

1. To list the purposes of the Constitution
2. 4 years
3. powers shared by the states and the central government
4. The thirteen states were so divided, and the country was so new and had so many difficulties the leaders thought the situation in the United States was hopeless.
5. These ideas make sure that the United States can never be ruled by a tyrant or that no one branch can take control of the country.

WORDS TO REMEMBER

1. change **2.** 2 houses **3.** power to refuse a law passed by the legislative branch **4.** a written statement of an idea for a new law **5.** each branch of government is given some power over the other two branches **6.** powers are divided between the state and federal governments

Chapter 9 SUMMARY

There were many political and economic problems in the United States by 1785 that caused the leaders of the country to worry. The states tried to solve some of these problems by holding meetings. At Mount Vernon and Annapolis, a few states met to discuss trade problems. The delegates at Annapolis called for another meeting to be held in Philadelphia.

Every state but Rhode Island sent delegates to this convention. The delegates realized that the problems of the country could not be solved by amending the Articles. A new government was needed.

Two plans were presented to the delegates. These plans were hotly debated. The Virginia Plan favored the large states. The New Jersey Plan favored the small states.

Finally, a compromise was worked out. This is called the Great Compromise. Along with several other compromises, it became the basis for the Constitution.

In the Constitution, the delegates divided or separated the government into three branches—the legislative, executive, and judicial. They also gave each branch a check over the powers of the others.

Special state conventions were set up to ratify the Constitution. Nine states were needed to put the government into effect. By the end of July 1788, all but two states had ratified the document. Three years later, the Bill of Rights was added to protect the rights of the individual against possible abuses by the federal government.

Chapter 9 TEST

WORDS TO REMEMBER

Write the definitions of the following special vocabulary words on your paper.

1. amendment
2. bicameral
3. veto
4. bill
5. checks and balances
6. federal

THINKING THINGS THROUGH

Indicate whether the following statements are true or false:

T 1. Some of the people of the United States were unhappy with the way the Articles of Confederation were working.

F 2. The small states were the most eager to set up a bicameral legislature.

F 3. Thomas Jefferson was so opposed to the Constitutional Convention that he refused to attend the meetings in Philadelphia.

T 4. The Virginia Plan favored the large states.

T 5. The people would elect the President of the United States under the Constitution through electors.

T 6. The Great Compromise set up a bicameral legislature.

F 7. The powers of the three branches of government under the Constitution were meant to blend together as they do in an absolute monarchy.

F 8. The people of the United States learned of the events at the Constitutional Convention each night after the meetings ended.

RELATED MATERIALS

Duplicator/Copy Masters: Quiz 15; Activities 17, 18
Workbook pages 26-28

WORKING WITH SKILLS
1. b, c **2.** a **3.** c **4.** b **5.** a **6.** b, c **7.** a **8.** b, c **9.** a

---

WORKING WITH SKILLS

In which of these sources would you look to find the following information? In some cases, more than one source can be used.

a. *Readers' Guide to Periodical Literature*
b. Encyclopedia c. Almanac

1. a complete version of the Constitution
2. an article in *Time* magazine concerning the role of the President
3. an up-to-date listing of the members of the Senate
4. a summary of how the states ratified the Constitution
5. a complete listing of magazines and their abbreviations
6. the names of the delegates who signed the Constitution
7. an article written about the Supreme Court
8. a listing of all Presidents and Vice Presidents of the United States
9. an article reviewing a particular book

ON YOUR OWN

1. Go to the library and find a magazine article about an American President. Write down the title of the article, the author, the volume number, the pages, and the date of the magazine. Read the article and summarize its main points.
2. Using an almanac as a source of information, complete the following chart by filling in the name of the person currently holding the office.

President	________
Vice President	________
Speaker of the House	________
Your two senators	________
	________
Your representative	________
Your congressional district	________

3. Look at the picture of the President's seal on this page. This seal is made up of many pictorial symbols—designs or drawings that represent deeper meanings and ideas. Some of the pictorial symbols are listed below. For each, write a sentence to tell what you think it means. Look at articles in the encyclopedia such as "President of the United States," "United States," and "Great Seal of the United States" for help.

circle of stars
eagle
eagle's shield
arrows in eagle's left talons
olive branches in eagle's right talons
pennant bearing *E Pluribus Unum*

QUESTIONS TO ANSWER

1. Howe, Clinton, Burgoyne, Gage **2.** Thomas Paine **3.** the battles for New York and New Jersey, August 1776 to January 1777; the battles to separate New England from the other colonies, July to October 1776; the war in the South, December 1778 to October 1781 **4.** George Rogers Clark **5.** the Treaty of Paris, 1783 **6.** Shays' Rebellion **7.** Roger Sherman **8.** four years 9. Supreme Court

Unit 3 TEST

WORDS TO REMEMBER

Choose the letter of the word or phrase that correctly completes each sentence.

a 1. Loyalists were Americans who were
 a. faithful to the king
 b. loyal to the American cause
 c. living in Great Britain

b 2. A feeling of pride in one's country is
 a. devotion
 b. patriotism
 c. unity

c 3. The Articles of Confederation was
 a. an ordinance
 b. a state document
 c. a constitution

b 4. The law that provided a means for adding new states to our country was
 a. the Land Ordinance of 1785
 b. the Northwest Ordinance
 c. the Articles of Confederation

c 5. The executive branch of government
 a. explains the laws
 b. makes the laws
 c. enforces the laws

a 6. An agreement to give up one thing in order to get something else is
 a. a compromise
 b. an amendment
 c. a majority

a 7. A preamble is
 a. a beginning
 b. an article
 c. an ending

b 8. Concurrent powers are those held by
 a. the states
 b. both the states and the federal government
 c. the federal government

c 9. A person who supported the Constitution was called
 a. an Antifederalist
 b. an elector
 c. a Federalist

QUESTIONS TO ANSWER

Answer these questions on your own paper.

1. Who were the British generals at Bunker Hill?
2. Who wrote *Common Sense?*
3. What three campaigns determined the outcome of the Revolutionary War?
4. The map on the next page shows the route of what American patriot fighter in the West?
5. In what document did the British recognize the independence of the United States?
6. What was the name of the rebellion that occurred in Massachusetts?
7. What delegate to the Constitutional Convention arranged the Great Compromise?
8. What is the term of office for the President of the United States?
9. Who has the power to declare the acts of the President unconstitutional?

RELATED MATERIALS
Duplicator/Copy Master Test 16–18

THINK THINGS THROUGH

1. because of the battles at Lexington and Concord 2. He wrote a pamphlet called *Common Sense* that argued for independence. 3. because of George Washington's leadership and the hope of eventual victory and independence 4. because the United States had obtained independence and generous boundaries 5. Land Ordinance of 1785; Northwest Ordinance of 1787 6. They thought the United States would split apart. 7. Each branch can serve as a check on the others. 8. After their experience under the Articles of Confederation, the delegates knew the country needed a fairly strong executive to run it; some delegates were afraid the President would become too powerful, like the king had been.

PRACTICE YOUR SKILLS

Paraphrases will vary.

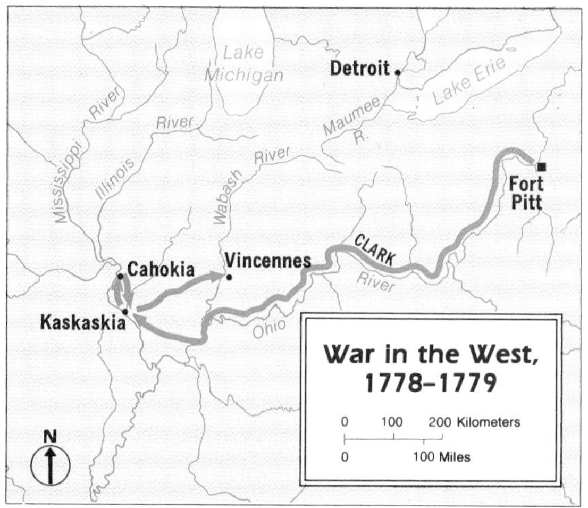

THINK THINGS THROUGH

1. Why did the delegates of the Continental Congress decide to hold another meeting?
2. How did Thomas Paine influence the fight for independence?
3. Why did Washington's soldiers stay together in spite of the hardships at Valley Forge?
4. Why were Americans generally pleased with the Treaty of Paris, 1783?
5. What were some accomplishments of the Articles of Confederation?
6. Why were Europeans surprised by the results of the Constitutional Convention?
7. What is the main advantage of having three separate branches of government?
8. Why did the delegates to the Constitutional Convention create the office of President? Why did having a strong executive worry some of the delegates?

PRACTICE YOUR SKILLS

Paraphrase the following selection from Thomas Paine's *Common Sense:*

In the following pages I offer nothing more than simple facts, plain arguments, and common sense; . . .

Volumes have been written on the subject of the struggle between England and America. Men of all ranks have embarked in the controversy, from different motives, and with various designs; but all have been ineffectual, and the period of debate is closed. Arms, as the last resource, decide the contest; the appeal was the choice of the king, and the continent hath accepted the challenge . . .

The sun never shined on a cause of greater worth. 'Tis not the affair of a city, a county, a province, or a kingdom, but of a continent . . . 'Tis not the concern of a day, a year, or an age; posterity are virtually involved in the contest . . . Now is the seed-time of continental union, faith and honor.

Betsy Ross, designer of the first American flag, displays it for George Washington (far left).

LAW AND THE CITIZEN

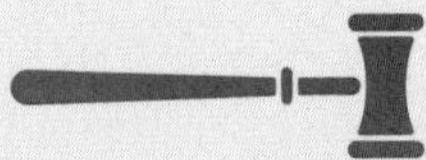

The Supreme Law of the Land

The Constitution, written in 1787, is the foundation of our government. The document has withstood many years with only twenty-six amendments—a remarkable accomplishment considering the vast changes which have occurred in the United States.

One branch in particular, the Supreme Court, has left its mark on the meaning of the Constitution. The role of the Supreme Court has changed dramatically over the years. Once thought to be the weakest of the three branches of government, the Supreme Court has gained in power. Today, Americans rely on the Supreme Court as the last word on matters related to the law.

The Court listens only to those cases which will have an effect on the entire nation. Beginning in October, the nine justices decide which cases they will hear. When the justices give their opinion in these cases, they make history. There is no place else where an appeal, or a request for review of an issue, can be made.

Sometimes the Supreme Court decides if a law passed by Congress is constitutional or unconstitutional, that is, does the law agree with the Constitution or does it conflict with the Constitution? If the law is unconstitutional, the Supreme Court can rule that the law must not be followed. This is a powerful check on Congress.

In each of the following units, The Law and the Citizen will present an important case brought before the Supreme Court. Read these cases carefully. Remember, history was made with these far-reaching decisions that the Court handed down.

Now you are ready to read one of the greatest documents of government ever written. The Constitution is printed in dark type and the paraphrase to help you understand the document is below it. The parts of the Constitution that are crossed out are no longer in effect owing to the passage of time or to an amendment. It is very important for citizens of the United States to understand how their government works, so read the Constitution carefully.

RELATED MATERIALS
Duplicator/Copy Masters Activities 19, 20

THE CONSTITUTION OF THE UNITED STATES

PREAMBLE:
The Purposes of the Constitution

We, the people of the United States, in order to form a more perfect Union, establish justice, insure domestic tranquility, provide for the common defense, promote the general welfare, and secure the blessings of liberty to ourselves and our posterity, do ordain and establish this Constitution for the United States of America.

We, the people of the United States, want to have a government that works better than the Articles of Confederation. We want to set up fair laws. We want to get along with one another and to have peace in our country. We want to defend ourselves against our enemies as a nation, not as separate states. We want our country to run smoothly and for our people to be happy. We want liberty for ourselves and our children, now and forever. These are reasons we are writing this Constitution for the United States of America.

ARTICLE 1
Congress, the Legislative Branch

The Power to Make Laws

SECTION 1. All legislative powers herein granted shall be vested in a Congress of the United States, which shall consist of a Senate and House of Representatives.

Only Congress can make the laws for the nation. The Congress will have two houses: a Senate and a House of Representatives.

How Representatives Are Elected

SECTION 2, CLAUSE 1. The House of Representatives shall be composed of members chosen every second year by the people of the several states, and the electors in each state shall have the qualifications requisite for electors of the most numerous branch of the state legislature.

Members of the House of Representatives are elected every two years by the voters in each state. The representative's term is for two years. Any citizen who can vote for state representatives, can also vote for members to the national House of Representatives.

Who May Be a Representative

SECTION 2, CLAUSE 2. No person shall be a Representative who shall not have attained to the age of twenty-five years, and been seven years a citizen of the United States, and who shall not, when elected, be an inhabitant of that state in which he shall be chosen.

To be a United States representative, a person must be at least twenty-five years of age, a citizen of the United States for seven years, and a resident of the state (and district) from which elected.

Representatives and State Populations

SECTION 2, CLAUSE 3. Representatives ~~and direct taxes~~ shall be apportioned among the several states which may be included within this Union according to their respective numbers, ~~which shall be determined by adding to the whole number of free persons, including those bound to service for a term of years, and excluding Indians not taxed, three-fifths of all other persons.~~

The number of representatives that each state can send to Congress depends on the population of the state. States with larger populations have more representatives than the states with smaller populations.

(Direct taxes—the amount of money that is given to the federal government—is no longer based on population. See the Sixteenth Amendment. Population for each state is no longer determined by adding three fifths of a slave to the number of free citizens. See the Fourteenth Amendment. All people living in the state, except Indians who pay no taxes, but can vote, are counted in full to decide how many representatives a state may have.)

Taking the Census

The actual enumeration shall be made within three years after the first meeting of the Congress of the United States, and within every subsequent term of ten years, in such a manner as they shall by law direct. ~~The number of Representatives shall not exceed one for every thirty thousand, but each state shall have at least one Representative; and until such enumeration shall be made, the state of New Hampshire shall be entitled to choose 3; Massachusetts, 8; Rhode Island and Providence Plantations, 1; Connecticut, 5; New York, 6; New Jersey, 4; Pennsylvania, 8; Delaware, 1; Maryland, 6; Virginia, 10; North Carolina, 5; South Carolina, 5; and Georgia, 3.~~

Congress decides how the population of the states is to be counted. A census or a count must be made every ten years to decide the number of representatives each state will have. Each state is allowed 1 representative for every 30,000 people; however, each state is allowed at least one representative no matter how small its population. (Since 1929, 1 representative is elected for every 470,000 people. The House of Representatives may have no more than 435 members.)

Filling Vacancies in the House

SECTION 2, CLAUSE 4. When vacancies happen in the representation from any state, the executive authority thereof shall issue writs of election to fill such vacancies.

When a state does not have the required number of representatives (someone dies or resigns), the governor of that state must call for a special election to fill the spot.

Officers of the House, Impeachment

SECTION 2, CLAUSE 5. The House of Representatives shall choose their Speaker and other officers; and shall have the sole power of impeachment.

The House of Representatives elects its own officers: the Speaker, the majority and minority leaders, the chaplain, and the sergeant-at-arms. Only the House can impeach, or accuse, an official from the executive or judicial branches of some misconduct or misuse of power.

The Senate

SECTION 3, CLAUSE 1. The Senate of the United States shall be composed of two Senators from each state, chosen ~~by the legislature thereof~~ for six years; and each Senator shall have one vote.

The Senate of the United States is made up of two citizens from each state, regardless of the population of the state. The senator serves for six years and has one vote. (The state legislators used to elect the senators, but this was changed by the Seventeenth Amendment in 1913. Now the people from each state elect their own senators. This is an example of the expansion of voting and greater power to the people to choose their own representatives in Congress.)

When the Senators' Terms End

~~SECTION 3, CLAUSE 2. Immediately after they shall be assembled in consequence of~~

~~the first election, they shall be divided as equally as may be into three classes. The seats of the Senators of the first class shall be vacated at the expiration of the second year, of the second class at the expiration of the fourth year, and of the third class at the expiration of the sixth year, so that one-third may be chosen every second year; and if vacancies happen by resignation or otherwise during the recess of the legislature of any state, the executive thereof may make temporary appointments until the next meeting of the legislature, which shall then fill such vacancies.~~

(The three different classes of senators ordered by this clause were intended only to get the Senate started. After the first four years of the Constitution, senators were no longer divided into classes; all senators now have six-year terms. Because of this "staggering system," there is never more than one-third of the senators who have just been elected—or reelected; one-third have served for two years, and one-third have served for four years. For this reason the Senate carries on its work without ever having a complete turnover in its membership.

The last part of this clause, describing how vacancies in the Senate were to be filled, has been changed by the Seventeenth Amendment.)

Who May Be a Senator

SECTION 3, CLAUSE 3. No person shall be a Senator who shall not have attained to the age of thirty years and been nine years a citizen of the United States, and who shall not when elected be an inhabitant of that state for which he shall be chosen.

In order to be a senator, a person must be at least thirty years of age, a citizen of the United States for nine years, and be a resident of the state from which elected.

The Vice-President

SECTION 3, CLAUSE 4. The Vice-President of the United States shall be President of the Senate, but shall have no vote unless they be equally divided.

The Vice President of the United States is the president of the Senate, or its chairperson. Because the Vice President is not an elected member of the Senate, he/she can only vote if there is a tie.

Other Officers of the Senate

SECTION 3, CLAUSE 5. The Senate shall choose their other officers, and also a President pro tempore, in the absence of the Vice-President, or when he shall exercise the office of the President of the United States.

The Senate chooses its other officers, for instance, its sergeant-at-arms and its chaplain. Because the Vice President of the United States sometimes is unable to serve as chairperson of the Senate, the Senate chooses a senator to be president pro tempore—president for the time being—who serves as chairperson in the absence of the Vice President, or when the Vice President becomes the President of the United States.

Impeachment Trials

SECTION 3, CLAUSE 6. The Senate shall have the sole power to try all impeachments. When sitting for that purpose, they shall be on oath or affirmation. When the President of the United States is tried, the Chief Justice shall preside; and no person shall be convicted without the concurrence of two-thirds of the members present.

Only the Senate can try officials after the House of Representatives has impeached, or accused the official of some misconduct or misuse of power. The Senate sits as a jury in this trial. When the Senate listens to the evidence against the President of the United States, the Chief Justice of the Supreme Court is the judge in charge. In all other impeachment cases, the president of the Senate sits as the judge. In an impeachment trial, the official is declared innocent unless two thirds of the Senate members present vote that the official is guilty. This is another check upon the executive branch (President) by the legislative branch.

Punishment in Impeachment Trials

SECTION 3, CLAUSE 7. Judgment in cases of impeachment shall not extend further than to removal from office and disqualification to hold and enjoy any office of honor, trust, or profit under the United States; but the party convicted shall nevertheless be liable and subject to indictment, trial, judgment, and punishment, according to law.

If the Senate declares an impeached official guilty it can punish the official in only one way, and that is by putting the official out of office and forbidding the person from ever holding another office in the national government. This does not mean that a national official can commit crimes without severe punishment. After being put out of office, an official can then be tried by a judge or jury in a regular court. If the court finds this person guilty, he/she can be punished like anyone else.

Members of Congress are never impeached, but they may be expelled by action of the house to which they have been elected. They can also be tried by a judge or jury in a regular court, where upon a finding of guilt, the official can be punished like any citizen. (See Section 5, Clause 2, on page 235.)

Elections to Congress

SECTION 4, CLAUSE 1. The times, places, and manner of holding elections for Senators and Representatives shall be prescribed in each state by the legislature thereof; but the Congress may at any time by law make or alter such regulations ~~except as to the places of choosing Senators.~~

The legislature of each state has the right to pass laws deciding when, where, and how senators and representatives are chosen, but Congress has the power to change those laws.

In each state, senators and representatives are elected on the first Tuesday following the first Monday in November of even-numbered years. (The last phrase is no longer in effect. See the Seventeenth Amendment.)

Meetings of Congress

SECTION 4, CLAUSE 2. The Congress shall assemble at least once in every year, ~~and such meeting shall be on the first Monday in December, unless they shall by law appoint a different day.~~

Congress must meet at least once a year. However, due to the great number of national issues with which Congress must deal, Congress meets much more often than required by the Constitution. It meets, often daily, for many months each year. (The date of the year's first meeting was changed in 1933 from the first Monday in December to January 3. See the Twentieth Amendment.)

Rules of Congress

SECTION 5, CLAUSE 1. Each house shall be the judge of the elections, returns, and qualifications of its own members, and a majority of each shall constitute a quorum to do business; but a smaller number may

adjourn from day to day and may be authorized to compel the attendance of absent members in such manner and under such penalties as each house may provide.

Each house of Congress has the right to decide if its members were properly elected and are qualified to hold office. A majority of members, or one half the members plus one, must be present to do any official business. Each house can make its own rules to require attendance.

More Rules of Congress

SECTION 5, CLAUSE 2. Each house may determine the rules of its proceedings, punish its members for disorderly behavior, and, with the concurrence of two-thirds, expel a member.

Each house has the right to make rules about its work and the actions of its members, and may punish its members for misbehaving. Each house has the right to expel a member by a two-thirds vote.

Records of the Actions of Congress

SECTION 5, CLAUSE 3. Each house shall keep a journal of its proceedings, and from time to time publish the same, excepting such parts as may in their judgment require secrecy; and the yeas and nays of the members of either house on any question shall, at the desire of one-fifth of those present, be entered on the journal.

Each house of Congress must keep a separate record of what goes on at its meetings and must publish the record periodically. The members may vote not to publish everything—that is, to keep some things secret. How each member votes on a particular question—whether yea (for) or nay (against)—is put into the record if one fifth of the members who are present wish this to be done.

Adjournments

SECTION 5, CLAUSE 4. Neither house, during the session of Congress, shall, without the consent of the other adjourn, for more than three days, nor to any other place than that in which the two houses shall be sitting.

During the period when Congress is meeting, neither house may suspend its meetings for more than three days unless the other house gives permission. Since the work of the two houses is closely related, neither house is allowed to move to another city unless the other house agrees.

Pay and Privileges of Members of Congress

SECTION 6, CLAUSE 1. The Senators and Representatives shall receive a compensation for their services, to be ascertained by law, and paid out of the Treasury of the United States. They shall in all cases, except treason, felony, and breach of the peace, be privileged from arrest during their attendance at the session of their respective houses, and in going to and returning from the same; and for any speech or debate in either house they shall not be questioned in any other place.

Members of Congress are paid out of the United States Treasury. The amount of their pay is decided by laws of Congress. Members of Congress may not be arrested at meetings of Congress or on their way to or from those meetings—unless they are suspected of committing serious crimes or disturbing the peace. They may not be arrested or be punished for anything they may say in Congress except by the house of which they are members. These privileges, called Congressional immunity, allow members of Congress to say, without fear of punishment, what they believe is for the good of the country.

What the Members of Congress May Not Do

SECTION 6, CLAUSE 2. No Senator or Representative shall, during the time for which he was elected, be appointed to any civil office under the authority of the United States which shall have been created or the emoluments whereof shall have been increased during such time; and no person holding any office under the United States shall be a member of either house during his continuance in office.

Members of the Senate and House of Representatives cannot be appointed to offices created during their term. They cannot take a job in which the salary for that job was increased during their term. They also cannot hold another government position during their term.

Bills for Raising Money

SECTION 7, CLAUSE 1. All bills for raising revenue shall originate in the House of Representatives; but the Senate may propose or concur with amendments as on other bills.

Only the House of Representatives can begin bills that deal with raising taxes. The Senate can make amendments or changes in these bills. This is a very important section. It places the power to tax in the hands of the people's representatives. The taxation issue was a major reason for the Revolution against British rule of the thirteen colonies.

How Bills Become Laws

SECTION 7, CLAUSE 2. Every bill which shall have passed the House of Representatives and the Senate shall before it becomes a law be presented to the President of the United States. If he approve, he shall sign it; but if not, he shall return it with his objections to that house in which it shall have originated, who shall enter the objections at large on their journal and proceed to reconsider it. If after such reconsideration two-thirds of that house shall agree to pass the bill, it shall be sent, together with the objections, to the other house, by which it shall likewise be reconsidered; and if approved by two-thirds of that house, it shall become a law. But in all such cases the votes of both houses shall be determined by yeas and nays, and the names of the persons voting for and against the bill shall be entered on the journal of each house respectively.

To become a law, a bill has to be passed by both the House of Representatives and the Senate. Then the President of the United States must see the bill. If the President approves and signs the bill, it becomes a law. If the President does not agree with the bill, it is returned to the Senate or the House (whichever began the bill) with a list of the reasons why the President is against it. This is called a veto. The House or Senate would then write these objections into their record. Then the bill is considered by both houses again. If two thirds of both the Senate and the House of Representatives vote yes on the bill, it becomes a law over the President's veto. The name and vote of each member is written in the record of each house.

The "Pocket Veto"

If any bill shall not be returned by the President within ten days (Sundays excepted) after it shall have been presented to him, the same shall be a law in like manner as if he had signed it, unless the Congress by their adjournment prevent its return, in which case it shall not be a law.

If the President receives a bill that has been passed by both the Senate and the House of Representatives, and keeps it for ten days (not counting Sundays) without signing it or vetoing it, the bill becomes a law. If Congress adjourns before the ten days are up, and before the President signs or vetoes the bill, it dies. This is called a pocket veto.

Other Actions of Congress

SECTION 7, CLAUSE 3. Every order, resolution, or vote to which the concurrence of the Senate and House of Representatives may be necessary (except on a question of adjournment) shall be presented to the President of the United States; and before the same shall take effect, shall be approved by him, or being disapproved by him, shall be repassed by two-thirds of the Senate and House of Representatives, according to the rules and limitations prescribed in the case of a bill.

If an order, resolution, or vote must be approved by both the Senate and the House of Representatives, the President's approval is also needed on these matters. If the President does not agree, like a bill, the order, resolution, or vote can be vetoed. Then two thirds of both the Senate and the House of Representatives would have to vote yes to override the President's veto. Congress does not need to get the President's approval to adjourn.

The Laying of Taxes

SECTION 8, CLAUSE 1. The Congress shall have power to lay and collect taxes, duties, imposts, and excises, to pay the debts and provide for the common defense and general welfare of the United States; but all duties, imposts, and excises shall be uniform throughout the United States.

Congress has the power to raise money by taxing. These taxes include duties—taxes on goods coming into or out of the country; imposts—also a tax on incoming goods; and excises—taxes on the making, selling, or using of goods. These taxes may be used to (1) pay the country's debts, (2) defend the country against its enemies, and (3) pay for services for the good of the people. Federal taxes must be the same throughout the country.

The Borrowing of Money

SECTION 8, CLAUSE 2. To borrow money on the credit of the United States.

Congress has the power to borrow money with the promise to repay the money at a later date.

Foreign and Interstate Commerce

SECTION 8, CLAUSE 3. To regulate commerce with foreign nations, and among the several states, and with the Indian tribes.

Congress has the power to pass laws about trade with foreign countries, between states, and with Indians.

Naturalization, Bankruptcy

SECTION 8, CLAUSE 4. To establish a uniform rule of naturalization, and uniform laws on the subject of bankruptcies throughout the United States.

Congress has the power to decide which citizens of a foreign country can become United States citizens, and the rules on how this can be done. Congress can also pass laws about bankruptcy to protect those people to whom money is owed. The laws must be the same for everyone.

Coinage, Weights and Measures

SECTION 8, CLAUSE 5. To coin money, regulate the value thereof and foreign coin, and fix the standard of weights and measures.

Congress has the power to print and coin money and to say how much it is worth. It can also set the value of how much foreign money is worth in United States money. Congress also sets up how weight and distance is measured so they will be the same in all parts of the country.

Counterfeiting

SECTION 8, CLAUSE 6. To provide for the punishment of counterfeiting the securities and current coin of the United States.

Congress has the power to make laws to punish people who counterfeit—make false money, bonds, or stamps.

Postal Service

SECTION 8, CLAUSE 7. To establish post offices and post roads.

Congress controls the postal system. It handles the post offices and builds some of the roads and highways over which the mail is delivered.

Rights of Authors and Inventors

SECTION 8, CLAUSE 8. To promote the progress of science and useful arts, by securing for limited times to authors and inventors the exclusive right to their respective writings and discoveries.

Congress encourages this country's art, science, and industry by means of laws helping artists and inventors of various kinds. Copyright laws protect authors, composers, and artists from having their writings, music, paintings, and other works copied without payment. Patent laws protect in the same way those who invent or discover new and useful manufactured articles or valuable new methods in science and industry.

National Courts

SECTION 8, CLAUSE 9. To constitute tribunals inferior to the Supreme Court.

Congress sets up national courts that have less authority than the United States Supreme Court, such as the United States District Courts and United States Circuit Court of Appeals.

Crimes at Sea, Crimes Against International Law

SECTION 8, CLAUSE 10. To define and punish piracies and felonies committed on the high seas, and offenses against the law of nations.

Congress rules what acts committed at sea are crimes and how they are to be punished. It may also make laws about crimes in which foreign countries or foreign citizens are involved.

Declarations of War

SECTION 8, CLAUSE 11. To declare war, grant letters of marque and reprisal, and make rules concerning captures on land and water.

Only Congress has the power to declare war. Private citizens can no longer wage war (letters of marque and reprisal). Only Congress can make laws about taking enemy property on land and sea.

The Army

SECTION 8, CLAUSE 12. To raise and support armies, but no appropriation of money to that use shall be for a longer term than two years.

Congress may create an army for the United States and vote the money to pay for it. But Congress must not give the armed forces at any one time more than enough for two years' expenses.

The Navy

SECTION 8, CLAUSE 13. To provide and maintain a navy.

Congress may create a navy for the United States and vote the money to pay for it.

Rules for the Armed Forces

SECTION 8, CLAUSE 14. To make rules for the government and regulation of the land and naval forces.

Congress may make the rules for the armed forces. (These now include the army, navy, air force, and marines.)

Use of the Militia

SECTION 8, CLAUSE 15. To provide for calling forth the militia to execute the laws of the Union, suppress insurrections, and repel invasions.

Congress may rule how and when the militias—that is, the citizen-soldiers in various states—are to be called to help the national government. The militias may be called on to enforce national laws, end rebellions, and drive out foreign enemies.

Control of the Militia

SECTION 8, CLAUSE 16. To provide for organizing, arming, and disciplining the militia, and for governing such part of them as may be employed in the service of the United States, reserving to the states, respectively, the appointment of the officers and the authority of training the militia according to the discipline prescribed by Congress.

Congress may organize the militias, furnish weapons to them, and make rules for those members of the militias who are in the service of the United States. Although the government of each state has the right to appoint the officers of its militia, it must train the militia as Congress directs.

The National Capital, Other National Property

SECTION 8, CLAUSE 17. To exercise exclusive legislation in all cases whatsoever over such district (not exceeding ten miles square) as may, by cession of particular states and the acceptance of Congress, become the seat of government of the United States; and to exercise like authority over all places purchased by the consent of the legislature of the state in which the same shall be, for the erection of forts, magazines, arsenals, dockyards, and other needful buildings.

Congress makes all the laws for governing the District of Columbia (containing the national capital—established in Washington). The capital is not under the control of any state or county government.

Congress also governs all other property belonging to the national government—post offices, national forests, national parks, etc.

Other Necessary Laws

SECTION 8, CLAUSE 18. And to make all laws which shall be necessary and proper for carrying into execution the foregoing powers and all other powers vested by this Constitution in the government of the United States, or in any department or officer thereof.

Besides the lawmaking powers given to Congress in clauses 1–17, Congress can make other laws which are needed to carry out the Constitution. This clause is called the "Elastic Clause" because it can be stretched to fit the changing needs of the country. This clause is also called the "Necessary and Proper" clause, because these laws made by Congress are supposed to be necessary (urgent and important), and proper (agree with the Constitution.)

The Slave Trade

SECTION 9, CLAUSE 1. The migration or importation of such persons as any of the states now existing shall think proper to

~~admit shall not be prohibited by the Congress prior to the year one thousand eight hundred and eight, but a tax or duty may be imposed on such importation, not exceeding ten dollars for each person.~~

(Congress could not stop slavery before 1808, but it could place a tax of up to $10 on each slave brought into the country. This clause is no longer in effect since the date 1808 is past and slavery is prohibited. This section was adopted as a compromise between the North and South.)

Habeas Corpus

SECTION 9, CLAUSE 2. The privilege of the writ of habeas corpus shall not be suspended, unless when in cases of rebellion or invasion the public safety may require it.

The national government is not allowed to take away the right of habeas corpus except when the country is in a state of rebellion or is being invaded. A writ of habeas corpus is a legal paper stating a person has the right to appear in court to hear the charges against him or her. The court must then decide if there is enough evidence to hold this person in jail. If not, the person must be released.

Bills of Attainder, Ex Post Facto Laws

SECTION 9, CLAUSE 3. No bill of attainder or ex post facto law shall be passed.

Congress cannot pass any bill intending to punish one particular person—a bill of attainder. Congress cannot pass any law that would punish a person for doing something that was not against the law at the time the person did it.

Direct Taxes in Proportion to Population

SECTION 9, CLAUSE 4. No capitation or other direct tax shall be laid, unless in proportion to the census or enumeration hereinbefore directed to be taken.

Congress cannot put a direct tax on any individual, unless the tax is in proportion to the population. The income tax is an exception. See the Sixteenth Amendment.

Export Taxes Forbidden

SECTION 9, CLAUSE 5. No tax or duty shall be laid on articles exported from any state.

Congress cannot put a tax on goods sent from one state to another or on goods sent from a state to another country.

Ports and Port Duties

SECTION 9, CLAUSE 6. No preference shall be given by any regulation of commerce or revenue to the ports of one state over those of another; nor shall vessels bound to or from one state be obliged to enter, clear, or pay duties to another.

Congress cannot favor the ports of one state over the ports of another state. Congress cannot put a tax on goods transported by ships traveling from one state to another.

Accounting for Public Money

SECTION 9, CLAUSE 7. No money shall be drawn from the Treasury but in consequence of appropriations made by law; and a regular statement and account of the receipts and expenditures of all public money shall be published from time to time.

Money can be paid out by the Treasury only if there is a law passed by Congress and signed by the President for that purpose. Statements showing how much money was received in the Treasury and how much was paid out must be made public from time to time.

Titles of Nobility, Gifts

SECTION 9, CLAUSE 8. No title of nobility shall be granted by the United States; and no person holding any office of profit or trust under them shall without the consent of the Congress accept of any present, emolument, office, or title of any kind whatever from any king, prince, or foreign state.

The government cannot give anyone a title (duke, earl, count, baron). This prevents our nation from ever being ruled again by a king or queen. No government official can accept any gift, money, position, or title from any foreign government unless Congress gives its permission.

Actions Forbidden to the States

SECTION 10, CLAUSE 1. No state shall enter into any treaty, alliance, or confederation; grant letters of marque and reprisal; coin money; emit bills of credit; make anything but gold and silver coin a tender in payment of debts; pass any bill of attainder, ex post facto law, or law impairing the obligation of contracts, or grant any title of nobility.

This section limits state governments' powers. State governments cannot make treaties or military agreements with foreign countries. They cannot become part of another country. State governments cannot give their citizens permission to fight against foreign countries. State governments cannot coin their own money or pass laws that make anything but gold or silver to be used as money.

State governments cannot pass laws that would punish a particular person or would punish people for things they did that were not against the law when they did them. State governments cannot pass any law that would destroy a legal contract between people, nor can state governments give people titles.

Taxation by the States

SECTION 10, CLAUSE 2. No state shall, without the consent of the Congress, lay any imposts or duties on imports or exports, except what may be absolutely necessary for executing its inspection laws; and the net produce of all duties and imposts, laid by any state on imports or exports, shall be for the use of the Treasury of the United States; and all such laws shall be subject to the revision and control of the Congress.

States must not interfere with commerce by taxing goods entering or leaving their territory—except that they may charge fees for inspecting such goods. Any money the states collect as inspection fees must be paid into the Treasury of the United States. Congress has the power to change the inspection laws of any of the states.

Other State Actions Forbidden

SECTION 10, CLAUSE 3. No state shall, without the consent of Congress, lay any duty of tonnage, keep troops or ships of war in time of peace, enter into any agreement or compact with another state, or with a foreign power, or engage in war, unless actually invaded, or in such imminent danger as will not admit of delay.

Unless Congress gives permission, no state may do these things: (1) charge a tax on ships that enter its ports, (2) have its own army—except the militia—or navy in peacetime, (3) make treaties with other states or with foreign countries, (4) make war except when it has been invaded or is likely to be invaded.

ARTICLE 2
The Presidency and the Executive Branch

Terms of the President and the Vice-President

SECTION 1, CLAUSE 1. The executive power shall be vested in a President of the

United States of America. He shall hold his office during the term of four years and, together with the Vice-President, chosen for the same term, be elected as follows.

The power to execute, or carry out, laws is given to a President of the United States. The President's term is for four years. The Vice President, who is elected with the President, also has a four-year term.

The Presidential Electors

SECTION 1, CLAUSE 2. Each state shall appoint, in such manner as the legislature thereof may direct, a number of electors, equal to the whole number of Senators and Representatives to which the state may be entitled in the Congress; but no Senator or Representative, or person holding an office of trust or profit under the United States, shall be appointed an elector.

The President and Vice President are chosen by a group of people called electors. Each state decides how its electors are to be chosen. The number of electors in each state is equal to the number of representatives and senators the state has in Congress. No person who has an office in the federal government can serve as an elector.

Duties of the Electors

SECTION 1, CLAUSE 3. The electors shall meet in their respective states and vote by ballot for two persons, of whom one at least shall not be an inhabitant of the same state with themselves. And they shall make a list of all the persons voted for, and of the number of votes for each, which list they shall sign and certify and transmit, sealed, to the seat of the government of the United States, directed to the president of the Senate. The president of the Senate shall, in the presence of the Senate and the House of Representatives, open all the certificates, and the votes shall then be counted. The person having the greatest number of votes shall be the President, if such number be a majority of the whole number of electors appointed; and if there be more than one who have such majority, and have an equal number of votes, then the House of Representatives shall immediately choose by ballot one of them for President; and if no person have a majority, then from the five highest on the list the said House shall in like manner choose the President. But in choosing the President, the vote shall be taken by states, the representation from each state having one vote. A quorum for this purpose shall consist of a member or members from two-thirds of the states, and a majority of all the states shall be necessary to a choice. In every case, after the choice of President, the person having the greatest number of votes of the electors shall be the Vice-President. But if there should remain two or more who have equal votes, the Senate shall choose from them by ballot the Vice-President.

(This clause is no longer followed. See the Twelfth Amendment.)

Election Day

SECTION 1, CLAUSE 4. The Congress may determine the time of choosing the electors and the day on which they shall give their votes, which day shall be the same throughout the United States.

Congress may decide on what day the electors are to be elected and the day when they are to cast their ballots for President and Vice President. This day is the same everywhere in the United States.

Who May Become President

SECTION 1, CLAUSE 5. No person except a natural-born citizen or a citizen of the United States at the time of the adoption of this Constitution shall be eligible to the office of President; neither shall any person be eligible to that office who shall not have

attained the age of thirty-five years and been fourteen years a resident within the United States.

Nobody may become President unless the person is a citizen of the United States by birth, is at least thirty-five years old, and has lived in the United States for fourteen years or more.

Succession to the Presidency

SECTION 1, CLAUSE 6. In case of the removal of the President from office, or of his death, resignation, or inability to discharge the powers and duties of the said office, the same shall devolve on the Vice-President, and the Congress may by law provide for the case of removal, death, resignation, or inability, both of the President and Vice-President, declaring what officer shall then act as President, and such officer shall act accordingly until the disability be removed or a President shall be elected.

(This clause is no longer in effect. See the Twenty-fifth Amendment.)

The President's Salary

SECTION 1, CLAUSE 7. The President shall at stated times receive for his services a compensation, which shall neither be increased nor diminished during the period for which he shall have been elected, and he shall not receive within that period any other emolument from the United States, or any of them.

The President receives a salary which cannot be made larger or smaller during his/her term in office. The President also cannot be given any other kind of salary from a state or the federal government.

President's Oath of Office

SECTION 1, CLAUSE 8. Before he enter on the execution of his office he shall take the following oath or affirmation: "I do solemnly swear (or affirm) that I will faithfully execute the office of President of the United States, and will to the best of my ability preserve, protect, and defend the Constitution of the United States."

Before the President can take office, he/she must take an oath. The President promises to do his/her job faithfully and to protect and defend the Constitution.

Military Powers, Pardons

SECTION 2, CLAUSE 1. The President shall be commander in chief of the Army and Navy of the United States, and of the militias of the several states when called into the actual service of the United States; he may require the opinion, in writing, of the principal officer in each of the executive departments, upon any subject relating to the duties of their respective offices, and he shall have power to grant reprieves and pardons for offenses against the United States, except in cases of impeachment.

The President is the commander-in-chief of the armed forces of the United States and of the militias when they are called into national service. The President can ask for written reports from Cabinet officers about the work of their departments. The President has the power to delay punishments and to pardon persons convicted of federal crimes. The President, however, cannot do this in cases of impeachment.

Treaties and Appointments

SECTION 2, CLAUSE 2. He shall have power, by and with the advice and consent of the Senate, to make treaties, provided two-thirds of the Senators present concur; and he shall nominate and, by and with the advice and consent of the Senate, shall appoint ambassadors, other public ministers

and consuls, judges of the Supreme Court, and all other officers of the United States whose appointments are not herein provided for and which shall be established by law; but the Congress may by law vest the appointment of such inferior officers as they think proper in the President alone, in the courts of law, or in the heads of departments.

The President may make treaties with foreign countries, but at least two thirds of the senators present must approve a treaty before it becomes a law. The President may appoint certain important officials only if the Senate approves the choices. Congress can pass laws that give to the President, to the department chiefs, or to the courts, control over the appointment of less important officials.

Filling Vacant Positions

SECTION 2, CLAUSE 3. The President shall have power to fill up all vacancies that may happen during the recess of the Senate by granting commissions which shall expire at the end of their next session.

If positions become vacant when the Senate is not meeting, the President may appoint persons to fill them. These are temporary appointments which end at the close of the next session of the Senate.

Other Duties of the President

SECTION 3. He shall from time to time give to the Congress information of the state of the Union, and recommend to their consideration such measures as he shall judge necessary and expedient; he may, on extraordinary occasions, convene both houses, or either of them, and in case of disagreement between them, with respect to the time of adjournment, he may adjourn them to such time as he shall think proper; he shall receive ambassadors and other public ministers; he shall take care that the laws be faithfully executed, and shall commission all the officers of the United States.

The President must speak to Congress concerning the condition of the country. During that speech, the President recommends laws that are necessary. This is called the State of the Union address.

The President has the power, in an emergency, to call a meeting of one or both houses of Congress. The President can also decide when the Congress should adjourn if Congress disagrees on a time for ending.

The President receives the representatives of other countries. The President sees that the laws of the country are carried out. The President also signs papers appointing people to federal government jobs.

Impeachments

SECTION 4. The President, Vice-President, and all civil officers of the United States shall be removed from office on impeachment for, and conviction of, treason, bribery, or other high crimes and misdemeanors.

The President, the Vice President, or any civilian official of the national government must be put out of office if he/she has been impeached and found guilty of disloyalty to his/her country, of bribery, or of other crimes.

ARTICLE 3
The Supreme Court and the Judicial Branch

Federal Courts, Federal Judges

SECTION 1. The judicial power of the United States shall be vested in one Supreme Court, and in such inferior courts as the Congress may from time to time ordain and establish. The judges, both of the Supreme and inferior courts, shall hold their offices during good behavior, and shall at

stated times receive for their services a compensation, which shall not be diminished during their continuance in office.

The power to decide cases is given to the Supreme Court of the United States and to lower courts which Congress sets up. The judges of all federal courts serve for life unless they are impeached and found guilty or voluntarily resign. The salaries of judges cannot be lowered while they are in office.

Kinds of Cases Tried in Federal Courts

SECTION 2, CLAUSE 1. The judicial power shall extend to all cases in law and equity arising under this Constitution, the laws of the United States, and treaties made or which shall be made under their authority; to all cases affecting ambassadors, other public ministers, and consuls; to all cases of admiralty and maritime jurisdiction; to controversies to which the United States shall be a party; to controversies between two or more states; ~~between a state and citizens of another state;~~ between citizens of different states; between citizens of the same state claiming lands under grants of different states, and between a state, or the citizens thereof, and foreign states, citizens, or subjects.

The cases tried by the federal courts are those concerning: (1) the Constitution and the nation's laws and treaties, (2) the representatives of foreign governments, (3) the laws controlling ships and sailors, (4) disagreements between our government and other governments or persons, (5) disagreements between states, (6) disagreements between citizens of different states, (7) disagreements in which citizens of the same state claim lands granted by different states, (8) disagreements between a state or its citizens and a foreign country or foreign citizens.

(The out-of-date part of Clause 1 was changed by the Eleventh Amendment, page 252.)

Jurisdiction of the Supreme Court

SECTION 2, CLAUSE 2. In all cases affecting ambassadors, other public ministers and consuls, and those in which a state shall be party, the Supreme Court shall have original jurisdiction. In all the other cases before mentioned, the Supreme Court shall have appellate jurisdiction, both as to law and fact, with such exceptions and under such regulations as the Congress shall make.

The Supreme Court has two kinds of jurisdiction—that is, authority to try cases. First, it can try new cases being brought to court for the first time, if those cases concern one of the states or a representative of a foreign government. This is the Supreme Court's *original jurisdiction.* Second, it can review cases again that have already been tried in lower federal courts—but only if one of the parties in the case objects to the decision of the lower courts and appeals the case. This is the Supreme Court's *appellate jurisdiction.* There is no higher court than the Supreme Court to which appeals can be directed.

Trial by Jury for Criminal Cases

SECTION 2, CLAUSE 3. The trial of all crimes except in cases of impeachment shall be by jury; and such trial shall be held in the state where the said crimes shall have been committed; but when not committed within any state, the trial shall be at such place or places as the Congress may by law have directed.

Every person accused of committing a federal crime has the right to a trial by jury. The trial must be held in the state where the crime was committed. If the crime was not committed in any state—in a territory or at sea, for example—Congress decides where the trial is to be held.

The Definition of Treason

SECTION 3, CLAUSE 1. Treason against the United States shall consist only in levying war against them, or in adhering to their enemies, giving them aid and comfort. No person shall be convicted of treason unless on the testimony of two witnesses to the same overt act, or on confession in open court.

Only these acts by a United States citizen may be considered treason: (1) making war against this country, and (2) helping this country's enemies. Nobody can be punished for treason unless two or more citizens both swear they saw the person commit the same act of treason or unless the person confesses in court.

The Punishment for Treason

SECTION 3, CLAUSE 2. The Congress shall have power to declare the punishment of treason, but no attainder of treason shall work corruption of blood or forfeiture except during the life of the person attainted.

Congress can pass laws which say how the crime of treason is to be punished. Only the person guilty of treason can be punished. The person's family cannot be punished.

ARTICLE 4
The States and the Nation

Official Acts of the States

SECTION 1. Full faith and credit shall be given in each state to the public acts, records, and judicial proceedings of every other state. And the Congress may by general laws prescribe the manner in which such acts, records, and proceedings shall be proved, and the effect thereof.

All states are required by Congress to accept the laws, records, and court decisions of the other states. Congress can pass laws to make sure the states let each other know about their laws, records, and court decisions. For example, couples married under the laws of Ohio would be considered legally married if they moved to any other state.

Privileges of Citizens

SECTION 2, CLAUSE 1. The citizens of each state shall be entitled to all privileges and immunities of citizens in the several states.

Citizens of one state who move into or do business in another state have the same rights and privileges as the citizens who live in that state.

Fugitives from Justice

SECTION 2, CLAUSE 2. A person charged in any state with treason, felony, or other crime, who shall flee from justice, and be found in another state, shall, on demand of the executive authority of the state from which he fled, be delivered up, to be removed to the state having jurisdiction of the crime.

A person accused of a crime in one state who goes to another state to escape punishment, must be returned if the governor of the state where the crime was committed asks it.

Runaway Slaves

~~**SECTION 2, CLAUSE 3. No person held to service or labor in one state, under the laws thereof, escaping into another, shall, in consequence of any law or regulation therein, be discharged from such service or labor, but shall be delivered up on claim of the party to whom such service or labor may be due.**~~

(This clause is no longer in effect. See the Thirteenth Amendment which abolished slavery.)

The Forming of New States

SECTION 3, CLAUSE 1. New states may be admitted by the Congress into this Union, but no new state shall be formed or erected within the jurisdiction of any other state; nor any state be formed by the junction of two or more states, or parts of states, without the consent of the legislatures of the states concerned as well as of the Congress.

New states may be added to the nation if Congress approves. But no new state may be made inside the boundaries of another state under any circumstance. Further, no new state may be made out of the lands of two states without the consent of Congress and of the legislatures of both those states.

National Territory

SECTION 3, CLAUSE 2. The Congress shall have power to dispose of and make all needful rules and regulations respecting the territory or other property belonging to the United States and nothing in this Constitution shall be so construed as to prejudice any claims of the United States, or of any particular state.

Congress has the power to govern and decide what to do with national territories and other lands which belong to the United States. Nothing in the Constitution favors one state over another state or one state over the United States in arguments over land claims.

Federal Guarantees to the States

SECTION 4. The United States shall guarantee to every state in this Union a republican form of government, and shall protect each of them against invasion; and, on application of the legislature, or of the executive (when the legislature cannot be convened), against domestic violence.

It is the responsibility of the federal government to make sure each state has a government in which the people elect their representatives. It is the duty of the federal government to protect states from invasion by enemies and to help a state by sending in the militia to put down riots, if the state requests this help.

ARTICLE 5
Amending the Constitution

The Congress, whenever two-thirds of both houses shall deem it necessary, shall propose amendments to this Constitution, or, on the application of the legislatures of two-thirds of the several states, shall call a convention for proposing amendments, which, in either case, shall be valid to all intents and purposes, as part of this Constitution, when ratified by the legislatures of three-fourths of the several states, or by conventions in three-fourths thereof, as the one or the other mode of ratification may be proposed by the Congress, provided ~~that no amendment which may be made prior to the year one thousand eight hundred and eight shall in any manner affect the first and fourth clauses in the Ninth Section of the First Article, and~~ that no state, without its consent, shall be deprived of its equal suffrage in the Senate.

The Constitution can be changed by amendments. An amendment can be proposed in either of two ways: (1) by the vote of two thirds of the Senate and two thirds of the House of Representatives, (2) by a special convention called together by Congress at the request of two thirds of the state legislatures. After an amendment has been proposed, it is adopted as part of the Constitution if it is approved (1) by the legislatures of at least three fourths of the states, or (2) by special conventions in at least three fourths of the states. But no amendment can be adopted that would take away any state's right to have two senators in Congress—unless the state gives its permission.

(A clause restricting the ability of Congress to amend Article 1 of the Constitution was set aside by the passage of time and by laws that were passed in 1808.)

ARTICLE 6
The Supreme Law of the Land

The National Debt

CLAUSE 1. All debts contracted and engagements entered into before the adoption of this Constitution shall be as valid against the United States under this Constitution as under the Confederation.

In this clause those who wrote the Constitution promised that the new United States government would pay the debts and carry out the agreements that had been made by the Congress that acted under the Articles of Confederation.

National Laws Are Above State Laws

CLAUSE 2. This Constitution and the laws of the United States which shall be made in pursuance thereof, and all treaties made or which shall be made under the authority of the United States, shall be the supreme law of the land, and the judges in every state shall be bound thereby, anything in the constitution or laws of any state to the contrary notwithstanding.

The Constitution, laws, and treaties of the United States are higher than the constitutions and laws of the states. Judges in each state must follow the laws of the United States, even if state laws conflict with those federal laws.

Oaths of Allegiance, Religious Tests

CLAUSE 3. The Senators and Representatives before mentioned, and the members of the several state legislatures, and all executive and judicial officers, both of the United States and of the several states, shall be bound by oath or affirmation to support this Constitution; but no religious test shall ever be required as a qualification to any office or public trust under the United States.

Members of Congress and the state legislatures and all other officials of the national and state governments must promise solemnly to uphold the Constitution and the form of government provided for by the Constitution. These officers do not have to be members of any particular religious group.

ARTICLE 7
Adoption of the Constitution

The ratification of the conventions of nine states shall be sufficient for the establishment of this Constitution between the states so ratifying the same.

Done in convention by the unanimous consent of the states present the seventeenth day of September, in the year of our Lord one thousand seven hundred and eighty-seven and of the independence of the United States of America the twelfth. In witness whereof, we have hereunto subscribed our names.

This constitution will go into effect when nine states meet and approve it in special conventions. This Constitution was written at a convention on September 17, 1787—in the twelfth year of the United States independence. Of course, the Constitution was adopted and went into effect. The names of all the signers of the Constitution appear on the next page.

George Washington—
President and deputy
from Virginia

New Hampshire
John Langdon
Nicholas Gilman

Massachusetts
Nathaniel Gorham
Rufus King

Connecticut
William Samuel Johnson
Roger Sherman

New York
Alexander Hamilton

New Jersey
William Livingston
David Brearley
William Paterson
Jonathan Dayton

Pennsylvania
Benjamin Franklin
Thomas Mifflin
Robert Morris
George Clymer
Thomas FitzSimons
Jared Ingersoll
James Wilson
Gouvemeur Morris

Delaware
George Read
Gunning Bedford, Junior
John Dickinson
Richard Bassett
Jacob Broom

Maryland
James McHenry
Dan of St. Thomas Jenifer
Daniel Carroll

Virginia
John Blair
James Madison, Junior

North Carolina
William Blount
Richard Dobbs Spaight
Hugh Williamson

South Carolina
John Rutledge
Charles Cotesworth Pinckney
Charles Pinckney
Pierce Butler

Georgia
William Few
Abraham Baldwin

AMENDMENTS TO THE CONSTITUTION

The Bill of Rights: Amendments 1–10

The first Congress began to meet in 1789. Many Americans felt that the new Constitution did not protect the rights of the people, so twelve amendments, or changes in the Constitution, were proposed. Ten of the twelve were accepted. These first ten amendments are known as the Bill of Rights. (The date beside each amendment is the date it was ratified.)

AMENDMENT 1. (1791)

Religion, Speech, Press, Assembly, and Petition

Congress shall make no law respecting an establishment of religion, or prohibiting the free exercise thereof; or abridging the freedom of speech, or of the press; or the right of the people peaceably to assemble, and to petition the government for a redress of grievances.

Congress cannot pass any law that would set up any religion as the official religion of the country or to keep people from following the religion of their choice. Congress cannot pass any law that would keep people from saying or printing what they choose. Congress cannot pass any law that would keep people from meeting together peacefully or from taking their complaints to the government.

AMENDMENT 2. (1791)

Right to Bear Arms

A well-regulated militia being necessary to the security of a free state, the right of the people to keep and bear arms shall not be infringed.

The federal government cannot interfere with the rights of the states to arm and drill their citizens in the state militia. This amendment does not guarantee that private citizens will be allowed to keep weapons for their personal use.

AMENDMENT 3. (1791)

Quartering Soldiers

No soldier shall in time of peace be quartered in any house without the consent of the owner, nor in time of war but in a manner to be prescribed by law.

In peacetime people cannot be forced to take soldiers into their houses and give them room and board. Even in times of war people cannot be forced to do this except according to laws passed by Congress. This was added to protect people from having to board soldiers in their homes as they were sometimes forced to do before the American Revolution.

AMENDMENT 4. (1791)

Search and Seizure

The right of the people to be secure in their persons, houses, papers, and effects, against unreasonable searches and seizures, shall not be violated, and no warrants shall issue, but upon probable cause, supported by oath or affirmation, and particularly describing the place to be searched and the persons or things to be seized.

No federal official can search a person, his or her home or papers, unless a warrant —an official order from a judge—gives an official the right to conduct this search. No judge can give out a warrant unless the official explains why the search is necessary, where the search will take place, and states what the official is searching for.

AMENDMENT 5. (1791)

Life, Liberty, Property

No person shall be held to answer for a capital or otherwise infamous crime unless on a presentment or indictment of a grand jury, except in cases arising in the land or naval forces, or in the militia, when in actual service in time of war or public danger; nor shall any person be subject for the same offense to be twice put in jeopardy of life or limb, nor shall be compelled in any criminal case to be a witness against himself, nor be deprived of life, liberty, or property without due process of law; nor shall private property be taken for public use without just compensation.

A person cannot be tried in a federal court for a serious crime unless a grand jury has examined the evidence and decided that the person should stand trial. A grand jury is set up to hear information from federal prosecutors. The grand jury will then decide whether there is enough information and evidence to formally charge that person with a federal crime for which he/she will then stand trial. The only people not covered by this rule are those serving in the armed forces in time of war or some other national emergency. If a person has been tried for a crime and found innocent, he or she cannot be tried again for that crime. A person cannot be forced to say anything at his or her trial that might help to prove the person guilty. A person cannot be executed, sent to jail, or fined unless it is the punishment handed down by a judge after a fair trial. Private property cannot be taken for public use unless the owner is paid a fair price for it.

AMENDMENT 6. (1791)

Rights of the Accused

In all criminal prosecutions, the accused shall enjoy the right to a speedy and public trial, by an impartial jury of the state and district wherein the crime shall have been committed, which district shall have been previously ascertained by law, and to be

informed of the nature and cause of the accusation; to be confronted with the witnesses against him; to have compulsory process for obtaining witnesses in his favor, and to have the assistance of counsel for his defense.

A person being tried in a federal court has the right to a prompt, public trial by jury. The citizens chosen as a jury must live in the state and district where the crime took place. The accused person must be told what the charges are and must be allowed to see and hear witnesses when they speak in court. The accused person also has the right to force witnesses that might prove him or her innocent to speak in court. The accused person has the right to a lawyer. If the person cannot pay a lawyer, the court will appoint one.

AMENDMENT 7. (1791)

Jury Trial

In suits at common law where the value in controversy shall exceed twenty dollars, the right of trial by jury shall be preserved, and no fact tried by a jury shall be otherwise reexamined in any court of the United States than according to the rules of the common law.

If a sum of money larger than $20 (which in 1789 was a relatively large sum) is involved in a lawsuit, the persons in the case may insist on a jury trial.

AMENDMENT 8. (1791)

Unreasonable Bail and Cruel and Unusual Punishments

Excessive bail shall not be required, nor excessive fines imposed, or cruel and unusual punishments inflicted.

Federal courts cannot force accused persons to put up an unreasonably large amount of bail. Bail is money or property an accused person gives to a court to ensure that the accused person will show up for the trial.

A person found guilty of a crime in a federal court cannot be punished by an unreasonably heavy fine or an unreasonably long prison sentence. The person also cannot be punished in cruel or unusual ways. Of course, punishment to fit the crime may be imposed by the courts.

One of the great benefits of the Constitution and its amendments is that certain procedures (methods of doing things) are uniform (standard). No single judge can do anything to take away constitutionally-guaranteed procedures and rights. Trial procedures are the same in all federal courts whatever state or part of the country they are located in. Many of these constitutional guarantees have been extended to include state and local court procedures and practices through the Fourteenth Amendment's "due process of law" clause.

AMENDMENT 9. (1791)

Rights of the People

The enumeration in the Constitution of certain rights shall not be construed to deny or disparage others retained by the people.

Certain rights are listed in the Constitution. This does not mean that these are the only rights the people have. It also does not mean that these listed rights are more important than the ones not listed.

AMENDMENT 10. (1791)

Rights of the States and of the People

The powers not delegated to the United States by the Constitution, nor prohibited by

it to the states, are reserved to the states respectively, or to the people.

All rights which have not been given to the federal government or denied to the state governments are rights the states and the people have. This permits individual states to regulate activities and matters not directly mentioned in the Constitution.

AMENDMENT 11. (1798)

Suits Against a State

The judicial power of the United States shall not be construed to extend to any suit in law or equity commenced or prosecuted against one of the United States by citizens of another state, or by citizens or subjects of any foreign state.

No federal court is allowed to try any case in which a state government is being sued by a citizen of another state or of a foreign country. Such a case must be tried in a court of the state that is being sued. This amendment changed a part of Article 3, Section 2, Clause 1.

AMENDMENT 12. (1804)

Presidential Elections

The electors shall meet in their respective states, and vote by ballot for President and Vice-President, one of whom, at least, shall not be an inhabitant of the same state with themselves; they shall name in their ballots the person voted for as President, and in distinct ballots the person voted for as Vice-President, and they shall make distinct lists of all persons voted for as President and of all persons voted for as Vice-President, and of the number of votes for each, which lists they shall sign and certify, and transmit, sealed, to the seat of the government of the United States, directed to the President of the Senate; the President of the Senate shall, in the presence of the Senate and House of Representatives, open all the certificates, and the votes shall then be counted. The person having the greatest number of votes for President shall be the President, if such number be a majority of the whole number of electors appointed; and if no person have such majority, then from the persons having the highest numbers, not exceeding three, on the list of those voted for as President, the House of Representatives shall choose immediately, by ballot, the President. But in choosing the President, the votes shall be taken by states, the representation from each state having one vote; a quorum for this purpose shall consist of a member or members from two-thirds of the states, and a majority of all the states shall be necessary to a choice. And if the House of Representatives shall not choose a President, whenever the right of choice shall devolve upon them, ~~before the fourth day of March next following,~~ then the Vice-President shall act as President, as in case of the death or other constitutional disability of the President. The person having the greatest number of votes as Vice-President shall be the Vice-President, if such number be a majority of the whole number of electors appointed, and if no person have a majority, then, from the two highest numbers on the list, the Senate shall choose the Vice-President; a quorum for the purpose shall consist of two-thirds of the whole number of Senators, and a majority of the whole number shall be necessary to a choice. But no person constitutionally ineligible to the office of President shall be eligible to that of Vice-President of the United States.

The electors meet in each state to vote for the President and Vice President after the "popular election." One of the candidates they vote for must not live in the elector's state. The electors cast two separate ballots, one for the President and one for the Vice President. The electors then make a list of the number of votes for each candidate. The lists must be signed by the electors, sealed, and sent to the president of the Senate in Washington, D.C.

The electoral votes are opened and counted by the president of the Senate in a meeting where both the members of the Senate and of the House of Representatives are present.

The presidential candidate having the most votes becomes the President, if the person has a majority (270) of all electoral votes cast (538). If no candidate receives a majority of electoral votes, the House of Representatives chooses the President. It chooses from the three candidates who received the most electoral votes. The House of Representatives votes by states, with each state having one vote. Two thirds of the states must be present to hold this election. A majority vote of the states is needed to win. If the House cannot choose a President by Jan. 20 (it used to be March 4), the Vice President takes over until the President is chosen.

The vice presidential candidate with the most votes becomes Vice President, if the person has a majority (270) of all electoral votes cast (538). If no candidate receives a majority of electoral votes, the Senate chooses the Vice President. It chooses from the two candidates with the most electoral votes. The Vice President must meet the same qualifications as the President.

AMENDMENT 13. (1865)

Slavery Forbidden

SECTION 1. Neither slavery nor involuntary servitude, except as a punishment for crime whereof the party shall have been duly convicted, shall exist within the United States or any place subject to their jurisdiction.

SECTION 2. Congress shall have power to enforce this article by appropriate legislation.

No one in the United States or its territories may be held in slavery. The only exception is when hard work is the punishment given by a court of law to a person who has committed a crime. Congress can make laws to enforce this amendment.

AMENDMENT 14. (1868)

Restrictions on the States

SECTION 1. All persons born or naturalized in the United States, and subject to the jurisdiction thereof, are citizens of the United States and of the state wherein they reside. No state shall make or enforce any law which shall abridge the privileges or immunities of citizens of the United States, nor shall any state deprive any person of life, liberty, or property without *due process* of law, nor deny to any person within its jurisdiction the equal protection of the laws.

All persons born or naturalized in the United States and ruled by this nation's laws are citizens—citizens both of the United States and of the state they live in.

No state may take away the rights of United States citizens or take any person's life, freedom, or property except according to law. All the laws of a state must affect everybody in the same way. This very important constitutional provision lies at the heart of the legal structure of the United States today. The phrase "due process of law" has been subject to many controversies decided over the years by the United States Supreme Court. Many of our existing legal rights and guarantees of equality, uniform treatment in court, and in dealing with local and state governments arise from the "due process" clause.

SECTION 2. Representatives shall be apportioned among the several states according to their respective numbers, counting the whole number of persons in each state, excluding Indians not taxed. But when the right to vote at any election for the choice of electors for President and Vice-President of the United States, Representatives in Congress, the executive and judicial officers of a state, or the members of the legislature thereof, is denied to any of the male inhabitants of such state, being twenty-one years of age, and citizens of the United States, or in any way abridged, except for participation in rebellion, or other crime, the basis of representation therein shall be reduced in the proportion which the number of such male citizens shall bear to the whole number of male citizens twenty-one years of age in such state.

The number of representatives a state may send to the House of Representatives is based on the number of peoplc in the state. (No longer were slaves counted as only three fifths of a person.) If a state refuses to allow any registered voter to vote in a state or federal election, the state will not be allowed to send as many representatives to the House of Representatives. The number of representatives will depend on the number of people who are not allowed to vote.

~~SECTION 3. No person shall be a Senator or Representative in Congress, or elector of President and Vice-President, or hold any office, civil or military, under the United States or under any state, who, having previously taken an oath as a member of Congress, or as an officer of the United States, or as a member of any state legislature, or as an executive or judicial officer of any state, to support the Constitution of the United States, shall have engaged in insurrection or rebellion against the same or given aid or comfort to the enemies thereof. But Congress may by a vote of two-thirds of each house remove such disability.~~

(According to this section, no person could ever become an official of the national government or a state government if he or she had ever held such an office in the past and then had rebelled against the national government. Congress could end this rule when two thirds of the senators and two thirds of the representatives voted to end it.

The effect of this section was to weaken the political power of the southern states and punish the leaders of the Confederacy. The section is long since out-of-date. Congress gave back full political rights to most of the Confederate leaders in 1872 and to the rest of them in 1898.)

~~SECTION 4. The validity of the public debt of the United States, authorized by law, including debts incurred for payment of pensions and bounties for services in suppressing insurrection and rebellion, shall not be questioned. But neither the United States nor any state shall assume or pay any debt or obligation incurred in aid of insurrection or rebellion against the United States, or any claim for the loss or emancipation of any slave; but all such debts, obligations, and claims shall be held illegal and void.~~

(The national government was ordered to pay back the money it had borrowed for the expenses of the Civil War. Neither the national government nor any state government was to be allowed to repay money that was borrowed by the Confederacy for fighting against the Union, or to pay slave owners for their slaves who had been set free. This, too, is now out of date. This section has served its purpose.)

SECTION 5. The Congress shall have power to enforce by appropriate legislation the provisions of this article.

Congress can pass laws to enforce this amendment.

AMENDMENT 15. (1870)

Negroes' Right to Vote

SECTION 1. The right of the citizens of the United States to vote shall not be denied or abridged by the United States or by any state on account of race, color, or previous condition of servitude.

SECTION 2. The Congress shall have power to enforce this article by appropriate legislation.

Neither the United States nor any state may keep a citizen from voting because of his/her race or color or because he/she was once a slave. Congress can pass laws to enforce this amendment. Acting upon this grant of constitutional authority, laws have been passed by Congress to make sure there is no discrimination or other obstacle to the rights of citizens to vote.

AMENDMENT 16. (1913)

The National Income Tax

The Congress shall have power to lay and collect taxes on incomes, from whatever source derived, without apportionment among the several states, and without regard to any census or enumeration.

Congress has the right to tax all kinds of incomes. The amount of money which the citizens of a state pay to the national government in the form of income tax does not have to be in proportion to that state's population.

AMENDMENT 17. (1913)

Election of Senators by the People

CLAUSE 1. The Senate of the United States shall be composed of two Senators from each state, elected by the people thereof, for six years; and each Senator shall have one vote. The electors in each state shall have the qualifications requisite for electors of the most numerous branch of the state legislatures.

The Senate of the United States is made up of two senators from each state. These senators are elected by the people for a six-year term. Each senator has one vote. Anyone who can vote for representatives to the state legislature, can vote in the election for senators. This amendment resulted in direct election of senators by the people instead of having them chosen by a select few persons in each state.

CLAUSE 2. When vacancies happen in the representation of any state in the Senate, the executive authority of such state shall issue writs of election to fill such vacancies: Provided that the legislature of any state may empower the executive thereof to make temporary appointments until the people fill the vacancies by election as the legislature may direct.

When a state does not have both senators in the Senate, the governor of the state must call an election to fill the vacancy. The governor can appoint someone to fill the vacancy until the election is held.

~~**CLAUSE 3. This amendment shall not be so construed as to affect the election or term of any Senator chosen before it becomes valid as part of the Constitution.**~~

(This amendment means that no person who is now a senator is affected in any way.)

AMENDMENT 18. (1919)

Prohibition (1919)

SECTION 1. After one year from the ratification of this article the manufacture, sale, or transportation of intoxicating liquors within, the importation thereof into, or the exportation thereof from the United States and all territory subject to the jurisdiction thereof for beverage purposes is hereby prohibited.

SECTION 2. The Congress and the several states shall have concurrent power to enforce this article by appropriate legislation.

SECTION 3. This article shall be inoperative unless it shall have been ratified as an amendment to the Constitution by the legislatures of the several states, as provided in the Constitution, within seven years from the date of the submission hereof to the states by the Congress.

(This amendment forbade the manufacture, sale, or shipment of intoxicating drinks, and it gave both to Congress and to the states the right to pass laws that would enforce the amendment. See the Twenty-first Amendment which repeals this amendment.)

AMENDMENT 19. (1920)

Women's Voting Rights

CLAUSE 1. The right of citizens of the United States to vote shall not be denied or abridged by the United States or by any state on account of sex.

CLAUSE 2. Congress shall have power to enforce this article by appropriate legislation.

Neither the federal government nor any state government may keep anyone from voting merely because of sex. Congress may pass laws necessary to carry out this amendment.

AMENDMENT 20. (1933)

Terms of Office

SECTION 1. The terms of the President and Vice-President shall end at noon on the twentieth day of January, and the terms of Senators and Representatives at noon on the third day of January, of the years in which such terms would have ended if this article had not been ratified; and the terms of their successors shall then begin.

The terms for the offices of President and Vice President end at noon on January 20 in the years following presidential elections. The terms of one third of the senators and all representatives end at noon on January 3 in the years with odd numbers. The new terms for these offices begin as soon as the old term ends.

SECTION 2. The Congress shall assemble at least once in every year, and such meeting shall begin at noon on the third day of January unless they shall by law appoint a different day.

Congress must meet at least once a year, beginning its meetings at noon on January 3 unless a law passed by Congress sets up a different day.

SECTION 3. If, at the time fixed for the beginning of the term of the President, the President-elect shall have died, the Vice-President-elect shall become President. If a President shall not have been chosen before the time fixed for the beginning of his term, of if the President-elect shall have failed to qualify, then the Vice-President-elect shall act as President until a President shall have qualified; and the Congress may by law provide for the case wherein neither a President-elect nor a Vice-President-elect shall have qualified, declaring who shall then act as President, or the manner in which one who is to act shall be selected, and such person shall act accordingly until

a President or Vice-President shall have qualified.

If the person elected President dies before January 20, when the term was to begin, then the person elected Vice President becomes President. If no President has been chosen by January 20, or if the person chosen does not meet the Constitution's requirements for the presidency, then the newly elected Vice President acts as President until a President who meets the requirements can be chosen. Congress may pass a law deciding what is to be done if neither the newly elected President nor the newly elected Vice President is able to meet the requirements for the presidency that have been clearly established in the Constitution.

SECTION 4. The Congress may by law provide for the case of the death of any of the persons from whom the House of Representatives may choose a President whenever the right of choice shall have devolved upon them, and for the case of the death of any of the persons from whom the Senate may choose a Vice-President whenever the right of choice shall have devolved upon them.

Section Four of the Twentieth Amendment permits Congress to pass laws deciding what to do in case of the death of any candidate chosen by either house of Congress to hold the office of President or Vice President.

SECTION 5. Sections 1 and 2 shall take effect on the fifteenth day of October following the ratification of this article.

(Section Five set the date on which the first two sections of this amendment were to go into effect.)

SECTION 6. This article shall be inoperative unless it shall have been ratified as an amendment to the Constitution by the legislatures of three-fourths of the several states within seven years from the date of its submission.

(Section Six of the Twentieth Amendment explained how and when the amendment was to be adopted.)

AMENDMENT 21. (1933)

Repeal of Prohibition

SECTION 1. The eighteenth article of amendment to the Constitution of the United States is hereby repealed.

The Eighteenth Amendment, the "Prohibition Amendment," is repealed by this amendment.

SECTION 2. The transportation or importation into any state, territory, or possession of the United States for delivery or use therein of intoxicating liquors, in violation of the laws thereof, is hereby prohibited.

Any states, territories, or possessions of the United States that want to prohibit alcoholic liquors have the right to do so by laws of their own.

SECTION 3. This article shall be inoperative unless it shall have been ratified as an amendment to the Constitution by convention in the several states, as provided in the Constitution, within seven years from the date of the submission hereof to the states by the Congress.

(Section Three of the Twenty-first Amendment ruled how and when this amendment was to be adopted.)

AMENDMENT 22. (1951)

Number of Terms for a President

SECTION 1. No person shall be elected to the office of the President more than twice, and no person who has held the office of President, or acted as President, for more than two years of a term to which some other person was elected President shall be elected to the office of President more than once. But this Article shall not apply to any person holding the office of President when this Article was proposed by the Congress, and shall not prevent any person who may be holding the office of President, or acting as President, during the term within which this Article becomes operative from holding the office of President, or acting as President during the remainder of such term.

No one may be elected to the office of President more than twice (eight years). If a President dies in office with more than two years remaining in the term, the new President who finishes out that term, may be elected for only one more term. If a President dies with less than two years remaining in the term, the new President who finishes out that term, may be elected for two more terms or a total of ten years.

This amendment did not apply to the President who was in office when it was ratified—Harry S Truman.

~~**SECTION 2. This Article shall be inoperative unless it shall have been ratified as an amendment to the Constitution by the legislatures of three-fourths of the several states within seven years from the date of its submission to the states by Congress.**~~

(This section ruled how and when the Twenty-second Amendment was to be adopted.)

AMENDMENT 23. (1961)

District of Columbia

SECTION 1. The District constituting the seat of Government of the United States shall appoint in such manner as the Congress may direct:

A number of electors of President and Vice-President equal to the whole number of Senators and Representatives in Congress to which the District would be entitled if it were a state, but in no event more than the least populous state; they shall be in addition to those appointed by the states, but they shall be considered, for the purposes of the election of President and Vice-President, to be electors appointed by a state; and they shall meet in the District and perform such duties as provided by the twelfth article of amendment.

The District of Columbia can appoint electors to vote for the offices of President and Vice President of the United States. The number of electors to be appointed is no more than the state with the fewest people. The electors of the District of Columbia shall select the President and Vice President in the same way as states do according to the Twelfth Amendment.

SECTION 2. The Congress shall have power to enforce this article by appropriate legislation.

Congress has the power to pass such laws as may be required to put this amendment into force.

AMENDMENT 24. (1964)

Poll Taxes

SECTION 1. The right of citizens of the United States to vote in any primary or other election for President or Vice-President, for electors for President or Vice-

President, or for Senator or Representative in Congress, shall not be denied or abridged by the United States or any state by reason of failure to pay any poll or other tax.

SECTION 2. The Congress shall have power to enforce this article by appropriate legislation.

Neither the federal government nor any state or local government may prevent any citizen from voting in national elections on the grounds that a tax of any kind was not paid. Congress has the power to make any laws necessary to enforce this amendment. The Twenty-fourth Amendment was another way to help secure the rights to vote to all persons in the United States. It forbade making people pay a special state tax before they were allowed to vote.

AMENDMENT 25. (1967)

Presidential Succession and Disability

SECTION 1. In case of the removal of the President from office or his death or resignation, the Vice-President shall become President.

If a President is impeached, resigns, or dies, the Vice President becomes President.

SECTION 2. Whenever there is a vacancy in the office of the Vice-President, the President shall nominate a Vice-President who shall take the office upon confirmation by a majority vote of both houses of Congress.

If the Vice President should leave office for any reason, the President can appoint a new Vice President who can take office if approved by a majority vote of both houses of Congress.

SECTION 3. Whenever the President transmits to the President pro tempore of the Senate and the Speaker of the House of Representatives his written declaration that he is unable to discharge the powers and duties of his office, and until he transmits to them a written declaration to the contrary, such powers and duties shall be discharged by the Vice-President as Acting President.

If the President is unable to carry out the duties of the office, the President can send a letter to the President pro tempore of the Senate and the Speaker of the House of Representatives. This letter will state the reasons why the President cannot carry out the duties of office. The Vice President will then act as President until the President sends another letter to the President pro tempore of the Senate and the Speaker of the House of Representatives saying that he/she can carry out the duties of office again.

SECTION 4. Whenever the Vice-President and a majority of either the principal officers of the executive departments, or of such other body as Congress may by law provide, transmit to the President pro tempore of the Senate and the Speaker of the House of Representatives their written declaration that the President is unable to discharge the powers and duties of his office, the Vice-President shall immediately assume the powers and duties of the office as Acting President.

Thereafter, when the President transmits to the President pro tempore of the Senate and the Speaker of the House of Representatives his written declaration that no inability exists, he shall resume the powers and duties of his office unless the Vice-President and a majority of either the principal officers of the executive department, or of such other body as Congress may by law provide, transmit within four days to the President pro tempore of the Senate and the Speaker of the House of Representatives their written declaration that the President is unable to discharge the powers and duties of his

office. Thereupon Congress shall decide the issue, assembling within 48 hours for that purpose if not in session. If the Congress, within 21 days after receipt of the latter written declaration, or if Congress is not in session, within 21 days after Congress is required to assemble, determines by two-thirds vote of both houses that the President is unable to discharge the powers and duties of his office, the Vice-President shall continue to discharge the same as Acting President; otherwise, the President shall resume the powers and duties of his office.

If a President cannot or will not write a letter to the President pro tempore of the Senate and the Speaker of the House of Representatives saying that he or she cannot carry out the duties of the office, the Vice President can write such a letter. The Vice President must have a majority of the President's Cabinet or a group appointed by Congress sign the letter, too. Then the Vice President becomes the President.

The President can write a letter to the leaders of Congress saying that there is no reason why he or she cannot carry out the duties of the office. The President will then return to office unless the Vice President and the Cabinet write to the leaders of Congress saying they feel the President still cannot carry out the duties of the office. This letter must be received in four days.

The Congress has to meet within 48 hours to consider the matter. The Congress has 21 days to discuss this. If two thirds or more of Congress votes that the President is unable to carry out the duties of office, the Vice President remains as Acting President.

Sections Three and Four are procedures setting forth how the executive branch of the federal government can continue to operate in the event of the President's disability.

AMENDMENT 26. (1971)

Eighteen Year Old Vote

SECTION 1. The right of citizens of the United States, who are eighteen years of age or older, to vote, shall not be denied or abridged by the United States or any state on account of age.

Neither the United States nor any state is permitted to keep citizens eighteen years of age or older from voting because of their age. This made eighteen years of age the uniform minimum voting age throughout the United States.

SECTION 2. The Congress shall have the power to enforce this article by appropriate legislation.

Congress can pass laws to enforce this amendment.

B. 1. 25 years old, citizen of United States for 7 years, resident of state and district from which elected **2.** 6 years **3.** the people, Seventeenth **4.** 35 years old, citizen of United States by birth, and resident of the United States for 14 years **5.** the Senate, two thirds **6.** executive branch **7.** Supreme Court **8.** life

THE CONSTITUTION TEST

A. Match each of the following words with its correct definition:

c **1.** preamble
f **2.** bill
h **3.** power
e **4.** Elastic Clause
a **5.** impeach
g **6.** Electoral College
d **7.** concurrent
b **8.** amendment

a. accuse an official of wrongdoing
b. addition or change
c. introduction
d. shared
e. Congress can make laws needed to carry out the Constitution
f. written proposal for a new law
g. electors who choose the President and Vice President
h. authority

B. Answer these questions:

1. What are the qualifications for a representative?
2. What is the length of a senator's term?
3. Who elects senators? What amendment changed the way senators were elected?
4. What are the qualifications for a presidential candidate?
5. Who must approve the President's treaties? By how large a margin?
6. Which branch of government carries out the laws?
7. Who heads the judicial branch?
8. How long may justices serve?

C. Fill in the blanks:

1. The preamble lists the ___six___ purposes of the Constitution.
2. There are ___435___ representatives in the House of Representatives.
3. ___Two thirds___ of both the Senate and the House of Representatives must vote to pass a law over the President's veto.
4. The President cannot serve more than a total of ___ten___ years.
5. Justices of the Supreme Court are appointed by the ___President,___ and approved by the ___Senate___.
6. The first ten amendments to the Constitution are called the ___Bill of Rights___.

D. Choose the correct answer:

b **1.** The age requirement for a senator is
a. 25 years **b.** 30 years **c.** 35 years

a **2.** A population count made every ten years is called a
a. census **b.** veto **c.** duty

c **3.** The Senate sits as the ____ in an impeachment trial
a. judge **b.** accusor **c.** jury

c **4.** The first ten amendments were added to the Constitution in
a. 1787 **b.** 1789 **c.** 1791

E. True/false

__T__ **1.** A representative must live in the state and district from which elected.
__F__ **2.** Only the Senate can impeach an official from the executive branch.
__F__ **3.** The membership of the Senate is based on the population of each state.
__T__ **4.** The President has the power to veto laws passed by Congress.
__F__ **5.** The Chief Justice of the United States gives the State of the Union address.
__F__ **6.** The Supreme Court decides how the crime of treason will be punished.

F. Essay Question

Explain the difference between the Supreme Court's original and appellate jurisdiction.

F. original jurisdiction: cases concerning a state or a representative of a foreign government **appellate jurisdiction:** cases that have already been tried in lower federal courts if one of the parties appeals the case

RELATED MATERIAL
Duplicator/Copy Master Test 19-20

Unit 4
A NEW NATION

Unit Four examines the early years of the new nation, from 1789 to 1850. The topics discussed in the unit include the following: George Washington's presidency, including the first Cabinet; President John Adams's differences with France; the Louisiana Purchase; tensions with Great Britain, which led to the War of 1812; the growth of roads, canals, and railroads; and the Industrial Revolution.

The "De Witt Clinton" on its first run

The United States Capitol in the 1830s

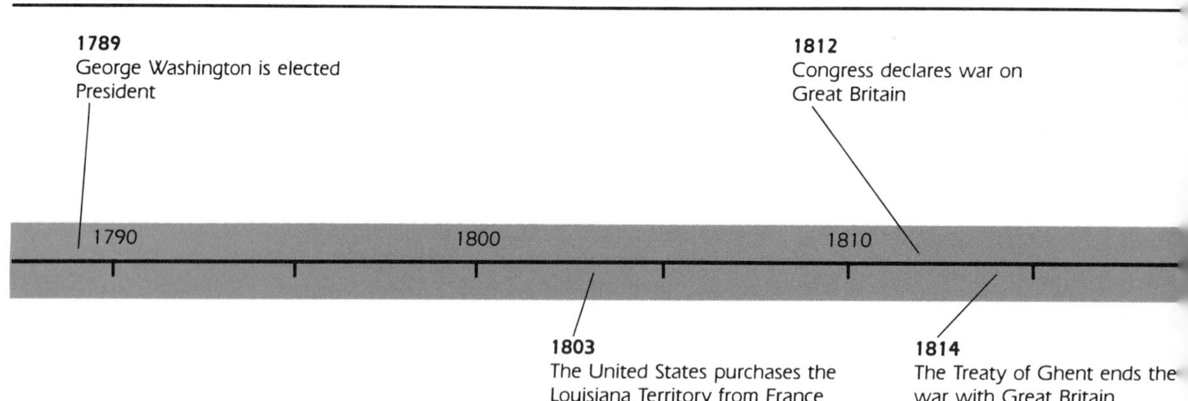
1789
George Washington is elected President
1812
Congress declares war on Great Britain
1790
1800
1810
1803
The United States purchases the Louisiana Territory from France
1814
The Treaty of Ghent ends the war with Great Britain

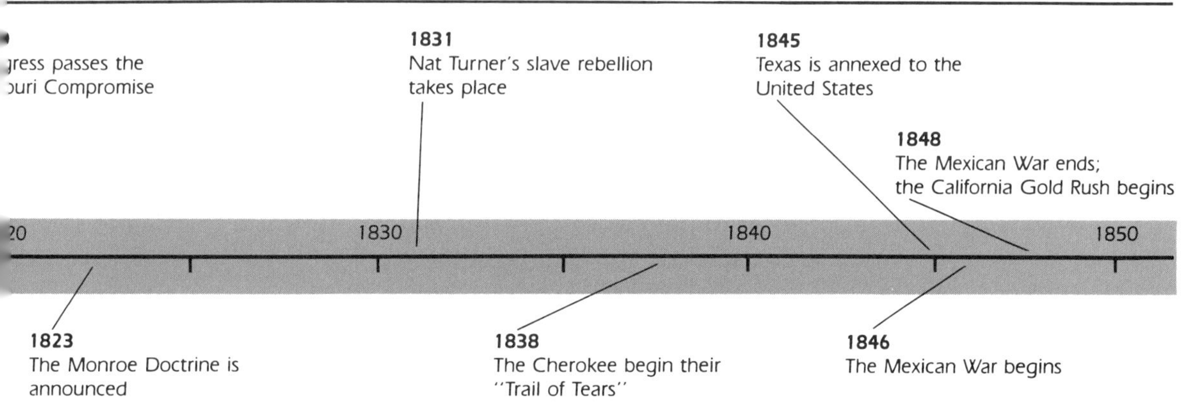

gress passes the
ouri Compromise
1831
Nat Turner's slave rebellion
takes place
1845
Texas is annexed to the
United States
1848
The Mexican War ends;
the California Gold Rush begins
20
1830
1840
1850
1823
The Monroe Doctrine is
announced
1838
The Cherokee begin their
"Trail of Tears"
1846
The Mexican War begins

Chapter 10
THE FEDERALIST PERIOD

Chapter 10 covers the administrations of the first two Presidents of the United States. Lesson 10-1 reviews the unanimous election of George Washington, Alexander Hamilton's plans for financial recovery, Washington's neutral foreign policy, and the development of political parties. Lesson 10-2 focuses on the administration of John Adams, which was plagued by foreign policy problems and domestic political strife.

CONTENT OBJECTIVES

After completing the lesson, students will know:

- that the establishment of a Cabinet was one of several precedents set by President Washington
- how Hamilton planned to pay the debts of the United States
- about the development of the first political parties
- why many Americans were angered by the settlement made by Jay's Treaty
- how Washington's insistence on neutrality had a long-term effect on United States foreign policy

VOCABULARY

administration: the President, the Vice President, and their advisers who set the policies of government
precedent: an example to be followed or referred to later
Cabinet: the official group of advisers to the President
bond: a paper that promises that the government will repay the money it borrows plus extra money that is called interest
assumption: taking over of debts
tariff: tax on imports
political party: a group of people with certain ideas about how government should be run and who try to get their candidates elected to government office
neutrality: not taking either side in a disagreement
impressment: forcing individuals to serve in a navy or army

10-1 The First Presidency

As you read, think about these questions:

Why did Washington's administration make careful decisions about even the smallest matters?

Why was Hamilton's financial plan important for the new nation?

Why were political parties formed?

What was the difference between Hamilton's view of the Constitution and Jefferson's?

Special Vocabulary	administration	bond	political party
	precedent	assumption	neutrality
	Cabinet	tariff	impressment

In February of 1789, the electors met in their own states to cast their votes for the first President of the United States. Each elector voted for two people—the one receiving the highest number of votes would be President; the one receiving the second highest number of votes would be Vice President. George Washington received all sixty-nine votes for President. John Adams, who received thirty-five votes, became Vice President.

Washington's journey from his home in Mount Vernon to New York City, the nation's capital, was a hero's parade. Cities and towns along the route held celebrations to honor their new leader. On April 30, 1789, thousands of people watched as Washington took the presidential oath on the balcony of Federal Hall in New York City.

Setting Examples

The new nation had a trusted and popular leader and a well-written plan of government. Many details concerning the day-to-day business of governing the United States still had to be determined by the first *administration*—the President, the Vice President, and their advisers who set the policies of the government.

Washington's administration made careful decisions about even the smallest matters. Anything the new government did could become a political *precedent,* an example to be followed or referred to later. A bad decision could lead the country in the wrong direction.

Some of the decisions Washington made dealt with the way he thought a President should act. Washington did not shake hands with people, he did not accept invitations, and he did not return visits. These ideas have certainly changed over the years. Some other decisions Washington made, however, have been followed by all Presidents since him.

The first President set up ways of dealing with Congress. On one occasion, Washington went to the Senate to seek approval for a treaty with the American Indians. Some senators, using their authority under the Constitution to offer advice and suggestions to the President, severely criticized the treaty. Washington became angry and left the Senate. To this day, no other President has gone to the Senate in person to seek advice or approval for a treaty.

As Washington boarded the boat that ferried him across the Hudson to his inauguration, the nation's first President declared that he had no wish beyond "the humble . . . lot of living and dying a private citizen."

Establishing Policies at Home

President Washington faced many difficult problems as the leader of a new nation, but he had two important advantages. He was respected by the people, and he had the help of some excellent advisers. In addition to these advantages, Washington began his term of office during a peaceful time. American business was improving somewhat, so the unrest in the states had quieted. Washington was able to concentrate on getting the government off to a good start.

Presidential Advisers. Congress created three departments to advise and inform the new President. They were the departments of State, the Treasury, and War. The leader of each department was called a secretary. The secretary of state handled the country's relations with other nations. The secretary of the treasury took care of the country's money. The secretary of war helped defend the country. The President also had two other official advisers—the attorney general and the postmaster general. The attorney general was a lawyer appointed to aid the government in legal matters. The postmaster general, who worked in the Treasury Department, made sure the mail traveled smoothly.

The first people who held these positions became known as the *Cabinet,* the official group of advisers to the President. With the President and Vice President, the Cabinet forms the executive branch of the government. The Constitution does not mention a Cabinet as part of the executive branch of government. Once again, Washington set a useful precedent that future Presidents would follow. See the chart below for a listing of the first Cabinet members.

WASHINGTON'S FIRST CABINET

Title	Name	Home State
Secretary of State	Thomas Jefferson	Virginia
Secretary of the Treasury	Alexander Hamilton	New York
Secretary of War	Henry Knox	Massachusetts
Attorney General	Edmund Randolph	Virginia
Postmaster General	Samuel Osgood	Massachusetts

The Federal Court System. The Constitution had given Congress the power to set up a system of federal courts. Congress had to decide how many courts to establish, the number of judges needed to run these courts, and the kinds of cases the judges would hear. The Federal Judiciary Act, one of the first laws Congress enacted, outlined the court system.

The Federal Judiciary Act of 1789 stated that there should be one Chief Justice to lead the Supreme Court and five associate justices. Washington appointed John Jay of New York to be the first Chief Justice. At first, few people thought the Supreme Court was very important. Jay even tried to get elected governor of New York while he was Chief Justice.

Congress also described a system of lower courts in the Federal Judiciary Act. It gave those courts specific duties. District courts were to hear most cases involving national laws. If people who lost a case in a district court could show that the judge's decision was questionable, they could appeal that decision. Then the case would go to the next higher court, the court of appeals. If that court's decision was still in question, the case could go to the Supreme Court. The decision of the Supreme Court was final.

John Jay, first Chief Justice of the Supreme Court, was once president of the Continental Congress. He lost his chance to be President of the country, however, by negotiating an unpopular treaty with the British.

Hamilton's Financial Program. The United States was heavily in debt. During the Revolution, the government had borrowed money from other countries, especially from France and the Netherlands. It had also borrowed money from American citizens. These citizens had loaned money to the government by buying *bonds.* Bonds are papers that promise that the government will repay the money it borrows plus extra money called interest. By 1790 the government had not paid back the money it owed. The states also owed money, which they had borrowed during the Revolution to buy supplies for their militias.

Alexander Hamilton, secretary of the treasury, prepared a financial plan for the government. His purpose was to strengthen the United States government by showing that it paid its debts. He hoped that it would in this way gain the respect of business people and of foreign governments.

Hamilton's plan included the following steps:

1) *Assumption,* taking over, of debts: Hamilton wanted the central government to pay back all money owed to American citizens and to foreign countries. In addition, he wanted the central government to pay back money owed by the states.

First secretary of the treasury and first leader of the Federalists, Alexander Hamilton was the son of a merchant. He believed the nation should be run by merchants, and he worked to protect their interests.

DISCUSSION

In a wide-ranging discussion, have the students answer this question and provide actual or hypothetical examples illustrating their position: How does the financial plan of the government of a democratic nation such as the United States show what is important to the people of that country?

2) Bank of the United States: Hamilton suggested setting up a national bank to take care of the government's money matters. The bank would hold the central government's money and pay its debts. It would lend money to private citizens to help make their businesses grow. Citizens would be able to buy shares in the bank. Hamilton thought that people who owned shares would be interested in helping the government succeed.
3) Taxes: In order to get the money to pay off the debts as he planned, Hamilton suggested a *tariff*, or tax on imports. Such a tax would add to the price of goods made in Europe. American goods would be cheaper than those from Europe. As a result, American manufacturing would be helped. Hamilton also suggested a tax on whiskey.

The First National Bank of the United States was established in 1791—not 1795, as the Roman numerals over its stately doors mistakenly proclaim. The coin shown here was in use at the time.

Opposition and Compromise. Congress passed much of Hamilton's plan. Not everyone agreed with Hamilton, however. Some farmers in western Pennsylvania refused to pay the tax on whiskey. These farmers used their corn to make whiskey because whiskey was easier to store and to sell than corn was. When these farmers rebelled in 1794, Washington sent soldiers to put down the so-called Whiskey Rebellion.

Hamilton and Jay, both New Yorkers, raised funds to have the Capitol moved to this site in New York. Hamilton probably hoped that government business would boost his law practice.

Some southern states had already paid their debts. People in those states were very upset about being taxed to pay the debts of other states. Two Virginians—Thomas Jefferson and James Madison—led the opposition to Hamilton's plan for paying state debts. Finally, Jefferson and Madison proposed a compromise. They promised to support Hamilton's plan if he would support a plan to move the capital to the South. Hamilton accepted the compromise. Jefferson and Madison helped get the assumption bill through Congress. Hamilton rounded up enough votes to move the capital from New York City. In order to get Pennsylvania's votes, Hamilton agreed that the capital would be in Philadelphia for ten years. In 1800 the capital of the United States was moved permanently to Washington, D.C.

Some further arguments over Hamilton's plan led to the beginning of America's first *political parties*. These are groups of people with certain ideas about how government should be run and who try to get their candidates elected to government office. Jefferson became the leader of the Republican Party, which favored a strict way of interpreting the Constitution. Jefferson felt that the government has only the powers that are exactly stated in the Constitution.

Hamilton became the leader of the Federalist Party, which favored a loose way of interpreting the Constitution. Hamilton felt that Congress has additional powers that are suggested, but not stated outright, in the Constitution. The following chart summarizes other differences between the Republicans and the Federalists.

AMERICA'S FIRST POLITICAL PARTIES	
Republicans	**Federalists**
Led by Thomas Jefferson	Led by Alexander Hamilton
Favored strict interpretation of the Constitution	Favored loose interpretation of the Constitution
Supported the interests of farmers	Supported the interests of business people
Believed in the ability of people to govern themselves	Believed in government by wealthy and educated people
Favored strong state governments	Favored a strong central government
Supported state banks	Supported a Bank of the United States

Facing World Problems

In 1792 George Washington was reelected President of the United States. Washington's first administration had withstood many problems at home, including the disagreements between Jefferson and Hamilton. During his second administration, Washington faced growing problems with some of the countries of Europe.

France had undergone its own revolution and had set up a new government. Early in 1793 France declared war on Great Britain, Spain, and the Netherlands. Americans began to take sides. Hamilton and the Federalists favored the British. They wanted to continue to trade with Great Britain. Jefferson and the Republicans favored France in the struggle. They feared that Great Britain and Spain could become a threat to the United States if France were defeated.

President Washington decided, however, that the United States should not get involved in Europe's problems. In 1793 Washington issued the *Neutrality* Proclamation. Neutrality means not taking either side in a disagreement. This statement remained an important guide to the United States' dealings with other countries for many years.

The first test of United States neutrality came later in 1793. Edmond Genêt, minister from France, tried to involve the United States in Europe's quarrels. Citizen Genêt, as he was called, began to arm ships and recruit Americans in United States ports. These acts clearly violated Washington's neutrality policy. The President took a firm stand and asked France to recall Genêt.

Jay's Treaty. The United States came close to war with Great Britain. One reason was that the British had remained in the Northwest Territory, where they controlled much of the fur trade. Another reason was that the British were stopping United States trade ships to look for British sailors who had left the navy without permission. Sometimes the British practiced *impressment*—that is, they forced American sailors to serve in the British navy.

In May of 1794 Washington sent Chief Justice John Jay to bargain with the British. Jay succeeded in working out a treaty that was signed in November of that year. In the treaty, the British promised once again to leave their trading posts in the Northwest. This time they kept their word. The United States allowed them to continue their fur trade in that area. The British agreed to let the United States trade with the West Indies on a limited basis, provided that the United States did not trade cotton, sugar, or molasses. The treaty asked very little of Great Britain. It did not even mention the American ships and sailors the British had taken. Americans were very angry over Jay's Treaty. Many people felt that the United States had given in to Great Britain. The treaty passed the Senate by a narrow margin. It did, however, prevent a war with Great Britain at that time.

ACTIVITY

Objective: To research information and summarize

Divide the class into groups of four. Have them use the school library to find information on one of the early leaders of America, such as Hamilton, Jefferson, Washington, Knox, or Jay. Tell them to investigate their subject's position on four issues: defense, taxation, state banks, and political parties. Each member of the group should be responsible for one issue. Students should use at least three sources. Each group will report their findings to the class and be ready to answer questions.

The British practice of impressing American sailors into the British navy was similar to the way Great Britain often forced its own citizens to serve in the navy.

Thomas Pinckney aided his country in many ways. He fought in the Revolution, served as governor of South Carolina, and was minister to Great Britain before becoming minister to Spain.

Pinckney's Treaty. In 1795 the Spanish feared that Great Britain might attack their New World empire. They, therefore, decided to become allies with the United States. Such a friend in the Americas might help discourage the British from attacking the Spanish.

Thomas Pinckney, the American minister to Spain, signed a treaty with the Spanish in 1795. This treaty, which was well-received in the United States, had four points:

1) American ships could travel on the Mississippi River without paying a tax to Spain.
2) For three years, Americans could use warehouses to store goods in New Orleans without paying a tax on them before shipping them elsewhere.
3) Spain would keep American Indians living in Spanish territory from attacking American settlers.
4) Spain accepted 31° north latitude as the boundary of West Florida.

Washington's Farewell Address. In 1796 Washington prepared to retire from political life. Although many people wanted Washington to run for a third term, he refused to do so. He wanted to give Americans some advice, however, so he issued a farewell address that was printed in several newspapers. Washington said that the United States would be wise not to get itself involved in a permanent alliance with any nation. He did not mean that the United States should keep itself separated from the rest of the world. He felt, however, that the United States should concentrate on handling its own affairs. He advised Americans to let Europeans handle their own problems. Washington's advice influenced the nation's leaders for many years.

ANSWER THESE QUESTIONS

1. Answers will vary. Washington did not shake hands, accept invitations, or return visits. He did not seek advice from the Senate in person. He appointed the first Cabinet.
2. Thomas Jefferson, Alexander Hamilton, Henry Knox, Edmund Randolph, and Samuel Osgood
3. Supreme Court, court of appeals, district courts
4. Jefferson thought states should have greater independence from federal government than Hamilton would have allowed.
5. because the United States was a new nation and so should concentrate on handling its own affairs

ANSWER THESE QUESTIONS

1. What were two precedents that George Washington set?
2. Who were the members of Washington's first Cabinet?
3. What were the different courts that made up the judicial branch of government as described in the Judiciary Act of 1789?
4. How did Jefferson and Hamilton differ in their beliefs about the power of the states and the power of the national government?
5. Why did President Washington believe in neutrality for the United States?

10-2 President John Adams

As you read, think about these questions:
Where did most people live in the 1790s?
What was the X Y Z Affair?
What were the Alien and Sedition Acts?
What were the Kentucky and Virginia Resolutions?

Special Vocabulary	naturalization	deport	nullify
	alien	sedition	

When George Washington decided that he would not run for a third term in office, the first political fight for the Presidency took place. John Adams of the Federalist Party and Thomas Jefferson of the Republican Party ran for the position. Although it was a close contest, Adams got a majority of the electoral votes. Thomas Jefferson, getting the second highest number of votes, became Vice President. As President, Adams was ready to govern the people and to try to solve the problems that Washington had left behind.

Life in the New Republic

In 1797 John Adams found that the nation had a growing population, an expanding economy, and a people with many

CONTENT OBJECTIVES

After completing the lesson, students will know:

- that the population and economy of the United States expanded rapidly in the 1790s
- why the United States fought an undeclared war with France in 1798
- the origin of the Naturalization, Alien and Sedition Acts
- the background of nullification

VOCABULARY

naturalization: the granting of citizenship to a person born in another country
alien: a person living in another country who has not become a naturalized citizen
deport: to send an alien out of the country who is thought to be dangerous to the peace and safety of the United States
sedition: the act of causing rebellion against the government in power
nullify: legally cancel

John and Abigail Adams were the first couple to live in the White House. Often separated by Adams's political duties, they exchanged many letters, which give us one of the liveliest and best-informed pictures of colonial life.

different lifestyles. Three new states—Vermont, Kentucky, and Tennessee—had been admitted to the Union. The expanding opportunities in industry and agriculture met most of the economic needs of the people. All people—except the slaves—could hope for a better life.

Population. In 1790 four million people lived in the United States. Ten years later, the population of the country had grown to five and one-half million, with nine out of every ten Americans living east of the Appalachian Mountains. By 1797 almost half of all Americans lived in the area from Maryland to Georgia.

Large cities, too, were growing in size. Philadelphia, New York, Boston, Charleston, and Baltimore were the nation's largest population centers. From 1790 to 1800 tens of thousands of people made these cities their homes. (Look at the chart below to compare the populations of American cities in 1790 and 1800.)

AMERICAN CITIES IN 1790 AND 1800

1790		1800	
1. Philadelphia, Pa.	44,000	1. Philadelphia, Pa.	69,000
2. New York, N.Y.	33,000	2. New York, N.Y.	60,000
3. Boston, Mass.	18,000	3. Baltimore, Md.	26,000
4. Charleston, S.C.	16,000	4. Boston, Mass.	25,000
5. Baltimore, Md.	13,500	5. Charleston, S.C.	20,000

Every part of the country seemed to be growing steadily. The northern states were becoming more populous. Even the western frontier saw an increase in settlers.

Economy. As the population of the United States grew, the economy of the country expanded to meet the needs of the people. Opportunities for many existed in farming, fishing, shipbuilding, and manufacturing.

In the South the cash crops of rice, tobacco, and indigo made many large plantation owners wealthy. Smaller farmers did not do as well because they did not own as much land. Slaves were worse off still, having to depend on others for their living.

These posters advertise the major crops of the Middle Atlantic and southern states—wheat and tobacco. The poster on the left is done in needlepoint.

In the Middle Atlantic states huge amounts of grain like corn and rye were produced. Grain products sold well in Europe at a good profit for the farmers. The iron industry also grew steadily in these states.

Most of the money that was made in New England was from trading with foreign countries. Farming, fishing, shipbuilding, and manufacturing also provided jobs for thousands of people.

Perhaps the most difficult way of making a living, besides being a slave, was farming on the western frontier. The farmers could sell their produce only by shipping it on flatboats down the Mississippi River to New Orleans. There it had to be unloaded and sold to the highest bidder.

Lifestyles. The people in each area of the country lived their lives in their own special way. Some customs and practices of the people were similar from area to area, but many sections of the nation had their very own lifestyles.

In the South the way people lived depended on whether they were slaves, small landowners, or large plantation owners. The slaves had a very difficult life. Their day was filled with work—often from sunrise to sunset. The pleasures that slaves received from their lives were few and of their own making. The small landowners found that the struggle to have enough to eat occupied most days of the

ACTIVITY

Objective: To make a graphic

Divide the class into groups of no more than four students. Direct them to research the lifestyles of one of the following groups living from 1790 to 1800: slaves, western and New England farmers, city dwellers, or plantation owners. After completing their research, each group should prepare a poster, mural, or other graphic representation of the information. Each group should present their graphic to the class.

Music was not only entertainment for slaves but also served as a link with their cultural heritage. Here slaves on a South Carolina plantation dance to the rhythm of African instruments.

week. There was little time for relaxing and having fun. The large plantation owners also worked hard. The large farms that these people owned demanded constant attention. The plantation owners, however, did have more money and time to enjoy a large home, family, and friends.

The people in New England also had a difficult life. They had to endure hardships caused by a harsh climate and rocky soil. These tough conditions produced a hardy people who could live through the terrible winters. These people spent a great deal of time trying to further their education. In fact, colleges and academies were first established in this region of the country.

The people who lived in the cities had their own problems, which were far different from those of their counterparts in the country. Cities were often dirty, and disease spread quickly. Many people died at a very early age because of this. Still, cities offered the people many opportunities not found elsewhere. Parties, dances, theater, and other social events brightened the lives of many. Museums and libraries gave the people a chance to enjoy learning and the past.

The western farmers found their lives filled with constant work. This work was often difficult and unpleasant. The

farmers had simple tools to work with and their one-room homes were built from logs. These cabins were cold and far from comfortable. Nevertheless, these people had given up much to come to the western frontier. Many wanted to be free from large cities and overcrowded areas. They owned the land they lived on and were free to live their lives the way they wanted. The western farmers did occasionally get together with neighbors, and these times were festive. The raising of a new barn or a log cabin brought everyone together for a good time.

The "American" log cabin actually was a Swedish invention. Swedish pioneers taught their neighbors on the American frontier how to notch logs together without nails.

Foreign Affairs

During George Washington's second term in office, he sent James Monroe to France. Monroe was to try to make the French understand that the United States wanted peace with all the nations of Europe. France, however, was very angry with the United States. In 1778 the United States and France had signed a treaty of alliance. When France later declared war on Great Britain, however, the United States refused to send France aid. This made French officials angry. They became even more furious with the United States when they learned about Jay's Treaty with Great Britain in 1794. When Adams became President, troubled relations with France remained a problem.

X Y Z Affair. Adams tried to improve relations between the United States and France by naming Charles Cotesworth Pinckney as minister to France. The French government refused to receive Pinckney as the minister when he arrived. Adams then sent John Marshall, Elbridge Gerry, and Pinckney to France to negotiate a treaty.

Four days after the American delegation arrived in France, it was received by the French foreign minister, Talleyrand. Talleyrand told the Americans that treaty negotiations could not begin immediately. More than a week passed before the Americans heard from the French again.

Three French secret agents called on the Americans. These agents wanted the United States to give France a large loan. The agents also said that before negotiations on a treaty could begin, the United States would have to pay France a bribe of $240,000. Marshall, Gerry, and Pinckney were furious. They quickly refused this request.

Three years before the X Y Z Affair, Charles Talleyrand fled to America to escape the revolution in France. He lived in the United States for two years.

When President Adams heard of these proposals, he made a full report to Congress. In the report Adams detailed what was being asked of the United States. He did not name the three French agents that had made these requests. Instead he called them X, Y, and Z. The newspapers of the time called the entire business the X Y Z Affair.

The American public was proud of its three ministers for refusing to give a bribe to the French government. Many people, including the Federalists led by Alexander Hamilton, wanted the United States to declare war on France. Adams did not feel that the United States was ready for another war. He was determined that if war came, France would have to start it. Adams asked Congress to create a new Department of the Navy. Congress did this and voted to increase the size and strength of both the army and the navy. Congress also repealed the treaty of alliance signed with France in 1778.

The war that was never declared between the United States and France nevertheless resulted in many sea battles. The American merchant ship emerged victorious from this seven-and-a-half-hour duel.

Undeclared War. President Adams stopped all trade between France and the United States. He also encouraged citizens who owned ships to fight against armed French vessels. These actions by the President and the military buildup by Congress led to an undeclared war with France lasting from 1798 to 1800.

The ships of the new United States Navy won many battles with French ships of the same size. The United States captured over eighty French ships, including naval and armed trading vessels. During the two-year war, however, the United States lost several hundred of its own ships.

This undeclared war between France and the United States pleased Great Britain. Great Britain gave the United States military supplies and sent naval officers to help train the new recruits. American neutrality was slipping away. It seemed as if the United States would become Great Britain's ally in its war with France.

French officials indicated that they were willing to discuss the problems between the United States and France. President Adams quickly sent a representative to France to meet with Talleyrand. In 1800 the United States and France signed a treaty that stopped the undeclared naval war.

Domestic Affairs

The undeclared war with France created many problems for President Adams at home. Members of his party, the Federalists, were upset with him for not officially going to war with France. Adams fired two of his Cabinet officers over this issue. French citizens living in the United States also attacked Adams over his stand on the war. These people supported Thomas Jefferson and the Republican Party. Adams searched for a solution to these domestic problems.

Adams and Legislation. Adams decided that the criticism from French citizens living in the United States had to be quieted. Adams proposed, and Congress passed, a series of laws that the President hoped would accomplish this goal.

The *Naturalization* Act was passed in 1798. Naturalization is the granting of citizenship to a person born in another country. This law lengthened the amount of time it took for a foreign citizen to become a United States citizen from five to fourteen years. This measure was passed to punish those foreign people who supported Jefferson.

The *Alien* Act also passed Congress. An alien is a person living in another country who has not become a naturalized citizen. This Alien Act allowed the President to *deport,* or send out of the country, any alien thought to be "dangerous to the peace and safety of the United States." The Federalists who controlled the Congress passed this law because they

In the Houſe of Repreſentatives,

NOVEMBER 10th, 1798.

THE HOUSE according to the ſtanding Order of the Day, reſolved itſelf into a Committee of the Whole on the ſtate of the Commonwealth,

Mr. CALDWELL in the Chair,

And after ſometime ſpent therein the Speaker reſumed the Chair, and Mr. Caldwell reported, that the Committee had according to order had under conſideration the Governor's Addreſs, and had come to the following RESOLUTIONS thereupon, which he delivered in at the Clerk's table, where they were twice read and agreed to by the Houſe.

I. RESOLVED, that the ſeveral ſtates compoſing the United States of America, are not united on the principle of unlimited ſubmiſſion to their General Government; but that by compact under the ſtyle and title of a Conſtitution for the United States and of amendments thereto, they conſtituted a General Government for ſpecial purpoſes, delegated

terfeiting the ſecurities and current coin of the United States, piracies and felonies committed on the High Seas, and offences againſt the laws of nations, and no other crimes whatever, and it being true as a general principle, and one of the amendments to the Conſtitution having alſo declared, "that the powers not delegated to the United States by the Conſtitution, nor prohibited by it to the ſtates, are reſerved to the ſtates reſpectively, or to the people," therefore alſo the ſame act of Congreſs paſſed on the 14th day of July, 1798, and entitled "An act in addition to the act entitled an act for the puniſhment of certain crimes againſt the United States;" as alſo the act paſſed by them on the 27th day of June, 1798, entitled "An act to puniſh frauds committed on the Bank of the United States" (and all other their acts which aſſume to create, define, or puniſh crimes other than thoſe enumerated in the conſtitution) are altogether void and of no force, and that the power to create, define, and puniſh ſuch other crimes is reſerved, and of right

This document is a copy of the original Kentucky Resolutions, read and passed by the state legislature in November 1798. The document was written by Thomas Jefferson in old style print and was left untitled.

wanted Republican newspaper editors who were aliens deported. President Adams did not put this law into effect; no one was deported.

The most widely enforced law passed by Congress was the *Sedition* Act. Sedition is the act of causing rebellion against the government in power. This law made it a crime to write or say anything "false, scandalous, or malicious" about the government. This law, like the Alien Act, was aimed at the Republican newspaper editors who supported Thomas Jefferson. Adams did enforce this law. Ten people were convicted of sedition—most received fines and jail sentences.

DISCUSSION

Discuss with the students the reasons why a President would support a law such as the Sedition Act, which restricted the writing or saying of anything "false, scandalous or malicious about the government." Ask students if they disapprove of any of the laws discussed in Chapter 10. How would people today feel if the government prevented them from discussing their disagreements?

Kentucky and Virginia Resolutions. Jefferson and Madison did not have the same ideas about government that John Adams did. They believed that the states, not the central government, should have most of the power. When Congress passed the Alien and Sedition Acts, Jefferson and Madison set forth their ideas of government in two resolutions. Jefferson wrote the Kentucky Resolutions, which were approved by that state's legislature in 1798. Madison authored the Virginia Resolutions, also passed in 1798.

These resolutions declared that the Constitution was an agreement between the states. In the Constitution, Jefferson and Madison argued, specific powers were given to each branch of government. These men believed that one branch of government could not pass a law or take an action that was not listed in the Constitution. If it did, the states had the right to decide if the law or action was constitutional.

Copies of the Kentucky and Virginia Resolutions were sent to every state in the Union. Jefferson and Madison wanted the states to join together to declare the Alien and

REPUBLICANS

Turn out, turn out and save your Country from ruin !

From an *Emperor*—from a *King*—from the iron grasp of a *British Tory Faction*—an unprincipled banditti of British speculators. The hireling tools and emissaries of his majesty king George the 3d have thronged our city and diffused the poison of principles among us.

DOWN WITH THE TORIES, DOWN WITH THE BRITISH FACTION,

Before they have it in their power to enslave you, and reduce your families to distress by heavy taxation. Republicans want no Tribute-liars—they want no ship Ocean-liars—they want no Rufus King's for Lords—they want no Varick to lord it over them—they want no Jones for senator, who fought with the British against the Americans in time of the war.—But they want in their places such men as

Jefferson & Clinton,

who fought their Country's Battles in the year '76

The campaign poster of Thomas Jefferson called on Republicans to fight against all restrictions of human freedom. Jefferson claimed that the country would be saved from ruin by electing men who had "fought their country's battles."

Sedition Acts unconstitutional, but none would. Instead, most northern states took the position that only the federal courts could declare laws and actions passed or taken by Congress to be unconstitutional.

Jefferson responded to this argument by saying that since the states were partners who agreed to the Constitution, the states had the right to decide whether something went against the Constitution. Jefferson wrote that states had the right to *nullify,* or legally cancel, any law they felt was unconstitutional. Both states—Kentucky and Virginia—however, declared that they were loyal to the Union and did not take any steps to nullify the Alien and Sedition Acts.

The presidential election of 1800 approached and once again John Adams and Thomas Jefferson were the opponents. Both sides had their supporters, but Adams was in political trouble. His own party was angry at him for his policy toward the war with France. Many Americans were upset with him over his enforcement of the Alien and Sedition Acts. Still, he was pleased with himself. He said he wanted his grave marker to read: "Here lies John Adams who took upon himself the responsibility for peace with France in the year 1800."

ANSWER THESE QUESTIONS

1. What were the five largest cities in the United States in 1790?
2. What three people did Adams send to France to negotiate a treaty?
3. What actions did Congress take after Adams explained the X Y Z Affair?
4. What was the difference between the Alien Act and the Sedition Act?
5. Why were the Kentucky and Virginia Resolutions so important?

ANSWER THESE QUESTIONS

1. Philadelphia, New York, Boston, Charleston, Baltimore
2. Marshall, Gerry, Pinckney
3. Congress created a Department of the Navy, increased the size of both the Navy and Army, and repealed the 1778 treaty of alliance with France.
4. The Alien Act allowed the President to deport aliens that were dangerous. The Sedition Act made it a crime to write or say things against the government.
5. This was the first time the idea of nullification was presented.

Objective: After completing this page, students should be able to take notes.

Taking Notes

When you write a note to a friend, you write down what you want to say in a few words or sentences. When you take notes from your textbook, you do the same thing. You write down the important ideas in a few words or sentences. Why take notes? Taking notes in class is one way of getting important information down quickly so that you can study it later when you have more time to do a good job. These notes that you take during a class can help you study for a test or even write a paper.

The hard part about taking notes is deciding which information is important enough to write down. How do you do this? Ask yourself these questions when you read a sentence or paragraph: Who or what is being talked about? What is happening? When did something happen?

When you answer these questions, most likely you will have the important information that you will need. Once you have the important ideas, write them down in a shortened form that you can understand. Read the following three sentences.

> John Adams of the Federalist Party and Thomas Jefferson of the Republican Party ran for the Presidency. Although it was a close contest, Adams got a majority of the electoral votes. Thomas Jefferson, getting the second highest number of votes, became Vice President.

What are the important ideas in these sentences?

- Adams—Federalist Party; Jefferson—Republican Party; Ran for President
- Adams—majority of votes
- Jefferson—second highest number of votes—became V. President.

Notice that these important ideas are in a shortened form that you can understand. Turn to page 278 and the section entitled X Y Z Affair, and take notes on the first four paragraphs. Remember to ask the three questions to help you decide what is important enough to write down.

Working with Skills

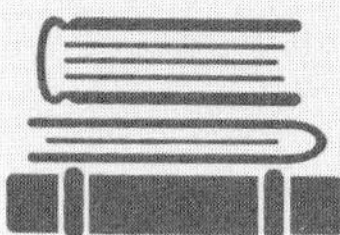

ACTIVITY

Objective: To take notes

Read aloud a passage from Lesson 10-2. As the lesson is read, have students write down the major points that are mentioned. Then have students compare what they have noted as important. Discuss these points with the class and try to determine with the students why there may be differences.

RELATED MATERIALS

Duplicator/Copy Master Activity 22

THINKING THINGS THROUGH

1. Federalists favored loose interpretation, while Republicans wanted to interpret the Constitution strictly. **2.** to prove that the new nation and its Constitution worked without any problems. **3.** They used Jefferson's argument that the Constitution gave the federal government only certain powers, and the states could nullify federal acts that went beyond those powers.

Chapter 10 SUMMARY

George Washington, the first President of the United States, understood that his administration had to make careful decisions or the nation could be led in the wrong direction. A Cabinet created by Congress helped Washington make these decisions.

Congress set up a federal court system during Washington's term. Congress said that six justices would form the Supreme Court. Washington chose John Jay to be Chief Justice.

Alexander Hamilton, Washington's secretary of the treasury, came up with a plan that would make the United States financially sound. Hamilton presented his plan to Congress, which passed most of it.

Not everyone agreed with Hamilton. Arguments over his plan led to the rise of political parties. Hamilton was the leader of the Federalist Party, and Thomas Jefferson was the leader of the Republican Party.

Washington felt that the United States should stay out of Europe's problems. He wanted the United States to remain neutral. When Washington left office after eight years, he warned Americans against becoming involved with any nation.

John Adams, the second President, agreed with Washington. However, France did not make it easy for Adams to remain neutral. France refused to accept Adams's minister and asked the United States for a bribe to begin discussing a treaty.

Adams also had problems at home. Congress passed the Alien and Sedition Acts in an attempt to quiet Adams's enemies.

Chapter 10 TEST

WORDS TO REMEMBER

Match each of the following words with the correct definition.

h	1. precedent	b	6. alien
g	2. assumption	i	7. deport
d	3. tariff	e	8. sedition
f	4. neutrality	c	9. nullify
a	5. impressment		

a. forcing American sailors to serve in the British navy

b. a person living in another country who is not a citizen

c. to legally cancel

d. a tax on imports

e. causing rebellion against the government in power

f. not taking either side in a disagreement

g. taking over

h. an example that may be followed later

i. to send out of the country

THINKING THINGS THROUGH

Answer the following questions.

1. How did the Federalists and Republicans differ in their feelings about the United States Constitution?
2. Why did Alexander Hamilton feel it was important for the United States to pay its debts?
3. How did the Kentucky and Virginia Resolutions reflect Jefferson's opinions about the Constitution?

RELATED MATERIALS

Duplicator/Copy Masters: Activities 21, 22; Quiz 21

Workbook pages 29-31

WORKING WITH SKILLS

sample notes:

Ben Franklin: liberty of press—goes too far, too much freedom to insult, lie, and condemn

Thomas Jefferson: liberty of press helps form public opinion, lets the people be interested in government

---

WORKING WITH SKILLS

Benjamin Franklin believed that the Constitution allowed newspapers too much freedom. He criticized the press on the following grounds:

It may make accusations of all kinds against all persons, judge, sentence, and condemn without a fair hearing. It favors about 1 citizen in 500. This five-hundredth part of the citizens can accuse and abuse the other 499 parts at their pleasure. If the *liberty of the press* meant merely the liberty to discuss news and opinions, I would be in favor of it. But if it means liberty to insult, lie about and condemn one another, I would cheerfully agree to trade my freedom of abusing others for the privilege of not being abused myself.

Thomas Jefferson strongly disagreed:

The basis of our government is public opinion. We must protect the right of the public to have opinions. Were it left to me to decide whether we should have a government without newspapers, or newspapers without a government, I should choose the latter. All people should receive newspapers and be taught to read them. If once the people lose interest in our government, then the country is lost.

What are the main ideas in each of these opinions? Write them down as if you were taking notes.

ON YOUR OWN

1. Ask five adults whether they think newspapers, radio, and television have too much freedom. Take down their answers in your notes and then discuss your findings with the class. Decide if the adults' opinions agree with those of Jefferson or Franklin.
2. Go to your school library and find an article in an encyclopedia that deals with George Washington. Take notes on Washington's major accomplishments while in office. Do the same for John Adams.
3. Look carefully at the picture below. It shows a detail from a painting of George Washington and the Marquis de Lafayette at Mount Vernon, Washington's home. Imagine that you lived on a southern plantation like Mount Vernon during the years just after the Revolution. Write a paragraph describing a typical day in your life. Use information from your textbook or an encyclopedia as well as any ideas you may get from the picture.

Chapter 11
THE VIRGINIA DYNASTY

Chapter 11 describes the political and economic changes that resulted from a rapid increase in the population and area of the United States in the early 1800s. Lesson 11-1 discusses the presidency of Thomas Jefferson. Lesson 11-2 focuses on James Madison and the events surrounding the War of 1812. Lesson 11-3 features James Monroe and the long-term significance for American foreign policy of the Monroe Doctrine, as well as the birth of two political parties.

CONTENT OBJECTIVES

After completing the lesson, students will know:

- the significance of the Louisiana Purchase
- about Lewis and Clark's successful expedition to the West
- that Jefferson's administration was confronted by many threats to the peace

VOCABULARY

dynasty: a group of rulers from the same family or line
unconstitutional: not allowed by the Constitution
expedition: an organized group of people making a trip
blockade: the closing off of an area to prevent people and supplies from going in and out

11-1 Thomas Jefferson

As you read, think about these questions:
How did Jefferson differ from his opponents, John Marshall and John Randolph?
How did the United States get the Louisiana Territory?
Who helped the explorers of Louisiana during their travels?
How did President Jefferson try to stop Great Britain from harming America on the seas?

Special Vocabulary	dynasty	expedition
	unconstitutional	blockade

The election of 1800 raised some new questions that the framers of the Constitution had not anticipated. Two members of the same party, Thomas Jefferson and Aaron Burr, both Republicans, had tied each other with the most votes. At first, it seemed that Jefferson had won the election. He had received 73 electoral votes to Adams's 65. Then it became known that Aaron Burr, another member of Jefferson's party, had also received 73 electoral votes. The electors had meant to choose Burr as Vice President, but instead a tie had resulted. The election would have to be decided by the House of Representatives. Burr had been expected to give way to Thomas Jefferson. Instead, Burr saw a chance to become President himself. He refused to step aside as agreed. Time after time, the members of the House voted. Each vote ended in a tie. Finally, Federalist Alexander Hamilton, believing Jefferson to be the better candidate, gave him his support.

The "Revolution" of 1800

On March 4, 1801, Jefferson became the first President to take the oath of office in the brand-new capital city of Washington, D.C. He had called his election "The Revolution of 1800," as though it had been a huge change in direction for America. Later events proved this claim to be overstated. In his inaugural address, he declared "We are all Federalists, we are all Republicans." These words sounded as if somehow the spirit of party had been erased by his election. In fact, as time passed, there seemed to be greater divisions than ever in American politics.

A Dynasty Begins. Thomas Jefferson was the first in a series of three Presidents from Virginia who served from 1801 to 1825. These leaders had played key roles in setting up the United States. They had begun as strong believers in the rights of the states, but slowly they swung some of their beliefs toward those of the Federalists. As time passed, people began to call the three Presidents the Virginia *Dynasty*. A dynasty is a group of rulers from the same family or line. Americans were playfully likening the Republican Presidents from Virginia to a hated royal family.

Thomas Jefferson is widely known as the author of the Declaration of Independence and the nation's third President. He was also an architect, farmer, inventor, scientist, musician, and student of languages.

Worthy Opponents. Some of Jefferson's toughest political opponents were also Virginians and related to him. One was his distant cousin John Marshall, the Chief Justice of the United States from 1801 to 1835. Marshall guarded the nationalist point of view of the Federalists. John Randolph, another cousin, was a powerful member of the House of Representatives. He guarded the states' rights views of the Republican Party. Marshall and Randolph often were in battle with the President.

The Nation Grows

In 1801 the French forced the Spanish to return New Orleans and all of Louisiana to France. The French seemed to be making plans to create a French empire in Louisiana. The first step in setting up this empire was to close New Orleans to American shipping.

In 1802 events in French Saint Domingue, today known as Haiti, ended French ideas about an American empire. Toussaint L'Ouverture, a black leader and a former slave, led a revolt against the French. L'Ouverture and the other former slaves defeated a huge French army in battle. Then war broke out in Europe. The French gave up their plans for a new American empire. Now they wanted to get rid of New Orleans and all of Louisiana.

Toussaint L'Ouverture died in a French prison in 1803. Yet his courageous leadership had made it possible for Haiti to declare its independence in 1804.

DISCUSSION

Explain to the students that Thomas Jefferson has often been called America's greatest statesman by historians. Yet he went beyond the powers granted to a President in the Constitution when he arranged the Louisiana Purchase. Have the students discuss whether they think the Louisiana Purchase was legal. Remind them that the Constitution does not forbid acquisition of new land but simply does not mention the topic. Ask if any agree with the Federalists that Jefferson's actions were unconstitutional. Ask if others think it is acceptable for Presidents to be innovative as leaders, so long as they do not directly go against the Constitution.

The Louisiana Purchase. Meanwhile, President Jefferson had sent American diplomats to France to try to buy New Orleans. Talleyrand, the French foreign minister, astonished the American ministers by offering to sell all of Louisiana to the United States for $15 million. The American ministers quickly accepted and signed a treaty in May 1803 to make the Louisiana Purchase.

Jefferson knew that the Constitution said nothing about buying new territory. The bargain, however, was too good to let pass. Jefferson, the supporter of a strict reading of the Constitution, decided to interpret the Constitution loosely. Some Federalists, fearing the impact of such a vast addition to the country, said the purchase was *unconstitutional*, or not allowed by the Constitution.

French soldiers fire a salute to the American flag in New Orleans on December 20, 1803. On that day, the United States took control of the Louisiana Territory.

Sacajawea interprets for Lewis and Clark in a meeting with Indians on the Columbia River. This Shoshone woman—whose name means "canoe pusher"—took her baby with her on the long expedition.

In spite of all the political arguments, Congress approved the purchase. The addition of Louisiana doubled the size of the United States. It provided rich new lands for pioneer farmers. It also brought lands around the Mississippi River under American control. Through the port of New Orleans, the United States could control trade on the Mississippi.

The Lewis and Clark Expedition. Jefferson appointed Meriwether Lewis, his private secretary, to lead a group to explore the land west of the Mississippi River. Lewis chose William Clark, an army officer, to be coleader of the *expedition*, or organized group of people making the trip.

The Lewis and Clark party of about forty explorers camped near the French village of St. Louis during the winter of 1803–1804. When spring came they set out to follow the Missouri River to its source. (Find the route of Lewis and Clark's expedition on the map on page 324.) By late autumn of 1804 the group, having traveled 1600 miles (2560 kilometers), settled in for the winter in what is now North Dakota. They named their settlement Fort Mandan after the friendly American Indians they met there.

At Fort Mandan, Lewis and Clark met a French fur trader, Toussaint Charbonneau, and his Shoshone wife, Sacajawea. Sacajawea proved most helpful. She knew the way across the Rocky Mountains and helped Lewis and Clark through lands that could have been dangerous. The Shoshone lived in western Montana and Idaho. Sacajawea's brother was their chief. The Shoshone, therefore, allowed the expedition to pass through their territory unharmed.

ACTIVITY

Objectives: To use reference materials and to locate information

Have the students research background information about the Lewis and Clark expedition. Have them find answers to one of the following sets of questions: (1) Who went on the expedition? How were they chosen? How did they prepare for the trip? (2) What obstacles were faced by the expedition in crossing the mountains? Were they prepared for them? (3) What were their relations, good and bad, with the Indians along the way? What role did Sacajawea play in these relations?

Finally, in November 1805, the Lewis and Clark expedition arrived at the Pacific Coast. There they built Fort Clatsop near present-day Astoria, Oregon. In the spring of 1806, the explorers began the trip home. They reached St. Louis in September 1806.

The Lewis and Clark expedition had been a great success. The explorers had mapped the entire length of the Missouri River from St. Louis to western Montana. They also had mapped the way from Montana to the Pacific Coast. Scientists with the explorers brought back samples of rocks and plants. Artists on the expedition returned with pictures of fish, plants, animals, and the countryside they had sketched along their route. The explorers had also been able to study the Native Americans they met.

Zebulon Pike. The Jefferson administration encouraged other explorers to examine western lands. In 1805 the army sent Lieutenant Zebulon Pike along with twenty soldiers to look for the source of the Mississippi River. Pike and his soldiers explored the banks of the Mississippi and visited lands that are parts of present-day Missouri, Illinois, Iowa, Wisconsin, and Minnesota.

A year later Pike went west along the Arkansas River and reached a spot near present-day Pueblo, Colorado. There he saw the huge mountain nearby which today bears his name, Pikes Peak.

Preventing War

President Jefferson won a second term in office in 1804. Early in this second term, troubles arose abroad which the young nation had to face, like it or not. The troubles arose from the British, the French, and North African pirates.

Barbary Pirates. Since the 1700s pirates from the north coast of Africa had been seizing foreign ships and crews, including Americans, sailing on the Mediterranean. These Barbary pirates—from Algeria, Tripoli, Tunis, and Morocco—held their captives until they received large payments.

In the 1790s the United States had agreed to pay Algeria and Tripoli "protection money" each year to leave American ships alone. In 1801 Tripoli declared war on the United States anyway. Jefferson responded by sending warships to the Mediterranean.

The Tripolitan War had little effect on life in the United States. Only a few warships were involved. Americans, however, were proud when they heard that Navy Lieutenant Stephen Decatur had led a daring raid into the harbor of Tripoli and that a group of young naval soldiers, called marines, had played a brilliant part in the fighting.

In 1805 Tripoli finally agreed to end the war. Tripoli signed a treaty agreeing to free its American prisoners for $60,000. The United States, however, continued to pay protection money to the other Barbary States until 1816.

Embargo Act. In 1803 the British and the French renewed their war against each other. In 1807 the British *blockaded* Europe to starve the French. A blockade is the closing off of an area to prevent people and supplies from going in and out. Any neutral ships that wanted to trade with France had

Stephen Decatur set the U.S.S. *Philadelphia* on fire in the Tripoli harbor to defeat the Barbary pirates. This battle is referred to in the lyrics of "The Marines' Hymn." The song begins with the words, "From the halls of Montezuma to the shores of Tripoli."

The wharf at Salem, Massachusetts, was quiet after passage of the Embargo Act in 1807. The embargo harmed the business of New England traders and shipbuilders.

to go to Great Britain first and pay for the right to carry their cargo to Europe. The British navy seized or destroyed any ships disobeying this law. In return, the French passed their own law in 1807 saying they would seize any neutral ship that stopped in Great Britain.

In December 1807, with Jefferson's approval, Congress passed the Embargo Act. The act forbade trading ships to enter or leave American ports. If the United States refused to send its ships to trade with the Europeans, Jefferson reasoned, the Europeans would not be able to attack them.

Unfortunately, the Embargo Act hurt Americans more than it did the Europeans. Europeans did not need American trade as badly as Congress thought they did. As a result of the embargo, people living in port cities such as Boston, New York, Baltimore, Philadelphia, and Charleston felt very hard times.

Randolph spoke for people who believed that the Constitution gave no President the power to make a national decision on issues like the Embargo Act. Congress finally repealed the Embargo Act after fourteen months. Jefferson signed the bill on March 1, 1809—just three days before he left office.

ANSWER THESE QUESTIONS

1. Randolph had a stronger belief in states' rights.
2. France
3. Mandan and Shoshone
4. Meriwether Lewis, William Clark, Zebulon Pike
5. It did not keep Great Britain and France from attacking American ships, and it hurt American trade.

ANSWER THESE QUESTIONS

1. How were John Randolph's ideas different from Jefferson's?
2. From what country was the Louisiana Territory purchased?
3. What two tribes of American Indians provided help to the Lewis and Clark expedition?
4. What three explorers were encouraged by Jefferson?
5. Why was the Embargo Act a failure?

Judicial Review

In the first years of Thomas Jefferson's presidency, most people considered the Supreme Court a weak part of the federal government. A decision by John Marshall helped strengthen the court. The decision was handed down in the court case *Marbury v. Madison* in 1803. Here are the facts of the case. President Adams had appointed many Federalist judges just before he left office. One was William Marbury. President Jefferson disapproved of a Federalist for this job. He ordered James Madison, the secretary of state, not to deliver the official appointment paper to Marbury. Marbury asked the Supreme Court to order the paper to be sent.

John Marshall worried about ordering the President to do something. What if Jefferson refused to enforce a court order? The Court had no way of forcing him to act.

With this problem in mind, all the judges of the Supreme Court reviewed the case. They asked three questions: Did Marbury have a right to the job? Could he take his case to a court? Was the Supreme Court the right court?

Marshall tried to avoid a battle with Jefferson as he answered the questions. He declared that Marbury had a right to the job and that he could bring the case to a court for settlement. Marshall said, however, that the Supreme Court did not have jurisdiction in the case. By this he meant that the Supreme Court had no right to hear and decide this case. He pointed out that the Constitution says that only certain cases may be heard by the Supreme Court. *Marbury v. Madison* was not one of those kinds of cases. (Read Article 3 of the Constitution on pages 244–245.)

In another part of his decision, Marshall increased the power of the court. Marbury had brought his case to the court because the Federal Judiciary Act of 1789, passed by Congress, said that the Supreme Court could issue the order Marbury wanted. Marshall, however, called the Judiciary Act unconstitutional because it gave the court powers not granted to it in the Constitution. By reaching this decision Marshall took power from the legislative branch. This set up the rule that the Supreme Court had the right to decide whether or not laws passed by Congress were constitutional. This rule is called the power of judicial review.

LAW AND THE CITIZEN

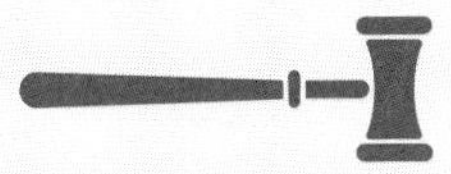

CONTENT OBJECTIVES

After completing the lesson, students will know:

- the events leading up to the War of 1812
- the role of the Indians in this war
- about the major battles that took place
- how the resolutions made at the Hartford Convention caused the Federalist Party to lose support
- that the Treaty of Ghent ended the war in 1814

VOCABULARY

War Hawks: legislators who favor war

ACTIVITY

Objective: To locate places on a map

Provide students with a United States outline map (Duplicator/Copy Master Activity 71.) Direct them to locate and label on the map the areas where the War of 1812 was fought. Include the following: New York state, Ohio, Northwest Territory, Canada, Pennsylvania, Louisiana, and Indiana. Within each of these geographic areas, specific battles were fought. Have students identify in red on the map the following cities, bodies of water, and geographic areas: Tippecanoe Creek, Wabash River, Niagara Falls, Lake Ontario, Lake Erie, Detroit, Presque Isle, Horseshoe Bend, Washington, D.C., and New Orleans.

11-2 James Madison

As you read, think about these questions:

What were the causes of the War of 1812?

Who was for and who was against the war?

What were some successes and failures of the American war effort?

Special Vocabulary War Hawks

The second President of the Virginia Dynasty was James Madison. By 1809 the behavior of Great Britain had grown into a huge problem for Madison and the United States. Britain continued to prevent American ships from trading in European ports. The British navy still bullied Americans at sea, taking sailors off ships and impressing them into the British navy. In addition, the British in Canada seemed to be waiting for a chance to cause trouble in the northwestern part of the United States.

Background to War

Like Jefferson, Madison did not want war with the British. He knew that the American army and navy were weak and poorly equipped to fight. Some Americans, however, especially a group of westerners and southerners, demanded war. Westerners and southerners in favor of war saw the American Indians building up strength. They feared that the British were supporting the Indians in the Northwest Territory and the Alabama country. Fighting the British and taking Canada from them would remove this threat.

The War Hawks. In 1810 a group of newly elected members of Congress arrived in Washington. Many of these new legislators favored war against the British. John C. Calhoun of South Carolina was a leader of the group. Other new legislators who favored war were Henry Clay of Kentucky, Felix Grundy of Tennessee, and Peter Porter of western New York. Not all southerners and westerners agreed with these views. John Randolph of Virginia, for example, angrily called these members *"War Hawks."*

The Battle of Tippecanoe. Unhappy events were also taking place on the American frontier in the early 1800s. Newcomers from the East were pressing westward from the original thirteen states into Indian lands. Native Americans like the Shawnee watched their lands disappear into the hands of the newcomers. At times the Indians fought back, at other times they signed treaties with the newcomers. Often one side or the other broke the treaties. To make matters worse, the British supplied guns to the Native Americans.

There seemed to be no peaceful outcome to their arguments. War seemed the only answer. Tecumseh, a leader of the Shawnee, tried to unite the Indian nations of North America to fight the newcomers. He and his brother, the Prophet, set up headquarters at a settlement called Tippecanoe, where the Tippecanoe Creek flows into the Wabash River in Indiana. In 1811 William Henry Harrison, governor of the Indiana Territory, attacked the Indians at Tippecanoe with about 1100 soldiers. After about two hours of hard fighting, Harrison and his troops drove the Indians into a swamp and destroyed their settlement. Tecumseh and thousands of his followers escaped to Canada.

James Madison, like Jefferson, was a scholar. His interest in constitutional history helped him play a major role in the Constitutional Convention.

The War of 1812

Just as the United States could see no peaceful way out of war against Tecumseh in 1811, it could find no peaceful way to end the abuses of the British. On June 18, 1812, therefore, Congress declared war on Great Britain.

The Invasion of Canada. The American generals made a plan that they believed would lead to victory against the British in Canada. The three-part plan called for one army, led by Henry Dearborn, to follow the route to Canada through the valley of Lake Champlain. A second army under Stephen Van Rensselaer would attack Canada across the Niagara River between Lakes Ontario and Erie. A third army under the command of William Hull would march through Detroit into Canada.

Tecumseh, whose name means "Shooting Star," led a brilliant but unsuccessful effort to resist American settlement of Indian lands.

Not one of the three parts of the American plan worked. In August 1812, Hull entered Canada for a time, but returned to Detroit. There a British force made up of Canadians and Tecumseh's Indians surrounded the Americans. Hull surrendered his entire army of 2200 soldiers. (Find Hull's route on the map on page 296.) In October, Van

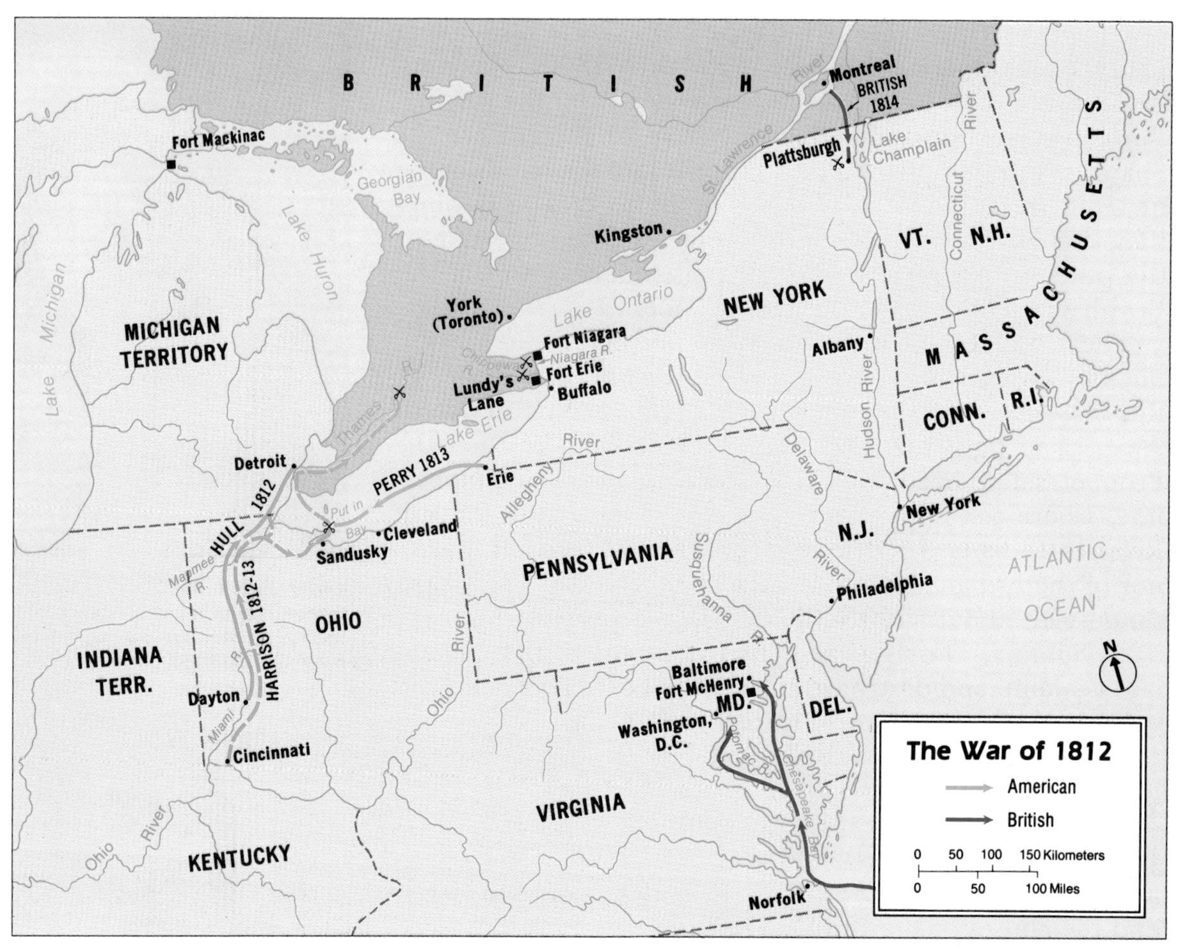

The American and British campaigns during the War of 1812 are marked on this map. Which two places did the British attack from Chesapeake Bay? Washington, D.C.; Fort McHenry

Rensselaer entered Canada across the Niagara River. The Americans expected help from the New York State militia. The militia, however, never arrived because the soldiers refused to leave the states and enter Canada. In November, Dearborn's assignment suffered the same end. When the Americans got to the Canadian border, the militia refused to go any farther.

The War at Sea. If not for the success of the United States Navy, the War of 1812 might have ended after a few months, with the United States as the loser. American warships, however, had several big victories. The American victories at sea proved to the British that they could not count on a free hand at sea; they would have to take some losses. Still, the British effectively blockaded the ports of the United States from 1813 until the end of the war.

The American ship *Constitution* defeated the British ship *Guerrière* near Newfoundland in 1812. Nicknamed "Old Ironsides," the *Constitution* became a symbol of American determination and courage.

Control of Lake Erie. One reason why the Americans could not win battles near the shores of Lake Erie was the presence of a small British fleet in the lake. The British fleet could transport soldiers and supplies from place to place quickly.

The United States Navy sent Captain Oliver Hazard Perry to Presque Isle (near present-day Erie, Pennsylvania) to build and command a lake fleet. Perry put together a small American fleet between March and June of 1813.

In September the two fleets met at Put-In Bay in the southwestern part of Lake Erie. They fought for three hours with Perry himself in command of the American fleet. At the end of the bloody battle, the Americans had a big victory. Then Perry sent a message to General William Henry Harrison, which afterwards was repeated all over the United States. It read, "We have met the enemy, and they are ours."

With Lake Erie in American hands, Harrison led his army of 4500 Kentucky volunteers to Detroit. From there the Americans chased the enemy into Canada, where the two sides fought the Battle of the Thames. In this October 1813 battle, Tecumseh was killed, the Americans gained control of their Northwestern Territory, and the British lost a spot from which they could attack the American frontier.

The Creek War. In 1813 the Creeks of the Alabama country joined the struggle against the newcomers on the frontier. In return, two thousand Tennesseans led by a frontier lawyer, Andrew Jackson, attacked and destroyed a number of Creek villages. They also fought a huge battle at Horseshoe Bend against the Creeks and the Cherokee. The outcome of the Battle of Horseshoe Bend was terrible for the Indians. More than nine hundred were killed.

DISCUSSION

Explain to the students that the burning of the White House was one low point of the War of 1812. Review for the class the definition of *symbol,* a thing that stands for something else. Have the class discuss whether they think symbols of national unity like the White House and the American flag are important to the nation and why. Have the students discuss specifically what they think makes up a nation—the land, the people, common history, or common goals? Ask if students think that symbols are mainly of sentimental value or if they provide a concrete focus for unity.

The Final Year. Between July and September of 1814, the Americans won the Battle of Chippewa across the Niagara River in Canada and the naval Battle of Lake Champlain. The British, however, made a surprise attack on Washington, D.C., and burned almost every public building there. They chased the American government, including President Madison, from the city. Dolley Madison, the President's wife, won a lasting reputation for bravery by staying at the White House until the last minute to save valuable documents.

After burning Washington, D.C., the British attacked Baltimore, Maryland, and nearby Fort McHenry. The British fleet pounded the fort with their cannon during a terrible night bombardment. Francis Scott Key, a Washington lawyer, witnessed the attack from the deck of an American ship. When daybreak came, he was overjoyed to see the American flag still flying over Fort McHenry. In inspired excitement he composed a poem, "The Star-Spangled Banner." Later put to an old English tune, it became the national anthem.

Treaty of Ghent. By the summer of 1814, neither side seemed to be gaining anything in the war. Representatives from Great Britain and the United States met in Ghent,

The ease with which the British captured and burned Washington in 1814 proved how weak American defenses were at the time.

Belgium, to begin peace talks. The Treaty of Ghent was signed on Christmas Eve, 1814. It ended the war, although it did not end the fighting immediately.

Battle of New Orleans. Before news of the treaty reached the United States, American soldiers won their greatest victory of the war. Late in 1814 Andrew Jackson led his frontier soldiers to New Orleans. There eight thousand British redcoats were preparing to attack the city. Jackson's force included militia soldiers, sailors, about four hundred thirty free blacks, and some pirates. In the Battle of New Orleans, January 15, 1815, the Americans killed or wounded more than two thousand of the enemy. Among Jackson's troops, only eight were killed and thirteen were wounded.

The Hartford Convention. From the very beginning of the War of 1812, many people in New England and New York City opposed the war. In fact, during the last weeks of the war, not knowing that peace was near, a group of Federalists from New England met in Hartford, Connecticut, to find a way to end "Mr. Madison's War," as the President's critics called it.

The delegates at the Hartford Convention, as the meeting was called, voted to accept a resolution which claimed that the states had a right to defy the national government in cases such as the War of 1812. To other Americans the words of the resolution at the Hartford Convention sounded like

Terrible slaughter occurred in the Battle of New Orleans. The British commander had insisted on marching his troops straight into strongly held American positions.

ANSWER THESE QUESTIONS

1. the British alliances with American Indians, impressment of American sailors, British refusal to permit American ships to trade in European ports
2. newly elected members of Congress who favored war with the British
3. the Battle of New Orleans
4. Delegates to the Hartford Convention, many of whom were Federalists, voted to accept a resolution which other Americans thought sounded like treason.
5. Both men successfully fought Native Americans.

treason. Since so many of those attending the meetings were Federalists, the Federalist Party lost much of its support outside New England. After the Hartford Convention, the Federalist Party was no longer a force in American politics as it had been in the past.

ANSWER THESE QUESTIONS

1. What were three causes of the War of 1812?
2. Who were the "War Hawks"?
3. What was the greatest American victory of the War of 1812?
4. Why did the Federalist Party lose its support outside New England?
5. How were William Henry Harrison and Andrew Jackson alike?

CONTENT OBJECTIVES

After completing the lesson, students will know:

- the roots of the Panic of 1819
- about the controversy surrounding the Missouri Compromise
- the main provisions of the Monroe Doctrine
- how the Democratic and Republican parties developed

VOCABULARY

sectionalism: the practice of holding one's own section of the country higher than other sections or than the country as a whole

free state: one without slaves

11-3 James Monroe

As you read, think about these questions:

What were the causes of the Panic of 1819?

Why did the argument over Missouri frighten many Americans?

Why was the Monroe Doctrine created?

How did the 1824 election lead to the formation of new political parties?

Special Vocabulary sectionalism free state

In 1816 the Republicans chose the third and—as it turned out—last member of the Virginia Dynasty, James Monroe, to be their candidate for President. Then fifty-eight years old, he had given more than forty years of service to the nation. He won the presidential election easily.

Era of Good Feelings

Before and during the War of 1812, some people of various sections of the country had developed mistrust of people from other sections. Many New Englanders felt they had been dragged into a useless war by westerners and southerners. Many westerners and southerners, on the other hand, believed that New Englanders had been traitors to the United States.

During the summer of 1817, the new President made a trip through the northern half of the country, hoping to bring his message of unity to the people. In Boston, one newspaper called Monroe's election the beginning of an "era of good feelings."

Panic of 1819. Things did not always go well during the era of good feelings. Sometimes the bad feelings overwhelmed the good feelings. A severe business depression called the Panic of 1819 upset many Americans.

During the depression, the Second Bank of the United States, created in 1816 and located in the North, gained the mistrust and hatred of many westerners and southerners. In the middle of the hard times, the bank made the people to whom it had loaned money pay it back right away. The bank's action led to the financial ruin of many farmers and business people in the West and South.

The Panic of 1819 worked against the unity that Monroe had hoped to create in his years as President. Now *sectionalism* once again showed itself throughout the country. Sectionalism is the practice of holding one's own section of the country higher than other sections, or even than the country as a whole.

Missouri Compromise. Another powerful issue in creating sectionalism was slavery. In 1803 Missouri came to the United States as part of the Louisiana Purchase. In 1818 Missourians asked Congress to make their territory a state. In 1819 the question arose, should Missouri enter the Union as a slave state or as a *free state*, that is, one without slaves. Many northerners believed the extension of slavery into new lands was wrong. They also saw that the number of slave states might grow faster than the number of free states, giving more power to the southern section in Congress. Of course, southerners saw a similar problem with allowing a new free state into the Union.

In 1820 Congress settled the question with a compromise. The Missouri Compromise allowed Maine to enter the Union as a free state in 1820 and Missouri to enter in 1821 as a slave state. This maintained an equal number of free and slave

James Monroe was the last President of the Revolutionary War generation. He continued to wear a three-cornered hat with his hair powdered and tied back long after these fashions had gone out of style.

DISCUSSION

One of the most important issues during Madison's administration was the threat of sectionalism. Have students explain why people's feelings about slavery created strong sectionalism. Ask the students if they can think of another time when sectionalism caused problems. An example is the War of 1812 when westerners and southerners wanted war and New Englanders did not. Ask students if they can think of more recent examples of sectionalism.

This is the way the House of Representatives looked at the time of the Missouri Compromise. After being lit, the big chandelier was hauled back up by rope and pulley.

states. The compromise drew an imaginary line across the Louisiana Purchase along the parallel 36° 30′ north latitude. Except in Missouri, slavery would not be allowed north of that line.

American Influence Abroad

President Monroe believed that the United States, like it or not, must be involved in affairs outside the national borders. John Quincy Adams, Monroe's secretary of state, understood this too, but worked to have the country involved only where the true national interest required it to be.

Revolutions in Latin America. The Spanish and Portuguese settlements in the New World directly concerned the United States. During the Napoleonic Wars in Europe, Spain and Portugal had neglected their American colonies. This neglect gave a chance to revolutionists throughout Latin America to work for the independence of their countries. Under the leadership of José de San Martín in Argentina, Chile, and Peru; Simón Bolívar in Venezuela, Colombia, and Bolivia; and Agustín de Iturbide in Mexico, one Latin American country after another fell away from European control. By 1825 eleven new nations had come into being in the Western Hemisphere.

At the end of the Napoleonic Wars, Americans worried that the Europeans would return to the New World and bring with them their systems of government. Great Britain worried that France might renew its strength and try to set

José de San Martín helped several nations of South America gain independence. Because he was disappointed with the political situation in South America, he spent the last years of his life in Europe.

up new colonies in the Western Hemisphere. Both the United States and Great Britain hoped to continue the trade with the new Latin American countries that they had developed during the years of war in Europe.

The Monroe Doctrine. In the summer of 1823, Great Britain asked the United States to join it in warning the nations of Europe not to attack the new Latin American countries in order to make them colonies again. Monroe and most of his advisers wanted to accept the British offer. Only Adams objected. Adams wanted America alone by itself to issue a warning to Europe. He argued that this would give the Americans a chance to form an independent foreign policy. Adams persuaded Monroe and the rest of the Cabinet to accept his view.

In his annual message to Congress on December 2, 1823, Monroe stated the policy that some years later became known as the Monroe Doctrine. The main part of the Monroe Doctrine warned European countries that the United States would not allow them to set up new colonies in the Western Hemisphere.

ACTIVITY

Objective: To recognize points of view

Divide the class into three groups representing (1) the United States and Great Britain; (2) Spain, Portugal, and France; and (3) Latin American nations including Argentina, Chile, Mexico, and Venezuela. Have the groups debate the meaning of the Monroe Doctrine and whether they think it fair. Let the group representing Spain, Portugal, and France speak first; have them point out they have the same right to colonies as the British do (and give examples). Have the group representing the Latin American nations discuss how they see the doctrine and whether they think it entitles the United States to take a hand in the affairs of their nations.

The End of the Dynasty

A custom had developed during the Virginia Dynasty. James Madison served as Thomas Jefferson's secretary of state. Then James Monroe served James Madison in the same way. John Quincy Adams, as Monroe's secretary of state, seemed in line to be the next President.

John Quincy Adams—son of John and Abigail—was the only President's son to be elected President.

John Quincy Adams, however, proved to be only one of several candidates. Henry Clay, from Kentucky, and Andrew Jackson, from Tennessee, also wanted to be President. So did William H. Crawford of Georgia and John C. Calhoun of South Carolina. All these candidates belonged to the Republican Party.

No candidate gained enough electoral votes to win the presidency. The members of the House of Representatives voted among the three candidates with the most electoral votes: Jackson, Adams, and Crawford. Henry Clay, now out of the race, gave his support to Adams.

Andrew Jackson was furious. He had won most of the electoral votes and hoped to win the presidency. After Adams won, the new President appointed Henry Clay secretary of state, giving him hope of some day becoming President as all recent secretaries of state had. Andrew Jackson charged that Adams and Clay had made a "corrupt bargain" with each other. The anger that followed caused a complete upset of the Republican Party. Jackson and his supporters started their own party and called themselves Democrats. The Democrats stressed a mild form of states' rights. They appealed to ordinary western and southern farmers and to skilled workers in the big city of New York.

Adams and Clay started the National Republican Party. The National Republicans appealed to former Federalists who believed in a strong national government. Those who had come to trust in the traditions established by the Virginia Dynasty tended to support the National Republicans. In 1828 the two new parties struggled for power. Jackson and the Democrats won a clear victory. The "people's choice" was in the White House at last.

ANSWER THESE QUESTIONS

1. the attempts at national unity begun with Monroe's election
2. the calling in of loans by the Second Bank of the United States
3. It allowed Missouri in as a slave state and Maine as a free one to maintain balance but banned further slavery north of the parallel 36° 30′.
4. to give America a chance to form an independent foreign policy
5. Democrats: western and southern farmers, skilled workers in New York city; National Republicans: former Federalists, strong nationalists

ANSWER THESE QUESTIONS

1. What was the "era of good feelings?"
2. What gained the hatred of westerners and southerners during the Panic of 1819?
3. How was the Missouri agreement a compromise?
4. Why did John Quincy Adams want the United States alone to warn Europe to stay out of the Americas?
5. What groups supported the Democrats and National Republicans?

Objective: After completing this page, students should be able to summarize facts from reading material.

Summarizing

As you know, the summary at the end of each chapter in this book briefly presents the important points from the chapter. Sometimes you may need to summarize information for your teacher, for a friend, or for your own notes. In your summary, you will want to include all the important points from your source and leave out the details.

In the following selection, Elias Pym Fordham, an English immigrant, describes his life in Illinois in 1818.

We are all in good health and spirits and are more accustomed to American manners—therefore more comfortable. It is useless for emigrants to think of retaining English manners or English feelings in this country of liberty and equality. But, to do the Americans justice, they respect the love which every man of generous feeling has for his native country. . . .

The western Americans generally feel great hostility to the British government but toward the English emigrants, they are . . . kind and hospitable. . . .

My little estate lies on and between two small hills, from which descend several small streams that unite in the valley and flow on through the prairie. . . . I have about 100 acres of meadow and 60 of timber land. The timber is white oak, walnut, and hickory. There are some persimmons, a most delicious fruit, growing on straight and rather hefty trees, a good many grapes, and hazels.

To summarize Fordham's impressions, first ask yourself the following questions: What are the main points of the selection? How can you put these points in your own words? What details can you leave out? Below is a sample summary of the first two paragraphs.

Fordham reports that he is doing fine in the West now that he is used to American manners. He says that Americans respect the immigrants' love of their native countries. Americans do not like the British government, but they are kind to the English immigrants.

On a piece of paper, write a summary of the third paragraph, describing Fordham's estate.

Working with Skills

READING SKILLS

ACTIVITY

Objective: To summarize

Have the class read the section The End of the Dynasty in Lesson 17-3. Have them write sentences that explain briefly the events leading up to the formation of the Democratic Party. For example: Starting with James Madison, the person appointed secretary of state later became president. Have at least five or six students read their summaries to the class.

ANSWER

Fordham says his estate is about 160 acres. Several kinds of timber, fruit, and nuts grow there.

RELATED MATERIAL

Duplicator/Copy Master Activity 24

THINKING THINGS THROUGH

1. more moderate; Marshall was a Federalist and Randolph an extreme states' rights supporter **2.** because the Constitution said nothing about buying new territory **3.** Answers will vary. If yes, because Embargo Act hurt American trade. If no, because nation was not ready for war. **4.** improved relations with Europe; increased American pride and independence from Europe; en-

Chapter 11 SUMMARY

From 1800 to 1825, the United States expanded rapidly in area and population. The Louisiana Purchase opened the area west of the Mississippi River. President Jefferson sent explorers to gather information about the area. A line of Presidents from Virginia served their country. They were Thomas Jefferson, James Madison, and James Monroe.

Americans fought the British in the War of 1812 to end British alliances with the Indians and naval attacks on American ships. The Treaty of Ghent in 1814 ended the war. Neither side gained any territory. After the War of 1812 relations with Europe improved. The war increased American pride and independence.

After the war, however, severe problems troubled the nation. In 1819 the United States suffered through a business panic. The Panic of 1819 caused a growth of sectionalism. In addition, sectionalism increased because of slavery. The Missouri Compromise ended the bitter debate over slavery for a time. In addition, the Monroe Doctrine, stated in 1823, began to create an independent American foreign policy.

In 1825 two new political parties formed. John Quincy Adams, the sixth President, led the National Republicans. Andrew Jackson, who defeated Adams in 1828, led the Democrats.

Chapter 11 TEST

WORDS TO REMEMBER

Match the following words with their definitions.

b 1. sectionalism
a 2. blockade
e 3. unconstitutional
d 4. dynasty
c 5. expedition

a. the closing off of an area to prevent people and supplies from going in or out

b. the practice of giving greater importance to the interests of the region rather than to those of the entire country

c. an organized group of people making a trip with a definite purpose

d. a group of rulers from the same line

e. not allowed by the Constitution

THINKING THINGS THROUGH

1. How was Jefferson's attitude toward government different from that of Marshall and Randolph?
2. Why did the Federalists claim that the Louisiana Purchase was unconstitutional?
3. Some have said that a war with Britain in 1807 would have been better than the Embargo Act. Do you agree? Why or why not?
4. How did the War of 1812 benefit the United States?
5. Why was sectionalism dangerous to the United States?
6. Was the term "dynasty" meant to praise the Presidents from Virginia or to anger them? Explain your answer.

RELATED MATERIALS

Duplicator/Copy Masters: Activities 23, 24; Quiz 22
Workbook pages 32-34

couraged American manufacturing **5.** because it could pull apart the Union **6.** to anger them; it suggested they were like a hated royal family

WORKING WITH SKILLS

The United States and Great Britain had developed trade with the new Latin American countries that achieved independence from Europe during the Napoleonic Wars. To protect this trade and keep Europe from recolonizing Latin America, the United States developed a policy warning Europe not to set up new colonies in the Western Hemisphere.

WORKING WITH SKILLS

Read the five paragraphs on pages 302–303 titled "American Influence Abroad." Write a one-paragraph summary entitled "The Monroe Doctrine." Make sure you tell how the doctrine came about and what it was supposed to do for Americans in the United States and in the rest of the hemisphere.

ON YOUR OWN

1. President Jefferson encouraged the exploration of the land west of the Mississippi. He wanted the explorers to bring back information about the land, the wildlife, and the people who lived there. Write a paragraph about what explorers would have found in your area in the early 1800s. Make sure you cover the following topics:
   a. geographical features
   b. wildlife
   c. people living on the land
2. Examine the map on page 324, Routes to the West. The solid blue line is the route Lewis and Clark took from St. Louis to Fort Clatsop. Now get a road map of the United States today. Plan an imaginary bus trip from St. Louis to Astoria, Oregon, taking roughly the same route as Lewis and Clark's. As you make your plans, decide which highways you would use, which towns you would visit, and what physical features you would see. Write a day-by-day log telling of your experiences on such an imaginary trip (assume that you could travel about 300 miles—480 kilometers—per day).
3. The Battle of New Orleans was fought in 1815 by a band of frontier soldiers led by Andrew Jackson. Read about the battle in an encyclopedia, then imagine you were one of those soldiers who fought the British. Write a letter home to your family describing what happened in the battle.
4. America's national anthem was written by Francis Scott Key during the British bombardment of Fort McHenry in September of 1814. Moved by the sight of the American flag flying in battle, he composed a poem that was later set to a song and printed as a handbill in the city of Baltimore. Use an encyclopedia to locate the complete "Star Spangled Banner." After reading the verses, compose your own version to describe feelings of pride in the American flag.

Chapter 12
THE DEVELOPING NATION

Chapter 12 focuses on the growth of the United States between 1820 and 1850, along with the many changes that resulted. Lesson 12-1 covers the movement of many people to the West and discusses the growing rift between the North and the South over the issue of slavery. Lesson 12-2 discusses nullification and President Jackson's attitude toward the Indians. 12-3 mentions the idea of manifest destiny and the discovery of gold in California.

CONTENT OBJECTIVES

After completing the lesson, students will know:

- why so many people began to travel west and why new modes of transportation were needed
- that steamboats and railroads were among the improvements made in travel
- about the expansion of cotton as a crop in the South and the corresponding increase in slavery
- about the growth of factories in New England, due largely to Eli Whitney's invention of interchangeable parts

VOCABULARY

canal: a waterway dug across land for ships to sail through
abolitionist: person who wanted to end slavery
interchangeable parts: standard parts that fit any gun (or other manufactured item)
union: an organization created to promote the interest of workers

12-1 A Nation on the Move

As you read, think about these questions:
Why were new means of transporting people and goods necessary after the War of 1812?
Why was the invention of the railroad important?
What invention had a dramatic effect on the American factory system?

Special Vocabulary	canal	interchangeable parts
	abolitionist	union

After the War of 1812, Americans turned their attention from the problems of Europe to the promise of a growing nation. Vast changes had begun to take place. One of the most exciting of these was the migrating of people into the region between the Appalachians and the Mississippi. One visitor to the United States said in wonder, "America seems to be breaking up and moving westward."

The National Road. A problem that faced every family deciding to move west was how to go. There was no easy, direct route to follow. Recognizable roads either did not exist or were of such poor condition that after a heavy rain, wagons and horses simply bogged down in the mud. On hot, dry days the dust in the air could be thick enough practically to blot out the sun.

In 1811 the construction of a road, called the Cumberland or National Road, began. This road would stretch from Cumberland, Maryland, to Wheeling, a town in western

Virginia. When the road opened seven years later, people by the thousands traveled on it, seeking a new life farther west. Conestogas, or covered wagons, filled with goods bound for market used the road in both directions.

As each part of the National Road was finished, hundreds of families in Conestoga wagons moved farther west. The road is now called United States Highway 40.

Canals. In the early 1800s shipping goods from one section of the country to another was expensive. The National Road had helped to lower this cost. Still, American business people searched for ways to move freight across the country even more cheaply. A way truly to link the East and the West had to be found. The answer, some thought, was the *canal*, a waterway dug across land for ships to sail through.

DeWitt Clinton, the governor of New York, began in 1817 to push for the construction of a canal linking the Great Lakes with the Atlantic Ocean. Many people considered

ACTIVITY

Objectives: To use reference materials and to make comparisons

Divide the class into three groups. Have one group do research in the library to find out more about the Erie Canal—how it was built, how many times it has been enlarged, and how the operation of the canal has affected nearby cities and towns. Have the other two groups do the same for the Suez Canal and the Panama Canal. Lead a class discussion in which students identify points of similarity and points of contrast regarding the three canals.

Boys walked alongside boats in the Erie Canal, guiding them with ropes to keep them from hitting the banks.

Clinton's "Big Ditch," as the project was nicknamed, doomed to failure. Finally the massive project got underway. Eight years later the canal stretched from Buffalo, New York, to Albany, New York, on the Hudson River. The Erie Canal, costing $7 million, paid for itself within nine years. Its immense success encouraged other states to begin canal projects.

Steamboats. Americans had always used the natural waterways to transport themselves and their goods from one place to another. When a boat was forced to sail against the current of a river, however, it was impossible to be sure how long the trip would take.

Several Americans worked on an invention—the steamboat —that would greatly aid river travel. They believed that a boat powered by steam engines would be able to move upstream readily against a strong current. When Robert Fulton's *Clermont* sailed up the Hudson River from New York City to Albany in 1807, a new age in travel and transport was born. What was also needed was a faster means of transportation across land.

Railroads. Some Americans were convinced that steam engines could also be used to move wagons faster on land. In 1828 investors in the city of Baltimore began to build a railroad to the Ohio River. The first spadeful of earth was turned by Charles Carroll, the last surviving signer of the Declaration of Independence. The merchants of Baltimore hoped that the railroad would give faster, cheaper service to the West than was then available.

By the 1840s railroad building was going on everywhere. During the 1850s, the amount of railroad track in the United States increased from 9021 miles (14,434 kilometers) to

With the connection between Baltimore and Wheeling, West Virginia, completed in 1853, the Baltimore & Ohio became the first passenger railroad in America. No north-south line was built until after the Civil War.

to distant places. Sometimes, however, an owner willingly bought a slave who had married one of his or her own.

Most slaves felt keenly about their hard lives. A group of them in Henrico County, Virginia, planned a rebellion in 1801. They were discovered, however, and many were executed. In 1822 another group of slaves from Charleston, South Carolina, led by Denmark Vesey, planned to take their freedom. They, too, were found out. The biggest slave rebellion was led by Nat Turner in Virginia in 1831. Before it was put down, fifty-seven white people and over one hundred blacks had died in the violence.

Owners saw to it that slaves up for auction were dressed in their best, but good clothes could not hide the slaves' anxiety. Many slaves spent most of their lives in cotton fields, which one slave said "seemed to stretch from one end of the earth to another."

Abolitionists. As the number of slaves in the United States grew, so did the voices against slavery. Many people, mostly from the North, openly encouraged slaves to revolt against their owners. Others lectured audiences and wrote newspapers explaining how evil slavery really was. These people were called *abolitionists*. An abolitionist was a person who wanted to end slavery.

One abolitionist was William Lloyd Garrison, a New Englander. Garrison printed his views in his abolitionist weekly, the *Liberator*. In his paper, Garrison demanded immediate and complete freedom for slaves. Garrison's views upset many southerners who were afraid that their slaves would rise in bloody rebellion. Two South Carolina sisters, Sarah and Angelina Grimké, wrote books, made

Former slaves Frederick Douglass and Sojourner Truth, leading spokespeople of the blacks in the 1800s, both talked with Abraham Lincoln about abolition. Douglass later became United States minister to Haiti.

DISCUSSION

Discuss with the students some changes in American life that occurred from 1815 to the early 1840s. Those they might mention include: movement of farmers to the cities, women working in factories, and increased production of goods. Ask students what changes have occurred recently that have made our lives very different. For example, the invention of the computer and TV changed ways of getting information. Ask whether they think change is always good, and why.

speeches, and supported the abolitionists with their money. They freed the slaves they inherited.

Free blacks also spoke out against slavery. Frederick Douglass, an ex-slave, was a persuasive speaker. He talked to many audiences about the hardships of slavery. A freed slave in New York named Isabella took the name Sojourner Truth and made remarkably effective abolitionist speeches against slavery, although she could not read or write. Bit by bit the abolitionists made millions of Americans aware of what slavery was actually like.

New England and the Industrial Revolution

In the 1800s small industries in New England grew larger to meet the needs of Americans and to lessen American dependence on foreign goods. The amount of factory products—household wares, clothing, and gadgets of every description—increased every year. This production soon would change people's lives beyond imagination.

Growth of Factories. The first factories in New England were small. They were located next to streams and rivers which provided them with water power. To some people, working in a factory at first seemed an escape from the labor and boredom of farming. Then they discovered they had exchanged one kind of boring work for another.

In 1798 a discovery by Eli Whitney changed the nature of the American factory for all time. This invention was the use of *interchangeable parts* in the making of muskets. Until Whitney's invention, guns were made one at a time in a gun maker's shop. In Whitney's gun factory, however, workers made all the parts of a musket in large numbers. Then many guns could be put together from the parts. An added benefit to this way of making a gun was this: every part of one gun fit any other gun made in the factory. This is what is meant by the phrase "interchangeable parts." So it was that the work of this one man revolutionized life in New England as well as in the South.

Lowell. During the period from 1830 to 1860, the largest industrial area in New England was the group of textile factories located in Lowell, Massachusetts. The factories turned raw cotton from the South into thread. The thread then was woven into cloth.

Most of the workers in Lowell were women from nearby farms. Parents often sent their daughters to Lowell to make extra money. In time, thousands of women lived and worked in Lowell. These women formed the first large group of factory workers in the United States.

Following the pattern of farm life, most factory work lasted from sunrise to sundown.

Economic and Social Consequences. As factories spread, the labor force also grew. Many people left their farms to move to the cities where most of the factories were located.

The conditions in many factories were poor. Bad lighting and little fresh air were common conditions. Factory workers realized that they had to find a way to make the factory owners change the terrible conditions. Workers began to form *unions*, or organizations created to promote the interests of the workers. One of the first union organizers was Sarah Bagley. Bagley spoke out forcefully to improve the wages and working conditions of the employees at the Lowell mills.

ANSWER THESE QUESTIONS

1. What city began the first railroad to the Ohio River?
2. What did the abolitionists fight against?
3. How did Eli Whitney influence both the southern and northern economies in the United States?
4. What happened as a result of the building of the Erie Canal?
5. Why did factory workers try to form unions?

ANSWER THESE QUESTIONS

1. Baltimore
2. slavery
3. His introduction of the cotton gin made it more profitable to grow cotton in the South. The invention of interchangeable parts led to the American factory system in the North.
4. It increased trade between the East and the West.
5. to force owners to improve bad working conditions

Working with Skills

MAP SKILLS

ACTIVITY

Objective: To compare maps

Have the students compare the slavery maps in this Map Skill with the map of England's Thirteen Colonies on page 85. Have them use the maps to answer the following questions: (1) Which states on the sites of the original colonies had a slave population of more than 30 percent in 1790? (2) more than 50 percent in 1840? (3) less than 30 percent in 1840?

Comparing Maps and Drawing Conclusions

Maps are an important source of information that is presented in a visual way. Comparing the information you can get from one map with information from another map can lead you to new conclusions.

A comparison of two maps is especially useful when they show how conditions in a specific area have changed over a period of years. Growth in total population of a state or nation can be shown in this way. Comparing maps can also reveal changes in the number of highways, of acres being farmed, or of towns established. For example, a map of the United States in 1776 would show few towns with more than 10,000 residents. A map of the United States today would show thousands of towns that size. Together the two maps would tell someone unfamiliar with American history that the country changed from rural to urban in nature over the last two centuries. Either map alone would not lead to that conclusion.

Look at the maps on the next page. The map on the left shows slavery in the United States in 1790. The map on the right shows slavery in 1840. Look at New York state on the 1790 map. Its color shows you that less than 30 percent of the total population were slaves. Now look at New York on the 1840 map. Its color has changed, showing that either there are no slaves in the state or that it is unsettled. You know that New York state was very much settled in 1840, so there must have been no slaves in the state. You can conclude from this evidence that something in New York changed during this period so that there were no longer slaves in the state. In fact, New York passed a law during this time ending slavery within its borders.

In addition to changes in the slave population, these maps show other changes that took place in the United States between 1790 and 1840. Compare the number of states shown on the 1790 map with the number of states shown on the 1840 map. How many states were added to the United States during that time?

ANSWER
ten

Study the maps that show slavery in the United States in 1790 and 1840. Then answer each of the questions.

RELATED MATERIAL
Duplicator/Copy Master Activity 26

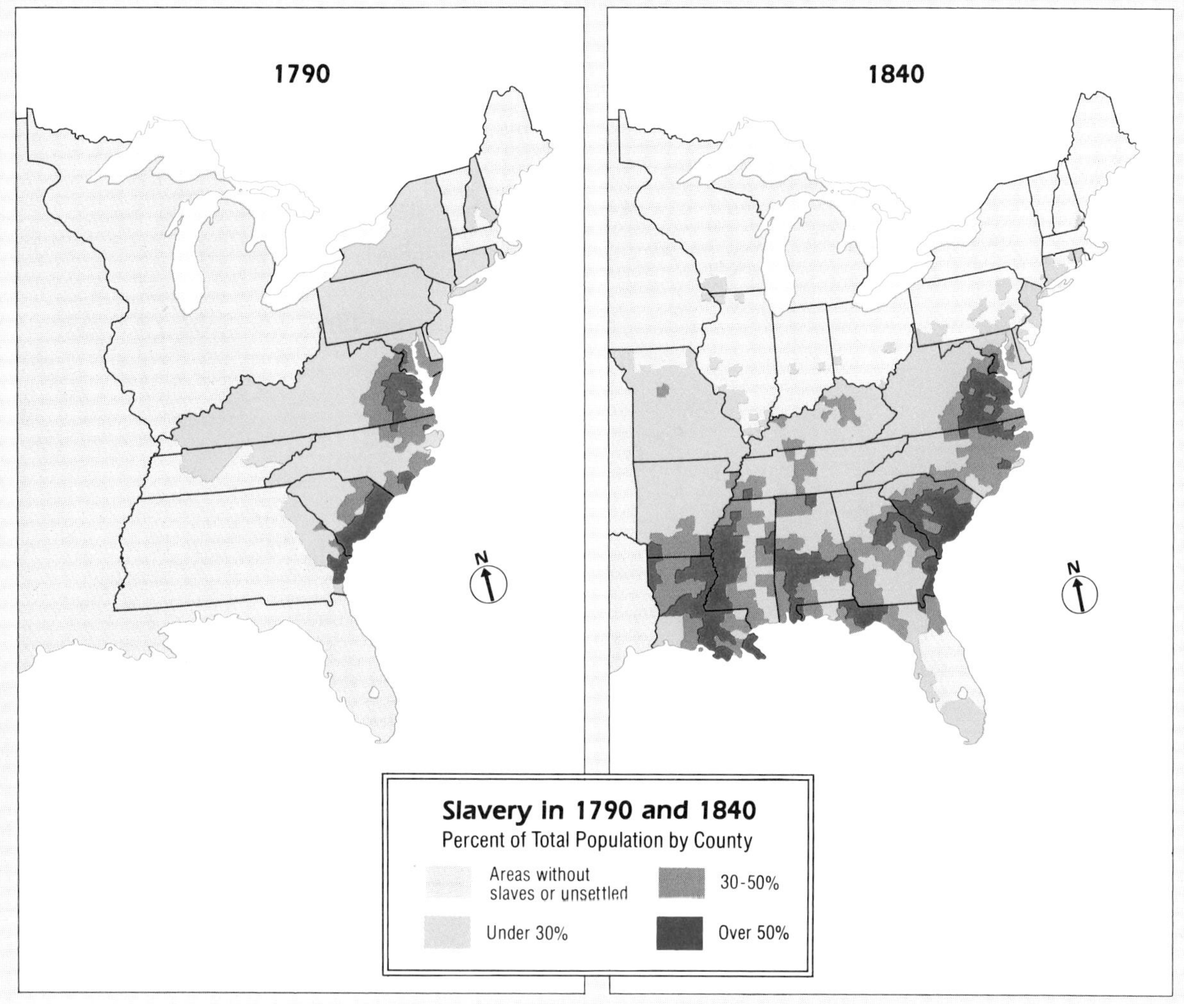

1. How did the percentage of slaves living in the North change between 1790 and 1840?
2. In what two directions did slavery expand between 1790 and 1840?
3. What states had areas with a slave population of more than 50 percent in 1790? In 1840?
4. What states that had slaves in 1790 did not have slaves in 1840?
5. What conclusions can you reach from comparing these two maps?

ANSWERS

1. reduced considerably—slavery has almost disappeared
2. south and west
3. 1790: Virginia, North Carolina, South Carolina, Georgia; 1840: Virginia, North Carolina, South Carolina, Georgia, Alabama, Mississippi, Louisiana, Arkansas
4. New York, New Hampshire, Delaware
5. Answers will vary; slavery had increased and expanded, thus the need for slaves must have seemed greater during this time.

CONTENT OBJECTIVES

After completing the lesson, students will know:

- how the issue of nullification increased tension between the North and the South
- President Jackson's attitude toward the Bank of the United States
- about the continued deterioration of relations between the United States government and the Indians

VOCABULARY

charter: official document

12-2 The Jacksonian Period

As you read, think about these questions:

How did voting requirements change from 1790 to 1828?

What was Jackson's stand on nullification?

Why did President Jackson attack the Second Bank of the United States?

How did the federal government deal with the American Indians?

Special Vocabulary charter

Andrew Jackson was a lawyer, a military hero, and senator before being elected President in 1828. Although Jackson was a wealthy plantation owner and slaveholder when he was elected President, he was admired as a self-made man. Unlike any President before him, Jackson was a westerner—with his home in Tennessee. As a popular Democratic Party leader, he pushed for laws and programs that helped many ordinary people.

Jackson had benefited from a change in voting rules. Starting in the 1790s the states had begun to drop all property requirements for voting. Eastern states were rewriting their constitutions to give all white men the vote. None of the new western states when they began to enter the Union in 1804 set property requirements for voting. In the election of 1828 twice as many adult white males voted as in 1824. Women and American Indians, nevertheless, had no voice in government. Very few states allowed free black men to vote.

Domestic Politics

Shortly after coming to office, Jackson and the Vice President, John C. Calhoun, found themselves disagreeing on serious matters. Mostly the two men disagreed about the Union. Calhoun believed that the North was growing at the expense of the South. To make matters worse, Secretary of State Martin Van Buren increased his own influence with Jackson by pointing out Calhoun's faults. In time the rivalry

Andrew Jackson, mocked as "King Veto" by some, expanded the power of the presidency. He introduced the "spoils system" into national politics, rewarding supporters with government jobs.

between the President and the Vice President caused Calhoun to resign his office after being reelected senator from South Carolina.

Nullification. Jackson and Calhoun had strongly disagreed on the tariff that Congress had passed in 1828. Southerners complained that the tariff was too high, raising considerably the cost of the manufactured goods they bought.

In 1828 Calhoun wrote a protest for the state of South Carolina. Unsigned, it said that states had the right to nullify laws that they felt were unconstitutional. South Carolina voted that after February 1, 1833, it would no longer collect the tariff for the United States. South Carolina also said it would withdraw from the Union if the federal government tried to force it to collect the tariff.

In answer, Jackson issued a Proclamation to the People of South Carolina. It said that no state could refuse to obey the laws passed by Congress. It also stated that no state could leave the Union. Jackson then asked Congress to pass a law allowing him to use federal troops to enforce the tariff. Congress passed the Force Bill in 1833.

ACTIVITY

Objective: To recognize points of view

Divide the class into two groups. Group 1 will represent John C. Calhoun and others from the South supporting the states' right to nullify laws that they felt were unconstitutional. The other group, led by Andrew Jackson, supports the laws of Congress with no right for nullification. Have each group prepare a brief statement of their views and present it to the class. Direct the discussion groups to answer these questions: Why did these different points of view increase sectionalism? What are some consequences of a state's support of nullification?

Congress tried to ease the situation by passing the Compromise Tariff of 1833. Jackson signed this bill which would lower the tariff gradually during the next ten years. Both sides claimed victory. The tension between the North and the South, however, had greatly increased.

Bank of the United States. Another cause of bad feelings was the Second Bank of the United States. Jackson, like many westerners, did not trust the BUS, as it was known. He believed that it favored the rich northeasterners over the farmers and pioneers of the South and West.

Jackson wanted to get rid of the bank. When a bill to give it a new *charter*, or the official document allowing it to do business, passed Congress in 1832, Jackson vetoed the bill. Jackson then put the government's money into state banks.

Indian Relations

Jackson's policy toward American Indians was a simple one. He wanted all Indians living east of the Mississippi River to move west of it to a special settlement. According to Jackson's plan, the federal government would provide land and food for the Indians. Most southerners and westerners approved of the President's policy. They wanted the Indian land for growing their crops. (See the map on page 321.)

DISCUSSION

Have the students discuss Andrew Jackson's actions in forcing the removal of the Cherokee even after the Supreme Court ruled in favor of the Native Americans. Remind the students that the principle of judicial review was established in the case of *Marbury vs. Madison.* Have them discuss how Jackson got away with ignoring the high court's ruling. Ask the students what they think can happen if a President does not obey the laws of the nation.

Indian Removal. In 1830 Congress passed the Indian Removal Act to do as Jackson wanted. When the Indians refused to leave their land, the federal government sent in troops to force them off it.

The Cherokee tried to fight the action by taking their case to the Supreme Court. The Cherokee claimed that the federal government had signed a treaty allowing them to keep their lands in the state of Georgia. Georgia, however, passed a state law taking the land from the Indians. The Supreme Court, led by John Marshall, ruled that the Cherokee could remain on their land because a federal treaty was higher than a state law. Jackson and the state of Georgia ignored the court's ruling. The Cherokee had to leave their homes. They were forced to travel west to the Indian Territory (now called Oklahoma) created by Congress in 1834. Thousands of Indians, including many women, children, and aged, died on this march. The suffering was so great that the Cherokee called the route they took the "Trail of Tears."

At the end of the Trail of Tears, the Cherokee were promised by the government that they would own their own lands "as long as grass shall grow and rivers run." Within twenty years, the promise was broken.

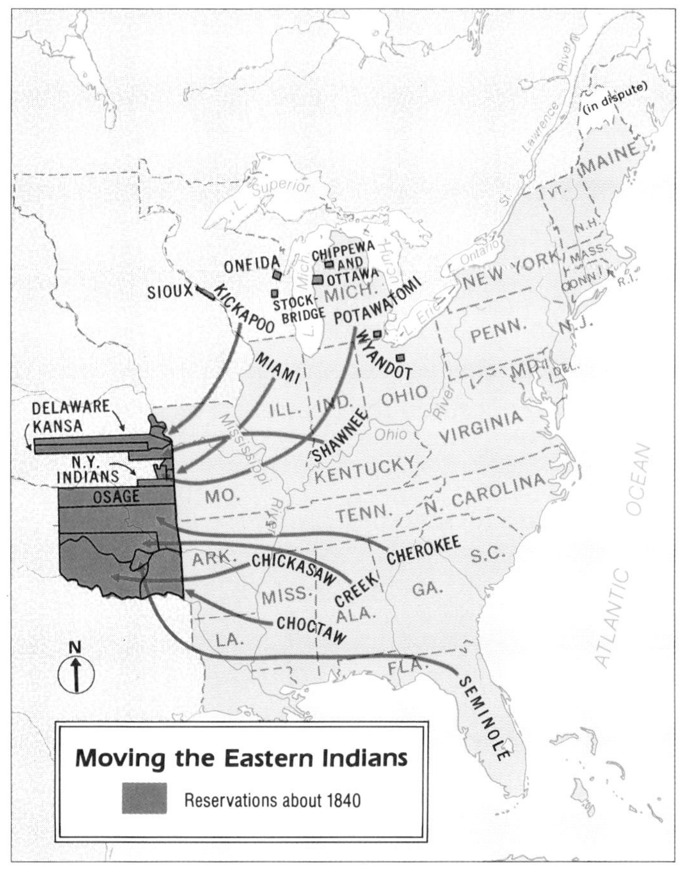

Oneida, Stockbridge, Chippewa, Wyandot, and Ottawa

This map shows the reservations the eastern Indians were moved to during the 1830s. Which groups were not moved west of the Mississippi River?

ANSWER THESE QUESTIONS

1. women and American Indians
2. nullify the law
3. He felt they supported the rich northeasterners over the farmers and pioneers of the South and West.
4. He wanted all Indians east of the Mississippi River to move west.
5. A federal treaty is higher than a state law.

Frontier Battles. Not all Indians left their homelands peacefully. In 1832 Chief Black Hawk led the Sauk and Fox into Illinois to reclaim their lands taken by white settlers. Black Hawk did not intend to fight the settlers, but he was forced into a battle by white soldiers. Most of Black Hawk's warriors were killed in this battle.

Battles also raged in the Southeast. The Seminole in Florida refused to obey a treaty of 1833 which said they had to leave their lands. Osceola, chief of the Seminoles, led his people in rebellion against the federal government. From 1835 to 1842 this Seminole War raged. Osceola was finally captured. Later he died in prison.

ANSWER THESE QUESTIONS

1. What two groups of people were not allowed to vote in 1828?
2. What did Calhoun want South Carolina to do about the Tariff of 1828?
3. Why did Jackson not trust banks?
4. What was Jackson's policy toward Indians?
5. Why did the Supreme Court rule in favor of the Cherokee nation?

CONTENT OBJECTIVES

After completing the lesson, students will know:

- the definition of manifest destiny
- how Texas went from being a part of Mexico to independence
- about the discovery of gold in California and about the "gold rush" that followed

VOCABULARY

manifest destiny: an expectation people think is guaranteed to come true

annexation: the adding of a new territory to a country

12-3 Expansion Into The Far West

As you read, think about these questions:
Why did people move to the Oregon Territory?
Where did the Mormons establish their new home?
Why did Texas rebel against Mexico?
What one event caused the population of California to boom?

Special Vocabulary manifest destiny annexation

During the 1840s, many Americans became convinced that the United States must expand and control the entire continent of North America. People began to refer to this hope as America's *manifest destiny*. Manifest destiny is an expectation that people think is guaranteed to come true. Thousands of settlers crossed the Mississippi River in search of new lands. For many, the final goal was Texas, California, or Oregon.

Trailblazers

The expeditions of Lewis and Clark and Zebulon Pike proved to be invaluable to the thousands of new settlers who headed west in the mid-1800s. These three explorers had mapped the United States from St. Louis, Missouri, to the Pacific Ocean. Wave after wave of settlers used these maps as guides. There were those brave, adventurous folks, however, who struck off on their own, hoping to find fresh routes and sights. These were the trailblazers, cutting new paths for others to follow.

ACTIVITY

Objective: To write original statements

Have students choose one of the trailblazers, explorers, scouts, traders, or religious leaders described in Lesson 3, or an explorer from Chapter 11. Have them write a paragraph describing the person's accomplishments, the states explored, the dates of his or her activities, and his or her contribution to the westward expansion of the United States. Ask for volunteers to read their paragraphs aloud to the entire class.

Jedediah Smith's band of trappers traveled across the Mojave Desert in 1826, proving that an overland route west was possible. At the time, much of the country was still unmapped.

Mountain Men and Trappers. The mountain men and trappers of the Far West were such trailblazers—heroic figures to many Americans. Among the most famous were Andrew Henry, Jedediah Smith, Kit Carson, and Jim Bridger. They seemed larger than life, accomplishing feats of personal courage few people could even dream of, let alone attempt.

These men and thousands like them came to know the wilderness and mountains of the Far West by heart. They established overland trails that would take later settlers through the rugged Rocky Mountains and Sierra Nevada.

Traders and the Santa Fe Trail. Santa Fe, 1000 miles (1600 kilometers) southwest of St. Louis, lay in Spanish hands. Spain refused to let any foreign people trade with this Mexican city. When Mexico declared its independence from Spain in 1821, a wave of American traders swept westward to seek their fortune in Santa Fe.

DISCUSSION

Have the students discuss some reasons why Americans moved west in the mid-1800s. Be sure to mention trading opportunities, religious freedom, lure of gold, and new economic chances. Ask students whether they would have left their homes to go west. To which area would they have gone? Why?

The first American to arrive in the town was William Becknell. Becknell, on his second trip to the city, had started out near Independence, Missouri. He had crossed through the Cimarron Desert controlled by the Comanche, passed through the Sangre de Cristo Range of the Rockies, and then entered Santa Fe. This overland route became known as the Santa Fe Trail. Other traders soon followed Becknell's route. The trip was forbidding, but the prospects of profits drove the traders on to their destination.

Santa Fe Trail, Oregon Trail

This map shows the routes used by pioneers to travel west. Which two trails started near the town of Independence, Missouri?

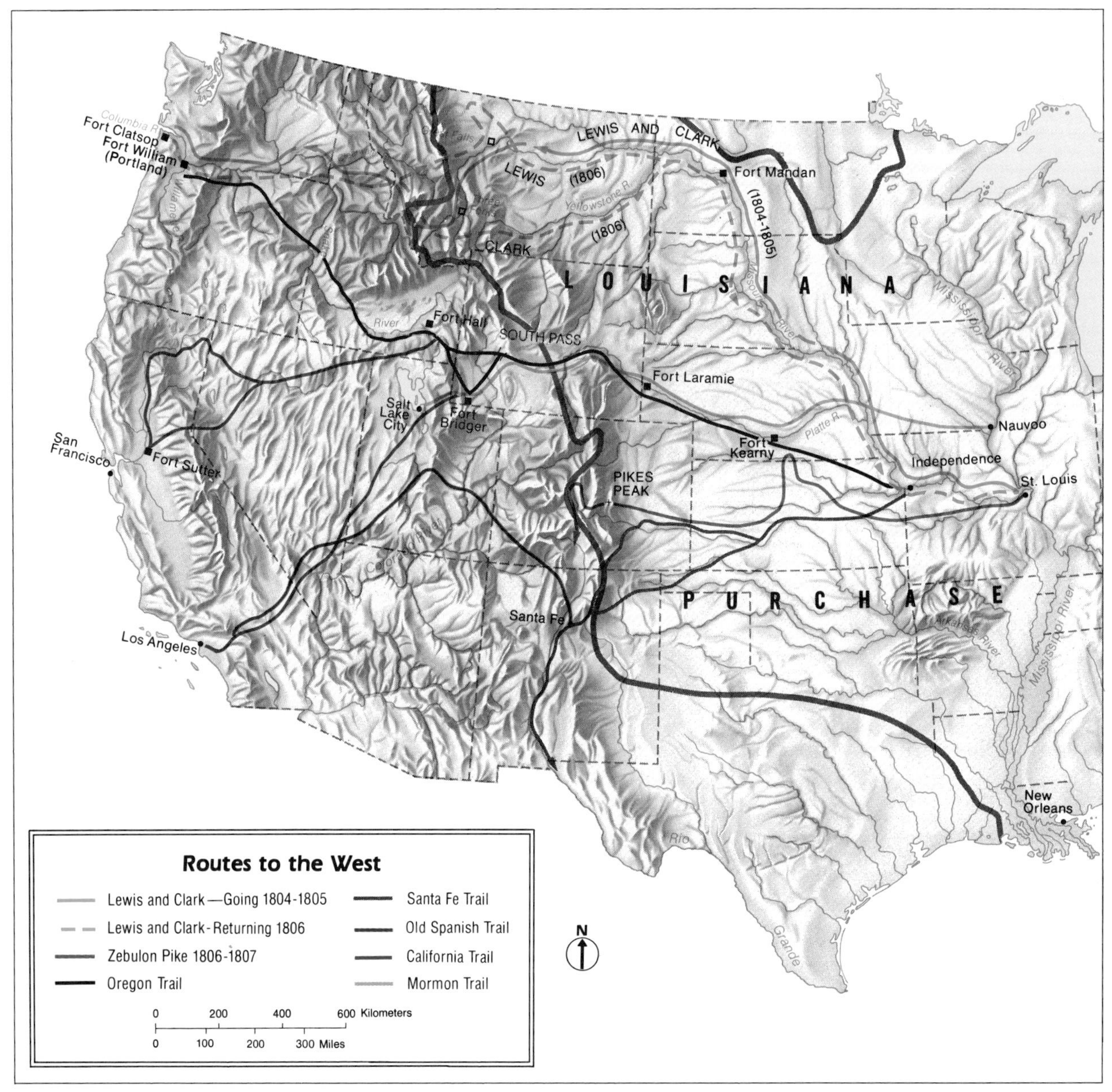

Women and children light fires as Mormon settlers pull their handcarts into camp along the Oregon Trail. The picture was painted by a member of the party.

Oregon Trail. Americans knew that the Oregon Territory held high promise for the fur industry. This part of North America also had river valleys with rich soil for farming. Many settlers hoped to live in the area permanently.

In the early 1840s Americans in ever increasing numbers began to make the difficult journey to the Oregon Territory. The constant traffic marked a road across the prairies, plains, and mountains that came to be known as the Oregon Trail.

The first settler to risk everything to get to Oregon was Dr. Marcus Whitman. Whitman became a Protestant missionary who went to the Oregon Territory to convert the Indians of the Pacific Northwest. Later he returned to New York and married. In 1836 Marcus and Narcissa Whitman began the long journey over the Oregon Trail. Narcissa Whitman was one of the first white women to endure the hardships presented by the journey.

The Mormon Trail. One significant group of settlers that followed a portion of the Oregon Trail in 1847 was the Mormons. The Mormons were a religious group who followed the teachings of Joseph Smith, their leader. This religion began in New York in 1830. Its followers soon moved westward, seeking to escape the keen opposition they met. They moved to Ohio and then to Illinois. In both states the Mormons were persecuted for their beliefs. In 1844 Smith was killed by a group of angry neighbors in Illinois.

Two years later Brigham Young, the new Mormon leader, took his followers across the Mississippi River. They hoped to find a site where they could live and worship in peace. On July 24, 1847, the Mormons saw the Great Salt Lake and surrounding mountains. Brigham Young declared this place, present-day Utah, the new home of the Mormons. Within two years the Mormon population had swelled to 8000.

From Republics to States

As more Americans moved from east to west, the new, independent government of Mexico became increasingly concerned. The rapidly expanding United States appeared to be inching ever closer to Mexican territory.

Texas. Texas was the part of Mexico that caused the government in Mexico City the most concern. The Mexicans hoped to set up a state that would be made up of both former Americans and of *Texanos*, a group that today might be called Mexican Americans. The Mexican government, therefore, encouraged settlers from the United States to come to Texas—if they would pledge their loyalty to Mexico and adopt the official religion of the country, Roman Catholicism. In 1822 Stephen Austin started the first colony in Texas made up of people from the United States. Soon the former Americans were calling themselves Texans.

The Texans tried to get along with the Mexican government. In 1832 many of them supported the election of Antonio López de Santa Anna as president of Mexico. They hoped that this leader would bring democracy to the country. Instead Santa Anna established a military government. After his election, the Mexican Congress passed a law ending the right of United States citizens to immigrate to Mexico. The law also forbade settlers to bring slaves into the territory.

The Texans tried to petition the government in an attempt to end the military rule that Santa Anna established. They then declared their independence from Mexico and appointed Sam Houston as commander of the army. Santa Anna organized his own army of 6000 troops and began a march to put down the Texas rebellion. Arriving at San Antonio, Santa Anna found the Texans and *Texanos* encamped in a mission called the Alamo. He began his attack. One hundred eighty-seven Texans and *Texanos* held off the Mexicans for thirteen days. Finally, on March 6, 1836, Santa Anna's soldiers broke through the Alamo's defenses. The defenders died to the last man. Among them were James Bowie, inventor of the Bowie knife, and Davy Crockett, the frontier scout and former member of the United States Congress.

Sam Houston led an army of angry Texans against Santa Anna. On April 20, 1836, Houston's forces surprised the Mexican army at San Jacinto. They killed half the Mexican soldiers and captured the other half, including Santa Anna. Houston offered to spare Santa Anna's life if he would give Texas its freedom. Santa Anna willingly agreed. In the spring of 1836, Texas became the Lone Star Republic.

Most Texans and many Americans wanted Texas to become part of the United States. But the members of Congress argued about Texas *annexation.* Annexation is the adding of a new territory to a country. Southerners such as John C. Calhoun wanted Texas annexed because it would be a slave state. Northerners opposed annexation for the same reason. Early in 1845 the Senate and the House of Representatives passed a joint resolution admitting Texas to the Union. The President quickly signed it. The antislavery members of Congress were furious. In December 1845, Texas joined the Union as a slave state.

General Winfield Scott rides victorious into the public square in Mexico City where the Aztecs once listened to Montezuma speaking.

The Mexican War. A dispute arose over the legal boundary between the United States and Mexico along the Texas border. The United States claimed that the border was along the Rio Grande. Mexico insisted that the border was farther north along the Nueces River.

In January 1846, President James K. Polk ordered General Zachary Taylor and his troops to camp along the Rio Grande.

In early May Mexican troops, making the first move, crossed the Rio Grande. The brisk fight that followed—the Battle of Palo Alto—convinced Congress to declare war on Mexico.

By December 1846, the United States had gained control over Texas, New Mexico, and California. When the Mexican forces under Santa Anna refused to surrender, Polk sent General Winfield Scott to capture Mexico's capital. General Zachary Taylor defeated Santa Anna at Buena Vista. Soon afterward, Scott and his troops entered Mexico City on September 14, 1847. Santa Anna had fled before the Americans arrived and resigned shortly afterwards.

The war was over. The Treaty of Guadalupe Hidalgo in 1848 gave the United States California and all of Mexico's land between California and the Rio Grande. The Rio Grande was set as the southern border of Texas. The United States paid Mexico $15 million and agreed to pay the money claims that Americans had made against Mexico.

The faces of these California prospectors give no hints of past achievements or future disappointments. They lived from day to day in hope of finding gold.

California Gold Rush. In January 1848 gold was discovered in California at a sawmill owned by a German-born adventurer named Johann Sutter. The event at Sutter's Mill soon became national, then international news. In 1849 "gold fever" brought eighty thousand people to California to mine. Some came by land, others came by sea. A few made lucky strikes, most of them were bitterly disappointed. Two years after the discovery of gold, California had enough people to enter the Union as a state.

A month after the discovery of gold, John Quincy Adams died. The leaders of the nation attended the elaborate funeral. No one would have guessed that thirty years would pass before America's chief voices would once again be as united as they were that cold day when they bade farewell to one who had served his country in so many ways.

ANSWER THESE QUESTIONS

1. to farm, to trap furs, to convert the Indians
2. a mission where Santa Anna attacked Texans
3. Mexican president
4. to escape persecution
5. boundary dispute between the United States and Mexico

ANSWER THESE QUESTIONS

1. For what reasons did Americans travel to Oregon?
2. What was the Alamo?
3. Who was Antonio López de Santa Anna?
4. Why did the Mormons move westward?
5. Why did the United States go to war with Mexico?

PEOPLE IN AMERICA

Levi Strauss

Not all those who made their fortunes in the gold rush during the 1840s and 1850s in California made them from gold. One, a Jewish immigrant from Germany, made his fortune out of denim.

Levi Strauss was eighteen years old when he left his home in the mountains of Germany in April 1848 and traveled to the port city of Hamburg. From there he boarded a ship that took him across the Atlantic to New York where he joined his two brothers, Willi and Jacob.

The Strauss brothers were peddlers who traveled the countryside selling needles, thread, and other sewing notions. After three months of roaming the small towns outside New York City, Levi was ready for adventure when he heard of the discovery of gold in far-off California.

Once again he boarded ship, this time a clipper ship that sailed from New York around the southern tip of South America to California. Levi Strauss landed at San Francisco in the spring of 1852. With him he carried the supplies he and his brothers had chosen so carefully in New York: large quantities of needles, thread, twine, scissors, thimbles, and several rolls of canvas and sailcloth.

Strauss had no trouble selling the goods he had brought. Everything had to be shipped to San Francisco at great cost by boat or wagon train, so prices there were high. Many miners paid Strauss in gold dust.

Strauss's canvas was another story. It had come from the French manufacturing town of Nimes and was called "serge de Nimes," or in the shortened form Americans had adopted, "denim." The denim was not strong enough for tents or sails and so it was difficult to sell. Finally, a miner coming from the gold fields offered to buy the denim if Levi Strauss would have it made into work pants for him. Strauss found a tailor who cut and sewed the pants as ordered. Strauss sold dozens of pairs of his work pants to the miners, especially after he added his special feature. He used copper rivets to strengthen the pockets of his pants.

Levi Strauss died in San Francisco in 1902, a wealthy man. Today, the company he founded sells clothes that bear his name to people all over the world.

THINKING THINGS THROUGH

1. Interchangeable parts made mass production possible. **2.** the trail of death and sorrow that the Cherokee traveled on when they were forced to leave their lands **3.** They thought he would bring democracy to the country. **4.** Many wanted to get rich quickly. **5.** It made the cultivation of cotton profitable. **6.** William Lloyd Garrison—published the *Liberator;* Sarah and

Chapter 12 SUMMARY

This period from the 1820s to the 1850s was a time of enormous expansion. New inventions and innovations in transportation—including the National Road, an extensive canal system, the steamboat, and the railroad—put Americans on the move. Northern manufacturing and southern cotton production greatly increased.

Andrew Jackson, a western hero, served as President from 1829 to 1837. Jackson set policies that aided many common people and the pioneers.

The size of the United States increased greatly during this era. Frontier settlements grew into cities; territories joined the Union as states. Americans reached these far-off territories by traveling on the Santa Fe, the Oregon, and the Mormon trails, as well as by ships that sailed around South America. War and treaties with Mexico added California, New Mexico, Arizona, and Texas to the Union. By 1850 the United States stretched completely across the continent.

Not all the results of expansion were good. Indian nations were torn from their tribal lands. Slavery increased and spread in the South. Relations with Mexico were severely damaged. North-South sectionalism increased. The gap between the industrial North and cotton-producing South widened dangerously.

Chapter 12 TEST

WORDS TO REMEMBER

Choose the correct word from the following list to complete each of the sentences below.

a. union
b. canal
c. charter
d. annexation
e. abolitionists

1. A __b__ is a waterway dug out of land.
2. Those people who wanted to end slavery were __e__.
3. A __a__ is an organization that promotes workers' interests.
4. The document allowing a bank to do business is called a __c__.
5. __d__ is the adding of a new territory to a nation.

THINKING THINGS THROUGH

Answer the following questions.

1. How did Eli Whitney's invention of interchangeable parts influence factories in the North?
2. What was the "Trail of Tears"?
3. Why did Texans support the election of Santa Anna?
4. Why did so many people head to California to search for gold?
5. Why was the invention of the cotton gin an important development in the South?
6. Who were some important abolitionists and how did they try to influence public opinion?
7. What were the main provisions of the Indian Removal Act?

RELATED MATERIALS

Duplicator/Copy Masters: Activities 25, 26, 27; Quiz 23
Workbook pages 35-37

Angelina Grimké—wrote books, donated money, spoke; Frederick Douglass and Sojourner Truth—made speeches **7.** all Indians to move west of the Mississippi to special settlements; the government to provide land and food

WORKING WITH SKILLS

1. larger **2.** that there were fewer slaves

WORKING WITH SKILLS

Compare the maps of slavery in 1790 and 1840 on page 317 to answer the following questions.

1. Did slaves make up a larger percentage or a smaller percentage of South Carolina's population in 1840 than in 1790?
2. Comparing the two maps, what can you say about the number of slaves in Pennsylvania in 1840 as compared with 1790?

ON YOUR OWN

1. Antonio López de Santa Anna was one of the most important political figures in Mexico during the mid-1800s. Using a book or other reference material from the library, look into his career as a soldier and politician. Write a few paragraphs telling how Mexicans regarded him during the 1800s and how they regard him today.
2. Davy Crockett was a legendary frontier settler of the American West. In the picture on this page painted in 1834, Crockett posed with the items of his trade. Make a list of the items and explain how each of them served him as a hunter and scout.
3. Settlers traveled to the West in long trains of wagons for safety. They faced bad weather, Indian attacks, and rugged land features that were new to them. Imagine you are traveling west on one of those wagon trains. Write a diary for at least a week (seven entries) of what you saw on that journey, what you felt and hoped about where you were going, and what you had left behind.

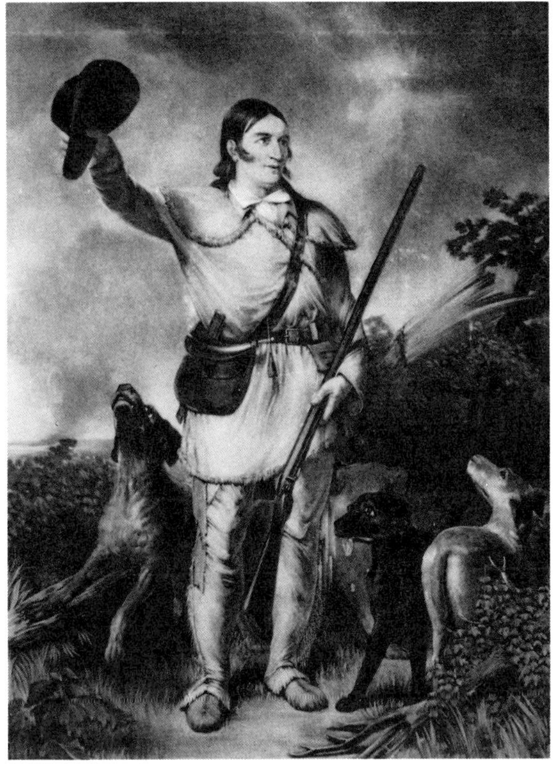

THINK THINGS THROUGH

1. the right of the Supreme Court to decide whether laws passed by Congress are constitutional
2. by denying free speech; Alien Act, allowed President to deport any alien he wanted; Sedition Act made it a crime to disagree with the government
3. because the French wanted the American ministers to bribe them in order to write a treaty
4. When no candidate gets a majority of electoral votes, the Constitution provides that the House of Representatives must select the President.
5. stopped trade with Europe, losing markets for American crops
6. Missouri entered the Union as a slave state and Maine entered as a free state, thus maintaining an equal number of slave and free states.
7. voting regulations changed, enabling white men without property to vote

Unit 4 TEST

WORDS TO REMEMBER

Match each of the following with the correct definitions.

a. abolitionist	e. neutrality
b. administration	f. nullify
c. annexation	g. secede
d. tariff	h. sectionalism

g 1. to withdraw from a group or organization

c 2. the addition of a new territory to a nation

e 3. not taking either side in a disagreement

b 4. the President, Vice President, and others who run the government

a 5. someone who believes slavery should be ended

f 6. to cancel legally

d 7. a tax on imported goods

h 8. the practice of giving greater importance to the needs of one region than to those of the entire country

QUESTIONS TO ANSWER

Choose the answer that best completes each of the following statements.

b 1. The Erie Canal is located in
   a. Ohio
   b. New York
   c. Pennsylvania
   d. California

c 2. As President, Andrew Jackson
   a. opposed the rights of pioneers
   b. supported the nullifiers
   c. opposed the rights of Indians
   d. supported the Bank of the United States

c 3. The most important factor that led to greater production in the United States was
   a. better workers
   b. railroads
   c. interchangeable parts
   d. cotton gin

c 4. The United States purchased the Louisiana Territory from
   a. Mexico
   b. Great Britain
   c. France
   d. Spain

c 5. The United States policy that warned European nations not to interfere in the Western Hemisphere was
   a. The Treaty of Ghent
   b. The Treaty of Guadalupe Hidalgo
   c. The Monroe Doctrine
   d. The Neutrality Proclamation

a 6. The United States gained Texas from
   a. Mexico
   b. Spain
   c. France
   d. Great Britain

a 7. An important factor that made it profitable to grow cotton throughout the South was
   a. the invention of the cotton gin
   b. the development of the railroads
   c. the use of steamboats
   d. the use of interchangeable parts

d 8. The first American to travel along the Santa Fe Trail was
   a. Brigham Young
   b. Sam Houston
   c. James W. Marshall
   d. William Becknell

RELATED MATERIAL
Duplicator/Copy Master Test 24-26

8. He thought the Indians prevented white settlers from expanding into new lands.
9. because of the slavery issue

WORKING WITH SKILLS

1. Wilmington, Charleston, New Orleans, Mobile; Virginia
2. McCulloch was a bank cashier at the Baltimore branch of the National Bank. At issue was the constitutionality of the act of Congress establishing the bank and the constitutionality of the tax imposed on the bank by the Maryland legislature.
3. Following the Louisiana Purchase, Jefferson appointed Meriwether Lewis and William Clark to lead an expedition to explore the land west of the Mississippi. Helped by Sacajawea, they mapped the river from St. Louis to Montana, then crossed the Rockies to Oregon, where they built Fort Clatsop. The three-year trip added to knowledge of the West and gave America its first claim on the Northwest coast.

THINK THINGS THROUGH

1. What right did the Federal Judiciary Act of 1789 give to the Supreme Court?
2. How did the Alien and Sedition Acts deny the First Amendment?
3. Why did the American public get angry about the X Y Z affair?
4. Why did the House of Representatives select the President in 1801?
5. How did the Embargo Act of 1807 harm Americans?
6. How did the Missouri Compromise maintain an equal number of free and slave states?
7. What change in voting regulations helped Andrew Jackson, who was a westerner, become President?
8. Why did Jackson want to move the Indians west of the Mississippi River?
9. Why did Congress fight over the annexation of Texas for so long?

As the nation expanded westward, rivalry sometimes developed among various forms of transportation.

PRACTICE YOUR SKILLS

1. Compare the map of Slavery in 1840 on page 317 with the map of the Cotton Kingdom on page 312. Which four coastal cities were in areas that had large numbers of slaves but produced no cotton? What state grew almost no cotton but used many slaves?
2. Look up the Supreme Court case *McCulloch v. Maryland* (1819) in the encyclopedia. Take notes on this case, making sure you write down who McCulloch was and what was at issue in this case.
3. Reread the section on the Lewis and Clark Expedition. It is on pages 289-290, Chapter 11 of your book. Then summarize the expedition in seventy-five words or less.

Unit 5

A PEOPLE IN CONFLICT

Chapter 13 An Era of Failed Compromises

Chapter 14 The Civil War

Chapter 15 Reconstruction

Unit Five examines the events leading up to the Civil War, the war itself, and the Reconstruction of the South after the war. Among the events discussed are the Compromise of 1850, the Lincoln-Douglas debates, the Dred Scott decision, major battles of the war, the Emancipation Proclamation, various plans for Reconstruction, and the effects of Reconstruction on the South.

The Confederate flag (left) and the Union flag (right)

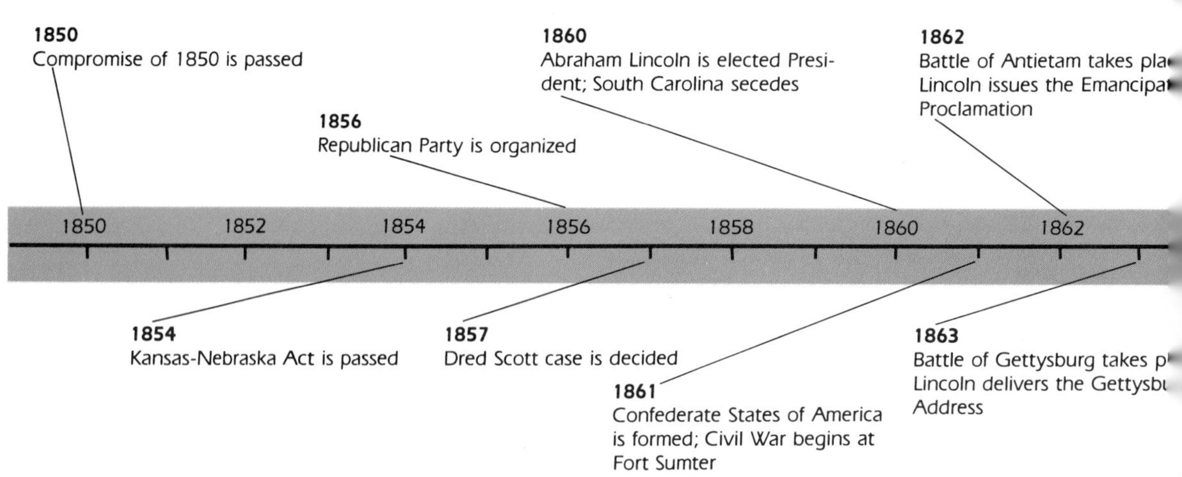
1850
Compromise of 1850 is passed
1856
Republican Party is organized
1860
Abraham Lincoln is elected President; South Carolina secedes
1862
Battle of Antietam takes pla
Lincoln issues the Emancipa
Proclamation
1850
1852
1854
1856
1858
1860
1862
1854
Kansas-Nebraska Act is passed
1857
Dred Scott case is decided
1861
Confederate States of America is formed; Civil War begins at Fort Sumter
1863
Battle of Gettysburg takes p
Lincoln delivers the Gettysb
Address

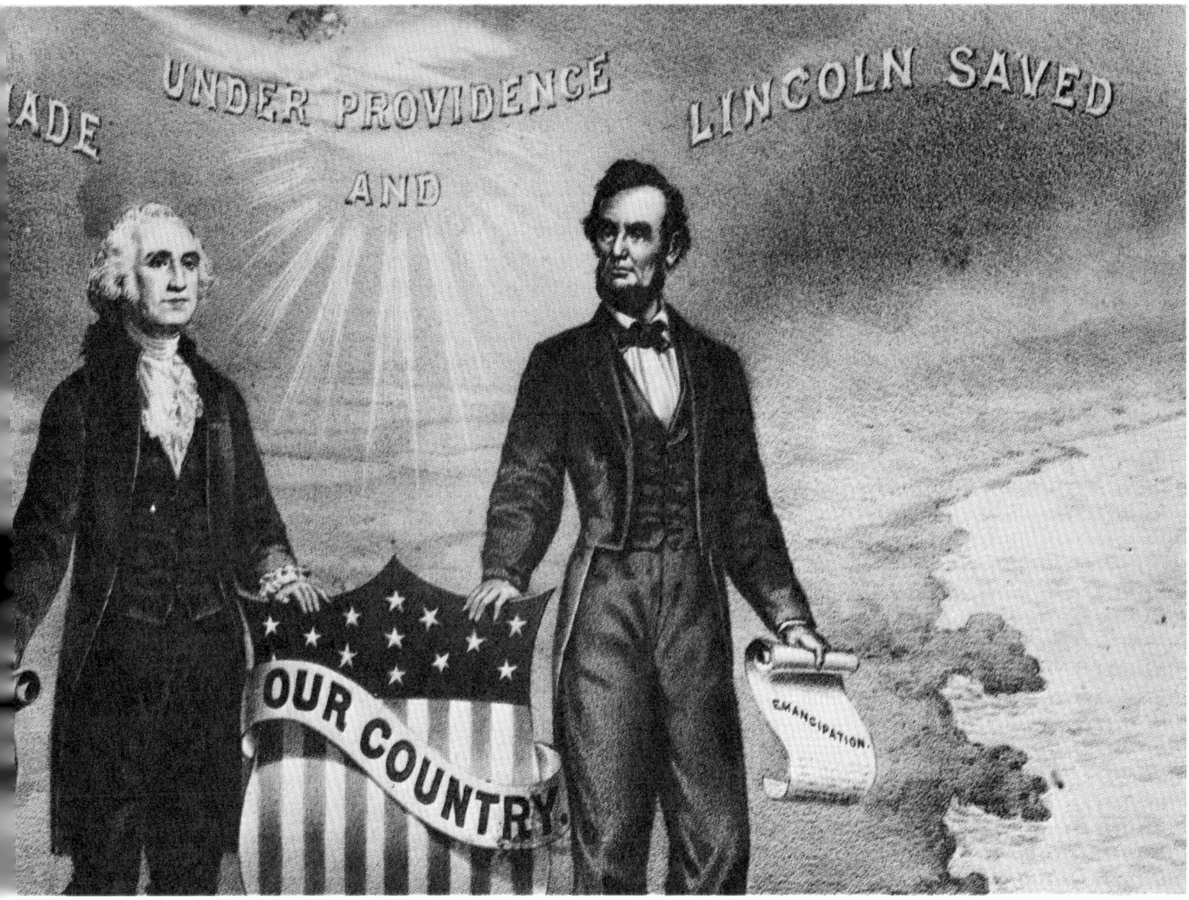

Washington and Lincoln guarding the national shield

1865
Lee surrenders at Appomattox; Lincoln is assassinated; Thirteenth Amendment is ratified

1870
Fifteenth Amendment is ratified

4 1866 1868 1870 1872 1874 1876 1878

1868
Most southern states are readmitted; Fourteenth Amendment is ratified; impeachment trial of Andrew Johnson takes place

1877
Compromise of 1877 is made; federal troops withdraw from South and Reconstruction ends

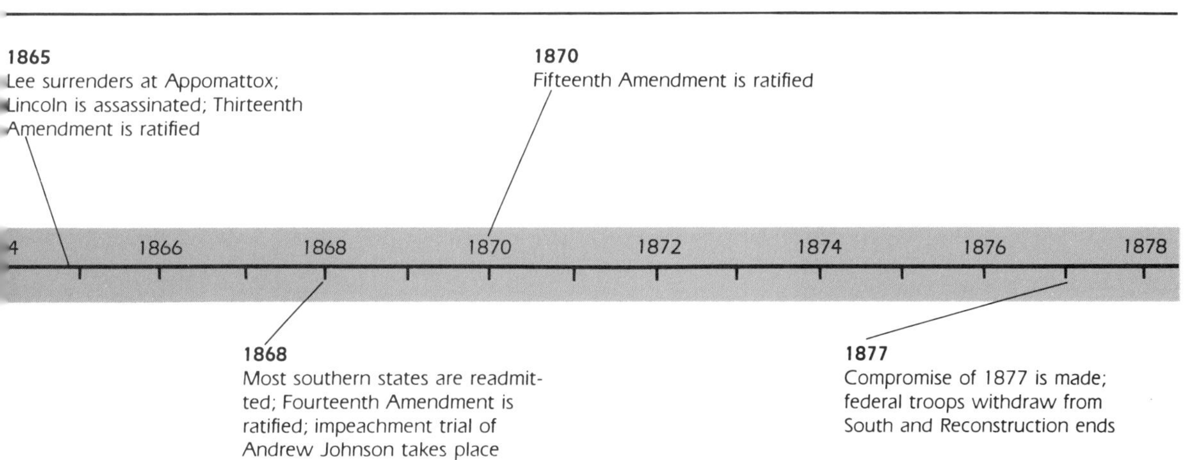

Chapter 13 discusses the events immediately preceding the Civil War. Lesson 13-1 focuses on the issue of the extension of slavery into new territories and explains how this issue increased tensions between the North and the South. Lesson 13-2 covers major events that increased the conflict between the two regions, including the Lincoln-Douglas debates, the Dred Scott decision, John Brown's raids, and the secession of South Carolina from the Union.

Chapter 13
AN ERA OF FAILED COMPROMISES

CONTENT OBJECTIVES

After completing the lesson, students will know:

- how the nation's growth aggravated the slavery issue in both the North and the South
- that the entry of California into the Union upset the balance established by the Missouri Compromise
- what was accomplished by the Compromise of 1850, though it failed to settle the slavery question
- that the issue of slavery caused the eruption of violence in Kansas

VOCABULARY

appropriation: a bill in Congress for spending money

popular sovereignty: voters in an area deciding for themselves whether to accept or reject slavery

omnibus bill: a single bill made up of several different proposals

13-1 Slave Versus Free States

As you read, think about these questions:

Why did the territory gained from Mexico cause problems in Congress?

Why did northerners and southerners have so much trouble coming to a compromise in 1850?

What events in the early 1850s helped drive the North and South farther apart?

Special Vocabulary appropriation, popular sovereignty, omnibus bill

You have learned that the economic differences in the country led to the development of three distinct sections—the North, the South, and the West. The people in each section had different needs and interests. For many years, however, people had been able to settle their differences peacefully. By 1850 things were changing. People began to put the interests of their section above the interests of the nation as a whole. Slavery became a key issue that led to a time of crises for the country.

Crisis and Compromise

The growth of the country widened the split between North and South. The United States was equally divided between slave and free states—fifteen of each—with an equal number of senators in Congress. In order to preserve this balance, Congress had to decide whether or not to allow slavery in newly acquired territories and in the states that would be carved out of these territories. Southerners were worried that the free states were growing faster in population than the slave states. They feared that people in the new territories would create more free states.

A Growing Crisis. The South's fears seemed to be coming true in 1846, when David Wilmot, a member of Congress from Pennsylvania, added an amendment to an *appropriation*, or spending, bill. The United States was involved in a war with Mexico. The Wilmot Proviso said that there could be no slavery in any territories the United States might gain from Mexico as a result of the war. Congress could not agree on the Wilmot Proviso. The northerners had a majority in the House of Representatives and passed the appropriation bill. The Senate, however, had the same number of southerners as northerners and voted against the bill. Because Congress was divided on the issue of slavery in new territories, it could not pass laws to deal with the area that the United States gained from Mexico in 1848. This area consisted of California and New Mexico. The problem became an issue in the presidential election of that year.

ACTIVITY

Objective: To summarize main ideas

Select three students and have each read one of the following sections, The Great Debate, Compromise of 1850, and The Fugitive Slave Act. Have each student in the class write a paragraph summarizing the main ideas in these paragraphs. Two main ideas that should be included are the provisions of the Compromise of 1850, and why the compromise failed to reduce tension over the slavery issue between the North and the South. Have two or three students read their paragraphs to the rest of the class. Discuss with the class the ideas mentioned and, with their suggestions, write the main ideas on the chalkboard.

These campaign posters from 1848 indicate some of the issues that separated the Whig candidates (left) from the Free Soil candidates.

The Whig Party chose General Zachary Taylor as its candidate for President. Although Taylor was a slaveholder from Louisiana, the Whigs hoped to avoid the issue of slavery. Because of Taylor's military victories, the Whigs expected him to win votes in the North as well as the South.

The Democratic Party was badly split. The Wilmot Proviso had driven a wedge between those delegates in favor of slavery and those against it. The antislavery Democrats left the convention and formed the Free Soil Party. They nominated former President Martin Van Buren, with a rallying cry of "Free soil, free speech, free labor, and free men."

The proslavery Democrats chose General Lewis Cass of Michigan. Cass campaigned on the idea of *popular sovereignty*. This meant that the voters in the new territories would decide for themselves whether or not to have slavery.

The split in the Democratic Party cost the Democrats the election. Zachary Taylor won by a large number of votes. The slavery question was beginning to decide the outcome of elections. The country looked to Taylor to settle the problem of slavery in the territories.

DISCUSSION

Ask students if they have ever felt so strongly about an issue that they would not listen to another point of view. Have them give examples from history of violence that occurred because two sides were unable to compromise. One example might be the Revolutionary War in 1776. Another is the fighting in "Bleeding Kansas." Have the students explain how Stephen Douglas attempted to provide a compromise in the Kansas-Nebraska Act.

The Great Debate. After gold was discovered at Sutter's Mill in 1848, the slavery crisis grew worse. Fortune seekers rushed into California. Soon there were 100,000 people in California, and President Taylor sent messengers to urge them to draw up a state constitution. The President said the settlers should decide the question of slavery for themselves.

In 1850 California asked to be admitted to the Union as a free state. Southerners were furious. The admission of another free state would upset the balance in the Senate. In addition, northerners wanted to end the slave trade in the District of Columbia. Some southerners began to call for the southern states to withdraw from the United States.

Henry Clay, now seventy-three years old and quite ill, returned to the Senate to propose a compromise. Clay needed all his many skills to steer his *omnibus bill*, a single proposal made up of several different bills, through Congress. President Taylor did not support Clay's compromise. John Calhoun, the senator from South Carolina, strongly opposed the plan.

Daniel Webster, another old Senate leader, spoke in favor of Clay's compromise. Webster, who was considered the greatest speaker of his time, gave a powerful address in support of the Union. He began: "I wish to speak today, not as a Massachusetts man, nor as a Northern man, but as an American and a member of the Senate of the United States. . . . I speak today because I do not wish the Union to break apart. Hear me for my cause." The Senate listened spellbound.

Even Webster could not change the minds of some senators. The debate dragged on. At the end of March, John Calhoun died. Then, unexpectedly, President Taylor fell sick after a Fourth of July celebration. A few days later, he was dead. The new President, Millard Fillmore, was a quiet man who hated fights. He threw his support behind Clay's proposal. At last, Congress passed the omnibus bill.

The Great Debate of 1850 brought three famous speakers to action in the Senate. In the picture, Henry Clay is shown addressing the group. Webster is seated at the left, head in hand. Calhoun is standing, third from the right.

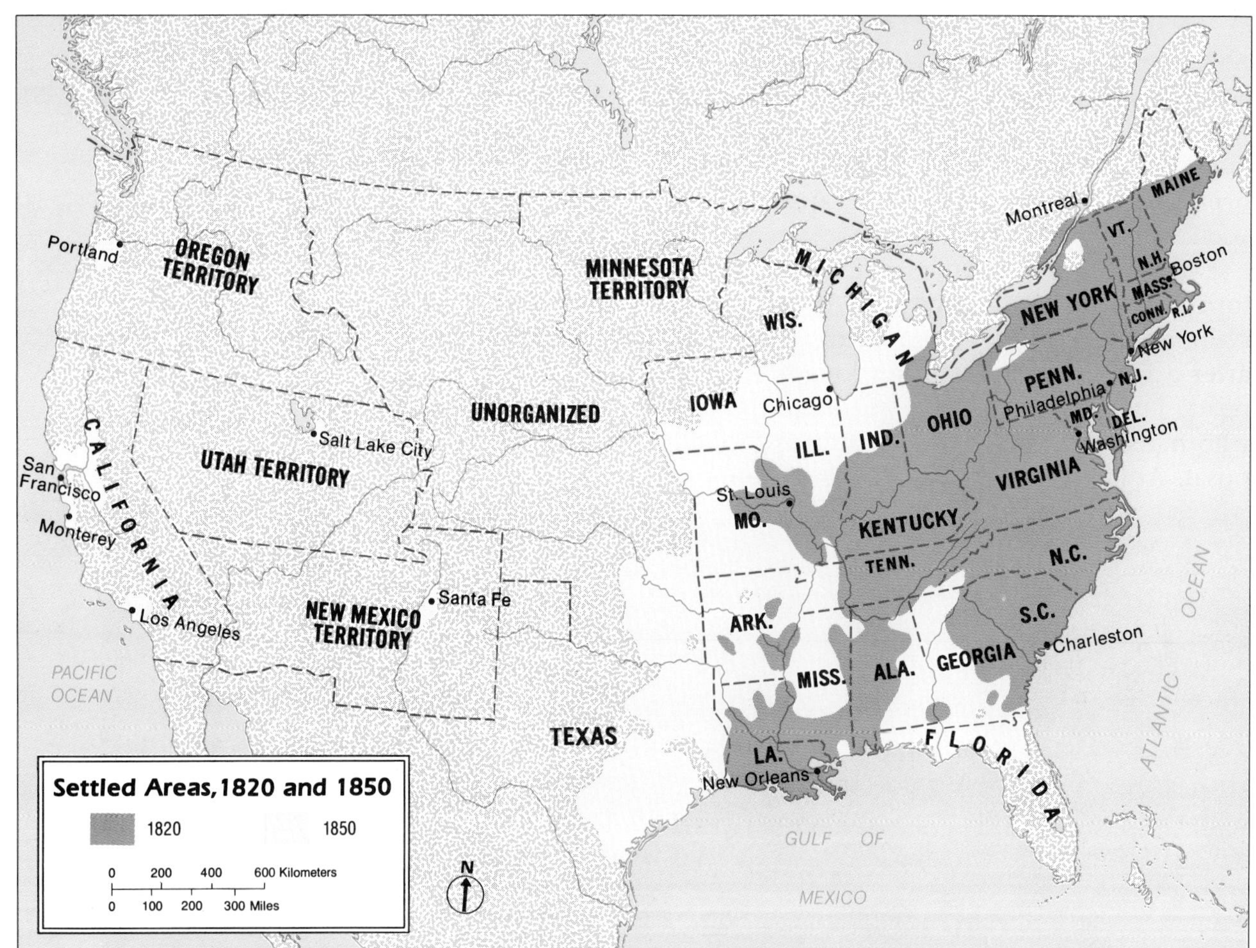

This map shows the areas which were settled by 1820. Which states that were *not* settled in 1820 had settled areas in 1850?

California, Florida, Iowa, Texas, and Wisconsin

Compromise of 1850. The Compromise of 1850 included most of the bills proposed by Henry Clay:

1) California was admitted as a free state.
2) Slave trade in the District of Columbia was ended.
3) New Mexico and Utah became territories in which the people themselves could decide on slavery.
4) A new fugitive slave law was passed to help slave-owners capture runaway slaves who had escaped to free states.
5) The boundary between Texas and New Mexico was adjusted. Texas lost some territory it had claimed, but, in return, the United states government paid Texas's state debt.

Both northerners and southerners were pleased over some parts of the compromise, but few people felt that the question of slavery in the territories had been settled. (See the map of Settled Areas, 1820 and 1850, above.)

Harriet Beecher Stowe was the daughter of a well-known antislavery preacher in New York. In Stowe's most famous book, the author combined her writing skills and her antislavery feelings.

The Fugitive Slave Act. It soon became clear that the question of slavery was far from settled. New social and legal forces attacked the compromise almost as soon as it became law. The Fugitive Slave Act angered northerners. This law allowed southerners to take back slaves who had escaped to northern states. Many people in the free states strongly opposed this law. Vermont became the first of several states to pass personal liberty laws, making it unlawful to capture former slaves.

Inspired by the Fugitive Slave Act, Harriet Beecher Stowe wrote *Uncle Tom's Cabin* in 1852. The story, which was directed against the injustices of slavery, became a best-seller. By mid-1853 about 1,200,000 copies had been published. The story also reached millions of people as a play. Others read *Uncle Tom's Cabin* in foreign languages. No one can say for certain how many people changed their minds about slavery because of *Uncle Tom's Cabin*, but it surely had a powerful effect.

The Kansas-Nebraska Act

The old leaders in Congress, Clay and Webster, died in 1852. Those who followed them cared less about compromise. William Seward, an antislavery senator from New York, had opposed the Compromise of 1850. Seward had made a

Although Stephen Douglas was Lincoln's longtime political opponent, he nevertheless supported Lincoln strongly in his efforts as President to preserve the Union.

speech during the crisis in which he said that there was a higher law than the United States Constitution. In other words, he believed that slavery was wrong even though the Constitution did not forbid people to have slaves.

The leader who seemed to have the best chance to fill Henry Clay's role as a voice for compromise was Senator Stephen Douglas of Illinois. Douglas had helped Clay get the Compromise of 1850 approved.

Additional Territories. After the Compromise of 1850, Stephen Douglas had said that he would never again bring up the question of slavery in the territories. He knew the anger it caused could only drive the North and the South farther apart. Because Douglas wanted to be President someday, he needed the support of southerners.

As leader of the Senate Committee on Territories, Douglas introduced a bill for organizing the territories of Kansas and Nebraska. The Kansas-Nebraska Act included the idea of popular sovereignty, thereby allowing settlers to decide if their territory would be free or slave. This part of the Kansas-Nebraska Act repealed the Missouri Compromise, which had forbidden slavery north of 36° 30′ north latitude.

Stephen Douglas thought that northerners as well as southerners would welcome the Kansas-Nebraska Act. He was badly mistaken. People in the North were furious when the act became law in 1854. Everywhere angry opponents of the Kansas-Nebraska Act burned effigies, or fake figures, of Douglas. Many northerners who opposed the act began to form political groups. Some of these people met in 1856 in Ripon, Wisconsin, to set up the Republican Party. Republicans hoped that Free Soilers, as well as antislavery Whigs and Democrats, would join them.

Bleeding Kansas. Both those in favor of slavery and those against it were eager to control the Kansas Territory. As it turned out, few settlers there actually owned slaves. Most people cared only about owning land. When elections were held in Kansas, however, the proslavery forces won a majority in the legislature. This was partly because proslavery people from Missouri crossed the border to vote in Kansas.

The new Kansas legislature began to draw up a constitution. It planned to ask Congress to make Kansas a slave state. In response, antislavery settlers elected their own legislature and governor and drew up an antislavery constitution.

Kansas now had two territorial legislatures and two state constitutions. Neither side seemed ready to back down.

In May of 1856, a group of Missourians attacked the antislavery town of Lawrence, Kansas. They burned the hotel, destroyed homes, and smashed the printing press. Antislavery people in Kansas—and throughout the country—were outraged.

Events turned even more violent. An abolitionist named John Brown took the law into his own hands. A very religious man, Brown thought that God meant for him to strike down slavery. Brown and a small group of followers attacked the proslavery town of Pottawatomie and killed five settlers.

Proslavery and antislavery forces exchange fire at Hickory Point in Kansas. The violence in Kansas marked the end of a period of compromise between North and South.

The shock waves from "bleeding Kansas" then reached the floor of the United States Congress. Senator Charles Sumner of Massachusetts rose to speak against slavery. He insulted the sponsors of the Kansas-Nebraska Act. One of the sponsors was Senator Andrew Pickens Butler of South Carolina.

Two days later Representative Preston Brooks, Butler's nephew, came up to Sumner after a meeting of the Senate. Brooks raised his cane and beat Sumner unconscious. In the North, newspapers attacked "Bully" Brooks for the savage event. Many white southerners, though, cheered Brooks for his act of revenge. The North and the South were drifting further apart.

ANSWER THESE QUESTIONS

1. What was the Wilmot Proviso?
2. What events led to the Compromise of 1850?
3. Who were some senators in favor of the Compromise of 1850?
4. Why did the idea of popular sovereignty not succeed in Kansas?
5. How did the growth of the country lead to problems over slavery?

ANSWER THESE QUESTIONS

1. an amendment to an appropriation bill saying there could be no slavery in territories gained from Mexico
2. the gain of new territories from Mexico; California's request to be admitted to the Union; the rise of abolitionists; the quarrels over slavery in Washington, D.C., and over fugitive slaves
3. Henry Clay, Daniel Webster
4. because the settlers in Kansas could not agree on the question of slavery and because outsiders interfered in their elections
5. by threatening to tip the balance between slave and free states in the Senate

PEOPLE IN AMERICA

Harriet Tubman

Harriet Tubman was an abolitionist and a former slave who led hundreds of other slaves to freedom on the Underground Railroad. The Underground Railroad was the name for the secret routes that slaves took and the stations, or hiding places, where they stopped on their way to freedom. Thousands of slaves escaped from the South during the 1840s and 1850s by the Underground Railroad. To make their escape, they needed the help of brave people like Harriet Tubman.

As a young woman, Tubman escaped from a plantation in Maryland when she learned that her owner was planning to sell her into heavy labor. Moving by night, she traveled through forests and across rivers. Both blacks and whites helped her along the way. At last she joyfully arrived in the free state of Pennsylvania.

Free herself, Tubman could not forget the unhappy people still in slavery. She began to make frequent trips back to Maryland to help other slaves escape, including her aged parents and nine brothers and sisters. Soon she was a "conductor" on the Underground Railroad. People called her "Moses" for her courage as a leader on the dangerous journey to freedom.

When the Fugitive Slave Act was passed in 1850, it became necessary to lead the slaves all the way to Canada so they could be safe from capture. Even so, Harriet Tubman never lost a single person who set out to freedom with her. In all, Tubman rescued about three hundred slaves in nineteen separate trips. Slave owners at one time put up a reward of $40,000 for her capture.

In later years, Tubman worked with those who were sick and in need. She was active in the women's rights movement in New England and New York. She also helped to set up two schools for blacks in the South and a home for old people in Auburn, New York, where she lived. The people of Auburn later put up a plaque to honor her deeds.

13-2 Prelude to War

As you read, think about these questions:
How was the Dred Scott case decided?
What was the Freeport Doctrine?
What was the result of John Brown's raid?
Who were the candidates in the presidential election of 1860?
What was the Confederate States of America?

Special Vocabulary	sue	due process	secede
	opinion	platform	

CONTENT OBJECTIVES

After completing the lesson, students will know:

- details of the Dred Scott decision
- the results of John Brown's raid on Harper's Ferry
- the reasons Abraham Lincoln won the election of 1860
- why the southern states decided to secede
- that the shots fired at Fort Sumter signaled the beginning of the Civil War

VOCABULARY

sue: start a lawsuit
opinion: statement of reasons for a decision by judges or justices
due process: the right to a trial in court
platform: formal statement of principles
secede: withdraw

Millions of people in both the North and South were proud of the Union. Most political leaders understood this feeling and tried to find ways that would keep the Union from breaking apart. Few people wanted to widen the split that already existed between North and South. The situation, however, was critical. If some solution to the nation's problems could not be found soon, it seemed that a war between these two sections of the country was certain.

Steps to Division

In 1856 Americans were sharply divided over the issue of slavery. The three major political parties were also split over this issue. The Republican Party and its candidate for President, John C. Frémont, were opposed to the spreading of slavery into the new territories. The American Party, made up of former Whigs, nominated Millard Fillmore. He tried to focus the attention of Americans not on slavery, but on immigration. The Democratic Party and James Buchanan supported the Compromise of 1850 and the Kansas-Nebraska Act. Buchanan tried to remain silent on the issue of slavery. With these political candidates having such different ideas, Americans had a wide choice for President.

Buchanan won this election. With this victory, the nation had a leader who wanted others to make the important decisions affecting the nation. Buchanan did not seem to be able to provide leadership when the country needed it most.

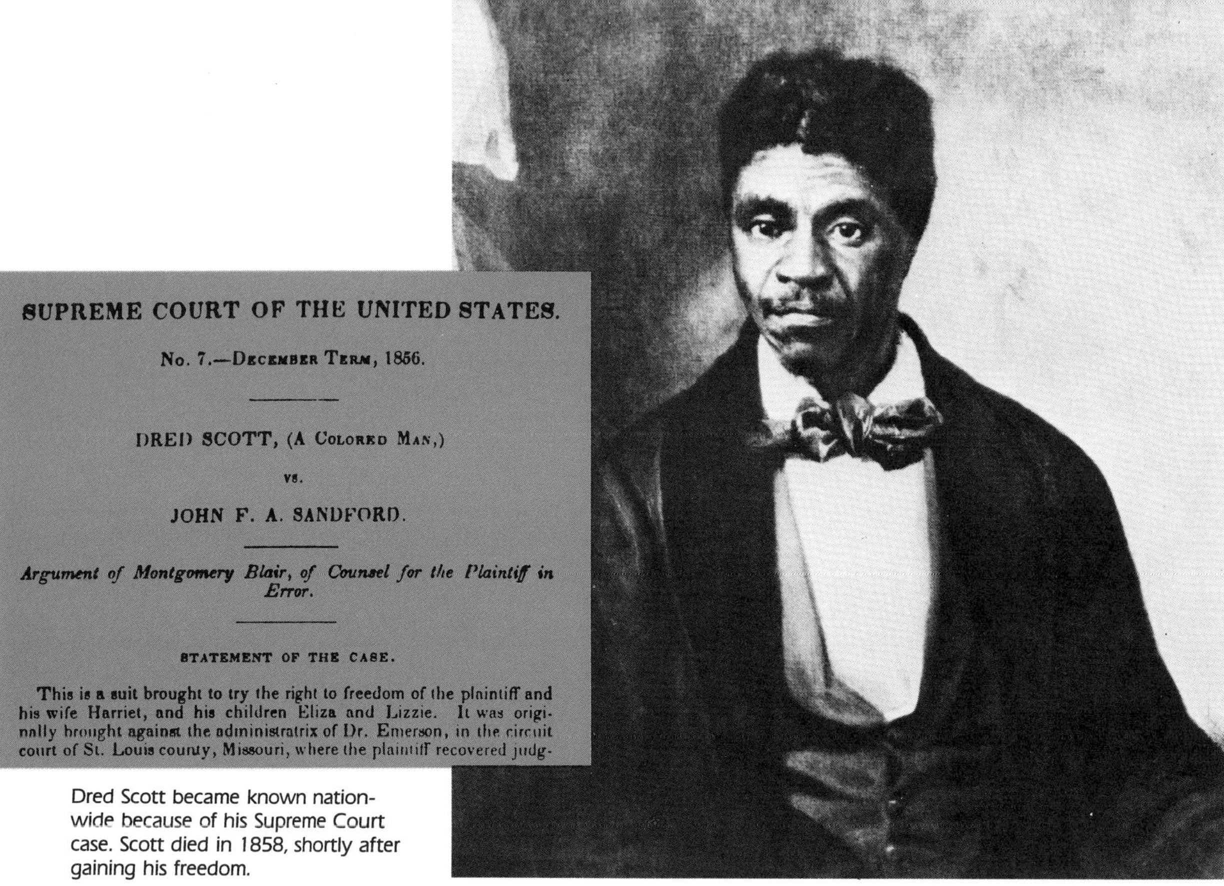

SUPREME COURT OF THE UNITED STATES.

No. 7.—December Term, 1856.

DRED SCOTT, (A Colored Man,)

vs.

JOHN F. A. SANDFORD.

Argument of Montgomery Blair, of Counsel for the Plaintiff in Error.

STATEMENT OF THE CASE.

This is a suit brought to try the right to freedom of the plaintiff and his wife Harriet, and his children Eliza and Lizzie. It was originally brought against the administratrix of Dr. Emerson, in the circuit court of St. Louis county, Missouri, where the plaintiff recovered judg-

Dred Scott became known nationwide because of his Supreme Court case. Scott died in 1858, shortly after gaining his freedom.

The Dred Scott Decision. President Buchanan hoped that the Supreme Court would settle the question of the spread of slavery into the territories. The Supreme Court had before it a case that could decide this issue. This case was called *Dred Scott v. Sandford.*

In 1834 Dred Scott, a slave, lived in Missouri, which was a slave state. Scott's owner, Dr. Emerson—a surgeon in the United States Army—took Scott to Rock Island, Illinois. The state of Illinois did not allow slavery. Later on, Dr. Emerson took Scott to Fort Snelling in the Wisconsin Territory, which also did not allow slavery. Scott lived in free territories for four years. Then he was returned to Missouri and slavery.

In 1846 Scott *sued,* or started a lawsuit, for his freedom in the Missouri courts. Scott said that because he had lived in free territories, he should be a free person, not a slave. The Missouri courts granted Scott his freedom, but this decision was overturned by the Missouri Supreme Court. Scott's case then went to a Federal District Court. From there, the case was appealed to the United States Supreme Court.

The Supreme Court said that there were three questions involved in the Dred Scott case:

1) Was Scott a citizen of the state of Missouri? If not, Scott did not have the right to sue for his freedom in the courts.
2) Did the fact that Scott had lived in free territories make him a free person and not a slave?
3) Was the Missouri Compromise, which made some territories free and others slave, constitutional?

Each of the justices handed down a separate *opinion*, or a statement of reasons for a decision. Chief Justice Roger B. Taney spoke for the majority of the Court. In answer to the three questions in the case, Taney said that Scott was not a citizen of the state of Missouri or of the United States. Therefore, Scott did not have the right to bring his case to court. Scott's four years in the free territories did not make him free. Scott's freedom was determined by the laws of the state that he lived in when he went to court—Missouri, a slave state. The Missouri Compromise was unconstitutional because Congress did not have the power to outlaw slavery in the territories. By outlawing slavery, Congress would be taking property—slaves—from the owners without the *due process* of law, or the right to a trial in court. The Fifth Amendment to the Constitution guaranteed this right.

This Supreme Court decision did not solve the problem of slavery in the territories as President Buchanan had hoped. Instead it only widened the split between the North and the South. As for Dred Scott, his friends raised enough money to buy his freedom in 1857.

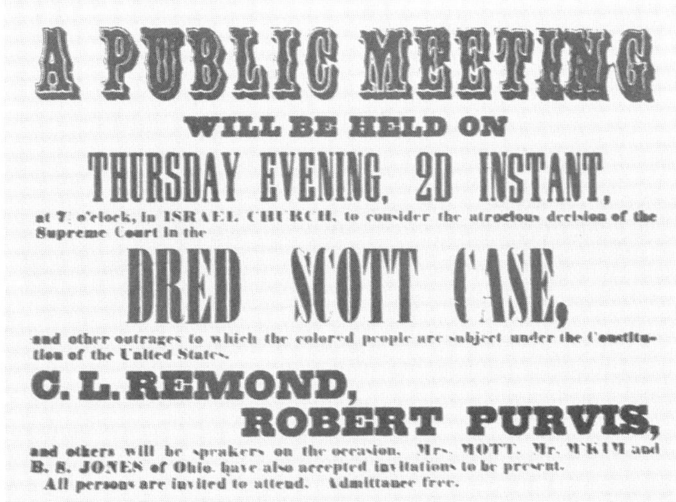

This poster shows how strongly people in the North reacted against the Dred Scott decision.

The Lincoln-Douglas debates of 1858 made the little-known Lincoln a national figure. Douglas had already won fame as a leader in the Senate.

Lincoln-Douglas Debates. In 1858 Stephen Douglas was running for reelection to the Senate from Illinois. If he won, he might become the presidential candidate of the Democratic Party in 1860. Many northerners, however, still blamed Douglas for the notion of popular sovereignty, which had led to the troubles in Kansas.

In the northern states, many people looked to the Republican Party to oppose the Dred Scott decision. In Illinois, the Republicans selected Abraham Lincoln to run against Douglas. At first, the lawyer from Springfield, Illinois, seemed no match for the clever, well-known Senator Douglas. A former Whig, Lincoln had served in Congress for one term during the war with Mexico. Most of the people in other states had never heard of him. All eyes were on Illinois, though. The election was a test of ideas on slavery.

Early in the campaign, Lincoln suggested that he and Douglas hold several debates in different spots around the state. Debates would help people from farms and small towns understand how he and Senator Douglas differed.

As it turned out, people who saw Lincoln could hardly imagine that he was running for the same office as Douglas. Tall and thin, Lincoln looked awkward in his poorly fitting clothes and high, stovepipe hat. While Douglas traveled on special trains, Lincoln rode as an ordinary passenger. Douglas, called the "Little Giant" because of his small height and great stature as a politician, rode in a coach at the head of parades. Lincoln got little attention as he walked with a few followers to the scene of the debate.

Douglas knew that Lincoln would not be an easy opponent. In Freeport, Illinois, Lincoln raised a shrewd question on slavery in the territories. He asked whether the people of a territory could decide against slavery before they became a state. If Douglas said no, the farmers who were against slavery in Illinois would vote against him. If he answered yes, he would be going against the Dred Scott decision, which was supported in the South.

Douglas replied that in spite of the Dred Scott decision, territories did not have to accept slavery if they did not want it. They could refuse to pass laws that would protect slaveowners. Douglas's reply became known as the Freeport Doctrine. The Freeport Doctrine helped Douglas win the election, but it hurt his chances of becoming President. He had said that the territories need not have slaves, and southerners never forgot that.

Although Lincoln lost the election, he had made his views known to the people. He believed that Congress must outlaw slavery in the territories. Although he did not actually attack slavery, he said "I believe this government cannot endure permanently half slave and half free." In other words, Lincoln thought that the country as a whole would have to decide the issue of slavery because the rights of all the people were concerned. Until the decision had been made, Lincoln insisted slavery should not be allowed to spread.

ACTIVITY

Objective: To identify points of view

Ask the class for two volunteers to play the roles of Abraham Lincoln and Stephen Douglas to reenact the Lincoln-Douglas debates. Divide the class into two groups—one to write a script for Douglas and the other to write a script for Lincoln. The scripts are to present each man's opinion on the issue of slavery. For Douglas, the script should include the Freeport Doctrine. Lincoln's script should include the statement, "This government cannot endure permanently half slave and half free." Have each volunteer read his or her statement to the class. Have the class decide which candidate made the most convincing presentation.

John Brown's Raid. By the end of 1857, law and order had returned to Kansas. The voters made it clear that they did not want proslavery laws or a proslavery constitution.

Then, in 1859, John Brown struck again. Brown attacked the federal arsenal at Harpers Ferry, Virginia. He hoped that the slaves in Virginia and the rest of the South would rise up to help him. They did not. After several days of fighting and fifteen deaths, federal troops under Colonel Robert E. Lee took John Brown prisoner.

Southerners were shaken by the violence of Brown's raid. The court in Virginia declared him guilty of murder and treason and sentenced him to die. On December 2, 1859, John Brown was hanged.

John Brown's trial caused strong feelings in the North and in the South. Some northerners thought that John Brown was a hero. Southerners thought Brown deserved to die. One thing was clear: northerners and southerners were no longer thinking like citizens of the same country.

John Brown, shown here on the way to his execution, hated slavery from childhood on. He helped many slaves escape to Canada before turning to violence.

DISCUSSION

Have students identify at least four characteristics of a good leader. Some attributes to consider might be self-confidence, respect for others and their ideas, and the ability to solve problems. Ask the students if they think the nation had good leadership during the period before the Civil War. Have them name at least two leaders, such as John C. Calhoun, Zachary Taylor, Henry Clay, or Stephen Douglas. Have the students explain why they were good or poor national leaders.

Point of No Return

By 1860 people were wondering if the Democratic Party could still make peace between the North and South. When the party met at Charleston, South Carolina, to select a candidate for President, a majority of the delegates favored Stephen Douglas. Try as they might, though, they could not get the two thirds of the votes needed to nominate him. Remembering the Freeport Doctrine, the southern Democrats refused to accept Douglas and left the convention.

In July the Democrats held another convention in Baltimore. This time they succeeded in nominating Douglas because the southerners were not there to oppose him. The southerners held their own meeting and nominated John Breckinridge of Kentucky.

The Election of Abraham Lincoln. The Republican Party met in Chicago in May. At first it seemed that William Seward might get the nomination. Most delegates, however, wanted a more moderate candidate, one whose views were not as harsh or one-sided. Since 1858 Abraham Lincoln had won the respect of many Republicans. These Lincoln supporters worked out a plan for the convention. The Lincoln "shouters," as they were called, packed the convention hall before Seward's supporters could arrive. On the third ballot, the Republicans nominated Lincoln. Reporter Murat Halstead wrote in the Cincinnati *Commercial* that the nomination of Lincoln was followed by shouts that sounded "like . . . a score of big steam whistles going."

The Republicans drew up a strong *platform,* or formal statement of principles, to appeal mainly to northerners. Hoping to please farmers, they called for cheap land in the West. To satisfy merchants, they called for a railroad to the West Coast and a higher tariff on goods imported from other countries. To draw the votes of foreign-born citizens, they opposed laws against immigrants. Above all, the Republicans called for a stop to the spread of slavery into the territories.

The Republicans' strategy worked. Every state in the North except New Jersey voted for Lincoln. He was elected by a clear majority of the Electoral College. Only forty percent of the voters actually marked their ballots for Lincoln. None of the slave states had voted for him.

Following the custom of the times, Lincoln did not campaign actively. He stayed home in Springfield after his nomination, letting his followers—and posters like these—speak for him.

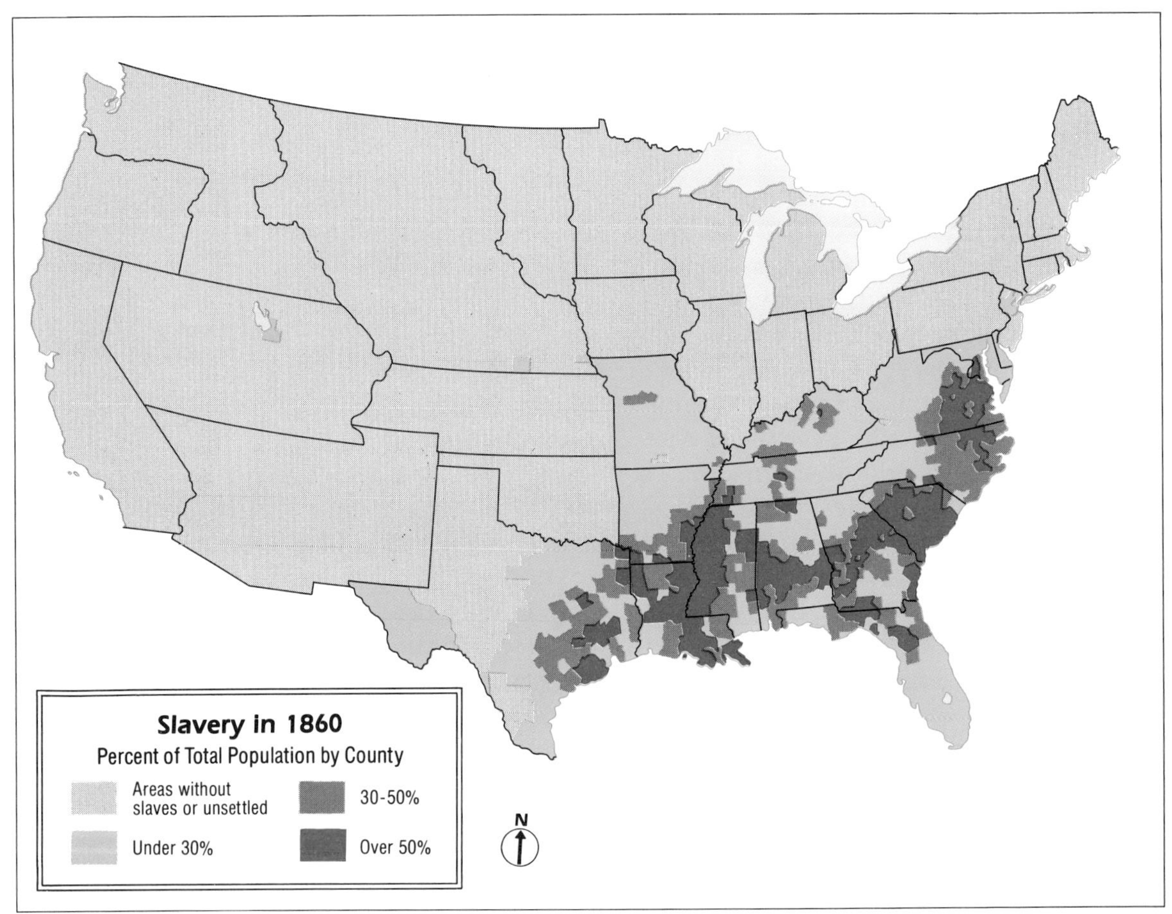

By 1860 slavery had become an important political issue. This map shows the areas in which there were slaves. Which color indicates areas with the largest percentage of slaves?

red

Formation of the Confederacy. Southerners had long worried, of course, that the North was growing more quickly than the South. They saw new states coming into the Union as free states. Sooner or later, the slave states would be in a minority. (See the map of slave states above.) They did not think that a southerner could ever be elected President again.

South Carolina quickly made plans to *secede,* or withdraw, from the Union. On December 20, 1860, a convention of South Carolinians met at Columbia, South Carolina. They eagerly voted in favor of secession. Every person at the meeting voted that South Carolina should leave the Union.

The action of South Carolina was the signal to other southern states. In the next six weeks, six of them voted to leave the United States. These states were Georgia, Florida, Alabama, Mississippi, Texas, and Louisiana. On February 4, 1861, their representatives met at Montgomery, Alabama. By the time the meeting was over, these southerners had formed a new country—the Confederate States of America. Soon after, they elected Jefferson Davis of Mississippi as their

An 1861 Currier and Ives cartoon pokes fun at the secession movement. The cartoon shows southern states as careless riders following South Carolina away from the Union and into danger.

President. Many people in both the North and the South looked at secession in horror. They hoped that something could yet be done to save the Union.

Lincoln's Inauguration. On a cold, gray day in March 1861, Abraham Lincoln stood before Chief Justice Taney and took the oath of office as President. Lincoln knew that the country was in grave trouble. The states of the Confederacy had already seized guns and forts lying within their borders.

In his inaugural address, Abraham Lincoln made it clear that secession was an unlawful act. He also appealed to the South to return to the Union. "We are not enemies," he declared. "We are friends. . . . Though passion may have strained, it must not break our bonds of affections."

Lincoln still hoped to settle the crisis without a war. He also wanted to keep the other southern states from seceding. Nine slave states, among them Virginia, had not yet made a decision. Lincoln did not want to recognize the Confederate States as a separate nation. Such recognition would make it appear that the United States approved of their acts. Above all, Lincoln wanted to make sure that the North did not attack the South.

When Lincoln was inaugurated, the thirty-four-year-old Capitol had not yet received its new dome. The dome was put in place in 1863 and topped with a statue of a woman symbolizing freedom.

Shots at Fort Sumter. In South Carolina, only Fort Sumter remained in the hands of United States troops. By April of 1861 these troops badly needed supplies. Supply ships were on the way, said Lincoln. The Confederate authorities decided to act quickly before the ships could arrive. They called on Major Robert Anderson, commander at Fort Sumter, to give up. They promised that his troops would be allowed to travel safely to the North. Major Anderson refused. On April 12, 1861, the Confederate guns began to thunder.

Once the Confederates attacked Fort Sumter, there was no turning back from war.

For thirty-four hours, the Confederate guns shelled Fort Sumter. Finally, the Confederates forced Anderson to surrender. When the supply ships at last arrived, they were used to take the troops back to New York.

The Confederate attack aroused people in the North. They held meetings and pledged their loyalty to the Union. President Lincoln wasted no time in calling for seventy-five thousand volunteers to join the army. Supporters of the Union in the North came forward eagerly to help put down the rebellion and save the Union.

The states of Virginia (except for the part that later became West Virginia), North Carolina, Tennessee, and Arkansas then joined the Confederacy. The terrible event that people had for many years tried to avoid was now taking place. Americans were going to war against one another.

ANSWER THESE QUESTIONS

1. Republican, Democratic, American
2. Illinois and Wisconsin
3. Territories could decide whether or not to pass laws to protect slave owners and slavery.
4. It overturned the legality of the Missouri Compromise and widened the split between the North and the South.
5. The North would get too much power; the South would not have enough representation in Congress; they believed the election signaled the end of their way of life.

ANSWER THESE QUESTIONS

1. What three political parties ran candidates for President in 1856?
2. In what free territories did Dred Scott live?
3. What was the Freeport Doctrine?
4. What effect did the Supreme Court decision on Dred Scott have on the United States?
5. Why did the Confederate States of America break away from the Union?

Objective: After completing these pages, students should know how to outline.

Outlining

An outline is one way of organizing information. An outline is a listing of main topics and the information that supports these topics.

In an outline the main topics and supporting information are organized according to the order in which they appear in a book. The main topic can be identified by placing a Roman numeral next to it. The supporting information can be identified by placing capital letters next to each piece of important information. Sometimes this important information is divided into subtopics. These are identified by Arabic numerals. Below is a portion of an outline of the information on page 351. Make sure to notice the structure of the outline. Each capital letter is placed directly under the first letter following the Roman numeral. Each Arabic numeral is placed directly under the first letter following the capital letters.

I. Election of Abraham Lincoln
   A. Republican Convention
      1. May 1860
      2. Chicago
      3. William Seward
      4. Lincoln wins on third ballot
   B. Platform
      1. Favored cheap land in the West
      2. Favored railroad to the West
      3. Favored higher tariff on imported goods
      4. Opposed laws against immigrants
      5. Called for a stop to the spread of slavery in the territories

Fill in the rest of the outline using the hints on the right.

C. Election

1. Won all northern states except New Jersey (who voted for Lincoln)
2. Majority in Electoral College (Electoral College)
3. 40 percent of voters (percentage of voters)
4. Won no slave states (slave states)

Working with Skills

STUDY SKILLS

ACTIVITY

Objective: To make an outline

Have students read the section of Lesson 2 beginning with "Point of No Return" to the end of the lesson. These paragraphs describe in detail the events leading directly to the Civil War. Have the students outline these events beginning with the failure of the Democratic Party to select a presidential candidate and ending with the outbreak of the Civil War. Direct them to outline the events in the order that they occurred.

RELATED MATERIAL

Duplicator/Copy Master Activity 28

THINKING THINGS THROUGH

1. an amendment to an appropriations bill, which would have prohibited slavery in the territory gained from Mexico
2. Northerners gained another free state in California; southerners gained popular sovereignty in New Mexico and Utah and a more severe fugitive slave law. 3. It repealed the part of the compromise that had forbidden slavery north of 36°30′ north

Chapter 13 SUMMARY

In the late 1840s and the 1850s, the issue of slavery began to cause more and more trouble. Southerners feared that the free states would gain a majority in the Senate.

Under the Compromise of 1850, California entered the Union as a free state, and the idea of popular sovereignty was applied to New Mexico and Utah. A Fugitive Slave Act was passed, and slave trade was ended in the District of Columbia.

In 1854 Congress passed the Kansas-Nebraska Act, based on the idea of popular sovereignty. War broke out in Kansas between proslavery and antislavery forces. The Supreme Court was unable to solve the trouble with its Dred Scott decision.

The Republican Party was organized and two years later nominated Abraham Lincoln for the Senate. After a series of debates, Lincoln lost the Illinois race to Stephen Douglas.

By 1860 the North and the South were acting like two different countries. Both groups were upset by John Brown's raid and trial in 1859. In the presidential election of 1860, Lincoln defeated Douglas and two other candidates.

After the election, South Carolina seceded from the Union. In February 1861 six southern states formed the Confederate States of America. On April 12, 1861, the Confederates opened fire on Fort Sumter. President Lincoln called for volunteers to save the Union.

Chapter 13 TEST

WORDS TO REMEMBER

Match each of the following words with the correct definition below.

e 1. due process
a 2. appropriation
d 3. popular sovereignty
b 4. platform
c 5. opinion

a. a bill in Congress for spending money
b. a formal statement of principles
c. the reasons given by judges or justices for making a decision
d. the principle that settlers in new territories could decide whether to have slavery
e. the principle that requires a court trial in order to take a citizen's property

THINKING THINGS THROUGH

Answer each of the following questions.

1. What was the Wilmot Proviso?
2. How did the Compromise of 1850 please both northerners and southerners?
3. How did the Kansas-Nebraska Act change the Missouri Compromise?
4. Why did Chief Justice Roger Taney think that Dred Scott was not entitled to be free?
5. How did the Freeport Doctrine help Douglas win reelection to the Senate from the state of Illinois?
6. What conditions helped Lincoln win the presidency?
7. Why did the South feel that secession was necessary?

RELATED MATERIALS

Duplicator/Copy Masters: Activities 28, 29; Quiz 27
Workbook pages 38-40

latitude. **4.** Scott was not a citizen of Missouri or of the United States, therefore had no right to bring his case to court.
5. Many Illinoisans were pleased with the idea that states could choose for themselves about slavery. **6.** Democrats were split; the Republican platform appealed to northerners, who were more numerous than southerners; Lincoln's views were well known because of the earlier debates; he was a moderate.
7. Southerners believed they would be a minority in the government and would be forced to give up their way of life, including slavery.

WORKING WITH SKILLS

Use the information in your textbook to fill in the missing topics in the following outline:

I. Laws Concerning Slavery
   A. Compromise of 1850
      1. Admitted California as a free state
      2. Ended slave trade in District of Columbia
      3. Allowed popular sovereignty in New Mexico and Utah territories
      4. Passed a new fugitive slave law
      5. Adjusted boundary between Texas and New Mexico
   B. Kansas-Nebraska Act
      1. Organized territories of Nebraska and Kansas
      2. Allowed popular sovereignty in Kansas and Nebraska
      3. Repealed Missouri Compromise

ON YOUR OWN

1. In December 1860 South Carolinians printed the poster at the right to announce their state's secession. By early 1861 seven states had seceded from the Union and formed the Confederate States of America. Imagine that you worked for a newspaper in 1861, when Tennessee had to decide whether to join the Confederacy. Write an editorial supporting or opposing secession. You may want to read some editorials in your local newspaper to see how writers try to persuade their readers to adopt a certain view. In your editorial, talk about slavery in the territories and Lincoln's election.

2. Of all the people you have read about in this chapter, which one would you most like to meet? Write a paragraph explaining why you chose the person you did and what three questions you would ask him or her if you had the chance.

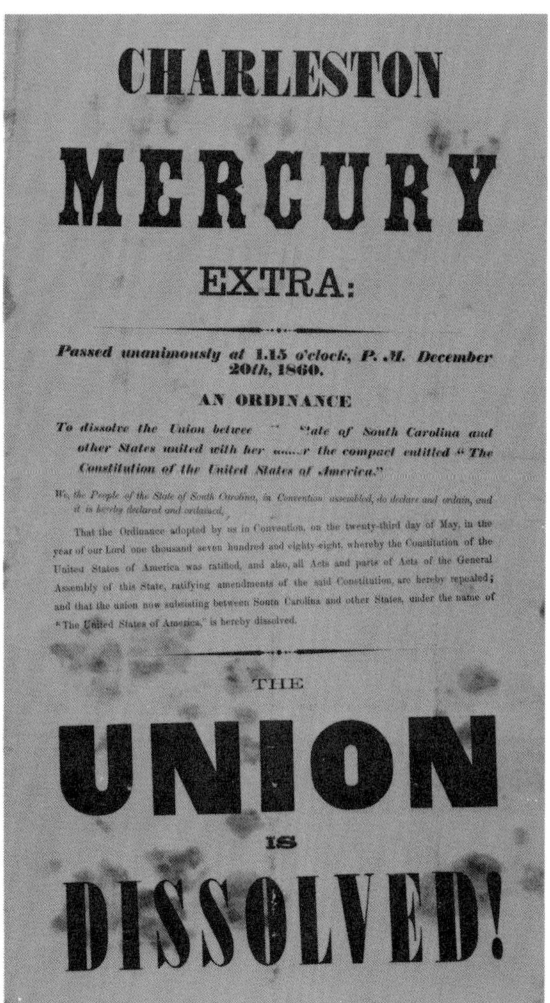

Chapter 14
THE CIVIL WAR

Chapter 14 covers the Civil War from the first battles to its conclusion. Lesson 14-1 outlines the resources each side had at their disposal, their leaders, and the early strategies of the war. Lesson 14-2 discusses the major battles that took place, the Emancipation Proclamation, the Gettysburg Address, and Lincoln's assassination.

CONTENT OBJECTIVES

After completing the lesson, students will know:

- the resources available to each side
- the leaders on each side and the way men and women in both the North and the South contributed to the war effort
- that new inventions made the Civil War the first "modern" war

VOCABULARY

offensive: the entering of enemy territory to fight

defensive: the defending of home territory against attack

conscription: drafting people for military service

14-1 The Sides Are Drawn

As you read, think about these questions:

What were the strengths and weaknesses of each side in the Civil War?

How did Lincoln and Davis differ as presidents?

In what ways did some people oppose the war?

How did modern inventions change the way war was waged?

Special Vocabulary offensive defensive conscription

A civil war—a war between two groups of people within the same country—can be more ferocious and full of hate than war between separate countries. The American Civil War was just such a fiery struggle between two sections of the country—the Union, or the North, and the Confederacy, or the South. Families were sometimes divided as members found themselves on opposite sides, and many relatives—even brothers—prepared to fight against each other.

General Robert E. Lee, a Virginian, was only one person who had the hard choice to make. Although he was a southerner, he did not support secession and had freed his slaves several years before. Still, when President Lincoln offered him command of the Union armies—one day after Virginia had seceded from the Union—he turned it down. He had decided, he replied, to offer his services to the South: "I cannot raise my hand against my birthplace, my home, my children."

Comparing the Union and the Confederacy

The following chart compares the North and the South at the start of the war. The numbers do not include the border states—Kentucky, Maryland, and Missouri. Those slave states, along with Delaware, remained loyal to the Union.

RESOURCES OF THE NORTH AND SOUTH

	North	South
Population	22 million	9 million
Railroads	20,000 miles (32,000 kilometers)	9000 miles (14,400 kilometers)
Factories	100,000	20,000
Money in Bank Deposits	$189 million	$47 million

Union Army volunteers often received a bounty, or payment, for volunteering. Some bounty jumpers enlisted several times under different names, deserting each time after being paid.

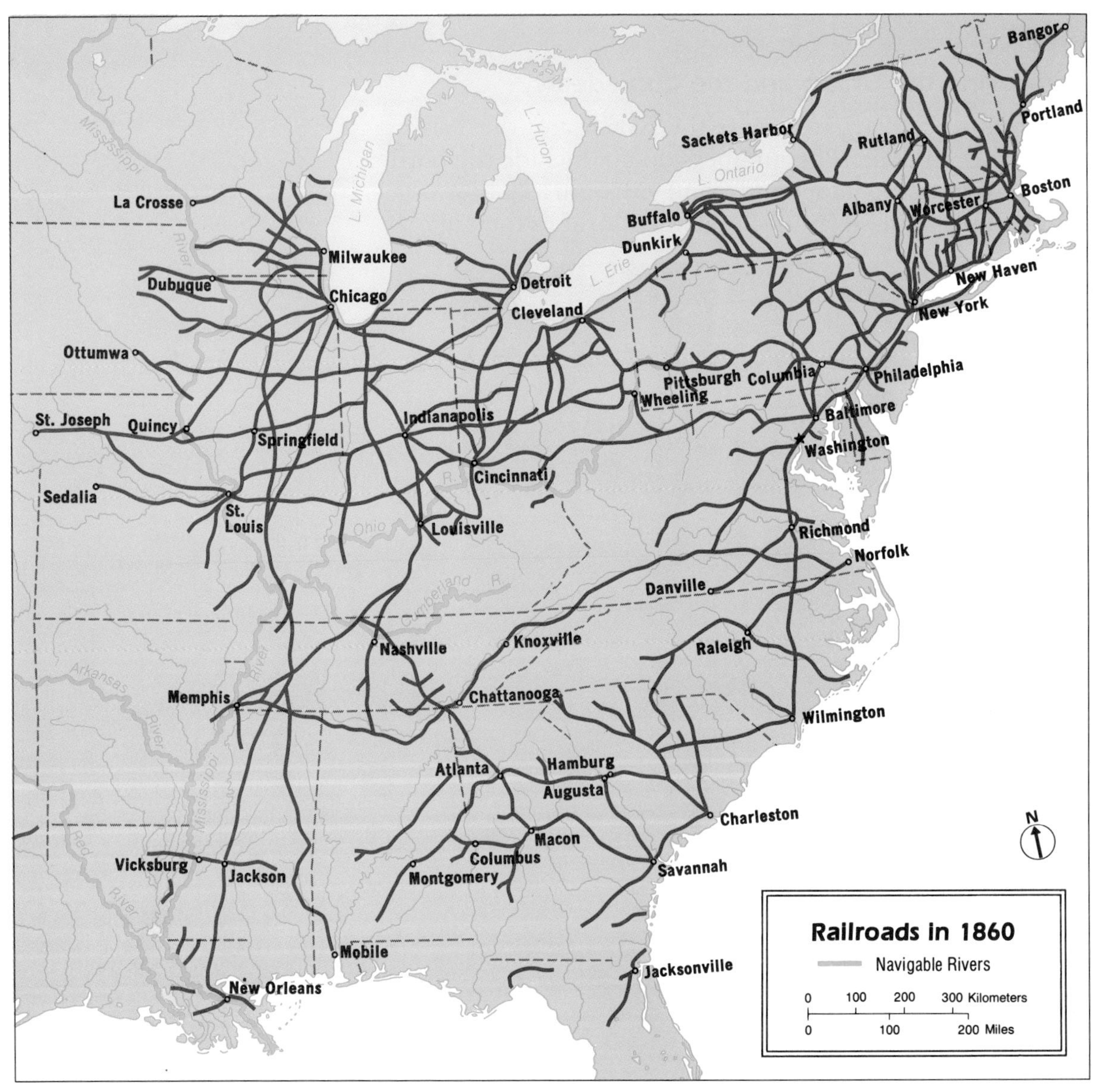

This map shows the network of railroads that existed in 1860. Which region had more railroads, the North or the South?

the North

Strengths of Each Side. We see that the Union would have many more soldiers than the Confederacy. It also had a navy. It had more money, more factories, and more railroads than the South. (See the map on this page.) These resources helped make the Union strong.

The South, on the other hand, had better military leaders. Many high-ranking officers in the United States Army were southerners. When the war came, most of those officers sided with the Confederacy.

The Union soldiers, wearing blue uniforms, would be fighting on the *offensive*, that is, they would be entering enemy territory to fight. The Confederate troops, dressed in gray, would be fighting on the *defensive*, that is, they would be guarding their own territory. People defending their own soil often find extra strength. In addition, the lifestyle in the South produced people who were especially skilled in the use of weapons and horses. As a group, Confederate soldiers were better prepared for battle than Union soldiers.

DISCUSSION

Discuss with the students their opinions of the advantages of each side at the start of the Civil War. Ask students if the Confederacy's advantages were as important as the Union's strengths (higher population; larger army; and more money, factories, and railroads). Have students explain why they feel the advantages of one side outweigh those of the other.

War Aims. The North had one goal: to save the Union. After 1862, however, the freeing of the slaves became a proud second goal. The South had a single goal: to win independence for the Confederacy.

The South was willing to risk war with the more powerful North partly because it believed that Great Britain and France would come to its aid. Almost all the cotton the British needed for their factories came from the southern states. The Confederates believed that the need for cotton would force the British to break the Union blockade of southern ports. As it turned out, the British got the cotton they needed from Egypt. Moreover, many people in Great Britain supported the Union because they opposed slavery. Great Britain, therefore, never came to the aid of the Confederacy. France also kept hands off the war.

The Home Front

Both the Confederacy and the Union had strong leaders. Jefferson Davis, of the Confederacy, had more political experience than Abraham Lincoln. A graduate of the United States Military Academy, Davis had been a senator from Mississippi and a secretary of war under President Franklin Pierce. He had trouble working with others, however. The people he chose for his Cabinet did not work well together.

In contrast, Abraham Lincoln, once in office, showed he had more wisdom and good judgment than most Americans expected to find in him. He had the ability to inspire great loyalty and he was skilled at balancing differences of opinion among members of his government.

Following the war, Jefferson Davis was charged with treason. He was imprisoned for two years but was never tried. His birthday is still celebrated as a holiday in seven southern states.

Support for the War. It was not just the leaders of government whose best efforts were needed. The war effort on both sides required the courage and hard work of ordinary men and women. Many women, North and South, worked in factories and at jobs that were formerly held by men. In the

Clara Barton (above right) was called the "Angel of the Battlefield" during the war. She later founded the American Red Cross. Sallie Tompkins (above) received the title of captain for her work in the Confederate army.

Confederacy women also helped their cause by running the farms and plantations. Many women produced cloth and other important goods in their homes. Several southern women were useful Confederate spies. Women in both sections cared for sick and wounded soldiers in hospitals.

No one knows for sure how many soldiers served in the Civil War. According to some sources, about 1,500,000 soldiers wore Union blue and about 900,000 the Confederate gray. From the beginning of the war, blacks in the North had tried to enlist in the Union army. At first Lincoln refused to let blacks fight. He feared losing the support of the border states, which had many slaveholders.

Resistance to War. Some people in the North wanted a peaceful settlement, even if it meant compromising with the South. Lincoln had a serious problem with northerners who were willing to see the southern states depart from the Union without a fight. "Peace at any price" was their goal. In order to restrict the influence of those people, who were called Copperheads, Lincoln agreed to certain policies that he would not have allowed in peacetime. For example, he ordered his generals to send people whom they considered dangerous to jail without a trial. After the war, the Supreme Court declared those policies unconstitutional.

Some northerners opposed *conscription*, or forcing people into military service. Congress passed draft laws during the Civil War when the supply of volunteers ran out. Angry crowds in New York City rioted against the war in 1863.

In the South few people openly opposed the war. The states, however, sometimes refused to pay their share of the cost of the Confederacy and were slow in supplying troops to

Mathew Brady, pioneering photographer, captured many scenes of the war on film, including this portrait of family life in the Thirty-First Pennsylvania Regiment.

the Confederate army. Confederate leaders believed strongly in states' rights. That is, they believed the states were more important than the central government. This greatly weakened the Confederacy at critical moments.

A New Kind of War

The Civil War is sometimes called the last of the old wars and the first of the new. At the beginning of the war, the armies fought much as they had fought for a hundred years. Modern inventions, though, were beginning to change things. Railroads and the telegraph made it easier for armies to move troops and supplies. Aerial balloons, introduced by the North, made it possible to spy out enemy positions. Weapons that were accurate at greater distances than before added to the horror of battle.

At first people in both the North and the South thought that the war would be short and easy. They could not imagine that hundreds of thousands of soldiers would die before it was over. They could not imagine, either, the suffering the wounded and dying would undergo in hospitals that were crude and unsanitary. The short, easy war turned into the nation's seemingly endless nightmare.

ANSWER THESE QUESTIONS

1. What were the advantages of the North at the beginning of the Civil War?
2. What major advantages did the South have?
3. What were the goals of each side in the Civil War?
4. How did people on the home front support the war?
5. Why is the Civil War considered the first of the new wars?

ACTIVITY

Objective: To recognize points of view

Obtain a recording of "Dixie," written by Dan Emmet as a minstrel tune (Burl Ives is one musician who has recorded this song), and "The Battle Hymn of the Republic," lyrics by Julia Ward Howe to the tune of "John Brown's Body" (Anita Bryant has recorded this song). Have students suggest why these songs captured the imagination of the American people during the Civil War period.

ANSWER THESE QUESTIONS

1. more soldiers, more money, more factories, more railroads, an army and a navy
2. better military leaders, defensive war, better prepared soldiers
3. North: to save the Union; South: the independence of the Confederacy
4. Many women took over jobs formerly held by men; women also worked in hospitals. Volunteers, including many blacks, served in the armies.
5. Modern inventions changed the way war was waged.

CONTENT OBJECTIVES

After completing the lesson, students will know:

- where the Civil War was fought
- the strategies of each side and details of the major battles that took place
- why the Union decided to change its strategy after Bull Run
- the text of the Gettysburg Address
- how the war was ended at Appomattox Court House
- about the assassination of Abraham Lincoln

VOCABULARY

peninsula: a piece of land surrounded by water on three sides
siege: the surrounding of a fort or a city by an army to starve it into submission
emanicipation: the freeing of those in slavery

14-2 The Battle Fronts

As you read, think about these questions:

How did the Union plan to defeat the Confederate armies in battle?

What early battles convinced the Union that the war would not be won quickly?

What battle was the turning point in the war for the North?

Special Vocabulary peninsula siege emancipation

The soil of the states that had seceded became the bloody battleground of the Civil War. The awful battles took place in an area reaching from the Atlantic Ocean to the Mississippi River, and from the Gulf of Mexico to southern Pennsylvania. Large cities and tiny churchyards alike witnessed the terrible fighting. Almost every area of the South learned the agony of war.

Early Strategies

The Union developed a strategy for winning called the "anaconda policy"—after the snake that crushes its victims. The plan was to capture Richmond, the Confederate capital, gain control of the Mississippi River, and blockade the Confederacy. The Confederacy aimed to fight off the attacks until it could get foreign help and invade the North.

The Border States. Lincoln understood how important Maryland, Kentucky, and Missouri were to the Union cause. If those border states joined the Confederacy, the Union might well lose the war. Lincoln tried hard not to do anything that would force them into the ranks of the South.

Western Virginia was also important to the Union hopes for victory. When Virginia seceded from the Union, people in the western part of the state talked of seceding from Virginia. A pro-Union government was set up at Wheeling, aided by federal troops. Shortly thereafter, West Virginia was admitted to the Union as a separate state.

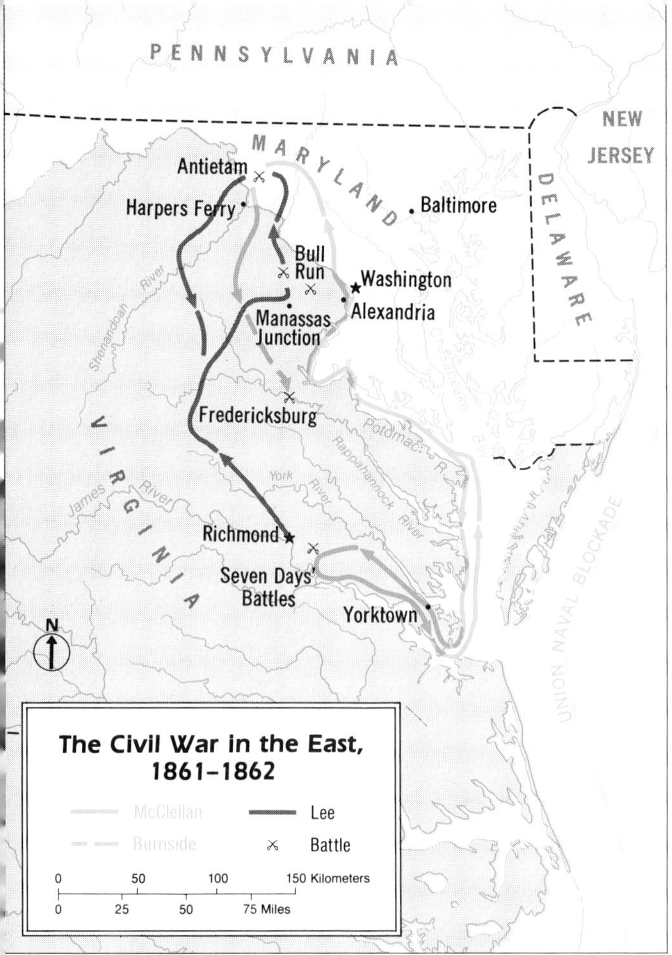

This map shows the movements of the northern and southern armies in the East during the early part of the Civil War. In what two states did the major battles take place?

Virginia and Maryland

The First Battle of Bull Run. In the summer of 1861, the Union had thirty thousand troops training near Washington, D.C. Most of them were not yet ready to fight. Still, the North was eager to smash the Confederacy. Early in July, General Irvin McDowell was ordered to advance on the Confederate position. The main force of the Confederate army was at Manassas Junction, near a stream called Bull Run, 25 miles (40 kilometers) from Washington. (See the map on this page.)

The Confederate general, P.T. Beauregard, knew that the Union army was advancing. He organized his troops along the Bull Run, hoping to attack before McDowell was ready. Meanwhile, another Confederate general, Joseph Johnston, slipped past the Union defenses in the Shenandoah Valley. He reached Beauregard with nine thousand more soldiers. On July 21, 1861, the first major battle of the war began.

Beauregard tried to carry out his plan to attack McDowell, but it failed. Instead, McDowell chose experienced divisions to lead the charge toward the Confederates. It seemed as if the Union forces would win the battle. The Confederates rallied. They gained a new hero, too: General Thomas J. Jackson. Someone had said of him during the attack: "There is Jackson standing like a stone wall." Ever afterward he was known as "Stonewall" Jackson. The South carried the day. The Union troops retreated in panic. The people in the North were shocked at the Union defeat.

Peninsular Campaign. The Union's goal, the capture of Richmond, remained unchanged. A new general, George B. McClellan, was put in command of the Army of the Potomac—the army stationed near Washington. McClellan waited months before he thought his troops were ready to go into action. At last, in April 1862, he ordered them forward.

McClellan's plan was to take his army by sea to Chesapeake Bay and to land on a *peninsula* near Yorktown. A peninsula is a piece of land surrounded by water on three sides. McClellan then planned to march up the peninsula to Richmond. He set out with ninety thousand troops.

It took McClellan more than a month to capture the cities of Yorktown and Williamsburg. Just 5 miles (8 kilometers) from Richmond, he faced Robert E. Lee, the general of the Army of Northern Virginia. For seven days the two forces

This wounded drummer boy symbolizes the courageous spirit of soldiers on both sides during the war. Youths in their early teens often lied about their age to fight, and die, alongside battle-seasoned soldiers.

On the day Yorktown surrendered following a month-long siege, Union gunners shelled a Confederate artillery unit. This sketch, made during the actual battle, was unsigned.

battled fiercely. On July 2, 1862, both broke off the fight. The Seven Days' Battle closed the Union's peninsular campaign. Soon after, Lincoln removed McClellan from his command and replaced him with General John Pope.

The Second Battle of Bull Run. Under General Pope, the Army of the Potomac once again moved toward Richmond. General Lee, on the Confederate side, did not wait for the Union forces to reach him. Instead, he attacked. On August 29–30, the two armies clashed near Bull Run. In this second Battle of Bull Run, Pope's army was badly beaten. Again northern hopes of taking Richmond had been dashed.

A Long War

Meanwhile, the Union forces fought elsewhere. The Union knew that supplies to the South from Europe would have to be cut off. The Union navy, therefore, tightly blockaded the southern ports. If the North could also gain control of the Mississippi River, it would place a tight iron ring around the Confederacy.

The War in the West. The Union decided to win the Mississippi by advancing up the Tennessee and Cumberland rivers. The campaign began in February 1862.

On February 6, General Ulysses S. Grant, with fifteen thousand troops, and Admiral Andrew Foote, with a fleet of ships, opened an attack on Fort Henry on the Tennessee River. Fort Henry fell quickly, and Grant moved on to Fort Donelson on the Cumberland River, which he took on

Confederate soldiers, thinking a victory at "bloody Shiloh" was theirs, wasted their energy raiding Union tents. After more than twenty-four hours, 24,000 soldiers lay dead or wounded.

February 16. General Grant and his troops had now achieved the first phase of the Union's western strategy. When word of these two victories reached the North, Grant became a hero. The struggle for the rivers was not yet over, however.

The Confederate army stationed at Fort Donelson had retreated to Corinth, where it regrouped. The two generals in command, Beauregard and Johnston, realized that Grant would soon receive more reinforcements from the Union forces fighting on the Mississippi River. While Grant marched to a stopping place for boats called Pittsburg Landing to await the reinforcements, Johnston made plans to attack Grant. On April 6, 1862, the Confederate army surprised the Union army as it rested near a little log church called Shiloh. A terrible battle began, and the Union forces were nearly defeated. During the night, however, Generals Buell and Wallace arrived to aid Grant. The next day, the tide of the battle turned. The Confederate army retreated once more to Corinth. Both sides had taken such heavy losses that people on both sides would always remember the battle as "bloody Shiloh."

Control of the Mississippi River. With the defeat of the Confederate forces at Forts Henry and Donelson, the Union held control of the Tennessee and Cumberland rivers. The upper Mississippi River was also in the hands of the Union. Only New Orleans, Louisiana, and Vicksburg, Mississippi, remained in Confederate hands. Once those cities fell, the Union would control the entire length of the river. (See the map on page 369.)

New Orleans could not offer much resistance to the combined forces of Admiral David Farragut and General Benjamin Butler. Vicksburg proved more difficult. The Union navy had tried unsuccessfully for a month, from May to June 1862, to bombard the city into submission. The Confederate flag—the Stars and Bars—continued to fly. In December and early 1863, land forces also failed to defeat General John Pemberton, the commander at Vicksburg. Shortly, Grant took up the effort.

On the night of April 16, 1863, with twenty thousand troops, he crossed the Mississippi River below the city. Twice he attacked it. Both times he was driven back. In May he began a *siege* of the city. A siege is the surrounding of a fort or city by an army to starve it into submission. The siege

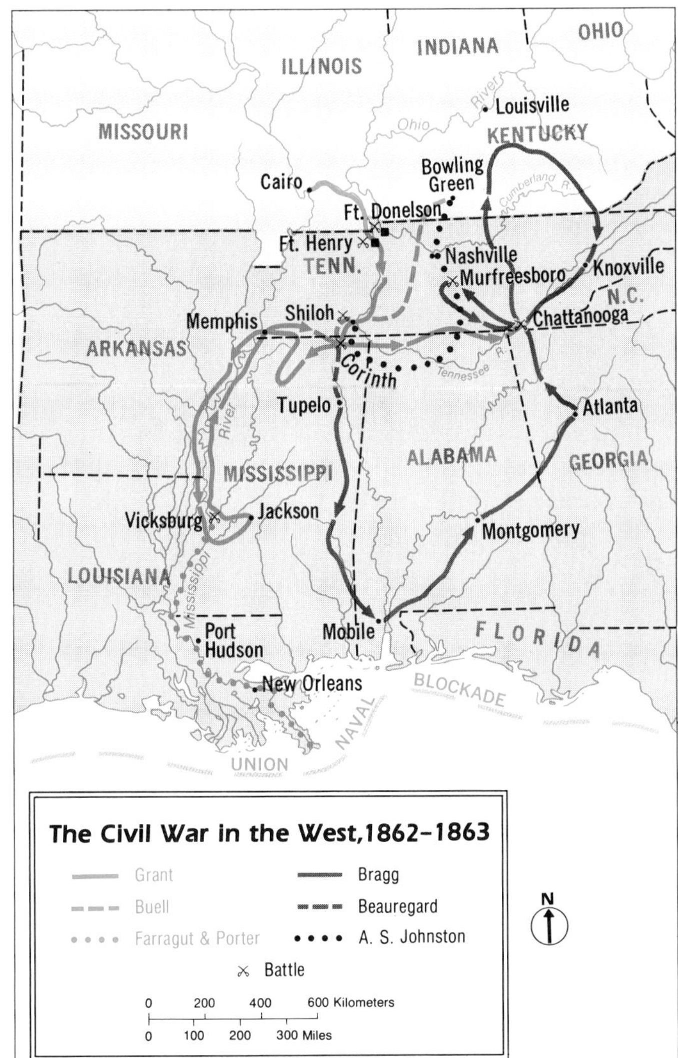

Illinois, Kentucky, Tennessee, Mississippi, Louisiana, Arkansas, and Alabama

This map shows the course of the war in the West. Trace the movement of Grant's forces from Cairo to Chattanooga. Which states did they pass through?

lasted more than six weeks. On July 4, Vicksburg finally surrendered. The Union now held the Mississippi River.

The U.S.S. *Monitor* (right) fought the former U.S.S. *Merrimac*—renamed *Virginia* by the Confederates—to a draw in the first naval battle between ironclad ships.

The Naval Blockade. The contribution of the Union navy was enormous. In addition to patroling the important rivers and bombarding targets from the sea, its ships blockaded more than 3500 miles (5600 kilometers) of Confederate shoreline. To enable the navy to carry out those missions, the North stepped up its production of ships. The Union blockade effectively cut off needed supplies to the Confederacy. As a result, the South suffered severe shortages of many goods—including salt, which was needed for preserving food.

The Confederate Charge

For the Confederacy to win in the end required that it go on the offensive. Lee would have to carry the war onto northern soil. He hoped to divide the North, seize badly needed supplies, and by his success obtain European help.

Antietam. In September 1862, Lee crossed into Maryland. For the first time Confederate forces had entered northern territory. McClellan was in charge of stopping Lee's advance. Luck was with McClellan. A Union soldier found a copy of Lee's plans. McClellan acted quickly to intercept Lee.

On September 17, McClellan and Lee met near Antietam Creek in Maryland. In the fierce battle that followed, the Union lost 2100 soldiers, the Confederates 2700. Lee retreated across the Potomac River, and McClellan failed to pursue him. The Confederates had escaped—to fight again another day. However, Antietam was the turning point in the war for the North. In forcing Lee's retreat, it had ended a long series of northern military defeats in the East.

The battle also had an important impact on Europe. Before the news of it had reached Europe, England and France had been planning to try to bring the Union and the Confederacy to peaceful terms. After the news of Antietam arrived, Europeans knew that the Union could end the war by itself.

Emancipation Proclamation. Antietam was important at home, too. President Lincoln had been waiting for a Union victory in order to make an announcement. Now Antietam provided the right moment. On September 22, 1862, he announced that all slaves in the Confederacy would be free on January 1, 1863. When New Year's Day arrived, he issued the *Emancipation* Proclamation. Emancipation means the freeing of those in slavery.

The Emancipation Proclamation did not apply to the border states. Lincoln was afraid that those states would secede if he freed their slaves. Actually, almost no slaves were freed simply by the proclamation because the Confederacy did not recognize Lincoln's authority. The proclamation did serve notice on the entire country that the fate of slavery would no longer be in the hands of the states but in those of the federal government.

The Emancipation Proclamation had a significant effect on the war effort. The Union army had already begun to enlist blacks as soldiers. Blacks could now see that the war had a new purpose: freedom for a whole race. Black soldiers, organized in black units, fought splendidly in several battles. By 1865 about 180,000 blacks had seized the chance to help fight for their people's freedom. Twenty-one of them earned the Congressional Medal of Honor for their bravery during the war.

A black Union soldier (below left) reads the news of the Emancipation Proclamation to his family, whose reactions range from celebration to disbelief. Although black soldiers were paid half as much as whites, about 68,000 blacks proudly gave their lives for the Union.

DISCUSSION

Have the students discuss what Lincoln meant when he said, "We here highly resolve that these dead shall not have died in vain; that this nation, under God, shall have a new birth of freedom. . . ." The discussion might include the Union soldiers' purpose for fighting, which was to reunite the nation. What might Lincoln have been referring to when he used the words, "a new birth of freedom"?

The Battle of Gettysburg. Jefferson Davis and General Robert E. Lee decided that the South had to strike a crushing blow to the Union. They planned a powerful invasion of Pennsylvania. In June 1863, Lee's army began to move northward.

Union generals were able to discover the movement of Lee's troops. General Joseph Hooker hoped to invade Richmond while Lee was marching north. Lincoln ordered him instead to keep his army between Lee's troops and Washington, D.C. Soon thereafter, Lincoln removed Hooker and gave the command to General George G. Meade. Meanwhile, Lee moved from his camp in Maryland to a new one in Pennsylvania. Meade followed him.

As Lee's army moved toward the town of Gettysburg, Pennsylvania, his advance force met Meade's advance force. The date was July 1, 1863. The bloodiest battle ever fought on the American continent was about to begin.

For two days Lee and his commanders ordered wave after wave of Confederate soldiers to go forward in attacks against Union strongholds on Cemetery Ridge and Culp's Hill. Meade's troops held firm. On the third day, Lee ordered General George Pickett to attack the enemy yet again.

Fifteen thousand "grays" moved across the rolling hills, their shining bayonets fixed. Almost instantly they met the deadly hail of Union gunfire. In a few minutes not a single mounted officer was left. Pickett's charge had led the Confederate forces as far north as they would ever get. The rebel army retreated into Virginia.

A few months after the battle, Lincoln attended the dedication of the Union cemetery at Gettysburg. In ten sentences known today as the *Gettysburg Address*, he expressed —perhaps better than anyone else has ever expressed—what

The handful of Confederate soldiers who managed to mount Cemetery Ridge struggled courageously to hold their position.

America stands for and what the Civil War was being fought to preserve.

> Fourscore and seven years ago our fathers brought forth on this continent, a new nation, conceived in Liberty, and dedicated to the proposition that all men are created equal.
>
> Now we are engaged in a great civil war, testing whether that nation, or any nation so conceived and so dedicated, can long endure. We are met on a great battle-field of that war. We have come to dedicate a portion of that field, as a final resting place for those who here gave their lives that that nation might live. It is altogether fitting and proper that we should do this.
>
> But, in a larger sense, we can not dedicate—we can not consecrate—we can not hallow—this ground. The brave men, living and dead, who struggled here, have consecrated it, far above our poor power to add or detract. The world will little note, nor long remember what we say here, but it can never forget what they did here. It is for us the living, rather, to be dedicated here to the unfinished work which they who fought here have thus far so nobly advanced. It is rather for us to be here dedicated to the great task remaining before us—that from these honored dead we take increased devotion to that cause for which they gave the last full measure of devotion—that we here highly resolve that these dead shall not have died in vain; that this nation, under God, shall have a new birth of freedom—and that government of the people, by the people, for the people, shall not perish from the earth.

Only five copies of the Gettysburg Address in Lincoln's handwriting remain in existence. The original was sold for the benefit of wounded Union soldiers.

The Final Campaign

The battles of Antietam and Gettysburg spelled the end of the Confederate plan to carry the war to the North. With the Mississippi River in Union hands (Vicksburg had fallen during the battle of Gettysburg), and the naval blockade growing ever tighter, the final stages of the war began.

Ulysses S. Grant. Early in 1864 President Lincoln brought General Grant east and placed him in charge of all the Union forces. Grant's work was cut out for him: to capture Richmond. As he moved south toward the Confederate capital, he had 100,000 soldiers. Lee had only 60,000. Another Union army—of 36,000 soldiers—under General Butler

ACTIVITY

Objective: To make inferences

Estimates establish that 540,000 people out of a total population of 31 million (1860) died as a result of the Civil War. The majority of the soldiers were under 21 years of age. Have the students imagine they are young soldiers writing a letter to their parents. They have just fought in an important battle. Have the students identify the battle, the state in which it was fought, and how they felt during the fighting.

Ulysses S. Grant, nicknamed "Unconditional Surrender" Grant for his refusal to compromise in battle, was the first West Point graduate to become President.

planned to march to Richmond up a bank of the James River in an attempt to cut Lee off from the rest of the South. To support Lee, General Beauregard had 30,000 soldiers.

On May 4–7, the two armies met at a stretch of woods called the Wilderness. Neither side won, but both sides lost thousands of soldiers in the battle. The next day, Grant pursued Lee to Spotsylvania Court House. Again, five days of bloody fighting produced no victor.

On June 1, Grant once more attacked Lee's forces, this time at Cold Harbor. For three more days Grant sent his troops against the Confederate army. In one month Grant had lost sixty thousand troops—the total number Lee had begun with. Lee had lost nearly half his army.

Grant now moved his troops to Petersburg, Virginia, 20 miles (32 kilometers) south of Richmond. He hoped to cut off all railroad and supply lines to Richmond. After four days of heavy fighting in an unsuccessful attempt to take the city, Grant began a siege that would last nine months.

March to the Sea. After the Mississippi River came under Union control, Union generals began a march into Tennessee. On September 19, 1863, Chickamauga fell to the "blues." On November 25, Chattanooga surrendered. The Union armies of the West, under William T. Sherman, were ready to march from Chattanooga to the Atlantic Ocean.

With 100,000 soldiers, Sherman left Chattanooga on May 7, 1864. On September 1, he reached Atlanta. His troops practically destroyed it by burning it. Then he set out on a bold march across Georgia, destroying everything in his path

Factories, cotton gins, railroads, warehouses, and bridges were deliberately destroyed during Sherman's march to the sea.

that the enemy might find useful. Sherman's unopposed advance left a wasteland 60 miles (96 kilometers) wide and 300 miles (480 kilometers) long. On December 10, 1864, Sherman entered Savannah, Georgia. From there, he marched northward into South Carolina. His soldiers continued to destroy what they could not take. The Confederacy's days were numbered.

John Wilkes Booth is believed to have shot himself when the barn where he was cornered by authorities was set afire.

Appomattox. Grant, meanwhile, was still laying siege to Petersburg. On March 25, 1865, Lee tried to break through Grant's lines. The superior Union forces held. Petersburg at last fell. Grant quickly pursued Lee and surrounded his forces. On April 3, Richmond surrendered. On April 9, 1865, Grant and Lee met at Appomattox Court House, where Lee surrendered in a simple ceremony. Grant allowed the Confederate officers to keep their guns and horses. In return, the soldiers pledged to fight no more. The ghastly Civil War was over.

Death at the Theater. Abraham Lincoln took the oath of office for the second time in March 1865. In his second inaugural, he urged all Americans to help heal the nation's wounds. On Friday, April 14, 1865, the President and Mrs. Lincoln went to Ford's Theater in Washington to attend a popular play. Suddenly a figure appeared behind the chair where Lincoln sat. A pistol was fired at the President's head. The man who shot Lincoln was John Wilkes Booth, a well-known actor who was greatly upset because the South had lost the war.

The President was carried to a house across the street from the theater. He died the next morning. His secretary of war, who was present, said softly, "Now he belongs to the ages." As people throughout the country mourned, they must have known that Lincoln would be remembered forever as the Savior of the Union and the Great Emancipator.

ANSWER THESE QUESTIONS

1. How did the Union hope to end the Civil War quickly?
2. What was the Union's western strategy?
3. How did the Emancipation Proclamation affect the war effort?
4. Why did the Union change its strategy for winning the war after the losses at Bull Run and in the Peninsular Campaign?
5. Why was the Battle at Antietam the turning point in the war for the North?

ANSWER THESE QUESTIONS

1. by capturing Richmond
2. to control the Mississippi, Tennessee, and Cumberland rivers
3. It added the cause of freedom for a whole race as a northern goal.
4. Union leaders realized that the Confederacy was far more capable of defending its territory than the Union had believed.
5. It stopped a series of losses for the North, kept Great Britain and France out of the war, and provided the chance for Lincoln to issue the Emancipation Proclamation.

Working with Skills

MAP SKILLS

ACTIVITY

Objective: To read special maps

Obtain a relief map showing the southern states and display it for the class. Have students refer to the map on page 365, "The Civil War in the East, 1861-1862." Have them identify on the relief map, and mark with a piece of colored tape, the places where battles of the Civil War occurred. Were they fought in hills or valleys? Ask the students if they see a relationship between the terrain and where the war was fought.

ANSWERS

1. Atlanta, Savannah, Charleston, and Raleigh
2. southwest
3. east

1. Chattanooga, Knoxville
2. Jackson, Atlanta, Macon, Savannah

1. Texas
2. Maine

Special Maps

Some maps give only a specific type of information. In the study of history, these special maps have many uses. For example, they can show the movement of armies, the means of transportation between different areas, or changes that occur over time. A special map shows only the information that is important for its particular purpose. It may leave out many features shown on general maps.

The map on the next page is an example of a map that shows the movement of armies. It uses lines and arrows to show the directions in which armies moved during the last three years of the Civil War. Study the map and then answer the following questions:

1. What cities did General Sherman pass through after leaving Chickamauga?
2. In what direction did Lee travel after Gettysburg?
3. In what direction did Grant go when he left Memphis?

Some transportation maps show the routes taken by explorers or early settlers. Others trace the building of roads and railroads. The map on page 360, "Railroads in 1860," is an example of this second type of transportation map. Use the map to answer these questions:

1. Suppose the Confederates had run a troop train from Memphis to Richmond. What cities would the train have passed through?
2. What cities would the North have had to capture to cut the shortest rail route between New Orleans and Charleston?

The map on page 340, "Settled Areas in 1820 and 1850," is an example of a map that shows change. On this map, you can see the various areas that were settled during the thirty years between 1820 and 1850. Use the map to answer the following questions:

1. Arkansas, Louisiana, Texas, and Mississippi were Confederate states. Which of them had the least amount of settled area in 1850?
2. Which New England state had unsettled areas in 1850?

RELATED MATERIAL

Duplicator/Copy Master Activity 31

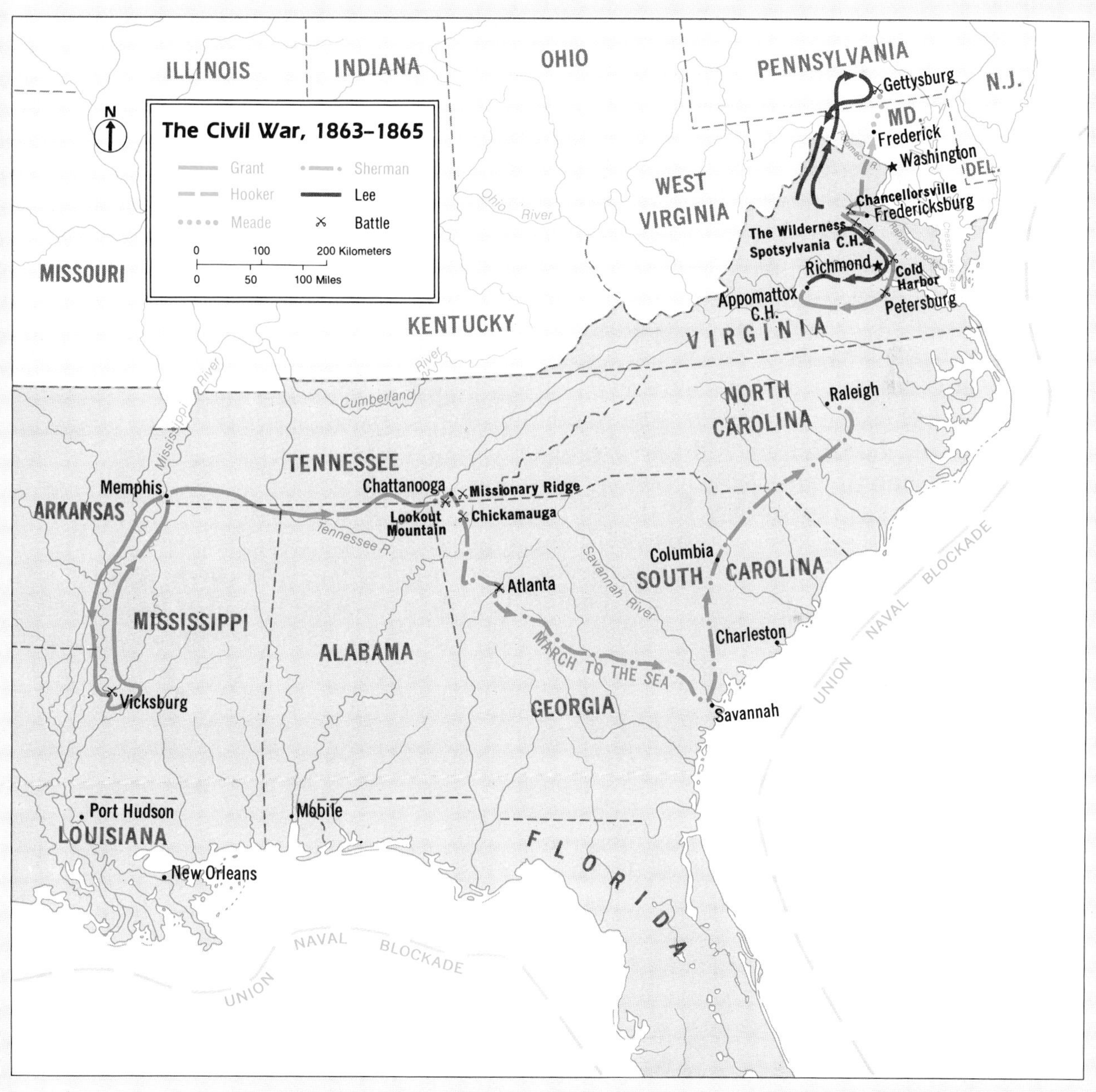
The Civil War, 1863–1865
Grant
Hooker
Meade
Sherman
Lee
Battle
0 100 200 Kilometers
0 50 100 Miles
N
ILLINOIS
INDIANA
OHIO
PENNSYLVANIA
N.J.
MD.
DEL.
WEST VIRGINIA
MISSOURI
KENTUCKY
VIRGINIA
NORTH CAROLINA
TENNESSEE
ARKANSAS
SOUTH CAROLINA
MISSISSIPPI
ALABAMA
GEORGIA
LOUISIANA
FLORIDA
Gettysburg
Frederick
Washington
Chancellorsville
Fredericksburg
The Wilderness
Spotsylvania C.H.
Richmond
Cold Harbor
Appomattox C.H.
Petersburg
Raleigh
Memphis
Chattanooga
Missionary Ridge
Lookout Mountain
Chickamauga
Columbia
Atlanta
Charleston
Savannah
Vicksburg
Port Hudson
Mobile
New Orleans
Ohio River
Cumberland River
Mississippi River
Tennessee R.
Savannah River
MARCH TO THE SEA
UNION NAVAL BLOCKADE
UNION NAVAL BLOCKADE

Chapter 14 SUMMARY

From 1861 to 1865, the Union and the Confederacy fought the Civil War. The North had more people, more money, more factories, and more railroads than the South. The South, however, had better military leaders and better prepared soldiers than the North.

The North fought on the offensive with the goal of saving the Union. The South fought on the defensive with the goal of independence for the Confederacy.

Even with its superior forces, the North was unable to win easily. At first, Lincoln could find no generals who were able to defeat Robert E. Lee. Finally, the Union stopped Lee at Antietam in Maryland.

In the West, General Ulysses S. Grant won several important victories. In July 1863, he captured Vicksburg, giving the Union control of the Mississippi River.

During 1863, Lee tried to invade the North. The Union and Confederate armies fought a three-day battle at Gettysburg in Pennsylvania. During 1864 and 1865, Grant hammered at the Confederate armies until Richmond fell.

Lee surrendered at Appomattox Court House on April 9, 1865. On April 14, 1865, Lincoln was assassinated by John Wilkes Booth.

Chapter 14 TEST

WORDS TO REMEMBER

Choose the correct word from the list below to complete each sentence.

a. siege
b. conscription
c. peninsula
d. emancipation
e. offensive
f. defensive

1. The North fought on the __e__ because it had to enter enemy territory.
2. The South fought on the __f__ because it was protecting its own territory.
3. Young people were forced to serve in the army through __b__.
4. Troops marched down the __c__, land surrounded on three sides by water.
5. The city surrendered after a four-month __a__, or attack by a surrounding army.
6. Abolitionists encouraged Lincoln to declare the __d__, or freedom, of the slaves.

RELATED MATERIALS
Duplicator/Copy Masters: Activities 30, 31; Quiz 28
Workbook pages 41-44

THINKING THINGS THROUGH

1. independence for the Confederacy. 2. North: some wanted peace; some supported Confederate cause; some were against conscription. South: some thought the states were more important than the central government. 3. Many British opposed slavery; Great Britain could get cotton from Egypt. 4. allowed the Union army to enlist blacks and to add freedom to their war goals. 5. The Confederates fought well; they were defending their homeland.

THINKING THINGS THROUGH

Answer each of these questions.

1. What were southerners fighting for in the Civil War?
2. Why did some people in the North and South refuse to support the war?
3. Why did Great Britain refuse to aid the Confederacy?
4. How did the Emancipation Proclamation affect the war effort in the North?
5. Why did it take the North so long to capture Richmond?

WORKING WITH SKILLS

Study the following maps: (a) "Settled Areas in 1820 and 1850," on page 340; (b) "Railroads in 1860," on page 360; and (c) "The Civil War, 1863–1865," on page 377. On which of these maps would you find this information:

1. the route that General Sherman took from Savannah to Raleigh
2. the most direct railroad route between Nashville and Chicago
3. the southern state with the largest area of unsettled territory in 1820
4. the location of the Battle of Chickamauga
5. the westernmost city served by a railroad in 1860

ON YOUR OWN

1. Pretend that you are a diplomat appointed to represent the Confederacy in Great Britain. Write a letter to the British prime minister explaining why you think Great Britain should help the Confederates win the war. Be sure to talk about the South's "cause," what kind of help is needed and what will happen if it is not given, and what the benefits of this aid will be for Great Britain.
2. Read Lincoln's Gettysburg Address on page 373. Now write a paragraph expressing in your own words what you think Lincoln meant.
3. The picture on the previous page shows guerrilla warfare carried out by Confederate soldiers during the Civil War. The word *guerrilla* means "little war" in Spanish and refers to small bands of fighters who use hit-and-run tactics to ambush the enemy. It was first used in the United States by Native Americans and, during the Revolutionary War, by patriot forces against the British. As the picture shows, guerrilla bands usually take advantage of natural features of the terrain, such as hills and trees, to conceal themselves behind enemy lines. Their chief weapon is surprise and the speed with which they can attack.

   Imagine that you are one of a small band of Confederate guerrillas carrying out raids on Union forces. Write a one-page story describing an ambush of unsuspecting troops who are resting during a long march. Include such details as how you managed to hide your position from the enemy and the effect of your attack.

Chapter 15 RECONSTRUCTION

Chapter 15 focuses on the difficulties of Reconstruction for the nation as a whole and the South in particular. Lesson 15-1 emphasizes various plans to readmit the southern states to the Union as well as Johnson's impeachment. Lesson 15-2 describes the effect of Reconstruction on blacks and whites in the South.

CONTENT OBJECTIVES

After completing the lesson, students will know:

- the plans of Lincoln, Johnson, and Congress to reunite the country
- the reasons for President Johnson's impeachment
- the effect of the Thirteenth, Fourteenth, and Fifteenth Amendments

VOCABULARY

reconstruction: the setting up of new state governments
amnesty: a pardon for offenses against a government
pardon: excuse someone from a past offense without punishment

15-1 Reuniting the Nation

As you read, think about these questions:

What was Andrew Johnson's plan for reuniting the nation?

What was Congress's plan to reunite the South with the Union?

What actions did Congress take to lessen the power of the presidency?

Why was Andrew Johnson impeached?

Special Vocabulary reconstruction amnesty pardon

In April 1865 when the guns had fallen silent, the North and the South both tried to total up the price they had paid. The North had lost 359,500 people, the South, 258,000. Some had died terrible deaths in prisoner-of-war camps. Hundreds of thousands had been permanently disabled. The cost in dollars was staggering. Many people on both sides wondered if their bitterness and anger would ever go away. They did not see how the Union could be made whole again.

Lincoln's Plan

Abraham Lincoln realized that when the Civil War was over a plan would be needed to bring the South back into the Union again. He knew that many people in the North wanted to punish the South severely—blaming it for bringing on the war. He was determined that the terms for reuniting the

Rebuilding had already begun in 1865 in this Charleston, South Carolina, neighborhood, which had been destroyed by fire and Union artillery.

nation be fair and just. In April 1863 Lincoln announced his plan for the *reconstruction,* or the setting up of new state governments, of the South.

Lincoln's plan was called the Ten Percent Plan. It provided that *amnesty,* which is a pardon for offenses against a government, be granted to those in the South who would take an oath of loyalty to the Constitution and the Union. There would be no amnesty, however, for high-ranking military officers, and political leaders of the Confederate government. Lincoln also thought of a way for states to regain their full rights, including the right to take part in elections for the United States Senate and House of Representatives. This would happen when at least ten percent of the people who had voted in the election of 1860—and who had also taken the oath of loyalty—voted to establish a new state government without slavery.

Other Plans

Abraham Lincoln's plan for the reconstruction of the South was criticized immediately. Lincoln hoped to find a group of people in each former Confederate state who would create a loyal government. Many northerners believed that this solution would make things too easy for the South.

Radical Republicans. Some of the fiercest opposition was in Congress. Members called "Radical Republicans" insisted that Congress, not the President, should decide how to deal with the South after the war. They were for harsh treatment of the South. They were eager to help the freed slaves and not yet willing to forgive the Confederates. If the South re-entered the Union readily, the Radical Republicans feared they would be quickly outnumbered in Congress. Then various laws, such as the tariff passed when the South was out of the Union during the war, might be repealed.

Leaders of the Radical Republicans. Thaddeus Stevens of Pennsylvania and Henry Davis of Maryland were leaders of the Radical Republicans in the House of Representatives. Charles Sumner of Massachusetts and Benjamin Wade of Ohio were leaders in the Senate. To punish the South, the Radicals came up with a harsh reconstruction plan.

The Radicals' plan, called the Wade-Davis Bill, required the majority of people in each southern state to take an oath that they had always been loyal to the United States and would remain so in the future. Each state would have to draw up a new constitution banning slavery and forbidding the payment of Confederate debts. The constitution would then have to be approved by Congress. Only then would the state be allowed to elect senators and representatives. No one who had held office in the Confederate government or who had voluntarily fought against the Union in the war could vote or hold office.

The President disliked this plan so much that he did not allow it to become a law. The Radical Republicans in Congress were furious with the President for going against the wishes of members of his own party.

Andrew Johnson's Plan. When Abraham Lincoln was assassinated, the Vice President, Andrew Johnson, became President. The Radical Republicans in Congress were sure that

Andrew Johnson proved to be one of the most unpopular of American Presidents. Many Americans, however, later realized that he had been treated unfairly.

Johnson would support their plan for reconstruction. Johnson, however, favored the milder policies of Lincoln. On May 29, 1865, the new President brought out his own plan. It was only slightly different from Lincoln's.

Under Johnson's plan most of the people who had participated in the rebellion would be pardoned. To *pardon* is to excuse someone from a past offense without punishment. But certain rich southerners would have to ask Johnson personally to pardon them. The plan also required that everyone who had been given a pardon take an oath of loyalty to the Constitution and the Union.

Most southern states quickly met the requirements. These states then elected senators and representatives to send to Congress. By December 5, 1865, all the states of the South except Texas had been reconstructed under Johnson's plan. Johnson declared the Union restored.

DISCUSSION

Discuss the reasons why members of Congress objected to President Johnson's plans for reconstruction. The students might cite revenge against the South, fear that the South would not help freed slaves, and the chance that Radical Republican laws might be repealed. Ask the students to describe what their feelings might have been toward the presidential and congressional reconstruction plans if they had been: a former slave, a former Confederate soldier, and a former Union soldier.

Congress's Reconstruction Plan. When Congress met on December 4, 1865, it refused to seat the senators and representatives from the southern states. Congress decided to put forth its own plan. Led by the Radical Republicans, it set up a Joint Committee of Fifteen to suggest new ideas about reconstruction. Six senators and nine representatives, both Republican and Democratic, were chosen for this committee.

The first action of the committee was to declare that the South had no state governments and that Congress would make the rules by which the South could come back into the

Union. Congress's plan, passed in three Reconstruction Acts in 1867, called for occupation of the South by the Union army. Blacks would take part in southern state governments and would have the right to vote. In short, southerners would have to recognize blacks as full United States citizens. In passing this law, Congress took over Southern reconstruction. It now set about forcing President Andrew Johnson to carry out the law.

Impeachment of Andrew Johnson. Congress's reconstruction plan widened the conflict between the President and Congress. The Radicals took other steps that made the conflict even worse. In 1867 they passed new acts limiting the President's powers. One act said that the President could only give military orders to the army through the commanding general—who happened to be Ulysses S. Grant. This arrangement severely limited the President's powers as Commander-in-Chief. The other law, the Tenure of Office Act, declared that the President could not dismiss Cabinet officers without the consent of the Senate.

Andrew Johnson did not believe that the Tenure of Office Act was constitutional. He challenged it—and the Radicals—by firing Edwin Stanton, the secretary of war. Johnson

President Johnson's impeachment trial, the only impeachment of a President in United States history, lasted two months.

appointed General Grant in his place. Congress refused to accept Johnson's dismissal of Stanton. Grant did not want to be caught in the middle of this argument between Congress and the President, so he resigned. Johnson appointed another general to be secretary of war.

The Radicals were furious that the President was breaking the Tenure of Office Act. Of course, their real anger was that Johnson had attempted to reconstruct the seceded states on his own. The Radicals drew up articles of impeachment against him. Articles of impeachment are formal statements accusing a high official of serious wrong-doing. If the House of Representatives voted to accept the articles accusing Johnson of "high crimes," he would be tried by the Senate. If two-thirds of the members of the Senate then voted against the President, he could be removed from office.

On February 24, 1868, the House of Representatives voted to impeach President Johnson. This was the first time a President had been impeached. On March 30, 1868, Johnson's trial in the Senate began. Presiding over the trial—in accordance with the Constitution—was the Chief Justice of the United States, Salmon P. Chase. Benjamin Butler of Massachusetts rose to press the charges against the President. Johnson was defended by his attorney general, who had resigned his position in the Cabinet to undertake this responsibility. Johnson himself was not present.

Some people wondered what would happen to the office of President if Johnson were found guilty and removed. The question never had to be answered. Johnson was saved from being put out of office by one vote. Seven Republican

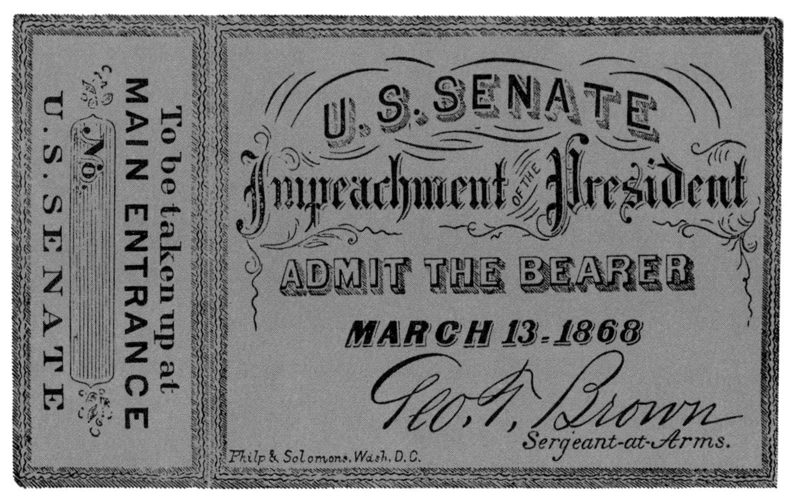

The impeachment trial was the biggest attraction in Washington in March 1868. Spectators jammed the Senate gallery every day.

senators broke with their party and voted to support the President and save the presidency from disgrace.

In 1868 the Republicans nominated the hero of the Union, General Grant, as their candidate for President. His Democratic Party opponent was Horatio J. Seymour, former governor of New York. During the campaign of 1868 the Republicans accused the Democrats of having begun the Civil War and of being disloyal to the Union. Such charges were called "waving the bloody shirt." Grant and the Republican Party won a sweeping victory, capturing twenty-six out of thirty-four states.

ACTIVITY

Objective: To summarize

Have students read contents of the Thirteenth, Fourteenth, and Fifteenth Amendments to the Constitution. Each student should write a short paragraph summarizing the three amendments. In the summary, have the students include the date of the amendment's adoption, the provisions of each section, and the branch to which the power was given to enforce these provisions.

Post-Civil War Amendments. When the Civil War ended, many in Congress questioned the legal position of the former slaves. Lincoln's Emancipation Proclamation had freed only the slaves in the rebel states. Something more was required to free *all* the slaves, including those in the border states. The freeing of *all* the slaves and the granting of citizenship and the vote to them was the work of the Radical Republicans. Through their efforts the Thirteenth Amendment was added to the Constitution in 1865. It formally abolished slavery in the United States forever. The Fourteenth Amendment gave the former slaves citizenship and the Fifteenth gave them the right to vote. Look at the chart

This poster celebrating the Fifteenth Amendment is framed with pictures of both black and white heroes of the day, including Abraham Lincoln and Frederick Douglass (top center).

below which lists the provisions of the Thirteenth, Fourteenth, and Fifteenth Amendments.

These amendments reversed the Supreme Court's decision in the Dred Scott case (see page 347). Blacks were now free citizens who could not be denied the vote because of their race. The door of democracy had finally been opened for blacks in the United States.

THE CIVIL WAR AMENDMENTS

Thirteenth	Fourteenth	Fifteenth
Ratified in 1865	Ratified in 1868	Ratified in 1870
Nobody in the United States or its territories may be held in slavery.	All persons born or naturalized in the United States and ruled by the nation's laws are citizens.	Neither the United States nor any state may keep citizens from voting because of their race or color or because they were once slaves.
Congress may make laws to carry out this amendment.	Such persons are citizens of the United States as well as of the state in which they live.	Congress may make laws to carry out this amendment.
	No state may take away the rights of United States citizens or take anyone's life, liberty, or property except by law.	
	All the laws of a state must affect everybody in the same way.	
	Congress may make laws to carry out this amendment.	

ANSWER THESE QUESTIONS

1. What was Lincoln's plan for reconstruction?
2. Who were the four leaders of the Radical Republicans?
3. What was the Tenure of Office Act?
4. Was Congress's or Johnson's reconstruction plan harsher on former Confederate states? Why?
5. Why did Congress pass laws limiting the powers of the President?

ANSWER THESE QUESTIONS

1. Lincoln's plan provided amnesty for southerners pledging loyalty to the Constitution and the Union. The only exceptions would be high-ranking Confederate military and political leaders. Full rights would be restored when ten percent of those taking the loyalty oath voted for a new state government without slavery.
2. Thaddeus Stevens, Henry Davis, Benjamin Wade, Charles Sumner
3. declared that the President could not dismiss Cabinet officers without the consent of the Senate
4. Congress's—military leaders were in charge of the South, states were forced to approve the Fourteenth Amendment. States had no choice but to comply.
5. Congress did not want the President to interfere with its reconstruction policies.

LAW AND THE CITIZEN

Citizens' Rights During Wartime

During the Civil War, President Lincoln decided that he must act forcefully to stop the actions of the Copperheads, the northerners who supported the Confederacy. To save the Union, he believed that it was necessary to suspend temporarily some rights guaranteed in the Constitution. For example, Lincoln ordered that in some cases Copperheads should be tried by military courts rather than by the regular civil courts. This controversial order became the subject of a Supreme Court case—*Ex parte Milligan*.

Lambdin P. Milligan was a teacher and lawyer in Indiana. The federal government accused him of planning to free Confederate prisoners and help them rejoin Confederate forces. Milligan was brought before a military commission established according to President Lincoln's orders. The commission found Milligan guilty and sentenced him to be hanged, and Lincoln personally approved the sentence. After Lincoln's death, however, President Andrew Johnson changed the sentence to life in prison.

Soon afterwards, Milligan asked the Supreme Court to determine whether he was being legally imprisoned. In 1866 the Supreme Court ruled unanimously that neither Congress nor the President has the power to establish military courts if civil courts are still operating. The Court further ruled that Congress can set up military courts only when an invasion or other grave emergency closes the civil courts. Milligan was thus a free man.

Chief Justice Salmon P. Chase and three other justices disagreed with the majority opinion in one respect. They said that Congress could have chosen to set up military courts, even though there was no invasion. However, since Congress had permitted civil courts to continue to operate, Milligan was entitled to be tried in one.

Ex parte Milligan was an important decision on the behalf of American citizens. The Supreme Court declared that "the Constitution of the United States is a law for rulers and people, equally in war and in peace, and covers with the shield of its protection all classes of men, at all times, and under all circumstances." Even in times of emergency, the President must respect constitutional rights.

15-2 Life During Reconstruction

As you read, think about these questions:

How did state governments in the South change during Reconstruction?

Why did some white southerners dislike the new state governments?

What events led to the end of Reconstruction?

Special Vocabulary sharecropping poll tax literacy test

CONTENT OBJECTIVES

After completing the lesson, students will know:

- about the black codes
- about the make-up of reconstruction governments
- how reconstruction governments affected the election of 1876
- how the Reconstruction period ended

VOCABULARY

sharecropping: a system under which a landowner allowed a farmer to live on and farm a piece of his or her land in return for the largest share of the crops raised

poll tax: a tax that a person has to pay in order to vote

literacy test: a test that determines whether a person can read and write

By June 1868 seven southern states had met the rules for reconstruction set by Congress. It appeared that the Union would at last be restored. Of the former Confederate states, Mississippi, Virginia, and Texas remained under military rule because they refused to satisfy Congress's requirements. Georgia was returned to military rule when it expelled blacks from the legislature. In 1870 these states finally returned to the Union.

During Reconstruction remarkable changes took place in the South. Black men voted and held office for the first time—as did many poor white men. The rich plantation owners who had controlled politics before the Civil War had lost their former power. Republican governors and lawmaking bodies were elected throughout the South.

Problems of Former Slaves

The former slaves, or freedmen as they were called, had little with which to rebuild their lives. Some stayed on the plantations, where they worked for their former owners. Some blacks, as well as many poor whites, made a living by *sharecropping*. Under this system, a landowner allowed people to live on and farm a piece of his or her land, lending them the money for the tools, seed, and animals they needed. The people farmed the land and turned over the largest share of their crop to the landowner in repayment. This system made it hard for farmers to save money and get ahead.

Other blacks traveled about, some of them looking for friends or relatives perhaps separated from them years earlier by being sold away. Some blacks moved to northern

Although slavery had ended, the South's economy was still based on cotton. Life for the field workers went on much as before.

cities, hoping for a chance to work and to learn to read and write. Almost all of them were poor.

ACTIVITY

Objective: To make inferences

Have the students discuss the black codes and explain how they limited the rights and the free movement of the blacks in the South after the Civil War. After the discussion have each student imagine how black southerners must have felt about the black codes. Have them write a letter to a white abolitionist society in the North telling about the effect of the black codes on their lives.

Black Codes. The former masters did not adjust easily, either. They almost immediately passed laws known as black codes. These were laws that limited the rights and even the movements of blacks. Mississippi and some other states said that blacks without jobs would be fined heavily or forcibly "apprenticed" to whomever the state chose. Blacks could not work in trades set aside for whites, except by special licenses. In effect, the former slaves were restricted to farming and household service jobs.

Other laws forbade blacks to carry guns and limited their right to sue in court. In Alabama, for example, blacks could not give evidence against whites. The codes, however, did recognize some of the rights blacks now had. They could now marry legally. They were also allowed to own property, although few could afford to do so.

The Freedmen's Bureau taught many former slaves to read and write and helped them adjust to freedom.

Uniformed agents of the Freedmen's Bureau helped maintain peace between white southerners and former slaves.

In 1866 Congress attempted to put an end to the black codes. It passed a bill to increase the powers of the Freedmen's Bureau. This was an agency that had been set up at the end of the war to help feed, clothe, and educate former slaves. Congress decided to give the bureau additional power in order to protect the civil rights, property, and lives of black people.

Johnson, however, vetoed the bill expanding the duties of the bureau. He insisted a new law was unnecessary because the state courts could take care of the problems that were arising. He also believed the new law would dangerously extend military rule. Congress, nevertheless, passed the bill over Johnson's veto.

The Ku Klux Klan. Many white southerners were determined to keep blacks out of politics. They formed "clubs" to strike fear into black voters. The best-known of these groups was the Ku Klux Klan. Members of the Klan, often riding in white robes at night, burned the houses of blacks and beat and even murdered those who tried to vote.

In 1870 and 1871 Congress passed acts to try to stop these lawless groups. Troops of the United States Army sometimes were ordered to protect black voters when they went to the polls, but violence against blacks did not cease.

DISCUSSION

Several different groups gained some power in the southern state governments and in Congress during the Reconstruction period. The most important ones to discuss with the class are the blacks, the carpetbaggers, and the scalawags. Discuss with the class the types of offices to which they were elected, southern attitudes toward the groups and reasons for these attitudes, and any changes in laws that resulted from the leadership provided by these groups.

Reconstruction Governments

The Republican state governments that took office in the South had a vast task. The new constitutions required the states to educate all children. Before the Civil War, the southern states had had few public schools. The states also had to repair the damage done by the war.

Blacks in Government. Blacks served in government positions for the first time. A few were elected to Congress or to high state offices. Two blacks from Mississippi—Hiram R. Revels and Blanche K. Bruce—served in the United States Senate. Revels, who had studied at Knox College in Galesburg, Illinois, had been a minister for black soldiers during the Civil War. Bruce was probably the greatest of the black politicians of his time. He worked in government for many years after leaving the Senate.

Many people later held the opinion that blacks dominated the reconstruction governments. This is not so. Many white southerners were simply distressed that people who had so recently been slaves were taking part in government at all. No black was elected governor. In South Carolina there were two lieutenant governors who were black, and there was a black judge on the state supreme court. Mississippi, Louisiana, and Florida had black lieutenant governors and superintendents of education. The only lawmaking bodies that

Robert Elliott, the speaker on the left, was one of the blacks who made up a majority in the South Carolina state legislature.

had more blacks than whites at any one time were in South Carolina and Mississippi. In some states, like Tennessee, blacks played only a very small part in the government.

Carpetbaggers and Scalawags. People in the South had names for some of the Republican state leaders. They called them "carpetbaggers" and "scalawags." The carpetbaggers were northerners who had come to the South after the Civil War. They got their name from a popular type of luggage made of carpet that they carried their belongings in. Many white southerners later charged that the carpetbaggers had come south only for personal gain, to take advantage of inexperienced black voters and troubled conditions.

In fact, many northerners moved to the South after the war for the same reasons many southerners moved to the West—to seek a new life. Some of those who went into public life were greedy or dishonest; but most of them were not.

Scalawags were white southerners who became Republicans. No one knows for sure how they got this name, which refers to worthless or dishonest people. Some scalawags were former Democrats or Whigs. They saw that the Radicals were in control of Congress and decided that it was wise to cooperate with them. Many of these people were in business and believed that the Republican Party would support laws to help them prosper.

Many southerners resented the carpetbaggers who came to the South after the war. The term *carpetbaggers* is sometimes still used to refer to outsiders who try to obtain political power.

End of Reconstruction

People in the North gradually began to lose interest in reconstruction. Their concern over the fate of the blacks had never been a burning one. After 1873 business was poor. Many northerners refused to continue to use money to support reconstruction.

In addition, many Republicans in the North no longer believed that they needed the black voters in the South. The election of 1872, in which Grant was reelected, had shown that there were enough Republican voters in northern states to win national elections. Many northern business people, looking for places to invest their money, turned their eyes to the South, where their help was badly needed. The business people hesitated to put their money there. They regarded the reconstruction governments as financially risky.

This political cartoon suggests that Grant rode to power on the backs of suffering southerners and that Hayes ignored the South's problems.

The Election of 1876. In 1876 the voters were upset by the discovery of corruption in the Grant administration. Both parties responded by nominating presidential candidates who were known as reformers. The Republicans nominated Rutherford B. Hayes, governor of Ohio. The Democrats chose Samuel J. Tilden, governor of New York.

The election of 1876 was very close, but neither candidate received a majority of electoral votes. A hot dispute developed over twenty of the electoral votes. Nineteen of them were in three southern states that still had reconstruction governments—South Carolina, Louisiana, and Florida.

In each of the three states rival groups of election officials —one Democratic and one Republican—reported the votes. The Democratic groups declared that Tilden had won the election. The Republicans said that Hayes was the winner. A situation like this had never happened before, and the Constitution said nothing about how to deal with it.

A Solution. As 1877 opened, Congress appointed an election commission to solve the problem. Seven members of this commission were Democrats and seven were Republicans.

The fifteenth member of the commission was a Supreme Court justice. In February the commission voted—eight to seven—to give all the votes to Rutherford B. Hayes.

The Democrats were furious over the commission's decision. The leaders of the parties made a secret bargain. It is now known as the Compromise of 1877. By its terms Hayes promised to appoint a southerner to his cabinet. He also promised to aid the South in obtaining railroads. Most important, Hayes promised to withdraw the last of the federal troops from the South. The withdrawal of troops from the South is considered the end of Reconstruction.

Most former slaves who tried city life ended up in the poorest neighborhoods. These Richmond, Virginia, residents were probably not much wealthier than they had been before emancipation.

Effects of Reconstruction. During Reconstruction the nation had been reunited and the rebuilding of the South had been started. Reconstruction, however, had failed to solve the problems of the blacks or of the South. Few blacks had acquired land. Most continued to work for white landowners. Agriculture remained the basis of the economy in the South because money to start industries was scarce.

After Reconstruction had ended, some southern states established a *poll tax*, a tax that a person had to pay in order to vote. Some states required voters to pass a *literacy test*, a test that determines whether a person can read and write. Since most blacks were poor and uneducated, these laws prevented them from voting. The laws thereby made it difficult for blacks to exercise the rights guaranteed by the Fifteenth Amendment.

As a result, many blacks left the South. They hoped to find a better life elsewhere. In the late 1870s large numbers of blacks began moving to the North and West.

Nevertheless, the three Civil War amendments are lasting monuments to Radical Reconstruction. One day, as we shall see, they would take on the full meaning their authors intended them to have.

ANSWER THESE QUESTIONS

1. no money; many stayed on plantations and worked for former owners; black codes limited their rights
2. to terrorize blacks and keep them from voting
3. northerners who entered southern politics and southern Democrats who became Republicans
4. Business was poor so many northerners did not want money used to reconstruct the South; some northern Republicans felt that black votes were no longer needed.
5. The withdrawal of federal troops from the South is considered the end of Reconstruction.

ANSWER THESE QUESTIONS

1. What were some problems of former slaves?
2. What was the purpose of the Ku Klux Klan?
3. Who were the carpetbaggers and scalawags?
4. Why did people in the North lose interest in reconstruction?
5. How did the Compromise of 1877 affect reconstruction?

Objective: After completing this page, students should be able to synthesize information.

Synthesizing Information

In trying to understand a period of history, it is sometimes helpful to have more than one statement on a single subject. By studying two or more statements made by different people or groups, you can see how the same issue looks from different viewpoints. Synthesizing, or combining, information from more than one source often gives you a fuller understanding than you could get from one source alone.

The following statements were adapted from ones made by former slaves many years after the Civil War.

D. Davis:

Yessir, the slaves fared well with Master Tom Davis, and there wouldn't have been a war over the slavery question if everybody had been like Master Tom. All his people were satisfied and . . . they weren't worried about freedom. . . . After freedom came they were glad to get it, but after they got it they didn't know what to do with it. . . . Master Tom called them all up and told them that they are as free as he is and they can leave if they want to. . . . Every one stayed, and I expect that a lot of them . . . are there yet. . . .

Robert Falls:

If I had my life to live over again, I would die fighting rather than be a slave. . . . But in those days, we slaves didn't know any better. All we knew was work, and hard work. . . . They didn't half feed us, either. Taught us to steal, that's what they did. . . . Then they'd whip us when we'd say we didn't know anything about it. . . . I remember so well how the roads were full of folks walking and walking along when the slaves were freed. Didn't know where they were going. Just going to see about something else some where else. . . .

Combine the information from the two statements to answer the following questions:

1. Did all former slaves feel the same way about slavery? About freedom? Explain your answers.
2. What did the slaves do when they were set free?
3. How does synthesizing information give you a better understanding of history?

Working with Skills

READING SKILLS

ACTIVITY

Objective: To synthesize information

Divide the class into two groups. Each group will prepare a presentation. Group 1 is to research and present information on the ways white southerners lived in the post–Civil War period. Group 2 is to do research and present descriptions of black southerners' lives after the Civil War. Have each group use the card catalogue to find sources describing their topic. At the conclusion of the two presentations, have each student write two or three paragraphs combining the descriptions of the lifestyles of the South after the Civil War.

ANSWERS

1. No, some had had more humane masters than others; most were glad to be free. Some did not know how to use their freedom.
2. Some stayed with former owners, many moved to other places to find work, still others roamed the countryside.
3. Answers will vary.

RELATED MATERIALS
Duplicator/Copy Master Activity 33

THINKING THINGS THROUGH

1. They wanted to punish the South. **2.** an agency to feed, clothe, and educate former slaves, and later to protect their rights **3.** that he broke the Office of Tenure Act by firing Stanton **4.** Thirteenth freed the slaves, Fourteenth made them citizens, Fifteenth gave them the right to vote **5.** with poll taxes and literacy tests and through secret societies like the Ku Klux

Chapter 15 SUMMARY

After the Civil War the government was faced with the problem of how to reunite the nation. President Lincoln had a plan for reconstruction, but Congress opposed Lincoln's mild policies. Radical Republicans wanted to punish the South.

Andrew Johnson formed his own plan, which was only slightly different from Lincoln's. Congress refused to approve Johnson's plan and put its own plan into effect by placing the South under military rule.

In 1868 Congress impeached Johnson. By a margin of one vote, the Senate allowed Johnson to remain in office. He was not asked to run for reelection. In 1868 Ulysses S. Grant won a sweeping victory.

Life was not easy for former slaves. Many remained on plantations where they worked for their former owners. Others moved to northern cities in search of work. Laws called black codes limited the rights of blacks. Groups such as the Ku Klux Klan terrorized blacks to keep them from voting.

Blacks were allowed to hold office for the first time in history. The new state governments in the South, however, were dominated by northerners called carpetbaggers and southerners called scalawags.

Reconstruction ended in 1877 when President Hayes withdrew federal troops from the South. Southern states made it difficult for blacks to exercise their rights. The Fourteenth and Fifteenth Amendments, however, remained lasting effects of Reconstruction.

Chapter 15 TEST

WORDS TO REMEMBER

Choose the correct word from the following list to complete each of the sentences below.

a. sharecropping c. pardon
b. amnesty d. poll tax
e. literacy test

1. Many southern states required that people pay a ___d___ in order to vote.
2. Lincoln proposed ___b___, the forgiving of past offenses, to those who would take a loyalty oath.
3. After the Civil War, many poor farmers made a living through ___a___.
4. A ___e___ determines whether a person can read and write.
5. Johnson required certain southerners to personally ask him to ___c___ them.

THINKING THINGS THROUGH

Answer each of these questions.

1. Why did the Radicals in Congress come up with their own reconstruction plan called the Wade-Davis bill?
2. What was the Freedmen's Bureau?
3. What were the charges brought against Johnson in his impeachment?
4. How did the three Civil War amendments affect blacks?
5. How did some southerners try to keep blacks from voting after Reconstruction?

RELATED MATERIALS

Duplicator/Copy Masters: Activities 32, 33; Quiz 29
Workbook pages 45-47

Klan that terrorized and murdered blacks

WORKING WITH SKILLS

1. Some never saw the northern armies, others had their lives threatened by Union forces. 2. No, some stayed on the land.

WORKING WITH SKILLS

Read the following paraphrased accounts of the Civil War by slaves. Then use what you learned about synthesizing information in this chapter to answer the questions below.

I remember plenty about the War, because the Yankees marched on Richmond. They killed every thing that was in the way. Everybody was scared. . . . The Master sent me to take the Missus to the mountain, but the Yankees captured me and said they were going to hang me. But the Master saved me. He sent his wife and mine to another place then, because the Yankees burnt his house.

We all heard one time that the Yankees were . . . on the way to burn Master Tom's mill, but they got on the wrong road. . . . They never did find it and do the damage I heard they did in other places around the state. . . . We sure were proud about that. . . . After the war, Master Tom had about four hundred bales of cotton on hand and the Yankee government took that and didn't pay him a bit.

1. Were slaves in personal danger during the war?
2. Did all southerners have to leave their homes when the enemy invaded?

ON YOUR OWN

1. Imagine that you are a senator at the trial of Andrew Johnson. Write a short speech in his defense. In your speech, be sure to cover the events that led up to the impeachment and how his removal would hurt the office of the President.
2. Make a chronological list of the bills passed by Congress that are discussed in Chapter 15. Include the amendments to the Constitution.
3. Look at the picture of black soldiers returning to their homes in Arkansas after the Civil War. Think of the challenges and hardships these people would have faced in the years following the war. Write a paragraph describing ways in which their lives might have improved or worsened during that time.

THINK THINGS THROUGH

1. Hayes became President and promised to appoint a southern Cabinet member and to help the South get railroads; federal troops withdrew from the South. **2.** to try to stop lawless groups from preventing blacks from voting **3.** It made it hard for the army to get the necessary men and money from the states. **4.** to capture Richmond; no **5.** It gained control of the Mississip-

Unit 5 TEST

WORDS TO REMEMBER

For each of the following words, choose the right definition.

b 1. due process
   a. the right of individual states to secede
   b. the right to a court trial
   c. the right to be readmitted to the Union

a 2. platform
   a. statement of principles
   b. political slogan
   c. judge's opinion

c 3. amnesty
   a. acceptance of the enemy's surrender
   b. shelter for fugitive slaves
   c. pardon for offenses against the government

c 4. conscription
   a. government seizure of large plantations
   b. enlistment in the army by former slaves
   c. forced military service

a 5. reconstruction
   a. the setting up of new state governments
   b. the rebuilding of war-damaged railroads
   c. the final step in the impeachment process

b 6. emancipation
   a. the granting of citizenship to slaves
   b. the freeing of those in slavery
   c. the guarantee of the right to vote

b 7. popular sovereignty
   a. the right to a trial by jury
   b. the right of voters to decide the question of slavery in the territories
   c. the right to support the candidate of your choice

QUESTIONS TO ANSWER

Indicate whether each of the following statements is true or false.

F 1. The Wilmot Proviso said that settlers of the new territories could decide for themselves about slavery.

F 2. The Supreme Court's Dred Scott decision settled the issue of slavery in the territories.

T 3. Every state in the North except New Jersey voted for Abraham Lincoln in 1860.

T 4. At the start of the Civil War, the North had more factories and more railroads than the South had.

T 5. The success of Grant's battle plan to control the Mississippi River made him a hero.

T 6. Andrew Johnson's plan for reconstruction was basically the same as Lincoln's.

T 7. Part of the reconstruction plan established by Congress called for the military occupation of the South.

THINK THINGS THROUGH

1. What were the terms of the Compromise of 1877?
2. What was the intent of the acts passed by Congress in 1870 and 1871?
3. What effect did the belief in states' rights have on the Confederate war effort?
4. What was the purpose of General McClellan's Peninsula Campaign? Did it succeed?
5. Why was the fall of Vicksburg important to the Union?
6. Why did southerners dislike the idea of popular sovereignty?
7. What was the Republican Party stand on slavery in the territories?

pi River and cut the Confederacy in two. **6.** because new territories might become free states, with the slave states in the minority in Congress **7.** It opposed slavery in new territories.

PRACTICE YOUR SKILLS

2. a. No. Some supported the Union, and others the Confederacy, depending on where they lived. **b.** Some were eager to take up arms, others were more reluctant to leave the life they had made for themselves. **c.** It made some of them sad and tense, it made others defiant.

PRACTICE YOUR SKILLS

1. In this unit you learned about three types of special maps: (1) maps that show transportation routes, (2) maps that show changes that occur over time, and (3) maps that show the movement of a person or group. Decide which kind of map(s) would best illustrate each of the following.
   2 a. the order in which the Confederate states seceded from the Union
   1 b. the stations on the Underground Railroad used by slaves escaping to free states
   1 c. the routes used by settlers moving into the western territories
   3 d. the western campaign of the Civil War, under General Grant
2. Using what you learned about synthesizing information in this unit, read the following excerpts dealing with the actions and feelings of immigrants to the United States during the Civil War. The first excerpt is from a German-language newspaper.

In St. Louis, the Germans held the secessionists in complete check. . . . Three thousand of these Germans enlisted under the Star-Spangled Banner, ready to defend the Union, the Constitution, liberty, and justice against the enemy. . . . The German hates the flag of the rebels and this hate knows no bounds.

The next excerpt is from a resolution issued by a Hebrew congregation in Shreveport, Louisiana.

Whereas, we received the "Jewish Messenger" . . . a paper published in New York in which an appeal has been made to support the stars and stripes, . . . Therefore be it *Resolved,* that we scorn and repel your advice. As law abiding citizens, we solemnly pledge ourselves to stand by, protect, and honor the . . . Constitution of the Southern Confederacy.

The last excerpt is from a letter that a Minnesota resident wrote home to Norway.

Last week we all had to leave our harvesting and . . . appear at the place of enlistment. A band played for a long time to . . . give us a foretaste of the joys of war. But we thought only of its sorrow. Now we are in a mood of uncertainty and tension, almost like prisoners of war in this formerly so free country. Perhaps I shall be a soldier next month and have to leave my home, my wife . . . and everything I have been working for over so many years.

Now answer these questions.

a. Did all immigrants to the United States support the same side during the Civil War? Explain your answer.
b. How did the immigrants feel about fighting in the war?
c. How did the war affect the mood of the immigrants?

RELATED MATERIALS
Duplicator/Copy Master Test 30-32

Unit 6
NATIONAL EXPANSION

Unit Six covers the opening of the West in the 1800s, the growth of the cities, and the rapid development of technology. The unit includes the following topics: a discussion of the role of the railroads in making the western states more accessible; an overview of the plight of the Indians as they were forced from their lands; an outline of the expansion of the cities; a discussion of the poor working conditions in many cities and reforms that were initiated.

The "Gramophone," 1877

John Gast's "American Progress," 1879

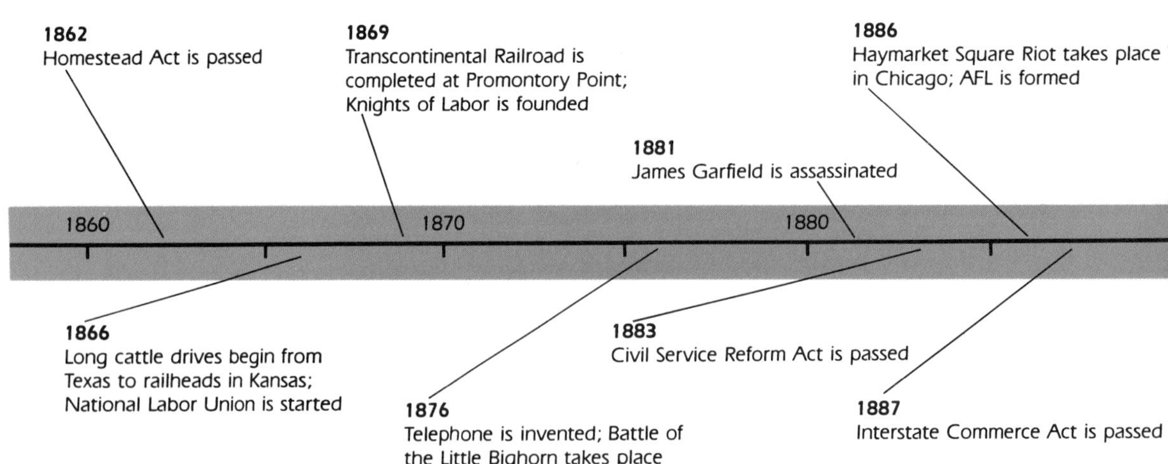
1862
Homestead Act is passed
1869
Transcontinental Railroad is completed at Promontory Point; Knights of Labor is founded
1886
Haymarket Square Riot takes place in Chicago; AFL is formed
1881
James Garfield is assassinated
1860
1870
1880
1866
Long cattle drives begin from Texas to railheads in Kansas; National Labor Union is started
1883
Civil Service Reform Act is passed
1876
Telephone is invented; Battle of the Little Bighorn takes place
1887
Interstate Commerce Act is passed

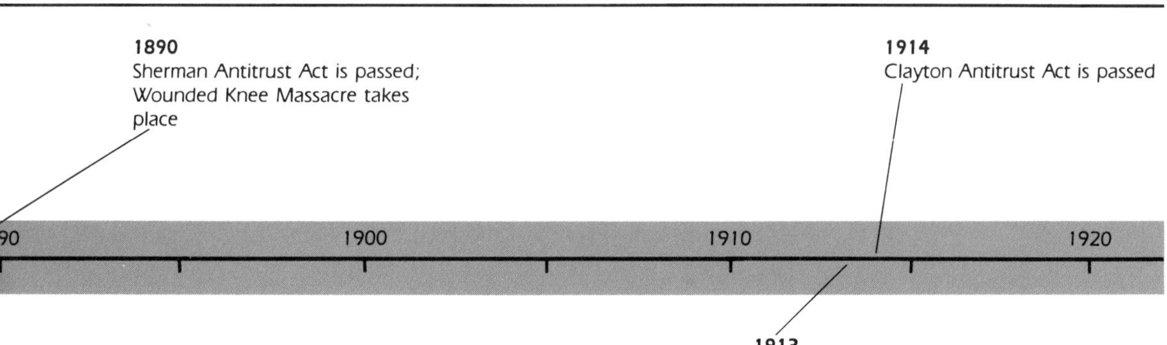
1890
Sherman Antitrust Act is passed; Wounded Knee Massacre takes place
1914
Clayton Antitrust Act is passed
90
1900
1910
1920
1913
Federal Reserve Act is passed

Chapter 16
THE MOVING FRONTIER

Chapter 16 outlines the challenges faced by new settlers to the West and the difficulties that arose between the settlers and the Indians. Lesson 16-1 discusses how the building of the railroads and the discovery of gold effected immediate changes in the West. Lesson 16-2 details the conflicts between the government and the Indians. It also discusses how and why farmers became a political force at the turn of the century.

CONTENT OBJECTIVES

After completing the lesson, students will know:

- that Congress helped the railroad companies build the first railroads across the continent
- the difficulties faced by cattle ranchers as they tried to move their herds east
- how the discovery of gold affected life in the West

VOCABULARY

transcontinental: crossing a continent
railhead: the end of the line
public domain: an area open for use by anyone
cattle baron: owner of a large ranch
vigilante: a citizen who maintains order and punishes criminals until law officers arrive

ACTIVITY

Objective: To trace routes and to analyze information from maps

Have the students look at a relief map of the United States. Have them imagine that they are planning the routes for the transcontinental railroad. Start from the west at Sacramento. Ask

16-1 Linking the Coasts

As you read, think about these questions:

What regions of the West did the transcontinental railroads cross?

How might the geography of each area make it difficult to construct a railroad?

Why did people want to come to the West?

Special Vocabulary	transcontinental	cattle baron
	railhead	vigilante
	public domain	

After the Civil War, many Americans were moving to places west of the Mississippi River. Travel to these areas was very difficult. Some people made the trip west in wagon trains on migrant routes such as the Santa Fe, the Oregon, and the Mormon trails. This form of overland travel took many months. Others took clipper ships to Central America, crossed the Isthmus of Panama, and boarded ships bound for California. This route was faster than wagon trains, but costly and dangerous. Faster, cheaper, and less dangerous means of transportation were needed.

The Transcontinental Railroad

Congress provided a solution to the problem of transportation to the West. In 1862 plans were made for a *transcontinental* railroad, or one that would cross the continent. This would allow people and goods to travel from coast to coast.

Building such a railroad would be difficult. It would involve laying tracks across 2000 miles (3200 kilometers) of empty plains, rugged mountains, and burning deserts.

Railroad Companies. Two companies set out to build the first transcontinental railroad. The Union Pacific began from Nebraska and built westward across the plains. A second company, the Central Pacific, started from Sacramento, California, and laid rails toward the East.

The national government gave the railroad companies huge amounts of land along the route. The companies then sold the land to pay for building the railroad and to make money before the trains began to run.

The Union Pacific hired many Irish immigrants who had come to the United States during the Civil War, as well as former slaves. Mormon workers joined the crews laying tracks across the Utah Territory.

In the West, Chinese workers helped build the Central Pacific Railroad. When the company advertised for workers in Asia, about ten thousand Chinese people came to the United States. These workers suffered great hardships working for the railroad. They were treated almost like slaves.

Spreading Web of Rails. The companies raced against each other to lay the most track. By 1869 the race to finish the railroad was over. The government decided to join the two lines at Promontory Point near Ogden, Utah. A grand ceremony was held to celebrate the great event. Important officials attended. Governor Leland Stanford of California pounded home a golden spike to fasten the linking rail in place. The East and the West were joined. The telegraph flashed the news to President Grant in Washington, D.C. Americans celebrated what became known as the "mountain wedding" all over the country.

One transcontinental railroad through the middle of the country was hardly enough. Soon, new lines joined together other parts of the country. Railroads such as the Southern Pacific and the Atchison, Topeka & Santa Fe spread like ribbons across the southwestern states and territories. To the North the Northern Pacific was built from Lake Superior toward Puget Sound in the territory of Washington. Smaller "feeder lines" reached out to towns and cities away from the main routes. Look at the map on page 406 to find the transcontinental railroads.

the students to identify physical barriers or problem areas as they plan to lay their track. Point out also that they might want to run their railroad near bodies of water and why.

Then reverse the process and start from Nebraska. Explain that planners for each railroad had to find the best route through their territory and also had to meet at a specific point.

All that the first transcontinental railroad lacked was passengers. The Union Pacific pushed westward faster than the population, so the railroad was forced to advertise its service.

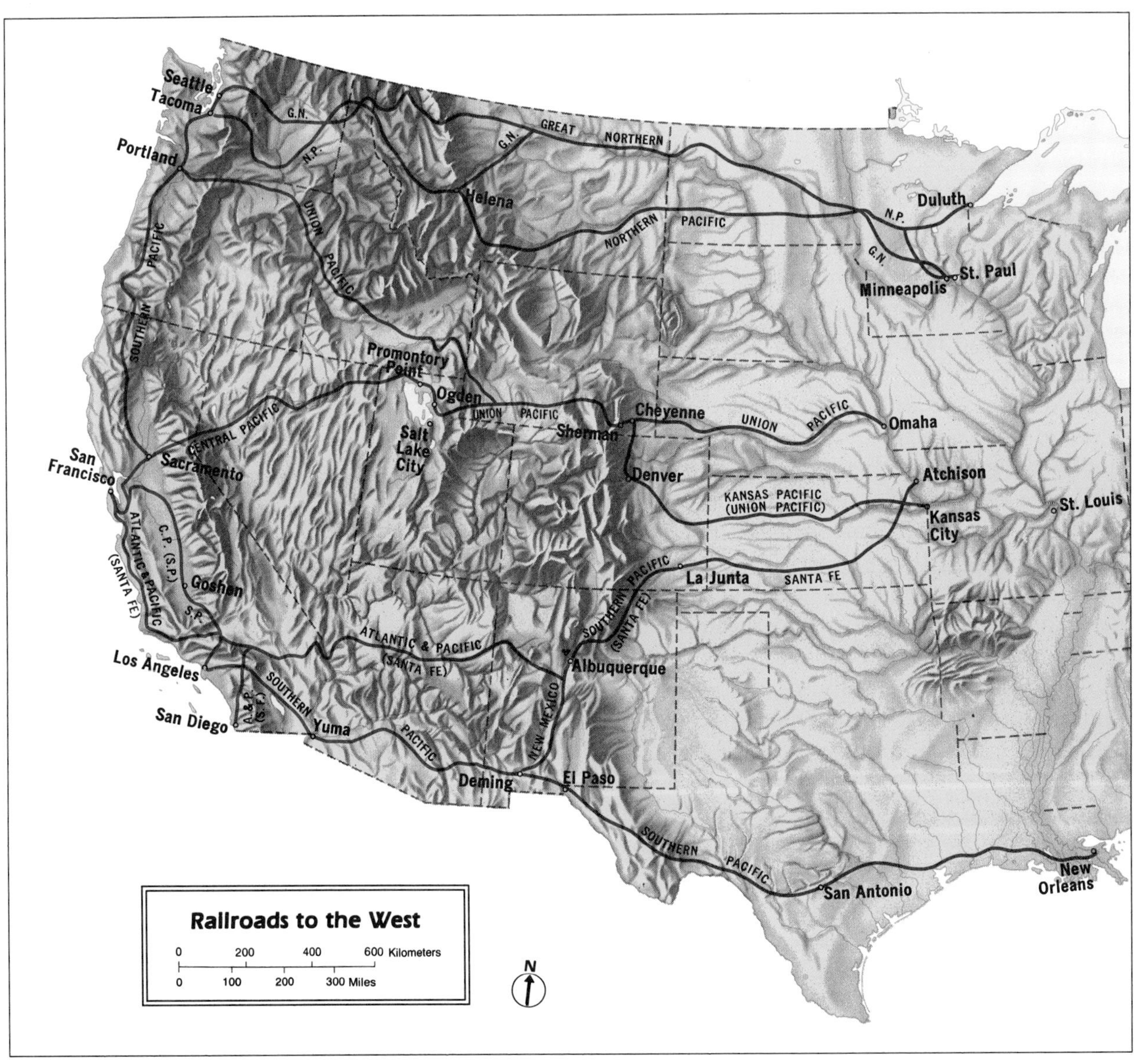

This map shows the routes of the first railroads to the West. Which six cities were the eastern starting points of these early railroads?

Duluth, St. Paul, Omaha, Atchison, Kansas City, and New Orleans

The Cattle Kingdom

For years, Spanish settlers in Texas and New Mexico had been raising Longhorn cattle. These hardy cattle fed on the range grass of the plains. They withstood the harsh conditions of this region. When the trains came to the West, people soon saw that cattle could be transported to market in the East by railroad.

The Long Drive. The long cattle drives began in the mid-1860s. Ranchers on horseback drove herds of cattle from Texas to the nearest point on the railroad. This point was often the *railhead,* or the end of the line. At first, ranchers made the long drive across Missouri to the railhead at Sedalia, Missouri. This route was called the Sedalia Trail. Later they drove the cattle along the Chisholm Trail to towns in Kansas. When the railroad later reached Denver, ranchers followed the Pecos Trail from Texas to Colorado.

In the spring, cowhands began to drive the cattle north to Kansas. Often they made a second trip in late summer. Both the cowhands, or drovers as they were sometimes called, and their herds faced dangers. Heavy rains flooded the streams. Dust clouds from the moving cattle nearly choked the riders. Angry farmers sometimes took shots at the drovers.

At first, most cowhands were either Mexicans or American Indians. Later in the 1860s, toughened soldiers from the Civil War became cowhands. About fifteen percent of cowhands were blacks.

Cow Towns. At the end of the long drive, the ranchers stopped to sell their herds and pay their cowhands. These stopping places became cow towns. Abilene, Kansas was the first such cow town. It developed in 1867 at the end of the Chisholm Trail. (Find Abilene on the map on page 413.) Law enforcers were hired to keep order in the cow towns. The people of Abilene chose "Wild Bill" Hickok, a friend of Buffalo Bill's, to protect their town. Even so, gunfights sometimes took place. Professional gamblers and outlaws tried to take money from the newly paid cowhands. After a few days, the cowhands left town. They returned to Texas to begin their work again.

The bustle of the cow town was short-lived. As new railroads were built, the railheads moved. The ranchers, cowhands, and even outlaws went to the new railheads. Some cow towns, such as Abilene, became quiet places.

The Open Range. By the late 1870s, cattle raising had spread from Texas to other parts of the West. Stronger breeds of cattle could stand the low temperatures on the northern Great Plains. This region included the eastern parts of Colorado, Wyoming, and Montana, as well as the Dakota Territory (North Dakota and South Dakota). Americans called the unsettled land in these areas the open range. The United States government owned the open range and let the ranchers treat it as *public domain.* A public domain is land open for use by anyone.

DISCUSSION

Have the students discuss the kinds of work done by people who settled the West. This should include a discussion of life as a railroad worker, cowhand, cattle baron, and prospector. Discuss the problems each had and the ways in which their jobs changed as conditions changed. For example, a prospector was always on the move setting up different camps. Point out that law and order was often absent and living conditions rough. Which job would the students have preferred? Ask them to explain their choices.

The *cattle barons*, or owners of large ranches, bought huge herds. Some of these owners lived as far away as England or France. Their herds could graze free of charge on the open government land. A single rancher sometimes had hundreds of thousands of cattle feeding on the grasses of the open range. Every year owners sold a large part of their herds for high prices.

Soon the cattle barons had too many animals on the open range. The price of cattle began to drop. Then the winter of 1885–1886 brought harsh blizzards. Snow covered the grass that the cattle needed for food. Because the cattle roamed free on the range, ranchers had a hard time finding them and bringing them food.

When the snow melted, eight out of every ten animals were dead. The next summer, scorching heat killed the range grass. In the brutal winter that followed, many of the

Not least among the hazards of a cowhand's life was a cattle stampede. With the help of a well-trained horse, a cowhand often had to head off hundreds of panicky animals.

remaining cattle died or became useless. They looked like walking skeletons.

Use of the open range came to an end after the bad winters of 1885–1887. An invention by Joseph Glidden, an Illinois farmer, helped ranchers develop a new way of raising cattle. This invention was barbed wire, which was used for fencing. It allowed ranchers to raise cattle in a closed-in area near the ranch. Ranchers and cowhands benefited greatly from this change. They would now be able to live and work in a set location.

The invention of barbed wire—here credited to Jacob Haish—had as great an impact on lifestyles and economy in the West as the cotton gin had had in the South.

The Mining Frontier

Gold was found at Sutter's Mill, California, in 1848. This was the first of many gold strikes. The California "Forty-Niners" were followed by the Colorado "Fifty-Niners." Rumors of gold and silver strikes sent prospectors rushing to rugged mountain areas all over the West. States like Colorado and cities like Denver began from the gold rushes.

The Gold Boom in Colorado. In 1858 word spread quickly that gold had been found in Colorado. Eager prospectors drove covered wagons across the country toward Pikes Peak, where gold had been found. Many of the wagons had the words "Pikes Peak or Bust" printed on them.

The miners set up camps near the gold strikes. Some mining camps grew so much and so fast that they became known as boom towns. A mining camp in Colorado became the boom town of Denver. (Find some other boom towns on the map on page 413.)

Some prospectors panned gold in streams and rivers. They used pans or shovels to take gravel from the river bottom. They swirled water around in the pan and spilled the water and gravel from the pan a little at a time. If there was gold in the gravel, it would remain in the pan because it is heavier than gravel. Other miners searched with picks and shovels, hoping to find a rich vein of gold or silver.

To protect their diggings, prospectors filed claims to the land at government offices. In spite of this, sometimes partners would fight over claims. Other times, "claim jumpers" would try to steal a mine from its rightful owner. To protect themselves, the miners set up *vigilante* groups. The vigilantes were citizens who maintained order and punished criminals until law officers arrived.

Chances are these California gold miners ended up as farmers in the Central Valley or as merchants in San Francisco. Very few prospectors actually struck it rich.

The gold boom in Colorado ended by 1862. By then prospectors had taken out all the gold that was easy to reach. Some gold and silver remained, but it was far beneath the surface. Only companies with machines and many workers could mine so deep in the earth. After Colorado, however, there were gold rushes in Nevada, Idaho, Montana, the Dakota Territory, and Alaska.

Boom Towns. In 1861 a man named Henry J. P. Comstock bragged about a mine discovered at Virginia City, Nevada. He bragged so much that people thought he had discovered it. In fact, he had not discovered the mine, but the mine became known as the Comstock Lode anyway. Both gold and silver came from the Comstock Lode. A fortune of $200 million was taken from this one mine.

The booming town of Virginia City, Nevada, grew up around the Comstock Lode and nearby mines. (Find Virginia City on the map on page 413). Twenty-three thousand people lived there at one time. Wealthy mine owners built

In its prime, Tombstone, Arizona, was an important center for silver mining. Tourists now visit the once bustling town.

large, fancy mansions. Virginia City had churches, saloons, and an opera house. Many young people came to Virginia City in search of both gold and adventure. One of these was the famous writer Mark Twain. He later wrote a book, called *Roughing It*, about the colorful life in Virginia City.

Like the cow towns, many mining camps and boom towns became today's western cities. Most mines, however, had too little gold or silver to keep people in a town. Virginia City became a ghost town, and so did Deadwood Gulch, South Dakota, and Central City, Colorado. Today some ghost towns have people again. The people are tourists who come to see where the rushes began.

ANSWER THESE QUESTIONS

1. Why was a transcontinental railroad needed?
2. Who were some of the people who worked to build the first transcontinental railroad?
3. How were cow towns and boom towns similar?
4. How did the use of barbed wire affect the cattle-raising industry?
5. What was the name of the book Mark Twain wrote about a boom town? What was the town?

ANSWER THESE QUESTIONS

1. Travel to the West by ship or wagon train was too slow.
2. Irish immigrants, former slaves, Mormon workers in Utah, Chinese workers in the West
3. Both sprang up quickly and sometimes died quickly when cattle drives moved away or mines dried up.
4. It allowed ranchers to fence in their land and so led to the end of the open range.
5. *Roughing It;* Virginia City, Nevada

Objective: After completing these pages, students should know how to measure distances on a map.

Working with Skills

MAP SKILLS

ACTIVITY

Objective: To measure distances on a map

Have the students look at a map of the United States with a distance scale. Have them find and write down the distance from Washington, D.C., to various towns and cities mentioned in this lesson—for example, Sacramento, California (2500 miles, 4000 kilometers); Ogden, Utah (1950 miles, 3100 kilometers); Denver, Colorado (1600 miles, 2500 kilometers); and Abilene, Kansas (1100 miles, 1750 kilometers). Tell the students to measure the distance in both miles and kilometers. After the students complete their measuring, point out that their answers show clearly how rapidly the country had grown in a short time.

Measuring Distances

Maps provide a way to measure distances. A distance scale is included on most maps, usually in both miles and kilometers. An inch on the map may equal hundreds of miles. A centimeter may equal hundreds of kilometers. Each map has a scale that tells the distances on that map. The map on the next page shows cow towns and boom towns in the West. Find the distance scale in the lower left-hand corner. It shows distances in both miles and kilometers.

You can use the scale and a ruler to measure distances on the map. Find out how many miles are represented by one inch. Do the same for kilometers and centimeters. Now use a ruler to measure the distance between Abilene and Kansas City. Multiply the number of miles or kilometers from the scale by the number of inches or centimeters between Abilene and Kansas City. Use the scale to express this value to the nearest 100 miles and nearest 100 kilometers.

Sometimes it will be necessary to estimate, or make a reasonable guess about, a distance. Suppose, for instance, that a distance falls three-fourths of the way between 200 and 400 kilometers. You will estimate that the distance is 350 kilometers. Here is how you might work out such a problem:

1. 400 km − 200 km = 200 km

2. 200 km × 3/4 = 150 km

3. 200 km + 150 km = 350 km

Now use the ruler and distance scale to answer each of the following questions. Give answers to the nearest 50 miles or 100 kilometers. Railroads are shown in black on the map. Cow trails are shown in red.

1. What is the distance from Chicago to San Francisco on the transcontinental railroad?

2. What town lies nearest San Francisco on the Union Pacific?

3. How does the Chisholm Trail compare with the other cow trails in length?

4. How far is Dodge City from the beginning of the Western Trail in Texas? How far is Ogallala from the same point? Notice that both towns are on a railroad. Which one do you think may have gotten more cattle business?

ANSWERS

1. 2150 miles, 3500 kilometers

2. Virginia City

3. It is shortest of the trails shown.

4. 600 miles, 1000 kilometers; 850 miles, 1400 kilometers; Dodge City

RELATED MATERIAL

Duplicator/Copy Master Activity 34

5. How far was the drive from the beginning of the Sedalia Trail in Texas to the railroad at Sedalia?

6. How far is Albuquerque from the nearest railhead? What problems might this distance have posed for Albuquerque?

5. 750 miles, 1200 kilometers;
6. 250 miles, 400 kilometers; it probably made transportation to and from Albuquerque difficult.

CONTENT OBJECTIVES

After completing this lesson, students will know:

- how the Plains Indians lived before settlers invaded their lands
- how the United States government made and broke promises to Indians
- about the Chivington massacre and the massacres that took place at Little Bighorn and Wounded Knee
- the difficulties of farming and homesteading in the Great Plains
- how the farmers joined together in the 1870s and became, for a time, a strong political force

VOCABULARY

massacre: the horrible killing of a large number of people
sacred: holy
sod: crust of the soil
homestead: settle on government lands

16-2 The Great Plains

As you read, think about these questions:

Why were the Great Plains once called the Great American Desert?

In what ways were the buffaloes important to the American Indians?

Why did the American Indians' way of life change?

What hardships did pioneers on the Great Plains face?

Special Vocabulary	massacre	sod
	sacred	homestead

West of the Mississippi River lay the Great Plains. "Buffalo grass" covered the gently rolling land as far as the eye could see. In summer, the heat baked the plains. During the winter, storms and bitter cold swept across the treeless land. In the 1800s, as today, less rain fell on the Great Plains than in most parts of the country. Because the region was so dry, trees grew only along the banks of rivers.

Indians of the Great Plains

Many Indian nations lived on the Great Plains. Among these were the Ute, Mandan, Cheyenne, Blackfeet, and Sioux. Other Indian groups moved to the Great Plains by order of the United States government in the 1830s. These groups included the Creek, Cherokee, Choctaw, and Chickasaw.

The government had once thought that the plains were useless. In fact, many maps referred to the region as the "Great American Desert." To government leaders, moving the Indians to this "desert" had seemed like a good idea. Lands that settlers wanted in the East would be opened. The Indians would have the Great Plains to themselves.

Lifestyle of the Plains Indians. Indians of the Great Plains used horses to hunt buffaloes and to fight battles. These horses were descendants of the ones brought to America by Spanish settlers. The use of horses allowed the Plains Indians to adopt a nomadic way of life. In other words, they moved their homes from place to place. Often they moved as they hunted. One of the Indian groups, the Sioux, used horses to take over the land of other Indian peoples. By the 1860s they held land in what is now South Dakota.

The Plains Indians used buffaloes for many of their needs. One buffalo weighed from 2000 to 3000 pounds (900 to 1350 kilograms). Such an animal provided enough food for the entire community. In addition, the Plains Indians used the buffalo's hide, or skin, to make tepees or other living quarters. They also used the buffalo's hide for robes to keep them warm in winter.

What the canoe was to the eastern Indians, the horse was to the Indians of the Great Plains. Here a horse pulls a *travois,* a platform stretched between poles, on which a family's belongings are piled.

Changes Come to the Plains. As early as the 1840s, the Indians' way of life began to change. Newcomers from the East killed buffaloes carelessly. The herds began to vanish rapidly. In the 1860s, there had been millions of buffaloes. By 1883 fewer than one thousand remained. For the Indians, it was as if their farms and factories had disappeared.

Ever since the 1830s, the United States government had planned to let the Indians keep the Great Plains as a place to live and hunt. The two sides even signed treaties in which the government promised to pay the Indians money and to stay out of their lands. The government, however, had trouble keeping its promises. Settlers moved to the plains. Soon the newcomers clashed with the Indians.

Fort Laramie, Wyoming, was located on the Oregon Trail. It helped protect hundreds of pioneers traveling west.

In 1864, with winter coming, one group of Indians wanted to make peace. Black Kettle, a Cheyenne chief, led his people to a camp on Sand Creek in what is now Colorado. After Black Kettle talked with an army officer, the chief thought that the war was over. Instead, a colonel of the militia was told to attack the Indians. Colonel J. M. Chivington led his troops against the camping Indians. Using guns and knives, the soldiers killed without mercy. When they were finished, 450 men, women, and children lay dead. This event became known as the Chivington *massacre*. A massacre is the horrible killing of a large number of people.

The Sioux and Cheyenne Wars. On the northern plains a similar story unfolded. During the Civil War, the Sioux attacked settlements on the northern Great Plains. This area stretched from Minnesota to eastern Montana and Wyoming. The Sioux warriors were skilled in fighting on horseback. Even so, the army gained the upper hand after the Civil War.

In 1868 the Sioux agreed to stop fighting. They accepted a treaty setting aside the Black Hills of South Dakota as a reservation. The Sioux were happy to live in the Black Hills, which they considered a *sacred*, or holy, place.

In 1875 miners disobeyed the law and sneaked into the Black Hills. There they discovered a large amount of gold. Soon hundreds of prospectors tramped through the sacred lands of the Sioux. The government refused to keep the miners out of the Indian lands. The Northern Cheyenne experienced the same kinds of broken promises. The Sioux and Cheyenne, therefore, followed their most respected leaders, Sitting Bull and Crazy Horse, off their reservations and into Montana.

The government of the United States ordered the army to force the Indians back to their reservations. Large cavalry scouting parties searched for the Sioux and the Cheyenne. One of the cavalry scouting parties of more than 265 soldiers was led by Colonel George Armstrong Custer. Custer hoped to win glory by fighting against the Indians. Soon Custer's scouts found evidence that the Indians were near. Thinking that the Sioux were few in number, Custer split his troops. He led his soldiers toward an Indian village on the Little Bighorn River. Without sending for the army as he had been ordered, Custer attacked. Suddenly 2500 Indians overwhelmed his small band. Custer and all his troops were killed. This was the Battle of the Little Bighorn or "Custer's Last Stand." It took place late in June 1876.

As a boy, Sitting Bull was known as Hukesni, meaning "slow." The great Sioux medicine man received his new name after he proved his bravery in battle.

Reservations. The victory of Sitting Bull and Crazy Horse was short-lived. In a few months, fresh army troops forced the Sioux to surrender. Most were returned to the reservations. Sitting Bull and a few followers escaped across the border to Canada. Finally in 1881, near starvation, Sitting Bull and his ragged band gave up to army troops.

George Armstrong Custer, who was killed during the Battle of the Little Bighorn, was the great-grandson of a Hessian soldier who remained in America after the Revolutionary War.

All over the West, the Indians had to accept life on reservations. Many of these areas were almost wastelands, not wanted by the settlers. The United States government promised to get food and blankets for the Indians. All too often, greedy government agents kept the money for supplies and gave the Indians spoiled food.

The Indians who had known a free life on the Great Plains suffered greatly on the reservations. In 1890, an Indian religious movement swept the West. The movement was called the "ghost dance." It helped spread the hope that the Indians would soon be delivered from the reservations. The movement frightened army leaders.

Then in late 1890, Indian police, fearing that Sitting Bull might use the ghost dance as a means of stirring up the Sioux, killed the great leader. This act caused a flurry of activity on some of the reservations. When some Sioux gathered to celebrate the ghost dance at Wounded Knee in present-day South Dakota, the army sent a group of soldiers to take guns and other weapons away from them. Somehow the soldiers started shooting at the ghost dancers with rapid-firing guns. When the smoke cleared, two hundred Indian men, women, and children lay dead on the frozen plains. This was the Wounded Knee Massacre.

DISCUSSION

Writers have often created a romantic picture of life in the old west—in books, film scripts, and television scripts. Have the students discuss the hardships the settlers actually faced in contrast to the glamorized version of their lives in the media. Ask the students to contribute inaccurate images they had formed from the media when younger. Ask them also to mention any stories, books, films, or television programs that they believe portray Western life more realistically.

Farming on the Great Plains

After the Civil War, a stream of settlers made their way to the Great Plains. People saw that thousands of small farms could be carved out of this huge frontier. Settlers arrived from many parts of the United States and from foreign countries. Veterans of the war came from North and South. Many who settled on the plains had farmed in other parts of the country that were no longer frontier. As the railroads were built, these men and women could come quickly and cheaply to the places where they planned to settle.

Challenges of the Plains. Many settlers who came to the plains were already farmers, but few of them were ready for the Great Plains environment. The soil, weather, animals, and resources there were different from those in other parts of the country. Farmers had to learn new ways of farming and even of living.

A settler who tried to plow the soil found that the *sod*, or crust of the soil, was very tough. Luckily, new metal plows had been invented that could cut the sod. In the 1830s, a blacksmith named John Deere had made the first steel plow. Farmers who came to him had complained that their wooden plows were hard to use. In 1877 a chilled iron plow, stronger than the steel plow, was sold to farmers on the plains.

The settlers on the plains soon found that there were not enough trees to build wooden houses. Lumber cost too much to bring by wagon or rail. Instead, the settlers used what they had all around them—sod. The farmers cut long strips of sod and then placed them in layers around a hole or dugout. Then they put grass or sod on poles overhead for a roof.

A family of Great Plains farmers poses in front of a house built of strips of sod instead of lumber, which was scarce and costly.

Above all, the farmers on the Great Plains needed water. The plains received only a half or even a third as much rainfall as the East. Though the soil was good, ways had to be found to get water. To their dismay, farmers found that water was deep underground. One way to draw water was through the use of windmills. Blades turned by the wind supplied the power to pump up water. The plains farmers also learned to keep the moisture in the soil by plowing deeper than they had in the past.

Pioneers on the Great Plains always had to struggle with the weather. In the winter, wild storms raged across the land. People sometimes froze to death going from the house to the barn in such blizzards. Some farmers even strung lines between their houses and barns so they would not lose their way. Just as suddenly as blizzards struck, "Chinooks," or warm westerly winds, could come up and melt the snow. Floods might then drive farmers from their homes.

Those settlers who won their struggle against the harsh environment could hope for rich harvests. In the Dakota Territory, some companies set up "bonanza farms." Using machines to farm thousands of acres, these companies proved that good crops were possible on the plains. In fact, machines could even help the small farmer who had less money and land. Wheat drills were used to plant seed. At harvest, farmers sometimes used horse-drawn reapers and threshers. By 1890 they used steam-powered threshers.

ACTIVITY

Objective: to write an original statement

Review for the class the facts of the Oklahoma land rush that started on April 22, 1889. Ask the students to imagine that they were there and they were later asked to write a personal account of what they did and saw for an eastern newspaper.

Divide the class in half. Have one group play the role of settlers and explain what they experienced that day. Have the other group play the role of Indians and explain what it felt like to be removed from their homes so that others could move in.

Homesteading. Many settlers came to the plains hoping to *homestead,* or settle on government lands. In 1862 Congress had passed the Homestead Act, a law that offered land to settlers. Under the Homestead Act, each settler had a right to take 160 acres (64 hectares). After living there and farming the land for five years, the settler would own the homestead or farm. Congress hoped that many workers from eastern cities would travel west and become landowners.

Sometimes the law failed to work out as planned. Congress gave some of the land to railroads and cattle companies. Land speculators often got the best land. These speculators bought land cheaply so that they could sell it later at a higher price. Others used dishonest ways of gaining land. People pretended to live on the land when they really did not. Few workers tried homesteading in the West.

Something like the gold rush happened on the plains in 1889. On April 22, thousands of settlers waited at the starting line to enter what had once been an Indian reservation in the Oklahoma Territory. The settlers were eager to claim land that the Indians had been forced to give up. At noon, an official fired a gun into the air, and the rush began. The "boomers" (called that because this was a land boom, something like a gold boom) went by wagon, horseback, and even bicycles. In a mad rush, they raced across the grassy plains to claim the government land. Towns like Guthrie, Oklahoma, sprang up in a single day.

Some Oklahoma settlers, called "sooners," staked out claims the day before the official opening of the territory. They rode their horses hard on April 22 to make it look as if they had taken part in the general rush.

Farmers Organize. Many farmers blamed the railroads for their problems. The railroads had been built quickly. They owed great amounts of money. For this reason, they charged the farmers high prices to ship their goods to eastern markets. As hard times squeezed the farmers, they began to look with anger at the railroads.

In the 1870s, farmers in states including Indiana, Illinois, and Wisconsin joined the Patrons of Husbandry (husbandry means farming). This group was also known as the Grange or Grangers. It had more than 1.5 million members. Oliver H. Kelley, the leader of the Grangers, knew how lonely farm life could be—especially in the West. He also understood the troubles of the farmer, because he was a clerk for the United States Department of Agriculture. The farmers gathered at their Grange Halls to try to find answers for what had gone wrong. For one thing, Grangers wanted states to pass laws to control the railroads. In time, the states began to listen to the Grangers. They passed laws that put limits on what the railroads could do. These laws were known as the Granger Laws. Later, Congress also passed a law to control the railroads.

The farmers on the Great Plains followed the lead of those in Indiana, Illinois, and Wisconsin and became more active in politics during the 1890s. This movement became known as the Populist Movement. Like the Grangers twenty years before, the Populists favored laws against the railroads and other companies that might be hurting the farmer. In 1892 some farmers and other reformers started the Populist Party. Meeting in Omaha, Nebraska, party members drew up a list

The Grange attracted members not only because of its political action but also because of the social and recreational activities it sponsored.

of actions the government could take and called the list the Omaha Platform. The Omaha Platform called for the government to own the railroads and telegraph companies. It also called for a secret ballot. Further, the Populists said that there should be free and unlimited coinage of silver. By this they meant that all the silver mined in the United States should be made into silver dollars. Like the Grangers before them, they hoped that more silver money would raise the prices of farm goods.

In 1892 three states elected Populist governors. The Populist Party even ran a candidate for president, General James Weaver. Soon, however, the Populists faded from sight. By 1900 higher prices and better rainfall had made the farmers less angry. Most of them began to vote for Democrats or Republicans. As it turned out, however, the two major parties helped pass many Populist reforms into law.

ANSWER THESE QUESTIONS

1. for food, shelter (tepees), robes to keep warm
2. tough sod, lack of trees for building houses, lack of water, violent weather
3. They found that money could be made from farming, cattle ranching, and mining.
4. The Indians learned to use horses to hunt buffaloes and fight battles; farmers made sod houses, used windmills, and plowed deeper.
5. The Granger movement was started to deal with the special problems of farming such as loneliness and troubles with the railroads.

ANSWER THESE QUESTIONS

1. How did the Plains Indians use buffaloes?
2. What were some problems faced by farmers on the Great Plains?
3. Why did people and the government change their minds about the value of the Great Plains?
4. How did various people, including Indians, adapt to the Great Plains environment?
5. For what reasons did farmers in the 1870s start the Granger movement (the Patrons of Husbandry)?

Chief Joseph

Chief Joseph of the Nez Perce Indians in Oregon was an exceptional leader. His Indian name, Hinmaton-Yalaktit, meant "thunder coming from the water up over the land."

In 1876 the government ordered the Nez Perce to give up their traditional lands. Joseph wanted to find a peaceful way to keep the lands, but settlers had moved into the area. Some of the Nez Perce began to make raids against the whites. Joseph decided to lead them into Canada.

Chief Joseph began his desperate march toward Canada in the early summer of 1877. Army troops pursued his band of two hundred warriors and many women and children. During the summer of 1877, Chief Joseph and his followers covered more than 1000 miles (1600 kilometers) through Idaho and Montana. They managed to escape from or defeat several armies.

Chief Joseph crossed the Yellowstone River and came to within 30 miles (48 kilometers) of Canada. Here General Nelson Miles caught up with him on September 30, 1877. Joseph and his warriors dug trenches and grimly prepared for battle. After five days of battle, Joseph saw that he could not win. He had only eighty-seven remaining warriors, almost half of them wounded. The many women and children made it harder to travel. Chief Joseph surrendered to General Milcs. Joseph spoke the following words to persuade his warriors to give up: "It is cold and we have no blankets. The little children are freezing to death. . . . Hear me, my chiefs. I am tired; my heart is sick and sad. From where the sun now stands, I will fight no more, forever."

After the surrender, the government sent Chief Joseph and his people to Indian Territory (Oklahoma). There the Indians lived under poor conditions, and many became sick and died. Later Joseph went to Washington, D.C., to plead for his people. At last some of the Nez Perce, including Chief Joseph, were sent to another reservation in the state of Washington. Chief Joseph died in 1904. He had kept his pledge never again to fight. He is remembered as a courageous and respected leader.

PEOPLE IN AMERICA

THINKING THINGS THROUGH

1. to transport goods to settlers in the West and to take goods they produced to market 2. They became nomadic. 3. because people from other parts of the country wanted to settle on the land 4. Abilene: founded on Great Plains after Chisholm Trail opened in 1867; declined as trails shifted westward; life was rough and rowdy. Virginia City: founded west of Rockies after

Chapter 16 SUMMARY

After the Civil War, Americans looked for new ways to travel west. In 1869 the first transcontinental railroad was built.

New kinds of frontiers appeared. On the Great Plains, cattle ranchers drove their herds north from Texas to the railheads. Later, ranchers raised cattle on the open range. Falling prices and bad weather ended use of the open range.

In mountain areas of the West, miners found gold and silver. Thousands of miners flocked to these areas. Boom towns sprang up near the mines.

The coming of settlers disrupted the Plains Indians' way of life. The Indians used buffaloes for food, clothing, and shelter. They fought for their hunting lands. By 1890, however, most Indians had been forced to live on reservations.

Farmers also came to the Great Plains. Some came to homestead govenment lands. There they learned to live and farm in a harsh and unfamiliar environment. Many farmers blamed the railroads for their troubles and formed a political party, the Populists. In 1892 they ran many candidates. Later, as farmers' lives improved, the Populist Party disappeared. Many of its stands were taken up by other parties.

Chapter 16 TEST

WORDS TO REMEMBER

Read each sentence below and decide which word belongs in the blank. Number your paper from 1 to 7. Then write the letter that stands for the correct word for each sentence.

a. massacre
b. homestead
c. public domain
d. railhead
e. transcontinental
f. vigilante

1. The job of the __f__ groups was to keep order until a sheriff was hired.
2. Cattle graze at no cost to their owners on land that is in the __c__.
3. Four hundred fifty people were unjustly killed in the __a__.
4. The train tracks ended at the __d__.
5. A railroad is called __e__ if it crosses the continent.
6. Congress passed a law allowing people to __b__ on the land.

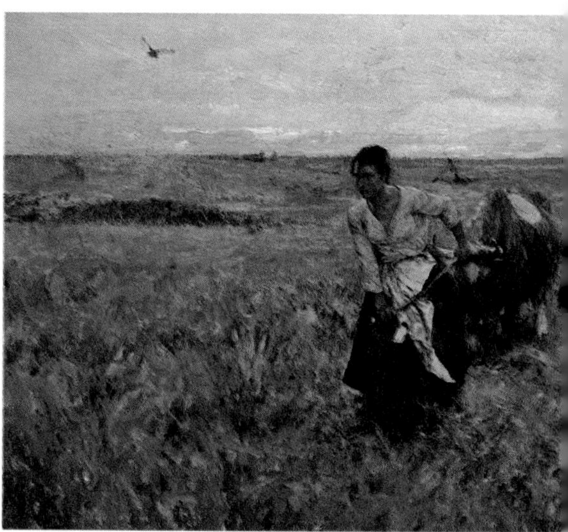

RELATED MATERIALS

Duplicator/Copy Masters: Activities 34,35; Quiz 36
Workbook pages 48-50

discovery of Comstock Lode in 1801; declined as mine dried up; much wealth in city. **5.** Cattle could be shipped to additional markets by railroad, so the cattle industry grew. **6.** steel plow for tough sod; stronger types of wheat and ways to keep moisture in soil in a harsh climate; machines to plant and harvest the crop

WORKING WITH SKILLS

1. 300 miles, 500 kilometers **2.** 350 miles, 600 kilometers **3.** 500 miles, 800 kilometers **4.** 950 miles, 1500 kilometers; it is very mountainous land. **5.** 100 miles, 200 kilometers (accept 150 kilometers)

THINKING THINGS THROUGH

1. Transcontinental railroads were needed to transport settlers to the West. For what other purposes were they needed?
2. How did the use of horses affect the lifestyle of the Plains Indians?
3. Why were the Plains Indians forced from their traditional lands to the reservations?
4. Compare a cow town such as Abilene, Kansas, with a boom town such as Virginia City, Nevada. Consider the following things:
   - where they were located
   - how quickly they started
   - the reasons they disappeared or kept growing
   - the quality of life in the towns
5. How did the completion of railroad lines affect cattle raising?
6. How did farmers on the Great Plains use new tools and farming methods to help solve the problems presented by the tough sod and harsh climate there?

WORKING WITH SKILLS

Look at the map on page 413 to answer these questions. Give answers to the nearest 50 miles or 100 kilometers.

1. On the distance scale of the map, 1 inch (2.5 cm) stands for how many miles? How many kilometers?
2. Find Dodge City and Cheyenne on the map. How many miles is Dodge City from Cheyenne? How many kilometers?
3. Measure the distance from Denver to Topeka. What is this distance in miles? In kilometers?
4. Measure the direct distance from Albuquerque to San Francisco in miles and in kilometers. What features on the map indicate that this would not be a likely route?
5. If you followed the Chisholm Trail from Wichita to Topeka, how far would you travel in miles? In kilometers?

ON YOUR OWN

1. Imagine that you are the owner of a general store in a mining boom town of the West. The year is 1875. What goods would you stock for sale? Think about the kinds of items people in such a community might need. You might ask some adults for ideas. Books, movies, or TV shows about the Old West may be helpful as well. Make a list of at least ten items you would sell in your general store.
2. The pioneer woman in the photograph on page 424 is farming on the Great Plains. Imagine that you are an early settler on the Great Plains. Using information from an encyclopedia and from your textbook, write a letter to your family back in New York City describing your new life. Tell them about the hardships you have met and how you have overcome them.

Chapter 17 discusses the changes in American life that came about as the cities expanded and industry developed. Lesson 17-1 discusses how a large number of people sought jobs in the cities and describes the living conditions they encountered. Lesson 17-2 focuses on the plight of the new immigrants, most of whom were poor, and other poor people. Lesson 17-3 reviews some of the important inventions of the 1800s and explains how they changed people's lives.

Chapter 17
URBAN AND INDUSTRIAL GROWTH

CONTENT OBJECTIVES

After completing the lesson, students will know:

- how the locations of some cities caused them to expand rapidly
- how improved transportation led to the development of suburbs
- some of the advantages and disadvantages of city life

VOCABULARY

urbanization: changing from a largely rural country to one in which many people live in cities
reaper: machine for cutting grain
tenement: a crowded apartment building
polluted: dirty
epidemic: an outbreak of disease that affects many people at the same time

17-1 Cities on the Move

As you read, think about these questions:
Why did cities grow rapidly after the Civil War?
What problems did cities face as they grew?
How was life in the city different from life on farms or in small towns?

Special Vocabulary	urbanization	tenement	epidemic
	reaper	pollute	

Someone once said that America was born in the country and later moved to the city. In the 1700s most people lived on farms or in villages. Only one out of twenty people lived in cities such as Boston, New York, and Philadelphia. Even these cities resembled small towns until the 1800s. Then some of them began to grow rapidly. They drew people from farms and villages. Immigrants from other countries also settled in urban areas. The United States was undergoing *urbanization*—that is, it was changing from a largely rural country to one in which many people lived in cities.

The Growth of Cities

Cities grew rapidly after the Civil War as thousands of people left farms and small towns to seek jobs in the factories in American cities. Good locations helped some cities grow. New York, for example, was built near the ocean and on the Hudson River, an important waterway. Railroads built shortly before the Civil War tied together the cities in the East. By linking these cities with other parts of the country, the railroads also helped the cities to grow. People could then easily reach these cities by train. Wheat, lumber, and other raw materials could arrive from outlying areas. Goods from factories in the cities could be sent to markets across the country.

Chicago's location made it an ideal place for the processing and shipping of American products, especially beef. The famous Union Stockyards processed about eighteen million head of cattle and other livestock every year.

In the 1860s Chicago was booming. The city stood at the point where the Chicago River flowed into Lake Michigan. A canal made it possible for boats to travel from Lake Michigan to the Mississippi River. Already Chicago was known as a railroad center. Farmers on the Great Plains sent their cattle and hogs to Chicago for slaughter. Wheat from the farmlands arrived in Chicago to be made into flour or bread. Cyrus McCormick, who had invented a *reaper*—a machine for cutting grain—in Virginia, built his factory in Chicago. He knew that he could ship his machines throughout the country and around the world from this excellent location.

Other cities also grew rapidly. Cleveland became a center for oil refining and Pittsburgh for steelmaking. Omaha and Kansas City prospered from meat packing and flour milling. In the Pacific Northwest, Seattle became a logging center.

By the late 1800s, New York City was already a huge urban center. Tall buildings held stores and offices. People, trucks, horsecarts, and carriages competed for space on the streets.

DISCUSSION

Review the information in the text on the building of elevated railroads in the cities. Have the students discuss the importance of public transportation in city and suburban life. Point out that funding for public transportation has become controversial in recent years. Ask the students whether they think public transit benefits an entire city or area, or just the people who use it. Have them explain their answers.

Cities Expand. Little towns called "suburbs" grew up around the cities during the years before the Civil War. The people of the suburbs, however, had limited connections with the people in nearby cities because of a lack of transportation.

After the Civil War, most American cities installed horse-drawn streetcars that ran on rails. New York City and a few other large cities also built elevated railroads or "els." These added means of transportation changed city and suburban life. People could now regularly travel from their homes in the suburbs into the cities. The downtown areas of the cities quickly became the homes of businesses, not of people.

Take New York City as an example. Until the 1880s New York City was limited to Manhattan Island. People lived near their work places and could easily walk to and from work.

Across the East River was Brooklyn, New York, a separate town. From 1834 until 1883 Brooklynites lived separate lives from their neighbors across the river. Then the Brooklyn Bridge was opened. People now could travel easily and often from Brooklyn to New York City and back. The streetcar was also a link in this improved chain of transportation. Just eleven years later, in 1894, Brooklyn had become so much a part of New York City life that it no longer was a suburb of New York. Now it was a part of the larger city.

Meanwhile across the Hudson River in New Jersey, 12 miles (18 kilometers) west of New York City, a country town had grown up. People from Orange, New Jersey, gave little thought to becoming a suburb of New York City. Transportation, however, changed that way of thinking. Just as the streetcar had changed Brooklyn from a suburb to a part of the city, so the railroad changed Orange from a sleepy country town into a suburb from which people could travel daily into and out of New York City. This kind of city growth took place all over the United States.

In most cities, the downtown was extremely crowded. City lots cost thousands of dollars. If buildings could rise skyward, thousands of businesses could be added to the downtown. In 1884 William Le Baron Jenney, an architect in Chicago, drew up plans for the first skyscraper. He used a steel frame to support the wood and concrete. The first skyscrapers had only ten stories, but later ones rose much higher. In Chicago, Louis Sullivan planned many of these buildings. Sullivan thought that the design of a building should show its purpose. He believed that large buildings could be both simple and beautiful.

New York's Central Park was designed by Frederick Law Olmstead and Calvert Vaux in 1858. Olmstead borrowed the idea of a city park from European cities. He wanted to provide an island of countryside in the city.

City Life

The cities that grew so quickly after the Civil War soon became awkward giants. Few people knew how to deal with urban problems. City dwellers had to learn to balance the advantages of city life against its disadvantages.

The horse derby was one of several spectator sports that developed in response to urban America's need for relaxation and entertainment.

Culture and Recreation. Museums, art galleries, and libraries allowed city people a chance to enrich themselves culturally. Visitors to the downtown areas could relax at theaters and restaurants. Families could visit the zoo, picnic in the park, or take boat rides. Men and women bicycled and played the new game of lawn tennis. Horse racing and boxing were popular pastimes as well. Beginning in 1869, professional baseball teams played before thousands of onlookers.

Slum dwellings appeared early in the history of cities. As cities became more industrial, the crowding and suffering of the people in the slums increased.

Housing. Wealthy people in cities lived very well. The families of lawyers and business leaders lived in "Victorian houses." These dwellings had rambling porches, tall chimneys, and lots of windows. The high-ceilinged rooms had cozy fireplaces and were furnished with large sofas and bright Oriental rugs.

Many skilled workers such as carpenters and brick masons lived in simple but comfortable houses. However, most poor people lived in wretched houses and apartments that contrasted sharply with the luxurious homes of the wealthy. Landlords who rented to poor families squeezed as many people into the buildings as they could. Many crowded apartment buildings called *tenements* had four apartments on each floor and were six stories high. Later, landlords divided these tenements into even smaller living quarters. People who lived in tenements had little air or light. The danger of fire was great in such buildings.

Health Problems. Many cities were unhealthy. The air and water were *polluted,* or dirty. In many cities, sewage from houses and factories flowed into rivers and other sources of water for drinking and washing. In 1881 the mayor of Cleveland called the Cuyahoga River "an open sewer through the center of the city." Other large cities had similar problems. Many people dumped their trash and old food in large boxes in the streets and alleys. It often rotted there for days. Polluted water and air often led to *epidemics* of typhoid and tuberculosis. An epidemic is an outbreak of disease that affects many people at the same time.

Crime. People in cities also had to worry about crime. Some people turned to crime because of poor living conditions. Robberies and killings took place in alarming numbers. Certain parts of cities were known as areas of gambling and other crimes. "Hell's Kitchen" in New York City was one such area. The "Barbary Coast" in San Francisco was another.

ANSWER THESE QUESTIONS

1. What is urbanization?
2. How did cities grow?
3. What cultural and recreational facilities existed in cities that were not present in rural areas?
4. What problems did cities face as they grew?
5. Why do you think housing conditions were made worse by the growth of cities?

ACTIVITY

Objective: To classify information

Point out to the students that most sections of American cities are in better condition than that described in the text for the 1800s. Explain that the term *public health* refers to the collective health of a city, town, or other unit. Ask the students to make a list of the occupations of those responsible for public health today in their city or town.

ANSWER THESE QUESTIONS

1. changing from a largely rural country to one in which many people live in cities
2. Industries located there; people went to the cities for jobs; improved transportation; good locations helped some grow even faster than others.
3. museums, art galleries, libraries, theaters, restaurants, zoos, parks, facilities for sports such as lawn tennis and baseball
4. poor housing, epidemics of disease, growth of crime
5. Cities grew so fast there was not enough housing for all the people who came; many landlords took advantage of this circumstance.

17-2 Migrants and Immigrants

As you read, think about these questions:

What were some of the reasons immigrants from Europe came to America's cities in large numbers during the late 1800s?

Why did some people want to pass laws to prevent people from immigrating to the United States?

In what ways did reformers work to improve the lives of immigrants and other city dwellers?

Special Vocabulary	mobile	ghetto	nativism
	anti-Semitism	sweatshop	

In the late 1800s, Americans became a *mobile* people—that is, more and more people moved from the place where they were born. Large numbers of immigrants continued to

CONTENT OBJECTIVES

After completing the lesson, students will know:

- the reasons why increasing numbers of Americans moved to the cities
- that "new immigrants" came from southern and eastern Europe
- about the working and living conditions encountered by the immigrants
- about reformers such as Jane Addams and Jacob Riis, who tried to improve conditions for city dwellers

VOCABULARY

mobile: being able to move from one place to another

anti-Semitism: the hatred and persecution of Jews

ghetto: a special section where Jews were forced to live

sweatshop: hot, crowded shop where immigrants worked for low wages

nativism: opposition to immigration

come to America from Europe. Much migration also took place within the United States. People migrated to the West to seek gold or new homes. Many others left farms or small towns to move to the cities.

From the Farm

People migrated from rural areas to cities for many reasons. As farmers used more machines, fewer workers were needed to raise the crops. Young men and women knew that they could find work in steel mills or clothing factories. By leaving the farm, they thought they could escape the drudgery of farm life. Those who were lucky might grow rich or at least have more money to spend.

Many young people from the rural areas of America and Europe left their families to make new lives in the growing cities. Many of them ended up living in tenements like the one pictured at the bottom of page 430.

Depression of 1873. Even more people left farms for the city because of a terrible depression that struck the United States in 1873. Farmers suffered badly because prices for farm

products fell to record lows. Many farmers decided to seek a new life in the cities. Life there was also uncertain, however. Thousands of workers lost their jobs as the depression dragged on into the 1880s. Almost one out of four workers in New York City was out of work.

Black Migration. The first migration of blacks took place during the 1870s. Many blacks moved from one part of the South to another. Some moved from rural areas to cities. Others moved from worn-out farmlands to rich farmlands. A few blacks moved to northern cities. However, they had difficulty finding jobs and often ended up living in conditions as poor as those they had left in the South. Most blacks who migrated in the late 1800s went west, where they became farmers or cowhands on the frontier.

From Abroad

In the 1880s immigrants came to the United States in larger numbers than ever before. Until that time, most immigrants had come from northern Europe. Most had left Great Britain, Ireland, Germany, or one of the Scandinavian nations. Sometimes these people are called the "old immigrants." After 1880 immigrants poured into the United States from southern and eastern Europe. These "new immigrants" came in largest numbers from Russia, Austria, Hungary, Italy, Greece, Romania, Poland, and Turkey. Many settled in the growing, industrial cities. This new immigration helped boost the population of these cities.

Reasons for Immigrating. Many of the "new immigrants" came from farms or rural villages in Europe. In these areas, the population was increasing faster than the need for workers. Many farmers who rented from landowners were forced off the land.

Some immigrants came to the United States to avoid being drafted into the military. Germany, Austria-Hungary, and Russia had large armies. Young men who lived in these empires could be forced to join the army. Often the young men or the whole family left to escape this hated policy.

Many Jewish people fled the problem of *anti-Semitism,* the hatred and persecution of Jews. In most European cities, Jews were forced to live in a special section known as the *ghetto.* In Russia, the government kept Jews from owning

Immigrants often had to sell whatever they owned in order to pay their passage to America. Many of them had to travel in very poor accommodations.

land or attending universities. The Russian government even allowed riots against the Jews. Russian Jews knew that the United States had no such policy. The promise of American life drew many such immigrants to the United States.

Almost from the moment they arrived, immigrants faced many hardships. Most immigrants came from farms and villages. To find jobs, they had to settle in cities. Most of them chose neighborhoods where people of their own culture lived. In these neighborhoods, they could speak their own language. They could attend their own theaters and buy newspapers printed in their native languages. Some immigrants never left these neighborhoods.

Some immigrants worked as laborers in factories. In fiery steel mills or noisy cotton factories, they sometimes worked as long as fifteen hours a day. Others made clothes, cigars, or other products in hot, crowded shops called *sweatshops*. They sometimes worked for as little as three or four dollars a week. Owners of these sweatshops knew that they could pay immigrants low wages. People who could not speak English would not protest.

Bessie Van Vorst worked at a series of different factory jobs and wrote about her experiences. In one such job, she stuffed pickles into jars for ten hours a day, six days a week.

Women such as these were handicapped by a lack of education. Frequently they did "piece work"—that is, they were paid for each piece of work completed rather than for the number of hours worked.

Her weekly pay was $4.20, of which $3.00 was spent for housing. Van Vorst wrote the following description of her first day on the job:

> My hands are stiff, my thumbs almost blistered. . . . Cases are emptied and refilled; bottles are labeled, stamped and rolled away . . . still there are more cases, more jars, more bottles. Oh! the monotony of it . . . ! Now and then someone cuts a finger or runs a splinter under the flesh . . . and still the work goes on.

Opposition to Immigration. Some people in the United States wanted to keep out immigrants. This opposition to immigration was called *nativism.* The nativists were alarmed by the large numbers of immigrants flocking to the United States. The unfamiliar customs of these newcomers upset them. Many immigrants from southern and eastern Europe seemed poorer than other immigrants. Most did not know how to read or write. Many of the immigrants were Jewish or Roman Catholic, while most opponents of immigration were Protestant. The Chinese, because of their appearance and customs, also faced discrimination.

Some Americans feared that their own way of life might be threatened if large numbers of immigrants kept coming. Members of labor unions also worried that thousands of poor workers from foreign countries might threaten their jobs or keep down their level of pay.

Nativist groups demanded laws against immigrants coming to the United States. In 1882 Congress passed the

DISCUSSION

Have the students discuss whether the United States should encourage or discourage immigration today. Point out that immigrants played a vital role in building the nation originally. Point out also that—as in the 1880s—some people now fear immigrants because of competition for jobs, language differences, and other reasons. Point out that discussions on such topics can be highly emotional and that it is important to separate facts from opinions.

Chinese Exclusion Act to keep Chinese workers from immigrating to the United States. Not until 1921 did Congress limit the number of immigrants from Europe who could enter the United States.

Toward a Better City

The promises of wealth and a better life had not come true for most immigrants. These people lived in overcrowded, dirty tenements. They were looked down upon by Americans who had come to this country as immigrants themselves only a few years before.

Every large city had its slums. Many Americans were shocked by the living conditions of the poor. How could the crowded neighborhoods and their pitiful inhabitants be helped? That was the question some reformers asked in the 1880s and 1890s.

Jane Addams recognized the special needs of those people who were suffering in the city. She established Hull House to serve as a bridge between foreign cultures and American ways of life.

Jane Addams. A young woman named Jane Addams had an answer. While in England, she had visited Toynbee Hall, a settlement house in the slums of London. In this house lived a group of well-educated young people from wealthy families. They helped people that no one else cared about. If a settlement house could work in London, why not try it in an immigrant neighborhood of Chicago? The idea for Hull House was born.

Jane Addams and her friend Ellen Starr established Hull House in 1889. They hoped to bring immigrants in touch with American life. Classes and clubs were begun at the settlement. Immigrants learned to read and speak English. Readings and concerts were held. Nurseries and kindergartens cared for the children of working mothers. Families in need received food and shelter.

Other Reformers. Churches also tried to help poor people in the city. Some church leaders wanted laws passed to help the poor. A few ministers and priests went into the worst neighborhoods to start churches or city missions. The Salvation Army was a church begun to help the poor. Its members opened missions in the cities to give food and shelter to those who had nothing.

Others tried to make the American people aware of poverty. In 1879 Henry George wrote *Progress and Poverty,* a book on economics. Henry George stirred many people by

ACTIVITY

Objectives: To identify main ideas and to make inferences

Review for the students the fact that Jacob Riis spent time at night in New York City's slums to gather material for his book *How the Other Half Lives.* Divide the class into three groups, representing Riis and his editors; poor people whom he interviewed as sources; and sweatshop owners and landlords whom he tried to interview and who were affected by his work. Have the group discuss the kinds of help they gave him, the obstacles he encountered, and the reasons why his work was important. Remind the students that Lessons 17-1 and 17-2 contain many clues to what Riis must have seen.

Schools for immigrant children were crowded and run-down. These children, photographed by Jacob Riis in the early 1890s, are being taught in a condemned building.

asking why there were so many poor people in a country that could produce so much. Jacob Riis, a newspaper reporter, visited the New York slums by night so that he could see the conditions at their worst. He used a camera and notebook to record what he found. In 1890 he wrote the book *How the Other Half Lives.* In this book, Riis tried to let people know how terrible conditions were for the poor in cities. Writers and reformers made Americans aware of the need to improve cities. In time, improvements were made.

ANSWER THESE QUESTIONS

1. What were some of the reasons why immigrants came to the United States in the late 1800s?
2. What hardships faced migrants and immigrants in the United States?
3. What changes did farm families have to make after moving to the city?
4. Why did immigrants face discrimination in this country?
5. How did writers and reformers help to bring about improvements in cities?

ANSWER THESE QUESTIONS

1. to find work, often after being forced off the land; to avoid the military; to escape religious persecution
2. long hours working in sweatshops, low pay, discrimination, tenement life
3. People who were accustomed only to farm life had to crowd into cities.
4. differences in religion, culture, language, and race; the notion that they were taking jobs away from other Americans
5. by making people aware of poverty and the need to improve cities, by starting missions, teaching English, feeding the needy

Objective: After completing this page, students should know how to make circle graphs and bar graphs.

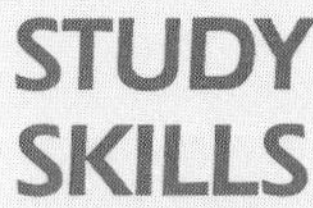

Working with Skills

STUDY SKILLS

ACTIVITY

Objective: To make graphs

Obtain statistics on the age distribution of the American population between 1860 and 1920 from an almanac or other reference source. Make these figures available to the class. Have the students construct a circle graph showing the percent breakdown by age groups for a particular year, such as 1900. Then have the students make a bar graph showing changes in one of the age groups every ten years.

ANSWERS

Questions in Paragraph
2 million and 3 million
the number of immigrants

Numbered Questions:
1. about 5,250,000
2. 1880s
3. 1860s; the Civil War

Reading Bar and Circle Graphs

A graph is a drawing that presents numerical information. Graphs help people see the relationships among numbers or amounts more clearly. Two major types of graphs are bar graphs and circle graphs.

The graph below is a bar graph. It shows the total number of immigrants who entered the United States for each decade, or ten-year period, between 1850 and 1900.

A bar graph compares information given on two axes, or straight lines that cross each other at a right angle. Look at the bar graph shown here. The vertical, or up-and-down, axis gives the number of immigrants. The horizontal, or left-to-right, axis gives the years.

Now look at the bar, or shaded-in area, above "1850–1859" on the horizontal axis. Between what numbers on the vertical axis does the bar stop? What do these numbers stand for? Now estimate the number of immigrants as closely as you can. You should conclude that the number of immigrants in the 1850s was about 2,800,000. Interpret the bar for each ten-year period in the same way. Use the graph to answer the following questions.

1. Look at the bar for the years 1880–1889. What was the immigration for the 1880s?

2. In what decade did the highest immigration occur?

3. In what decade did the lowest immigration occur? What might be a reason for this?

IMMIGRATION TO THE UNITED STATES, 1850–1899

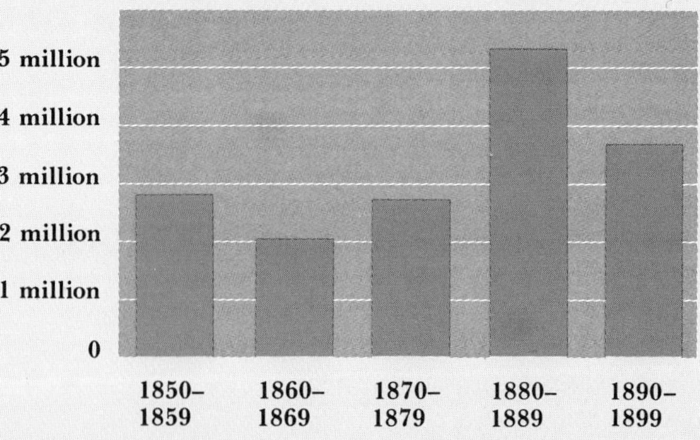

RELATED MATERIAL
Duplicator/Copy Master Activity 37

A circle graph shows information by dividing a circle into slices like a pie. For this reason it is often called a "pie graph." Look at the circle graph below. It shows the percentage of total immigration from several European countries to the United States between 1820 and 1900.

The main advantage of a circle graph is that it shows how parts relate to the whole. In the graph below, the whole circle stands for the total European immigration to the United States. Each "slice" stands for immigration from a particular country. A label gives a name and a percent figure for each slice. You can judge how one country's figures compare with another's by comparing the size of the slices. Look at the graph. Which country contributed more immigrants, Germany or Russia? It is clear that more immigrants came from Germany, because its slice is larger. Now look at the slices for Italy and Austria. Which country sent more immigrants? The graph shows you that these two countries sent about the same number. Study the circle graph, and answer the following questions.

EUROPEAN IMMIGRATION TO THE UNITED STATES, 1820–1900

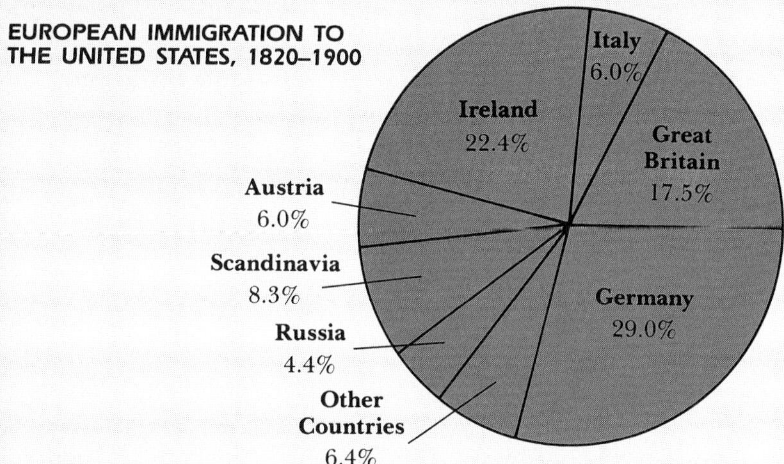

4. From what country did the most immigrants come to the United States between 1820 and 1900? What percent of the total did this country supply?

5. What country provided the next highest total of immigrants? What was its percentage?

6. What region provided about eight percent of all immigrants? Judging by sight only, how does this share compare with Great Britain's? With Russia's?

4. Germany; 29.0%
5. Ireland; 22.4%
6. Scandinavia; smaller than Great Britain's; larger than Russia's

CONTENT OBJECTIVES

After completing the lesson, students will know:

- about some of the important American inventors of the 1800s
- how their inventions changed the way Americans lived
- who were the "captains of industry" and how they made their money
- about the development of corporations and large monopolies

VOCABULARY

patent: the right of an inventor to use and sell an invention

corporation: an organization that can own property and make contracts as if it were an individual

stockholder: person who owns shares of a corporation

limited liability: protection for stockholders of a corporation from having to pay its debts if it goes out of business

trust: an arrangement through which one company owns or controls a number of other companies

17-3 Technology and Industry

As you read, think about these questions:

How did inventions made after 1850 lead to the development of new industries?

What is needed to turn an inventor's dream into goods that people use?

How did the captains of industry change the ways of doing business?

Special Vocabulary patent, corporation, stockholder, limited liability, trust

In 1838 the clerk of the United States Patent Office resigned from office. He sadly announced that all useful inventions had been discovered. Yet from 1850 to 1860, inventors in the United States registered about twenty-eight thousand *patents*. A patent is the right of an inventor to use and sell an invention. Little did the clerk of patents know that in 1838 America was about to enter a great period of invention.

The Age of Invention

Many inventions made during the 1800s were improvements of things already in use. For example, people had for some time used lifts to move heavy loads between floors. If the ropes that raised such a lift broke, however, the lift would crash to the floor below. People were afraid to ride anything that might suddenly fall. In 1852 Elisha Otis, a worker in a bed factory, invented an elevator with a safety device to catch the car if the ropes broke. Otis's elevator was safe for people as well as freight.

Other inventions of the 1800s provided better ways of producing much-needed materials. For example, during the 1850s, Henry Bessemer of Great Britain found a cheap and fast way to make steel.

Another important group of inventions opened the door for the use of new forms of energy. In 1859 Edwin Drake, a retired railroad conductor, built the first steam-powered oil drilling rig. Within four months his first oil well in western Pennsylvania was producing twenty-two barrels of oil a day.

Petroleum soon became a cheap and abundant source of energy. Similarly, electricity became widely used after Thomas Alva Edison invented the electric light bulb in 1879.

Some inventions of the late 1800s brought great advances to American industry. Others, such as the vacuum process for canning food invented by Amanda Jones, helped change the way people lived, both in the United States and in other countries. For more information on American inventors, see the chart below.

DISCUSSION

Have the students discuss how the major inventions mentioned in the text further accelerated the growth of cities. Point out, for example, that elevators made possible the development of large office buildings in cities. Have the students discuss which invention of the period was most important and why. Then point out the ways in which one invention may complement another.

OUTSTANDING AMERICAN INVENTORS

Inventor	Invention	Date	Importance
Elisha Otis	Safety elevator	1853	Otis's elevator provided the first safe means of transporting people and heavy loads between the floors of a building. Elevators later became an essential part of skyscrapers.
Edwin Drake	Oil drilling rig	1859	Drake's invention made it possible to drill wells to tap America's vast reserves of petroleum. This new source of energy later provided power for industries and modern forms of transportation, such as automobiles and airplanes.
Alexander Graham Bell	Telephone	1876	The telephone enabled people to communicate across great distances. The telephone industry became a major business and provided reliable communication that helped other industries.
Thomas Edison	Electric light bulb	1879	Electric lighting improved living and working conditions for Americans. It also helped promote the use of electricity, which later powered industrial equipment and home appliances.
Charles Martin Hall	Hall-Héroult process	1886	This process, developed independently by Hall and Paul Héroult of France, made it possible to produce aluminum quickly and inexpensively.
George Eastman	Box camera	1886	Eastman's simple and inexpensive camera helped make photography a popular hobby.

Captains of Industry

An invention was only the first step in bringing an idea to life. Money had to be found to make and sell the product. A factory had to be set up and workers hired. Some inventors turned out to be clever business people. Thomas Edison and Alexander Graham Bell, the inventor of the telephone,

Alexander Graham Bell opens the New York to Chicago line in 1892. As a teacher of the deaf, Bell studied the way speech sounds are made and heard. His training helped him develop the telephone, which was patented in 1878.

helped begin companies bearing their names. George Eastman made millions of dollars from the Kodak camera.

Many industries sprang to life from the bold acts of business leaders known as "captains of industry." The captains of industry were tough and sometimes even ruthless in their efforts to build an industry and keep it alive. Being in business could be risky as well as profitable. Some captains of industry fought each other as if business were a matter of life and death. Many of them wanted to make their company the largest one or even the only one in their industry. As a result, they forced small companies out of business.

Most of these captains of industry stood at the heads of large *corporations*. A corporation is an organization that can own property and make contracts as if it were an individual. A charter from a state gives the corporation the right to raise money. It can raise money either by borrowing money or by selling shares of stock. People who buy these shares of stock are called *stockholders*. They become the owners of the company. The stockholders of a corporation have *limited liability*. This means that if a corporation goes out of business, the stockholders do not have to pay the company's debts. Because of limited liability, many people were willing to invest their money in corporations during the 1800s.

Railroad Empires. The first captains of industry combined several railroads to form networks that stretched from one part of the country to another. In 1862 Cornelius Vanderbilt bought the New York Central Railroad. The "Commodore," as he was called, wanted his railroads to go as far west as possible. He believed a larger system of rails could provide better service and make more money. Before Vanderbilt died in 1877, the New York Central reached from New York City to Chicago.

To build his rail empire, Vanderbilt had to buy smaller railroads. Some of these railroads ran to the same cities as the New York Central. In 1866 Vanderbilt tried to buy one such railroad, the Erie. A fierce struggle took place between Vanderbilt and the owners of the Erie. It was known as the "Erie War." Many Americans were upset when they read about the tricks and even the dishonesty of these railroad owners in the "Erie War."

In the late 1890s, Edward H. Harriman tried to put together a railroad empire that would run from coast to coast. In 1901 he battled James J. Hill of the Great Northern Railroad for control of the Northern Pacific Railroad. Both men had the help of important banks in the East. When neither was able to win the struggle, they joined their companies in the Northern Securities Company. With little or no competition, the Northern Securities Company could charge whatever price it wished for its services.

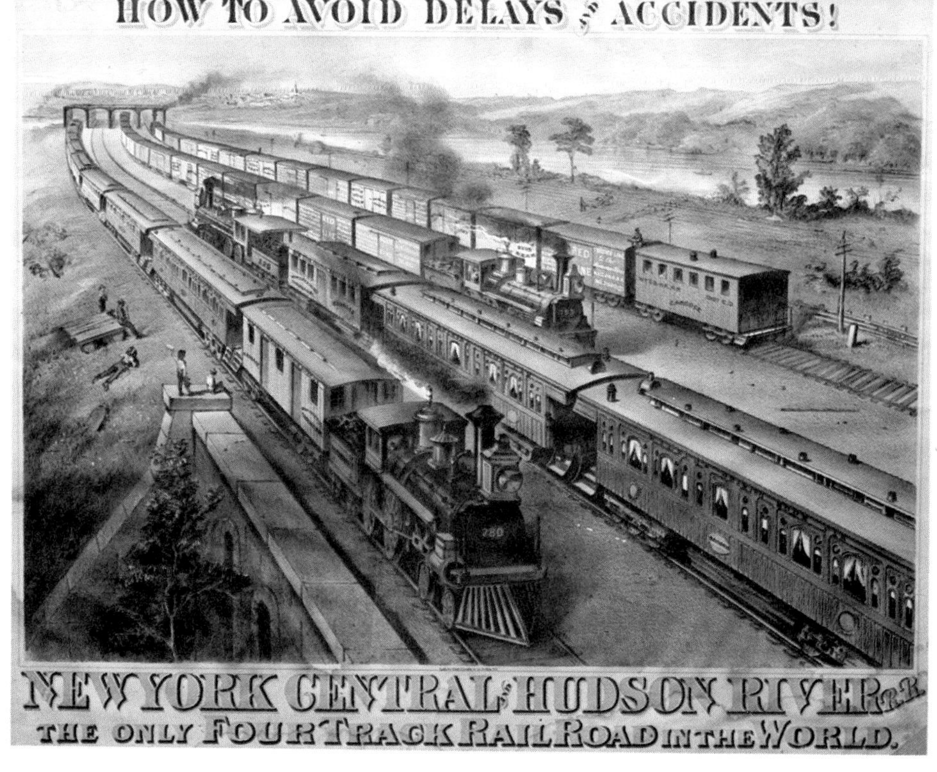

HOW TO AVOID DELAYS & ACCIDENTS!
NEW YORK CENTRAL & HUDSON RIVER R.R.
THE ONLY FOUR TRACK RAIL ROAD IN THE WORLD.

Four-track rail lines made it possible for Cornelius Vanderbilt to run passenger and freight trains on separate tracks in both directions.

For many years, John D. Rockefeller controlled everything that had to do with buying and selling oil. He later used part of his fortune to establish foundations that continue to benefit people around the world.

The Standard Oil Monopoly. When Edwin Drake drilled his first oil well, John D. Rockefeller was already on his way as a business leader. Rockefeller saw that he could become an even bigger success still by getting into the oil business. In 1862 Rockefeller invested in an oil refinery in Cleveland. Refineries converted petroleum into kerosene. Step by step, he learned the oil industry, from buying petroleum from the drillers to selling kerosene in grocery stores.

To Rockefeller, the oil business in the 1860s seemed filled with waste. More than twenty refineries operated in Cleveland alone. Making money from oil was still risky. Rockefeller hoped that his company, Standard Oil, would become the only large company refining oil. In 1870 he called upon the other companies to sell out to Standard Oil. Those companies that agreed to sell received Standard Oil stock. Companies that tried to hold out were soon forced out of business. By 1880 Rockefeller held the entire oil industry in his hands.

Many people were alarmed by Standard Oil's great economic power and its ability to drive other companies out of business. Standard Oil was the first corporation set up as a *trust.* A trust is an arrangement through which one company owns or controls a number of other companies. As Rockefeller bought up companies, he used the trust to hold them. "Trust" soon became another word for monopoly. People thought of Standard Oil as a giant monopoly.

In 1889 Andrew Carnegie wrote an essay about wealth. In it he said that a rich person should use any extra money for the general good. Carnegie lived by his own rule.

Sultan of Steel. Andrew Carnegie came to the United States from Scotland at the age of thirteen. He soon joined his father working in a cotton mill for $1.20 a week. Two years later, he got a job as a telegraph messenger for the Pennsylvania Railroad. Soon he was secretary to the vice president of the railroad and later a railroad official. With money made in clever investments, he bought shares in an iron company.

In 1873 Carnegie made a trip to Great Britain, where he met Henry Bessemer. Carnegie became convinced that the Bessemer process was the best way to make steel. When he returned to the United States, he built the largest Bessemer steel mill in the world.

In time Carnegie brought together much of the steel industry. He owned the boats for hauling ore and the rights to ore fields. He even bought railroads for transporting iron and steel. Throughout his life in business, Carnegie hired talented people. He always found the most modern ways of making and selling steel.

In 1901 Carnegie faced a steel war with the other companies. At the age of sixty-five, he longed to retire. He wanted to spend his time writing books and giving away his money. J.P. Morgan, a New York banker, stepped forward to buy Carnegie's steel company. Out of this and other companies, Morgan set up the United States Steel Corporation. The bankers led by Morgan paid Carnegie $492 million for his company. In turn, United States Steel became the first company worth a billion dollars.

Great Fortunes. Most captains of industry left large sums of money when they died. Much of the money went to their children and grandchildren. Some families of tycoons spent large amounts of money to amuse themselves. Yet few captains of industry spent large amounts on themselves. Though they lived well, they had more interest in making money than spending it. Both Rockefeller and Carnegie gave large sums of money for good causes. Rockefeller called his money "God's gold." He said that God had allowed him his money to do good. Andrew Carnegie thought that people should spend the first half of their lives making money and the second half giving it away. Carnegie gave away much of his fortune to build Carnegie libraries across the country. Rockefeller's gifts helped wipe out the dread disease of hookworm in the South. He and his family also gave money for black schools. These gifts helped soften the distrust that some people felt for the captains of industry.

Most Americans could see that the development of industry gave them more comforts than ever before. Americans were beginning to talk proudly of their "standard of living," which was marching steadily upward.

This view of the inside of a steel mill shows a Bessemer converter in operation. The new process helped America become an industrial giant.

ACTIVITY

Objectives: To use reference materials and to write a report

Have each student do research on the life of one of the major captains of industry mentioned in the text—Vanderbilt, Rockefeller, Carnegie, or Morgan. Have the students find the answers to the following questions: How did each make his start in life? What kind of innovation, or new approach—if any—did the person use to get ahead? Specifically, what kinds of misconduct was each accused of? Did the person donate money to charity?

ANSWER THESE QUESTIONS

1. What was the "Erie War"?
2. How did Elisha Otis's safety elevator differ from the lifts that were used earlier?
3. In what ways did the captains of industry use their fortunes to help people?
4. Why were many people upset by the power of Standard Oil and other trusts?
5. How did a corporation help turn an invention into a product for people to use?

ANSWER THESE QUESTIONS

1. a power struggle in which Cornelius Vanderbilt tried to take control of the Erie railroad
2. It had a safety device to catch the car if the ropes broke.
3. Carnegie: to build libraries; Rockefeller: to fight disease and educate blacks
4. because they drove other companies from business and raised prices
5. by raising the money to make and sell the product

THINKING THINGS THROUGH

1. They were not used to city life or to working in factories; both groups were often poor. **2.** Cities used the elevator to help them grow upward; electricity served city people as a source of energy to light buildings and streets and to run machines; canned food

Chapter 17 SUMMARY

After 1860 people from farms and small towns migrated to the cities to find jobs and a more exciting life. Els and skyscrapers allowed cities to grow both outward and upward. City planners helped make urban life more pleasant by designing parks and buildings to fit the environment.

Cities had both advantages and problems. Pollution of water and air harmed the health of city dwellers. The poor lived in crowded and unsafe tenements. The crime rate was also high.

In the 1880s the "new immigrants" began to arrive in large numbers. They settled in the cities. Many had trouble adjusting to life in the United States. Luckily, some churches and settlement houses tried to help these immigrants.

After the Civil War, inventions sprang one after another from the minds of inventors. Drake's oil well and Edison's electric light changed life in the United States. The age of invention also led to new industries that produced steel, oil, electric lights, and telephones.

The captains of industry built huge corporations that provided goods and services to Americans. In some industries, one company grew so large that few other companies were left. In later years, many business leaders gave some of their money to help people in the United States and around the world.

Chapter 17 TEST

WORDS TO REMEMBER

Match each of the following words with the correct definition below.

c	1. urbanization	g	5. ghetto
d	2. polluted	h	6. mobile
f	3. patent	b	7. corporation
a	4. tenement	e	8. nativism

a. a crowded apartment building
b. an organization that can own property and make contracts as if it were an individual
c. a change from a largely rural country to one in which many people live in cities
d. dirty
e. opposition to immigration
f. the right of an inventor to use and sell an invention
g. a special section of a city where Jews were forced to live
h. capable of moving from place to place

THINKING THINGS THROUGH

Answer each of the following questions.

1. In what ways were the migrants from farms to cities similar to the "new immigrants" from Europe?
2. How did cities use inventions and new ideas to solve some of their problems?
3. Why do you think the United States did not limit the number of immigrants coming into the country in the late 1800s and early 1900s?

RELATED MATERIALS

Duplicator/Copy Masters: Activities 36, 37; Quiz 37
Workbook pages 51-53

allowed city people to maintain a healthful diet. **3.** Businesses were eager to have a large labor supply of people to work in the factories; many Americans felt that there was enough room and opportunity for all. **4, 5.** Answers will vary.

WORKING WITH SKILLS

1. 1900-1920; 1880-1900
2. 1860
3. 1920

---

4. Should there have been more laws to control the actions of companies in new industries? Why or why not?
5. What things that you use in everyday life can be traced back to the inventions of the late 1800s?

WORKING WITH SKILLS

The table below shows the number of people who lived in cities in the United States as measured every twenty years from 1840 to 1920. It also shows what percentage of the nation's total population consisted of city dwellers in each of these years.

Year	Number	Percentage
1840	1,800,000	11%
1860	6,200,000	20%
1880	14,100,000	28%
1900	30,200,000	40%
1920	54,200,000	51%

Review the bar graph on page 438. Then study the graph on this page. It shows the number of city dwellers for each year listed in the table. Draw a similar graph that shows the percentage given for each year. Use the graphs to answer these questions:

1. What time period had the largest increase in numbers? In percentages?
2. In what year did one out of five people live in the urban areas?
3. In what year did more people live in urban than in rural areas for the first time?

NUMBER OF AMERICANS LIVING IN CITIES, 1840-1920

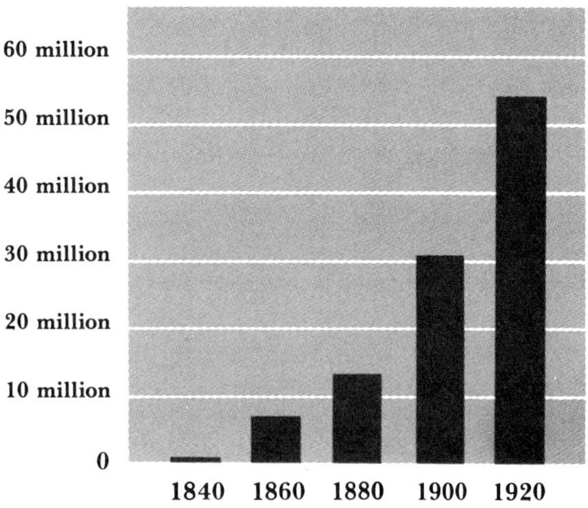

ON YOUR OWN

1. Imagine that it is 1880 and you have just inherited $1000. You decide to invest your money by purchasing stock in a corporation. Which of the following types of companies would you choose to invest in: (a) an oil company, (b) a steel company, or (c) a railroad? Write a paragraph explaining your choice. Tell why you think people will want to buy the product or service provided by the company you are investing in.
2. On a sheet of poster paper draw a time line for the period from 1850 to 1900. Mark on your time line the dates for the inventions discussed in the chapter. Add any other dates you wish from the chapter, for developments such as the skyscraper. Illustrate your time line with your own drawings or with photographs taken from old magazines.

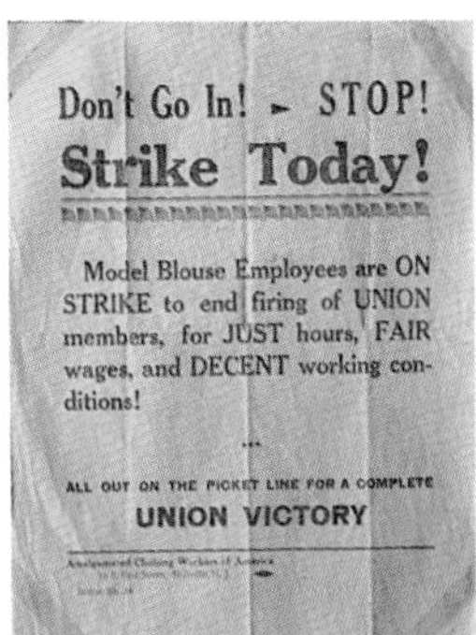

Don't Go In! - STOP!
Strike Today!
Model Blouse Employees are ON STRIKE to end firing of UNION members, for JUST hours, FAIR wages, and DECENT working conditions!
ALL OUT ON THE PICKET LINE FOR A COMPLETE
UNION VICTORY

Chapter 18
POLITICS AND REFORM

Chapter 18 focuses on labor problems and the progressive movement in the late 1800s and early 1900s. Lesson 18-1 describes the grim working conditions, the beginning of unions, and the reactions of business and government. Lesson 18-2 discusses political corruption, reforms, and the division of the Democrats over the gold standard. Lesson 18-3 introduces reforms associated with the "Wisconsin Idea" of Robert La Follette and summarizes important national reforms during the Roosevelt, Taft, and Wilson administrations.

CONTENT OBJECTIVES

After completing the lesson, students will know:

- that working conditions were extremely harsh in the 1800s
- when the first labor unions evolved and some of the problems confronting them
- Samuel Gompers's role in creating a successful, powerful federation of workers
- how the Triangle Fire helped focus public attention on the problems of workers

VOCABULARY

trade union: an organization of workers who work at a single skilled trade
cooperative: a business that the workers own together
federation: an association of groups that have a common goal or purpose
anarchist: one who is against all forms of government
injunction: a court order that prohibits a specific action

18-1 Labor Reform

As you read, think about these questions:

What conditions in factories led to the need for labor unions?

Why was it difficult for workers to organize unions?

Why did union actions sometimes lead to violence?

Special Vocabulary	trade union	federation	injunction
	cooperative	anarchist	

In the years right after the Civil War, factories grew in number and size as never before. Thousands of young people came from the farms to fill jobs in them, as did millions of immigrants. Factory life was generally very difficult. Many factories had dim lighting and little fresh air. Workers had to be at their machines for up to fifteen hours a day. Adults earned as little as five cents an hour. The conditions surrounding child labor, or the working of children in factories, were especially tragic.

A reformer who became known as Mother Jones gathered information on child labor. She described what she saw in the cotton mills:

> Little girls and boys, barefooted, walked up and down between the endless rows of spindles, reaching thin little hands into the machinery to oil it. They replaced spindles all day long. . . . Tiny babies of six years old with faces of sixty did an eight-hour shift for ten cents a day. If they fell asleep, cold water was dashed in their faces. . . .

Not until 1938 did Congress make it illegal to employ children under age sixteen in factories.

Labor Unions Begin

Workers increasingly joined together in unions to get better working conditions. The first unions were *trade unions*. A trade union is an organization of workers who work at a single skilled trade such as plumbing or carpentry.

National Labor Union. In 1866 William Sylvis, an iron worker from Pennsylvania, tried to bring the trade unions together in a single organization. He named it the National Labor Union. Its chief goal was to get an eight-hour day for workers. In 1868 the federal government and five state governments agreed to let their employees have the eight-hour day. After Sylvis died in 1869, the National Labor Union quickly faded from view.

Labor leader Terence Powderly (center), here being introduced to a Knights of Labor convention, had begun working as a laborer at the age of thirteen.

The Knights of Labor. In 1869 Uriah S. Stephens, a garment cutter in Philadelphia, began a union called the Knights of Labor. During the 1870s the membership of the Knights of Labor grew slowly but steadily. Terence V. Powderly, of Carbondale, Pennsylvania, became leader of the Knights in 1879. He supported equal pay for men and women and opposed child labor and the selling of liquor. Powderly hoped that, in time, workers could set up *cooperatives*. A cooperative is a business that the workers own together. Most of all, the Knights under Powderly tried to bring all workers—skilled and unskilled, black and white, male and female—into a single union. Anyone could join who was not a lawyer, a liquor dealer, a gambler, or a banker. Under Powderly's leadership, the Knights of Labor began to grow rapidly. By the mid-1880s, it had about 700,000 members. Many new members looked to the Knights to win them higher pay and better working conditions.

The Knights of Labor, however, had only a short taste of success. Soon membership dropped off. The skilled and unskilled workers did not get along well. Many workers thought the Knights should be in favor of strikes, which it firmly opposed. By 1900 the union had almost disappeared.

Samuel Gompers served as president of the AFL from 1886 until his death in 1924. He was considered the head of the American labor movement during those years.

The AFL. Samuel Gompers, an immigrant from Great Britain, helped organize a successful *federation* of trade unions in 1881. A federation is made up of several groups that have a common goal or purpose. In 1886 Gompers's federation became the American Federation of Labor, or AFL.

As leader of the AFL, Gompers pressed for step-by-step improvement in pay and work conditions for union members. He tried to bargain with employers and to reach a contract, or written agreement, with them regarding wages and hours. He put into effect the rule: "No contract, no work." By 1924 the AFL had more than 3 million members.

The AFL was a trade union and therefore open only to skilled workers. It did little to help the unskilled workers. In fact, after the Knights of Labor declined, there was no large union for most unskilled workers for over forty years.

Labor Struggles

Labor unions were hard to organize and to keep alive. Many working people were afraid to join them, knowing they might be fired if their employers found out. Factory owners depended on this fear. They also knew they could quickly replace anybody who was a "troublemaker." Immigrants and other people kept coming to the cities looking desperately for jobs. Large numbers of workers remained unorganized, or outside the unions.

Business and government leaders did not understand the outlook of working people. Owners felt that they could act as they pleased with their businesses. Government officials believed their job was to help the owners protect their property and maintain order. Several times when workers tried to strike, government leaders sent troops against the strikers. Violence broke out during the hard times of the 1870s and of the 1890s.

DISCUSSION

Review for the students Terence V. Powderly's goal of uniting skilled and unskilled workers in the Knights of Labor. Explain that today most unions are very specialized, organizing workers who do one type of work in an industry. Have the students discuss the advantages and disadvantages of a union for all workers versus many specialized unions. Ask students if they think "a super union" of all skilled and unskilled workers is possible or desirable today.

Railroad Strike of 1877. In 1877 railroad workers in many parts of the country went on strike. They were angry because the railroads had cut their wages. In Pittsburgh, twenty-five strikers died in a battle with state troops. Then furious railroad workers joined other workers in a growing mob. They attacked the soldiers with firearms. As the troops fled, the mob took over railroad property. Finally, President Rutherford B. Hayes sent federal troops to Pittsburgh and other cities where riots were taking place. Only then did the strike come to an end.

The Haymarket Square riot and bombing gave the labor movement a bad reputation. Many people believed that an increase in organized labor would mean an increase in violence.

Haymarket Square. Again in 1886 labor troubles took a violent turn. The workers at Cyrus McCormick's harvester factory in Chicago went on strike. They were demanding an eight-hour day. The large numbers of strikers were enough to frighten the police. In addition, however, the workers had read newspaper articles written by a small group of *anarchists.* An anarchist is someone who is against all forms of government. Some anarchists advocate violence to achieve their aims. In this case, the anarchists urged the workers to take violent action during the strike.

On May 3, 1886, after days of battling angry mobs, police killed several strikers during a riot. Anarchists called a meeting in Haymarket Square that evening to protest the shootings. The police arrived at the meeting to break it up. Suddenly someone hurled a bomb, killing seven police and wounding many others. Eight leaders of the meeting were

ACTIVITY

Objective: To use reference materials

John Peter Altgeld was governor of Illinois from 1893 to 1897. Have the students research his term as governor, specifically his controversial actions regarding the Haymarket defendants and the Pullman Strike. Once the research is completed, have the students discuss Altgeld's political career.

arrested. The court found all eight guilty, though there was no direct evidence against them. Four were hanged.

Pullman Workers' Strike. Another example of labor unrest also took place in Chicago. The city was the center of the railroad industry in the 1880s and 1890s. Many manufacturers of railroad equipment built their factories there. George Pullman, for example, located the factory for making his sleeping cars, or Pullmans, there.

Pullman made many millions of dollars on his inventions, which included the dining car and the chair car. He decided to move his factory to a new location south of Chicago. There he built around his factory a whole new town, which he named after himself.

In the town, completed in 1881, workers lived in company homes, shopped in company stores, and worshipped in a company church. During the good years, the rents and prices paid by the workers to Pullman seemed fair. George Pullman seemed to be one of the best employers in the United States and the rest of the world as well.

In the 1890s, however, a deep economic depression hit the country. Pullman ordered a cut in the wages of his workers. At the same time, however, people living in Pullman had to continue to pay the same rents and prices to the company as before. They could not move to the less expensive towns nearby for fear of losing their jobs.

Pullman, Illinois, was the scene of much violence during the strike by Pullman employees who lived there. Damages to company property totaled $80 million.

When a group of forty-three workers asked to talk to Pullman about their troubles, he refused to see them. In fact, he fired all of them and threw them out of the town. Eventually he fired 3000 workers out of a work force of 5800.

In 1894, Pullman workers decided to strike. They had the support of the American Railway Union—a newly organized union headed by Eugene V. Debs. It refused to handle trains with Pullman cars. By the summer of 1894, the strike had become so widespread that the whole railroad system of the country was upset. George Pullman refused to negotiate to settle the strike. The railroad operators finally persuaded the federal government to help.

The railroads went to court and got an *injunction*, a court order that prohibits a specific action. The courts ordered Debs and his union members to end their strike. Debs refused and went to jail. President Grover Cleveland then sent government troops to end the strike, using the excuse that the mails were being held up. In the end, thousands of workers lost their jobs and their homes.

The tragic Triangle fire led New York City to enact a strict building code. Many labor laws were also revised as a result of this fire.

The Triangle Fire. One of the saddest events in the history of American working people occurred in New York City in 1911. On a hot summer's day, a fire broke out in the Triangle Shirtwaist Factory, a New York City sweatshop. When it was over, 146 young women had lost their lives. Many of them had been unable to get out of the building because the fire escapes were locked. New York City conducted an investigation into the Triangle Factory. The investigation exposed some of the terrible conditions in sweatshops. Soon afterwards, the city passed strict laws for factory fire safety. The public now paid more attention to the welfare of workers.

ANSWER THESE QUESTIONS

1. What workers' benefit did the National Labor Union aim for?
2. Why did the Knights of Labor finally disappear?
3. How did Gompers work for better pay and conditions for AFL members?
4. What action led to the Pullman strike of 1894?
5. What did the Triangle Factory fire in New York do for the conditions under which people worked?

ANSWER THESE QUESTIONS

1. an eight-hour day
2. The skilled and unskilled workers quarreled; people thought the union should organize strikes but the union refused.
3. He tried to get contracts for workers by bargaining with employers.
4. George Pullman cut the workers' wages without lowering rents or prices in company stores.
5. It led to an investigation that exposed the bad work conditions in sweatshops.

CONTENT OBJECTIVES

After completing the lesson, students will know:

- the extent of local and federal political corruption in the late 1800s
- how business and economic reforms were enacted and regulatory commissions set up
- the difference between the "silver" and "gold" Democrats

VOCABULARY

political machine: an organization set up to get and keep political power
ward: city voting district
regulatory commission: a government body set up to control the actions of certain industries
bimetallism: the use of two metals for money
gold standard: the use only of gold to back the nation's money supply

ACTIVITY

Objective: To identify main ideas

Find examples in reference books of Thomas Nast's cartoons attacking Boss Tweed and share them with the class. Also, have the students bring in political cartoons from the daily newspaper, or have them find the cartoons in news magazines in the library. Ask the students to state clearly the point of each cartoon. Explain that you need background about a news story to understand some cartoons and why. Ask the students to discuss whether they think cartoons are a good political weapon and why.

18-2 Political Reform

As you read, think about these questions:
How did a political machine get and keep power?
What reforms were passed in the late 1800s by the United States Congress?
How does the election campaign of 1896 demonstrate the public's concern for reforms?

Special Vocabulary	political machine	bimetallism
	ward	gold standard
	regulatory commission	

During the late 1800s, dishonesty touched many levels of government and business. Some politicians used their positions for personal gain. They found ways, often corrupt, to keep political power. In business, some large companies took over smaller ones and became monopolies or trusts. With little or no competition, the trusts set prices at will.

Citizens began to demand an end to abuses in government and business. The demands for change led to powerful reform movements.

Corruption in Politics

Early *political machines* were organizations set up to get and keep power in government. In a city or state, the machine made sure that voters turned out on election day and voted as the machine directed.

At the head of the city machine stood the political "boss." Often the boss filled an important office such as mayor. In the 1860s one of strongest city political machines appeared in New York City. Its head was Mayor William Marcy Tweed. Boss Tweed and other members of the machine lived grandly at the people's expense.

In the early 1870s, the *New York Times* started attacking Tweed. Thomas Nast, a cartoonist for *Harper's Weekly*, a magazine, made people see Tweed's greed through witty drawings. Samuel J. Tilden, a New York lawyer, also worked against the Tweed machine. Tilden gathered enough evidence to convict Tweed of stealing money from the city. The

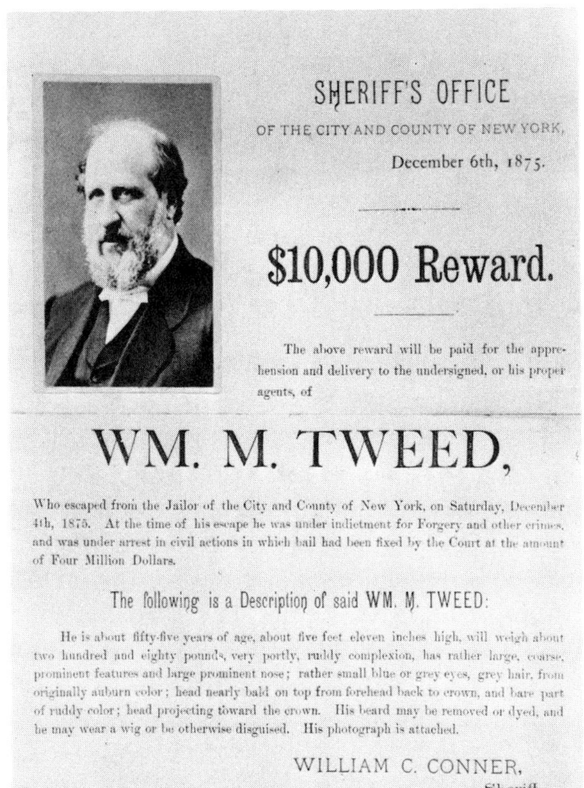

SHERIFF'S OFFICE

OF THE CITY AND COUNTY OF NEW YORK,

December 6th, 1875.

$10,000 Reward.

The above reward will be paid for the apprehension and delivery to the undersigned, or his proper agents, of

WM. M. TWEED,

Who escaped from the Jailor of the City and County of New York, on Saturday, December 4th, 1875. At the time of his escape he was under indictment for Forgery and other crimes, and was under arrest in civil actions in which bail had been fixed by the Court at the amount of Four Million Dollars.

The following is a Description of said WM. M. TWEED:

He is about fifty-five years of age, about five feet eleven inches high, will weigh about two hundred and eighty pounds, very portly, ruddy complexion, has rather large, coarse, prominent features and large prominent nose; rather small blue or grey eyes, grey hair, from originally auburn color; head nearly bald on top from forehead back to crown, and bare part of ruddy color; head projecting toward the crown. His beard may be removed or dyed, and he may wear a wig or be otherwise disguised. His photograph is attached.

WILLIAM C. CONNER,
Sheriff.

As this arrest warrant shows, Boss Tweed escaped from prison in 1875. He made his way to Spain but was returned to America by the Spanish government and died in prison.

fact that Boss Tweed went to jail, however, changed very little. Other bosses took his place, and other cities had bosses much like him.

Ward Bosses and Immigrants. Like an octopus, a machine reached its arms into every neighborhood of the city. In a *ward*, or city voting district, the ward boss acted as the city boss did for the whole city. The ward boss's job was to make sure that the people he was "in charge of" helped the political machine win on election day.

For all its evils, a political machine served a useful purpose too. When immigrants arrived in a city, the ward boss sometimes dropped by to lend them a hand. The boss might also help to get firewood for a poor family in the winter. In the summer the boss might run a picnic, with ice cream and candy for the children. Sometimes it seemed that the ward boss was the only one who cared for people in need. No wonder the boss found it easy to get out the vote.

The Spoils System. Questionable political behavior was not limited to the local political machine. Even national government officials had a way of rewarding loyal workers with

DISCUSSION

Have the students discuss whether government jobs should be filled only by those passing qualifying tests. Explain that this is still an issue today in many cities and states because the Pendleton Act covers only federal employees. Have the students discuss whether party workers or relatives of elected officials should be able to hold government positions. To encourage debate, ask the students to imagine themselves volunteers who have spent hundreds of hours working for a candidate. Should they be denied government jobs because they are "patronage workers"?

government jobs. From the beginning, political parties rewarded their members through the spoils system. Andrew Jackson had made it the expected thing. Under the spoils system, party members who helped win elections could expect Presidents to give them good government jobs, regardless of whether they were qualified for those jobs.

By the 1880s the spoils system had become a heavy burden to Presidents. In fact, on July 2, 1881, President James A. Garfield was shot at Union Station in Washington, D.C., by a disappointed office seeker unable to get a job from the Garfield administration. Garfield lived through the summer, but died in September. His tragic death persuaded the country that there must be a better way to fill government jobs. In 1883 Congress passed the Pendleton Act. The act set up a commission to make rules for the hiring of government employees. Under the new rules, workers had to pass a test to qualify for certain jobs.

Business and Economic Reforms

In 1884 Grover Cleveland, a Democrat, had been elected President. As mayor of Buffalo and governor of New York, he had won a reputation as a reformer. As President, he

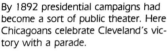

By 1892 presidential campaigns had become a sort of public theater. Here Chicagoans celebrate Cleveland's victory with a parade.

worked to reduce the tariff, which he believed made some prices too high. Though he lost the election in 1888 to Benjamin Harrison, Cleveland was elected again in 1892. He became the only President to serve two terms separated by the term of another President.

Interstate Commerce Act. Various states had passed Granger laws after the Civil War to make the railroads charge fair rates. In 1886, however, the Supreme Court canceled these laws, saying that the Constitution reserved to the federal government the right to make laws on interstate commerce.

For a while, it seemed that some railroad companies would have a free hand in charging unfair rates. Then, during Cleveland's first term, Congress passed the Interstate Commerce Act. The act attempted to force railroads to charge fair rates. It also forbade the railroads to give special rates to large companies in return for business. Railroads could no longer charge more for short distances than for long ones. The law also created the Interstate Commerce Commission (the ICC). This arm of the government was the first of many *regulatory commissions*, or government bodies set up to control the actions of certain industries. It was empowered to look at the records of companies involved in interstate transportation and communications.

Sherman Antitrust Act. The success of the government against the big railroad companies led reformers to demand laws against the trusts. In 1890 Congress passed the Sherman Antitrust Act. It allowed the government to break up trusts that were "combinations in restraint of trade." In other words, companies could not join together in order to interfere with free and open commerce.

Neither the Interstate Commerce Act nor the Sherman Act worked very well at first. The Supreme Court prevented the laws from being used as they were intended. The courts sometimes used the Sherman Act against labor unions. Even the Interstate Commerce Commission could do little to restrain the railroads. In the early 1900s other acts were passed to help strengthen these two laws.

The Silver Issue and the Election of 1896. A terrible depression starting in 1893 made life harder for many Americans. Some people began to believe that coining silver freely would raise the amount of money people could spend and thus

Bryan was only thirty-six when he won the Democratic presidential nomination with a fiery speech he had actually given many times before.

improve economic conditions. Many Democrats and Populists from the South and West called for *bimetallism*, or the use of two metals, gold and silver, for money. They felt that such a policy would not only increase the amount of money in use but also allow them to increase the prices of farm goods. Many other people, however, believed in having only a *gold standard*, or the use only of gold to provide backing for the nation's money supply.

"Silver" and "gold" Democrats struggled against each other for control of their party in 1896. Then William Jennings Bryan, a "silver" candidate, went before the party convention and gave a moving speech in favor of the free and unlimited coinage of silver. The excited delegates nominated Bryan as the Democratic candidate for President. William McKinley, the governor of Ohio, won the Republican party's nomination. The election campaign became a battle of gold against silver, East against West, city against country. Farmers generally supported bimetallism, while many urban dwellers favored the gold standard. Furthermore, many important leaders in business and industry supported McKinley.

Though Bryan campaigned hard, McKinley and the Republicans won the election. Bryan did well in the South and West, but McKinley swept much of the North and East. As a result of this victory, the Republicans also kept control of Congress. Republicans would hold the White House for the next sixteen years. The fire of reform on the national level had been set. It would become much easier after 1896 for a President to be a reformer, and to argue for reform.

ANSWER THESE QUESTIONS

1. local: bosses and political machines stole or used city money; national: the spoils system of rewarding party workers with jobs
2. They realized that needy immigrants would show appreciation to a generous machine by voting for its candidates at election time.
3. new rules for hiring government employees; laws to regulate trusts and railroads; bimetallism
4. It would raise prices and therefore increase the value of farm produce.
5. They were the first federal laws that attempted to control railroads and trusts.

ANSWER THESE QUESTIONS

1. What forms did political corruption take at the local and national levels of government?
2. What did the machine bosses realize about the political power of the immigrants?
3. What were some important reforms that people wanted in the 1880s and 1890s?
4. How did farmers believe that bimetallism would help them?
5. Why were the Interstate Commerce Act and the Sherman Antitrust Act important?

Objective: After completing this page, students should understand the difference between fact and opinion.

Distinguishing Between Fact and Opinion

In a political speech, the speaker tries to get the listeners to accept certain ideas. Often the speaker cites a few facts to make an argument sound convincing. A careful listener must learn to separate facts from opinions.

In 1896 William Jennings Bryan delivered what became famous as the "Cross of Gold" speech to the Democratic convention. Read the part of Bryan's speech given here.

> It is the issue of 1776 over again. Our ancestors, when but three millions in number, had the courage to declare their political independence of every other nation; shall we, their descendants, when we have grown to seventy millions, declare that we are less independent than our forefathers? No, my friends, that will never be the verdict of our people. . . .If they [supporters of the gold standard] say bimetallism is good, but we cannot have it until the other nations help us, we reply that . . . we will restore bimetallism and then let England have bimetallism because the United States has it. . . . Having behind us the producing masses of this nation and the world . . . we will answer their demand for a gold standard by saying to them: You shall not press down upon the brow of labor this crown of thorns, you shall not crucify mankind on a cross of gold.

William Jennings Bryan knew that his listeners would accept certain facts. For example, Bryan quotes the population for the nation in his time: "when we have grown to seventy millions." Census figures show that the population of the United States stood at around 70 million in 1896. On the other hand, when Bryan claims to have "behind us the producing masses of the nation and the world," he is stating an opinion. Only a scientific poll could determine whether these people really supported Bryan. Read each statement below and decide whether it is a fact or an opinion.

1. "It is the issue of 1776 over again."
2. "Our ancestors, when but three millions in number, had the courage to declare their political independence. . . ."
3. "No, my friends, that will never be the verdict of our people. . . ."

Working with Skills

READING SKILLS

ACTIVITY

Objective: To distinguish between fact and opinion

Divide the class into several groups. Have each group make a poster taking a side in one of the major issues mentioned in this lesson—for example, reform politics versus machine politics, or labor versus management. The poster should refer to a specific event and take a specific point of view. Review each completed poster with the class and discuss the use of facts and opinions in each.

ANSWERS

1. O
2. F
3. O

RELATED MATERIAL

Duplicator/Copy Master Activity 39

CONTENT OBJECTIVES

After completing the lesson, students will know:

- how the Wisconsin Idea inspired reform on a national level
- about the reforms promoted by Theodore Roosevelt and William Taft
- about Wilson's "New Freedom," a progressive program

VOCABULARY

initiative: a way for voters to start a new law through a petition

referendum: a way for voters to decide on certain bills brought up in the state legislature

recall: a way for the voters to remove a bad official from office before the end of a term

conservation: the wise use of natural resources

ACTIVITY

Objective: To summarize information

Have the class identify the important reforms initiated by Mayor Tom Johnson of Cleveland and Governor Robert La Follette of Wisconsin. List the reforms on the chalkboard as the students supply them. Then ask the students which of these changes they think are most important and why. Also ask them which, if any, of these reforms they would like to see enacted in their community or on a national level today.

18-3 The Progressive Movement

As you read, think about these questions:

What problems in American life did the Progressives seek to solve?

What new ideas did the Progressives have to offer?

How did the Presidents in the Progressive Era (1900–1917) help bring about reforms?

Special Vocabulary	initiative	recall
	referendum	conservation

In the 1880s and 1890s, as you have read, a period of reform had already begun. Yet many conditions still cried out for a remedy. Writers known as "muckrakers" called attention to what was wrong. The muckrakers were so named because they were said to rake through the muck looking for nothing but abuses in business and politics. They covered many subjects, including trusts, city government, drugs, child labor, and violence against black people. The muckrakers' articles increased the demand for reform.

The Populists had worked for change in the 1890s. Now the progressives took up the cause of reform. While Populists were from farms and small towns, many progressives lived in cities. They were often lawyers, members of the clergy, writers, merchants, and politicians.

Local and State Politics

The progressives saw a need for change at all levels of government. On the local level, the progressive reformers began to upset urban political machines around 1900. Tom Johnson, a reformer, was elected mayor of Cleveland in 1901. He was able to lower streetcar fares and raise the taxes paid by railroads and companies that provided gas, water, and electricity. While Tom Johnson was mayor, reformers called Cleveland the best-governed city in the country.

Reforming State Government. At the state level, reformers supported *initiative, referendum,* and *recall.* Initiative allows the people themselves to take steps for a new law if it has enough supporters. The people would sign a petition presenting their proposal, then the state legislature has to consider passing it into law. Referendum requires a state legislature to bring before the people for a vote certain laws they hope to pass. If the people vote "yes," the bill can become a law. If they vote "no," the bill is dead. Recall provides voters with a chance to remove a bad official from office before his or her term is finished.

In Wisconsin, a young reformer named Robert La Follette was elected governor in 1900. Under his leadership, the state lawmakers passed a number of reform laws. These included creating commissions to regulate railroads and big business, allowing the state to tax businesses, providing for initiative and referendum, and starting a program to conserve the state's natural resources. The reform program that La Follette sponsored became known as the "Wisconsin Idea."

The Wisconsin Idea quickly spread to other states. Soon one state after another elected a reform governor. In New York Charles Evans Hughes, who had investigated abuses in the insurance business, became governor. Californians chose as their governor Hiram Johnson, another reformer. New Jersey elected Woodrow Wilson governor, also as a reformer.

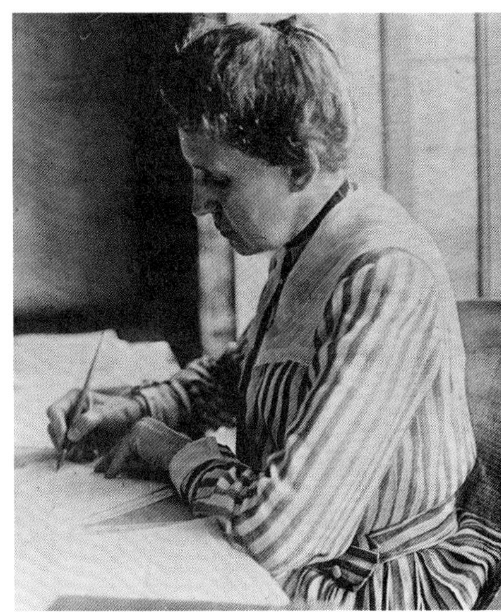

Author Ida M. Tarbell was a pioneer in the field of investigative reporting. Her *History of the Standard Oil Company* strengthened the movement against monopolies.

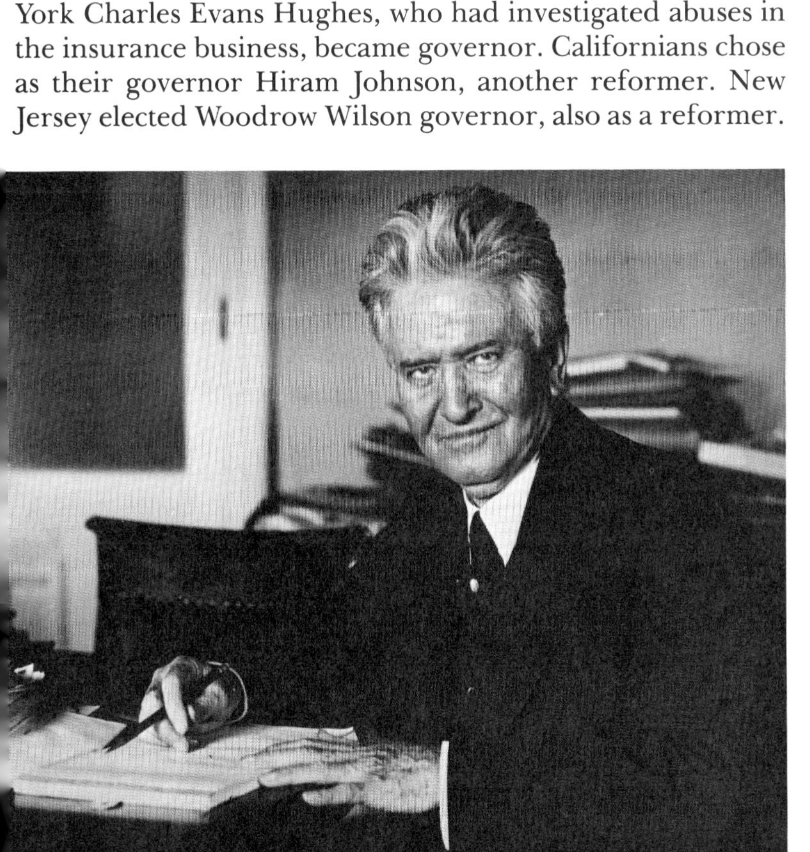

Wisconsin Governor Robert La Follette later served as a Progressive leader in the Senate. In 1924 he received five million votes for President.

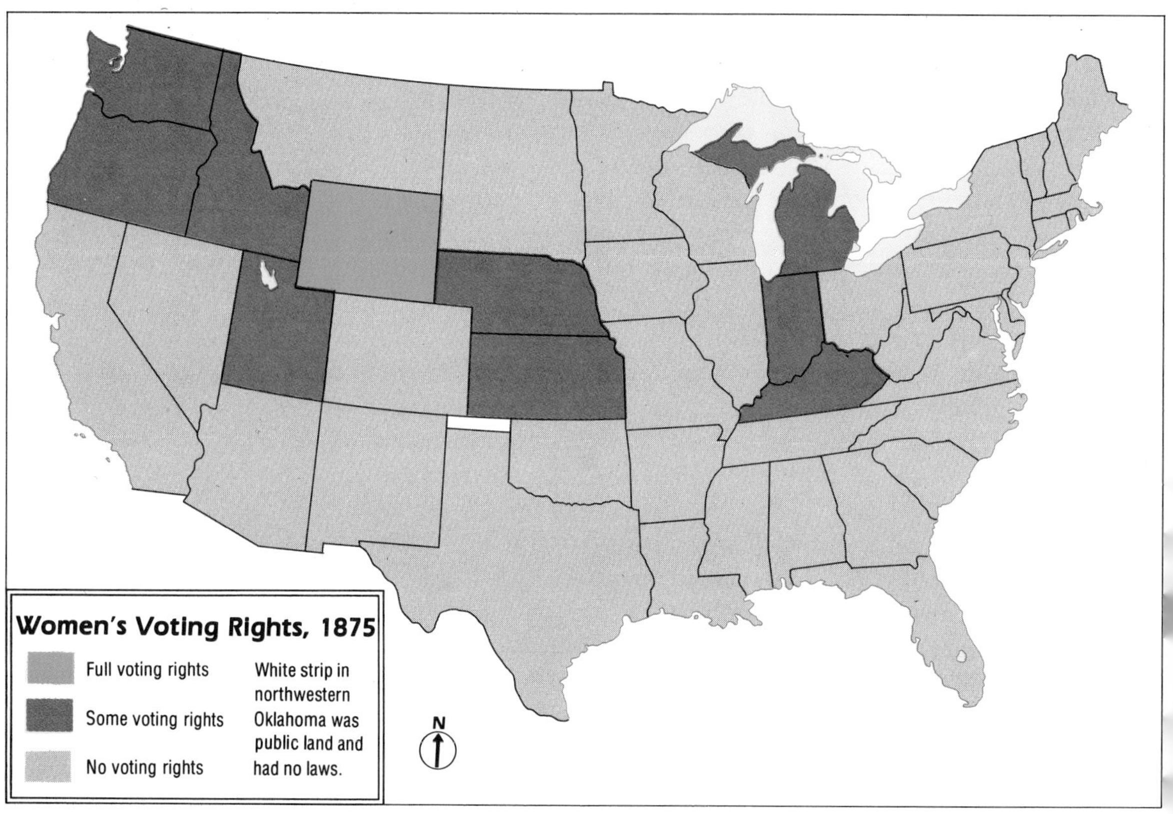

This map shows the states and territories that had given women at least partial voting rights by 1875. Were women's voting rights more common in the East or in the West?

the West

States and Woman Suffrage. Many progressives took up the cause of woman suffrage, or the right of women to vote. For many years the states alone determined whether women could vote or not. The states varied widely in how they handled the matter. In 1869 the territory of Wyoming became the first government to grant full voting rights to women. By 1915 many states had granted women some voting rights. Look at the maps on pages 462 and 463 to compare women's voting rights by states in 1875 and 1915.

National Politics

In September 1901 President McKinley was shot by an assassin as he greeted people at the Pan-American Exposition in Buffalo. When he died two weeks later, Theodore Roosevelt became President.

Roosevelt in the White House. Theodore Roosevelt, whom many Americans called "Teddy" or "TR," was a powerful personality. He believed that the President should act boldly.

President Roosevelt attacked the trusts. Using the Sherman Antitrust Act, he ordered the attorney general to break

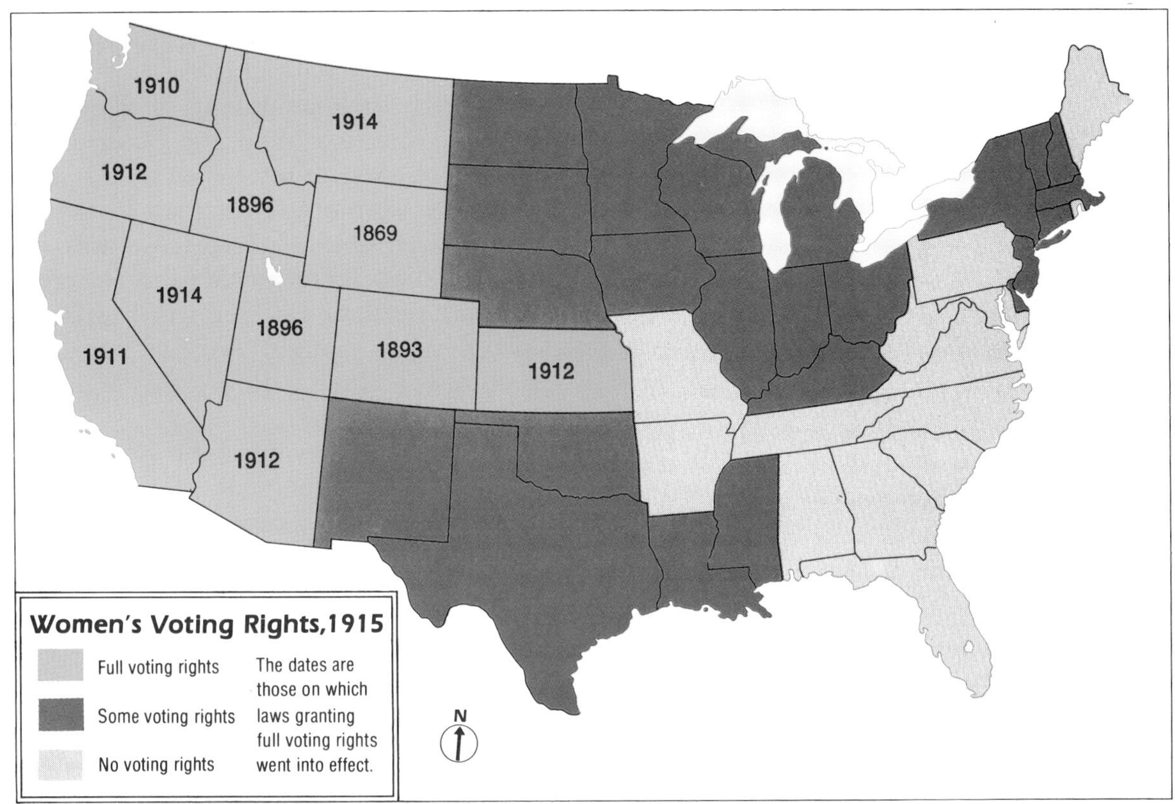

up James J. Hill's Northern Securities Company in 1902 (see page 443). This company was a trust that owned many railroad companies. Roosevelt believed it was too large and operated without competition. Yet Roosevelt left other large companies alone. He believed that trusts should be broken up only if they acted against the public good.

In 1906 the President also helped get a new railroad law. The Hepburn Act expanded and strengthened the Interstate Commerce Commission. The ICC now set railroad rates.

Roosevelt used the powers of the presidency to promote *conservation*, or the wise use of natural resources. The President ordered the Department of the Interior to take charge of government lands, especially forests. Most important of all, Roosevelt made conservation a popular subject.

Taft as President. In 1908 Roosevelt decided not to run for another term. Instead, he urged William Howard Taft, his good friend and secretary of war, to accept the Republican nomination. In the election, Taft defeated William Jennings Bryan, the Democratic candidate once again.

Taft had promised to work for Roosevelt's goals. After the election, he tried to keep his promises. While Taft was

Compare this map with the one on the previous page. How many states had granted full voting rights to women by 1915?

eleven

President, Congress started an amendment to allow the direct election of senators. Until that time, the Constitution required that members of the Senate be elected by the state legislatures. Taft also broke up more trusts than Roosevelt had during his term in office. One of these trusts was the Standard Oil Company of New Jersey, which the Supreme Court broke up in 1911 as a result of Taft's efforts. In spite of these efforts, some progressives thought Taft had not done enough. Some Republicans, including Roosevelt, began to make speeches attacking Taft.

In 1912 both Taft and Roosevelt wanted the Republican nomination. In primary elections, or state elections held before the convention to choose party candidates, Roosevelt won more votes than Taft. The delegates to the convention, however, nominated Taft.

Taft—shown here with his family—is the only person to have held the nation's two highest offices: President and Chief Justice of the Supreme Court.

A group of progressive Republicans decided to break away and form their own party, the Progressive Party. They nominated Roosevelt. Before their convention Roosevelt declared, "I feel as strong as a bull moose." The Progressive Party was nicknamed the Bull Moose Party. The "Bull Moosers" called for many reforms. They demanded laws against children working in factories. They also wanted to

In this 1912 campaign poster, the familiar image of Roosevelt's hat from the Spanish-American War reminded voters of his past courage.

help women workers in America's factories earn a fair wage. The party favored woman suffrage and government regulation of the trusts.

Wilson and the "New Freedom." The Democrats chose Woodrow Wilson, the governor of New Jersey, as their candidate. The Democratic platform called for what Wilson described as the "New Freedom"—a program of widespread reforms. Wilson opposed all trusts, while Roosevelt only wanted to control the ones that harmed the public. On election day, the Republicans split their votes between Taft and Roosevelt. Wilson won the White House.

Wilson proved to be a strong President. In 1913 he got Congress to pass the Federal Reserve Act. This act, creating a Federal Reserve System, set up a central bank for the first time since Andrew Jackson's day. It established a Federal Reserve Bank in each of twelve districts of the United States. Each district bank had power over the loan practices of member banks within the district. People hoped that this system would help the country avoid economic depressions.

Wilson had promised to break up the big corporations. As President, however, he seemed to agree with Roosevelt that it was only possible to control them. In 1914 Wilson helped set up a Federal Trade Commission to keep an eye on the way that large companies did business.

DISCUSSION

Review with the class the provisions of the Clayton Antitrust Act and why it was passed. Have the students discuss whether government should regulate business and how much. Ask the students to consider the advantages and disadvantages of big business, in terms of both internal operating efficiency and the public welfare. Have them discuss the concept of business regulating itself. Mention the consumer movement and ask students if they think that pressure from consumers is strong enough to cause businesses to alter their practices.

Wilson's campaign themes were designed to show the public that he understood national problems.

The Clayton Antitrust Act aimed at preserving competition in business. This law assured that businesses would not secretly try to keep prices high or control other companies. Businesses would have to compete honestly with one another through prices, quality, service, and advertising.

In 1916 Wilson worked to get other progressive laws through Congress. One of these laws gave railway workers an eight-hour day. Another aimed at improving working conditions on American ships. Still another made possible easier loans for farmers. Congress also passed a child labor law to end some abuses of children in industry.

By 1917 the Progressive Era was drawing to a close. People had become tired of reform. Their attention was being riveted on a war in Europe. Wilson aimed high for a place in history. He hoped to have the role of peacemaker in the awful struggle abroad.

ANSWER THESE QUESTIONS

1. Who were the muckrakers?
2. Was the "Wisconsin Idea" most useful at the local, state, or federal level of government?
3. Why did Roosevelt act to break up some trusts but not others?
4. What did the Hepburn Act accomplish?
5. How did Wilson's actions show him to be a strong President?

ANSWER THESE QUESTIONS

1. writers who called attention to many abuses in business and politics
2. state level
3. He believed that only those trusts that harmed the public good should be broken up.
4. The act expanded the ICC and made it stronger, allowing the ICC to set railroad rates.
5. He got the Federal Reserve Act and the Clayton Antitrust Act passed, helped set up the Federal Trade Commission, and got other progressive laws through Congress.

Regulation of Monopolies

LAW AND THE CITIZEN

During the late 1800s, many Americans became concerned about the power of trusts. In 1890 Congress passed the Sherman Antitrust Act. This act declared unlawful any trust or other combination that restrained trade or commerce. Congress, however, did not clearly define terms such as "combination" or "commerce." The courts would have to determine how the Sherman Antitrust Act could be used.

The Supreme Court had its first chance to interpret the Sherman Act in 1895. The E. C. Knight Company and four other companies had sold their stock and property to the American Sugar Refining Company in exchange for stock in American Sugar. These deals gave American Sugar control of more than ninety percent of the sugar refining in the United States. The federal government charged that the purpose of these deals was to create a sugar monopoly. The government went to court to break up this monopoly.

In the case of *United States v. E. C. Knight Company*, the Supreme Court ruled that the government could not use the Sherman Act to break up American Sugar. Chief Justice Melville Fuller made a distinction between manufacturing and commerce. The Constitution only gave Congress the right to regulate commerce, claimed Fuller, but American Sugar was engaged in manufacturing.

Chief Justice Fuller believed that manufacturing should be regulated by the states. However, the Supreme Court had already limited the right of the states to regulate large companies. Any company that sent its goods to other states could be controlled only by Congress. The Court's decision in *United States v. E. C. Knight* meant that certain companies could escape government control completely.

Justice John M. Harlan strongly disagreed with the majority of the Court. He thought that manufacturing should be regarded as commerce or trade, since it too may involve interstate agreements.

The E. C. Knight case left the Sherman Act without any teeth. During the 1890s it was used mainly against labor unions. Only after 1900 did the Supreme Court slowly accept the idea of using the Sherman Act against the trusts. Then the act began to get the kind of results that Congress had originally intended.

THINKING THINGS THROUGH

1. People were afraid to anger their bosses; there were many others waiting who might take their jobs. **2.** People associated labor unions with anarchy and violence. **3.** They helped people in need, especially immigrants, in return for votes. **4.** It meant that government jobs would not always go to the most qualified people. **5.** Most Populists were farmers or people from small

Chapter 18 SUMMARY

After the Civil War, many more people than ever went to work in factories. Conditions in the factories were bad, and workers began to join labor unions. The Knights of Labor, an early union, had about 700,000 members in the 1880s. It was open to unskilled as well as skilled workers. The American Federation of Labor was formed in 1886. It was a trade union for skilled workers. The AFL grew steadily.

Corruption in politics was widespread after the Civil War. Political bosses organized city machines. The machines were often dishonest, but they sometimes helped the immigrants.

People began to demand political reforms during the later 1800s. After President Garfield was shot by an office seeker, Congress passed the Pendleton Act in 1883. Later, Congress passed the Interstate Commerce Act and the Sherman Antitrust Act. These laws attempted to regulate the railroads and the trusts.

The years from 1900 to 1917 are known as the Progressive Era. Progressives were reformers who tried to clean up government, help working people, and regulate business practices. Robert La Follette set the model for progressive reforms at the state level in Wisconsin. At the national level, several Presidents achieved progressive goals. Theodore Roosevelt attacked the trusts and got the Hepburn Act passed. Woodrow Wilson persuaded Congress to pass the Clayton Anti-trust Act, the Federal Reserve Act, and child labor laws.

Chapter 18 TEST

WORDS TO REMEMBER

Choose the correct word from the following list to complete each sentence below.

a. conservation
b. bimetallism
c. cooperatives
d. injunctions
e. political machine
f. regulatory commissions
g. initiative

1. Theodore Roosevelt believed in the __a__ of natural resources.
2. An organization set up to get and keep power in a government is a __e__.
3. Congress has set up __f__ to watch the actions of railroads and other corporations.
4. Early unions such as the Knights of Labor were interested in forming __c__ in which workers could own the businesses.
5. People may suggest laws through __g__.
6. William Jennings Bryan called for a policy of __b__, or the use of both gold and silver to back money.
7. Courts used __d__ to force unions to return to work.

THINKING THINGS THROUGH

Answer each of the following questions in a complete sentence.

1. Why were early unions in the United States slow to make gains for workers?
2. Why did the Haymarket Riot of 1886 hurt the labor movement?
3. How were city bosses able to gain and keep political power?
4. How did the spoils system conflict with good government?
5. What were some differences between the Populists and the Progressives?

RELATED MATERIALS
Duplicator/Copy Masters: Activities 38, 39; Quiz 38
Workbook pages 54-56

towns; many progressives lived in cities and were professionals such as lawyers and members of the clergy.

WORKING WITH SKILLS

Read the following statements about a strike. Statement *A* is by the leader of the union representing Penn Factory workers. Statement *B* is by the manager of the factory.

A. Workers at the Penn Factory walked off the job at 11:00 A.M. today. The workers are demanding higher wages and stricter safety rules. It has been obvious for a long time that safety standards at the factory are very low. Last year five workers suffered injuries on the job.

B. Workers at the Penn Factory went on strike at 11:00 A.M. today. The workers' demands for higher pay are unreasonable. Furthermore, Penn's safety record is outstanding. In the last year, only 5 out of 980 employees were injured.

Now read the items below. They are taken from statements *A* and *B*. Decide whether each is a fact or an opinion. Write *F* or *O* beside each number on your paper.

1. Workers at the Penn Factory went on strike at 11:00 A.M. today.

0 2. Safety standards at the Penn Factory are very low.

F 3. Five workers suffered injuries at the Penn Factory last year.

0 4. Penn's safety record is outstanding.

0 5. The workers' demands for higher pay are unreasonable.

ON YOUR OWN

1. In 1948 *Life* Magazine conducted a poll of American historians to rank the Presidents. They decided whether each President was great, near great, below average, or a failure. Imagine that you are one of these historians and judge each of the Presidents from 1885 to 1921. Judge their handling of responsibilities. Use an encyclopedia if you need additional information. List the standards by which you are judging them (leadership, ideas, honesty, etc.). How does your ranking compare with those of other members of the class?
2. Imagine that you are a muckraker in a big city in the 1890s. Where would you go to look for a story? Consider aspects of government and industry in which you might expect to find abuses. Make a list of at least five sources you would investigate in order to write your articles.
3. The picture on this page shows women who worked for woman suffrage and other reforms in the late 1800s. A great leader of the woman suffrage movement, Susan B. Anthony, is seated second from the left. Seated and fourth from the left is Elizabeth Cady Stanton, another crusader for woman suffrage. Look up both women in an encyclopedia. Write a short paragraph on each.

Unit 6 TEST

WORDS TO REMEMBER

Replace the words in italics in each sentence with a word from the following list that has the same meaning.

a. massacre
b. tenements
c. railhead
d. sod
e. conservation
f. patent
g. ward
h. sweatshops
i. injunction

c 1. Cattle were driven from Texas to the *end of the railroad.*

f 2. The inventor obtained a *right to use and sell an invention.*

e 3. The President and the people worked for *wise use* of energy.

a 4. The Indians were victims of a *horrible killing* by the army.

d 5. Settlers used a strong new plow to turn the *crust of the soil.*

b 6. Some city people lived in *run-down apartment buildings.*

h 7. Many workers made clothes and cigars in *hot, crowded factories.*

i 8. The owner of a factory could get a *court order* to end a strike.

g 9. Even a *city voting district* had a political boss.

QUESTIONS TO ANSWER

Choose the letter of the word or words that correctly answer each question.

a 1. Which city began as a gold rush town?
a. Denver
b. Omaha
c. Dallas
d. St. Louis

c 2. Which was the site of an Indian massacre in 1890?
a. Sand Creek
b. Little Big Horn
c. Wounded Knee
d. Minnesota

d 3. Which problem did settlers on the Great Plains *not* face in the 1890s?
a. falling prices
b. drought
c. harsh winters
d. crowded cities

b 4. Who invented the first practical elevator?
a. Samuel Morse
b. Elisha Otis
c. Wilbur Wright
d. Cornelius Vanderbilt

d 5. Who started Chicago's Hull House?
a. William Jenney
b. Helen Hunt Jackson
c. Jacob Riis
d. Jane Addams

b 6. Who helped improve the process of making steel?
a. John D. Rockefeller
b. Henry Bessemer
c. George Eastman
d. Edwin Drake

a 7. Which President served two terms that were separated by four years?
a. Grover Cleveland
b. Rutherford Hayes
c. William McKinley
d. Benjamin Harrison

RELATED MATERIAL
Duplicator/Copy Master Test 39-41

THINK THINGS THROUGH

1. chilled iron plow (accept steel plow), windmill 2. The settlers wanted the Indians' land. 3. Austria, Greece, Hungary, Italy, Poland, Romania, Russia, Turkey 4. to find jobs 5. business: Andrew Carnegie; labor unions: Samuel Gompers

PRACTICE YOUR SKILLS

1. a. 975 miles, 1500 kilometers b. 1450 miles, 2300 kilometers c. 700 miles, 1200 kilometers d. 1000 miles, 1650 kilometers e. 650 miles, 1000 kilometers 2. a. Cleveland; Weaver b. Harrison; Cleveland c. circle graph d. bar graph e. bar graph

THINK THINGS THROUGH

1. What were two of the most important inventions used on the Great Plains?
2. Why were the Plains Indians and the new settlers unable to live peacefully together?
3. From what countries did the "new immigrants" come?
4. Why did many of the immigrants settle in the cities?
5. Who were some immigrants who were successful in the business world or in labor unions?

PRACTICE YOUR SKILLS

1. In this unit you learned how to measure distances on a map. Use the map, "Railroads to the West," on page 406 to measure the rail distances indicated below. Use the scale given on the map. Give answers to the nearest 100 miles and the nearest 200 kilometers.
   a. from Duluth to Helena on the Northern Pacific
   b. from St. Paul to Seattle on the Great Northern
   c. from Atchison to Albuquerque on the Santa Fe
   d. from New Orleans to El Paso on the Southern Pacific
   e. from Promontory Point to San Francisco on the Central Pacific
2. In this unit you learned to read circle graphs and bar graphs. The two graphs on this page give data for the three presidential candidates in the election of 1892. You know that Grover Cleveland won. Study the graphs. Then answer the questions.
   a. Which candidate received the most votes? Which received the least votes?
   b. Which candidate was the middle vote getter? To which other candidate was the middle vote getter's total closer?
   c. Which graph best shows how well the candidates did in terms of the total vote cast?
   d. Which graph best shows the closeness of the vote totals of two of the candidates?
   e. Which graph gives more information?

ELECTION OF 1892

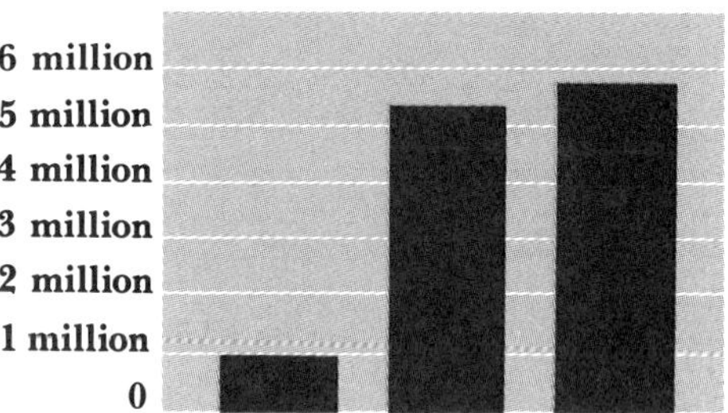

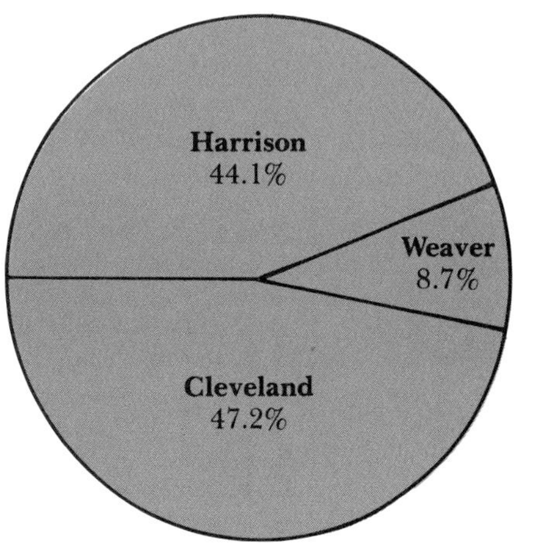

UNIT 7
A RELUCTANT INTERNATIONAL POWER

Unit Seven examines the period from 1890 to 1929, in which the United States became a major international power. The topics discussed in this unit include the following: the Spanish-American War, the building of the Panama Canal, the "big stick" foreign policy of Theodore Roosevelt, World War I, the League of Nations, changes in American society after the war, and the growth of the consumer economy and stock market speculation.

A detail from a World War I recruiting poster

Thomas Hart Benton's mural "The Changing West"

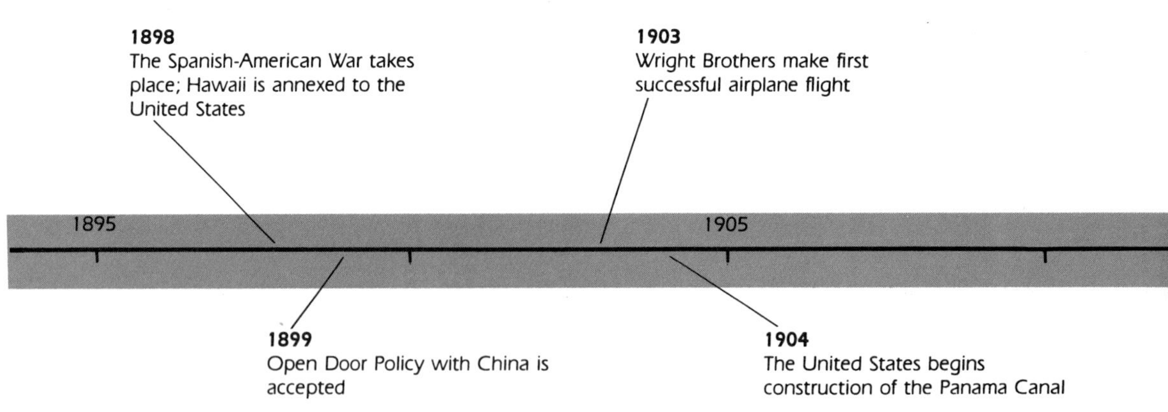

1898
The Spanish-American War takes place; Hawaii is annexed to the United States

1899
Open Door Policy with China is accepted

1903
Wright Brothers make first successful airplane flight

1904
The United States begins construction of the Panama Canal

1914
World War I breaks out in Europe

1918
Germany signs the armistice ending World War I

1920
Women win the vote; prohibition becomes law

1915 1925

1917
The United States enters World War I

1919
The peace conference is held at Versailles; the United States refuses to join the League of Nations

1927
The first "talkie" is released; Charles Lindbergh flies nonstop from New York to Paris

Chapter 19
LOOKING TO THE PACIFIC

Chapter 19 focuses on the growth of American influence in the Caribbean and Pacific regions during the late 1800s. Lesson 19-1 describes the annexation of Hawaii, the Spanish-American War, American acquisitions as a result of the war, and the China trade. Lesson 19-2 discusses the Roosevelt Corollary to the Monroe Doctrine, the construction of the Panama Canal, and Theodore Roosevelt's role in mediating peace between Russia and Japan.

CONTENT OBJECTIVES

After completing the lesson, students will know:

- the events leading to the annexation of Hawaii
- the events leading to the Spanish-American War
- details of the war in the Philippines, Cuba, and Puerto Rico
- about the Boxer Rebellion and the Open Door Policy in China

VOCABULARY

imperialism: the practice of gaining control over other lands and peoples
isolationism: the practice of a country that has little to do with any other countries
guerrilla warfare: hit-and-run raids by small armed bands
atrocity: an extremely cruel action
yellow journalism: a kind of reporting that gets the reader's attention with big headlines and pictures of crimes, accidents, or wars
anti-imperialist: a person who opposes imperialism
spheres of influence: the control of some part of a country by a foreign country

19-1 United States Expansion Overseas

As you read, think about these questions:

By what means did the United States gain control of lands overseas?

What events led the United States into a war with Spain?

What reasons did some Americans use to justify American control of foreign lands?

What reasons did other Americans give against such control?

Special Vocabulary	imperialism	yellow journalism
	isolationism	anti-imperialist
	guerrilla warfare	sphere of influence
	atrocity	

Throughout the 1800s Great Britain continued to be viewed with suspicion, yet it was also greatly admired by Americans It provided a model in government, industry, and culture Many Americans were impressed by the new empire tha Great Britain assembled from the 1870s on. This practice o gaining control over other lands—usually at a great distanc from home—is called *imperialism.*

By the late 1800s France, Germany, and other Europea countries were also building empires. Some Americans wa s ed an empire of their own. They wanted their nation to gr in territory and wealth as the European countries w of Some wanted this in order to gain markets for Amer en growing industries. Others wanted to spread their wa of

ase. Outside the camps the guerrillas fought on. News of Weyler's *atrocities,* or extremely cruel actions, brought cries of protest from Americans. Newspapers carried reports of the atrocities to American readers. Weyler was called "the Butcher." The Spanish government recalled Weyler and sent another general to replace him.

0,000 REWARD.—WHO DESTROYED THE MAINE?—$50,000

NEW YORK JOURNAL
AND ADVERTISER.

FIRST EDITION

DESTRUCTION OF THE WAR SHIP MAINE WAS THE WORK OF AN ENEM

$50,000!

$50,000 REWARD!
For the Detection of the Perpetrator of the Maine Outrage!

Assistant Secretary Roosevelt Convinced the Explosion of the War Ship Was Not an Accident.

The Journal Offers $50,000 Reward for the Conviction of the Criminals Who Sent 258 American Sailors to Their Death. Naval Officers Unanimous That the Ship Was Destroyed on Purpose.

$50,000!

$50,000 REWARD!
For the Detection of the Perpetrator of the Maine Outrage!

NAVAL OFFICERS THINK THE MAINE WAS DESTROYED BY A SPANISH MINE.

Hearst's *New York Journal* offered $50,000 reward for information leading to the person responsible for the "*Maine* Outrage."

The Role of the Press. During the 1890s most Americans got their information from daily newspapers. Some newspapers used a kind of reporting called *yellow journalism.* This sort of reporting got the reader's attention with big headlines and pictures of crimes, accidents, or wars. The name came from "The Yellow Kid," a comic strip in two New York papers, the *World* and the *Journal.* Joseph Pulitzer owned the *New York World.* William Randolph Hearst, Sr., owned the *New York Journal.* The turmoil in Cuba was made to order for the yellow journalists. Pulitzer and Hearst tried to outdo each other by printing more and more shocking reports of conditions in Cuba, which stunned American readers. A war spirit began to build in America.

"Remember the Maine!" Many Americans felt that a war with Spain was needed to free Cuba. But President McKinley moved cautiously. He hoped that new officials in Spain would end the violence in Cuba. Throughout 1897 he waited while the push for war mounted about him. Then two unexpected events dashed hopes for peace.

The first event involved a stolen letter. Dupuy de Lôme was a Spanish diplomat in Washington, D.C. In December 1897, he sent a letter to a friend in Havana, Cuba. In the letter he described McKinley as a weakling who listened only to those who called for war. The letter was stolen from a Havana post office. It was translated into English and printed in Hearst's newspaper. Americans were angry because their President had been insulted.

American tempers had not cooled over the De Lôme letter when a more serious event took place. The United States had sent the new battleship *Maine* to Cuba to protect American interests. On the night of February 15, 1898, it was anchored in Havana Harbor. (See the map of Cuba on page 478.) Suddenly an explosion tore the *Maine* apart. The ship sank and two hundred sixty American sailors died. The American people could hardly believe the news. Everywhere people raised the cry, "Remember the Maine!"

DISCUSSION

Review for the students the sinking of the United States battleship *Maine* and the escalation of public opinion in favor of war. Stress that slogans like "Remember the Maine!" have been important in rallying public opinion. Have the students contribute other slogans from other wars they have studied. Ask the students what other factors they think go into the forming or changing of public opinion. Also, have them discuss why a government thinks it important to have the support of public opinion before going to war.

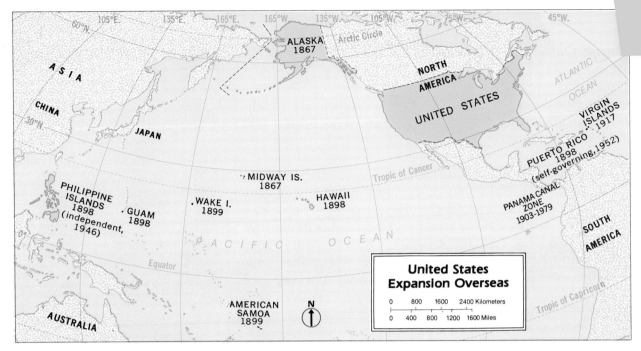

This map shows the new territories the United States began to acquire in the late 1800s. According to the map, what were the first new territories?

Alaska, Midway Island

In the Battle of Manila Bay, Commodore Dewey (center, with mustache) destroyed or captured ten ships.

Public pressure mounted for President McKinley to do something about the Spanish in Cuba. On April 11, the President placed the matter before Congress. On April 25, the United States declared war on Spain. Congress also said that Cuba would become an independent country.

War in the Philippines. The day before war was declared, Commodore George E. Dewey's fleet was already steaming from Hong Kong to Manila in the Philippine Islands. (See the map of the Philippines on page 481.) His orders from the President were short and clear, "Capture or destroy the Spanish squadron at Manila." On the night of April 30, 1898, Dewey's fleet slipped into Manila Bay. Battle came with the dawn. By sunset Spanish power in the Pacific was ended.

Americans rejoiced at the news, but many were puzzled. They expected to read of war news from Cuba. Some did not even know where the Philippine Islands were. As Americans studied their maps, some wondered if the United States would become an imperial power.

War in Cuba. Throughout most of May 1898, the United States Navy hunted the Spanish Atlantic fleet with no success. Admiral Pascual Cervera's Spanish fleet arrived safely at Santiago de Cuba and entered the harbor. Commodore Winfield S. Schley quickly headed for Santiago. On May 28, he stationed United States ships outside the harbor. With the

Spanish fleet bottled up, the United States Army could be safely transported to Cuba. On June 22, troops under the command of General William Shafter landed a few miles east of Santiago.

The Spanish had fortified the hills around Santiago. Spanish fire kept the Americans pinned down. Among those units pinned down were the Rough Riders, a volunteer cavalry unit. Theodore Roosevelt was in command of the Rough Riders. He had resigned as assistant secretary of the navy to form a cavalry unit made up of college students, cowhands, public officers, miners, stagecoach drivers, and Native Americans. The Rough Riders were a cavalry unit, but they fought on foot because their horses never arrived.

About noon on July 1 Roosevelt gave the order to attack, and the Rough Riders quickly took Kettle Hill. Next the

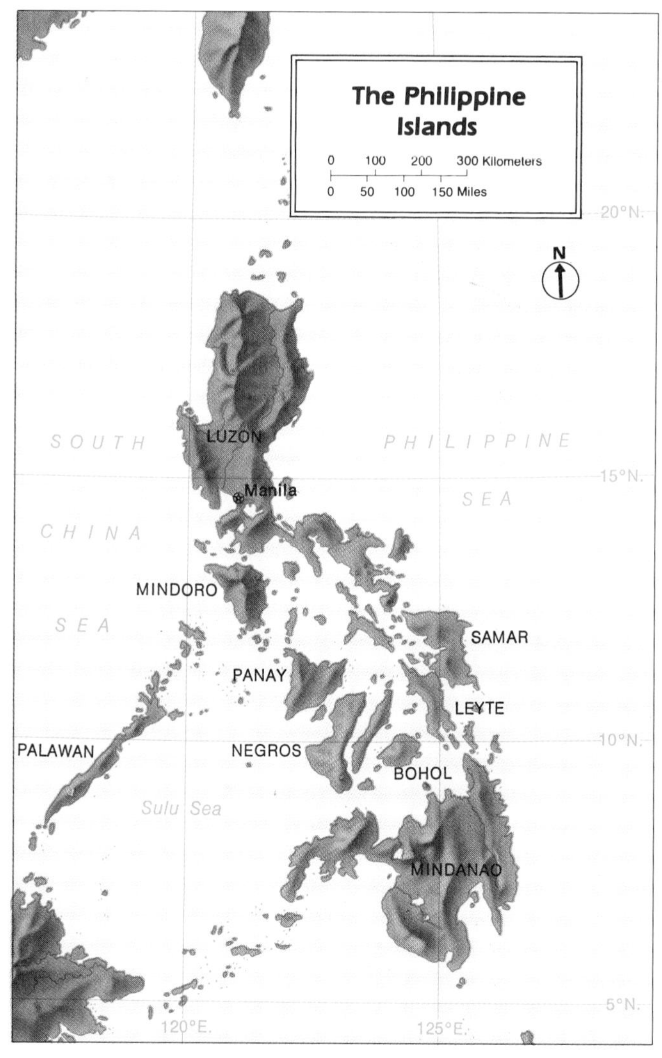

Luzon

The first battle of the Spanish American War was fought at Manila in the Philippine Islands. On which of the islands is Manila located?

The fame earned by Teddy Roosevelt (center) as deputy commander of the Rough Riders opened a new phase in his political career.

Americans advanced slowly through the tall grass into heavy Spanish fire. The black troops of the Ninth and Tenth Cavalries were heroes of the day. Colonel Roosevelt and other commanders praised them for their bravery. Blacks, whites, and Native Americans went up San Juan Hill and took it. America had another victory and new heroes.

The most important battle of the war took place two days later. On Sunday morning, July 3, 1898, Admiral Cervera tried to move his fleet out of Santiago harbor. The American battleships *Iowa, Texas, Indiana,* and *Oregon* chased the fleeing Spanish. The Americans closed in and began firing. Volley after volley ripped into the Spanish fleet. All the Spanish ships were destroyed, while the Americans lost only one sailor. On July 17, 1898, Santiago surrendered. With the fall of Santiago, the rest of the Spanish in Cuba surrendered.

The day following the surrender of Santiago, the United States ordered General Nelson A. Miles to occupy Puerto

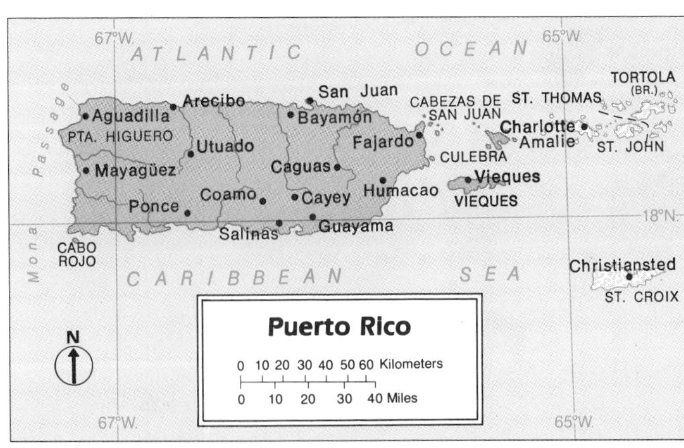

about 100 miles (160 kilometers)

Puerto Rico was the scene of the last battle of the Spanish American War. To get an idea of the size of the island, measure the distance from Mayagüez to Fajardo.

President McKinley, shown here (fifth from the right) at the signing of the Treaty of Paris of 1898, had learned to hate war during the Civil War. He felt that he was forced into the Spanish-American conflict.

Rico. General Miles landed in Puerto Rico on July 25 and began a victorious advance. Fighting ended on August 12. General Miles raised the American flag over Puerto Rico. Unlike Cuba, Puerto Rico had not been promised independence. The island came under the control of the United States. (See the map of Puerto Rico on page 482.)

Peace and Problems. Spain's island empire went to the United States under the Treaty of Paris of 1898–1899. The Spanish gave up Cuba. The United States was to occupy Cuba for a time and then leave. The United States received Puerto Rico and Guam, an island in the Pacific. In addition, the Spanish ceded the Philippine Islands to the United States for $20 million.

When the peace treaty with Spain was signed, Americans wondered if the United States should hold the conquered lands. Many did not like the idea of an American empire. They said the Americans once lived in colonies and won their independence. Americans, therefore, should not hold other lands as colonies. People who opposed imperialism were called *anti-imperialists*. In 1899, President McKinley accepted the ideas of the imperialists. The United States kept control of its new possessions.

The issue of imperialism divided the nation in the election of 1900. The Republicans nominated William McKinley for a second term. Roosevelt was nominated as Vice President. Republicans supported the ideas of imperialism. Democrats supported the ideas of the anti-imperialists. They nominated William Jennings Bryan as President. The election was hard fought. When the votes were counted, McKinley had won.

American Relations with China

The location of the United States had long influenced its dealings with other countries. Americans felt protected from Europe and Asia by oceans. They thought the problems of Europeans and Asians were none of their concern. From the safety of their location, Americans saw no need for alliances with other countries.

As American industry grew, merchants began to trade more and more with other countries. When other nations became buyers of American products, Americans became interested in the affairs of those nations. In reaching out into the world, the United States became involved with the empire of China.

Spheres of Influence in China. China is an ancient, large, and populous country in eastern Asia. Throughout the 1800s European powers had forced China to give them special trading rights in particular areas of the country. These areas were called *spheres of influence.* A sphere of influence exists when a foreign country has control over some part of another country. European powers even annexed Chinese territory. For example, China was forced to give Hong Kong to Great Britain. Bit by bit, China was carved up into spheres of influence of Great Britain, France, Germany, and Russia.

The United States had a small but profitable trade with China. In 1844 a treaty with China gave the United States trading rights like those given to European powers. The United States, however, did not annex territory or set up a sphere of influence in China. In the late 1800s American merchants became more interested in trading with China.

Secretary of State John Hay did not like the growing spheres of influence in China. They choked off American trade. In 1899 Hay persuaded the European powers to accept an Open Door Policy for China. This policy allowed all nations to trade on equal terms at any port in China. In doing so, it also preserved China's independence.

The Boxer Rebellion. Of course, the Chinese were enraged that parts of their country had come under the influence of foreign powers. As time went on, their hatred grew toward the "foreign devil." Thousands of Chinese joined secret societies whose goal was to chase the foreigners out of China. The most powerful secret society was called the Society of

American marines help put down the Boxer Rebellion. The United States accepted only $4 million of $24 million owed it by China for damages. The rest went to educate Chinese students in America.

Harmonious Fists. Foreigners called its members "Boxers" because they practiced exercises that resembled shadowboxing. The Boxers urged the Chinese to drive all foreigners from their land and to return to more traditional ways.

In June 1900 the Boxers struck. They destroyed foreign-owned property. They killed foreign missionaries, business people, and diplomats. Even children of foreigners were killed. They swept into the capital city of Peking and cut off escape of the Europeans and Americans who lived there. On June 20, Europeans and Americans fled to the protection of the British diplomatic headquarters.

An international army was assembled and sent to rescue the people trapped in Peking. Austrian, French, German, British, Italian, Japanese, Russian and United States troops marched on Peking. On August 14, 1900, they defeated the Boxers and freed the captives.

With the Boxers defeated, the European powers wanted to divide China among themselves. However, Secretary of State Hay held firm to his idea of an "Open Door" for China. He insisted that China remain independent. He also said that China should keep all its territory, but should pay the foreign governments for the deaths and damage caused by the Boxers. The powers agreed.

ANSWER THESE QUESTIONS

1. What did the United States want to use Pearl Harbor in Hawaii for?
2. Why were Hearst and Pulitzer so interested in Cuba?
3. Why did Pulitzer and Hearst practice "yellow journalism"?
4. How did imperialists feel about the United States acquiring overseas possessions? How did anti-imperialists feel?
5. How did the Open Door Policy help preserve China's independence?

ANSWER THESE QUESTIONS

1. as a naval base and coaling station
2. the situation in Cuba was made for "yellow journalism"
3. to get the readers' attention in hopes of outdoing each other in the competition for readers
4. Imperialists wanted the nation to gain overseas possessions, but anti-imperialists were opposed to such possessions.
5. It allowed all nations to trade on equal terms in China and so prevented the European powers from dividing China.

Objective: After completing this page, students should be able to understand and interpret political cartoons

Working With Skills

STUDY SKILLS

ACTIVITY

Objective: To understand political cartoons

Make available to the class several examples of political cartoons, some historical and some contemporary. Include an equal number of cartoons that satirize social trends, individual foibles, or the like—for example, some cartoons from *The New Yorker.* Explain that cartoons are used as a form of social commentary, as well as political commentary. For each sample, ask the students to identify the cartoon as political or not—and to explain clearly the point of the cartoon.

ANSWERS

Answers to questions in running copy: sticking American flags on the globe; Spanish-American War

1. *Rocky Mountain News*
2. because some Americans were hoping to gain those islands
3. The cartoonist probably felt that the United States should be an imperialist power.
4. It shows the United States taking control of other countries; answers will vary.
5. yes; answers will vary

Understanding Political Cartoons

Political cartoons comment on the news of the day. They often exaggerate reality in a humorous way to express an opinion. Cartoons can play an important role in shaping public opinion on current events. With few words and a little space, a skillful cartoonist can make a powerful point.

Political cartoonists use symbols to help express their message quickly. For example, the man in the cartoon on this page is Uncle Sam, who stands for the United States. What is Uncle Sam doing in the cartoon? The credit, or small print under the cartoon, tells when the cartoon first appeared in print. What war was the United States fighting at that time?

Use the cartoon and the information you have learned in this chapter to answer the following questions.

1. In what newspaper did this cartoon first appear?
2. When this cartoon was published, the United States had not annexed Cuba or Puerto Rico. Why do you think American flags have been placed on these islands nonetheless?
3. The caption published with the cartoon read, "By gum, I rather like your looks." What do you think the cartoonist viewed as the United States' role in world affairs?
4. How does this cartoon express the idea of imperialism? Do you think words could express this idea as well? Why or why not?
5. Do you think this cartoon expressed an idea that was popular in 1898? Why or why not?

"Rocky Mountain News," May 15, 1898

RELATED MATERIAL
Duplicator/Copy Master Activity 41

19-2 Theodore Roosevelt's Foreign Policy

As you read, think about these questions:

How did Theodore Roosevelt use the Monroe Doctrine to justify his actions in Latin America?

What policies did Theodore Roosevelt use to increase United States participation in world politics?

Why did the United States want to build a canal across the Isthmus of Panama?

Special Vocabulary	foreign policy	corollary
	duty	mediator

Theodore Roosevelt was elected Vice President in 1900. He became President in September 1901, following the assassination of President McKinley. Roosevelt had a strong *foreign policy*. Foreign policy is the plan of action a nation uses in dealing with other nations. Roosevelt spoke out for his country and acted fast when the situation demanded it. The United States began to play a leading role in world politics.

Action in the Americas

President Roosevelt's foreign policy was called "big stick" policy. This name came from one of his favorite sayings, "Speak softly, and carry a big stick; you will go far."

The Roosevelt Corollary to the Monroe Doctrine. Roosevelt's "big stick" was felt in the Dominican Republic. The Dominican Republic lies on the eastern end of the island of Hispaniola in the Caribbean. The country of Haiti occupies the western end of the island. In 1904 the Dominican Republic was deep in debt. It owed more than $32 million to European countries. European powers threatened either to blockade the Dominican Republic or to take over the collections of its *duties*. Duties are charges made by a government on goods people bring in or take out of the country.

By collecting duties in the Dominican Republic the European nations planned to recover their money. President Roosevelt saw this plan as another threat to the Monroe

CONTENT OBJECTIVES

After completing the lesson, students will know:

- what the Roosevelt Corollary to the Monroe Doctrine is
- how the United States came to build the Panama Canal
- Theodore Roosevelt's role as a peacemaker in the Russo-Japanese War
- about the "Gentlemen's Agreement" between Japan and the United States

VOCABULARY

foreign policy: the plan of action that a nation uses in dealing with other nations

duty: charges made by a government on goods people bring in or take out of the country

corollary: a statement that follows or adds to the meaning of a statement made earlier

mediator: one who acts as a go-between to bring arguing parties together to settle their differences

DISCUSSION

Review for the students that Theodore Roosevelt expanded the Monroe Doctrine by saying the United States would be a "police officer" in the Western Hemisphere. Have the students discuss how the Latin Americans reacted to this and why. Have them discuss how Americans might react if another nation appointed itself "police officer" in this hemisphere. Ask the students if they have the impression that the Roosevelt Corollary is still in effect.

Doctrine. His idea was for the United States to be a go-between. The United States would collect the duties in the Dominican Republic. Part of the money would go to repay the loans. The rest would be used to help run the government of the Dominican Republic. Roosevelt placed a collector in the Dominican Republic. He then sent the navy and marines to protect the collector. The arrangement worked. The duties were collected and paid out as promised.

Theodore Roosevelt, shown here with Edith Roosevelt and their six children, was the youngest man ever to become President. His energy and enthusiasm were admired by many Americans.

President Roosevelt's decisions about the problems of the Dominican Republic added something new to the Monroe Doctrine. The Monroe Doctrine stated that the United States would not allow foreign countries to interfere in the affairs of countries in the Western Hemisphere. Now Roosevelt added the idea that the United States had the job of seeing that countries in the Western Hemisphere behaved in a way that avoided trouble with European nations. He said the United States would be a kind of "police officer" of the Western Hemisphere and solve the problems that arose in the Americas. This addition to the Monroe Doctrine is called the Roosevelt Corollary to the Monroe Doctrine. A *corollary* is a statement that follows or adds to the meaning of a statement made earlier.

Teddy Roosevelt's "big stick" foreign policy was criticized in many political cartoons like this one, called "The World's Constable."

Most Latin American leaders were unhappy about the Roosevelt Corollary. They did not want to be bullied by their northern neighbor any more than they wanted to be bullied by European powers. In spite of Latin American feelings, the United States became involved in the affairs of Haiti, Honduras, and Nicaragua. Marines were sent to bring order to these countries.

Panama and the Canal. After the Spanish-American War Americans felt the need to build a canal between the Atlantic and Pacific oceans. They realized such a canal was necessary to allow the navy to travel quickly from one ocean to the other. The canal would also be important to American trade. Ships could avoid the long voyage around South America. This would reduce shipping costs as well as travel time.

A French company had failed in an attempt to build a canal across Panama during the 1880s. In 1902 this company sold its rights and machinery in Panama to the United States for $40 million. At that time Panama was controlled by Colombia, the South American country that borders Panama. The United States needed Colombian permission to begin construction. The United States offered Colombia $10 million for a narrow strip of land across Panama. This strip would be called the Canal Zone. In addition, the United States would pay Colombia $250,000 a year. Colombia rejected the offer, hoping to get a much better deal.

Panama had revolted against Colombia several times in the past. Rebels in Panama were sure of American support if they were to revolt again. On November 3, 1903, another revolt took place. It was nearly a bloodless revolution. One person was killed. A new government of Panama was organized overnight, and the nation declared its independence.

Teddy Roosevelt was the guiding spirit of the Panama Canal project, the greatest national undertaking since the building of the first transcontinental railroad.

The new government of Panama made a treaty with the United States. According to the treaty, the United States leased, or rented, the Canal Zone forever. The Canal Zone was 10 miles (16 kilometers) wide. Construction on the canal began in 1904 and took ten years to finish. One of the first tasks was to solve the problem of yellow fever and other diseases that were killing many of the workers. William C. Gorgas of the United States Army Medical Corps did the job. Dr. Gorgas knew that yellow fever and malaria were carried by mosquitoes. Under his direction, workers drained swamps, the breeding grounds of mosquitoes. Dr. Gorgas also supervised the construction of hospitals and sewage systems. When he finished, the Canal Zone was as healthy a place as most cities in the United States.

A canal using locks was to be built 85 feet (26 meters) above sea level in central Panama. In 1907 Roosevelt put Colonel George W. Goethals, an army engineer, in charge of construction. The work moved forward rapidly. Earth was removed; locks and a dam were built. More than forty thousand workers dug their way between the Atlantic and Pacific oceans. When finished, the "big ditch," as many called the canal, stretched 50 miles (80 kilometers) across Panama.

World Involvement

President Roosevelt enjoyed world politics. He and his opinions were respected by the leaders of other nations. "TR," as many Americans referred to him, was best known to Americans as the hero of San Juan Hill, but he also enjoyed the role of peacemaker in differences between nations.

TR helped establish the United States as a world leader. Many Americans, however, including some in Congress, did not want the United States cast in such a role. Imperialism was starting to lose favor. People learned that world leadership brought problems. They felt that problems at home needed solving before those overseas. They lost interest in overseas colonies. Cuba, as the United States had promised, became independent. Congress also made plans for the Philippines, Puerto Rico, and Hawaii to move toward governing themselves.

Roosevelt the Peacemaker. At the beginning of the twentieth century, Russia and Japan were both trying to control Manchuria and northern China. The United States followed the contest closely. Because of the Open Door Policy, Americans did not want any country to become too powerful there.

Northern China and Manchuria were not the only issues that caused problems between Russia and Japan. The two nations disagreed about the ownership of Sakhalin Island, north of Japan. The Russians held the island, but the Japanese thought of it as part of their island nation.

In 1904 a war broke out between Russia and Japan. Roosevelt felt the victor might become strong enough to take over part of China. He watched the progress of the war with interest. In 1905 Roosevelt suggested to both sides that he bring them together for peace talks. He offered to serve as *mediator.* A mediator acts as a go-between to bring arguing parties together to settle their differences. Finally, both Russia and Japan agreed to meet with President Roosevelt in the United States. They met at Portsmouth, New Hampshire. The President was at his best. He kept the difficult negotiations going, even when they might have broken down. The

Roosevelt's reputation as a world leader was made greater by his role as mediator in the Russo-Japanese War.

ACTIVITY

Objective: To identify issues and questions

Have the class review the material on Japan's relations with the United States in the early 1900s. Start a list on the chalkboard of "Problems" and another of "Solutions." You might start the list with "War with Russia" and "Mediation by President Roosevelt." Have the students contribute items to the lists from their reading in this lesson.

Russians and the Japanese finally reached an agreement. Russia agreed to turn over the southern half of Sakhalin Island to Japan. The Japanese agreed not to call for Russian payments to make up for damage to life and property during the war.

Tensions Between the United States and Japan. The Japanese were not completely happy about Roosevelt's part in ending the war. They felt they had been winning the war when the peace talks began. They blamed Roosevelt for their getting only half of Sakhalin Island. Partly because of this anger the Japanese continued to increase their power in Manchuria. In 1910 Japan also annexed Korea. By the early 1900s Japanese growth took place at sea as well as on land. Japan had become the leading naval power in East Asia.

The outcome of the Russian-Japanese peace talks in 1905 was not the only cause for anger between the Japanese and the Americans. The treatment of Japanese immigrants in California contributed to ill feelings between the United States and Japan. Many state and local laws in California treated Asians unfairly. Californians felt that laborers from China, Japan, and Korea would take American jobs because the Asians would work for less pay. In 1906 the San Francisco school board refused to allow Chinese, Korean, and Japanese children to attend regular public schools. Instead, the board sent them to separate schools.

President Roosevelt was upset over the action taken by the San Francisco school board. He invited the mayor and the school board to the White House. He persuaded them to cancel their order to keep the Asian children separate from the other school children. He also got Japan to agree to stop laborers from leaving Japan for the United States. This arrangement between the United States and Japan was known as the "Gentlemen's Agreement." In 1908 the United States and Japan signed a treaty that said both countries would recognize the Open Door in China. Tensions then began to ease.

The Great White Fleet. Theodore Roosevelt believed that the United States should have a strong navy. As a young man he had written a book about the role of the navy in the War of 1812 and had served as assistant secretary of the navy. When he became President, the navy had only nine battleships. Roosevelt urged that more be built. He wanted a large navy

The sixteen battleships of the "Great White Fleet" leave port on their 1907 goodwill tour. The fleet got its name because the ships were painted white.

to defend the coast of the United States, to protect China's Open Door, and to enforce the Roosevelt Corollary to the Monroe Doctrine. Within a few years, Roosevelt had built up a large, modern navy for the United States.

Because of the tensions between Japan and the United States, Roosevelt decided to show off his new navy to Japan and the rest of the world. He announced that he was sending the new battle fleet on a goodwill cruise around the world. Others felt Roosevelt wanted to show the Japanese that the peacemaker still carried a "big stick."

The Great White Fleet, as Roosevelt's new navy was called, left its base in Virginia in 1907. The fleet was made up of sixteen battleships. The Great White Fleet was warmly received at every port of call, even at Yokohama, Japan. Fourteen months after leaving Virginia, the Great White Fleet returned. The trip had both demonstrated goodwill and showed off America's large, modern navy.

ANSWER THESE QUESTIONS

1. What name was given to the idea that the United States had the right to intervene in the affairs of Latin American countries?
2. In what way did Dr. William C. Gorgas help make the construction of the Panama Canal possible?
3. Why did some Americans object to the United States becoming a world leader?
4. Why did President Roosevelt want to settle the war between Russia and Japan?
5. What was the Great White Fleet? Why did President Roosevelt send it on a cruise around the world?

ANSWER THESE QUESTIONS

1. the Roosevelt Corollary to the Monroe Doctrine
2. He eliminated yellow fever and other diseases so that the workers building the canal could survive.
3. They felt that problems at home needed solving before those overseas.
4. He feared that the victor in the war might become powerful enough to take over part of China.
5. a fleet of 16 American battleships; to demonstrate goodwill and to show off America's large, modern navy

THINKING THINGS THROUGH

1. by printing sensational stories about Spanish atrocities in Cuba and thereby stirring up public opinion against Spain 2. the Philippine Islands, Guam, and Puerto Rico 3. They thought that the United States should not hold colonies because the nation had once been a colony and had won its independence. 4. He said the United States would see that

Chapter 19 SUMMARY

During the late 1800s the United States began to extend its power. In 1898 the United States annexed Hawaii after a revolt by American sugar planters there.

In 1895 Cubans revolted against Spanish control. American newspapers printed sensational stories about Spanish atrocities in Cuba. After the battleship *Maine* was sunk by a mysterious explosion, Congress declared war on Spain in 1898. The United States quickly defeated Spain and gained Spain's island empire.

In 1899 Secretary of State John Hay opened the ports of China to all nations. Hay thus kept China from being cut up into spheres of influence by Japan and the European powers.

President Theodore Roosevelt's "big stick" policy kept European powers from intervening in the affairs of Latin American countries. He also used the Monroe Doctrine to justify intervening in the affairs of Latin American countries if they could not manage their affairs.

A canal linking the Atlantic and Pacific oceans was needed. President Roosevelt gained rights to a strip of land across Panama. In 1904 construction on the Panama Canal began.

President Roosevelt served as a mediator to end the Russo-Japanese War in 1905. In 1907 he sent the new United States battle fleet on a world cruise both to show American might and as a gesture of goodwill.

Chapter 19 TEST

WORDS TO REMEMBER

Match each of the following words with the correct definition below.

b 1. isolationism
f 2. foreign policy
i 3. corollary
a 4. imperialism
c 5. yellow journalism
e 6. anti-imperialist
g 7. mediator
d 8. atrocity
h 9. duty

a. the practice of gaining control over other lands and people

b. the policy of a country that has little to do with other countries

c. newspaper reporting that gains readers' attention with big headlines and pictures of crimes, accidents, and wars

d. an extremely cruel action

e. a person who opposes empire-building and holding overseas possessions as colonies

f. the plan of action a nation uses in dealing with other nations

g. a person who serves as a go-between to bring disputing parties together to settle their differences

h. charges made by a government on goods coming into or going out of the country

i. a statement that follows or extends the meaning of a previous statement

THINKING THINGS THROUGH

1. How did yellow journalism help create tensions between the United States and Spain?
2. What territories did the United States gain as a result of the Spanish-American War?
3. Why did the anti-imperialists oppose the

RELATED MATERIALS

Duplicator/Copy Masters: Activities 40, 41; Quiz 42
Workbook pages 57-59

countries in the Western Hemisphere fulfilled their obligations to other nations, so that other nations would have no cause to interfere in the Western Hemisphere. **5.** They were both trying to gain control over Manchuria and northern China. **6.** to aid trade and to enable the navy to move ships between the Atlantic and Pacific oceans more quickly **7.** by persuading the San Francisco school board not to segregate Asian children and by sending the Great White Fleet on a goodwill cruise **8.** to drive foreigners out of China; Boxers **9.** They were unhappy, because they did not want to be bullied by the United States any more than they wanted to be bullied by European nations.

WORKING WITH SKILLS

1. in a police officer's uniform **2.** the "new diplomacy"; that Roosevelt is threatening other nations as part of his new policy **3.** people from Latin America, Turkey and Afghanistan, Europe, and Japan; to keep Europeans and Asians from getting involved in the countries of the Western Hemisphere

United States' holding power over conquered lands?

4. What new meaning did Theodore Roosevelt give to the Monroe Doctrine?
5. Why did a war break out between Russia and Japan in 1905?
6. Why did the United States want to build and control the Panama Canal?
7. In what ways did President Theodore Roosevelt improve relations between the United States and Japan?
8. What was the goal of the Society of Harmonious Fists in China and what name did foreigners give members of the society?
9. How did most Latin American leaders react to the Roosevelt Corollary to the Monroe Doctrine?

WORKING WITH SKILLS

Study the cartoon on page 489 to answer the following questions.

1. How is Theodore Roosevelt dressed in the cartoon?
2. What is written on the "big stick"? What does this say about Roosevelt's foreign policy?
3. What groups of people is "TR" keeping apart? Why?

ON YOUR OWN

1. Watch the news on your favorite television station for a few days, comparing the way in which news is reported on television today with the way it was reported by newspapers in the late 1800s. What kinds of stories do newscasts begin with? What kinds of stories do they end with? Where in the telecasts does the station place local news, national news, and international news? Do you think that the newscasts use any of the techniques of sensationalism that the yellow journalists practiced? Why or why not?
2. The picture on this page shows Commodore Matthew C. Perry and his flagbearer arriving in Japan in 1854. Read about this expedition in an encyclopedia and write a paragraph describing how Perry persuaded the Japanese to open trade with the United States.

Chapter 20
WORLD WAR I

Chapter 20 is an overview of World War I. Lesson 20-1 describes the strong nationalistic feelings in Europe in the early 1900s and discusses many of the events that ultimately led to war. Lesson 20-2 outlines United States participation in the war, summarizes some of the major battles, and explains how the peace was finally made.

CONTENT OBJECTIVES

After completing the lesson, students will know:

- how tensions built between nations until war was unavoidable
- the importance of imperialist, nationalist, and militarist sentiments in causing the war
- why people expected the war to be a short one and why this was not the case
- how the United States was drawn into the war

VOCABULARY

nationalism: strong devotion to one's nation or national group
militarism: a strong emphasis on military preparedness
mobilize: assemble armies and make them ready for war
ultimatum: a set of severe demands
trench warfare: a war in which soldiers fight from long ditches dug in the ground
contraband: war materials bound for the enemy
diplomatic ties: formal international relations

20-1 Storm Clouds Over Europe

As you read, think about these questions:
What conditions in Europe led to the outbreak of World War I?
What benefits did neutrality offer Americans?
Why did many Americans sympathize with the Allies?
Why did the United States finally enter the war?

Special Vocabulary: nationalism, militarism, mobilize, ultimatum, trench warfare, contraband, diplomatic ties

When 1914 began few people anywhere expected a general war in Europe. There had not been such a war for nearly a hundred years. Yet a widespread war did come. Still, as the armies of Europe marched off to the battlefields, Americans did not expect to be involved in the fighting. In 1917, however, against its best hopes, the United States was drawn into the combat. The war had became a *world* war, the first such war in history.

From an Uneasy Peace to War

From the late 1890s on, the people of Europe had lived under a shaky peace. The nations competed with each other for foreign markets and for control of colonies in far places. An arms race heated up as the nations built their armies and constantly increased their stock of weapons. By 1914 tensions in Europe were near the breaking point.

Increasing Tensions. Three powerful forces caused world tensions to increase at the beginnning of the twentieth century: imperialism; *nationalism,* or strong devotion to one's nation or national group; and *militarism,* a strong emphasis on military preparedness. Europeans believed that they had a right and a need to establish far-flung empires throughout the world. The British, French, Russians, and Austro-Hungarians all had their own empires. The Germans and Italians wanted to begin theirs, but unclaimed lands were scarce.

Competition for markets and overseas colonies led to other rivalries. In the years after 1900, for example, a furious naval race developed between Great Britain and Germany. The British argued that Germany's naval competition was a serious threat to peace.

Europeans felt very strong ties to people sharing their particular language and heritage. Such feelings led to increased nationalism. Some national groups, however, were not allowed to govern themselves. They lived in countries ruled by other people. Most of these small national groups were in central and eastern Europe. Austria-Hungary, for example, included Germans, Magyars, Bosnians, Czechs, Slovaks, Croatians, Serbs, Slovenes, Italians, and Poles. Many such national groups were demanding independence.

Each nation kept its armies ready to fight. Militarism was a tradition in Germany, especially in the region known as Prussia. The Prussians had unified Germany by war in the 1860s and 1870s. One leader had said proudly that Germany was made of "blood and iron."

DISCUSSION

Review for the students the definition of *nationalism.* Have them discuss the fine line between national pride and the kind of nationalist feeling that leads to wars. Ask the students to consider how far a nation should go in defending its interests when those interests seem to conflict with those of other nations. Have the students contribute recent examples from the news of nationalism that resulted in military incidents.

Displays of military strength, such as this Prussian cavalry unit, were an increasingly common sight in Europe just before World War I began.

Militarism appeared in other countries as well. Each major nation made plans to *mobilize*, or assemble armies and make them ready for war on short notice. The large standing armies of drafted soldiers gave people a sense of security in a very dangerous world.

European Alliances. European countries tried to protect themselves by forming alliances. By 1914 there were two major alliances in Europe. One was called the Triple Alliance. It was made up of Germany, Austria-Hungary, and Italy. Italy later left the alliance, but the Ottoman Empire (now Turkey) joined it. This alliance was also known as the Central Powers because of the countries' location in central Europe. The second alliance, called the Triple Entente, was made up of France, Russia, and Great Britain. This alliance was also known as the Allies, or the Allied Powers. Find the members of the two alliances on the map on page 505.

Assassination in Sarajevo. On July 28, 1914, Archduke Francis Ferdinand, heir to the throne of Austria-Hungary, made a state visit to Sarajevo. This small town was the capital of Bosnia, a province that Austria-Hungary had controlled for thirty years. Many people in Bosnia were unhappy under Austrian rule. They wanted to be a part of Serbia, a neighboring country. The people of Bosnia and Serbia shared a common heritage and language.

A small group of Serbian patriots mingled with the crowd watching the procession in Sarajevo. Suddenly one of the patriots fired a gun at the archduke and archduchess and killed both of them. The government of Austria-Hungary

Police arrest a member of the group responsible for the assassination of the archduke and archduchess in Sarajevo. This event led to the outbreak of World War I.

insisted that the government of Serbia had helped in the assassination. Austria-Hungary sent an *ultimatum*, a set of severe demands, to Serbia. Serbia's response was unacceptable to Austria-Hungary. It went to war against Serbia.

Immediately, Russia, which was Serbia's ally, mobilized its army and came to Serbia's assistance. Austria-Hungary, thereupon, asked its ally Germany to help fight the Russian army. Germany mobilized its army and declared war on Serbia and Russia. It then declared war on France, because France was an ally of Russia. The European alliance system had helped turn a local conflict into a general war.

The Fighting Begins. Germany had long worried about having to fight Russia and France at the same time. The Germans, therefore, planned to knock France out of the war quickly and then turn on Russia. On August 3, 1914, the Germans invaded Belgium on their way into France. Belgium's plains offered an easy route for the German army. Great Britain had pledged to protect the borders of Belgium, which was a neutral country. Germany's entry into Belgium therefore brought Great Britain into the war.

The Germans expected to defeat France in about six weeks. The French planned to strike into Germany and move toward Berlin, the German capital. The Russians believed they could defeat Austria-Hungary and then drive deep into Germany, too. The Austrians planned to occupy Serbia. None of these plans worked.

The German army rolled through Belgium and France toward Paris, the French capital. The French army finally stopped the advance at the Marne River, just 15 miles (24 kilometers) from Paris. The front became deadlocked in *trench warfare*. Trenches were long ditches dug in the ground

ACTIVITY

Objective: To analyze relationships

Have the students review the sections "European Alliances," "Assassination in Sarajevo," and "The Fighting Begins." To help the students understand the web of relationships and alliances that led to war, have them make a diagram or flow chart of the sequence of events that started the war and involved most European countries. Have them start their diagram with the assassination, then draw an arrow to the next major event. As each nation enters the war, the student should briefly note the reason—for example, "attacked by Germany" or "ally of Belgium."

Life in the trenches was made up of long stretches of uncomfortable boredom broken by moments of terror. Here, French troops prepare to go "over the top."

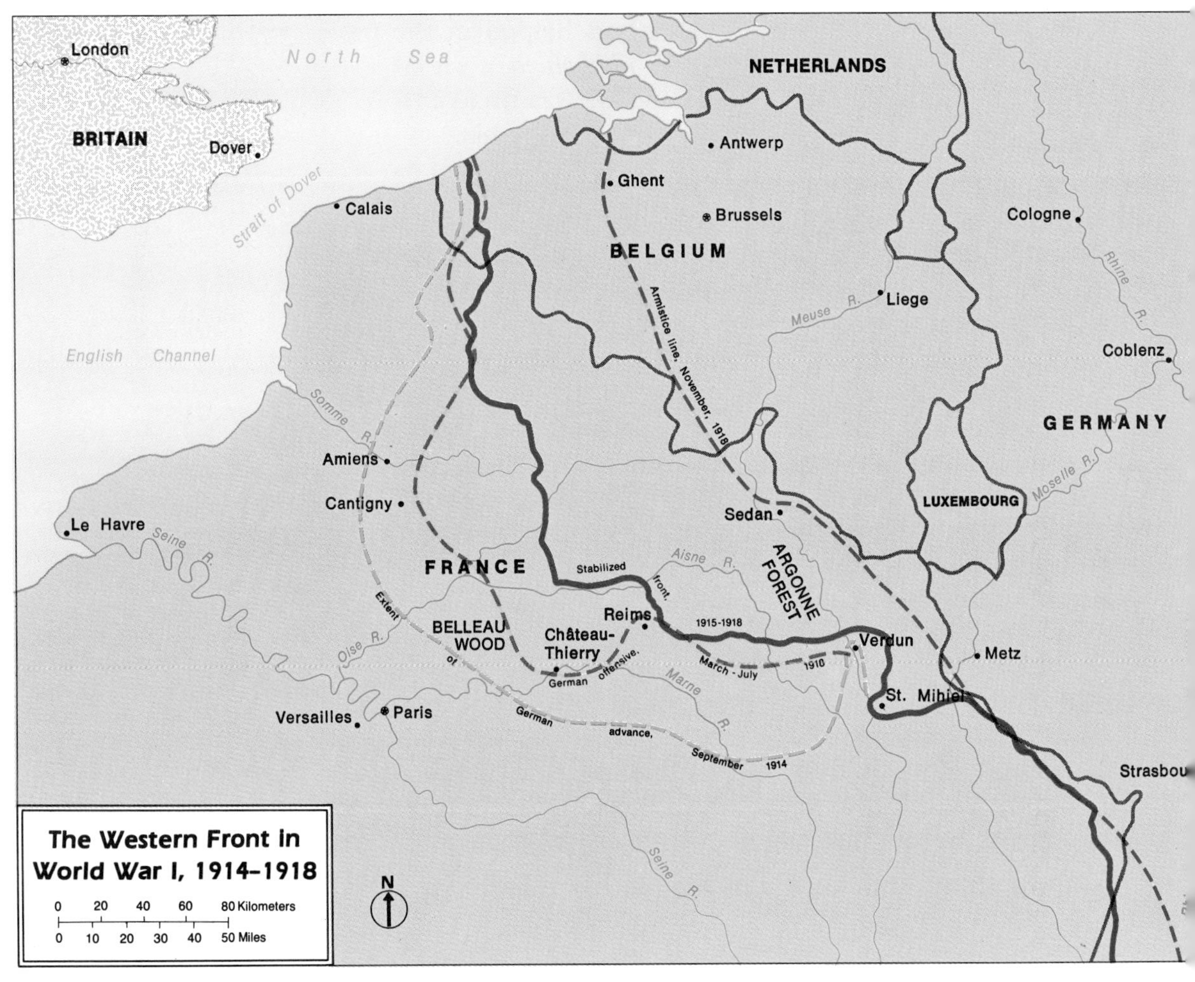

This map shows the main battle lines of the western front. Which line shows the German army's western-most position?

dashed blue line

for the protection of troops. The trenches zigzagged for hundreds of miles across France and Belgium. This line of trenches became known as the western front. (See the map above.) As troops went "over the top" of their trenches, seeking to make gains in territory, barbed wire snarled them. Armies on both sides used machine guns, poison gas, and other terrible new weapons. Overhead, the first military airplanes reported troop movements and fought battles called "dogfights."

On the eastern front the war did not bog down in trenches. The eastern front ran between the Baltic Sea and the Black Sea. There the Germans smashed the Russian army, though the Russians had some success against Austria-Hungary. When Italy joined the Allies and attacked Austria in 1915, the war in Europe also had a southern front.

American Neutrality. President Woodrow Wilson issued a proclamation of neutrality in August 1914. It stated that the United States must remain neutral in the European war. While few Americans wanted to become involved in it, many people sympathized with the Allies. Americans recognized ties of language and tradition with the British. They also remembered France as a friend that had aided the thirteen colonies during the American Revolution.

As long as the United States remained neutral, it could do business with both sides. Business boomed as American supplies poured into Europe. Yet trade with the warring countries also caused trouble. They claimed the right under international law to stop and search neutral ships on the high seas. They sought to seize any *contraband*, or war materials bound for their enemy. The British navy was able to blockade Germany. The British insisted that even food being shipped to the Germans was contraband. The United States protested seizure of its ships, but the British were determined to starve Germany out of the war.

The United States Is Drawn Into War

The blockade was Great Britain's major strategy to defeat Germany. Germany had a similar plan to prevent supplies from reaching the Allies. It used a new weapon, the submarine, or U-boat, for this purpose. Germany's use of submarine warfare eventually pulled the United States into the war.

Submarine Warfare. Warships had always given warning to cargo or passenger ships before capturing or sinking them. Such warning allowed passengers to get to safety in lifeboats. Submarines, however, were designed for surprise attack. They could easily be sunk themselves. U-boats simply lost the element of surprise if they surfaced to warn a ship.

Early in 1915 Germany announced that a war zone existed in the waters around the British Isles. Neither enemy ships nor neutral ships would be safe in the war zone. The United States sent a warning to Germany. It would hold Germany responsible for any loss of American ships and lives.

On the night of May 7, 1915, the British passenger ship *Lusitania* was off the southern coast of Ireland. Suddenly, without warning, a U-boat torpedoed it. The *Lusitania* sank in minutes, taking the lives of 1198 men, women, and children—128 of them Americans.

CUNARD
EUROPE VIA LIVERPOOL
LUSITANIA
Fastest and Largest Steamer
now in Atlantic Service Sails
SATURDAY, MAY 1, 10 A. M.
Transylvania, Fri., May 7, 5 P.M.
Orduna, - - Tues., May 18, 10 A.M.
Tuscania, - - Fri., May 21, 5 P.M.
LUSITANIA, Sat., May 29, 10 A.M.
Transylvania, Fri., June 4, 5 P.M.
Gibraltar–Genoa–Naples–Piraeus
S.S. Carpathia, Thur., May 13, Noon

NOTICE!

TRAVELLERS intending to embark on the Atlantic voyage are reminded that a state of war exists between Germany and her allies and Great Britain and her allies; that the zone of war includes the waters adjacent to the British Isles; that, in accordance with formal notice given by the Imperial German Government, vessels flying the flag of Great Britain, or of any of her allies, are liable to destruction in those waters and that travellers sailing in the war zone on ships of Great Britain or her allies do so at their own risk.

IMPERIAL GERMAN EMBASSY

WASHINGTON, D. C., APRIL 22, 1915.

The captain of the *Lusitania* was so confident of the strength of his ship that he ignored German warnings. His decision not to sail a zigzag course across the Atlantic led to the loss of many lives.

The *Lusitania,* although not armed as the Germans claimed, was carrying a shipment of rifles when it was sunk.

Some Americans demanded war against Germany. President Wilson, however, moved carefully. He sent notes of protest to Germany. Germany finally accepted the blame for the loss of American lives on the *Lusitania*. It agreed to pay damages and promised not to sink passenger ships again without warning.

Submarine warfare nevertheless continued. In March 1916 a U-boat torpedoed the *Sussex*, an unarmed French cargo ship. Two Americans were killed. President Wilson warned the German government that such submarine attacks must stop. If not, he said, the United States would break *diplomatic ties*, or formal international relations, with Germany. Germany gave in. It promised to sink no more cargo ships without warning.

The Zimmermann Telegram. Arthur Zimmermann was Germany's secretary of foreign affairs. In January 1917 he sent a telegram to the chief German diplomat in Mexico City. The telegram urged that Mexico be encouraged to form an alliance with Germany. Zimmermann told the diplomat to offer Germany's support in helping Mexico regain the states of New Mexico, Arizona, and Texas in exchange for Mexico's support in the war against the United States. Zimmermann's telegram was intercepted. When American newspapers published the text of the telegram on March 1, 1917, Americans were furious.

The United States Declares War. Germany meanwhile had returned to unrestricted submarine warfare. President Wilson had been reelected in 1916 on the slogan, "He kept us out of war." Now, however, he broke off diplomatic ties with Germany. German U-boats sank ships at an alarming rate. Between February 3 and April 1, 1917, German U-boats sank eight American ships.

On April 2, 1917, the President called the members of both houses of Congress together to address them. He asked them to understand that war had been forced upon the United States. He said the United States would be fighting to make the world "safe for democracy." On April 6, 1917, Congress declared a state of war with Germany.

ANSWER THESE QUESTIONS

1. What event triggered war in Europe in 1914?
2. What were the two opposing alliances in Europe in 1914?
3. What type of warfare developed on the western front?
4. What policy did the United States follow when fighting broke out in Europe?
5. How did submarine warfare help bring the United States into the war?

ANSWER THESE QUESTIONS

1. the assassination of the Archduke Francis Ferdinand of Austria-Hungary at Sarajevo
2. the Central Powers, or Triple Alliance, and the Allied Powers or Allies, also called the Triple Entente
3. trench warfare
4. neutrality
5. Submarine attacks on American ships forced Wilson and Congress to declare war on Germany.

Objective: Once students have completed these pages, they will understand how to analyze relationships on maps.

Working with Skills

MAP SKILLS

ACTIVITY

Objective: To analyze relationships on maps

Have the students look at the map The Western Front in World War I, 1914-1918, page 500. Remind the students that the soldiers dug into trenches along the front. Ask them a series of questions designed to elicit an understanding of why the front was so important to Britain and its allies, such as: (1) What important river in France is west of the front? (Seine River) (2) Why was it important to protect Calais and Dover? (important ports) (3) Why did Britain pledge to protect Belgium? (If the Germans controlled Belgium and northern France, they would be too close to England.)

ANSWERS

QUESTIONS IN TEXT

green
orange
Russia
red

Analyzing Relationships on a Map

The map on the next page shows the European alliances and neutral countries in 1914. This political map uses color to indicate the alliances. Look at the map key in the upper right corner. What color stands for the countries allied to Germany? Find Germany and its allies on the map. These countries were known as the Central Powers because of their location in central Europe. On the map you can see that the Central Powers were bordered on the east and the west by countries allied to Great Britain. What color is used for these countries? They were known as the Allied Powers or Allies. Find the large country to the east of the Central Powers. What is it? Find the Allied Powers to the west of the Central Powers.

The way in which a nation's geographic position determines how it will fight a war is called its strategic position. Look again at the map. Compare the strategic positions of the two alliances. Think about the advantages and disadvantages of each alliance's strategic position. One advantage of the Central Powers' strategic position was closer communications between member countries. On the other hand, this alliance's central position meant that it had to fight on two fronts. One advantage of the Allied Powers' strategic position was that these countries were in a better position to control Atlantic shipping than the Central Powers were. On the other hand, a great distance separated France and Great Britain from Russia, another Allied Power.

Some countries in Europe remained neutral during the war. What color in the map key stands for the neutral countries? Find the neutral countries on the map. Some nations were able to remain neutral because of their geographic location. Look at each neutral nation and think how its geographic position may have helped it stay out of the war. Notice Switzerland's position. A landlocked country, Switzerland was completely surrounded by warring countries. Yet it remained neutral. Switzerland is a nation that has a history of neutrality going back many centuries. Furthermore, most of the country is made up of rugged mountains. Armies would not have found Switzerland easy to invade. On the other hand, Belgium desired to remain neutral, but it could not. Germany invaded Belgium at the start of the war.

RELATED MATERIAL
Duplicator/Copy Master Activity 43

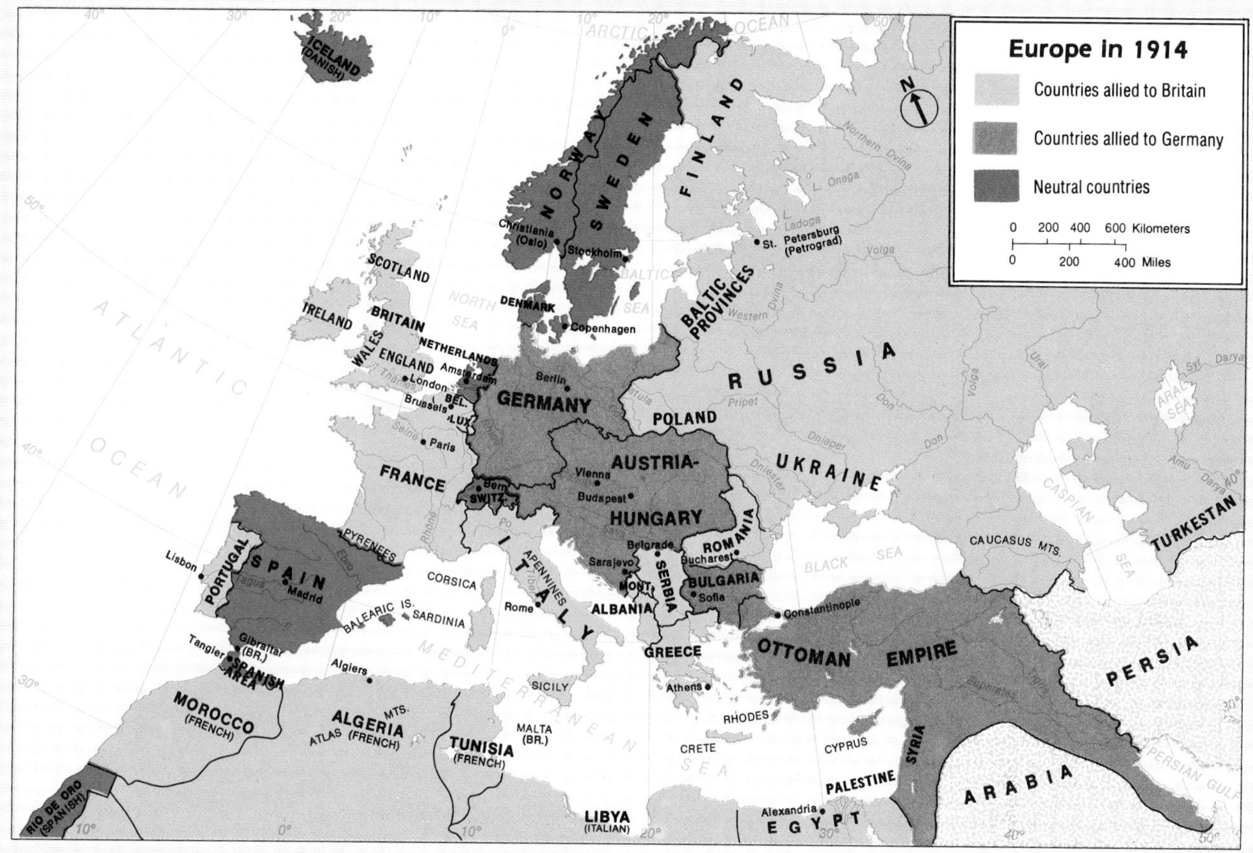

Study the geographic relationships between countries on the map to answer the following questions:

1. Before the war broke out, Germany claimed that it was being "encircled." What do you think the Germans meant by this?
2. How did Great Britain's geographic position protect it from invasion by an army?
3. Why did most of the fighting in France take place in the northeastern part of the country?
4. How did Italy's geographic position aid the Allies in defeating Austria-Hungary? How did Austria-Hungary's military position become similar to Germany's after Italy joined the Allies?
5. Why did the Allied Powers have a better chance of receiving American supplies than the Central Powers did?
6. Why was it easier for Great Britain to use a naval blockade of Germany than for German U-boats to sink ships headed for Great Britain?

ANSWERS

1. that countries were forming alliances against it to the east and to the west
2. Invading Great Britain would have meant crossing the English Channel.
3. because Germany invaded France through Belgium in the north
4. Italy shared a border with Austria-Hungary; Austria-Hungary had to fight on two fronts.
5. France and Great Britain are located on the Atlantic coasts and so are closer to the United States.
6. Germany's only outlets to the ocean are through the North Sea or the English Channel. England's geographic position enabled it to control these outlets.

CONTENT OBJECTIVES

After completing the lesson, students will know:

- what people on the homefront did to assist the war effort
- some American military strategies that helped to win the war
- details of the Treaty of Versailles
- about the start of the League of Nations and why the United States did not join it

VOCABULARY

propaganda: communications used to make people think a certain way
convoy: cargo ships traveling in groups, escorted by warships
casualty: a soldier killed or wounded
armistice: cease-fire

20-2 Americans at War

As you read, think about these questions:

What steps did Americans take to prepare for war?

How did the home front help the battlefront?

In what battles did American troops fight?

How did President Wilson's ideas of a peace treaty differ from those of the other Allies?

Why did the United States not join the League of Nations?

Special Vocabulary	propaganda	casualty
	convoy	armistice

When the United States went to war against Germany in 1917, President Wilson dreamed of a postwar world in which nations would work together to solve problems without war. In the meantime, the President knew that Americans would have to sacrifice in order to win the war.

Americans on the Home Front

When the United States entered the war, it had an army of only a little more than 200,000 soldiers. The navy was still being rebuilt. Few factories were set up to produce war materials. The nation had an enormous job ahead.

Supporting the War Effort. In May 1917 Congress passed the Selective Service Act. All men between the ages of twenty-one and thirty had to register for possible military service. Of the twenty-four million who registered during the war, nearly three million were selected for service.

The war cost the United States over $33 billion. The government needed a special way to raise money. It sold Liberty bonds. Millions of citizens who bought these bonds were, in effect, lending money to the government. Later, the government repaid the value of the bonds plus interest.

The war effort required many supplies, including food, clothing, and equipment. Factories were soon operating around the clock. Americans also learned to help by conserving resources. The President put Herbert C. Hoover in

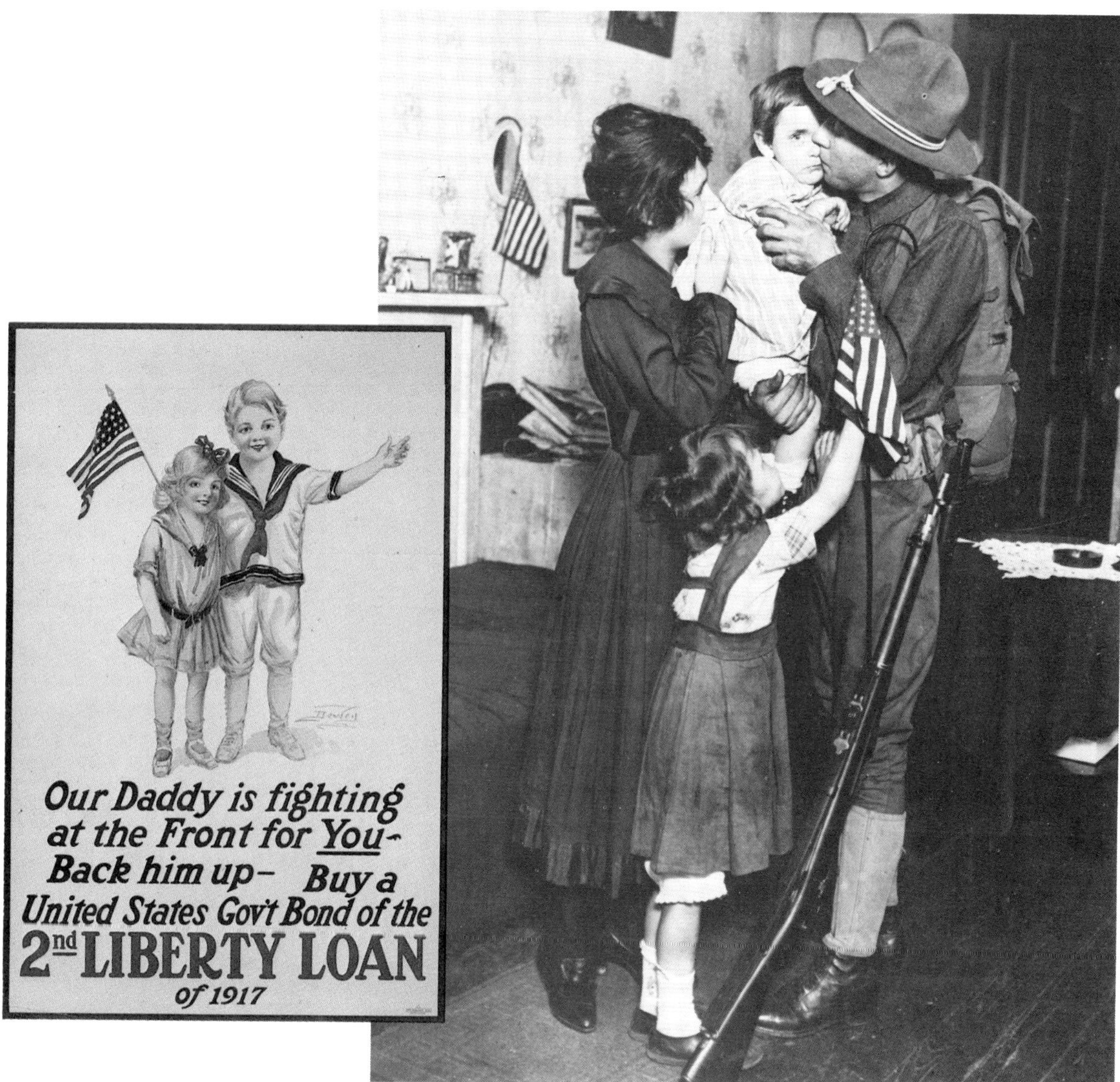

Our Daddy is fighting
at the Front for You-
Back him up- Buy a
United States Gov't Bond of the
2nd LIBERTY LOAN
of 1917

An advertisement for Liberty bonds (left) reminded Americans that thousands of soldiers had said farewell to their families and gone off to war.

charge of the Food Administration. Under Hoover's guidance, Americans began to cut down on waste of food. Many city people planted their own vegetable patches, known as "liberty gardens." The government also had a Fuel Administration to help save coal and oil.

Help from Industry, Labor, and Farms. The federal government set up agencies called boards to help workers and farmers produce more. The War Industries Board controlled factory production. Bernard Baruch, an industrial leader, ran this board.

A War Labor Board was created to guarantee a supply of workers where they were needed. The board gave labor unions the right to bargain with employers. In return, labor leaders promised not to strike. The War Labor Board promised men and women equal pay.

Farmers raised more food than ever before. The increase in wheat production was spectacular. The government bought the extra wheat and sent it to the needy Allies.

Although women and blacks provided support for the war effort, neither group was properly appreciated. Blacks fought in segregated units as they always had. Women performed jobs formerly done by men, but they received less pay than the men had.

The Roles of Minorities and Women. Most Americans helped as they could to win the war. The role of minorities was vital to victory. Thousands of blacks were in the armed forces. About 100,000 of them served overseas. More than 1300 blacks were officers. Although it was a war "to make the world safe for democracy," black soldiers fought in all-black units. One such unit, the 370th Infantry Regiment, won honors in some of the toughest fighting of the war.

Blacks also took jobs in factories. Thousands left the South and moved to northern cities seeking work. Their arrival in large cities led to the growth of such black communities as New York's Harlem and Chicago's South Side.

When America went to war, so did American women. Some went to the battlefront as nurses and to drive ambulances. On the home front, thousands of women sought work—many for the first time—in factories and offices. Women produced ammunition, drove trucks, and delivered the mail. Women as well as men sold Liberty bonds at rallies. They rolled bandages for the Red Cross.

Intolerance and Opposition. As the nation went to war, a *propaganda* campaign urged citizens to hate the enemy. Propaganda is communications used to make people think a certain way. Posters and movies depicted German cruelty. Many people refused to listen to German music or read German books. Anti-German feelings easily got out of hand. Some German Americans lost their jobs or were even beaten in the streets.

Congress passed strict laws banning opposition to the war. Some people spoke out against it anyway. Eugene V. Debs received a jail sentence for speaking against the war. In all, about 1500 persons were jailed for their antiwar views.

ACTIVITY

Objective: To identify issues and questions.

Divide the class in half. Have the first group create a propaganda campaign for the Allies, including posters, handbills, newspaper stories, and cartoons. Advise them that they can use songs like George M. Cohan's "Over There!" and slogans like "make the world safe for democracy." Then have the second group portray a group of German-Americans during World War I. While the first group is creating propaganda, the second group should write a brief paragraph about how they feel having their loyalties questioned. When the propaganda is done, have the second group evaluate it and explain which items are fair and which are not.

Americans on the Battlefront

In June 1917 the first American troops arrived in France. Their commander was General John J. Pershing, known as Black Jack because he had commanded all-black troops. Pershing wanted the Americans to fight as separate units. He resisted using American troops simply as replacements for Allied losses. By the spring of 1918, American forces were ready to help turn the tide of battle.

The arrival in England of "Pershing's Crusaders"—fresh, if untested, American troops—boosted the morale of war-weary Europeans.

The destroyer USS *Allen* escorts the troopship USS *Leviathan* across the North Atlantic in 1917. Safe delivery of soldiers and goods was a major problem for the navy.

Role of the Navy. Naval action in World War I was a contest between Allied ships and German U-boats. In early 1917 Germans were winning the battle for the seas. U-boat captains were sinking Allied ships faster than they could be built. Great Britain was running out of food.

Then William S. Sims, an American admiral, devised the *convoy* system. In this system, cargo ships traveled in groups escorted by warships. A convoy moved slowly, but its ships could be protected by destroyers. Destroyers were slim, fast warships that patrolled the edge of the convoy. They could destroy U-boats with explosives called depth charges.

American shipyards were busy night and day. They soon were building two ships for every one that was sunk. The war was being won on the production line no less than in the field. Furthermore, American and Allied shipping losses dropped sharply as the convoy system began to work.

Stopping the German Advance. In the fall of 1917, the government in Russia was overthrown in a revolution. As a result, Russia withdrew from the war. German troops, which were no longer needed in Russia, were shifted to France in the spring of 1918. They enabled Germany to mount a major attack on the western front. Once again the German army reached the Marne River. General Pershing offered American troops to Marshal Ferdinand Foch, the Allied commander, to stem the enemy tide.

In May and June of 1918, American soldiers turned back the Germans at Cantigny and at Château-Thierry. (See the map on page 500.) A short distance from Château-Thierry was a place called Belleau Wood. The wood, less than 2 square miles (5.1 square kilometers) in size, was a German stronghold. United States Marines attacked it in June. The marines suffered nearly eight thousand *casualties*, or troops killed or wounded, but they drove the Germans out.

In July 1918 the Germans attacked again along the Marne River. Again they almost succeeded, but eighty-five thousand American troops helped save Paris. Americans spearheaded a counterattack that stalled the German advance. The Second Battle of the Marne was over.

The Battle at St. Mihiel and the Argonne Forest. Next the Americans were given the job of reducing the bulge in the battle line at St. Mihiel. Early in September an American army of 550,000 attacked St. Mihiel from two sides. They gradually eliminated the bulge, and captured 15,000 German soldiers along with hundreds of guns.

In late September 1918, the Americans had to fight their way through the Argonne Forest. This battle was one of the fiercest ever fought by Americans. About one in every ten soldiers was killed or wounded. All along the battlefront now the Germans were falling back. The end of the war was near.

A bombed-out church provides shelter for wounded soldiers during the American advance in the Argonne.

Armistice—the Central Powers Defeated. As the main German defenses along the western front were pierced, the Central Powers crumbled. Bulgaria surrendered in September, the Ottoman Empire in October, and Austria-Hungary in November. Germany was in a desperate situation. The Germans reorganized their government hoping to get better peace terms. Then they asked for an *armistice*, or cease-fire. The armistice was signed on November 11, 1918. The bloodiest and most costly war in world history to that time was over. Ten million people had been killed in battle. Even during the short time the United States had fought in the war, fifty thousand Americans had lost their lives.

Britain and France put the punishing of Germany at the top of their list of aims. The British believed they would never feel safe until the German navy was reduced. The French wanted to make sure a German army could never again invade their country. Both nations wanted to make Germany pay for the war. President Wilson, on the other hand, believed that harsh terms would lead Germany to seek revenge.

Wilson's Fourteen Points. President Wilson had given much thought to the kind of peace he wanted. In January 1918 he presented his "Fourteen Points" to Congress. These points contained his plan for building a peaceful world. The President was most interested in the last, or fourteenth point. It called for a "league of nations" that would protect the independence of all nations.

The Treaty of Versailles. The Allies did not like Wilson's plans, but they were exhausted from the long war. The peace talks were set to begin at Paris, in January 1919. President Wilson decided to go there himself and help write the peace treaty alongside the other Allied leaders. They included David Lloyd George of Great Britain, Georges Clemenceau of France, and Vittorio Orlando of Italy. These leaders and President Wilson became known as the "Big Four."

After months of hard work, the "Big Four" completed the treaty in June 1919. It contained much of what France and England wanted. Germany was made smaller. France regained the province of Alsace-Lorraine and the Saar Basin. The German navy was reduced. Germany was allowed to keep only a small army. Germany was forced to take sole blame for starting the war and to pay the enormous cost of

President Wilson (fifth from left) is seated between Lloyd George (left) and Clemenceau at the signing of the peace treaty in the magnificent Hall of Mirrors at the Palace of Versailles.

damages it caused. These terms enraged the Germans. The seeds of revenge had been planted exactly as Wilson had feared.

The Senate Rejects the League. In July 1919 Woodrow Wilson came home. He asked the Senate to approve the Treaty of Versailles, which provided for his beloved idea of a League of Nations. Wilson knew he was going to have a tough fight. One article in the League's charter required member nations to protect each other. Since only Congress can declare war, some senators were afraid that the League could, in effect, take away this power. Many also resisted the notion that the United States ought to have permanent international obligations such as the League might create. The United States, they said, ought to remain isolated from the world.

Wilson's most powerful opponent was Republican Senator Henry Cabot Lodge of Massachusetts. Lodge was chairman of the Senate Committee on Foreign Relations. Republican Senator William E. Borah of Idaho was another. Lodge and Borah were the leading supporters of isolation.

Senator Lodge was at the head of the fight to weaken the League. He wanted to keep the power to make war and

DISCUSSION

Review for the students the fact that there was a strong isolationist sentiment in the United States in 1919, which kept the nation out of the League of Nations. Have the students discuss whether the United States has an obligation to take part in world organizations like the league. Have them discuss whether the United States government should give up any of its powers (for example, to wage war) to such a body.

A car ride in March 1920 provided the public with one of its first—and last—glimpses of President Wilson following his stroke. Edith Wilson helped take care of presidential business during his illness.

peace decisions in the Congress. He proposed certain compromises with Wilson's views. Wilson refused to compromise. He said the Senate must accept the treaty as it stood.

The President decided to take his case directly to the people. In September 1919 he set out on a speaking trip. Addressing crowds in city after city, Wilson said that without the League of Nations, there would be another world war.

Late in September the President became ill in Pueblo, Colorado. The President's doctor and the First Lady, Edith Wilson, persuaded him to return to Washington, D.C. A few days later Wilson suffered a stroke. His left side became paralyzed. The First Lady allowed only a few close friends to see the President. She brought him important papers and guided his hand in signing them. Some people even said that she was acting as President.

Meanwhile, the Senate debated the Treaty of Versailles. In November 1919 it failed to ratify the treaty. Later, the Senate turned it down a second time. Wilson had failed to get the United States to join the League. Americans were unwilling to accept the responsibility of world leadership.

ANSWER THESE QUESTIONS

1. How did the United States raise a large army?
2. How did the United States raise money to pay for the war?
3. How did Britain and France want to treat Germany after the war? Why was Wilson opposed to punishing Germany?
4. What was President Wilson's plan for peace called?
5. Why were some senators against joining the League of Nations?

ANSWER THESE QUESTIONS

1. through the Selective Service Act (accept the draft)
2. higher taxes and the sale of Liberty Bonds
3. They wanted to punish Germany; Wilson believed that such treatment would cause Germany to seek revenge.
4. the Fourteen Points
5. They did not want to give up any congressional powers, such as the power to declare war; they did not want the United States to take on international obligations.

LAW AND THE CITIZEN

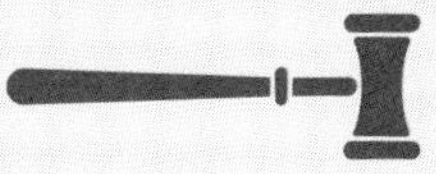

Freedom of Speech

Most Americans supported World War I. Some people, however, were very much opposed to it. Congress passed laws in 1917 and 1918 making it a crime to speak or write anything against the war. Interference with the sale of war bonds and speaking against the draft were also crimes. It was unlawful to use disloyal language in talking about the country, flag, or Constitution.

Among the people arrested for such crimes were Eugene V. Debs and Charles Schenck. Both of these men were leaders of the Socialist Party. During the war Debs made a speech before party members. In it he criticized the draft. He stated his opposition to the war with Germany. As a result he was arrested, tried, and convicted. After serving two years in prison, Debs was pardoned, or released from his sentence, by President Warren G. Harding.

Charles Schenck distributed thousands of leaflets opposing the wartime draft. He insisted that the draft was unfair. He also encouraged others to speak out against the draft. Schenck was arrested and tried. The court found Schenck guilty and sentenced him to prison. Schenck appealed, and the case of *Schenck v. United States* went to the United States Supreme Court.

The Supreme Court upheld Schenck's conviction in a unanimous decision. Justice Oliver Wendell Holmes wrote the decision for the court. He pointed out the difference between speech that must be protected and speech that could be dangerous to the country. Holmes wrote, "The character of every act depends upon the circumstances in which it is done. The most stringent [strict] protection of free speech would not protect a man in falsely shouting fire in a theater and causing a panic." He went on to say that Schenck's activities presented "a clear and present danger" to the nation. Holmes believed Schenck's leaflets might cause men to resist the draft. Such action on a large scale would harm the nation's war effort. Many later judges have based their decisions on Justice Holmes's "clear and present danger" test for free speech.

THINKING THINGS THROUGH

1. militarism, nationalism, imperialism 2. to defeat France quickly and then fight against Russia; the quick war in France became deadlocked in trench warfare 3. It did not have to fight and could trade with both sides. 4. American merchant ships often went to Great Britain; Americans often traveled on British ocean liners. Attacking American ships and foreign ships on

Chapter 20 SUMMARY

Europe went to war in 1914. On one side were the Central Powers, including Germany, Austria-Hungary, and Bulgaria. On the other side were the Allied Powers—Great Britain, France, Russia, and later, Italy.

At first, the United States remained neutral. Americans traded with both sides. Soon, however, German U-boats were destroying American shipping and lives. Then in 1917 the Zimmermann telegram increased bad feelings against Germany. In April 1917 the United States entered the war.

On the home front, an all-out war effort began. The draft was started to raise a large army. Citizens bought Liberty bonds to raise billions of dollars for the war. Americans produced more goods and food while using less. Blacks, women, and other minorities rallied to defend the nation.

The United States Navy used convoys to protect merchant and troop ships from U-boats. American troops arrived in France and began to turn the tide of battle. They helped turn back several German offensives in 1918. Finally in November 1918 the Germans agreed to an armistice.

President Wilson called for a just peace in his Fourteen Points. Britain and France, however, wanted to punish Germany. The Allies completed the Treaty of Versailles in June 1919. It set harsh terms for Germany but included plans for a League of Nations to keep world peace. At home, Wilson campaigned hard for the League, but the Senate rejected the treaty and the League.

Chapter 20 TEST

WORDS TO REMEMBER

Match each of the following words with its correct definition below.

e 1. militarism
g 2. diplomatic ties
a 3. trench warfare
b 4. propaganda
f 5. convoy
d 6. armistice
c 7. nationalism

a. fighting from long ditches dug in the ground
b. communications used to persuade
c. devotion to one's nation or national group
d. a cease-fire or end to combat
e. a strong emphasis on military preparedness
f. ships grouped together and escorted across the ocean by warships
g. formal international relations

THINKING THINGS THROUGH

1. What conditions caused tension in Europe before the war?
2. What was Germany's strategy at the beginning of the war? Why did it break down?
3. What advantages did the United States have as a neutral nation?
4. Why did Germany risk bringing the United States into the war by carrying on unrestricted submarine warfare?
5. Who were the "Big Four" and what countries did they represent?
6. What did President Wilson think might happen if Germany were punished?

RELATED MATERIALS

Duplicator/Copy Masters: Activities 42, 43; Quiz 43
Workbook pages 60-63

which Americans traveled risked the anger of the American government. **5.** Wilson, United States; Clemenceau, France; Orlando, Italy; Lloyd George, Great Britain **6.** Germany might start another war for revenge.

WORKING WITH SKILLS

1. the Allied Powers **2.** Germany could control the Baltic Sea, and the Ottoman Empire could control the Black Sea. **3.** the Allied Powers; Italy, France, Greece, and all of North Africa were Allies

---

WORKING WITH SKILLS

Study the map of Europe in 1914 on page 505. Then answer the following questions.

1. Which European alliance had more nations as members?
2. How could two of the Central Powers have blocked Russia's access to the seas?
3. Judging from the map, which alliance probably controlled the Mediterranean Sea? Why?

ON YOUR OWN

1. The illness of President Wilson raised questions about who should run the executive office when the President cannot. Read Article 2, Section 1, Clause 6 of the United States Constitution on page 243. Make a list of the officials who stand in line to take on presidential responsibilities. Then study the Twenty-fifth Amendment on pages 259–260. How does it clarify when other elected officials can act for the President? When was this amendment made part of the United States Constitution?
2. Look up President Wilson's Fourteen Points in an encyclopedia. Which points do you agree with? Are there any points that you do not agree with? Why?
3. A number of new weapons were introduced during World War I. Among these were tanks, Zeppelins, airplanes, poison gas, machine guns, and submarines. Use the card catalog to find a book about World War I and read about one of these weapons. Then write a paragraph or two explaining the role it played in the war. Also tell what steps were taken to protect people and property against the weapon. For example, soldiers used gas masks to avoid breathing poison gas.
4. The picture on this page shows French pilots practicing dropping bombs from airplanes just before World War I. After some thought, write a paragraph explaining how aircraft would change the nature of war—especially for populations behind the battle lines.

Chapter 21
THE ROARING TWENTIES

Chapter 21 focuses on the changes in American life after World War I and explains how the 1920s became known as "the Roaring Twenties." Lesson 21-1 discusses social change in American life, as automobiles provided more mobility, women won the vote and other freedoms, and organized crime capitalized on Prohibition. Lesson 21-2 describes the apparent prosperity of the 1920s, the growth of big business, and the extent of speculation on the stock market.

CONTENT OBJECTIVES

After completing the lesson, students will know:

- about the influence of automobiles and airplanes on American life
- about the leisure activities that became popular in the 1920s
- how women's roles changed
- the problems caused by Prohibition
- about the Red Scare and discrimination against blacks and immigrants

VOCABULARY

assembly line: a system in which workers put together goods in stages
prohibition: the national effort to ban the production, sale, and consumption of alcoholic beverages
temperance: keeping from drinking alcoholic beverages
communism: an economic system in which the government owns the factories and other means of production
quota: a certain number of each group

21-1 American Society Changes

As you read, think about these questions:

What changes in American life took place during the 1920s?

What inventions influenced many of these changes?

How did the role of women change?

What problems troubled people during the roaring twenties?

Special Vocabulary assembly line, prohibition, temperance, communism, quota

In 1919 the doughboys were home from their "great crusade" in Europe. The American people looked forward to easier times during the 1920s. They believed that they deserved them.

Leisure Activities

Returning soldiers, as well as those who had stayed home, counted up the war's terrible cost in human life. Many Americans made up their minds to enjoy themselves in the years to come. For their part, American business people decided to give people exactly what they wanted—automobiles, airplanes, motion pictures, radios. What Americans seemed to want most of all during the 1920s was noise— the roar of motors, the roar of loud music, the roar of crowds. Perhaps this was why some have called this period "The Roaring Twenties."

Known affectionately as the "Tin Lizzie," the Model T could be almost totally assembled in just ninety-three minutes.

Automobiles. Nothing altered American life more than the automobile. In 1900 there were only about eight thousand automobiles registered in the United States. They were too expensive for most people to buy. By the end of the 1920s, there were over 23 million automobiles on the road. Average Americans owned practically all of them.

More than anyone else, Henry Ford put America on the road. In 1903 Ford formed the Ford Motor Company. He wanted to build cars that were cheap enough for the ordinary person to buy. Later he described his reasoning:

> The design which I settled upon was called "Model T." The important feature of the new model—which, if it were accepted, as I thought it would be, I intended to make the only model and then start into real production—was its simplicity. There were but four constructional units in the car—the power plant, the frame, the front axle, and the rear axle. All of these were easily accessible and they were designed so that no special skill would be required for their repair or replacement.

The Model T was built on an *assembly line*. On an assembly line, products moved past workers on tracks. Each worker performed a single job over and over. At the end of the track, the product was finished. Because the Model T could be assembled so quickly, it cost only $300.

The first regular airmail service began in 1918 with a flight between Washington, D.C., and New York. Here mail is transferred from plane to train in Minnesota.

Soon automobile manufacturing became the most important American industry. Many workers built cars. Many others worked at manufacturing the glass, rubber, leather, and metals needed in cars.

Airplanes. For some years people had flown in balloons and gliders as a sport. Then two brothers from Dayton, Ohio—Orville and Wilbur Wright—became the first to fly a craft that was heavier than air. Their airplane was powered by a lightweight engine. On December 17, 1903, they got it into the air for twelve seconds at Kitty Hawk, North Carolina. The air age had begun.

World War I helped show how useful airplanes could be for military purposes. After the war, airplanes began flying passengers and mail. Commercial flying grew slowly.

Then a young American—he was twenty-five years old—by the name of Charles A. Lindbergh decided to fly across the Atlantic Ocean. He had his eyes on a $25,000 prize that a New Yorker was offering to the first flier who crossed the ocean nonstop to or from New York. Some business people in St. Louis had helped him buy and equip a suitable plane, which he named *The Spirit of St. Louis*. On May 20, 1927, Lindbergh took off from Long Island, New York, for Paris, about 3600 miles (5760 kilometers) away. Thirty-three and a half hours later, he put his plane down at the Paris airport. Wildly cheering crowds greeted him. People all over the world thought of Lindbergh as their hero. They called him "Lucky Lindy."

The stories of America's two most famous aviators had very different endings. Charles Lindbergh became an adviser to the airplane industry through the days of supersonic jets. Amelia Earhart vanished over the Pacific Ocean in 1937 while trying to fly around the world alone.

Lindbergh's achievement convinced Americans that there was a future in air travel. In 1927, 8661 passengers traveled by air. The next year the number jumped to 47,800. In 1930 United Airlines was formed, creating the first transcontinental air route. Rival organizations that became TWA and American Airlines came into being soon afterward.

Women also pioneered the skyways. Amelia Earhart was the most famous woman in the skies. Earhart was the first woman to fly across the Atlantic, first to fly it alone, and the first to fly alone from Hawaii to the West Coast.

Movies. Motion pictures had been invented in the late 1800s. In the early 1900s movie makers began to make long movies with plots rather than just scenes with action.

Going to the movies became a favorite pastime of Americans in the 1920s. They went to "movie palaces" where they could see silent pictures. Piano or organ players provided mood music to match the action on the screen. Performers such as Clara Bow and Rudolph Valentino became idols to millions of fans. Then in 1927 a new movie revolutionized the film industry. It was *The Jazz Singer*—the first talking picture. "Talkies" were an immediate sensation. Their stars became public heroes whose doings off as well as on the screen became everybody's business.

Radio. In the 1920s Americans also fell in love with the radio. Millions of Americans listened to programs such as "The Happiness Boys," "The A & P Gypsies," and "Roxy and

Through the magic of radio, John Coolidge and some neighbors listen to his son, President Calvin Coolidge, accept the nomination of the Republican Party in 1924.

His Gang." Also for the first time, millions of people heard their leaders speak. President Calvin Coolidge became the first President to broadcast an inaugural address—on March 4, 1925. By 1929 nearly half of America's homes had radios.

Radio stations made their money by selling air time for commercials. Station WEAF in New York broadcast the first such commercial in 1922. The National Broadcasting System was formed in 1926. Others followed, as broadcasting became big business.

ACTIVITY

Objective: To use reference materials

Divide the class into five or six groups. Have each group produce a ten-minute radio show on one of these topics: silent films, Babe Ruth's baseball career, Langston Hughes's poetry, or Bessie Smith's music. Have the students do research on their chosen topic, and ask them to make their presentations informative as well as interesting. If possible, obtain and play for the class beforehand a sample of an actual 1920s radio broadcast to give them an idea of the style that was used.

Sports. More Americans than ever before followed sports in the 1920s. The radio helped create new fans. Baseball was the "national pastime." The greatest figure was George Herman Ruth—the legendary "Babe"—who revolutionized the game with his home-run hitting. But every sport had its giants: golf had Bobby Jones; football, "Red" Grange; boxing, Jack Dempsey; and tennis, Bill Tilden and Helen Wills.

The Arts. The arts also had many stars during the 1920s. Three authors notably captured the spirit of the times. F. Scott Fitzgerald showed what upper-class society was like in *The Great Gatsby*. Sinclair Lewis portrayed life in small towns of the Midwest in *Main Street* and *Babbitt*. Ernest Hemingway wrote about the effects of the war on young Americans in *The Sun Also Rises*.

In the 1920s the arts flourished in Harlem, the black community of New York City. This period is known as the Harlem Renaissance, or revival. Langston Hughes was a leading poet of the Harlem Renaissance. He published *Weary Blues* in 1926. In this collection of poems, Hughes expressed the sadness that many blacks felt about their lives.

One of the greatest contributions that black people have made to American art is the music known as jazz. It became popular generally in the 1920s. For this reason, the period is sometimes called "The Jazz Age." Jazz combined African and European influences to produce a truly American form of music. Most of all, jazz featured lively, irregular rhythms. In one style of jazz called the blues, singers related sad stories through slow, soulful melodies. Black performers, including Louis Armstrong, Eubie Blake, and Bessie Smith, became outstanding jazz artists.

The Missourians were typical of the jazz bands that flourished in the 1920s. Bessie Smith, however, was one-of-a-kind because of her distinctive voice and singing style.

New Roles for Women

Women gained new freedom and independence in the 1920s. They joined the work force in larger numbers than ever. Many freed themselves from restrictions that society had long placed on women.

Women Win the Vote. Women had been campaigning for suffrage, or the right to vote, since the mid-1800s. During World War I the cause of woman suffrage received an added boost. Millions of women had worked hard to help win the war. Politicians realized that the time had come to grant women their full rights as citizens.

In 1919 Congress passed an amendment to the Constitution at last giving women the right to vote. By 1920 three fourths of the states had ratified what then became the Nineteenth Amendment. This amendment said that neither the federal government nor any state may deny a woman citizen the right to vote merely because she is a woman.

Unlike the man on this 1926 cover of *Life* magazine, most older people thought they had little to learn from flappers.

Wider Freedom for Women. Some young women led the way in breaking with traditional roles. Called "flappers," they had their hair bobbed, or cut short, and wore short dresses. They learned how to drive automobiles. They listened to jazz and danced the Charleston. The flappers shocked many of the older generation who shook their heads in amazement.

Wider freedom for women took other, more serious forms. Many families were able to have new inventions like refrigerators and washing machines. These appliances shortened the work day for homemakers. Women joined the work force in greater numbers than ever before. Many had to work in order to help support their families. Others volunteered their time to charity work.

In the past, most women who worked outside the home were factory hands. By the 1920s women were taking other kinds of jobs, too. Many became secretaries. School teaching had become a profession open to women in increasing numbers. Other opportunities were opening, however slowly. Women earned one third of all graduate degrees in the 1920s. Nevertheless, few women were able to obtain high paying jobs.

Social Problems

The 1920s were exciting and prosperous for many Americans. Behind the glittering appearance, however, lay serious social problems.

Prohibition and Crime. Some of these problems grew out of the *prohibition* movement, the national effort to ban the production, sale, and consumption of alcoholic beverages. The movement had started with the crusade for *temperance* in the United States in the 1830s. Temperance means keeping from drinking alcoholic beverages. Some women's groups had worked hard for temperance.

By World War I nineteen states had adopted prohibition. In 1919 the nation as a whole adopted it in ratifying the

DISCUSSION

Have the students discuss prohibition and how organized crime profited from it. Have them talk about whether government can or should make legislative changes in the ways people live. To stimulate debate, ask students if government has a responsibility to deal with the problems caused by drinking, such as drunk drivers.

By 1933, public opinion agreed with these antiprohibition marchers. The Twenty-First Amendment, ending prohibition, was ratified in December of that year.

Eighteenth Amendment. This amendment forbade "the manufacture, sale or transportation of intoxicating liquors."

Rural Americans generally supported prohibition. Most city dwellers did not like the law. Americans who wanted to, easily found ways to get around prohibition. People called bootleggers illegally sold liquor that had been smuggled into the country or made in secret. Some made alcoholic beverages at home. Others did their drinking at secret clubs called "speakeasies," where "booze" was sold illegally.

Bootlegging was highly profitable. Organized crime soon began to take it over. Rival gangs competed for the illegal liquor market in violent struggles. Often gangsters sought protection from the law by making deals with dishonest public officials.

The automobile greatly aided organized crime and helped make it a national problem. The Bureau of Investigation of the Justice Department was expanded in the 1920s to deal with the crime that prohibition caused. The Bureau later became the Federal Bureau of Investigation.

Rise of Intolerance. Black people were disappointed after the war "to make the world safe for democracy." The returning black veterans found an America brimming with intolerance. Race riots broke out in many American cities in the summer of 1919. In addition, the Ku Klux Klan (see page 392) was reborn in 1915. The new Klan was as violent as the one that had terrorized blacks after the Civil War. Besides blacks, the Klan turned its hatred on Catholics, Jews, foreigners, and minorities in general.

As you have read, a revolution took place in Russia during World War I (see page 510). The new rulers established a government based on *communism*, an economic system in which the government owns the factories and all other means of production. The communists aimed to spread their revolution all over the world. Many Americans reacted with deep concern. Some business leaders blamed communists for starting labor strikes in 1919. Then came a wave of bombings by anarchists in 1919 and 1920. People began to believe that the bombings were part of a plot by communists to overthrow the government.

The public's fear of communist plots was called the "Red Scare." Attorney General A. Mitchell Palmer insisted that communists were planning to destroy America. His agents rounded up and arrested thousands of foreigners. Some of them were sent out of the country for reasons that were very hard to defend. In time the fear of communists died down. Most of those arrested by Palmer were released.

Restriction of Immigration. Some Americans feared that millions of people would come to the United States. They wanted America to close its doors to immigrants. Congress responded by placing limits on the number of immigrants to the United States. It set national *quotas* for immigrants. This means that only a certain number of each group could come to America. Countries in northern and western Europe received large quotas. Those in eastern and southern Europe received small ones. Congress excluded Asian and African people altogether. By 1929 Congress was allowing only 150,000 immigrants into the United States per year, less than one quarter the number of just eight years before.

Immigration laws did not apply to Canadians or Latin Americans. Indeed, during the 1920s, many Mexicans came to the United States. A revolution in Mexico caused over 450,000 Mexicans to become American immigrants.

ANSWER THESE QUESTIONS

1. by using an assembly line to produce cars cheaply
2. by becoming the first person to fly solo nonstop across the Atlantic Ocean
3. gave women the right to vote
4. secretary, teacher, and other professions
5. helped lead to growth of organized crime, paved the way for violence among criminals and bribery of public officials

ANSWER THESE QUESTIONS

1. How did Henry Ford help make it possible for average Americans to own automobiles?
2. How did Charles Lindbergh become a hero to Americans?
3. What did the Nineteenth Amendment do?
4. What jobs did women begin to fill during the 1920s?
5. What were some of the bad effects of prohibition?

"Fats" Waller

PEOPLE IN AMERICA

Thomas Wright "Fats" Waller was born in Harlem on May 21, 1904. His parents had moved from Virginia to New York City to provide their children with more opportunites. They hoped their son Thomas would become a minister. For this reason, they encouraged his early love of hymns and music. They sacrificed to buy him a piano.

Waller became the pianist for his elementary school. To celebrate the honor, his father took him to Carnegie Hall to hear the great Polish pianist, Ignace Paderewski. The young boy never forgot the thrill.

One day Waller bought a ticket to the local movie house, the Lincoln Theater. The silent film did not interest him nearly as much as the live music that accompanied it. He moved up for a closer look at the piano player. Soon Thomas was a regular at the theatre. He would watch the hands of the piano player and then go home and play the same piece.

Because of his hefty size, Thomas was given the nickname "Fats" by schoolmates. One day the manager of the Lincoln Theatre offered Fats a chance to fill in for the regular piano player. Fats loved performing. The audience encouraged him by yelling "Make it rock, Fats! Make it rock!" He knew that he wanted to be a professional musician.

Living in Harlem after World War I, Fats could not help but be influenced by jazz. It was lively and exciting music. Soon Fats was considered an excellent jazz piano player. By 1924, he was a well-known musician in Harlem.

In the 1920s, Fats recorded over 100 songs. His music was regularly played over the radio. He traveled not only in the United States but also in Europe. His personality and musical talent made him famous.

Fats also helped write several Broadway shows. The most famous was *Hot Chocolate*, which opened in 1929. The show included his popular song, "Ain't Misbehavin'."

During the 1930s, his popularity soared. He appeared in the movie *Stormy Weather*. Fats looked forward to enjoying the wealth which his career was finally reaping. Unfortunately, he never got the chance. He died on his way home to New York from California in 1943. He left behind a wealth of songs and recordings for all Americans to enjoy.

CONTENT OBJECTIVES

After completing the lesson, students will know:

- about the growth of the consumer economy and consumer credit
- that farmers and workers did not benefit from the new prosperity
- about the Teapot Dome scandal
- how Americans made fortunes on paper in the stock market

VOCABULARY

consumer: a person who spends money on goods or services

standard of living: the total amount of goods and services that an individual or group consumes

credit: a system of buying goods and paying for them later

stock market: a place where shares of stock in companies are bought and sold

21-2 Republicans In Power

As you read, think about these questions:

Why did Americans buy so many consumer goods during the 1920s?

Which groups of people did not share in the prosperity of the 1920s?

Why did so many average Americans become speculators in the stock market?

What signs that the economy was not strong appeared by 1929?

Special Vocabulary	consumer	credit
	standard of living	stock market

Three Republicans in a row—Warren G. Harding, Calvin Coolidge, and Herbert C. Hoover—served as President during the 1920s. These Presidents were not strong leaders like Wilson and Roosevelt. They generally believed that government should do as little as possible. They maintained that government must not interfere with business. They were sympathetic to the problems of farmers, but, in general, they ignored the needs of labor.

The Republicans won a smashing victory in the election of 1920. It brought Harding to the presidency with more than sixty percent of the popular votes. People were tired of war and progressive causes, tired of active chiefs like TR and Wilson. Harding promised a return to "normalcy." He had made up the phrase. It sounded like a promise to go back to simpler times.

The Postwar Economy

The time of the Republican Presidents was one of general prosperity. After a short postwar setback, business boomed. The amounts of goods and services produced increased sharply compared to before World War I. Companies making automobiles, household appliances, and building materials enjoyed especially rapid growth.

For millions of American citizens things kept getting better. There were some important exceptions, however, including particularly farmers, unskilled workers, and coal

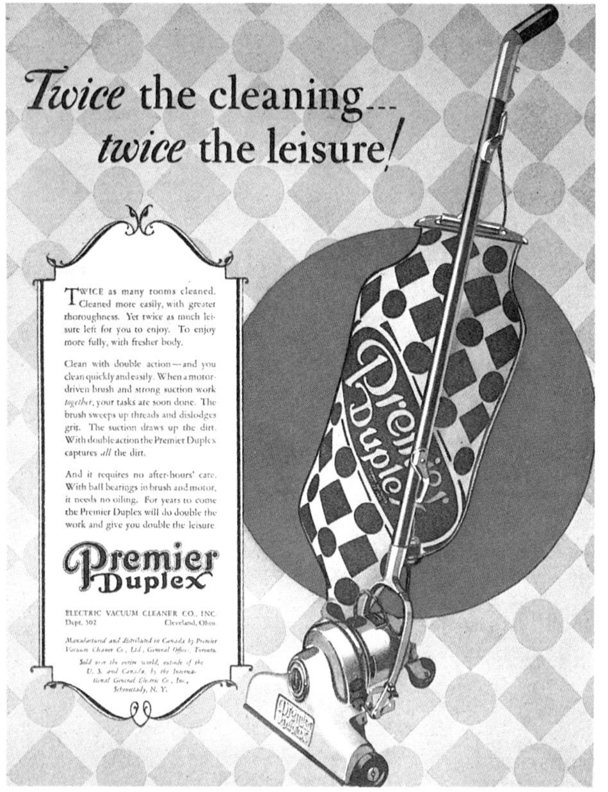

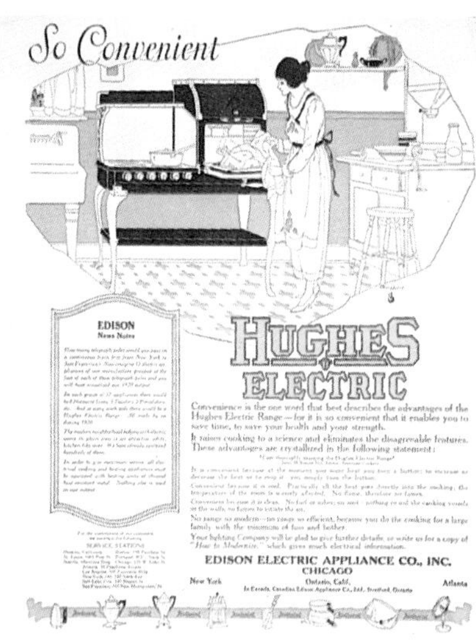

The power of advertising in magazines and on radio helped to heighten the demand for more consumer goods during the 1920s.

miners. Black people also failed, for the most part, to share in the good times.

Consumer Economy. People can either save, invest, or spend income. A person who spends money on goods or services is called a *consumer*. During the 1920s America became a nation of consumers.

People's incomes were increasing steadily. By 1929 the total income of Americans was $30 billion higher than it had been in 1920. Many workers chose to use their extra income to buy consumer goods. These are goods—such as automobiles or clothing—that consumers use. Thanks to inventions and mass production, many more consumer goods were available in the 1920s than ever before. Millions of people wanted items like automobiles and radios. They also wanted washing machines, electric stoves, and refrigerators.

Factories turned out more goods as people consumed more. Manufacturers used the assembly line and new electrical machinery to produce whatever Americans wanted. They put lessons learned on World War I production lines to work. The map on page 530 shows the locations of industrial areas in the United States in 1919.

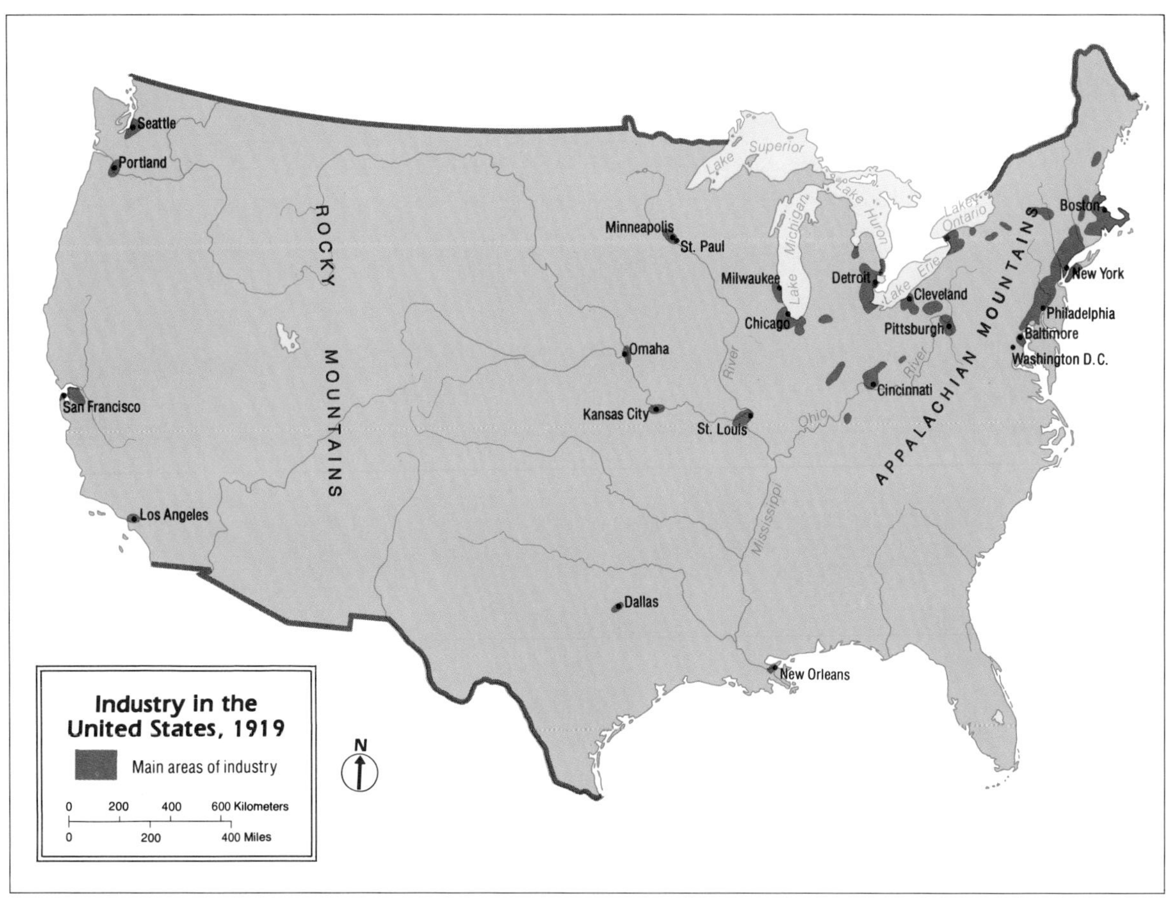

This map shows the main industrial centers of the United States in 1919. What geographical characteristic do almost all of them have in common?

They are located on a body of water.

Americans achieved a higher *standard of living* in the 1920s than ever before. The standard of living is the total number of goods and services that an individual or group consumes. Not everyone in the United States shared in the growing wealth. Taken as a whole group, however, Americans were living very well.

Consumer Credit. People bought consumer goods beyond the limits of their income in the 1920s. They were able to do so by using *credit,* the system of buying goods and paying for them later. In return for this privilege, the buyer pays interest on the amount of the purchase.

Credit, wisely used, has advantages. It increases the consumer's purchasing power and helps producers increase sales. Credit has disadvantages, too. Sometimes consumers buy too much on credit. By 1929 credit had gotten out of hand. Consumer debt was a staggering $75 billion. Consumers were betting that times would stay good and that they would always have their jobs.

The system of buying on credit raised false hopes for the good life among people who could not afford the new luxury items.

Workers and Farmers. The groups who were left out of the good times felt shortchanged and angry, because they saw so clearly what they were missing. The average worker's wages were increasing only slowly. Unions were weak and hard to organize. In 1919 about four million workers had gone on strike for higher wages. These strikes had met with strong opposition. A steel strike had been broken by force. Meat packers, textile workers, and railroad workers all had had their wages cut.

Farmers were also greatly discouraged. They had to continue to pay for land they had bought during the war at high prices even though the return on their crops had fallen sharply. Many were deep in debt.

Blacks were not hopeful about the future. In the South they worked mostly at low-paying farm jobs. The migration of blacks to northern and western cities continued. About 500,000 blacks left the South in 1923. They did not always find work where they went. By 1929 more blacks were unemployed than any other group.

Big Business and Government

During the 1920s many Americans respected business. They felt that business leaders were responsible for the nation's prosperity. Many people could agree with President Coolidge's statement: "The business of America is business."

The Business of Government. Presidents Harding and Coolidge tried to make running the government more businesslike. They believed in spending as little government money as possible.

In 1921 Harding appointed Andrew Mellon to be secretary of the treasury. Mellon, a Pittsburgh millionaire, believed taxes should be cut to encourage business. Between 1924 and 1929 Congress cut taxes substantially. Business leaders and wealthy people were especially pleased.

In 1921 the Congress set up a Bureau of the Budget within the Treasury Department. It allowed the government to compare its income with the money it spent. The United States now had its first national budget system.

Warren G. Harding was the first President to be elected while a senator. His election was also the first in which all women could vote and in which the results were broadcast over radio.

Teapot Dome Scandal. Harding found it hard to say no to his friends. The President's weaknesses soon led to serious problems in his administration.

Some of the friends that Harding had appointed turned out to be dishonest. Scandals began to come to the surface. The worst of them was called the Teapot Dome affair. This scandal began in 1922, but Americans did not learn of it until 1924. Albert B. Fall, the secretary of the interior, had persuaded Harding to give him control of certain public lands in the West. These lands contained rich oil deposits that were reserved for the use of the navy.

One oil deposit north of Casper, Wyoming, was called Teapot Dome. Fall secretly gave oil companies drilling rights on the navy reserves at Teapot Dome and elsewhere. In return for his favors, the oil companies gave Fall money bribes. The plot was discovered, and Fall stood trial. The court found him guilty of taking a bribe and sentenced him to prison. He was the first Cabinet member in American history to be sent to jail.

Harding had become aware of some of the shady deals of his so-called friends. He knew that these people had betrayed him and the public. In 1923 the President went on a political trip to Alaska and the West Coast. He became ill and

DISCUSSION

Review for the class the facts of the Teapot Dome affair. Have the students discuss why it is wrong for a public official to profit from his position. Explain the concept of "public trust." Have the students discuss whether laws and regulations can keep public officials honest. Do citizens have to depend on the integrity of the individuals holding office? How do citizens obtain information about those individuals and what they are doing?

died on August 2 in San Francisco. Harding never knew of some of the worst wrongdoings in his administration.

"Silent Cal." When Harding died, Vice President Calvin Coolidge became President. People came to know him as "Silent Cal" because he was a man of few words. He was personally honest, stingy with his own money as well as the public's. He had an appreciation of hard work and simple virtues. Because people had confidence in him, he rescued the presidency and the Republican Party from the disgrace that Harding had brought them. Coolidge served as President for the remainder of Harding's term and was elected for a term of his own in 1924, with the slogan "Keep Cool with Coolidge."

Calvin Coolidge was a man of much common sense and few words. His most famous statement was "I do not choose to run for President in 1928."

Under Coolidge there was little government regulation of business dealings. The President believed that business would prosper if left alone. Sooner or later, everyone would share in business prosperity. As the good times spread, Republicans called them the "Coolidge prosperity." Coolidge also reduced government spending, and he worked to reduce the national debt. In 1920 the national debt had been more than $24 billion. By the end of the 1920s it had fallen to only about $16 billion. The national debt has never been that low again.

Like the stock exchanges, the exchanges where crops and other commodities were traded were busy in the late 1920s. These men are buying and selling cotton.

Prosperity and the Gambling Spirit

While Calvin Coolidge was hunting ways to save money, some Americans were spending as never before. Millions of them were investing, too. For many, no moneymaking scheme seemed too risky. They could not imagine being wiped out in a sudden downturn of the economy.

A feeling of optimism, or hope in the future, swept America in the 1920s. People believed that the average person could get rich—fast. Tomorrow, they were sure, would be better than today.

Objective: After completing this page, students should understand how to relate ideas to a main concept.

Relating Ideas to a Main Concept

In most speeches, there is one main concept that the speaker wishes to get across to the audience. Many of the ideas in the speech are offered to support the main concept or to explain the concept further. The following excerpt comes from a 1928 campaign speech by Herbert Hoover. Its main concept is Hoover's understanding of the American system.

> During one hundred and fifty years we have builded up a form of self-government and a social system which is peculiarly our own. . . . It is the American system. . . . It is founded upon a particular conception of self-government in which . . . local responsibility is the very base. . . . It is founded upon the conception that only through ordered liberty, freedom, and equal opportunity to the individual will . . . initiative and enterprise spur on the march of progress. . . .
>
> When the war [World War I] closed, the most vital of all issues . . . was whether governments should continue their wartime ownership and operation of many instrumentalities [means] of production and distribution. We were challenged with a peace-time choice between the American system of rugged individualism and a European philosophy of diametrically [completely] opposed doctrines. . . . The acceptance of these ideas would have meant . . . the undermining of the individual initiative and enterprise through which our people have grown to unparalleled greatness.
>
> . . . When the Republican Party came into full power, it went at once resolutely back to our fundamental conception of . . . the rights and responsibilities of the individual. Thereby it restored confidence and hope in the American people.

This speech became known as the "rugged individualism" speech. That phrase seemed to summarize Hoover's main concept—that the American system is based on the freedom of the individual and on local responsibility. Carefully reread Hoover's words and then answer the following questions.

1. How does Hoover relate his opposition to government ownership of business to his concept of the American system?

2. According to Hoover, how did the Republican Party restore confidence and hope?

Working with Skills

READING SKILLS

ACTIVITY

Objective: To relate ideas to a main concept

Have the students reread the section "Workers and Farmers" on page 531. Ask them to state the main idea of the text in a sentence. Then ask them questions about how the main idea is developed, such as (1) What happened in the steel strike? How does that reinforce the main idea? (2) What were many farmers paying for? (3) What kinds of jobs did most blacks have in the South in the 1920s?

ANSWERS

1. He says that government control of business would destroy the American system through the undermining of individual initiative.
2. by returning to a system based on the rights and responsibilities of the individual

RELATED MATERIAL

Duplicator/Copy Master Activity 44

THINKING THINGS THROUGH

1. It convinced people that there was a future in air travel. 2. Answers will vary but may include the independence of the flappers; more women at work, more women earning college degrees, the vote for women 3. revival of the Ku Klux Klan; the Red Scare; immigration quotas 4. because of the assembly line, production lessons learned during World War I, new electrical

Chapter 21 SUMMARY

The Roaring Twenties were a period of change. Automobiles altered ways of work and leisure. Radio and movies became part of the American scene. More and more people traveled by airplane.

People enjoyed many kinds of entertainment in the 1920s. Most of all, the black American music known as jazz captured the spirit of the times.

Roles of women changed in the 1920s. The Nineteenth Amendment gave women full voting rights in 1920. Many women joined the work force.

Prohibition began in 1920. It led to a rapid growth of organized crime.

Intolerance increased in the 1920s. The new Ku Klux Klan appeared after 1915. A "Red Scare" after World War I led the attorney general to arrest thousands with little or no cause. Also, Congress set tight limits on immigration after 1920.

The Republicans were in power during the 1920s. They favored business. Congress lowered taxes and reduced government spending. Scandals rocked the Harding administration, but Coolidge restored confidence in government.

The 1920s were boom times. American consumers bought many goods, often on credit. Blacks, farmers, and factory workers did not share in the prosperity.

A wave of optimism swept over America. Millions invested in the stock market. The nation elected Herbert Hoover President in 1928, expecting continued prosperity.

Chapter 21 TEST

WORDS TO REMEMBER

Choose the correct word from the following list to complete each sentence below.

a. prohibition
b. temperance
c. quota
d. consumer
e. standard of living
f. credit
g. stock market

1. A __d__ is a person who uses money to purchase goods and services.
2. By using __f__ people can buy goods and pay for them later.
3. A place where shares of stock are bought and sold is called a __g__.
4. People who consume many goods and services have a high __e__.
5. Congress set a __c__ to limit the number of immigrants who could enter the United States.
6. A person who practices __b__ does not drink alcoholic beverages.
7. Many city dwellers opposed __a__, which outlawed the selling and drinking of alcoholic beverages.

THINKING THINGS THROUGH

Answer each of the following questions.

1. How did Lindbergh's flight across the Atlantic in 1927 help the cause of air travel?
2. How did the roles of American women change in the 1920s?
3. What are some examples of the ways intolerance increased in America in the 1920s?
4. Why were factory workers able to produce more goods in the 1920s than previously?

RELATED MATERIALS

Duplicator/Copy Masters: Activities 44,45; Quiz 44
Workbook pages 64-66

machinery in factories **5.** advantages: allows people to extend buying power, increases sales; disadvantages: allows people to accumulate debts **6.** People were optimistic; they had had prosperity for almost a decade and thought that it would continue.

WORKING WITH SKILLS

1. state purchase and sale of liquor, agricultural relief, and the development of hydroelectric power **2.** Valid problems exist, but putting government into business is not an appropriate way of solving them.

---

5. What are some advantages and disadvantages of credit?
6. Why were people willing to take risks with money in the late 1920s?

WORKING WITH SKILLS

Read the following excerpt from Hoover's rugged individualism speech and then answer the questions.

> There has been revived in this campaign . . . a series of proposals which, if adopted, would be a long step toward the abandonment of our American system and a surrender to the destructive operation of governmental conduct of commericial business. Because the country is faced with difficulty and doubt over certain national problems—that is, prohibition, farm relief, and electrical power—our opponents propose that we must thrust government a long way into the businesses which give rise to these problems. . . . It is proposed that we shall change from prohibition to the state purchase and sale of liquor. If their agricultural relief program means anything, it means that the government shall directly or indirectly buy and sell and fix prices of agricultural products. And we are to go into the hydroelectric power business. In other words, we are confronted with a huge program of government in business

1. What three proposals by the opponents does Hoover oppose?
2. How does he relate his opposition to the main idea of his speech?

ON YOUR OWN

1. The 1920s have been called the golden age of sports. Sports stars won fame in boxing, baseball, football, swimming, tennis, and golf. Choose one of these sports and find everything you can about it for the period 1920–1929. Use encyclopedias and other books for your research. Then make a chronological list of the outstanding achievements in the sport during the 1920s. Some athletes and coaches of the period are given below to help you.

   Boxing: Jack Dempsey, Gene Tunney, Jack Johnson

   Baseball: George Herman "Babe" Ruth

   Football: Harold "Red" Grange, Knute Rockne

   Swimming: Clarence "Buster" Crabbe, Gertrude Ederle, Johnny Weissmuller

   Tennis: William Tilden, Helen Wills

   Golf: Walter Hagen, Robert Jones
2. Imagine that you are investing in the stock market in 1929. You buy $10,000 worth of stock on margin. To do this, you pay $1000 down, and your broker loans you the other $9000. Now imagine that stock prices fall suddenly. How much will you have to pay your broker if the stock value falls to $7000? to $5000? Now pretend that 999 other people have also bought the same amount of stock as you have on margin. How much money will come due if the value of $10,000 worth of stock falls to $7000? if it falls to $5000? Make a chart to compare the totals for yourself alone and for 1000 people.

Unit 7 TEST

WORDS TO REMEMBER

Match each of the following words with its correct definition below.

a. imperialism	e. temperance
b. isolationism	f. propaganda
c. foreign policy	g. consumer
d. quota	h. stock market

f 1. communications used to make people think a certain way

d 2. a specified share of a total amount

a 3. a policy of gaining control over other lands and peoples

g 4. a person who purchases goods and services

c 5. a plan of action a nation uses in dealing with other nations

h 6. a place where shares of stock, or ownership, in companies are bought or sold

b 7. the practice in which a country has little to do with other countries

e 8. refraining from drinking liquor

QUESTIONS TO ANSWER

Choose the letter of the word or words that correctly answer each question.

b 1. From what country did the United States purchase Alaska?
   a. Canada
   b. Russia
   c. Spain
   d. Great Britain

a 2. In what year was the Spanish-American War fought?
   a. 1898
   b. 1901
   c. 1896
   d. 1894

d 3. Which country did *not* belong to the Triple Alliance?
   a. Italy
   b. Turkey
   c. Germany
   d. Russia

a 4. Who was the most powerful American opponent of the League of Nations?
   a. Henry Cabot Lodge
   b. Woodrow Wilson
   c. Arthur Zimmerman
   d. Bernard Baruch

a 5. With which subject did the Eighteenth Amendment deal?
   a. prohibition
   b. woman suffrage
   c. civil rights
   d. the stock market

c 6. Which president said "The business of America is business"?
   a. Herbert Hoover
   b. Franklin Roosevelt
   c. Calvin Coolidge
   d. Warren Harding

b 7. Who was the first person to fly nonstop across the Atlantic Ocean?
   a. Bill Tilden
   b. Charles Lindbergh
   c. Amelia Earhart
   d. Langston Hughes

b 8. What is the lowest the national debt has been in this century?
   a. $10 billion
   b. $16 billion
   c. $30 billion
   d. $24 billion

RELATED MATERIAL
Duplicator/Copy Master Test 45-47

THINK THINGS THROUGH

1. the policy that allowed all nations to trade on equal terms with China 2. Latin America 3. militarism, imperialism, nationalism 4. Germany's policy of unrestricted submarine warfare 5. automobiles, airplanes, movies, radios 6. They felt that giving business free rein was good for the whole country. 7. workers, farmers, blacks 8. the spread of communism in other nations, labor strikes, anarchist bombings

PRACTICE YOUR SKILLS

1. a. a soldier (doughboy); label on soldier's helmet (U.S.) b. The cartoonist was saying that the United States was stronger than Germany. c. that Germany was trying to take over the world 2. a. Americans became a nation of consumers. b. Incomes were increasing steadily; consumers chose to spend extra income on consumer goods. c. The higher standard of living is a result of having more money to buy goods that people want or need.

THINK THINGS THROUGH

1. What was the Open Door Policy?
2. In what region of the world did Theodore Roosevelt use his "big stick" policy?
3. What were some major causes of World War I?
4. What led the United States to declare war on Germany in World War I?
5. What inventions began to change the way Americans lived in the 1920s?
6. What was the attitude of American Presidents toward business during the 1920s?
7. What groups of Americans did not share in the general prosperity of the 1920s?
8. What factors contributed to the "Red Scare" in the United States?

He Did.

PRACTICE YOUR SKILLS

1. In this unit you learned to interpret political cartoons. Study the cartoon on this page. Then answer the questions.
   a. The cartoonist uses Wilhelm—the German Kaiser, or ruler—to represent Germany. What does the cartoonist use to represent the United States? What clue is given?
   b. Why do you think the cartoonist has made the American soldier look bigger than the German Kaiser?
   c. What do you think is the cartoonist's attitude toward Germany's war aims?
2. In this unit you learned to relate ideas to a main concept. Reread the text section under the heading "Consumer Economy" on pages 529–530. Then answer the questions below.
   a. The main concept in this section is stated in the last line of the first paragraph. What is the concept?
   b. The second paragraph gives two facts about incomes that help explain how America became a nation of consumers. What are these facts?
   c. The last paragraph explains that Americans achieved a high standard of living during the 1920s. How is this idea related to the main concept of the section?

Unit 8
DEPRESSION AND WAR

Unit Eight examines the Great Depression, World War II, and the Cold War period. A brief description of the subject matter of this unit includes the following topics: a discussion of the stock market crash; a discussion of the rise of dictators in Europe; survey of World War II in Europe and Asia; an overview of Cold War policies; and a discussion of the attempted invasion of Cuba at the Bay of Pigs.

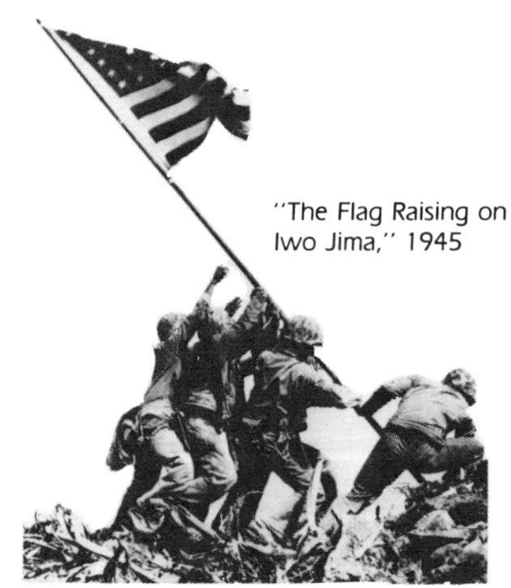

"The Flag Raising on Iwo Jima," 1945

A bank closing during the Great Depression

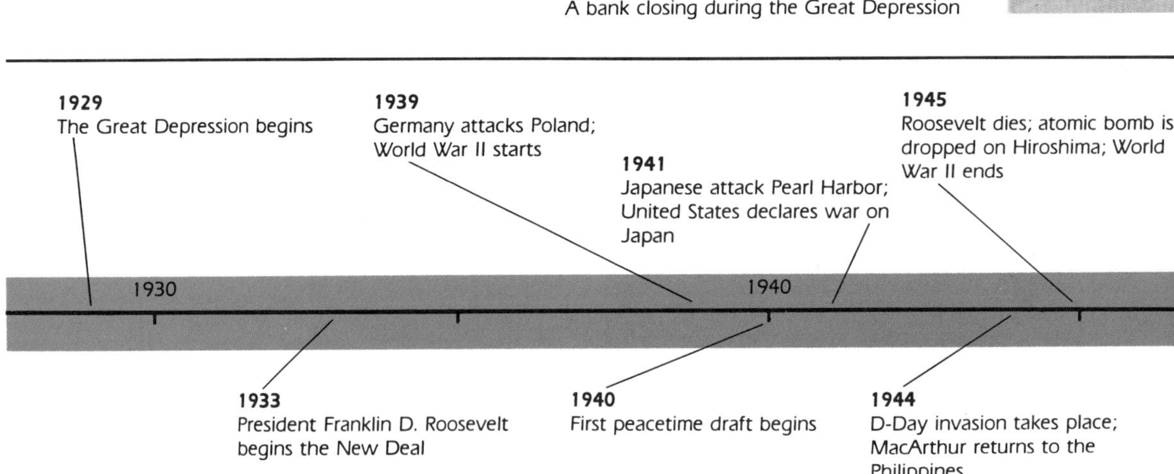
1929
The Great Depression begins
1939
Germany attacks Poland; World War II starts
1941
Japanese attack Pearl Harbor; United States declares war on Japan
1945
Roosevelt dies; atomic bomb is dropped on Hiroshima; World War II ends
1930
1940
1933
President Franklin D. Roosevelt begins the New Deal
1940
First peacetime draft begins
1944
D-Day invasion takes place; MacArthur returns to the Philippines

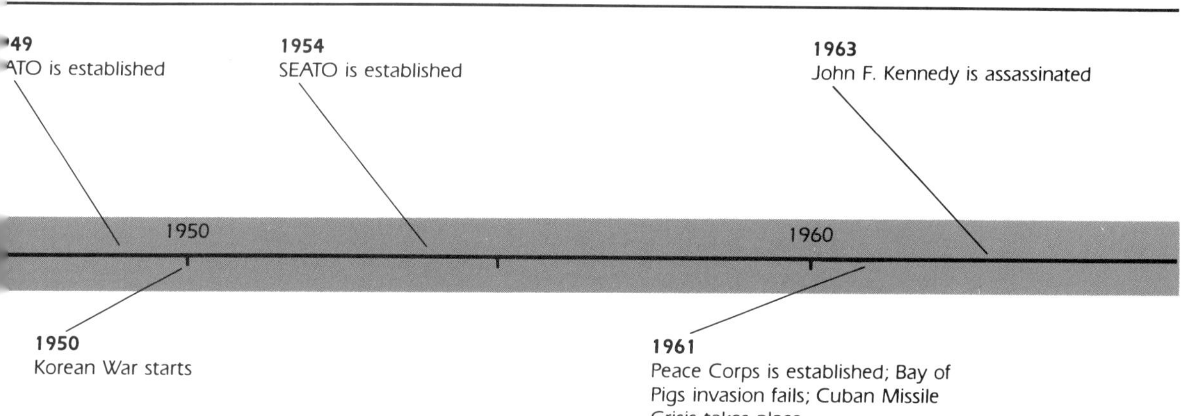
'49
ATO is established
1954
SEATO is established
1963
John F. Kennedy is assassinated
1950
1960
1950
Korean War starts
1961
Peace Corps is established; Bay of Pigs invasion fails; Cuban Missile Crisis takes place

Chapter 22
THE GREAT DEPRESSION

Chapter 22 covers the Great Depression, which lasted from 1929 to 1939. Lesson 22-1 describes the stock market crash, the drought that created a dustbowl in the Middle West, and how President Hoover tried to find solutions to these problems. Lesson 22-2 covers President Franklin D. Roosevelt's administration, several of his New Deal programs, and the signs of trouble in Europe.

CONTENT OBJECTIVES

After completing the lesson, students will know:
- the causes that most historians agree led to the stock market crash
- how the Great Depression affected people's lives
- that drought caused many farmers to leave their farms and to set out for California
- the measures Hoover took in his attempts to make conditions better

VOCABULARY

direct relief: money or a job given to people by the federal government

22-1 End of Prosperity

As you read, think about these questions:
What event marked the beginning of the Great Depression?
What were the causes of the depression?
What did President Hoover do to try to end the Great Depression?
How did the dust bowl make life even harder for many victims of the depression?

Special Vocabulary direct relief

Herbert C. Hoover took office in 1929 with high hopes. The 1920s had been a period of general prosperity. Most people, including the President, thought prosperity would surely continue. In his inaugural address, President Hoover said that the future was bright with promise.

Some people predicted difficulty ahead. They warned of a weakening economy. These people, however, were few in number, and their warnings went unheeded. Most Americans had faith in the words of the new President.

The Great Crash

Some people wondered how much longer the stock market could continue to boom. Early in 1929 the economy had showed some signs of slumping. Automobile sales had fallen off. Home construction also had slowed down. More goods had been produced than could be sold for profit.

Wall Street turned into "Disaster Street" on October 24, 1929, a day that become known as Black Thursday. The stock prices fell sharply as more than 13 million shares were sold. During the following days, the prices of stocks dropped so low that many stocks became almost worthless.

By the middle of November, investors had lost over $30 billion. People who had been millionaires a few weeks earlier had been wiped out. The stock market crash marked the beginning of a long and difficult time in American history. Americans entered a ten-year period (1929–1939) called the Great Depression. The causes of the depression were complicated. Most historians, however, agree on several.

First, the effects of World War I helped create the severe trouble. The Allied countries had had to borrow billions of dollars from the United States to win the war. In addition, for many years European factories had been producing war goods rather than products people could use. Europeans thus needed the goods American factories could make. Yet they had no money with which to buy them. Europeans wondered how they could pay their war debts to Americans *and* buy the goods they needed from American factories.

At first Americans attempted to keep trade going by lending more money to the Europeans. But the lending stopped when the Americans saw they could make greater profits in the stock market. The Europeans suddenly had to reduce their purchases from America. This caused many American factory workers to be laid off.

Second, trouble on American farms also hurt the economy. The nation's farmers were one group that did not share

For black sharecroppers in the South, the drop in farm prices meant a deepening of the poverty that had always been part of their lives.

ACTIVITY

Objective: To use reference materials

Thousands of banks in the United States failed in 1930, 1931, and 1932. The Banking Act of 1933 was intended to prevent massive numbers of bank closings in the future. Have the students research in the library the key provisions of the act. Have each student answer these two questions: What are reserves? What is the role of the Federal Deposit Insurance Corporation in protecting bank deposits?

in the prosperity of the 1920s. By the end of the 1920s, the average income of farmers was less than one third of the average other workers received.

During World War I the United States sold huge quantities of farm crops to the English and French. This trade benefited farmers. As a result many farmers borrowed money to buy additional land in order to raise more crops. After the war, however, European countries bought far less food from the United States as they returned to full production themselves. The prices for farm goods declined. The incomes of American farmers dropped, even though the cost of things they needed kept rising. The reduced buying power of farmers hurt the economy.

Third, too much credit, usually in the form of installment buying, was another factor contributing to the depression. Installment buying allowed people to pay for purchases over a long period of time. Payments were usually made in equal monthly amounts. More than two thirds of the automobiles sold in 1928 were bought this way. After the stock market crashed on Black Thursday, millions of people did not have enough money to make their installment payments. Banks and businesses could not recover the money that was owed them. These "bad debts" forced many to shut their doors.

Fourth, factories with modern machines produced more goods than people could buy. The joblessness caused by a slowdown in orders for manufactured goods by Europeans and by trouble on American farms further reduced buying power in America.

Hard Times

When the crash came, business leaders were afraid to build new factories or take a chance on new products. Storekeepers and other business people often found it impossible to borrow the money they needed to stay in business. Ben Isaacs, who was in the clothing business at that time, remembers how it was:

All of a sudden, in the afternoon, October, 1929 . . . I was going on my business and I heard the newspaper boys calling, running all around the streets and giving . . . [the] news: stock market crashed, stock market crashed. It came out just like lightning.

We lost everything. It was the time I would collect four, five hundred dollars a week. After that, I couldn't collect fifteen, ten dollars a week. I was going around trying to collect enough money to keep my family going. It was impossible. Very few people could pay you. Maybe a dollar if they would feel sorry for you or what.

We tried to struggle along living day by day. Then I couldn't pay the rent. I had a little car . . . I sold it for $15 in order to buy some food for the family. . . .

The lines at soup kitchens grew longer as more and more people found themselves unable to buy food for their families.

Unemployment. When people lost their money in the stock market crash, they stopped buying goods. Many factories closed or reduced the number of workers greatly. Millions of people lost their jobs. Many jobless workers suffered nervous illnesses. Their families suffered, too. President Hoover tried to encourage the nation, but conditions got worse. Fear had gripped the people.

During the worst of the depression, in 1932 and 1933, the country had between 12 and 13 million unemployed workers. In city after city, people lined up outside soup kitchens to get a handout of a cup of watery soup and a piece of bread. People of all types and backgrounds, including college graduates, sold apples on street corners for a nickel. (See the graph on page 552 for information on unemployment.) The song "Brother, Can You Spare a Dime?" caught the mood of the times.

Shanty towns where people, unable to pay rent, lived in wooden crates and cardboard boxes sprang up around large cities. Blaming the President for the country's condition, people called these collections of shanties Hoovervilles.

Hardest hit of all were blacks and Spanish-speaking people. Discriminated against because of their skin color, they were often the first to be fired and the last to be rehired. Women were also discriminated against. Many women who had work were criticized for holding a job that, it was said, could better go to a man.

"I'm counting the Kansas farms as they go by," said one Nebraska victim of the dust bowl.

The Dust Bowl. In addition to the hardship caused by the vast numbers of unemployed, large parts of the country suffered from a severe drought in 1930. As the ground dried out, the soil turned to powder. Strong winds whipped up dust storms as blinding as blizzards. A large area of the United States extending from the Texas panhandle to the Dakotas became known as the "dust bowl." (See the map on page 548.)

John Steinbeck, the novelist, wrote, "Every moving thing lifted the dust into the air; a walking man lifted a thin layer as high as his waist, and a wagon lifted the dust as high as the fence tops, and an automobile boiled a cloud behind it." Dust was everywhere. It seeped through tightly closed windows and doors. On a single day in the early 1930s, western wheat fields lost 300 million tons (270 million metric tons) of topsoil because of heavy winds. From the farmlands of the West, dust found its way 2000 miles (3200 kilometers) to the East Coast. Some even turned up on the decks of ships far out on the Atlantic Ocean!

Farmers in Kansas, Colorado, Oklahoma, northeastern New Mexico, and the plains of Texas were hit hardest. Some of the farmers sold or lost their farms and had to become tenant farmers. Tenant farmers work the land but do not own it. They pay rent or share their crops with the owner. Although this arrangement has a long history, it is usually very discouraging for the tenant. During the depression many farmers had no choice. (See the map on page 549.)

because the West is subject to longer droughts than the East

Some parts of the United States suffer from dry spells more than others do, as this map shows. Why are dust storms more likely to occur in the western part of the country than in the eastern part?

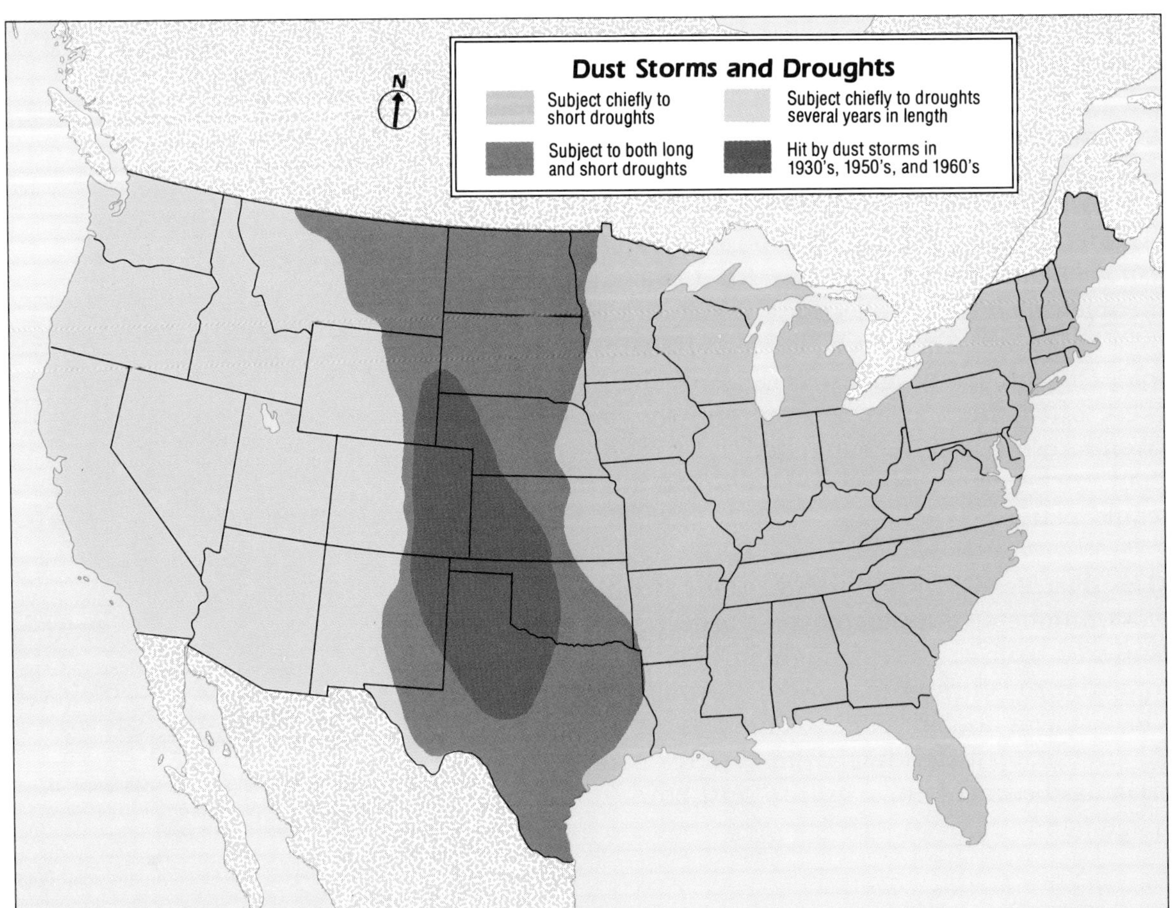

California Dream. Thousands of farmers felt hopeless. With their land ruined by the drought and with no chance of paying off their debts, great numbers simply left. Along with their workers, they became migrants.

Many of these migrant farmers headed for California. Word had reached them that the lush valleys of California offered ready employment. Many dreamed of making a fresh start there on the West Coast. They packed their automobiles or trucks with everything they could and set out.

For most of the migrants, the California dream became a nightmare. Jobs proved very scarce. The migrants moved from place to place and lived in camps along the roadside. When they did work, wages were low and the hours long.

For many migrant farmers, the journey to California was a long and difficult one.

Searching for Solutions. President Hoover told the country that prosperity was just around the corner. Past depressions had seemed to end by themselves. Hoover took what he believed was strong action. He met with business leaders to urge them to enlarge their companies and not to fire workers. He also called for lower taxes. He encouraged cities and states to create jobs by constructing public buildings.

four

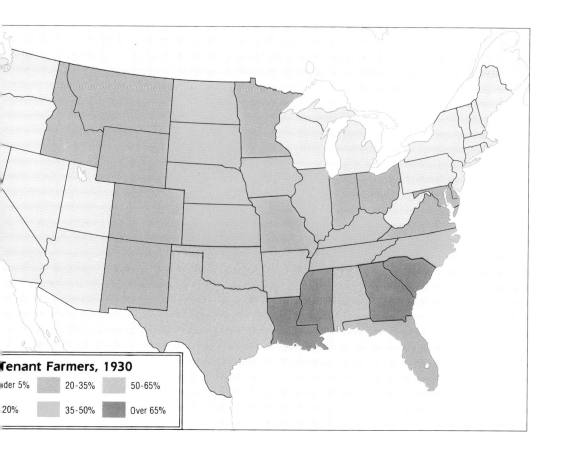

This map shows the percentage of farmers in each state who were tenant farmers in 1930. In how many states did tenant farmers make up more than sixty-five percent of the farm population?

enant Farmers, 1930

der 5% | 20-35% | 50-65%

20% | 35-50% | Over 65%

DISCUSSION

Have the students discuss some solutions that President Hoover tried. They should mention: Hoover's encouraging states and cities to create public construction jobs and to reduce taxes; his urging business and industry to expand and not to fire workers. Ask the students why these steps failed. Urge the students to think of other steps that could have been taken to alleviate the nation's economic distress.

The results Hoover hoped for did not come about. Business leaders spent as little money as possible, in order to stay in business. Cities and states tried to give relief to the unemployed, but this aid left little money for public construction projects.

The Reconstruction Finance Corporation. Late in 1931, the President recommended the establishment of the Reconstruction Finance Corporation (RFC). Congress voted for it immediately. The RFC provided loans to banks, businesses, and local governments. The aim was to aid the economy—particularly through construction projects. About $2 billion was provided through the RFC.

The government also tried to help farmers. Between 1929 and 1932 farmers' income dropped by fifty percent. Farmers were still producing great surpluses. The government bought and stored huge quantities of grain and other crops.

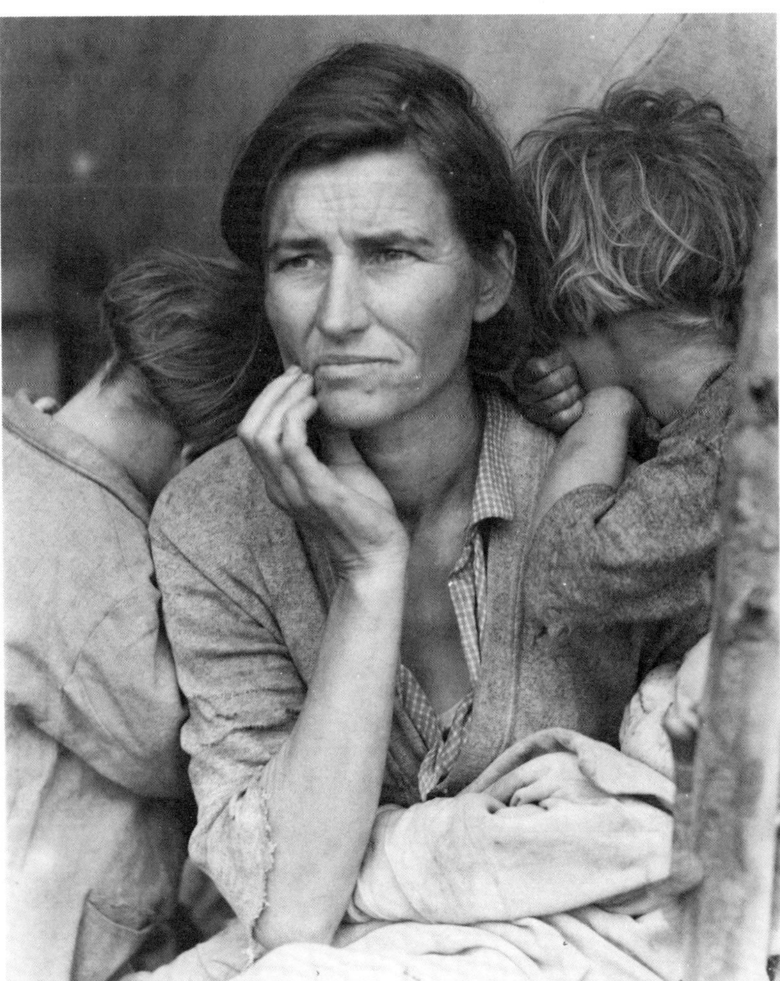

Dramatic photographs like this one by Dorothea Lange captured the expressions on the faces of poor Americans during the Great Depression.

Yet, it did not help raise prices for farmers. In fact, prices fell even lower as the surpluses increased. Wheat prices in 1932 were only about a third what they had been four years earlier. Corn was so cheap that many farmers used it for fuel.

The Bonus Marchers had fought to "make the world safe for democracy," but now they found their government unwilling to help them.

The Question of Direct Relief. An increasing number of people thought the government should provide *direct relief* for the jobless. Direct relief meant the federal government would give money or jobs to people. Hoover could not bring himself to accept this idea. He thought that private groups should help people. People in a position to help others had proved very generous. There appeared to be a limit, though, to what private groups could do to improve the economy.

City governments all over the country tried to help their suffering people. But many cities were practically broke. They could hardly pay their police officers, firefighters, and other city workers, let alone take care of the unemployed. States also helped, but they soon ran out of funds, too. Until the very end of his administration, however, Hoover resisted giving direct relief to people.

Bonus Marchers. In the summer of 1932 about 1500 veterans of World War I marched on Washington, D.C. They were seeking an immediate bonus. Ex-soldiers had been promised a sum of money, payable in 1944. Because of the hard times, these bonus marchers wanted the money paid sooner.

The demonstration, which eventually included nearly 17,000 veterans, was a peaceful one, but Congress and the President would not grant the marchers' wishes. After several weeks most of them left the city, but the stubborn ones remained. President Hoover ordered an army division to remove them. General Douglas MacArthur, the chief of staff, moved in with armed soldiers. They scattered the marchers—many with their families—with tear gas. This awful scene made the President less popular than ever.

ANSWER THESE QUESTIONS

1. What happened on the day remembered as Black Thursday?
2. How many Americans were unemployed during the worst period of the depression?
3. Which states were hardest hit by the drought of the early 1930s?
4. Who were the bonus marchers? What did they demand from Congress?
5. Why did President Hoover oppose giving direct relief to people?

ANSWER THESE QUESTIONS

1. The stock market crashed and the Great Depression began.
2. 12 to 13 million
3. Colorado, Kansas, New Mexico, Oklahoma, and Texas
4. World War I veterans who marched on Washington, D. C., in 1932; payment of the money they were due to receive in 1944
5. He believed that private groups—not the government—should help people

Objective: After completing this page, students should know how to make a line graph.

Working with Skills

Study Skills

Reading Line Graphs

In Chapter 17 you learned how to read and interpret two types of graphs—bar graphs and circle graphs. The graph on this page is an example of another important type of graph called a line graph.

A line graph provides a good way to show changes in quantity over a period of time. The graph below, for example, shows how the number of unemployed Americans changed between 1929 and 1939. The years are shown along the bottom of the graph, and the number of unemployed people appears along the left side. Points on the graph indicate how many people were unemployed during each year. These points are connected with a line to provide a picture of the overall trend of unemployment during the period from 1929 to 1939.

Use the graph below to answer the following questions.

1. How many people were unemployed in 1929?
2. How many people were unemployed in 1939?
3. In what year was the number of unemployed people largest?
4. After reaching its highest point, unemployment declined but then rose again. In what year did it reach its second peak?

UNEMPLOYMENT DURING THE DEPRESSION

Millions

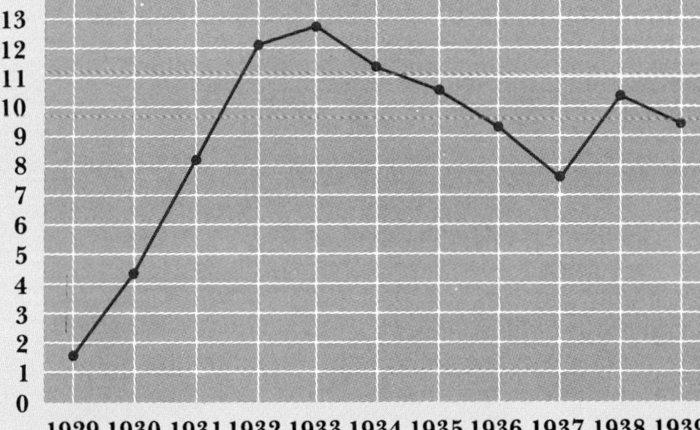

ANSWERS

1. about 1,500,000
2. about 9,500,000
3. 1933
4. 1938

ACTIVITY

Objective: To make a line graph

Have the students choose a stock from the New York Stock Exchange listings in a daily newspaper. Explain to them the meaning of the various numbers following the company's abbreviated name. Have students record the changes in their stock every day for one school week. Then ask them to draw a line graph to plot these changes. Provide a sample on the blackboard, using the price numbers as a vertical axis and the days of the week as a horizontal axis.

RELATED MATERIAL

Duplicator/Copy Master: Activity 47

22-2 Changes at Home and Abroad

As you read, think about these questions:

What types of programs did President Roosevelt propose to help solve the problems of the depression?

How did the New Deal expand the role of the federal government in the United States?

How did economic problems contribute to changes in the governments of other nations?

Special Vocabulary collective bargaining dictator appeasement

CONTENT OBJECTIVES

After completing the lesson, students will know:

- that President Franklin D. Roosevelt began his term with a positive spirit, a strong plan of action, and excellent advisers
- some specific facts about New Deal programs
- about international problems, economic and political alike, that developed into signs of war by the 1930s

VOCABULARY

collective bargaining: the process through which workers negotiate as a group with employers for better wages, hours, and conditions

dictator: a ruler who has complete control of a nation

appeasement: keeping peace by satisfying potential enemies at any cost

The depression hit Americans hard, but other peoples also suffered. The times were ripe for change, and important changes in government occurred both in the United States and in foreign countries.

The Election of 1932

By 1932 Herbert Hoover had lost the confidence of the American people. Many blamed him for the depression. Still, the Republicans renominated him. The Democrats chose Franklin D. Roosevelt. Four years earlier he had been elected governor of New York. In 1930 his reelection by a large vote had proved his popularity.

As Roosevelt traveled around the country, he spoke of plans to restore prosperity. In one of his speeches he pledged "a new deal for the American people."

Hoover said Roosevelt was dangerous. He insisted that Roosevelt's ideas would lead to the decay of America itself. Roosevelt's smile and hopefulness appealed to people everywhere. On election day Roosevelt gained an easy victory, winning forty-three of the forty-eight states.

Inauguration Day. On March 4, 1933, Franklin D. Roosevelt was sworn in as the thirty-second President of the United States. The cold, cloudy weather matched the mood of the past few years. In addition to the shivering crowd on the steps of the capitol, millions listened to his words on radio. No President had ever spoken to so many people at one time.

Roosevelt—the only child of a wealthy couple—is pictured at right as a teenager. On the way to his inauguration, Roosevelt barely spoke to Hoover, whom he disliked.

Roosevelt's strong voice rang out, "This is a day of national dedication." Then he declared with assurance, "Let me assert my firm belief that the only thing we have to fear is fear itself." He pledged to take firm steps to revive the stricken country. The United States, he said, must act as boldly as if it had been invaded by a foreign army.

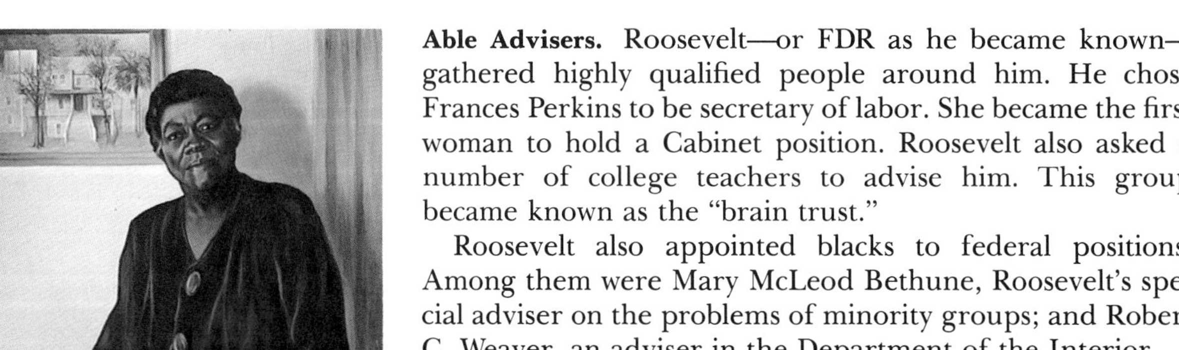

Able Advisers. Roosevelt—or FDR as he became known—gathered highly qualified people around him. He chose Frances Perkins to be secretary of labor. She became the first woman to hold a Cabinet position. Roosevelt also asked a number of college teachers to advise him. This group became known as the "brain trust."

Roosevelt also appointed blacks to federal positions. Among them were Mary McLeod Bethune, Roosevelt's special adviser on the problems of minority groups; and Robert C. Weaver, an adviser in the Department of the Interior.

The seventeenth child of former slaves, Mary McLeod Bethune founded the National Council of Negro Women.

The New Deal

Roosevelt wasted no time in launching his program to restore prosperity, which he called the New Deal. The program had three major goals—relief, recovery, and reform. The first goal was to give immediate aid to Americans in need. The second goal was to help restore prosperity to Americans. The third goal was to provide new laws that would prevent a severe depression in the future.

The First Hundred Days. Roosevelt's first action after taking office was to close all the country's banks for four days. He wanted to have experts examine their records. These experts were to make certain that only the healthy ones stayed in business. When most of the banks opened their doors again, the people had fresh confidence in the future. Some of the fear that had gripped them had begun to vanish.

Roosevelt persuaded Congress to act on his programs in record time. Within one hundred days of his inauguration, Roosevelt pushed several major programs through Congress. People often referred to New Deal programs by using only letters. They thus became known as "alphabet programs." (See the chart below.)

DISCUSSION

Have the students discuss the differences between the New Deal goals of relief, recovery, and reform. Have the students define these goals as they relate to the New Deal programs discussed in the text, especially the Civilian Conservation Corps, the National Recovery Act, the Tennessee Valley Authority, and the Social Security Act.

ROOSEVELT'S NEW DEAL PROGRAMS

Program	Initials	Date Begun	Date Ended	Description
Civilian Conservation Corps	CCC	March 1933	1942	Employed young people (18–25) to work on conservation of forests, parks, and reservoirs
Tennessee Valley Authority	TVA	May 1933	*	Provided electricity, flood control, conservation of land for seven southern states
Federal Emergency Relief Administration	FERA	May 1933	1935	Provided direct relief to needy
Agricultural Adjustment Administration	AAA	May 1933	1934	Paid farmers to destroy certain crops or not to raise them
National Recovery Administration	NRA	June 1933	1935	Set rules for business—weekly hours, hourly wages
Public Works Administration	PWA	June 1933	1939	Constructed hospitals, roads, and schools
Federal Deposit Insurance Corporation	FDIC	June 1933	*	Insured all deposits up to a certain amount in Federal Reserve Banks
Federal Housing Authority	FHA	June 1934	*	Insured loans on home repair or construction
Works Progress Administration	WPA	April 1935	1943	Employed workers for public construction; also paid artists, writers, and musicians
Social Security	SS	August 1935	*	Provided payments to the elderly, the blind, the unemployed, and orphans

*Still operating

The blue eagle of the NRA was a special symbol of hope in a dark time. It was the proud badge of people working together for democracy.

The Civilian Conservation Corps (CCC) was formed to put to work young people between the ages of 18 and 25. They made up the largest group of the unemployed. These people were sent outdoors, planting trees, fighting forest fires, building reservoirs, and cutting forest trails. For their work they received thirty dollars a month plus food, clothing, and shelter. Each member had to send twenty-five dollars home each month.

One of the most important programs started under Roosevelt was the National Recovery Administration (NRA). It was intended to help business and workers. The NRA sought to reduce unemployment, raise wages, reduce the number of work hours, and eliminate child labor. A committee was appointed to write codes, or rules, for business to follow. Manufacturers who followed the codes displayed a blue eagle for everyone to see. Parades, fireworks, and speeches greeted the beginning of the NRA. Business people became hopeful again.

Most New Deal programs were created to help the country's economy recover immediately. Some, however, would continue to affect the country for a long time. One such program, the Tennessee Valley Authority (TVA), was set up to control floods in the Tennessee Valley and to provide electricity. The Tennessee Valley covers large sections of seven southern states. The TVA's powers included the right to buy land, to construct dams, to build recreation areas, and to sell electricity.

Opponents of the TVA maintained that the government was hurting private business by going into business itself. Private electric companies complained that the TVA set rates too low to compete with. Whatever its weaknesses, however, the TVA did much to help the area. The dams it built prevented floods. People got electricity. Other conservation measures saved land and increased agricultural production.

Later Programs. In 1935 Congress created the Works Progress Administration (WPA) to provide work for the unemployed. During the next six years, the WPA spent $11 billion to carry out a wide range of projects. WPA workers built schools, roads, parks, playgrounds, airports, and football stadiums. Artists, writers, and musicians were paid to paint, write, or perform. WPA bands provided popular entertainment in elementary schools across the nation.

Also during 1935 Congress passed what Roosevelt considered the most important of all New Deal reforms, the Social Security Act. This act still affects millions of Americans. The Social Security Act provided monthly payments to retired Americans. It also gave states money to provide help to blind persons and orphans who required it. Another part of the law provided funds for the unemployed. Funds for Social Security came from taxes on workers and their employers.

The WPA helped keep alive the skills of artists who painted many murals like the one pictured here.

Advances for Workers. Under the Roosevelt administration, working conditions for large numbers of Americans improved rapidly. In 1935 Congress passed the Wagner Act, named for Senator Robert F. Wagner of New York, its leading sponsor. The Wagner Act gave workers the right to join unions and to practice *collective bargaining*. Collective bargaining happens when workers negotiate as a group with employers for better wages, hours, and conditions.

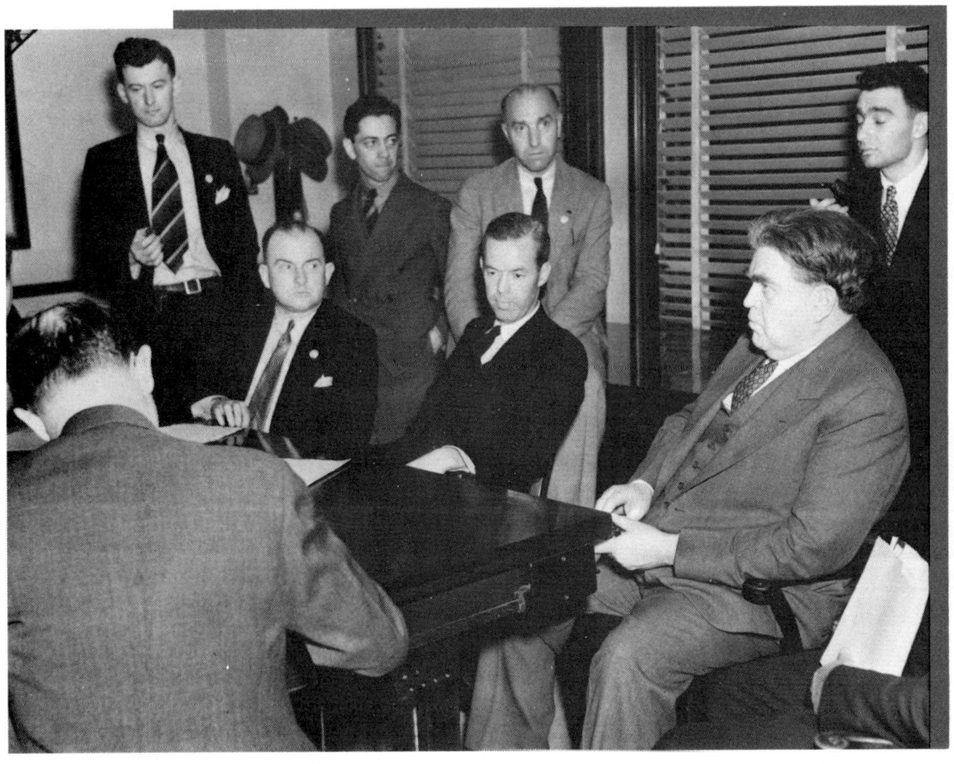

Labor leader John L. Lewis (seated right) learned about organizing at an early age. His father had been a miner and an active member of the Knights of Labor.

The Wagner Act encouraged the establishment of unions made up of all workers in an industry. The AFL, made up only of craft unions, opposed such organizations. In 1935 John L. Lewis, head of the United Mine Workers, helped form a group within the AFL to build up industry-wide unions. In 1938 this group broke away from the AFL and formed the Congress of Industrial Organizations (CIO). Many workers in the steel and automobile industries joined the CIO.

Following successful attempts to gain more benefits for workers, unions began to grow. Under the protection of the Wagner Act, other unions sprang up. By 1939 about 9 million workers belonged to unions.

The Election of 1936. Following four years of the New Deal, the Democrats enthusiastically renominated Franklin D. Roosevelt. He faced Alfred M. Landon, the popular Republican governor of Kansas. In his campaign, Roosevelt pointed to the accomplishments of his administration. These included relief for the jobless, help for the farmers and workers, and a legal guarantee of the right to join unions.

Republicans attacked the New Deal. They insisted that Roosevelt's program hurt private business. In addition, they criticized Roosevelt as one who enjoyed power too much. In the election, however, Roosevelt won all but two states, Maine and Vermont.

A Plan to Pack the Court. Shortly after his second inauguration, Roosevelt presented a plan to change the Supreme Court. He and others thought that the older justices on the Court were preventing progress. In 1935 the Supreme Court had ruled that the National Industrial Recovery Act, which had created the NRA, was unconstitutional. The Court similarly had struck down the Agricultural Adjustment Act in 1936.

Roosevelt wanted to add one new judge for every one over seventy years of age who did not retire. Even some Democrats strongly opposed the President's plan. They believed that the the President wanted to pack the court with people he could control. Roosevelt's plan failed, and in proposing it, he damaged his reputation.

International Problems

European and Asian peoples—many with fewer resources than Americans had—also looked for new leaders. Sadly, some of these leaders were opposed to and even hated democracy. They tried to unite their people by building powerful military machines and looking for enemies to wage war against. Italy, Germany, and Japan became international troublemakers and then peacebreakers.

Italy and Mussolini. Following World War I, there was much confusion in Italy. Soldiers could not find work. Industrial strikes were common. Poverty was everywhere. Italians looked to the leadership of a strong personality. Such a person was Benito Mussolini, who had been a teacher, a writer, and a soldier.

ACTIVITY

Objective: To analyze relationships

Have the class make a list of the qualities necessary for a strong leader and the qualities that make a dictator. Point out that there is often a fine line between the desirable qualities of a positive leader and the negative qualities of a dictator. Start a list on the blackboard with examples to make clear that good and bad can be two sides of the same coin—such as "Positive: strong opinions of what should be done" and "Negative: refuses to consider others' viewpoints."

Mussolini, a brilliant leader, used violence to gain power in Italy.

In 1922 Mussolini became prime minister of Italy. Soon he set himself up as a *dictator*, or a ruler who has complete control of a nation. Mussolini appealed to many Italians who dreamed of a new and powerful Italy. He believed he could make his country rich by taking over other lands.

Germany and Hitler. While Mussolini was rising to power in Italy, Adolf Hitler dreamed of a powerful Germany with himself as its leader. He brooded much over Germany's defeat in World War I. Germany lost the war, Hitler said, because of the enemies within the country. He picked on Jews and communists especially.

In fiery speeches, Hitler won to his side millions of Germans, promising them they would rule the world. His followers came to be known as Nazis. In the same month that Franklin Roosevelt became President of the United States, Hitler became chancellor (leader) of Germany.

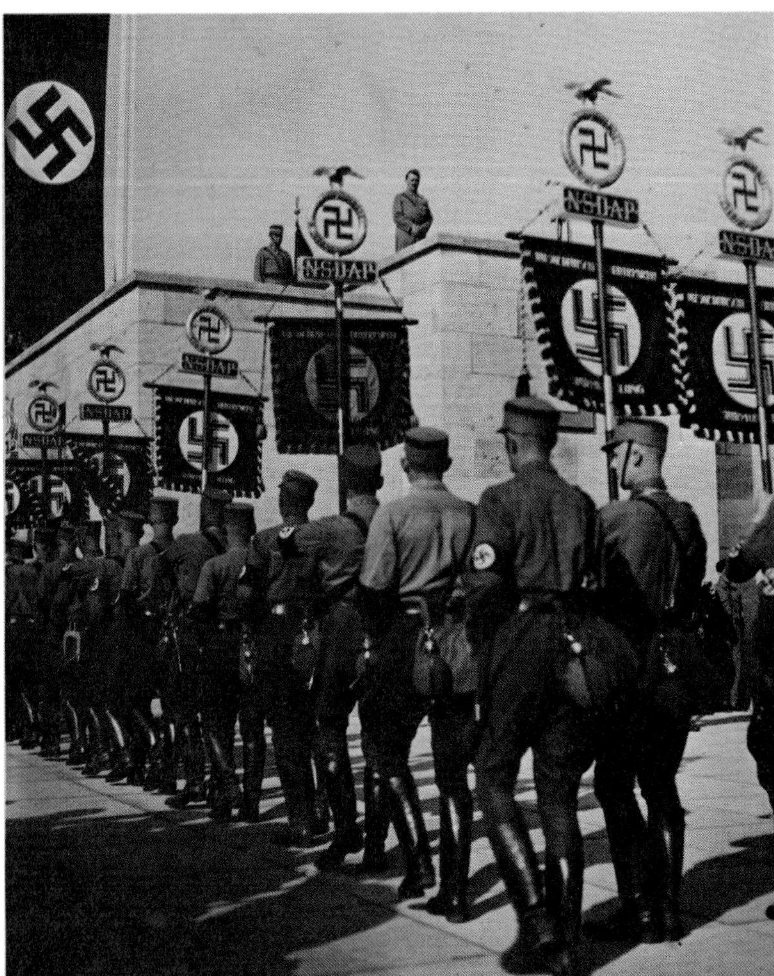

Hitler used military power as a substitute for any real solution to Germany's economic problems.

Stalin and the Soviet Union. While Hitler and Mussolini came to power in Germany and Italy, the Soviet Union was also undergoing vast changes. After communists overthrew the Russian czar in 1917, they changed the name of the country to the Union of Soviet Socialist Republics (USSR), or the Soviet Union. V. I. Lenin took control of the country and ruled as a dictator until his death in 1924. After Lenin died, Joseph Stalin, who had been the head of the Communist Party, forced his way to the head of the government.

Militarism in Japan. In the 1930s a group of army leaders became important in Japan. They wanted to rule all of Asia, but they lacked the raw materials necessary for building a strong military machine. To get these essential resources they intended to take over other countries that had them.

In 1931 Japan attacked and conquered Manchuria, a northern region of China. The military leaders soon laid plans for invading other territory. In 1937 Japan moved south from Manchuria. By the end of the 1930s, most of eastern China had been taken over by Japan.

Signs of War. The European dictators were also planning to take more land for their own countries. Mussolini's army invaded Ethiopia in Africa in 1935. Many countries denounced this move. No nation did anything about it, though, and the Ethiopians suffered a terrible defeat.

If a new general war started, Americans wished to stay out of it. The results of World War I were not what people had expected or hoped for. The war had not "made the world safe for democracy." When some European countries failed to repay their war debts, many Americans considered them ungrateful. Never again, many Americans said, should the United States waste its strength and wealth on foreign military adventures.

Congress knew the feeling of the country. Therefore, in 1935 and 1936 Congress passed three Neutrality Acts to keep the United States out of foreign wars. These acts prohibited the sale of arms to countries at war. In addition, the neutrality acts forbade loans to nations at war, forbade Americans to travel on ships belonging to such nations, and said that goods sold to them had to be paid for in advance.

France and Great Britain also wanted to avoid war. Both had suffered much during World War I. They wanted to stop the dictator nations from taking over other countries, but

British Prime Minister Neville Chamberlain returned from meeting with Hitler in Munich to promise "peace in our time." His name became forever associated with the hated policy of appeasement.

they did not want to go to war to do so. Their policy became known as *appeasement*. Appeasement means keeping peace by satisfying potential enemies at any cost.

At a conference in Munich, Germany, in 1938, French and British leaders agreed to allow Germany to take over a part of Czechoslovakia. Hitler promised them he would not take over any other nation. Soon, however, Germany and Italy took over other countries. They believed that the United States, France, and Great Britain would not oppose them.

ANSWER THESE QUESTIONS

1. He closed all the banks for four days.
2. to join unions and to practice collective bargaining
3. Social Security
4. to put people on the court who agreed with his views
5. Many people were disillusioned by the aftermath of World War I; it did not prove to be "the war to end all wars" and some of the former allies seemed ungrateful for the efforts of Americans.

ANSWER THESE QUESTIONS

1. What was the first action President Roosevelt took to help restore prosperity in the United States?
2. What rights did the Wagner Act guarantee to American workers?
3. Which of the New Deal reforms still affects millions of retired and needy Americans?
4. Why did President Roosevelt want to increase the number of justices on the Supreme Court?
5. Why might Americans have wanted to stay out of the war that was threatening to break out during the late 1930s?

Delegation of Powers

LAW AND THE CITIZEN

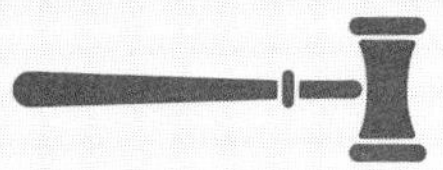

In 1933, Congress—at the request of President Roosevelt—set up the National Recovery Administration (NRA). The NRA was intended to help build up industry and to give employment to jobless workers. This law required industry and business to follow rules and regulations which dealt with wages, the length of the work week, and other matters. Congress gave the President the power to appoint the people who set up these rules and regulations and to make sure they were followed. One company, the Schechter Poultry Corporation of New York, challenged the NRA.

Joseph Schechter and his three brothers ignored the rules set up in the Live Poultry Code, which regulated their business. Schechter refused to pay his employees the fifty-cent-an-hour minimum wage, and he made his employees work more than the maximum forty hours per week. The company was also accused of selling sick chickens. The Schechter Corporation was brought to court on these charges. This case is often referred to as the "sick chicken" case. The Federal District Court in New York convicted the Schechter Corporation. Eventually the case reached the Supreme Court.

The Schechter Corporation argued that the NRA was unconstitutional because Congress had given the President powers that the Constitution said belongs to Congress alone. Schechter's lawyers also said that the NRA tried to regulate intrastate trade, that is, trade within a state. Congress can only regulate interstate trade, trade between states.

Chief Justice Charles Evans Hughes and a majority of Supreme Court justices agreed with these arguments. Hughes said that Congress could not give away powers that the Constitution gives it. The NRA, therefore, was unconstitutional. Hughes also ruled that the poultry company was doing all its business in the state of New York. So, only New York had the power to regulate the Schechters' business.

With the NRA declared unconstitutional, a major part of Roosevelt's plan to help the nation recover from the depression had been eliminated. The administration would have to seek new solutions to the nation's economic problems.

THINKING THINGS THROUGH

1. Many Allied nations had huge war debts. Their factories had been making war goods, so they had no consumer goods to sell. Europeans had no money, so could not buy American goods. 2. blacks, Spanish-speaking people, and women 3. monthly payments to the retired, money for the blind and orphans, funds for the unemployed 4. Answers will vary. If yes, need for govern-

Chapter 22 SUMMARY

The period from 1929 to 1939, known as the Great Depression, was one of the most difficult times in American history. A stock market crash wiped out the savings of millions of people.

Unemployment was widespread. Overproduction of goods led to surpluses on the market. In part this was due to the lack of income among Americans to purchase products. Millions of Americans had bought things on the installment plan and could not keep up their payments.

A tremendous drought throughout several western states ruined much of the farmland. Unable to make a living, many farmers and their families left their homes.

President Hoover was against direct relief for Americans, but he tried to help them. He hoped to get businesses to enlarge their companies, and he pushed for the establishment of the Reconstruction Finance Corporation.

By 1932 the country wanted new leadership in the White House. Franklin D. Roosevelt won a smashing victory over President Hoover. Upon his inauguration, Roosevelt began his program, already called the New Deal. President Roosevelt lifted the spirit of the nation and gave America confidence again. Not all of his programs worked. A few, like Social Security, have had a long-lasting effect.

The problems of the depression contributed to the rise of dictators in other nations. Adolf Hitler in Germany and others prepared for war.

Chapter 22 TEST

WORDS TO REMEMBER

Match each of the following words with the correct definition below.

a. dictator
b. collective bargaining
c. direct relief
d. appeasement

a 1. a ruler who has complete control of a nation

c 2. money or jobs given to needy people by the government

b 3. the process through which unions and employers agree on wages, hours, and working conditions

d 4. maintaining peace by giving potential enemies what they want

THINKING THINGS THROUGH

Answer each of the following questions.

1. What effects of World War I helped lead to the depression?
2. Which groups of people were hardest hit by unemployment during the depression?
3. What benefits did the Social Security Act make available to Americans?
4. Do you believe the government should run projects such as the Tennessee Valley Authority? Why or why not?
5. Why did France and Great Britain follow a policy of appeasement with the war-like nations during the late 1930s?

RELATED MATERIALS

Duplicator/Copy Masters: Activities 46, 47; Quiz 48
Workbook pages 67-70

ment action; if no, government should not compete with business. **5.** They did not think it worth fighting another war to stop the warring nations.

WORKING WITH SKILLS

1. 1929 **2.** 1933 **3.** 1931 and 1932

WORKING WITH SKILLS

Study the line graph on page 552. Then use the information below to draw a line graph of the percentage of Americans who were unemployed during the depression.

Year	Percentage Unemployed	Year	Percentage Unemployed
1929	1.3%	1935	8.3%
1930	3.5%	1936	7.1%
1931	6.5%	1937	6.0%
1932	9.7%	1938	8.0%
1933	10.2%	1939	7.2%
1934	9.0%		

Use your graph to answer the following questions.

1. In what year was the percentage of unemployed Americans smallest?
2. In what year was the percentage of unemployed people largest?
3. Between what two years did the percentage increase most?

ON YOUR OWN

1. Talk with two neighbors, grandparents, or other people about their experiences during the Great Depression. Ask them how unemployment and other economic problems affected daily life. Also ask them whether any of the New Deal programs helped them or their friends directly. Take notes on your conversations and share them with the class.
2. On an outline map of the United States indicate the areas listed below. Use an atlas if you need help.
   a. the dust bowl
   b. the area served by the Tennessee Valley Authority
3. The picture on this page was taken in New York City in February 1932. Imagine that you are one of the people waiting in the "hunger line," hoping to be one of the lucky twenty to receive a free meal. Write a diary entry in which you describe the experience. Include conversations you had with other people in line. Be sure to tell whether you got a meal and to mention your plans for looking for a job.

Chapter 23
WORLD WAR II

Chapter 23 describes World War II beginning with the Nazi attack on Poland and continuing through to the Allied victories in Europe and the Pacific. Lesson 23-1 outlines the German and Soviet attacks in Poland, German attacks in western Europe, and the Japanese attack on Pearl Harbor, which brought the United States into the war. Lesson 23-2 covers Germany's invasion of the Soviet Union, major battles in Europe, the war in the Pacific, and the aftermath of the war.

CONTENT OBJECTIVES

After completing the lesson, students will know:

- that the *Blitzkrieg* gave Germans control over a large part of Europe by June 1940
- how the United States tried to remain neutral as the war intensified
- that the United States declared war on Japan after the attack on Pearl Harbor

VOCABULARY

Blitzkrieg: quick, destructive form of warfare used by Germans in World War II; it means "lightning war" in German

infantry: foot soldiers

rationing: limiting the amount of goods that people can buy

23-1 The Struggle Begins

As you read, think about these questions:

What new type of warfare did the Germans use in their invasion of Poland?

How did the United States aid Great Britain and France during the early months of the war?

What effect did the attack on Pearl Harbor have on Americans' attitudes toward the war?

Special Vocabulary *Blitzkrieg* infantry rationing

Until 1936 Germany, Italy, and Japan had each acted alone in invading other countries. In 1936, however, Adolf Hitler and Benito Mussolini signed a treaty making their two nations allies. Mussolini said the line between Rome and Berlin—the capitals of their countries—would be the axis, or center line, upon which the world would turn. Italy, Germany, and later Japan became known as the Axis powers.

The Nazi Invasion

Ever since the beginning of Nazism, Hitler had cursed the communists of the Soviet Union. Joseph Stalin, the head of the Soviet Communist Party, had for years spoken against Hitler and the Nazis. In the summer of 1939, Hitler and Stalin stunned the world. They signed a treaty saying that Germany and the Soviet Union would not fight each other. The rest of the world wondered what these two leaders were planning.

The answer came on September 1, 1939. On that day, Hitler sent his armies into the western part of Poland. The Soviet Union moved into Poland from the east. This attack began World War II.

Great Britain and France had promised earlier to help the Poles if their country was invaded. They kept their word and declared war on Germany. Eager not to widen the conflict, they did not go to war against the Soviet Union.

Lightning War. The Nazi attack on Poland was swift and deadly. German troops, supported by tanks, artillery, and dive bombers, sped into action. Hitler's army moved so fast that its attack was called a *Blitzkrieg*, which means "lightning war" in German. After breaking through the Polish defenses, the armored divisions destroyed supply centers, communication lines, and transportation routes. Meanwhile, the bombers pounded Poland's cities. When the Polish army was completely disorganized, the Nazi *infantry*, or foot soldiers, moved in and finished the job. Warsaw, the capital of Poland, fell within three weeks.

Hitler used his new kind of warfare—the *Blitzkrieg*—again in the early spring of 1940, this time in Scandinavia. Denmark quickly surrendered. Then Hitler's armies rolled

Using horses and sabers, the Poles were totally unable to stop the advancing German tanks. The complete German success in Poland convinced Adolf Hitler that his plans for conquering the world could not fail.

On May 27, 1940, the German air force bombed Dunkirk, putting the harbor out of use for large ships. At this point, the British navy pressed small boats into service.

through Norway. Before this takeover was even completed, Hitler attacked the Netherlands, Belgium, and northern France. In a matter of days, both Holland and Belgium fell.

With the invasion of Belgium, the Nazi armies finally met the French and British. The *Blitzkrieg* worked as well against them as against its other victims. In a short time, the Nazis drove a confused British army to a French town on the English Channel named Dunkirk. They appeared to have 300,000 British caught helpless on the beach.

The English people rose to the desperate need. Fishing and pleasure boats—and anything else that would float—by the hundreds rushed across the English Channel to Dunkirk from almost every coastal village in Britain. They took the trapped army home to England. Over ninety percent of the British army survived to fight another time.

The British army had been driven off the continent. With the French army also in retreat, nothing stood in the way of the advancing Germans. They turned south, occupied Paris, and forced the French to surrender on June 22, 1940. The Germans took a million French prisoners of war. As the last of the French were giving up, Mussolini also declared war on France. (See the map on page 569.)

ACTIVITY

Objective: Solving problems

Divide the class into small groups of three to five students. Have the students do role playing, imagining that they are the people of southern England trying to rescue the British troops at Dunkirk. Point out that the actions of the British people at Dunkirk took great courage as well as skillful planning. Have half the groups plan the actual sea rescue. Have the other half plan what to do on the coast when the troops arrive. All should consider what supplies they would need, what they would have to do specifically, and what problems they would expect to encounter. One person from each group should report its conclusions to the class.

The Bombing of Britain. Less than three weeks after France fell, the Battle of Britain began. Nazi bombers began pounding southern England. Hitler was convinced this bombing would pave the way for an invasion by the Nazi armies across the English Channel. The British proved to be a stubborn people. Winston Churchill, the prime minister, inspired his nation with his words:

> . . . we shall defend our island, whatever the cost may be, we shall fight on the beaches, we shall fight on the landing grounds, we shall fight on the fields and in the streets, we shall fight in the hills; we shall never surrender.

Only a few thousand British fighter pilots stood between England and defeat. Day after day, the pilots flew their

German, Italian, and Soviet expansion are shown on this map. What countries did Italy take over?

Albania and Ethiopia

planes against the mighty force of German bombers. The British were helped by the fact that they were able to learn daily Germany's secret military orders. The struggle in the skies was fierce. By the end of October 1940, the British had lost more than 900 fighter pilots. During the same time, however, the Germans had lost between 1700 and 2700 aircraft. The Battle of Britain was over. The British pilots had turned back a German invasion of their island. Churchill thankfully said of the brave pilots, "Never have so many owed so much to so few."

DISCUSSION

Have the students discuss their views on American neutrality in the first stage of the war. Explain that the Lend-Lease Act was controversial. Some people thought that aiding the European allies was a major step toward war and condemned such aid. Others thought that the Lend-Lease Act was just a halfway measure and the United States should enter the war to aid the allies decisively. Have the students explain which view they agree with and why.

American Neutrality. After the invasion of Poland in 1939, Congress passed a Neutrality Act. The law permitted countries to buy arms from the United States as long as they paid cash and transported the weapons on foreign ships. This law mainly helped Great Britain since its ships could most easily get to American ports.

Roosevelt, who was pro-British, feared that war might come despite America's attempts to stay out of it. He therefore proposed the country's first peacetime draft law. All men between the ages of twenty-one and thirty-five were required to register for the draft. This meant that they could be required to serve in the military for one year.

In November 1940 Roosevelt became the first President to be elected for a third term. Following his reelection, Roosevelt took steps to help the European allies. He got Congress to pass the Lend-Lease Act. This act of March 1941 permitted the United States to lend, rent, or sell ships, airplanes, and weapons to nations fighting against the Axis powers.

"The Way of a Stork," a cartoon about the Lend-Lease program, shows the American eagle flying weapons and aircraft to Britain. President Roosevelt once said that Lend-Lease was like lending a neighbor a hose to put out a fire.

The President also sent naval ships to protect the ships of friendly nations against attack from German U-boats in the North Atlantic. As a defense measure, the United States signed a treaty with the free Danish government in which the United States received the right to build air and naval bases in Greenland, a possession of Denmark.

In August 1941 Churchill and Roosevelt met aboard a British ship near Newfoundland. They agreed to a set of goals called the Atlantic Charter. The charter was not a treaty. Neither the United States nor Great Britain had to honor anything written in it. The two nations simply agreed to work for the right of all people to choose their own form of government, and to enjoy economic security. By all the steps taken from 1939 to 1941, Roosevelt was making it clear that America was on the side of those defending freedom.

General Douglas MacArthur briefs Filipino soldiers during a campaign to halt Japanese invasion of the tiny island of Corregidor.

In the Philippines, Japanese forces quickly drove an army of Americans and Filipinos onto the Bataan Peninsula. General MacArthur took thousands of his troops from the peninsula to an island in Manila Bay called Corregidor.

For three months, MacArthur and his troops withstood a steady bombardment. Finally, with defeat near, the general and his family escaped to Australia in a submarine. As MacArthur departed he promised grimly, "I shall return."

Detention Camps. Following the sneak attack on Pearl Harbor, a deep distrust of Japanese Americans developed in the United States. People worried that Americans of Japanese descent might help the enemy. With the agreement of Earl Warren, governor of California, President Roosevelt disgracefully ordered the army to move the Japanese Americans from the Pacific Coast to inland detention camps.

Two thirds of these people forced to move were American citizens. They became prisoners in their own country. They lost their homes and businesses. Japanese Americans in other parts of the country suffered from discrimination. The episode remains a stain on American democracy.

In 1943 the American military finally agreed to accept Japanese Americans into service. Thousands of them enlisted, including 1200 men from detention camps. Their war record was outstanding. None of the Japanese Americans in the camps were ever found to pose a threat to the country.

In 1941 there were more than 100,000 people of Japanese descent in the United States. About 71,000 of them were *Nisei* (American born). Early in 1942 all those living on the West Coast were moved to relocation camps.

By 1943 more than two million women were working in factories and shipyards doing jobs that had formerly been done by men.

Mobilizing Resources. To help defeat the Axis, the United States had to mobilize its resources fast. All Americans were called on to do their part. Through voluntary enlistments as well as the draft, the number of people in the military soared. Training programs were rapidly organized to teach the recruits to be effective soldiers, sailors, and fliers. By war's end more than 15,000,000 Americans had served in uniform. The total included over 200,000 women.

American industry, organized by a government agency known as the War Production Board, began to produce war goods at an incredible pace. For example, automobile factories stopped making cars for civilian use in 1942. Later the same year they began manufacturing airplanes, trucks, rifles, and other materials of the war. By 1944 over 100,000 planes a year were being produced in American factories.

Employment opportunities rose as industries kept their plants open twenty-four hours a day and put on three shifts of workers. Because many employees worked longer than an eight-hour shift, income rose dramatically during the war. Women took their places alongside men as workers in factories and shipyards. The economic misery of the Great Depression had ended at last.

Millions did volunteer work. Children collected scrap metal and paper for recycling. Older people became air raid wardens or airplane spotters for civil defense units.

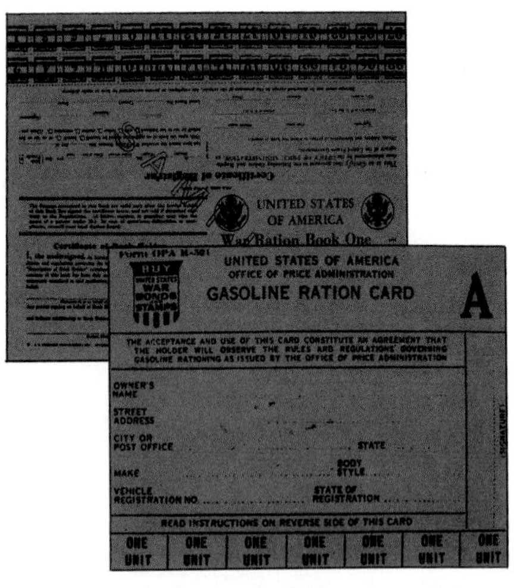

UNITED STATES OF AMERICA
War Ration Book One

UNITED STATES OF AMERICA
OFFICE OF PRICE ADMINISTRATION
GASOLINE RATION CARD
A

BUY UNITED STATES WAR BONDS AND STAMPS

THE ACCEPTANCE AND USE OF THIS CARD CONSTITUTE AN AGREEMENT THAT THE HOLDER WILL OBSERVE THE RULES AND REGULATIONS GOVERNING GASOLINE RATIONING AS ISSUED BY THE OFFICE OF PRICE ADMINISTRATION

OWNER'S NAME
STREET ADDRESS
CITY OR POST OFFICE .... STATE ....
MAKE .... BODY STYLE ....
VEHICLE REGISTRATION NO. .... STATE OF REGISTRATION ....
(SIGNATURE)

READ INSTRUCTIONS ON REVERSE SIDE OF THIS CARD

ONE UNIT | ONE UNIT | ONE UNIT | ONE UNIT | ONE UNIT | ONE UNIT | ONE UNIT

Rationing made civilians part of the total war effort. The first ration books, issued in 1942, had stamps for the purchase of sugar.

Rationing. To make sure that certain supplies and food were available for the military, the government began *rationing* them to civilians. Rationing means limiting the amount of goods people may purchase. The Office of Price Administration distributed books of ration stamps. Americans could buy such items as coffee, sugar, butter, meat, canned goods, and oils only by using stamps as well as money. Gasoline, rubber tires, and woolen and cotton clothing were also rationed.

ANSWER THESE QUESTIONS

1. the alliance of Italy, Germany, and Japan
2. the attack of Hitler's army; because it was so swift and deadly
3. Women worked in factories, children collected scrap metal and paper, and seniors served in civil defense units.
4. a program of lending, renting, or selling war materials to the Allies; it allowed them to continue the war
5. because it was a complete surprise and because 8 battleships and 150 planes were destroyed and more than 2000 military personnel were killed

ANSWER THESE QUESTIONS

1. What were the Axis powers?
2. What was the *Blitzkreig*? Why was it so successful?
3. How did women, children, and old people help the war effort?
4. What was the Lend-Lease Act? How did it help America's allies?
5. Why was the attack on Pearl Harbor such a great blow to the United States?

23-2 Americans Join the Fight

As you read, think about these questions:

Why did the United States decide to concentrate its war effort at first in Europe?

What shocking brutality of the Nazis became fully public when the war in Europe ended?

What conditions led to the Allied victory in the Pacific?

What were some of the purposes for establishing the United Nations?

Special Vocabulary amphibious force concentration camp liberate

CONTENT OBJECTIVES

After completing the lesson, students will know:

- that winning in Europe was America's first priority when it entered the war
- how the German decision to attack the Soviet Union turned the tide of the war
- that Allied forces eventually won decisive battles in the Pacific
- about the horrors of the Holocaust
- that the United States dropped two atomic bombs on Japan, killing many thousands of people and bringing an end to the war

VOCABULARY

amphibious force: a military force that can travel on both land and water
liberate: to free
concentration camp: camps for political prisoners

When the United States entered the war, President Roosevelt quickly put into effect plans to concentrate on defeating the Axis powers in Europe first. The war in the Pacific would come second. The reasons were sound. In Europe, the British seemed near defeat. If Great Britain fell to the Germans, Americans would stand alone against the victorious Axis powers across both the Atlantic and the Pacific. General George C. Marshall, the chief of staff, and the military chiefs of Great Britain worked closely together. They agreed on the strategy of "Europe first."

War in Europe

The year 1941 had been a successful one for the Axis in Europe and Africa. Hitler's armies made Greece and Yugoslavia their victims in April. In May a Nazi invasion by air drove the British from the island of Crete.

With these victories, the Axis gained new air bases that tightened their hold on the Mediterranean area. With the Mediterranean Sea under their control, the Germans could stop the British from using the Suez Canal. This would cut the British off from easy reach of important parts of their empire—including the Middle East and India.

Morocco

Allied and German invasion routes are indicated on this map. Which country was invaded directly from the United States?

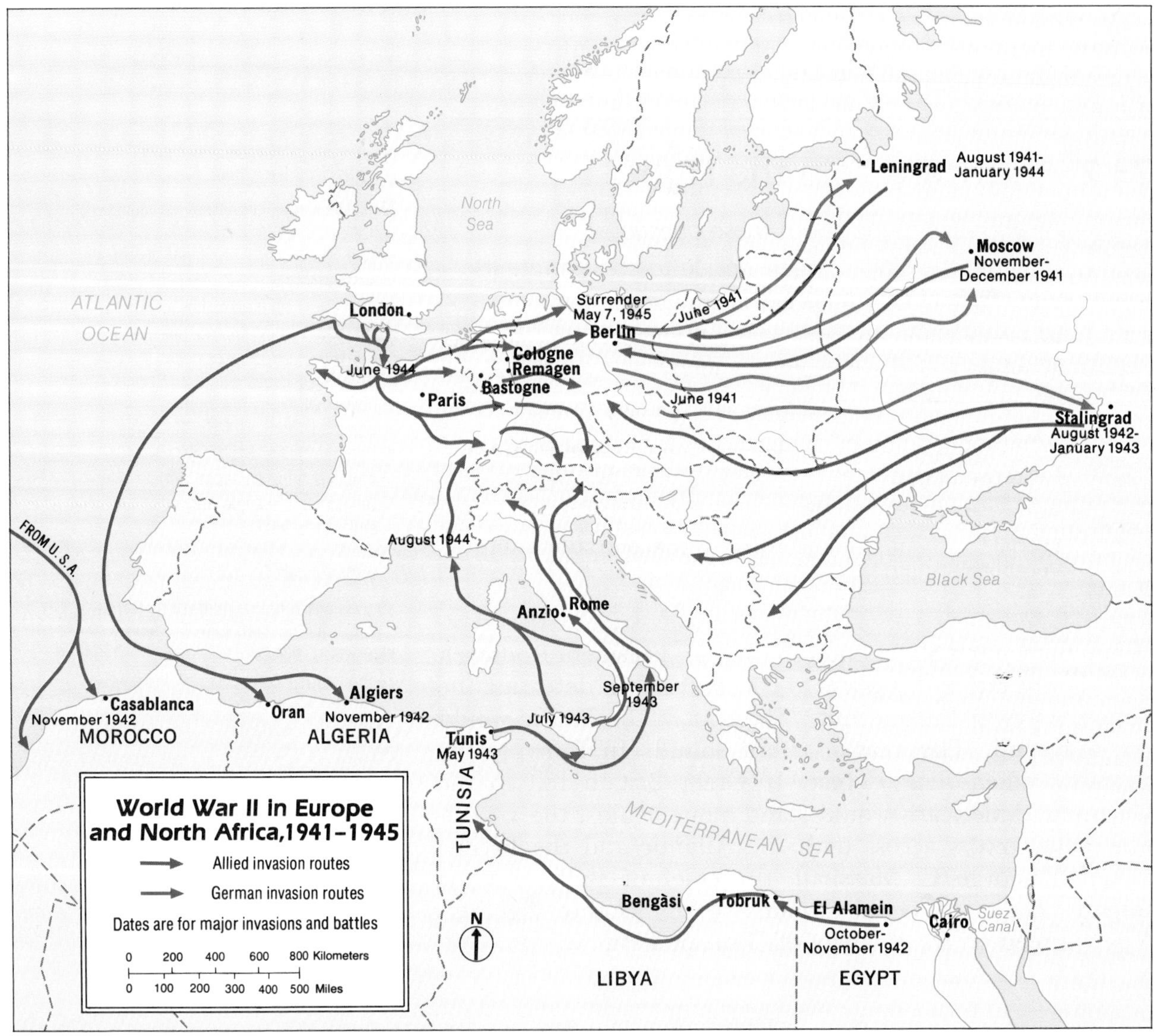

World War II in Europe and North Africa, 1941–1945

Squeezed on three sides—with Montgomery to the south, Free French forces in the southwest, and Eisenhower's forces led by General George S. Patton to the west—the Axis army of about 250,000 troops was bottled up in Tunisia. In early May of 1943 they surrendered.

Italy. With the victories in North Africa, British and American fortunes began to change. In July 1943 the Allies invaded Sicily, which fell after thirty-eight days of furious fighting. At about the same time, Italians turned against their dictator Mussolini, and drove him from power.

On September 3, 1943, the Allies invaded Italy. Five days later, Italy, the southern end of the Axis, surrendered. The fighting in Italy continued. The Germans, who had quickly occupied most of Italy, still fought stubbornly and fiercely. Rome did not fall to the Allies until June 4, 1944.

D-Day. In the early morning hours of June 6, 1944—a day that is known as D-Day—a huge Allied force crossed the English Channel and landed on the Normandy coast of France. The invasion, commanded by General Eisenhower, involved more than a million soldiers, sailors, and fliers. Immense numbers of planes, ships, tanks, transports, guns, food, clothing, and medical supplies supported the attack. It was the greatest *amphibious force* ever assembled. An amphibious force is one which can move on both land and water.

The Germans aimed to hurl the invaders into the sea, but the Allies gained a toehold on the European continent. In

General Eisenhower talked with these paratroopers before they were dropped into France behind the German lines. Paratroopers were trained to parachute from airplanes into combat areas, where they cut railroad lines, blew up bridges, and seized airfields.

the first forty-eight hours, 107,000 troops and 14,000 vehicles poured onto the French beaches. By July 2, one million Allied troops were beginning to fan out over France. In August Paris was *liberated*, or freed, from Nazi control.

All summer long Allied bombers struck at Germany. The goal was to smash German industry and make it impossible for Germany to wage war any further. About one million German civilians were killed or wounded in the attacks. Still, Hitler was determined to fight on.

Battle of the Bulge. After liberating France, the Allies moved northward. By September 1944 they were tearing into the Rhineland region of Germany. The Germans, however, had one more blow to deliver. In a surprise attack they drove the Allies back 45 miles (72 kilometers) from their farthest advance. The line bulged along a 60-mile (96-kilometer) stretch. The Germans, it appeared, might recapture Antwerp in Belgium, but the Americans held. When Germans demanded the surrender of a unit at Bastogne, the general replied in one word: "Nuts!" Over 8000 Americans were killed and 48,000 wounded in the Battle of the Bulge. The Germans had only delayed the end of the war in Europe.

The War in the Pacific

Following the attack on Pearl Harbor, the Japanese dominated the war in the Pacific and in Asia. President Roosevelt's decision to try first to win in Europe had its price.

Japanese Victories. In 1942, after storming the Philippines, Japanese troops invaded Borneo and the Celebes. In February they crushed the Allies in a naval battle in the Java Sea. By the end of March, the Japanese had taken over the Netherlands East Indies from which they acquired oil and other important war materials.

On the Asian mainland, the Japanese had similar successes. They had already pushed the Chinese army and government far into western China. The Chinese Nationalist leader, Chiang Kai-shek, could get American lend-lease supplies only on trucks that came to China on the Burma Road. The Japanese quickly closed the Burma Road in April 1942. Not until 1945, when the war was ending, did American and British soldiers cut through the dense jungles of Burma and reopen the road to China.

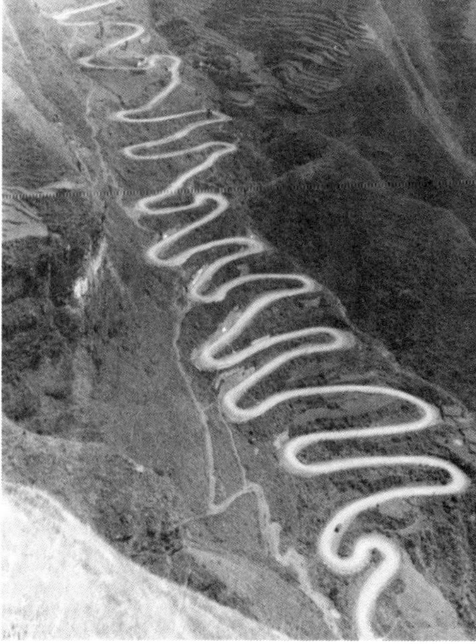

The winding Burma Road was a major target for the Japanese during the war in Asia. After they had succeeded in blocking the road, supplies to China had to be airlifted over the Himalaya Mountains.

A Shift in the War. Many Americans were impatient with the "Europe first" strategy. They wanted to fight Japan, too. At last, in April 1942, the United States Army Air Corps performed a bold feat. They sent over Tokyo a fleet of bombers flown off an aircraft carrier. The planes led by General James H. Doolittle dropped their deadly cargo on an unsuspecting city. The war had come to Japan.

One of the first big Allied victories came in June of 1942. A Japanese force headed for Midway Island, a crucial spot in the middle of the Pacific. The Americans had occupied Midway and planned to use it as a jumping-off point for the attacks on Japan. Fortunately for the Americans, they had figured out the secret code used by the Japanese fleet. The United States Navy picked up the enemy messages and learned that a big attack was coming somewhere in the Pacific. Soon the Navy guessed that Midway was the target. The American Pacific fleet, under Admiral Chester W. Nimitz, met the Japanese and destroyed four carriers and nearly three hundred planes. The Battle of Midway was the turning point of the Pacific fighting.

ACTIVITY

Objective: Using reference materials

Have the students find biographical information in the school library on General Douglas MacArthur. Have the students write a brief report on his life that should cover these three points: MacArthur's background and training, the major achievements of his military career, and the reason why he became controversial.

Beginning late in 1942 American troops, led by General Douglas MacArthur, began to strike toward Japan by fighting northward from Australia. These forces would wind up in the Philippine Islands by hopping from island to island through the South Pacific. In October 1944 MacArthur stormed ashore on Leyte Island in the Philippine Islands. "People of the Philippines!" he declared, "I have returned."

A second American force pushed through the central Pacific Ocean heading for the Mariana Islands, Iwo Jima, and the island of Okinawa. This force was under the command of Admiral Nimitz. Shortly after MacArthur won back the Philippines, Nimitz's forces won very cruel battles on Iwo Jima (4189 Americans killed; 15,308 wounded) and Okinawa (11,260 Americans killed; 33,769 wounded). By May 1945 the path to Japan lay open.

The War Comes to a Close

In the fall of 1944, Franklin Roosevelt was elected President for an unprecedented fourth time. Less than four months later, this towering leader of the free world suffered a stroke and died in Warm Springs, Georgia. The Vice President, Harry S Truman of Missouri, became President. He pledged to carry out Roosevelt's war plans.

Germany Surrenders. With the Battle of the Bulge behind them, total victory was in sight for the Allies. In March 1945 the Allies crossed the Rhine into Germany. Meanwhile, the Soviet army knifed through the enemy homeland from the south and east. Shortly, the Soviets were on the outskirts of Berlin. Their artillery pounded the city to rubble.

On May 1 reports came that Hitler had committed suicide in his Berlin bomb shelter. About one million Nazis surrendered the next day in Germany and Italy. In less than a week, Nazi forces in other countries also gave up. On May 8, 1945, Germany surrendered unconditionally. That day became known as V-E Day (Victory in Europe Day).

Concentration Camps. When the war in Europe ended, news of the shocking brutality of the Nazis became fully public. The Allies discovered many *concentration camps*, or camps for political prisoners throughout German-occupied Europe. The Nazis had crowded millions of people inside these camps. The largest group of victims were Jews from all over Europe, whom the Nazis were determined to destroy.

The Nazis had the idea that Germans were a "super race." All other people the Nazis regarded as inferior. Jews were singled out. Young and old Jews—including even infants—were subjected to unbelievable brutality. Thousands died of

When the United States 7th Army marched into Dachau, a concentration camp, the inmates cheered their liberators. Only a small number of those in concentration camps survived the Nazi brutality.

DISCUSSION

Have the students discuss whether it is ethical for scientists to develop weapons like the atomic bomb. Point out that some scientists think that science and technology should be used to improve life for all humanity, not to kill people. Point out that other scientists think that they have a responsibility to help defend their country—and that even if they refuse to develop weapons, scientists from other nations will develop them.

J. Robert Oppenheimer, head of the Manhattan Project, recognized the horror of atomic warfare. After the war, he helped develop plans for international control of atomic energy.

starvation and disease. Others were packed into trains and transported to special gas chambers where they were murdered. Horribly, Germany, which called itself a civilized country, sent about six million Jews and many Poles to their death. We call this terrible mass destruction the Holocaust.

The Manhattan Project. As early as 1939 President Roosevelt had been warned by the scientist Albert Einstein that the Germans were working on a new weapon. Such a weapon would have much more destructive power than anything ever developed before.

Acting on this information, the President organized a group to build a similar weapon for the United States. Their undertaking became known as the Manhattan Project. In total secrecy the scientists designed and built an atomic bomb, based on the power released by splitting atoms of a type of the metal uranium. On July 16, 1945, the bomb was tested successfully at Alamogordo, in New Mexico. The gigantic explosion had the energy of many thousand tons of TNT. A new era in human history had begun.

Hiroshima and Nagasaki. Truman decided he would not hesitate to use the new weapon against Japan. Japan appeared to be losing the war. Still, the resistance its remaining soldiers put up was fierce. If the United States did not use the atomic bomb, the President believed, vast numbers of American and Allied soldiers would still have to die.

On July 26, 1945, Truman, therefore, sent word to the Japanese to give up or suffer terrible destruction. When the Japanese did not reply, he ordered the Army Air Force to drop an atomic bomb on the Japanese city of Hiroshima. On August 6, 1945, nearly all of that port city was wiped out. Between seventy thousand and eighty thousand people were killed. Thousands more suffered from injuries and radiation sickness that the bomb produced. A second atomic bomb was dropped on the city of Nagasaki on August 9, 1945, killing an additional forty thousand people.

The Japanese decided to surrender. The papers that officially ended the war against Japan were signed on September 2, 1945, aboard the battleship *Missouri*. Church bells all over America rang out. People danced in the streets everywhere. The war—"it"—was over at last. The joy of victory was dimmed by the knowledge that 322,000 Americans had been killed and 800,000 had been wounded.

The UN Security Council meets in the Council chambers. The delegates and their aides sit at the horseshoe-shaped table. Interpreters at the center table translate speeches as they are given.

Establishing the United Nations. Many national leaders wanted to establish a world organization after the war. They hoped that such an international institution might help prevent war in the future. The League of Nations had failed. Now the world had a second chance. Many countries agreed to send representatives to San Francisco on April 25, 1945, to establish a new world body.

After two months of discussion the United Nations Organization came into existence. A General Assembly where all nations—big and small—had an equal voice would debate issues, but would have no power to decide them. A Security Council of eleven members would examine critical questions and take action on them if members of the council agreed to do so. The United States, China, the Soviet Union, Great Britain, and France would be permanent members of the council. Other countries would take turns filling the additional six positions. An international court of justice would also be available to settle arguments between nations.

Would the Allies stick together now that the desire to defeat the Axis was no longer present? No one guessed the kind of road the United States would have to travel in the postwar world.

ANSWER THESE QUESTIONS

1. When did Germany invade the Soviet Union?
2. Where did the Soviets win big victories?
3. What was D-Day?
4. What was the strategy for finally winning the war in the Pacific?
5. Why did President Truman decide to use the atomic bomb against Japan?

ANSWER THESE QUESTIONS

1. June 22, 1941
2. at Moscow and Stalingrad
3. the Allied invasion of Normandy on June 6, 1944
4. to move northward and westward from Australia and Midway Island to Japan, island by island
5. to avoid a vast loss of Allied lives in the fight for Japan

Objective: After completing these pages, students should understand how to read and interpret symbols and legends used on a map.

Working with Skills

MAP SKILLS

ACTIVITY

Objective: To use symbols and legends to interpret a map

Pass out an outline map of the United States to each student (Duplicator/Copy Master 71). Have each student devise a symbol to indicate the states he or she has visited or lived in. Have each devise another symbol to indicate the five states they would most like to visit, based on what they have read and heard. Have them mark these symbols on their map and write a legend that clearly and briefly explains the symbols.

ANSWERS

1. Battle of the Coral Sea, May 1942
2. Solomon Islands
3. August 6 and 9, 1945
4. February-March 1945
5. 800 miles (1200 kilometers)
6. Battle of Midway
7. Okinawa

Using Symbols and Legends to Interpret a Map

Most maps use symbols to help provide information. A symbol may be a line, a series of lines, a color, or even a small picture. Mapmakers use symbols to give information because symbols take up less space than words. Once you understand how to interpret, or get meaning from, symbols properly, you can fully understand what a map shows.

Most maps have a legend to help you understand the symbols on the map. The legend is a list of symbols and what they stand for. The legend may also include the map scale and other information. Mapmakers generally enclose the legend in a box somewhere on the map.

Look at the map on the next page. This map shows the progress of World War II in the Pacific from 1942 to 1945. The legend indicates that one of the symbols used on this map is a series of diagonal, or slanted, lines. Mapmakers frequently use such a symbol to provide information about a certain area on a map. Here they show the area of the Pacific that the Japanese controlled in August 1942.

This map uses several other symbols. The solid line on the map marks the boundary of the Allied advance westward by March 1945. Solid lines are commonly used to show boundaries. A dot, on the other hand, is a useful way to mark the spot where a specific event took place or to show where a city is located. Some of the dots on this map have stars at their centers. They stand for United States naval victories.

The legend for this map also indicates that the dates in black are when the United States captured certain islands. The dates in red indicate when atomic bombings took place. All dates appear under the name of the place where the event they refer to took place.

Study the placement of the symbols of this map carefully. Then answer the following questions.

1. What was the first victory of the Allies in the Pacific after the Japanese bombed Pearl Harbor in Hawaii on December 7, 1941?

2. In what group of islands is Guadalcanal located?

3. What are the dates of the atomic bombings of Japan?

4. When did the Battle of Iwo Jima take place?

RELATED MATERIAL

Duplicator/Copy Master: Activity 49

5. How far from the coast of Indochina were the Allies in March 1945?

6. Which battle shown on this map took place outside the area that Japan controlled in August 1942?

7. Which island did the United States gain control of in June 1945?

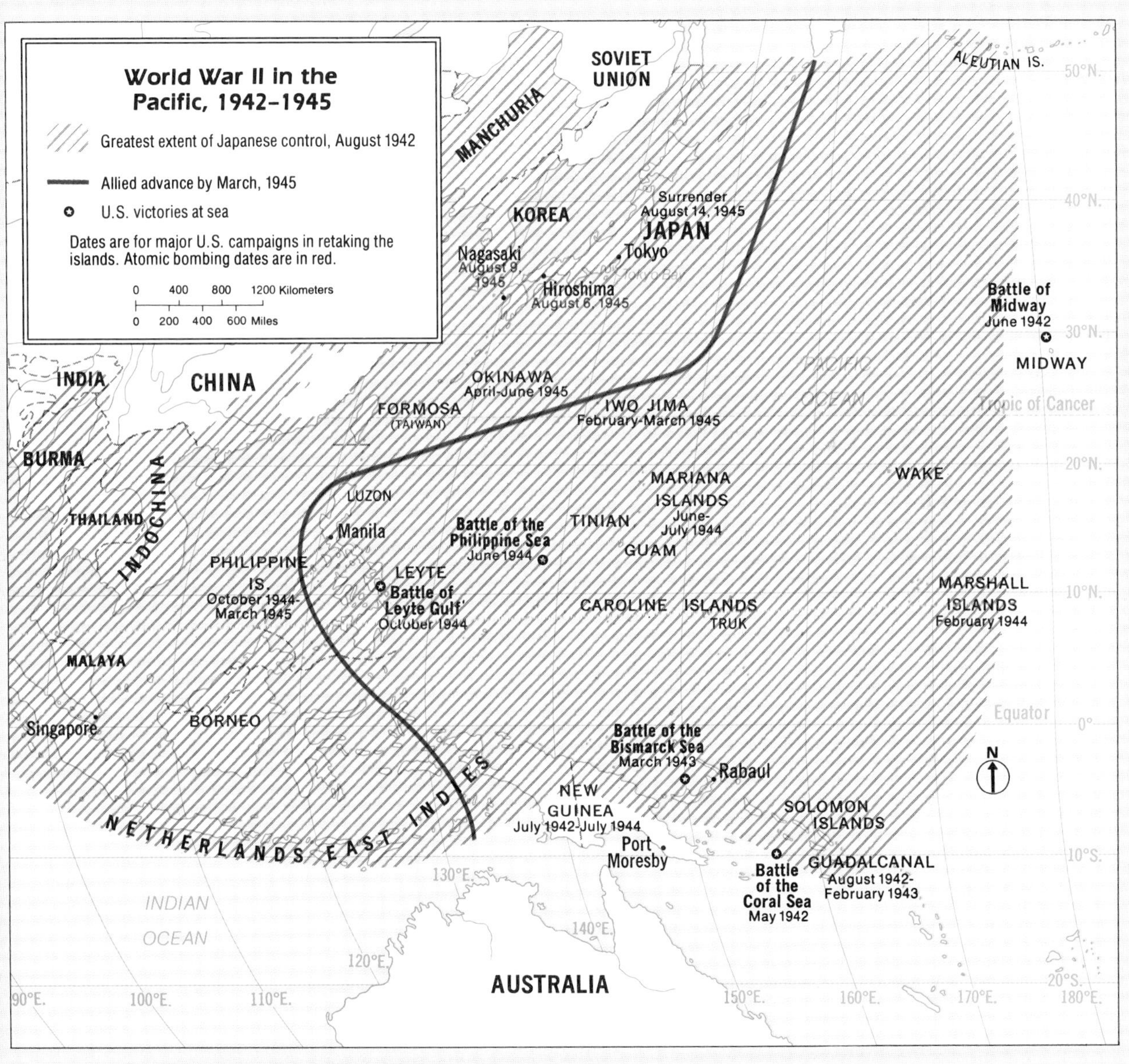

THINKING THINGS THROUGH

1. Factories worked around the clock producing war goods; they hired many workers and income rose. **2.** The British seemed near defeat. **3.** The United States planned to use it as a base to attack the Japanese; also, it was a major Allied victory in the Pacific after many defeats. **4.** The Allies landed their troops

Chapter 23 SUMMARY

On September 1, 1939, World War II began when Adolf Hitler's Nazi armies attacked Poland. Great Britain and France came to Poland's aid. In spite of this help, Germany defeated Poland and took country after country in Europe. Soon the British stood alone as enemies of the Nazis.

The United States tried to remain neutral while still supplying the Allies with war goods and food. Finally, on December 7, 1941, the United States came into the war when the Japanese attacked the American naval base at Pearl Harbor, Hawaii. Americans mobilized their industries and people for war. President Roosevelt, meanwhile, had decided to help defeat Germany before dealing with Japan.

The fortunes of the Allies turned in 1942 and 1943. In the Pacific, the Americans halted the Japanese string of successes at Midway Island. In Africa, Generals Montgomery and Patton defeated the Germans. In the Soviet Union, German drives failed at Moscow and Stalingrad.

The fate of the Nazis was sealed when the allies landed in Europe on D-Day 1944. The end of the war in Europe came in 1945 when Soviet troops attacked Berlin.

In the Pacific, the Allies recovered island after island from the Japanese. Finally, to avoid a bloody battle for Japan, President Truman ordered the dropping of atomic bombs on Hiroshima and Nagasaki. On August 14, 1945, the war ended. The Allies signed an agreement creating the United Nations to help avoid future wars.

Chapter 23 TEST

WORDS TO REMEMBER

Match each word with its definition.

c 1. *Blitzkrieg* a. foot soldiers
b 2. liberated b. freed
d 3. rationing c. lightning war
a 4. infantry d. a system limiting purchases

THINKING THINGS THROUGH

1. How did World War II end the Great Depression?
2. Why did the United States concentrate its greatest forces on the Nazis first?
3. Why was the Battle of Midway so important to the United States?
4. What was the effect of D-Day?
5. What caused Japan to surrender without being invaded?

WORKING WITH SKILLS

Look at the map, "Aggression in Europe, 1935–1940" on page 569. Use the symbols in the map key to answer these questions:

1. What color stands for Germany?
2. What symbol stands for lands controlled by Germany?
3. What color stands for the Soviet Union?
4. What symbol stands for lands controlled by the Soviets?
5. How does the map show the relationship between aggressor nations and the lands they controlled?

RELATED MATERIALS

Duplicator/Copy Masters: Activities 48, 49, 50; Quiz 49
Workbook pages 71-73

onto European soil. **5.** the atomic bombs dropped on Hiroshima and Nagasaki

WORKING WITH SKILLS

1. yellow **2.** diagonal yellow lines **3.** red **4.** diagonal red lines **5.** aggressors took over lands closest to them in most cases

ON YOUR OWN

1. Use an encyclopedia to do research on air power used in Europe in World War II. Concentrate on the struggle between Britain's Royal Air Force and the German *Luftwaffe*. Try to learn how each air force protected its home country and how each waged war against the enemy. Compare the role of air power in World War II with that of World War I. Write a short report to present your findings.
2. Make a large poster in whatever shape you want. Show the foods and materials rationed during World War II. Put as much information as possible on the poster. Show prices of goods during that time; indicate the amounts people could get and how often. Display any stamps or pictures used during the war. You may wish to ask older people who lived during the war to help you.
3. The black soldier pictured at the right, Colonel Benjamin Davis, Jr., commanded the 332nd Fighter Group, which destroyed more than two hundred enemy planes in Europe during World War II. Use the card catalog to find books on black history. From the information in these books, make a list of some of the outstanding accomplishments of black soldiers during the war.

Chapter 24
THE COLD WAR

Chapter 24 discusses the growing involvement of the United States as a world power in the period after World War II known as the cold war. The chapter includes the foreign policies of Presidents Truman, Eisenhower, and Kennedy and ends with the assassination of Kennedy. Lesson 24-1 describes how the USSR and the United States became rivals after World War II and how this rivalry was carried to the brink of war. Lesson 24-2 covers the presidencies of Eisenhower and Kennedy, focusing on international relations.

CONTENT OBJECTIVES

After completing this lesson, students will know:

- how Soviet actions after the war caused tension with the United States
- that the United States responded to Soviet expansionism with a policy known as containment
- how President Truman followed a policy of "limited war" in Korea, turning away from the possibility of a wider conflict
- how the Cold War fostered a fear of communism that was exploited by Senator Joseph McCarthy

VOCABULARY

censor: control what is said or written
iron curtain: the invisible border between the communist and noncommunist worlds
cold war: a bitter economic and political rivalry
containment: a policy of preventing Soviet influence from spreading beyond areas already controlled by the USSR
condemn: officially express disapproval of behavior

24-1 Postwar Conflicts

As you read, think about these questions:

What did the Soviets do to make Americans distrust them after World War II?

How did the development of nuclear weapons affect foreign policy in the 1950s?

Why did President Truman reject General MacArthur's plans for the Korean War?

Special Vocabulary	censor	cold war	condemn
	iron curtain	containment	

Recalling V-E Day, Secretary of State James F. Byrnes said, "As a result of our sufferings and sacrifices in a common cause, the Soviet Union then had in the United States a deposit of goodwill, as great, if not greater than any other country." Only a short time later, however, American goodwill turned to distrust.

Soviet Expansion

The communists had always insisted that their form of government would spread throughout the world. In 1940 shortly after World War II began, the Soviets took over Lithuania, Latvia, and Estonia. These lands became part of the Union of Soviet Socialist Republics (the USSR).

The Big Three Conferences. In February 1945 Roosevelt, Churchill, and Stalin met in Yalta on the Black Sea in the southern USSR. The "Big Three," as these leaders and their nations were called, talked about how to end the war and what to do with the liberated nations. Roosevelt and Churchill thought that by cooperating with Stalin at Yalta they would win his cooperation on a postwar peace plan.

At that time, the Allies mistakenly believed that Soviet arms would be useful in defeating Japan. Stalin agreed to fight against Japan after Germany surrendered. In return, he asked for control of North Korea and other territory in Asia. The Soviet dictator promised Churchill and Roosevelt that he would allow free elections in the eastern European countries then occupied by Soviet troops.

The Big Three agreed to divide Germany into four parts after the war, one part for each of their countries and one part for France. The leaders at the Yalta Conference also decided to set up the United Nations (see Chapter 23).

Another important meeting took place in July 1945 in Potsdam, outside Berlin. By this time Roosevelt had died, and Churchill no longer held office. Harry Truman spoke for the United States. Clement Attlee, the new British prime minister, spoke for England. Joseph Stalin, the last of the Big Three, spoke for the Soviet Union. The Allied leaders drew up the Potsdam Declaration, an agreement for postwar Japan. The plan did away with the Japanese armed services, set up a way to punish Japan's wartime leaders, and called for a democratic form of government in Japan.

ACTIVITY

Objective: To summarize information

Have the students list the agreements made at the Yalta and Potsdam conferences. Then have the students indicate which of these agreements were broken during the Cold War period and by whom. Using this list as a source of information, have the students write a paragraph summarizing the reasons why the United States government felt compelled to oppose the Soviet Union in the Cold War.

The Big Three—(from left to right) Winston Churchill, Franklin Roosevelt, and Joseph Stalin—made agreements at Yalta that remained secret until after the war.

In the eyes of the western world, the Soviet Union was a giant bear grabbing all of Germany for itself.

Dividing Germany. When the war had ended, Germany was divided into four parts, as had been agreed upon at Yalta. The Soviets moved into eastern Germany and set up a communist government. It became known as East Germany. The United States, Great Britain, and France took over running their parts of western Germany.

The capital city of Berlin was in the Soviet part of Germany. The Allies divided the city of Berlin into parts—like the country. The Soviets ran one section, the other Allies ran the other sections. Not long after taking over the eastern half of Berlin, Soviet troops sealed off their part of the city from the rest. In fact they practically cut off the western half of the city from the outside world. Only one road connected Berlin with western Germany. The Soviets clearly hoped that the United States, Great Britain, and France would give up West Berlin to East Germany.

In 1947 the United States and Great Britain decided to combine their parts of Germany to form West Germany. Later France added its part. Finally, in 1949, the western Allies allowed West Germany to set up a republic and adopt a new constitution. With the help of the United States, the new nation's economy grew in the next several years. The USSR, however, refused to cooperate in carrying out the Yalta provision that called for treating Germany as an economic unit. East Germany remained a separate country.

The Iron Curtain. Stalin also broke his word about allowing free elections in eastern Europe. He refused to recognize any eastern European government that was not communist. Since the Soviet armies controlled the countries, they could easily set up communist governments wherever they liked. They did so in Poland, Yugoslavia, and Romania in 1945; in Albania and Bulgaria in 1946; in Hungary in 1947; and in Czechoslovakia in 1948. (See the map on page 591.) The Soviets argued that they needed friendly countries on their borders to protect the USSR from France and Germany, its traditional enemies.

The communist governments of eastern Europe had much in common. They would not allow free popular elections. They *censored* the press and speech. Censoring means controlling what is said or written. They discouraged travel from place to place. They refused to allow private ownership of business and industry. Church attendance was frowned upon, and religious leaders were persecuted.

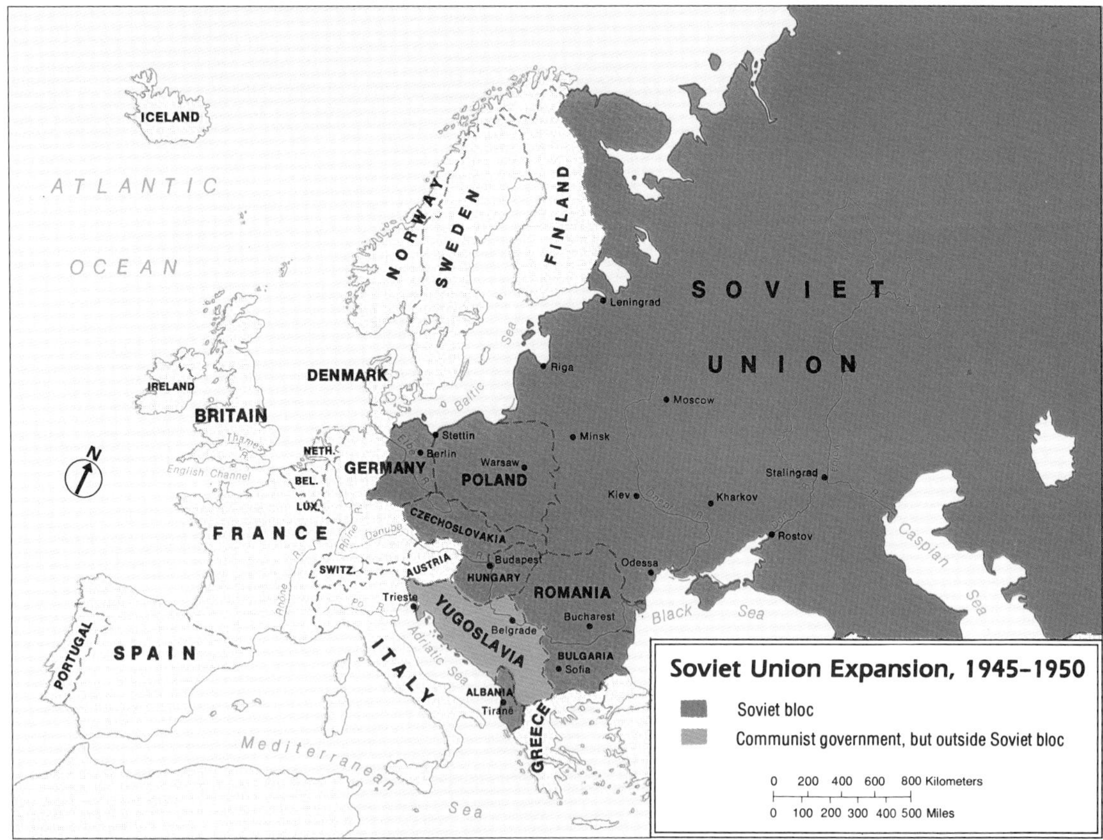

This map shows the area controlled by the Soviet Union in 1950. Which communist country was not controlled by the Soviets?

Yugoslavia

The Soviets had made it clear that they wanted a new period of history to begin in eastern Europe. Some western leaders were confused by how quickly the Soviet Union had ceased cooperating. Winston Churchill, however, was not. In a speech in March 1946, Churchill declared: "From Stettin in the Baltic to Trieste in the Adriatic, an iron curtain has descended across the Continent." Churchill used the words *iron curtain* to describe the invisible wall between the communist and noncommunist worlds.

By late summer 1949, the USSR announced that it had successfully exploded an atomic bomb. Now the two great rival nations had this terrible weapon.

America Responds

The feelings between the United States and the Soviet Union continued to harden. The shooting war that some people had feared happily did not break out. The two countries definitely fought each other, however, in a *cold war*. Cold war was a new phrase to describe economic and political rivalry that stops short of a shooting war.

DISCUSSION

Have the students discuss Truman's policy of containment. Have them find Greece and Turkey on a map. Ask them why the location of these countries seemed critical in containing the Soviets. How did the Marshall Plan help contain Soviet expansion in Europe? Refer the students to Chapter 22 and draw a parallel to the period after World War I when dictators took control of several countries suffering from widespread poverty.

The Truman Doctrine and the Marshall Plan. President Truman wanted to stop Soviet expansion without going to war. He and his advisers came up with a strategy that became known as *containment*. By containment the Americans meant preventing Soviet influence from spreading beyond areas already controlled by the USSR. Truman wanted to stop the spread of communism by giving economic aid to countries to help them recover from World War II.

The American policy of containment through economic and military aid got its first test in 1947. In that year Greece and Turkey were in danger of being taken over by local communist parties supported by the Soviets. If these countries slipped behind the Iron Curtain, too, the USSR would have control of the eastern Mediterranean and probably the Suez Canal as well. To prevent this disaster from occurring, Truman asked Congress for money to help Greece and Turkey defend themselves. During the next three years the United States spent $650 million to aid the two countries. As a result, the Greeks and Turks successfully strengthened their governments and their armed forces. The communist threat in the eastern Mediterranean soon ended. Truman's ideas of containment through economic and military aid became known as the Truman Doctrine.

Soon Truman saw that other nations besides Greece and Turkey needed American aid. Europe would require a long-run solution to its problems. In June 1947 Secretary of State George C. Marshall proposed that the United States

After Truman signed the Marshall Plan into law, Europe was able to set about the huge task of reclothing and rehousing its people.

help European countries help themselves. Truman supported this idea. Enacted into law in 1948, it became known as the Marshall Plan. Its goal was to get western European countries to rebuild their economies with American aid. Under the plan, the United States contributed billions of dollars to Europe's recovery during the next four years.

The Berlin airlift was one of the greatest triumphs in the history of aviation. It also represented a high-point of American power in the world.

Berlin Blockade. In the summer of 1948 the Soviets blocked all roads and railroads running from West Germany to Berlin. They hoped to drive the western powers out of the city completely. The world waited fearfully to see whether the Allies would try to run the blockade with tanks and guns.

Finally, Truman and the British and French leaders agreed on a course of action—an airlift. The United States Air Force, aided by Great Britain and France, would carry food, fuel, and other supplies to West Berlin. Day after day, for months huge cargo planes carried in goods—in all, over 2 million tons (1.8 million metric tons) of supplies. After more than ten months the Soviets ended their blockade. The western air forces had won the gratitude and respect of the people of Berlin and West Germany.

North Atlantic Treaty. President Truman believed that all the western nations should join together to face the Soviet Union in case of war. In April 1949, therefore, western European nations joined Canada and the United States in forming the North Atlantic Treaty Organization (NATO). Members agreed that "an armed attack against one or more of them in Europe or North America shall be considered an attack against them all."

Congress ratified the treaty in the summer of 1949. Truman made General Eisenhower NATO's first supreme commander. Eisenhower's task was to organize the forces of the NATO nations (including West Germany, which joined in 1954) into a common defense.

Developments in the Far East

President Truman had placed General Douglas MacArthur in charge of the American occupation forces in Japan. The general was also to take on the work of rebuilding Japanese society. With the help of the United States, the Japanese wrote a new constitution which promoted civil rights and permitted women to vote. Trade unions were encouraged, and school children learned to value democracy. In 1951, having fulfilled the provisions of the Potsdam Declaration, Japan signed a peace treaty with most of its recent enemies.

Likewise, progress was made in the Philippines. To restore prosperity and repair war damages, the United States gave the Filipinos more than $600 million. On July 4, 1946, the Philippines achieved their independence.

Mao Tse-tung (right) and Chiang Kai-shek were both part of the revolutionary tradition in China. Chiang helped overthrow the ancient Manchu dynasty. Mao was an original member of the Chinese Communist Party.

Communists Take Over China. Two groups had been fighting for control in China even before World War II. One was the Nationalist Party, led by Chiang Kai-shek.The other was the Communist Party, under Mao Tse-tung. Before the war with Japan, Chiang Kai-shek had almost united China. During the war, however, the communists gained wide support.

In 1947 civil war broke out in China. Despite $2 billion in American aid to the Nationalists, the communists began winning the important battles. By 1949 the communists had driven the Nationalists off the mainland of Asia onto the island of Formosa (also called Taiwan). In the fall of 1949, the communists set up the People's Republic of China and ruled over its half billion people.

The Korean War. Under the terms of the Yalta agreement, the Soviets occupied Korea north of the 38th parallel north latitude. The Americans took over the area to the south of

The Soviet Union as an Ally. On June 22, 1941, the uneasy peace between Hitler and Stalin came to an end. Despite his agreements with Stalin, Hitler ordered an attack on the Soviet Union. Two days later the United States announced that the lend-lease program, which had provided ships and other war machinery and weapons to Great Britain and to China, would be extended to the Soviets.

Many historians believe that Hitler's decision to conquer the Soviet Union was the turning point in the European war. First of all, it provided Great Britain with some temporary relief in its battle with the Nazis. More important, it paved the way for the Soviet Union to join its strength with that of Great Britain and the United States. The Nazis quickly drove hundreds of miles into the Soviet Union. For a brief time, they had little standing between them and Moscow, the Soviet capital city. Then in October, the Russian winter arrived. The bitter cold temperatures froze the oil in the German tanks. Nazi soldiers suffered frostbite.

On November 28, 1941, the German armies were within 20 miles (32 kilometers) of Moscow. The Soviet defenders stopped them in a fierce battle. Finally, the Germans felt forced to give up hope of taking the Soviet capital.

In the summer of 1942, the Germans moved on Stalingrad in the south of the Soviet Union. This proved to be an even greater failure. Beginning in August 1942 the Soviets held firm and fought without letup in one of the decisive battles of history. By the end of the struggle in January 1943, 247,000 Germans lay dead, and 94,000 had surrendered. After that, the Soviets began to roll the Nazi tide out of their country.

During the German invasion of the Soviet Union, nature's forces—mud and frost—were on the side of the defenders. These German soldiers had marched into the USSR confidently. Within a few months, they were suffering bitterly.

North Africa. Early 1942 was a time that had belonged to the German Field Marshal Erwin Rommel and his Africa Korps. His successes in desert fighting had earned him the nickname "The Desert Fox." Autumn, however, brought a new desert hero. He was British General Bernard L. Montgomery. In November "Monty" and his troops won a gigantic victory over Rommel at El Alamein in Egypt. Then the British forces pushed the Germans westward 2000 miles (3200 kilometers) into Tunisia.

A few days after this stunning triumph, British and American troops landed in Morocco and Algeria. Hundreds of warships had brought more than 300,000 troops to the North African coast under the overall command of the American General Dwight D. Eisenhower.

"Monty's" victory over "The Desert Fox" at El Alamein came at a low point in the British war effort. This victory made General Montgomery (left) a hero.

the parallel. In the South, an election was held under the supervision of the United Nations (the UN) in 1948. The Soviets, however, refused to allow the UN officials to enter the North to hold elections there. The Soviets set up instead a communist-run People's Republic of Korea. The People's Republic then built a powerful army.

The UN recognized the South Korean government as the legal one. In 1949 the United States withdrew almost all its troops from the South but continued giving economic aid to the new government there.

On June 25, 1950, North Korea invaded South Korea. The UN Security Council held a meeting to discuss the Korean problem. The Council voted to send an army to Korea as a kind of police unit to restore order there. The Soviet Union did not attend the meeting and therefore could not veto the Council's decision. Several member nations of the UN decided to send help to South Korea. The largest number, however, would come from the United States. With UN approval, Truman named General MacArthur commander of the UN forces.

If the Soviets had been present when the United Nations voted to send troops to Korea, they would certainly have vetoed the operation.

The situation was at first grim for the UN "police action." By early August, the UN forces had been pushed south to the very tip of the Korean Peninsula. It seemed that communist forces would drive them into the sea.

In mid-September, however, General MacArthur began his plan to fight his way back, up the peninsula. He sent the army into an attack on the communist lines. At the same time, he landed UN troops on the west coast at the port of Inchon near South Korea's capital city, Seoul. The plan succeeded. UN troops—mainly American—pushed the communists back across the 38th parallel, chasing them toward the Yalu River, Korea's border with China. China warned the UN troops to leave North Korea. The UN Security Council ignored the warning.

Then on November 26, 1950, Chinese communist troops charged across the Yalu and attacked the UN forces. MacArthur was forced to retreat with heavy losses. The UN army held but was once again near the 38th parallel.

MacArthur demanded that the United States respond with strength against the Chinese. He wanted to 1) blockade the Chinese coast, 2) bomb military bases in Manchuria, and 3) assist Chiang Kai-shek in invading mainland China.

Truman and his advisers believed that MacArthur's plan could lead to World War III. The American and UN policy in Korea was to fight only a "limited war," one confined to Korea. For this reason, Truman vetoed McArthur's plan.

Many Americans grew impatient as the fighting in Korea dragged on. In April 1951 MacArthur wrote a letter to the Speaker of the House, Joseph W. Martin. In it MacArthur openly disagreed with the President's strategy. Truman felt he could do nothing else but remove the famous general from his command. Most Americans accepted the judgment that to fight China "would involve us in the wrong war, at the wrong place, at the wrong time, and with the wrong enemy."

McCarthyism. America's cold war with the communists had a chilling effect at home. As the 1950s began, many Americans feared that communism was gaining strength in the United States. Republican Senator Joseph R. McCarthy of Wisconsin took advantage of this fear.

According to Senator McCarthy, communist agents were everywhere—in the military, in corporations, in universities. Leaders in many walks of life dismissed employees McCarthy branded as communists. McCarthy was taking advantage of

Senator McCarthy—seen here (right) during a radio broadcast—lost the support of many Americans because of his conduct in a series of televised hearings in 1954.

the public's frustration with the boldness of the Chinese and the Soviets. Some whom McCarthy attacked as doing the work of traitors were former President Truman and the hero-general George C. Marshall. McCarthy charged that President Eisenhower had been tricked by communist lies.

Members of the Senate finally decided to end the wave of fear and suspicion that became known as "McCarthyism." Late in 1954 the United States Senate voted to *condemn* McCarthy. This means that the Senate officially expressed its disapproval of his behavior.

The Senate vote in 1954 ended McCarthy's influence. He had sown the seeds of distrust and mistrust among Americans. He had also damaged many people by his falsely labeling them communists.

ANSWER THESE QUESTIONS

1. Who were the "Big Three" at the Yalta Conference? At the Potsdam Conference?
2. How was Germany divided after World War II?
3. What was the policy expressed in the Truman Doctrine?
4. Why did the United Nations send troops to Korea in 1950?
5. What is McCarthyism? How did it hurt some people?

ANSWER THESE QUESTIONS

1. Roosevelt, Churchill, Stalin; Truman, Atlee, Stalin
2. into four zones: British, American, French, Soviet
3. to stop communism by providing economic and military aid to help countries recover from World War II
4. to stop the invasion of South Korea by North Korean communists
5. a series of false accusations of communism; many people lost their jobs and reputations

PEOPLE IN AMERICA

Tsung Dao Lee

One result of the cold war was a spurt of scientific research in the 1950s and 1960s. In an effort to win the arms race with the Soviets, the United States government increased its support of scientists who were working on new weapons systems, space exploration, and other kinds of important research. One of those scientists was Tsung Dao Lee.

Tsung Dao Lee was born in Shanghai, China, on November 24, 1926. He especially enjoyed reading as a child. His parents encouraged him to read books of all kinds. In high school Lee became interested in science, particularly physics. After high school he studied at the National Chekiang University, as well as at Southwest Associated University in K'un-ming.

Following graduation, Lee was one of two Chinese students that year to be offered a scholarship to study in America. He enrolled at the University of Chicago in 1946. Four years later he received the Ph.D. degree.

Soon Lee took a teaching position at the University of California. He later became a professor at Princeton University. Already he had begun to distinguish himself in the field of physics. In 1953 Lee moved to Columbia University in New York City. Over the next four years his achievements in physics were outstanding.

Lee was only thirty years old when he was awarded the Nobel prize in physics in 1957. The award was for a discovery he and an associate had made that proved a certain "law" of nature to be false. It was a complicated principle, which for thirty years had been considered true. Called the "conservation of parity," it dealt with the behavior of atoms.

Such discoveries are important because they reveal to us the workings of things close to us, like our bodies themselves, or of things far away from us, like the makeup of the sun and other stars. It was scientists like Tsung Dao Lee who made possible, for better or for worse, the development of nuclear weapons and new medicines, as well as the long strides people have taken into space.

24-2 Other Postwar Presidents

As you read, think about these questions:
What was the Eisenhower Doctrine?
What new programs did President Kennedy start to deal with problems in poor nations?
How did the Cuban missile crisis threaten the safety of the world?

Special Vocabulary brinkmanship summit conference

CONTENT OBJECTIVES

After completing the lesson, students will know:

- that the arms race heated up in the early 1950s, so that by 1953 the United States and the Soviets had both created hydrogen bombs
- how the Middle East became the focus of international attention
- some of the programs President Kennedy developed to solve problems in the world
- about President Kennedy's assassination in 1963

VOCABULARY

brinkmanship: the practice of pushing a dangerous situation to the limit of safety in order to obtain the greatest advantage

summit conference: a meeting attended by heads of government

The Korean War was the great handicap for the Democrats in the presidential election of 1952. Peace talks had begun, but the fighting continued. Republicans took advantage of the widespread unhappiness over what some were calling "Truman's War"—a war the President could not win and could not end.

The Eisenhower Years

The Republicans nominated the popular war hero, General Dwight D. Eisenhower. He promised to go to Korea immediately, if elected, and find a way to end the war. Eisenhower won the election and flew at once to Korea. It took seven months, though, before a peace settlement was signed. The settlement left the communists in control of North Korea.

The Arms Race. The United States and the USSR became more distrustful of each other. Both nations began building increasingly powerful weapons. This competition produced a dangerous arms race.

Following the explosion of the Soviet's atomic bomb in 1949, the United States had begun work on an even bigger bomb. On November 1, 1952, America tested the first hydrogen bomb. It was a thousand times more powerful than the bombs that had fallen on Hiroshima and Nagasaki. About a year later, the Soviets also had a hydrogen bomb.

New ways to launch these bombs were being developed. Supersonic planes, atomic submarines, and guided missiles would soon be able to deliver nuclear bombs great distances.

Great success as a general was an important asset for Eisenhower—shown here in his military dress uniform—in his campaign for the presidency.

Brinkmanship. As the arms race quickened, local conflicts around the world continued to challenge American leaders. For example, Chiang Kai-shek's Nationalist government in Formosa still controlled a few islands close to mainland China. Early in 1955 Chinese communists attacked one of these islands, Ichiang, and they threatened the islands of Quemoy and Matsu.

In January 1955 President Eisenhower asked Congress for the authority to use military power to defend Formosa. Congress granted Eisenhower's request by passing the Formosa Resolution. To keep the communists off balance, the resolution was purposely vague about the defense of the islands other than Formosa. Unsure of America's intentions, the communists finally decided against an all-out attack.

Writing about such crises as these in 1956, John Foster Dulles, Eisenhower's secretary of state, said, "The ability to get to the verge [edge] without getting into war is the necessary art. If you cannot master it, you inevitably get into war. If you try to run away from it, if you are scared to go to the brink, you are lost."

Dulles's foreign policy, therefore, became known as *brinkmanship*—that is, the practice of pushing a dangerous situation to the limit of safety in order to obtain the greatest advantage. This strategy frightened many people; they believed it placed the nation and the world in unnecessary danger. Others, however, believed that Dulles's strong stands had helped prevent communism from expanding.

John Foster Dulles is shown here (third from left) in the first televised Cabinet meeting. Such telecasts gave Americans a better view of their government in action.

The Eisenhower Doctrine. In 1956 peace was again disturbed, this time in the Suez Canal area. Israel, France, and Great Britain invaded Egypt, aiming to take over control of the canal. The USSR threatened to force the invaders out of Egypt and the canal area. Eisenhower angrily told the invaders that he was opposed to their way of solving international problems. The invading soldiers withdrew and a United Nations peace-keeping force stepped in.

Following this episode, in January 1957, President Eisenhower asked for Congressional approval, in advance, of any military action he might need to take in the Middle East. Congress again gave Eisenhower what he asked for. It adopted what became known as the Eisenhower Doctrine. This doctrine had two parts. 1) It authorized the President to use military force to stop Soviet aggression in the Middle East. 2) It provided $200 million to be used to assist any Middle East country that wanted American help.

Nikita Khrushchev's visit to Washington was the first such visit by a Soviet leader. It raised American hopes that the cold war was ending.

The U-2 Incident. In 1959 Nikita Khrushchev, the head of the Soviet government, and President Eisenhower agreed to hold a *summit conference* of the "Big Four" in Paris in May 1960. A summit conference is a meeting attended by the heads of government, in this case the governments of the United States, the USSR, France, and Great Britain.

On May 5, 1960, Khrushchev shocked the world by announcing that an American plane, called a U-2, had been shot down over Soviet territory. The United States eventually admitted that the U-2 was a spy plane. Eisenhower announced the United States would cancel future U-2 flights. When he arrived in Paris on May 16, however, he found that Khrushchev wanted him to apologize for the U-2 incident. When Eisenhower refused to do this, the summit conference was canceled.

The Kennedy Years

In 1961 America had a new President, John F. Kennedy. The new President continued the foreign aid programs started by Truman and Eisenhower. He was also eager to try some new solutions to the problems of the world.

John Kennedy was the first President born in the twentieth century. Like Lincoln, the first President born in the nineteenth century, he took office in the sixty-first year of the century.

Alliance for Progress. One of the first problems the new President tackled was the poverty of Latin America. In March 1961 Kennedy called for "a decade of democratic progress" to develop a prosperous Latin America, free of communism. Nineteen Latin American countries joined the United States in forming an "Alliance for Progress."

By the end of four years the United States had given more than $4 billion to the Alliance. Latin America itself put up over $20 billion. The work of the Alliance, nevertheless, was disappointing. Much of the money found its way to the rich and powerful, rather than into the hands of the poor. In later years, Congress gradually reduced the level of support for the program.

The Peace Corps. Also in 1961 President Kennedy established the Peace Corps. Under this program, the United States government sent American men and women "to help foreign countries meet their urgent needs." During the first year, more than nine hundred volunteers—teachers, students, doctors, engineers, and business people—worked in sixteen countries in Latin America, Asia, and Africa. They lived in the homes of the local people, helping them to build roofs, hospitals, schools, and sanitary systems. By 1964 colleges and universities were training ten thousand participants to work in forty-six countries. The work of the Peace Corps helped create understanding and goodwill between the United States and many other nations.

This Peace Corps teacher in Kenya reflects the hopefulness with which America entered the 1960s. Through the work of the Peace Corps, the United States gained goodwill in many nations.

The Bay of Pigs. A revolution in 1959 had placed the government of Cuba in the hands of Fidel Castro. He was a communist, and he received support from the Soviets. Thousands of anticommunist Cubans fled their island and settled in the United States, mostly in Florida (see Chapter 25).

These immigrants, though they had found a new home in the United States, still wanted to overthrow Castro. For nine months near the end of Eisenhower's administration, the United States had been giving military training to several hundred anti-Castro Cubans.

Kennedy learned of the anti-Castro forces when he came into office in 1961. Several advisers urged him to continue training and supporting the anti-Castro Cubans. Other advisers urged him to drop the project, fearing what might happen if the force tried to invade Cuba. Kennedy decided to go ahead with the invasion project. He refused, however, to allow American troops to take part in it.

On April 17, 1961, about 1500 anti-Castro Cubans landed in Cuba at the Golfo de Cochinos, or Bay of Pigs. Without United States military support, the invaders were no match

DISCUSSION

Have the students discuss the Bay of Pigs invasion. Ask them to think about the advantages and disadvantages of participation by the United States government in the overthrow of a foreign government. They should weigh the dilemma of having a communist government so close to the United States and the natural inclination of the American people to allow the Cuban people to select their own form of government.

for Castro's forces, who easily smashed the effort. Kennedy was angry that he had been led to believe that the invasion could succeed. Still, he accepted full blame for its failure.

ACTIVITY

Objective: To use reference materials and to write a report

Have the students do library research to write a brief report on West Berlin during the Kennedy years. The report should answer these questions: (1) What crises did West Berlin face during the Kennedy years? (2) When did President Kennedy go to West Berlin and why? (3) What was the effect of his famous statement, "I am a Berliner"?

The Berlin Wall. West Berlin had troubled the Soviets since the late 1940s. In 1961 the Soviets threatened to sign a peace settlement with East Germany. This move would allow the German communists to claim that their country, including the area of West Berlin, should no longer be occupied by any foreigners. Kennedy, like Truman and Eisenhower before him, made it clear that the United States intended to stay in Berlin.

The Berlin Wall became known in Germany as the "wall of shame." It cut off families and friends from one another and from freedom.

One reason for the continuing Soviet concern over West Berlin was that almost 1700 East Berliners were fleeing to the West every day. The Soviets and East Germans, on August 13, 1961, began building a barbed wire fence. Later the fence was replaced by a high cement-block wall. The wall sliced the city in two.

The building of the Berlin Wall broke the Yalta agreements, and every rule of decency. It certainly ended the large number of escapes. The wall became a sign to all the world that communists must use force on their own people to turn off their natural desire for freedom.

The world held its breath as American ships inspected Soviet vessels for weapons during the Cuban missile crisis. For the first time, the world was on the brink of nuclear war.

The Cuban Missile Crisis. In the fall of 1962, Kennedy faced the most serious crisis of his presidency. On October 16, a United States spy plane discovered that the Soviets were building missile bases in Cuba. This meant that Cuba would soon have the ability to destroy many cities in the eastern and southern United States. Immediately Kennedy assembled his Cabinet and other advisers. He wanted to get the missiles out of Cuba without causing a nuclear war.

On October 22, 1962, Kennedy ordered a naval blockade of Cuba to stop the Soviets from shipping any more weapons to Cuba. He also demanded that Khrushchev remove the missiles. As the tension mounted, Khrushchev suddenly indicated he had decided not to challenge the blockade. The Soviet Union promised to remove the missiles. The United States promised not to invade Cuba.

Test Ban Treaty. The scare of the Cuban missile crisis deepened the desire of Americans to make the world a safer place for all. In June 1963 Kennedy proposed that the USSR, Great Britain, and the United States limit their testing of nuclear weapons. After many meetings among representatives of the three countries, a limited nuclear test ban treaty was finally signed in Moscow on August 5, 1963.

Under the test ban treaty, no more test bombs could be exploded above ground or under water. Only underground tests would be allowed. Secret testing was stopped altogether.

One hundred nations agreed to the treaty. As he signed it on behalf of the United States, President Kennedy said, "It offers to all the world a welcome sign of hope."

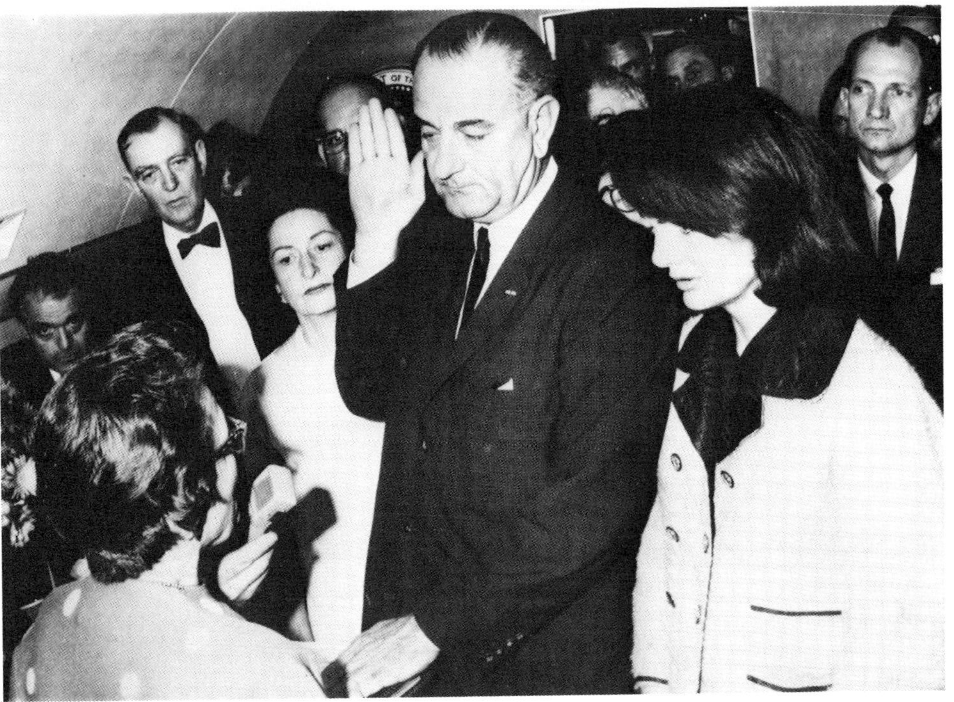

Lyndon Johnson took the oath of office on the plane that carried Kennedy's body back to Washington for burial. Jacqueline Kennedy (right) and Lady Bird Johnson stand with the new President.

Assassination. On the morning of November 22, 1963, the President and Mrs. Kennedy flew to Dallas, Texas. There the President hoped to strengthen his support before the next election. The Kennedys rode in an open car with Governor John Connally and Mrs. Connally on the trip from the airport. Crowds lined the streets. The people cheered and waved. Without warning, bullets hit Kennedy. His automobile sped to a hospital where he was pronounced dead. Two days later, Lee Harvey Oswald, the person accused of killing the President, was himself shot to death while being moved from one jail to another.

Lyndon B. Johnson, the Vice President, became the new President. He was keenly aware of how much the world in a short time had come to love and admire Kennedy. Johnson hoped to be loved and admired, too.

ANSWER THESE QUESTIONS

1. competition over powerful weapons between the United States and the USSR
2. invasion of Egypt's Suez Canal area by Israel, France, and Great Britain
3. in 1961
4. The missiles could be used to attack cities in the southern and eastern United States.
5. no more test bombs above ground or underwater; no secret tests; underground tests only

ANSWER THESE QUESTIONS

1. What was the arms race?
2. What conflict led to the Eisenhower Doctrine?
3. When was the Peace Corps established?
4. Why did Kennedy insist that the Soviets remove their missiles from Cuba?
5. What were the provisions of the nuclear test ban treaty?

Objective: After completing these pages, students should know how to skim reading material to collect information.

Skimming to Collect Information

You will recall that in Chapter 3 you learned about the skill of skimming a document. Put that skill to work again and read the following excerpts from President Kennedy's inaugural, given on January 20, 1961. Then answer the questions below by skimming the material to locate the necessary information quickly. (If you need to, reread the information in "Working With Skills" on page 62 in Chapter 3.)

. . . The world is very different now. For man holds in his mortal hands the power to abolish all forms of human poverty and all forms of human life. And yet the same revolutionary beliefs for which our forebears fought are still at issue around the globe—the belief that the rights of man come not from the generosity of the state but from the hand of God.

We dare not forget today that we are the heirs of that first revolution. Let the word go forth . . . to friend and foe alike, that the torch has been passed to a new generation of Americans . . . unwilling to witness or permit the slow undoing of those human rights to which this nation has always been committed, and to which we are committed today. . . .

To those peoples in the huts and villages of half the globe struggling to break the bonds of mass misery, we pledge our best efforts to help them help themselves, for whatever period is required—not because the communists may be doing it, not because we seek their votes, but because it is right. . . .

In the long history of the world, only a few generations have been granted the role of defending freedom in its hour of maximum danger. I do not shrink from this responsibility—I welcome it. I do not believe that any of us would exchange places with any other people or any other generation. The energy, the faith, the devotion which we bring to this endeavor will light our country and all who serve it—and the glow from that fire can truly light the world. . . .

1. Why is the world different now?
2. For what belief did our forebears fight?
3. To what is the nation committed?
4. Why do we pledge our help to those in misery?

Working With Skills

READING SKILLS

ACTIVITY

Objective: To skim material to collect information

List these dates on the chalkboard: 1956; 1960; April 17, 1961; August 13, 1961; and 1962. Have the students skim Lesson 24-2 to find the foreign policy crisis associated with each date. Ask the students to make a brief list of the crises, putting the date first.

ANSWERS

1. because humans have the "power to abolish all forms of human poverty and all forms of human life"
2. the belief that humanity's rights come from God, not from "the generosity of the state"
3. "human rights"
4. because "it is right"

RELATED MATERIAL

Duplicator/Copy Master Activity 52

THINKING THINGS THROUGH

1. a plan to help Western European nations rebuild after the war **2.** The United States tested the first hydrogen bomb in 1952. **3.** to enable all western nations to face the Soviet Union together in case of war **4.** MacArthur wanted to invade China; Truman thought this would lead to World War III. **5.** He took advantage of people's fears of China and the Soviets to accuse

Chapter 24 SUMMARY

After World War II, the Soviet Union set up communist governments in eastern European countries and kept East Germany separate from the rest of Germany. These actions helped start the cold war.

Between 1948 and 1951, the United States sent billions of dollars in aid to western Europe under the Marshall Plan. This aid helped European nations recover from war damage and resist the influence of communism. The North Atlantic Treaty Organization, formed in 1949, strengthened western Europe's military defenses.

In 1950 United Nations forces, most of whom were American, fought against communist North Korean forces in the Korean War. The North Koreans were aided by China, which had become a communist country in 1949. American dissatisfaction with the war helped Dwight D. Eisenhower become President in 1952.

Fear of communism in the United States led to a wave of mistrust called McCarthyism after Senator Joseph McCarthy. McCarthy damaged the lives of many Americans by falsely calling them communists.

Soon after his election in 1960, President John F. Kennedy started the Peace Corps to help the poor of the world. Kennedy's position in foreign policy was weakened by his support for an unsuccessful invasion of Cuba in 1961. In 1962, however, Kennedy forced the Soviets to remove their missiles from Cuba. Kennedy was assassinated on November 22, 1963, and Lyndon B. Johnson became President.

Chapter 24 TEST

WORDS TO REMEMBER

Match each of the following words with the correct definition given below.

b 1. brinkmanship
d 2. containment
f 3. summit conference
a 4. censor
e 5. iron curtain
c 6. cold war

a. to control what is written or said
b. pushing a dangerous situation to the limit
c. economic and political rivalry that stops short of a shooting war
d. stopping the spread of communism
e. the imaginary wall separating communist and noncommunist countries
f. meeting of world leaders

THINKING THINGS THROUGH

1. What was the Marshall Plan?
2. What developments in the arms race followed the explosion of the first Soviet atomic bomb?
3. Why was NATO organized?
4. Why did President Truman remove General MacArthur from command?
5. How did Senator McCarthy contribute to American fears of communism?
6. How did President Kennedy handle the Cuban missile crisis?

RELATED MATERIALS
Duplicator/Copy Masters: Activities 51, 52; Quiz 50
Workbook pages 74-76

such leaders as former President Eisenhower of being tricked by the communists. **6.** He ordered a naval blockade of Cuba and demanded that the USSR remove its missiles.

WORKING WITH SKILLS

1. "our sister republics south of the border" **2.** to assist free people in "casting off the chains of poverty" **3.** oppose aggression or subversion anywhere in the Americas **4.** masters of their own houses

---

WORKING WITH SKILLS

Skim the following excerpt from Kennedy's inaugural to find the answers to the questions below.

> To our sister republics south of our border, we offer a special pledge—to convert our good words into good deeds—in a new alliance for progress—to assist free men and free governments in casting off the chains of poverty. But this peaceful revolution of hope cannot become the prey of hostile powers. Let all our neighbors know that we shall join with them to oppose aggression or subversion anywhere in the Americas. And let every other power know that this Hemisphere intends to remain the master of its own house.

1. To whom does Kennedy offer a special pledge?
2. What is to be the purpose of the "alliance for progress"?
3. What will Americans join with their neighbors to do?
4. What do the countries of the Western Hemisphere intend to remain?

ON YOUR OWN

1. If you know a Peace Corps veteran, interview him or her and write a brief report about the purpose and outcome of his or her project. Otherwise, use the card catalog or *The Readers' Guide to Periodical Literature* to find information about the Peace Corps. Make a list of five Peace Corps projects in five different countries.
2. Imagine that you were living in East Berlin in 1961 when the Berlin Wall was built. Write a short story describing how your life would have changed overnight as communication with the West was cut off. Remember that families and friends were suddenly separated, and travel outside the city was not permitted.
3. The cartoon by Bill Mauldin on this page shows Lincoln weeping after the Kennedy assassination. The cartoonist seems to be suggesting parallels between Lincoln and Kennedy. Using an encyclopedia, try to find some similarities between these two Presidents. Write your conclusions in a short paragraph.

QUESTIONS TO ANSWER

1. 1929, 1939 **2.** TVA **3.** Stalin **4.** War Production Board **5.** Montgomery, Rommel, El Alamein **6.** Hiroshima, Nagasaki **7.** Marshall Plan **8.** Mao Tse-tung **9.** Bay of Pigs

THINK THINGS THROUGH

1. American factory workers were laid off when Europe was forced to reduce its American purchases in order to pay its war debts. **2.** He ordered the Army to remove the marchers from Washington. **3.** Poverty and defeat made their people vulnerable to the promise of power and revenge. **4.** the draft, the Lend-Lease Act, the building of bases in Greenland **5.** It revived the economy—unemployment fell and wages rose as factories converted to war production. **6.** It was a turning point, in that it gave Great Britain some relief and joined the USSR's strength to the Allies. **7.** the secret effort by Allied scientists to build the

Unit 8 TEST

WORDS TO REMEMBER

Match the words listed on the left with their definitions on the right.

d	1. brinkmanship	b	5. *Blitzkrieg*
f	2. rationing	g	6. containment
e	3. collective bargaining	c	7. appeasement
a	4. liberate	h	8. direct relief

a. free
b. lightning attack
c. keeping peace at almost any cost
d. strategic risk taking
e. negotiating as a group
f. limiting the purchase of goods
g. stopping Soviet expansion
h. money or a job

QUESTIONS TO ANSWER

Fill in the blanks in the following statements.

1. The Great Depression lasted for ten years, from ________ to ________.
2. One New Deal program provided electricity long after the depression ended. It was the ________.
3. After Lenin died, ________ used force to take control of the government of the USSR.
4. The ________ organized American industry to produce goods needed by the Allies.
5. In autumn 1942, British General ________ defeated German Field Marshal ________ at ________ in Egypt.
6. Truman forced Japan to surrender by dropping atomic bombs on two cities: ________ and ________.
7. The United States policy of helping war-damaged European countries help themselves was known as the ________.
8. ________ led the Chinese communists to power and set up the People's Republic of China.
9. On April 17, 1961, fifteen hundred Cuban revolutionaries were defeated by Castro's forces at the ________.

THINK THINGS THROUGH

1. In what way did World War I help cause the depression?
2. How did President Hoover respond to the Bonus Marchers's demands?
3. How did the defeat of Italy and Germany in World War I help to lead to the rise of dictatorships in those countries?
4. What actions did the United States government take to prepare for war before the attack on Pearl Harbor?
5. What was the effect of the war on the economy of the United States?
6. How did Hitler's decision to attack the Soviet Union affect the progress of the war in Europe?
7. What was the Manhattan Project?
8. What methods did the communist governments in eastern Europe use to maintain firm control of their countries?
9. What was the Alliance for Progress?

RELATED MATERIAL
Duplicator/Copy Master Test 51-53

atomic bomb **8.** censorship, no free elections or private ownership of businesses, limitations on travel and worship **9.** a program of economic aid to Latin America to help it develop democratically

PRACTICE YOUR SKILLS

1. a. four—Leningrad, Moscow, Stalingrad **b.** 500 miles (800 kilometers) **c.** November 1942 **d.** the battle of Leningrad—two years, five months **2. a.** a flashlight **b.** clean socks **c.** a bottle of anti-mosquito dope **d.** a hunting knife **3. a.** the horizontal line along the bottom **b.** along the vertical line on the left **c.** eleven **d.** up

---

PRACTICE YOUR SKILLS

1. Study the map of World War II in Europe and Africa, 1941-1945, on page 576. Use the legend on that map to answer these questions.
   a. How many German invasion routes are shown? What major cities are these invasion routes aimed at?
   b. How many miles (kilometers) are represented by one inch?
   c. In what month were Allied forces fighting in Algiers?
   d. Of the major battles fought in the USSR, which went on the longest? How long was that battle?

2. Skim the following excerpt from an article in the army magazine *Yank*. It offers advice to soldiers going to fight in the Pacific, by a reporter named Bill Steele.

   Probably the handiest item to bring along is a hunting knife with a good stout blade. And you never have too many pairs of clean socks. Swim trunks —don't forget 'em! And bring rubber soled sneaks for boxing, baseball, or just hitting the sack for a few minutes before chow. And flashlights are swell to have and impossible to buy around here. Plus, there's many a man who'd hock his PFC [Private First Class] stripe for a bottle of anti-mosquito dope.

   a. What item is "swell" to have and "impossible" to buy?
   b. What can you never have too many of?
   c. What item is worth a man's PFC stripe?
   d. What is the handiest item to bring along?

3. Suppose that you want to draw a line graph showing how many American workers belonged to unions each year from 1930 to 1940.
   a. Where on the graph would you write the years?
   b. Where would you indicate the number of union members?
   c. How many points would you need to plot on the graph?
   d. Based on what you have learned about the union movement during the depression, in what direction would you expect the line to move?

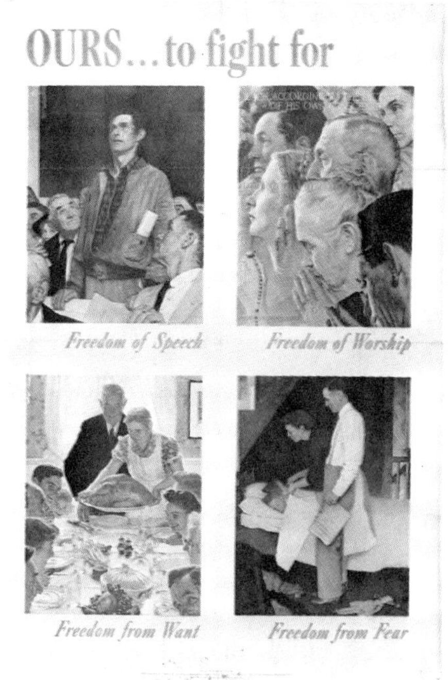

Famous Norman Rockwell posters like this expressed the spirit of the 1940s and 1950s in America's struggle to preserve democracy.

Unit 9
NEW DIRECTIONS

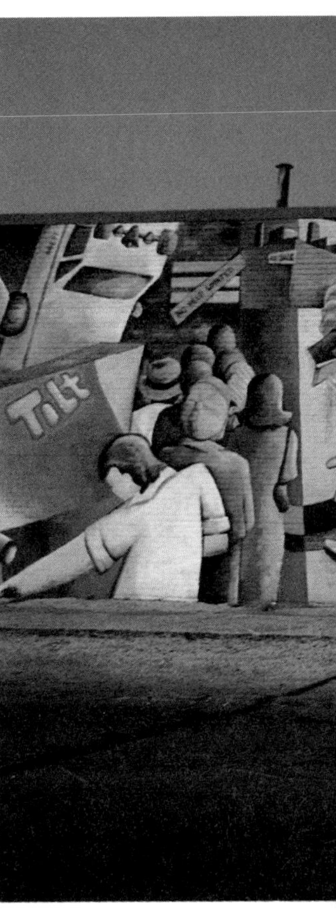

Unit Nine discusses the period from 1950 to 1973, in terms of domestic events and foreign policy. The topics discussed in the unit include the following: the Civil Rights Movement, the Women's Liberation Movement, the Vietnam War, the Watergate scandal, tensions in the Middle East, and migration to the suburbs and to the Sun Belt.

A peace demonstration in Washington, D.C.

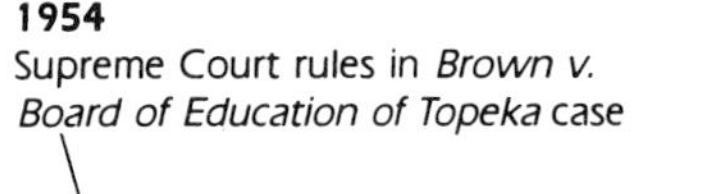

1954
Supreme Court rules in *Brown v. Board of Education of Topeka* case

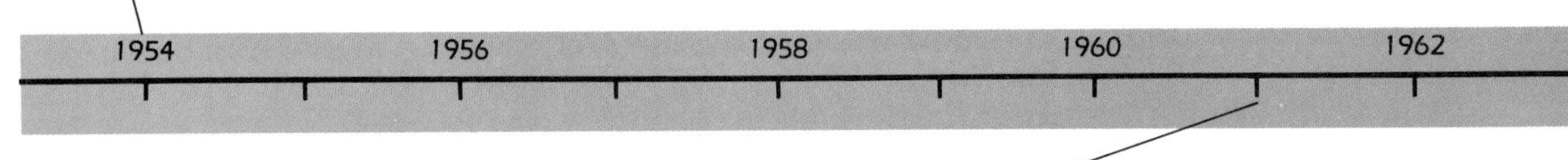

1961
Alan Shepard becomes the first American to enter space

A Chicago neighborhood mural

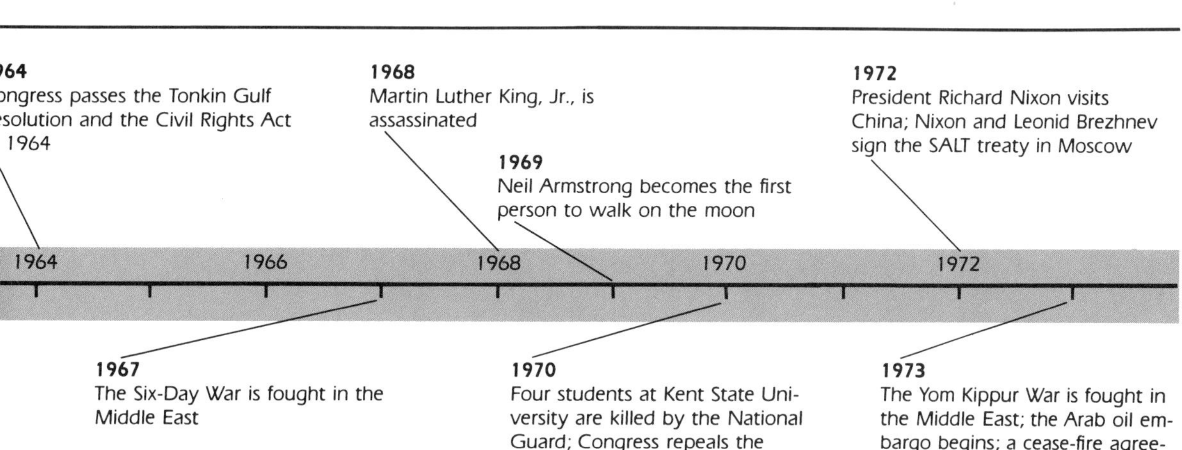

Chapter 25
FIGHTING DISCRIMINATION

Chapter 25 discusses the movements after World War II for equal rights for women and minorities. Lesson 25-1 recounts the efforts of the Civil Rights Movement to gain equal rights for blacks and discusses the violent opposition with which the movement was met. Lesson 25-2 details the efforts of Hispanics, Native Americans, and women to achieve equal opportunity.

CONTENT OBJECTIVES

After completing the lesson, students will know:

- that segregation and discrimination were part of American life through the late 1940s
- about the decision reached by the Supreme Court in *Brown v. Board of Education of Topeka*
- how 200,000 "Freedom Marchers" in Washington, D.C., in 1963 brought national attention to the civil rights cause
- the details and impact of the three civil rights acts passed in the 1960s
- about the assassination of the Reverend Martin Luther King, Jr., and its aftermath

VOCABULARY

civil rights: the rights guaranteed by a government to protect persons against unjust acts by government or individuals
segregation: the system of forcing a certain group of people to live and conduct their affairs separately from the majority of people
prejudice: the judging of a group on the basis of limited information
stereotype: a false mental picture of a whole group from knowing only one or two of its members
discrimination: mistreating people of another group
desegregation: ending of segregation
integration: the blending of races or groups

25-1 The Civil Rights Movement

As you read, think about these questions:
What was segregation?
What caused discrimination?
How were America's schools desegregated?
How did Martin Luther King, Jr., influence the Civil Rights Movement?
What were some improvements brought about by the Civil Rights Movement?

Special Vocabulary civil rights, segregation, prejudice, stereotype, discrimination, desegregation, integration

After World War II—in which America had made freedom its goal—many minority groups were actively determined to put an end to the violation of their *civil rights*. Civil rights are the rights guaranteed by a government to protect persons against unjust acts by the government or by individuals.

Segregation

Ever since the Reconstruction period, black Americans had struggled to make real in practice the rights guaranteed them in the Constitution. These rights included equal treatment and the right to vote. In spite of these efforts, white people imposed on black Americans a special way of life. This way of life was called *segregation*. Segregation was the system of forcing a certain group of people—in this case blacks—to live and conduct their affairs separately from the majority of people. Black Americans had to live in separate parts of town, go to separate schools, ride in separate parts of trains and buses, and do a hundred other everyday things separately from the majority of Americans.

In the South, governments passed laws enforcing segregation. In the North, segregation was not enforced by law, but segregation existed anyhow. This was so because black people usually could not afford to live in white parts of town. In addition, they knew that white people did not generally welcome them outside the black sections. They, therefore, went to their own schools and churches, ate in their own restaurants, and generally kept to themselves. Over the years, every northern big city developed its own black neighborhood.

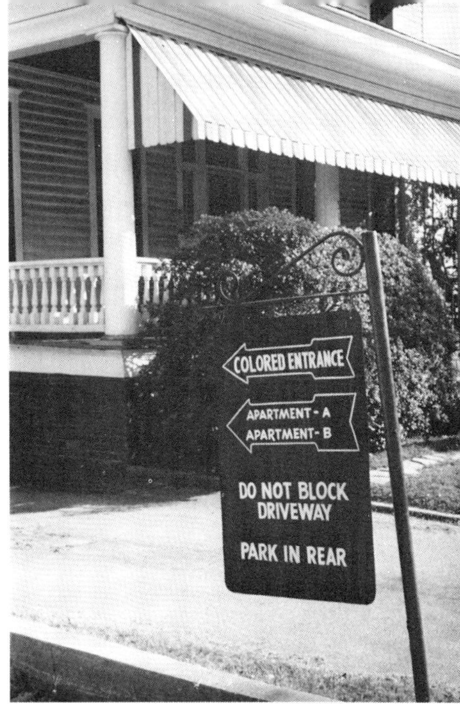

During the 1950s signs like this one constantly reminded blacks that they were expected to remain separate from whites.

Separate but Equal. In 1896 the Supreme Court of the United States gave its blessing to segregation. It declared that the states could practice segregation as long as public facilities used by blacks were equal in quality to those used by whites. This was called the "separate but equal" ruling.

Such a decision neglected two important problems in American life. First, social groups often are *prejudiced* against each other. This means that people sometimes judge a group unfavorably, even if they do not know very much about its members. They often get a false picture in their minds about the group from knowing only a few of its members, or none at all. This false mental picture is called a *stereotype*.

Discrimination. The second important problem in American life which insured that the idea of separate but equal could not work well was *discrimination*. Discrimination occurs when people from one group mistreat people of another group because they regard them as inferior or undesirable.

Discrimination against blacks sometimes was violent, as when whites beat up a black for being in the "wrong part of town." It sometimes was nonviolent, as when a restaurant refused to serve food to black people.

By 1945 segregation was firmly planted in the American way of life. Furthermore, over the years, discrimination had guaranteed that the segregated way of life was not equal to the dominant way of life. Segregated schools, for example, were supposed to be equal in quality to others. Discrimination, however, caused some school officials to send the oldest

DISCUSSION

Have the students discuss the concept of "separate but equal" facilities for blacks and whites. Does the concept seem fair? Stress that an idea can seem reasonable but have unforeseen consequences in everyday life. The text gives examples of two ways in which black schools were not treated equally (sent the oldest books and least prepared teachers). Have the students offer examples of other ways in which the black schools may have been shortchanged.

books and the least prepared teachers to the older school buildings frequently assigned for use by black students.

Americans had succeeded in making life separate for black people, but they had not made it equal. Because of discrimination, segregation had inequality built into it.

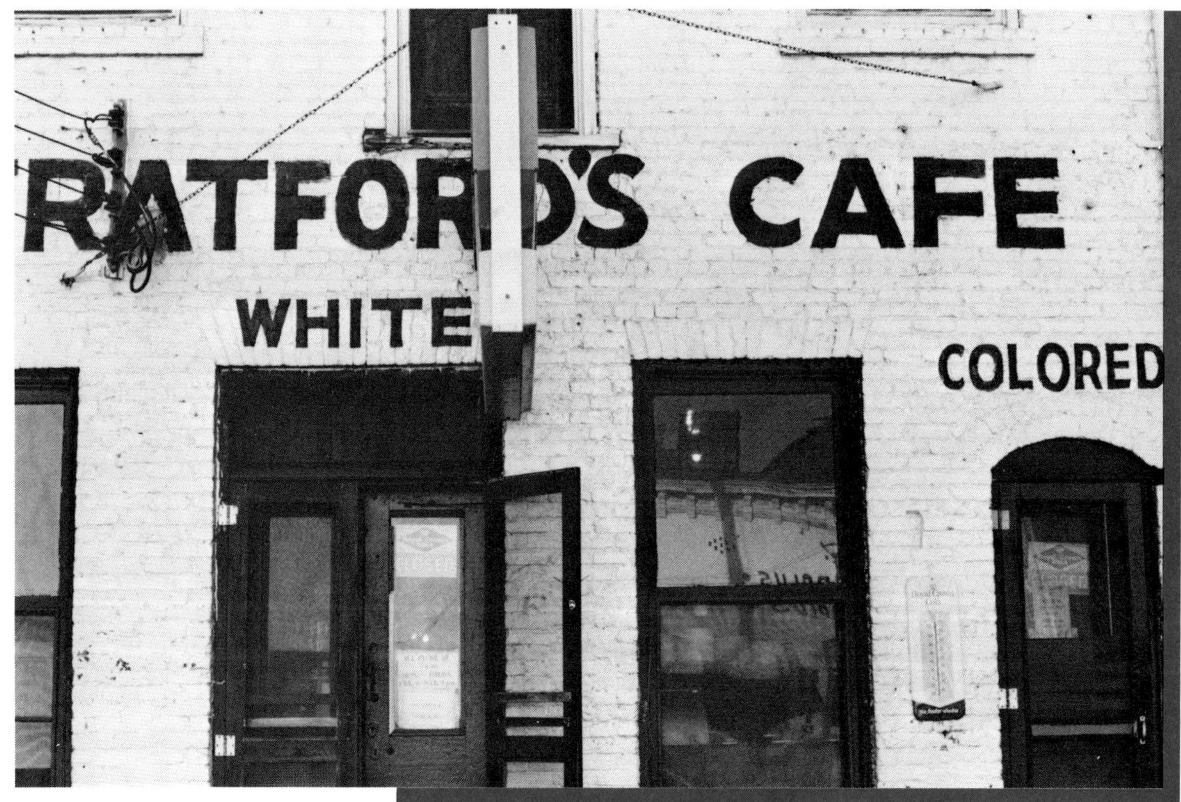

As late as 1968, the National Advisory Committee on Civil Disorders stated that America was moving toward separate but unequal societies.

The War Against Segregation

President Harry S Truman began *desegregation*—the ending of segregation—in the armed forces in 1948. He ordered the *integration* of the armed forces—the blending of all races in all military units. The biggest battles against segregation, however, were still to be fought.

Desegregating the Schools. Linda Brown, a black girl from Topeka, Kansas, wanted to attend a white school near her home. The school board refused to let Linda enroll there, saying that she belonged in the black school across town.

Oliver Brown, Linda's father, with the help of the National Association for the Advancement of Colored People (NAACP), sued the Board of Education of Topeka. The case

These children were the first blacks to attend Little Rock's Central High School in 1958. Here they are sitting with two officials of the NAACP at the Supreme Court.

finally reached the Supreme Court of the United States. There, in 1954, the justices, with Chief Justice Earl Warren as their leader, ruled that Linda Brown was indeed entitled to attend the all-white school. (For more about this subject, see **Law and the Citizen,** page 624.)

Many Americans in the North and the South hated the idea of desegregation. Organizations like the Ku Klux Klan threatened to fight integration with violence. Other organizations came into being, like the White Citizens' Councils. They insisted that all-white schools would be ruined by integration. These people refused to do business with people who opposed segregation.

In the North, some white people felt sure that desegregation would never touch their communities. Since segregation there was not laid down by law, northerners felt that the court's ruling had little to do with them. In time, however, they learned differently. The 1954 Supreme Court decision was aimed against all segregated schools, no matter how the segregation came about.

One of the toughest battles against segregated schools anywhere in the nation was fought by President Dwight D. Eisenhower in Little Rock, Arkansas, in 1957. There the governor of Arkansas, Orval Faubus, was determined to bar blacks from attending white schools. As a result, President Eisenhower had to order state and national troops to force the governor and some of the people in Little Rock to obey the federal desegregation laws. Because of the federal action,

Little Rock's Central High School, which had been all-white, began to admit black students.

The Montgomery Boycott. The schools were not the only places where battles were fought against segregation. On the public buses of Montgomery, Alabama, desegregation won another major victory. On December 1, 1955, a black woman named Rosa Parks stepped aboard a crowded bus after a hard day's work. At that time buses in Montgomery, as in most cities in the South, were segregated. Parks sat down in the white section of the bus. This was no problem until all the other seats in the white section were filled. Then a white man boarded the bus and wanted a seat. The driver told Parks to move to the black section. Parks refused and was arrested for breaking a segregation law.

The black community of Montgomery was outraged. The NAACP took up Parks's cause. Parks also got help from a young Montgomery minister, Martin Luther King, Jr.

King organized and led a protest against the bus company and the segregation laws of Montgomery. He got black people to stop using the buses, which cost the bus company a lot of money. Meanwhile, the NAACP went to the Supreme Court and asked it to review the Montgomery law allowing segregation on the city's buses. The high court ruled that such segregation was illegal and must cease.

Again a segregation law had been struck down. Now a hero, Martin Luther King, Jr., had also come out of the battle. He would lead people, black and white alike, who wanted to fight in further struggles against segregation. In 1957 King helped set up a new organization to battle for civil rights. This organization was the Southern Christian Leadership Conference (SCLC).

Sit-ins and Freedom Rides. The first successes in the fight against segregation led to new crusades. Throughout the states where segregation was practiced, black and white people conducted what were called sit-ins. At a sit-in black people went to a segregated restaurant and took seats. Usually they were ignored or told that the restaurant was segregated. They, nevertheless, remained seated. The restaurant owners then called the police who came and arrested the blacks. Such an event often caused the black community to begin a boycott of businesses. One after another, stores gave in to the pressure created by the loss of business.

never approved of the riots that had taken place in America's cities. He had preached that the most effective protest is that which is nonviolent. In fact, in 1964 he had been given the Nobel Peace Prize, an award given only to those few people who help bring people together in dignity and justice.

As word of King's murder spread, the grief of millions of black people and white people as well told of King's enormous contribution to American life. More than any other figure, he had made Americans understand what a terrible evil racism is. In cities all over the country, black people in fury over King's death struck out at the world around them. Between April 4 and April 11, riots occurred in 125 cities in 29 states.

Shirley Chisholm was elected to the United States House of Representatives in 1969. She campaigned for the Democratic presidential nomination in 1972.

Improvement. During the 1960s, President Johnson began what he called a "war on poverty" aimed at relieving the distress of the poor. Laws were passed that helped poor people—black and white alike—get training for better jobs and get better housing. Since so many blacks were poor, they benefited from the antipoverty laws that were passed.

Black people gained much political power during the 1960s. Many talented black people obtained public office. Thurgood Marshall, appointed by President Johnson, became the first black justice of the United States Supreme Court. Robert C. Weaver, also appointed by Johnson, became the first black member of a President's Cabinet. Carl Stokes in Cleveland, Ohio, and Richard Hatcher in Gary, Indiana, became the first black mayors of major American cities. Shirley Chisholm of New York entered the House of Representatives as its first black woman member. In 1966 Julian Bond took a seat in the Georgia state legislature, a "first" for a black since Reconstruction days. These are only a handful of the black people who became leaders because of the efforts made in the 1950s and the 1960s to end segregation and discrimination in American society.

ANSWER THESE QUESTIONS

1. Who was Linda Brown?
2. What happened to Rosa Parks in 1955?
3. What were three laws that helped black people gain their civil rights in the 1960s?
4. How did each of the three branches of the federal government help blacks during the 1950s and 1960s?
5. Why did some black people riot in the cities between 1965 and 1968?

ANSWER THESE QUESTIONS

1. the girl for whom the suit *Brown v. the Board of Education of Topeka, Kansas* was filed
2. She was arrested for sitting in the white section of a bus; this led to the Montgomery boycott.
3. Civil Rights Act of 1964; Voting Rights Act of 1965; Civil Rights Act of 1968
4. The judiciary overturned the separate but equal doctrine; the executive under President Eisenhower supported integration in Little Rock, Ark.; the legislature passed civil rights laws in 1964, 1965, 1968.
5. segregation, discrimination, prejudice; poverty; to protest the assassination of Martin Luther King, Jr., in 1968

LAW AND THE CITIZEN

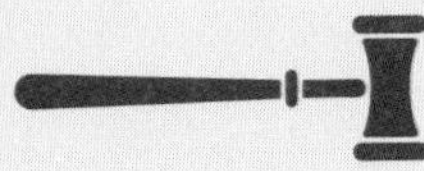

Separate but Equal

After Reconstruction several southern states passed laws that segregated blacks from whites in public places. In 1892 Homer Plessy, a black citizen of Louisiana, challenged a law saying that blacks and whites had to use separate railroad cars when traveling in Louisiana. In court he argued that the law was unconstitutional because it violated the "equal protection of the law" clause of the Fourteenth Amendment. Judge John H. Ferguson upheld the Louisiana law. Plessy appealed the decision to the Supreme Court.

In *Plessy v. Ferguson* the Supreme Court was asked to rule if Plessy's rights as a citizen had been violated by the law providing for segregation. The Supreme Court said that states had the right to make segregation laws—as long as the facilities for blacks and for whites were equal in quality. This ruling put the court's blessing on segregation.

In 1952 many states still had segregation laws. Kansas had a law that allowed separate schools for black children and white children. One family in Topeka, Kansas, the Browns, decided to challenge this law.

Linda, the Browns' eight-year-old daughter, had to go to the all-black school twenty-one blocks from her home. The school was old, overcrowded, and short of teachers. Just five blocks from the Brown home was the all-white school, which had none of these problems. It was against the law, however, for Linda to attend this school. The Browns took their case to a federal court in Topeka. The judge ruled that the Kansas law allowing these separate schools was constitutional because the schools were nearly equal. The Browns appealed the case to the Supreme Court.

The case, *Brown v. The Board of Education of Topeka*, was heard in 1954. The Court was asked to decide if separate but equal facilities, such as schools, were legal. All the justices readily agreed with Chief Justice Earl Warren who presented the ruling in favor of Linda Brown. Warren declared, "In the field of public education the doctrine of separate but equal has no place. Separate educational facilities are unequal." In cases later, the Court ruled that all laws that permitted separate but equal facilities were unconstitutional. The *Plessy v. Ferguson* decision had been overturned.

25-2 Other Social Movements

As you read, think about these questions:

What organizations were formed to help Mexican Americans fight against discrimination?

How did the reservation system affect the lives of Native Americans?

In what ways did some women feel they were discriminated against in the 1960s and 1970s?

Special Vocabulary *barrio*

CONTENT OBJECTIVES

After completing the lesson, students will know:

- that Hispanics made up a growing percentage of the population, though they had little political power
- about some Hispanic groups, including Mexican Americans, Puerto Ricans, and Cubans
- the problems faced by Native Americans and some political action initiated to improve their lives
- a brief history of the women's liberation movement

VOCABULARY

barrio: Spanish neighborhood

Blacks were not the only Americans who suffered the effects of discrimination. Spanish-speaking people and Native Americans had also felt its force. Because of their sex, women too had been denied opportunity and full freedom.

Hispanics

Spanish-speaking Americans, sometimes called Hispanics, make up the second largest minority group in the United States. In 1973 eleven million Hispanics lived in the United States. They were about 5.2 percent of the entire population.

In spite of their large numbers, Hispanics had a small voice in American political affairs. In part this weak role was due to the fact that Hispanics were not a single group. There were, in fact, several groups, the largest being Mexican Americans, Puerto Ricans, and Cuban Americans.

Mexican Americans. Three fifths of the Spanish-speaking people in the United States are Mexican Americans. Some of these people are from families that have lived in the American Southwest since it was under the Spanish or, later, the Mexican flag.

Many Mexican Americans came to the United States from Mexico during World War II when there was a great demand for workers. They usually settled in the cities of California and Texas. Very often Mexican Americans continued to speak only Spanish. They therefore tended to settle in neighborhoods in which Spanish was the main language. These Spanish neighborhoods were called *barrios*.

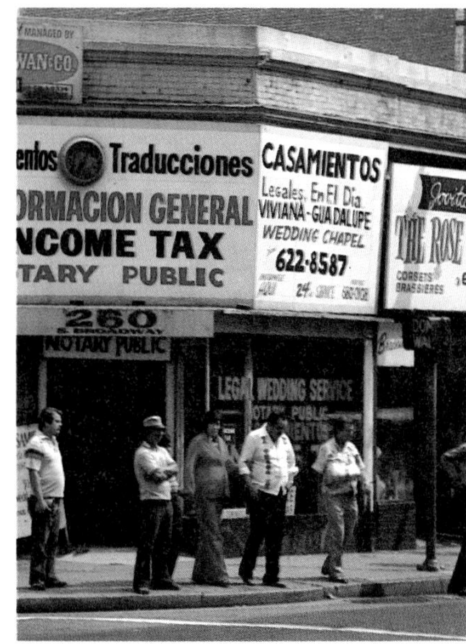

By 1970 eighty percent of Mexican Americans were living in cities. Spanish-speaking neighborhoods grew rapidly in most major metropolitan areas.

Mexican Americans faced discrimination in education, housing, and jobs. One reason for this discrimination was language. Most of the schooling in the United States took place in English. Most jobs called for workers who knew how to speak, read, and write English. Yet the Mexican Americans were proud of their heritage and refused to give up something as important to them as their language.

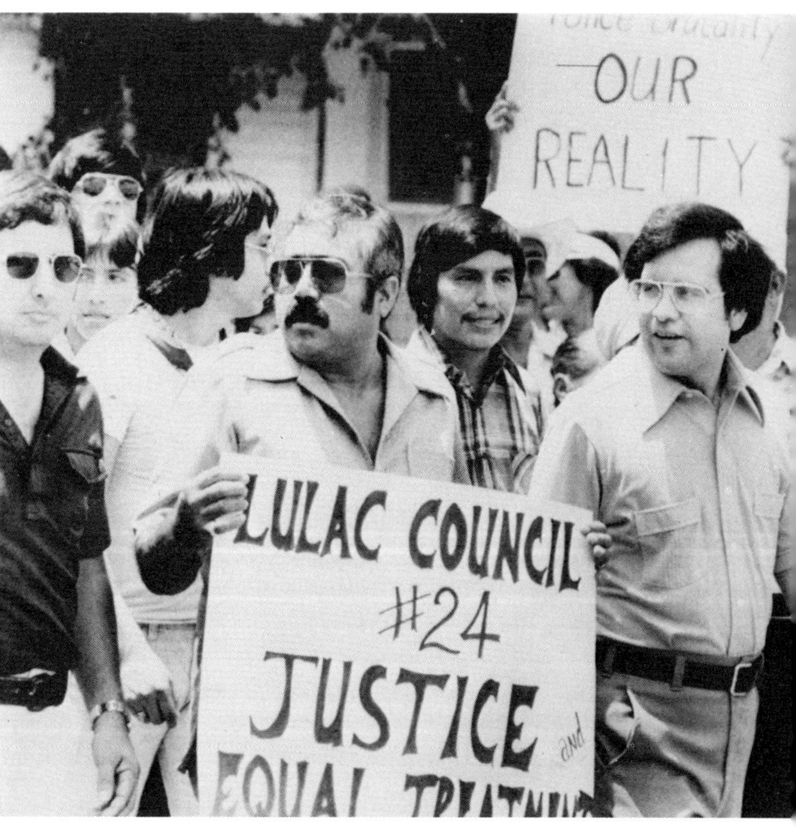

A group of Mexican Americans takes part in a protest march, a familiar practice for minorities during the 1960s and 1970s.

The Mexican American struggle for civil rights began during the 1960s and 1970s. During those years, many Mexican Americans realized that they needed to gain political power in order to improve their lives. In several cities and states, the Mexican Americans started organizations to help those in need and to gain political power. In 1965, for example, Rodolfo Gonzales founded the Crusade for Justice in Denver. The Crusade worked to provide social services and develop job opportunities for Mexican Americans. In California, César Chávez started the United Farm Workers Union in order to improve pay and working conditions of migrant workers. In Texas, Mexican Americans set up *La*

Raza Unida (the United People), a political party. Quickly the party spread to the Mexican American communities of other southwestern states. During the 1970s candidates of *La Raza Unida* won election to positions in city governments in many western states.

During the 1960s and 1970s, hope for a more powerful voice in public affairs grew. From Texas, Eligio De La Garza and Henry B. Gonzales were elected to the House of Representatives. Edward R. Roybal went to the House from New Mexico. Vincente T. Ximines became commissioner of the Equal Opportunity Commission in Washington. Then in 1981 Henry Cisneros became the mayor of San Antonio, Texas. He was the first Mexican American mayor of a big American city.

Former Attorney General Robert F. Kennedy breaks bread with César Chávez to mark the Mexican American leader's first meal after a twenty-three day protest fast. Kennedy was a strong supporter of the United Farm Workers.

Puerto Ricans. Puerto Ricans are American citizens who live either in Puerto Rico or in cities on the mainland. On the island of Puerto Rico, people adopted their own constitution in 1952. The Puerto Ricans, therefore, govern themselves. Because Puerto Rico is not a state, the islanders do not have a voting member in Congress. They do, however, send a nonvoting member to speak for them.

In the early 1940s, with United States aid, Puerto Ricans developed a program called "Operation Bootstrap." It was designed to improve industry, agriculture, and education. Luis Muñoz Marín, the Puerto Rican most responsible for "Operation Bootstrap," was elected governor of Puerto Rico in 1948. He was reelected for three terms.

By 1970, as a result of "Operation Bootstrap," Puerto Rico's per person income was greater than that of any Latin American country. Compared with income of other citizens of the United States, however, Puerto Rican income was low. Unemployment was three times that of the United States. Because of poverty on the island, large numbers of Puerto Ricans came to the United States during the 1950s to look for work. By the 1970s, over 1,500,000 Puerto Ricans were living on the mainland. About half of them lived in New York City. In fact, New York City had more Puerto Rican residents than San Juan, Puerto Rico's capital.

Puerto Ricans faced many of the same problems that troubled other Hispanics. They lived in *barrios* which were often run-down. Unemployment in the Puerto Rican *barrios* was as much of a problem as it was in the Mexican American *barrios*. Language was also a difficult barrier to overcome in an effort to improve their lives. Even so, Puerto Ricans on the mainland took steps to organize for gaining a voice in political affairs. *La Raza Unida* had spread to the Puerto Rican *barrios* and was getting some of the same results as it did elsewhere. In 1970 the Puerto Ricans of New York City elected Herman Badillo to Congress.

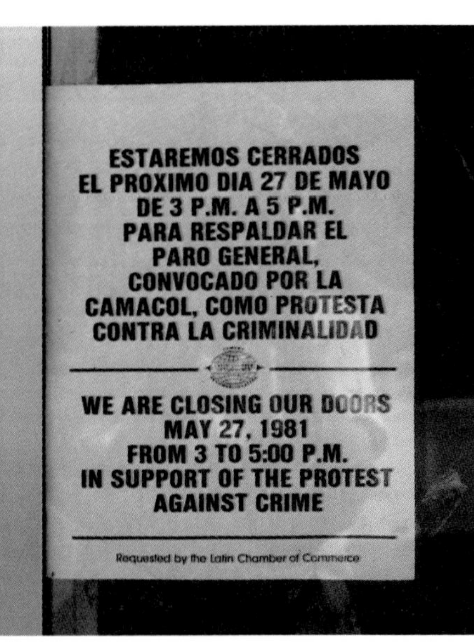

ESTAREMOS CERRADOS
EL PROXIMO DIA 27 DE MAYO
DE 3 P.M. A 5 P.M.
PARA RESPALDAR EL
PARO GENERAL,
CONVOCADO POR LA
CAMACOL, COMO PROTESTA
CONTRA LA CRIMINALIDAD
WE ARE CLOSING OUR DOORS
MAY 27, 1981
FROM 3 TO 5:00 P.M.
IN SUPPORT OF THE PROTEST
AGAINST CRIME
Requested by the Latin Chamber of Commerce

This sign posted in a Miami business by the Latin Chamber of Commerce illustrates one community's response to the problems of violence.

Cubans. A huge emigration from Cuba to the United States occurred after the Cuban Revolution of 1959. As a result, the state of Florida and the city of Miami gained a very large Cuban population. Some of the Cuban neighborhoods of Miami suffered from many of the problems that troubled Mexican American and Puerto Rican *barrios*.

One group of Cuban Americans arrived on the mainland in the late 1950s shortly after Fidel Castro's revolution. Many of these newcomers were highly educated and well-to-do. Fiercely opposed to Castro, they created many businesses in Miami, providing jobs for thousands.

A second group of Cubans arrived during the early 1980s when Castro allowed thousands of Cubans to leave their island on small boats. Many of these people left Cuba with nothing but the clothing they wore. They arrived in the United States with little more than a hope that someday they might find a good job and make a comfortable living.

Native Americans

In 1960, sixty-four percent of all Native Americans, about 500,000 people, lived on reservations. The effects of reservation life on Native Americans may have been even worse than the effects of segregation on blacks and Hispanics. The people living on reservations had the lowest income and the highest unemployment rate of any group in the United States. Compared to other Americans, Native Americans also had the least education, the poorest health, and the shortest life span.

Government Action. In the 1950s, Congress recognized that the federal government had not done a good job running the reservations. It therefore began a new policy called "termination." Termination, Congress hoped, would end the federal government's responsibility for Indians. From then on, according to the plan, the states would make decisions for the reservations. Termination only increased Indian problems. Few states could provide the health, education, and welfare services needed by the Native Americans.

Soon the federal government recognized that the new reservation system was also failing to help the Native Americans. Congress, therefore, urged them to leave the reservations and relocate in cities. By 1970 forty-five percent of all Indians lived in urban areas. Unfortunately, this arrangement also had many shortcomings. Most urban Indians lived in the poorest sections of America's cities. In addition to the poverty in which they lived, many Native Americans found city life unlike anything they had known before. They did not adjust to it. In time, a large number of Native Americans returned to the reservations on which they had lived before.

For those Indians who remained in the cities, working together to improve their lives seemed the only answer. In several cities, Native Americans set up Indian Centers. Such centers helped new arrivals and gave Native Americans a chance to practice their customs, especially teaching Indian children about their heritage. The centers existed in many cities, including Chicago and Los Angeles.

Political Power. Many Native Americans recognized that few other Americans even knew about their problems. In 1968 therefore, a small group of Native Americans organized the American Indian Movement (AIM) to work for equal rights

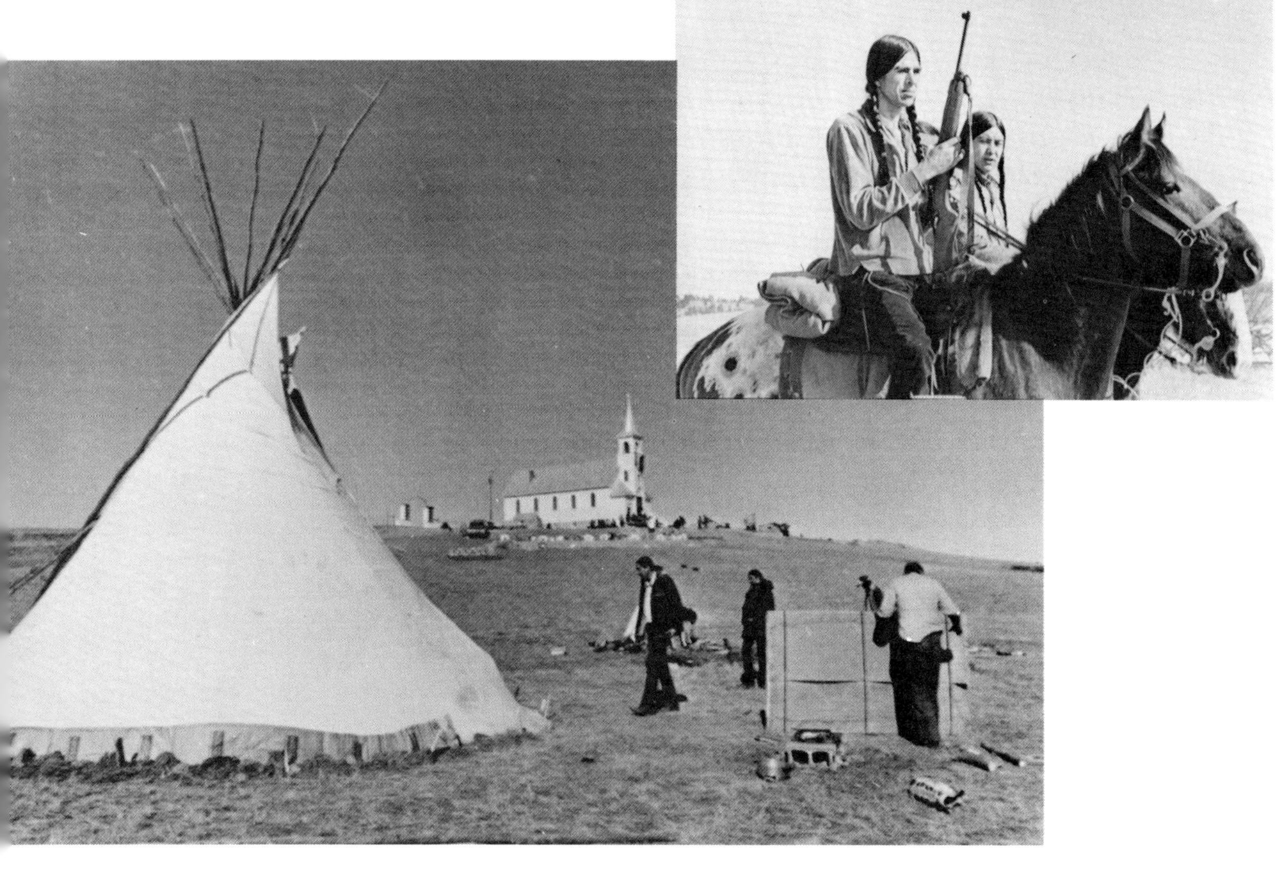

The church shown here stands on the site of the 1890 massacre of two hundred Indians by United States troops at Wounded Knee. AIM members (upper right) keep guard during their 1973 takeover of Wounded Knee.

ACTIVITY

Objective: To use reference materials

Have the students research in library sources their choice of the following groups: the American Indian Movement, the United Farm Workers, *La Raza Unida*—or, from Lesson 25-1, the NAACP, Congress of Racial Equality, or the Southern Christian Leadership Conference. Have the students find out what the goals and programs of each group were and what techniques they used to meet their goals. Then have the class discuss and compare their findings.

for Native Americans and to call attention to the problems of Indians.

In 1972 AIM members took over the offices of the Bureau of Indian Affairs in Washington, D.C. They demanded that all the promises made by the United States government in treaties with Indians be kept. The next year a group of AIM members took over the village of Wounded Knee in South Dakota. They hoped once again to call attention to the problems of Native Americans in the United States. The Indians occupied Wounded Knee for seventy-one days before leaving.

Finally other Americans seemed to be listening to Native Americans. In 1975 Congress passed the Indian Self-Determination and Education Assistance Act. This law gave the Indians a voice on their own reservations and in their educational programs.

Human and Natural Resources. In very recent years, Native Americans have made great strides in improving their lives. Much of the credit goes to a large number of Indians who began leading their people in the 1960s: Diego Abieta, Anne Dodge Wauneka, Juana Lyon, John W. Stevens, and William J. Hensley, to name only a few. Native American writers such as Vine Deloria (*Custer Died for Your Sins*) and N. Scott Momaday (*House Made of Dawn*) tried to tell all the American people about the past of the Native Americans and of their feelings today.

Women and Discrimination

During the 1960s many Americans recognized that women, too, suffered from discrimination. These feelings prompted a rebirth of feminism. Feminism had been part of American society for more than one hundred years. During the 1960s and 1970s, however, the movement took on a new name. It came to be known as the Women's Liberation Movement.

Spokespersons for the Women's Liberation Movement, such as Betty Friedan and Gloria Steinem, pointed out that women, on the average, earned about half as much as men, often for doing the same jobs. They rarely held high-level jobs in business. Women also held little political power, compared with their numbers. By the mid-1960s, the United States Senate still had only one elected woman member. She was Margaret Chase Smith of Maine. Up to the mid-1960s, no woman had ever been elected governor of any state or mayor of any large American city. Only two women had ever been appointed to a President's Cabinet (Frances Perkins by FDR and Oveta Culp Hobby by Dwight Eisenhower). No woman had ever been elected President.

The National Organization for Women. In 1966 about three hundred women and men formed the National Organization for Women (NOW). NOW became the largest organization in the feminist movement in the United States. In addition to hundreds of other activities meant to educate people to feminist ideas and protest against discrimination, NOW helped organize a nationwide Women's Strike for Equality. On the day of the strike women picketed, marched, and made speeches on behalf of equal rights.

Some changes were made during the 1970s. In 1972 federal officials began enforcing Title VII of the Civil Rights Act of 1964. This section of the act outlawed job discrimination based on race *or* sex. The federal government ordered companies working on government contracts to set up plans

DISCUSSION

Have the students discuss to what extent discrimination against women is based on stereotypes. Have them focus on these questions: What are some of the stereotypes about women, and how did they get started? How do stereotypes about a group harm individuals in the group? The last question can be broadened to compare the experiences of women to those of blacks, Hispanics, Native Americans, and other minorities.

Governors Dixy Lee Ray of Washington (left) and Ella Grasso of Connecticut were among the first women elected to high political office.

for hiring women and minorities. Congress also passed the Equal Opportunity Act of 1972. This law required employers to pay equal wages for equal work. It also forbade discrimination against women who applied for credit.

Feminists had some influence in increasing the political power of women. Between the late 1960s and the 1980s, many women took public office. Ella Grasso in Connecticut and Dixy Lee Ray in Washington became governors; Jane Byrne in Chicago and Dianne Feinstein in San Francisco became mayors of large cities; Patricia Harris and Juanita Kreps became Cabinet members under President Carter. President Ronald Reagan appointed Sandra Day O'Connor to be the first woman justice of the Supreme Court (see **People in America,** page 745).

The Equal Rights Amendment. Feminist groups worked for the passage of an amendment to the Constitution that would outlaw discrimination based on sex. They argued that there would not be complete equality until all people stood equally before the law. The Equal Rights Amendment (ERA) passed Congress in 1972. Its declaration was: "Equality of rights under the law shall not be denied or abridged by the United States or any state on account of sex." After passage in Congress, the proposed amendment was sent to the states to be ratified.

At first, many states quickly ratified it. In the late 1970s and early 1980s, however, the ERA met with opposition.

Phyllis Schlafly and feminists disagreed strongly about the ERA during the 1970s. The amendment was first introduced in Congress in 1923 but was not passed until forty-nine years later.

Some said that the Civil Rights Act of 1964 already protected women's rights. They also feared that the ERA might require women to be subject to the military draft in case of a national emergency.

In 1972 Phyllis Schlafly of Illinois founded and became the national chairperson for Stop ERA. She saw the ERA as likely to be damaging to family life. By 1982 the ERA had still not been ratified by the required number of states.

Not all the hopes of minorities and women were fulfilled by the new laws and changed atmosphere of the years since World War II. Still, most Americans could more comfortably speak of the United States as a leader in the worldwide movement for greater human freedom.

ANSWER THESE QUESTIONS

1. What is a *barrio*?
2. Who were some Hispanics who helped their people during the 1960s and 1970s?
3. What was "termination"?
4. Was the reservation system better or worse than other forms of segregation? Explain your answer.
5. Why did some women support ERA? Why did some oppose ERA?

ANSWER THESE QUESTIONS

1. a Hispanic, or Spanish, neighborhood
2. Rodolfo Gonzales, César Chávez, Eligio De La Garza, Henry B. Gonzales, Edward R. Roybal, Vincente T. Ximines, Henry Cisneros, Luis Muñoz Marín, Herman Badillo
3. the end of federal involvement in Native American reservations
4. one of the worst; on reservations Native Americans had the worst statistics on employment, health, and education of all American minority groups
5. Some women claimed discrimination against them, including low pay and lack of political power; some claimed the ERA would endanger the family.

Objective: Once the students have completed these pages, they will know how to compare points of view.

Working with Skills

READING SKILLS

Comparing Points of View

Throughout history, certain issues have aroused strong and conflicting viewpoints. Often the written word has been used as a powerful tool in the fight for or against a controversial measure. It is important for readers to be able to compare different points of view on one subject, in order to clearly understand all the issues and come to a sensible conclusion for themselves.

One controversial issue in recent years was the Equal Rights Amendment (ERA). Both supporters and opponents of ERA worked hard to influence public opinion and state legislatures. Here is the point of view of Melissa Thompson of the National Organization of Women:

What does the Equal Rights Amendment really mean? Money! Money in the pockets of women. The heart of all discrimination against women is money, whether it is state marriage property laws giving ownership . . . to the male spouse or federal laws limiting a woman's access to the military and its training and jobs. . . .

The only right *constitutionally* guaranteed women is the right to vote! Other constitutional rights have been allowed to cover women but [they have] been limited to a case-by-case judicial ruling. . . .

The [ERA] would also act to reinforce all the anti-discrimination statutes [laws] that feminists have gotten enacted in the last fifteen years—statutes that can easily be legislated away by the whim of Congress or state legislatures otherwise.

The ERA will mean that both spouses will have the same legal rights and responsibilities. This does not mean that both spouses will or can be required to pay fifty percent of the marital expense. It does mean that either spouse could be held liable for the support of the other based on individual ability.

Now read the point of view of Phyllis Schlafly of Stop ERA:

The Equal Rights Amendment pretends to be an advance for women, but actually it will do nothing at all for women. It will not give women equal pay for equal work or any new employment advantages, rights or benefits. There is no way it can extend the rights

ACTIVITY

Objective: To compare points of view
Explain to the students that the rights movements discussed in this chapter were possible only after the decline of McCarthyism (which they read about in Chapter 24). Find and make available to the students statements by Senator Joseph McCarthy and one of his opponents—for example, special counsel to the army Joseph N. Welch or Senator William Benton of Connecticut. (This material should be available in *Vital Speeches* or history texts.) After they read these passages, ask the students questions to bring out the particulars of each point of view.

RELATED MATERIAL
Duplicator/Copy Master Activity 54

> already guaranteed by the Equal Employment Opportunity Act of 1972. Under this act . . . women have already won multi-million-dollar back-pay settlements against the largest companies in our land.
>
> . . . There is no law that discriminates against women. What ERA will do is to require us to "neuterize" all federal and state laws, removing the "sexist" words such as male, female, man, woman, husband and wife, and replacing them with sex-neutral words such as person and spouse. . . .
>
> At the federal level the most obvious result would be on the draft and military combat. ERA will take away a young girl's exemption from the draft in all future wars. . . . The Selective Service Act would have to read "all persons" instead of "all male citizens."
>
> When the laws pertaining to family support are neuterized, this will void [eliminate] the husband's obligation to support his wife, to provide her with a home, and to support their minor children.

In comparing these two points of view, you will find total disagreement on the benefits of the ERA. Yet both Schlafly and Thompson raise the same issues. For instance, Thompson believes that discrimination against women is built into all laws except where courts have ruled otherwise. Schlafly believes that no law discriminates against women.

Your job as a careful reader is to separate the issues one by one and see what each writer thinks about each issue. Compare the two quotes and answer the following questions.

1. Thompson identifies money—more money for women—as the real meaning of ERA. In Schlafly's view, what is the real meaning of ERA?
2. Thompson says that ERA would equalize rights and responsibilities in marriage, so that a husband and wife each contribute to the partnership what they can afford. Schlafly sees ERA's effect on marriage differently. What is her view?
3. Schlafly is worried that ERA would force women to register for the draft and fight in wars. How does Thompson view ERA's impact on women in the military?
4. How do Schlafly and Thompson disagree about which rights are guaranteed to women?

ANSWERS

1. It would "neuterize" all laws.
2. that a husband's obligation to support his wife and children would be eliminated
3. It would allow women equal access to opportunity—training and jobs—in the military.
4. Schlafly says that job rights are guaranteed by Equal Employment Opportunity Act of 1972. Thompson says that the only right constitutionally guaranteed is the right to vote, whereas other rights could be legislated away by Congress.

THINKING THINGS THROUGH

1. in schools, buses, and restaurants **2.** sit-ins, boycotts, freedom rides **3.** Separate schools had inequality built into them because of discrimination. **4.** Several different groups made up the Hispanic population, therefore their power was divided and lessened. **5.** to draw attention to the plight of the American Indian and to work for equal rights

Chapter 25 SUMMARY

After World War II, American minority groups made efforts to fight against segregation and discrimination. The first group to make progress against segregation was the black Americans. Blacks fought against segregation in the schools, on buses, in restaurants, in other public facilities, and in housing. Out of the fight against segregation came a major American leader, the Reverend Martin Luther King, Jr.

Hispanics also began fighting against discrimination. The Hispanic minority was made up of several Spanish-speaking groups, including Mexican Americans, Cubans, and Puerto Ricans.

Native Americans suffered some of the worst effects of discrimination. They lived on reservations where poverty, unemployment, and sickness troubled them more than any other American minority group. The federal government tried to solve the problems of Native Americans, but with little success. Finally, the Indians themselves organized to protest against discrimination and to force other Americans to become aware of their needs.

Some women also could show that others in American society discriminated against them in business, in politics, and in their social relationships. After organizing and protesting, those who felt discriminated against pressured the federal Congress to pass the Equal Rights Amendment. The ERA had many supporters, but also met with powerful opposition.

Chapter 25 TEST

WORDS TO REMEMBER

Match each of the following words with the correct definition below.

f 1. civil rights d 4. desegregation
a 2. prejudice e 5. integration
b 3. stereotype c 6. *barrio*

a. judging a person or group without knowledge
b. a false mental picture of a group
c. Spanish neighborhood
d. ending segregation
e. the blending of races
f. rights of citizens

THINKING THINGS THROUGH

1. Where were the biggest battles against desegregation fought?
2. What tactics did groups such as the SCLC and CORE use to fight segregation?
3. Why did the Supreme Court rule that the principle of separate but equal was a false notion?
4. Why did Hispanics have such a small voice in American politics despite their large numbers?
5. Why was the American Indian Movement begun?

WORKING WITH SKILLS

Here are two additional arguments about the ERA. The first is from Melissa Thompson and the second from Phyllis Schlafly.

Don't ever let anyone tell you that the ERA is a federal power grab, because it gives the federal government no additional power. . . . This is clearly a federal issue affecting every U.S. citizen. State ERA's are inadequate because they do not cover federal action.

RELATED MATERIALS
Duplicator/Copy Masters: Activities 53, 54; Quiz 54
Workbook pages 77-79

WORKING WITH SKILLS

Thompson believes that the issue affects all citizens of all states and that discrimination should be outlawed at the federal level. Schlafly believes that the federal government has too much control of Americans' private lives and cannot solve the problems it already has.

Probably the greatest danger in ERA is . . . the provision that Congress will have the power of enforcement. This will transfer into the hands of the federal government the last remaining aspects of our life that [it hasn't] yet got . . . into, including marriage, divorce. . . . Why anyone would want to give the federal politicians more power, when they can't solve the problems they have now, is difficult to understand.

Why does Thompson believe federal control is important in terms of the ERA? Why does Schlafly believe it would be harmful?

ON YOUR OWN

1. Here is a list of ten famous Asian Americans: John Aiso, Chi Cheng, Reignson Changtun Clen, Dorothy Gee, Samuel Ichiye Hayakawa, Daniel Ken Inouye, Tomi Kanazawa, Dai Keong Lee, Patsy Takemo Mink, Jade Snow Wong. Go to your school or community library and find out what each person is most noted for.
2. You have studied about a few minority, or ethnic, groups in this chapter. Other minorities, such as Jews, Italians, Poles, Irish, and Koreans, also make up the American people. Write a biography about a member of one of these ethnic groups who has made a lasting contribution to society.
3. Some special groups of new Americans began coming to this country in the late 1970s. These refugees from Vietnam, Cuba, and Haiti are called "boat people" because they risked their lives sailing to the United States in small boats. Find out about the "boat people" and write a paragraph about their search for freedom.
4. The photograph on this page shows Martin Luther King, Jr., leading a protest march through Selma, Alabama, in 1963. Research King's civil rights activities from the 1955 bus boycott through his death in 1968. Use the information you find to make a time line of events in his life.

Chapter 26
THE AFFLUENT SOCIETY

Chapter 26 discusses the quality of life in America from the 1950s to the 1970s. Lesson 26-1 covers the migration to the suburbs and the Sun Belt and the growth of mass culture. Lesson 26-2 describes the impact of television and computers, and the significance of America's successes in space exploration.

CONTENT OBJECTIVES

After completing the lesson, students will know:

- why Americans began to move to the suburbs after World War II
- some of the problems of suburban living
- the reasons for the migration to the Sun Belt, and how this migration affected the nation

VOCABULARY

affluent: rich
commuter: person who travels a distance to work
metropolitan area: a city and its suburbs
megalopolis: an almost continuous urban area made up of several cities and their suburbs
census: the count of the American population taken every ten years

ACTIVITY

Objective: To identify trends by making a graph

Assign each student one of the states. Using a world almanac as a source, have them prepare a bar graph showing population changes in their assigned states during the period beginning with 1930 and ending with 1970. Using ten-year periods, have students compare their findings in each period and calculate the total increase in population. Have them note the decade that shows the greatest increase in population. Then discuss with the students why there was an increase in almost every state.

26-1 People on the Move

As you read, think about these questions:

Why did so many Americans move to the suburbs after World War II?

What made suburban housing affordable?

What factors caused the migration to the South and West?

Special Vocabulary affluent, commuter, metropolitan area, megalopolis, census

Beginning in the late 1940s, the United States entered a period of widespread prosperity. Americans became a more *affluent*, or rich, people. Wage earners expected to have higher take-home pay every year than the year before—maybe even though working a shorter day. People also expected that with their money they could buy more and more comforts that would make their lives constantly easier and more enjoyable. A law known as the GI Bill had provided money for veterans to attend college, buy houses, train for jobs, and start businesses. The eager veterans, assisted in this fashion, helped to spark the good times.

During the bad times of the 1930s and early 1940s, people had tended to have small families. During the prosperity of the postwar years, tremendous growth in population took place. Families began to have more children. This so-called baby boom of the late 1940s and 1950s created a demand for more goods and services than ever before.

Two major population shifts resulted from the prosperity of this period: a move from the cities to the suburbs and a move from the northern and eastern parts of the country to the southern and western parts. These shifts that began in the 1950s have continued to influence American life.

Move to the Suburbs

The vigorous growth of the suburbs during the 1950s and 1960s resulted from two forces in American society. One was the demand for new housing created by the fact that during the war there had been practically no home-building. The other was the eagerness of city dwellers to escape the growing crowds, noise, and pollution of the cities.

Reasons for Moving. People moved to the suburbs in search of a better life for themselves and their children. A ranch house (one-story house) with a garage for the family station wagon and a lawn for the backyard barbecue became part of the "American dream."

Railroad lines and cheap, mass-produced cars, together with low-cost gasoline, turned thousands of Americans into *commuters*, people who travel some distance to work. These forms of transportation made it possible for people to work in the city and live in the suburbs.

Affordable housing added to the attraction of the suburbs. Builders bought large tracts of land and erected dozens or even hundreds of similar houses, row upon row. Crews of workers moved from house to house, each doing a single job.

Many suburban developments, like this one, featured curved or winding streets rather than the regular system of square blocks found in most cities.

One crew poured the concrete. Another built the frame of the house. Then came electricians, plumbers, and roofers. Whole blocks of houses became ready for sale at the same time. New "developments" consisting of such houses seemed to spring up overnight.

Houses built in this way were much cheaper than custom-designed houses. Moreover, government programs enabled many people to buy houses for the first time. In the 1950s and 1960s, because jobs were plentiful, even working people found it easy to obtain credit. Home buyers made only a small down payment and had twenty or thirty years to pay off the balance of the purchase price plus the interest.

Other factors contributed to the shift in population to the suburbs. Many young families sought good neighborhood schools. Most suburban schools were built to educate the children of the postwar baby boom, so they were usually newer than the ones in the cities. Often they also provided smaller classes. Most important, they usually were set amid trees, grass, and flowers.

Convenient shopping also attracted people to the suburbs. Cities had a central downtown business district, often increasingly inconvenient to reach. The suburbs had shopping centers, and later, malls. Such places provided a variety of stores and plenty of parking, although they did not always have the selection of goods available downtown.

A Changing Suburban Lifestyle. The suburbs, during the 1950s and early 1960s, were not only a new *place* to live but also a new *way* to live. Homeowners took pride in their lawns and gardens, purchased new household appliances, and enthusiastically took part in community activities. Practically all suburban children enrolled in organized activities, such as Little League and scouts. Many attended dancing classes and took music lessons. People did not seem to mind that they lived in single-family houses that were practically alike and led lives that were all pretty much the same.

The automobile that made suburbs possible remained an important part of the suburban lifestyle. People used their cars to shop, to go to drive-in movies, to visit friends, and to drive children to school and to other activities. Most suburban families owned at least one automobile, and many owned two or more.

In the mid-1960s and 1970s, however, suburban living began to change, becoming for many people considerably

The shopping mall became a center of suburban life. It served as a place where people met for entertainment as well as for shopping. In some places, the mall came first and later attracted home builders.

less attractive. The cost of services rose rapidly, raising taxes to record levels. Suburban residents also felt keenly the rising cost of gasoline. Some commuters formed car pools to save energy and money. Still, the decline of the cities made the suburbs continue to be desirable places to live in.

Many city merchants followed former customers to the suburbs and opened branch stores. In the 1970s clusters of light industry and offices called industrial parks were built in suburban areas, creating jobs for people in the suburbs.

Problems in the Suburbs. Suburban living filled many needs. People found the space, clean air, and good schools they wanted—for a while. There were problems, however, which grew worse as the suburbs became more populated.

Workers faced a daily trip to the city that took longer and longer as railroad services decreased and traffic jams increased. Shopping centers and industrial parks required acres of land for parking. The large asphalt parking lots were often eyesores. Housing developments that had been constructed so rapidly did not have adequate facilities for the large number of people who moved into them. Suburban schools—particularly the smaller ones—did not have the variety of courses that good city schools had. The suburban crime rate increased alarmingly, and local police protection could not deal with it. Indeed, many of the problems city people hoped to escape followed them to the suburbs. Some suburbanites also complained about a lack of cultural activities and about missing the city's ethnic neighborhoods.

In some parts of the country *metropolitan areas*—cities and their suburbs—began to overlap one another. It was difficult to distinguish cities from suburbs as they became part of a sprawling urban area known as a *megalopolis*. This was an almost continuous urban area made up of several cities and their suburbs. One such area, known as Boswash, spread from Boston to Washington—450 miles (724 kilometers) along the East Coast and 100 miles (160 kilometers) inland. Another megalopolis grew on the West Coast from San Francisco to San Diego. It is known as Sansan.

DISCUSSION

Population shifts have many effects on a nation. America has experienced many population shifts in its history. Discuss with the students some of these. They might mention the movement across the Appalachian Mountains after the French and Indian War, the settlement of California after the gold rush, and the Mormons's settlement of Utah for religious reasons. Most recently, Americans in great numbers have moved to the Southwest. Have the students discuss several reasons why people move to different areas. Ask them if they can think of any disadvantages to moving to new areas. Have the students discuss some reasons they might like to move to a new area.

Move to the Sun Belt

The move from the North and Northeast to the South and Southwest was in full swing by the 1970s. The 1980 *census*—the count of the American population taken every ten years—showed this unmistakable trend. The southern states, from Florida to Arizona, became known as the Sun Belt.

Reasons for Migration to the Sun Belt. One group of Americans—senior citizens—began the movement to the Sun Belt in the 1960s. The reason for this move was the growing popularity of retirement communities in the South, where the winters are milder than in the North, often called the Snow Belt. Communities such as Sun City, Arizona, offered retired people a variety of activities and a comfortable lifestyle in pleasant surroundings.

Retired people were not the only Americans attracted to the warm climate of the South. Some visited first as vacationers to relax in the region's many resorts. Later, these people sold their homes in the North and moved to the Sun Belt where heating costs and taxes were lower.

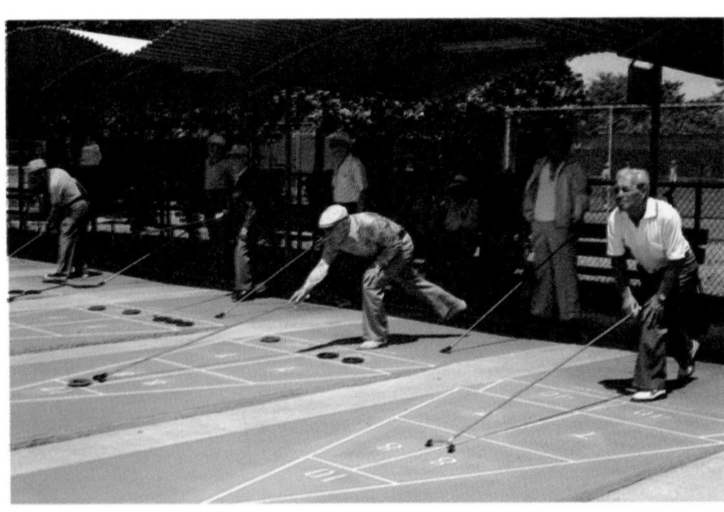

Retirement communities like this one in Florida enabled senior citizens to relax with other people of the same age and interests as themselves.

Many of these same factors attracted businesses and industries to the South. Labor costs tended to be lower in the South because labor unions were weaker there than in the

North. Many textile industries relocated in the South. Most oil, gas, and petrochemical industries built their headquarters there. More recently, the space industry made its headquarters in Florida, Alabama, and Texas.

People migrated to take jobs in these flourishing industries. Other businesses followed because a growing population meant customers for their goods and services. Large corporations opened branch offices and stores to serve the region. The chart below shows how the movement to the Sun Belt affected the populations of states in the North and in the South during the 1970s.

POPULATION GAINS AND LOSSES BASED ON MIGRATION 1970–1979

North		South	
Connecticut	−37,000	Alabama	75,000
Illinois	−542,000	Arizona	464,000
Indiana	−150,000	Arkansas	136,000
Massachusetts	−92,000	Florida	1,848,000
Michigan	−300,000	Georgia	128,000
New Jersey	−131,000	Louisiana	34,000
New York	−1,823,000	Mississippi	7,000
Ohio	−565,000	New Mexico	94,000
Pennsylvania	−406,000	Texas	1,045,000

Results of Migration to the Sun Belt. One result of the population shift to the South was the emergence of "modern boom towns." Houston, Texas, is an example of a city that grew tremendously during the 1960s and 1970s. It became one of the world's leading oil centers and the home of the Lyndon B. Johnson Space Center. Thousands of people moved to this city each week during the 1970s, quickly turning Houston into the fifth largest city in the United States. Atlanta, Georgia, during the 1960s became the center of another of the nation's fastest-growing urban areas.

The migration to the South and Southwest had several major effects on the nation as a whole. A larger population living in the Sun Belt put a heavy demand on the region's natural resources. In the Southwest especially, water, which

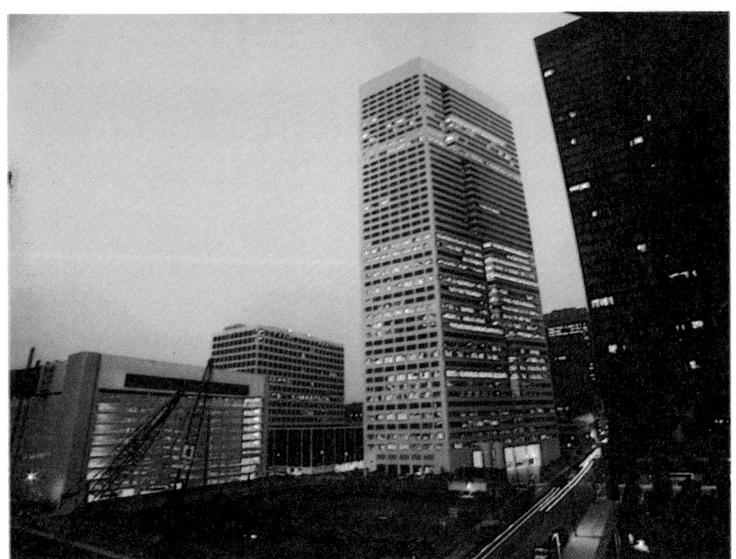

Automobiles provide the main means of transportation in many of the modern boom towns, such as Houston, shown here.

was always scarce, became scarcer. Moreover, as the growing Sun Belt cities sprawled outward, they took over much valuable farmland.

The loss of industries, jobs, workers, and taxes was deeply distressing to the northern states. When plants were closed in the automobile and steel industries for instance, many workers were laid off. Some of them headed for the booming cities of the Sun Belt. Understandably, a certain amount of friction developed between the political leaders of the Sun Belt and those of the Snow Belt. Some voices in the energy-rich states resented the restrictions placed on the use of energy in the interest of aiding the North.

The shift in population also meant a shift in political power in Congress. Remember that the number of representatives from a state to the House of Representatives depends on the number of people living in the state. The Sun Belt, with its growing population, increased its power in Congress. For example, Florida gained four seats in the House of Representatives as a result of the 1980 census.

ANSWER THESE QUESTIONS

1. They were searching for a better life for themselves and their children; housing was more affordable; good neighborhood schools were being built; and more convenient shopping was available.
2. cost of services rose, long daily trips to work, lack of cultural activities, some housing developments did not have adequate facilities for large numbers of people
3. a city and its suburbs
4. lower labor costs because labor unions were weaker; milder weather, lower energy costs; increase in population resulted in more customers and a large source of workers
5. The shift in population to the Sun Belt resulted in an increase in the numbers of representatives in Congress for the Sun Belt area. Political support for northern interests decreased.

ANSWER THESE QUESTIONS

1. What were some reasons why people moved to the suburbs?
2. What were some problems in the suburbs?
3. What is a metropolitan area?
4. What are two reasons why many industries moved to the Sun Belt?
5. Why might a bill favorable to the northern states have a more difficult time passing Congress in the 1980s than previously?

26-2 New Technology

As you read, think about these questions:

How did television help create a mass culture?

How did television and computers contribute to the information revolution?

What technological inventions used in ordinary life were an outgrowth of the space program?

Special Vocabulary	media	computer
	mass culture	miniaturization

CONTENT OBJECTIVES

After completing the lesson, students will know:

- the impact, both positive and negative, that computers and television have had on American society
- about the advances made in space travel during the 1950s, 1960s, and 1970s by the Soviets and Americans
- how sophisticated space travel affected the lives of ordinary people

VOCABULARY

media: means of mass communication

mass culture: a culture in which the vast majority of people share the same values and ways of living

computer: an electronic device designed to perform mathematical tasks

miniaturization: making parts smaller and smaller

At the same time that the migrations of the mid-1900s were changing *where* Americans lived, advances in technology were changing *how* Americans lived. New inventions speeded travel and communication, provided new conveniences, and made an ever-growing amount of information available to Americans.

A Mass Consumer Society

Americans have long received most of their information through various *media*, or means of mass communication. Included among these media in the past were newspapers, magazines, movies, and the radio. During the 1950s and 1960s, people began to receive more information faster than ever before, thanks mainly to television.

Television: The Mass Medium. During the 1950s television became the most influential of all the media. Because of television's power to reach masses of people, it changed American life more than any invention other than the automobile. It altered the character of the living room, family life, sports and entertainment, and national politics.

After World War II, television became widely available to American families. By the early 1950s there were millions of television sets—black and white—in American homes. In the 1960s color television began replacing black and white. By the 1970s ninety-seven of every one hundred households in the United States owned at least one set.

Television viewing, a popular American pastime since the 1950s, began to change during the 1970s. Cable television and subscription television systems became very popular.

DISCUSSION

Have the students discuss the ways some products are advertised on television, for example, computer games and blue jeans. Some types of presentations that they might cite include an endorsement by a famous person, a demonstration of the way the product operates, or a cartoon character or comedian talking about the product. Discuss with the students how they think they are affected by the advertising on TV. Ask them if they believe the commercial messages that advertise their favorite programs. Do they purchase the products advertised on these programs?

Mass Culture. Gradually, regional differences among Americans gave way before the influence of television. People in every corner of the country watched the same programs. Their view of the world—their knowledge and their opinions—were shaped by the same newscasters and the same entertainers. As a result, people tended to laugh at the same jokes, dress in the same kinds of clothes, and admire the same public figures.

Television spread fads across the country within a few days. Just as quickly, it could create national heroes—actors, sports personalities, or ordinary people caught by the camera. In short, television helped create a *mass culture,* or one in which the vast majority of people share the same values and ways of living. No one could doubt that people in all walks of life became better informed about their country and their world through television.

In the same way that television popularized actors, it also popularized products. National advertising campaigns on television became the most effective way for manufacturers to sell their goods. This mass advertising soon led to mass consumption—more people spending more money to buy more goods than ever before. This system provided many benefits. More goods were produced to satisfy demand, thus creating more jobs. Many of the products were useful and made life more pleasant. Some people, however, could see that the power of television commercials led many Americans to confuse their needs and wants.

By the 1970s many Americans began to point out some other negative effects of television. Some feared that television made viewers passive and unable to use their own imaginations. Other observers were concerned over the large amount of violence that television viewers witnessed. Still others argued that the rich diversity of American life was being whittled away as television programs and commercials inspired the same desires and tastes in so many people.

During the 1970s improved technology helped provide solutions to some of these problems. Cable television systems supplied special interest programs to people whose tastes differed from those of most viewers. For example, these systems brought programs on the arts and other special subjects to those who valued them. Some people were even enabled to continue their education by watching courses specially produced for television.

The Computer Age. Like television, *computers* also helped revolutionize American life during the 1950s. A computer is an electronic device designed to perform mathematical tasks. It cannot think, but it can carry out the instructions, called a program, given to it by human beings.

The first computer available to consumers was UNIVAC I, introduced in the early 1950s. Gradually advances in technology made it possible to build computers that were much smaller, much cheaper, and much faster. Computers of the 1970s could carry out instructions in fractions of a second.

Univac I filled a large room, but by the 1970s advances in electronics had made it possible to build computers small enough for use in the home.

The computer's immense speed at processing huge amounts of information soon made it useful in almost every field. Computers were used by stores to send out bills to customers, by manufacturers to operate machinery, by airlines to make reservations, and by scientists to conduct research. Computers set type for newspapers and even helped design bridges. Law enforcement officials used computers to keep track of information about criminals.

During the late 1970s, some Americans began to buy personal computers for use in their homes. These machines kept household accounts, checked security systems, and even played chess.

During the 1970s many people became concerned about the large quantity of information on American citizens stored in computers by government and businesses. They feared that such information could be used by the wrong people for unlawful purposes. As a result, laws were passed to limit the use of computer information.

The Space Program

"We have lift-off!" With those words, the National Aeronautics and Space Administration (NASA) has launched a series of rockets into space. The United States space program is one of the glamorous success stories of modern technology. Millions have watched as each mission took off to expand our knowledge of earth, moon, solar system, and even the universe beyond.

Background. For years science-fiction writers dealt with the possibility of space travel. Jules Verne, a French writer, wrote about a trip to the moon in 1865 in a book he called *From the Earth to the Moon*. Real space exploration was made possible by Robert H. Goddard, a college professor in Massachusetts, and other scientists who developed liquid-fuel rockets.

Goddard in 1926 fired the first successful liquid-fuel rocket. It rose 184 feet (56 meters) before crashing to earth. Almost single-handedly Goddard moved rocket research forward in the 1920s and 1930s. His remarkable research became the basis for modern rocketry.

Milestones in Space. The space age actually began in 1957. In that year, the Soviet Union launched *Sputnik I*. The United States, not far behind the Soviets at that point, was determined to be the leader in exploring space. *Sputnik I* was a small satellite that orbited about 140 miles (224 kilometers) above the earth. On January 31, 1958, the United States sent a small satellite, *Explorer I,* into orbit. In 1961, however, the Soviets came up with another first. Yuri Gagarin became the first person to achieve orbital flight.

A month later Alan B. Shepard, Jr., in *Freedom 7,* became the first American to enter space. *Freedom 7* was one in a series of rocket launches called Project Mercury. A major Mercury milestone took place on February 20, 1962. John H. Glenn, in *Friendship 7,* became the first American to orbit the earth. Sixty million Americans, glued to their television sets, cheered Glenn's lift-off. He returned to a hero's welcome.

An American Goal. With the Mercury Project a success, America looked forward to new triumphs in space. President John F. Kennedy set America's goal: to place an American on the moon by the end of the 1960s. Preparations for the journey to the moon involved two space projects named Gemini and Apollo. The first "space walk" was made by Edward White on the Gemini 4 mission. The Apollo 8 team successfully orbited the moon in 1968. Finally, the day arrived for Apollo 11—the mission to the moon.

On July 20, 1969, Neil A. Armstrong stepped onto the surface of the moon and said, "That's one small step for man, one giant leap for mankind." Buzz Aldrin joined him as

The spot where Neil Armstrong first stepped onto the surface of the moon is marked by a plaque that reads, "We came in peace for all mankind."

the second human being to walk on the moon. They set an American flag in place. Meanwhile Michael Collins circled the moon in the command ship *Columbia*.

Armstrong and Aldrin carried out a number of scientific experiments on the lunar surface. They collected samples of moon rocks, which scientists could study for clues to the origin of the moon. One hundred and four years after Jules Verne wrote his novel about a moon trip, science fiction had become reality. Americans had won the "race" to the moon.

In this painting of the joint United States-USSR space mission, the Apollo spacecraft is on the left. The mission tested techniques for rescuing crews in space.

Beyond the Moon. Other important space missions followed Apollo 11. In 1973 the space station Skylab was sent into orbit 270 miles (432 kilometers) above the earth. Three crews operated the laboratory for periods of twenty-nine, fifty-nine, and eighty-four days. Each crew performed a number of experiments. They also kept a careful watch of each other's health. Besides gaining much information about the earth and sun, the Skylab mission proved that human beings could live in space for long periods.

In July of 1975, the two competitors in the space race cooperated on a space mission. The Soviet Soyuz spacecraft and the American Apollo spacecraft docked in outer space.

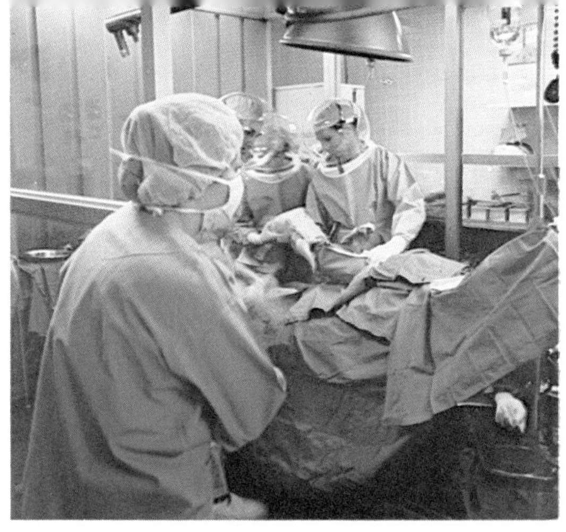

Surgeons perform an operation in a portable "clean room," which lessens the danger of infection. The technique and the astronaut-type helmets the surgeons are wearing were developed by NASA.

The two crews worked together to conduct experiments. Once again the world was awed by pictures from space as the astronauts and cosmonauts visited each other's spaceships.

Two unmanned American spaceships, *Voyager 1* and *Voyager 2,* were launched in 1977. After three years of travel time, these spaceships began returning spectacular images to earth, first of Jupiter and its moons and then of Saturn and its mysterious rings. *Voyager 2* will travel near Uranus in 1986 and Neptune in 1989.

On April 12, 1981, NASA launched a different kind of spacecraft. *Columbia* was the first of several space shuttles that will become the space transport ships of the future. The shuttles are designed to enter and return from space over and over again. Such spacecraft can travel between earth and stations, such as Skylab, that would be in permanent orbit.

ACTIVITY

Objective: To learn to use several sources of information

Take students to the school library. Have them choose one of the following topics: cable TV; NASA; or one of the astronauts on the Apollo, Soyuz, or Columbia space projects. Using at least two sources—encyclopedias, history books, magazines or almanacs—have each student write two paragraphs describing the topic they have chosen.

Effects on Ordinary Lifestyles. In solving problems related to space travel, scientists helped to solve problems on the earth. Flame retardant materials developed by NASA engineers later protected mass transit riders from some of the dangers of fire. The space program also was responsible for methods of collecting and storing solar energy that can heat homes, offices, and factories. Freeze-dried foods became popular with hikers and campers. Such by-products of research are called "spin-offs."

Many spin-offs resulted from NASA's efforts at *miniaturization*, or making parts smaller and smaller. While outer space appears limitless, the area inside a spacecraft is limited. Parts must be as small and light as possible. One useful spin-off of miniaturization was the pocket calculator.

Despite the spin-offs and the vast amount of scientific information which resulted from the space program, many people opposed it. They objected to the billions of dollars it cost. They believed that tax money should be spent to solve difficult problems on earth rather than to explore space.

Americans will constantly have to balance what needs to be done on earth against what can be done in space. There is no doubt, however, that the United States space program has been a technological triumph. Americans have again been pioneers—pioneers in the exploration of space.

MILESTONES IN THE UNITED STATES SPACE PROGRAM

Year	Project	Astronauts	Achievement
1958	Explorer I		First American satellite
1961	Mercury (Freedom 7)	A. Shepard, Jr.	First American in space
1962	Mercury (Friendship 7)	J. Glenn	First American to orbit the earth
1965	Gemini 4	E. White J. A. McDivitt	First "space walk" by an American
1968	Apollo 8	F. Borman J. A. Lovell, Jr. W. A. Anders	First human orbit of the moon
1969	Apollo 11	N. Armstrong M. Collins E. Aldrin, Jr.	First human on the moon
1973	Skylab		Space station established
1977	Voyagers I and II		Planetary exploration
1981	Columbia	J. Young R. Crippen	First reusable space shuttle

ANSWER THESE QUESTIONS

1. by transmitting the same information and same programs to millions of Americans thus creating national values
2. their immense speed at processing huge amounts of information and their capability to carry out instructions in fractions of seconds
3. to keep household accounts, to check security systems, and even to play games
4. Soyuz-Apollo programs
5. flame retardant materials used on mass transit cars; the development of the pocket calculator; new methods of collecting and storing solar energy to heat homes and offices; freeze-dried foods

ANSWER THESE QUESTIONS

1. How has television helped create a mass culture?
2. What makes computers useful to so many people?
3. How are computers used in homes?
4. On what space project did the United States and the USSR cooperate?
5. What are two of the contributions made by the space program to ordinary life?

Objective: After completing this page, students should be able to write a simple report.

Simple Written Reports

A written report is a useful way to present information about a person, place, event, or other topic. It may describe the workings of an airplane, the population patterns of a country, or a marathon race. You can gather information for a report through personal observation, through asking questions of experts, or through research in books and other written sources. Sometimes you may use all three methods.

A simple report has three main parts. The first is the introduction, which explains what your subject is and what your readers can expect to learn about it. The introduction should stimulate the readers' curiosity to make them want to continue reading. It should state the purpose of the report and raise questions that you will answer later.

Next comes the body of the report. In the body, you should present the facts about your subject, explained with details and examples. The writing should be clear and simple, with the major topics and subtopics arranged in a logical order. The body is the place to answer questions raised in the introduction. You should carefully leave out facts that are not really necessary to an understanding of the subject. Otherwise, the report will be too long to keep the readers' interest.

Finally, a report has a conclusion. Here you should restate, in different words, the purpose of the report and summarize the information presented in the body. In this way, you remind the readers why the report is important and what they have learned from it. The conclusion serves as a quick review of the entire subject.

In a short report, the introduction might be one paragraph, the body five paragraphs, and the conclusion one paragraph. Whether your report is on trout fishing or on the economy of Greece, it should be just long enough to tell the reader the necessary facts in an interesting manner.

Select one of the following topics and write a two-page report about it.

1. the invention of television
2. personal computers
3. the *Apollo 11* mission
4. Skylab

Working with Skills

STUDY SKILLS

ACTIVITY

Objective: To write a simple report

Have each student think of their favorite TV program. From their observations of this program, have them write a simple report about the type of program it is, a description of the characters who appear each week, the story line, and some reasons why they enjoy the program. Be sure the students understand that a simple report consists of three sections, and that it should not be too long.

RELATED MATERIAL

Duplicator/Copy Master Activity 56

THINKING THINGS THROUGH

1. to find a better life for themselves and their children especially affordable housing, better schools and convenient shopping 2. oil, gas, petrochemical industries, textile and space industries 3. made information available to more people, more quickly 4. made viewers passive, unimaginative, presented too much violence, created a mass culture reducing diversity of

Chapter 26 SUMMARY

After World War II, America became an affluent society. Americans also became highly mobile and began to rely heavily on technology to maintain their lifestyles.

Two major migrations of Americans took place after World War II—one to suburbs, and the other to the Sun Belt. As a result of these shifts in population, many cities in the South boomed. Meanwhile, cities in the North had to struggle to overcome problems caused by a loss of jobs and tax money. Southern states gained population while northern states lost population.

Television and computers together created an information revolution. The power of television resulted in a mass culture, in which regional differences among Americans became blurred. American consumers were greatly influenced by the power of commercials. They also became more informed about world events through television. The computer's ability to store vast amounts of information and retrieve it quickly made it a valuable tool in government, industry, education, and science, as well as in the home.

The United States space program, administered by NASA, conquered the problems of space travel in a series of missions. The landing of astronauts on the moon on July 20, 1969, was a great accomplishment of modern technology. During the 1970s the space program continued with new missions to explore the planets and to develop reusable space vehicles.

Chapter 26 TEST

WORDS TO REMEMBER

Match the following words with the definitions given below.

b 1. miniaturization c 4. census
d 2. megalopolis e 5. mass culture
a 3. affluent f 6. media

a. wealthy
b. the process of making parts smaller and smaller
c. population count
d. super-city
e. people share most of the same values
f. means of mass communication

THINKING THINGS THROUGH

1. Why did so many people move to the suburbs after World War II?
2. What is the economic base of the Sun Belt?
3. What two changes did television and computers make in the way Americans receive information?
4. What do some people consider harmful effects of television?
5. How are computers used by scientists? By airlines? By law enforcement agencies?
6. How did Robert Goddard advance the exploration of space?

RELATED MATERIALS
Duplicator/Copy Masters: Activities 55, 56; Quiz 55
Workbook pages 80-82

American life **5.** by scientists to conduct research, by airlines for reservations, by law enforcement agencies to keep track of information about criminals **6.** by developing liquid-fuel rockets and launching the first successful liquid-fuel rocket

WORKING WITH SKILLS

1. personal observation; through asking questions of experts; or through research in books, magazines, and other written sources **2.** introduction **3.** body **4.** should be just long enough to explain the necessary facts in an interesting way

---

WORKING WITH SKILLS

Reread the feature on simple reports on page 653. Use the information you learned there to answer these questions.

1. What are three methods of gathering information for a written report?
2. Where should you look in a report to find a statement of its purpose?
3. Where in a report would you expect to find quotes from experts on the subject?
4. How can you be sure that a report is the right length?

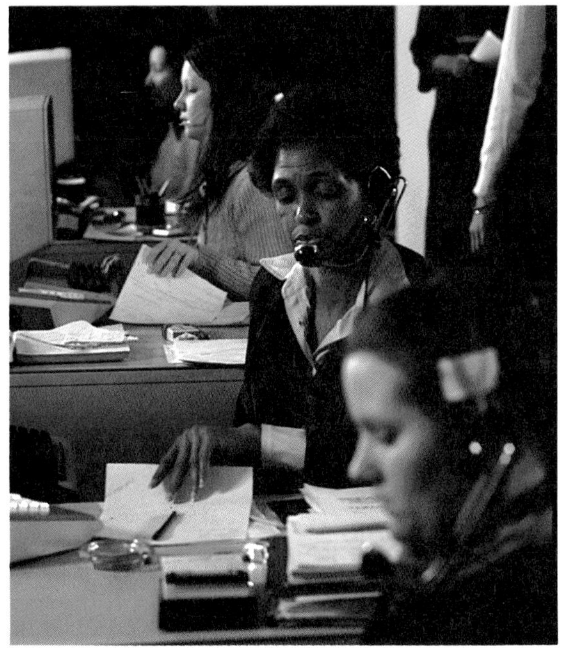

ON YOUR OWN

1. A century or so after Jules Verne wrote *From The Earth to The Moon,* the United States actually landed a man on the moon. Write a short science-fiction story about space exploration a hundred years from now. Use your imagination to describe what space missions will be taking place then, drawing on what you know about the space shuttle, satellites, unmanned space vehicles currently in use, and computers.
2. Keep a record of your television-viewing patterns for one week. List the amount of time you spend watching television each day. List the progams you watch and the kinds of commercials that are presented. Compare your record with those of your classmates. What conclusions can you make regarding viewing patterns of people?
3. The office workers in the picture on the left are using computers to aid in job performance. This illustrates only one way in which computers are used. Look up computers in the encyclopedia to learn about other uses for the computer in the home, in school, or in fields of science and research. Organize your information in a chart and share it with the class.

Chapter 27
THE SEARCH FOR PEACE

Chapter 27 reviews United States history from the war in Vietnam through the growing difficulties in the Middle East. Lesson 27-1 explores the reasons the United States became involved, and stayed involved, in the Vietnam war. Lesson 27-2 discusses the presidency of Richard Nixon and the Watergate scandal. Lesson 27-3 focuses on the Middle East, including Israel's birth, the struggle between the Arab nations and Israel, and the changing relationship between the OPEC nations and the industrial nations.

CONTENT OBJECTIVES

After completing the lesson, students will know:
- the history of American involvement in Vietnam
- why opposition to the war began in 1966 and grew steadily
- President Nixon's role in expanding the American involvement in Vietnam
- about the formal peace talks in 1973

VOCABULARY

domino theory: a theory that if one country fell to the communists, its neighbors would also fall
Vietnamization: American policy during the Vietnam War to reduce United States troop strength in Vietnam and train the South Vietnamese to take over the fighting themselves
incursion: raid

27-1 Southeast Asia

As you read, think about these questions:

How did the United States become involved in the war in Vietnam?

Why did Presidents Lyndon Johnson and Richard Nixon widen the war?

How and why did American public opinion toward the war change from 1964 to 1972?

Special Vocabulary domino theory, Vietnamization, incursion

Since the beginning of the 1900s, America has felt forced to try to influence events in several parts of Asia. Shortly after the disappointing outcome of the war in Korea, the United States became involved in Southeast Asia, especially in the nations of Vietnam, Laos, and Cambodia (today called Democratic Kampuchea).

Background

France had controlled Indochina from the mid-1800s until it fell to the Japanese during World War II. After the war ended, the French tried to regain control of the area. The Vietnamese, however, resisted the return of the French. A civil war began which lasted eight years, from 1946 to 1954. China supported the Vietnamese, and the United States and other Western nations supported France.

General Earle Wheeler addresses a conference of SEATO military advisers. Unlike NATO, SEATO has no unified military force and did not develop into a strong alliance.

The Beginning of American Involvement. In May 1954 the Vietminh—Vietnamese nationalists and communists—overpowered the French fortress of Dien Bien Phu. The French wanted the United States to bomb communist bases in response. Eisenhower, however, wanted no part of active American participation in a war on the mainland of Asia. Soon after their defeat, the French withdrew from Vietnam.

In 1954 the concerned parties signed the Geneva Agreements on Indochina, dividing Vietnam into two parts. The part of the country north of the 17th parallel north latitude became North Vietnam. It was controlled by communists, led by Ho Chi Minh. He was backed by the Soviet Union and China. South Vietnam's government was headed by Ngo Dinh Diem. It was strongly supported by the United States. President Eisenhower sent aid, arms, and military advisers.

The United States had long feared that the communists would try to take over Southeast Asia. It therefore formed the Southeast Asia Treaty Organization (SEATO) in 1954. The members—the United States, Great Britain, France, the Philippines, Australia, New Zealand, Pakistan, and Thailand—agreed to fight the spread of communism in Southeast Asia. According to the Geneva Agreements, Vietnam was to hold a national election in 1956, reuniting the country. Ngo Dinh Diem opposed the election. He declared South Vietnam a republic with himself as president. Diem's failure to follow the Geneva Agreements angered the communists in North Vietnam. They believed that they would have won the election. Under Ho's leadership, the North Vietnamese encouraged communist rebels in South Vietnam, called Viet Cong, to oppose Diem. Together, they waged guerrilla warfare against the South Vietnamese government.

The Domino Theory. President Eisenhower based his decision to send aid and advisers to South Vietnam on what was called the *domino theory*. This theory held that if one country fell to the communists, its neighbors would also fall, in turn. If Vietnam went, so too would Thailand, Laos, and Cambodia. The United States was determined to prevent such a result. President Kennedy sent the first American combat troops to South Vietnam. By mid-1963 about 16,300 American soldiers were in South Vietnam.

The Tonkin Gulf Resolution. In August 1964 America's role in the conflict grew. President Lyndon B. Johnson reported to Congress that North Vietnamese ships had attacked two United States destroyers in the Gulf of Tonkin. The President asked Congress to allow him to "take all necessary measures" to turn back any attack against United States forces. Congress granted the request in what became known as the Gulf of Tonkin Resolution. It gave the President great freedom to send money and troops to Southeast Asia.

American military involvement in Vietnam now increased rapidly. By March 1965 American planes were bombing North Vietnam regularly. In April, American troops began to carry out offensive actions against the Viet Cong. With no public announcement, American troops began patrolling the jungles of Vietnam.

By 1967 the United States was deeply involved in the war in Vietnam. Hundreds of thousands of United States soldiers were fighting there. Thousands were being killed or wounded. The cost in dollars was in the billions.

The Tet Offensive. In 1968, on the Vietnamese New Year's holiday called Tet, Viet Cong and the North Vietnamese started the largest offensive battle of the war. They attacked cities and villages throughout Vietnam. Even the United States embassy in Saigon, South Vietnam's capital city, came under assault.

As the Americans struck back, the physical destruction of Vietnam was fearful. The casualties of the North Vietnamese were enormous. The communists could not hold the cities they had taken—and they were eventually driven out of them. Still, when William C. Westmoreland, the commanding general, called it an American victory—and also asked for 206,000 more American troops—public opinion turned sharply against continuing the war.

Opposition to the War. The war in Vietnam was the first war ever reported regularly on television. Until 1967, the American public had received generally favorable reports about the war through the press. In late 1965 surveys of public attitudes showed that sixty-six percent of the country approved of President Johnson's policies in Vietnam. By October 1966, however, the level of approval had dropped to forty-four percent.

More and more Americans thought that the United States should not be fighting in Vietnam at all. Some people argued that the conflict was actually a civil war in which the United States should not take sides. Others pointed out that democracy was not at stake, because the government of South Vietnam was not a democracy but a dictatorship.

At first, most antiwar protesters were young people, including college-age men eligible for the draft. By 1968, however, it was no longer just the young who opposed the war. Mass demonstrations by war protesters took place in the streets of almost every major city in the United States. Some Americans refused to pay taxes to support the war. Thousands of young men went to prison or left the country rather than serve in the army. The movement to get the United States out of Vietnam grew stronger and stronger.

In the spring of 1968, President Johnson made two decisions in response to the growing mood of distress and anger in the country. He announced that he was halting the bombing of North Vietnam—and that he would not run for reelection. He could not unify the people. He would seek to end the war.

DISCUSSION

Have the students discuss how far citizens can go in protesting government actions that they consider to be wrong. Remind the students that some —but not all—of the protests against the Vietnam War took the form of illegal activity, such as refusing to pay taxes. Have the students talk about whether people are justified in such protests if they consider the government's actions to be illegal and immoral.

Americans took to the streets to try to bring soldiers home from Vietnam. When the veterans did come home, however, they were largely ignored by a nation that had trouble accepting defeat.

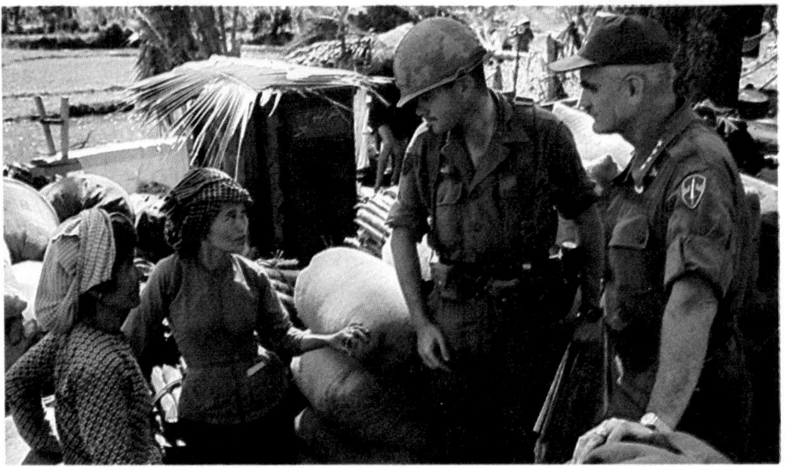

William C. Westmoreland (right) served as commanding general during most of the Vietnam War. After returning to the United States, he became the Army chief of staff.

The Policy of Vietnamization

President Richard Nixon was elected in 1968. He had promised to end the war in Vietnam without a defeat. His goal was an honorable peace that would assure an independent, noncommunist South Vietnam. His plan for achieving this goal was a policy called *Vietnamization*. Under it, the United States would gradually reduce its troop strength in Vietnam and train the South Vietnamese to take over the fighting themselves. Eventually, it was hoped, the Vietnamese would protect themselves without United States help. In June 1969 Nixon announced that 25,000 American troops would leave Vietnam by the end of August.

ACTIVITY

Objective: To make inferences

Review for the students the fact that Congress repealed the Gulf of Tonkin resolution in 1970. The original resolution empowered the President "to take all necessary measures to repel any armed attack against forces of the United States and to prevent further aggression." Ask the students to write one or two paragraphs explaining their theory of whether Congress will be more cautious about granting such broad power to a President in the future. Have them explain their answer.

The War Spreads. In the spring of 1969, however, Nixon had ordered the bombing of suspected Viet Cong bases in Cambodia. Nixon kept these raids a secret from the American public because he feared even greater opposition. Most people wanted to end the war, not widen it to include other countries.

During 1970 the South Vietnamese gradually began to assume more of the burden of combat, as Nixon had planned. In April the President announced plans to return 150,000 more troops from Vietnam. On April 30, however, Nixon also announced that American troops had entered Cambodia. Nixon said that the purpose of the *incursion*, or raid, was to destroy supplies and capture a communist headquarters in Cambodia.

The spread of the war to Cambodia touched off fresh protests throughout the country. At one college campus, Kent State University in Ohio, the governor called out the National Guard to help control the crowds. Tragedy struck when some members of the National Guard fired their guns at students, killing four of them.

The events at Kent State shocked many Americans and increased the antiwar activities throughout the country. By December of that year, Congress voted to repeal the Gulf of Tonkin Resolution. America's attitude toward the war had completely reversed itself since 1964.

The End of the War. In 1971 the South Vietnamese entered Laos. They hoped to cut off the Ho Chi Minh Trail, a series of communist supply routes through the jungle. When Laos was added to the area of fighting, Congress began to insist on a definite date for ending the war. By early 1972 United States forces were down to 40,000. By December of that year, the number was 24,200.

In March 1972 the North Vietnamese and Viet Cong decided to test Vietnamization by joining forces and attacking once again. To assist the South Vietnamese, the United States resumed the bombing of North Vietnam.

Since 1968 formal peace talks between the United States and North Vietnam had been going on in Paris without success. In 1972, however, Nixon announced that Henry Kissinger, his national security adviser, had been secretly conducting a successful series of meetings with North Vietnam's representatives. The efforts finally led to a cease-fire agreement signed on January 27, 1973. The agreement stated that American forces would leave South Vietnam and that American prisoners of war would be returned by the North Vietnamese.

The last American troops left Vietnam at the end of March 1973. The efforts at Vietnamization had not been successful in stopping the Viet Cong. By April 1975 communist forces controlled all of South Vietnam, as well as Laos and Cambodia. The longest and most unpopular war in American history was finally over.

Henry Kissinger—shown here just after signing the cease-fire agreement in 1973—had come to the United States from Germany in 1938 to escape persecution by Hitler.

ANSWER THESE QUESTIONS

1. What were the provisions of the Geneva Agreements?
2. What was the domino theory?
3. Why did the American public begin to question American involvement in Vietnam?
4. How was the policy of Vietnamization supposed to work?
5. How did the spreading of the war to Cambodia help speed the end of the war?

ANSWER THESE QUESTIONS

1. Vietnam was divided in two; the communists controlled the North; national elections that would reunite the nation were scheduled for 1956.
2. If one country fell to the communists, so would its neighbors.
3. Thousands of American soldiers were being killed; billions of dollars were being spent; some believed it was a civil war and not in the American interest to take sides.
4. The South Vietnamese would be trained to fight for themselves; Americans would withdraw.
5. Massive protests against the bombing caused new protests and led to repeal of the Gulf of Tonkin Resolution by Congress.

Objective: After completing these pages, students will know how to collect information from a map.

Working with Skills

MAP SKILLS

ACTIVITY

Objective: To collect information from a map

Have the students look at the map of "Southeast Asia" on these pages, with an eye toward increasing their understanding of the area. Ask them questions such as the following: (1) Which countries, in addition to Vietnam, border on the South China Sea? (Malaysia, the Philippines, China) (2) If the "domino theory" were true, which nation would have become Communist after Vietnam? Why? (Answers will vary.) (3) How far is it from Phnom Penh, Kampuchea, to Ho Chi Minh City, Vietnam? (125 miles, 200 kilometers)

ANSWERS

1. Saigon
2. Rangoon, Jakarta, Bangkok, Manila
3. 0° latitude (equator)
4. 800 miles, 1300 kilometers
5. 450 miles, 700 kilometers
6. Vietnam, Laos, Burma, India
7. Celebes and Borneo

Collecting Information from a Map

In this book you have learned eight ways of working with maps: (1) tracing a route, (2) using latitude and longitude, (3) understanding map scale, (4) comparing maps, (5) understanding different types of special maps, (6) computing distances on maps, (7) analyzing relationships on maps, and (8) using symbols and legends. Each of these skills will be useful at some times and not at others.

When you study a new map, you should first figure out which skills will be helpful in interpreting that particular map. Knowing which questions are appropriate to ask about a specific map and finding the answers will tell you all you need to know to understand the map.

Look at the map of Southeast Asia on the next page. You can see right away that it does not show routes or identify relationships. The only symbol that you must interpret is a circle with a star inside. This symbol marks the location of capital cities. Study the map and decide which of the other skills listed above you can use to collect information from this map.

Many maps offer additional bits of helpful information, which you should take time to look for. The map of Southeast Asia, for example, shows in parentheses the former names of cities and countries that have recently changed their names. The nation of Kampuchea, for instance, was formerly called Cambodia.

Study the map to find the answers to the following questions.

1. What is the former name of Ho Chi Minh City?
2. What is the capital of Burma? Of Indonesia? Of Thailand? Of the Philippines?
3. Near what latitude is Singapore located?
4. Approximately how far from the equator is the capital of Kampuchea in miles? In kilometers?
5. How far is it between Viangchan and Rangoon in miles? How far is it in kilometers?
6. What countries on this map share a border with China?
7. Between what two islands does the Makassar Strait lie?

RELATED MATERIAL
Duplicator/Copy Master Activity 58

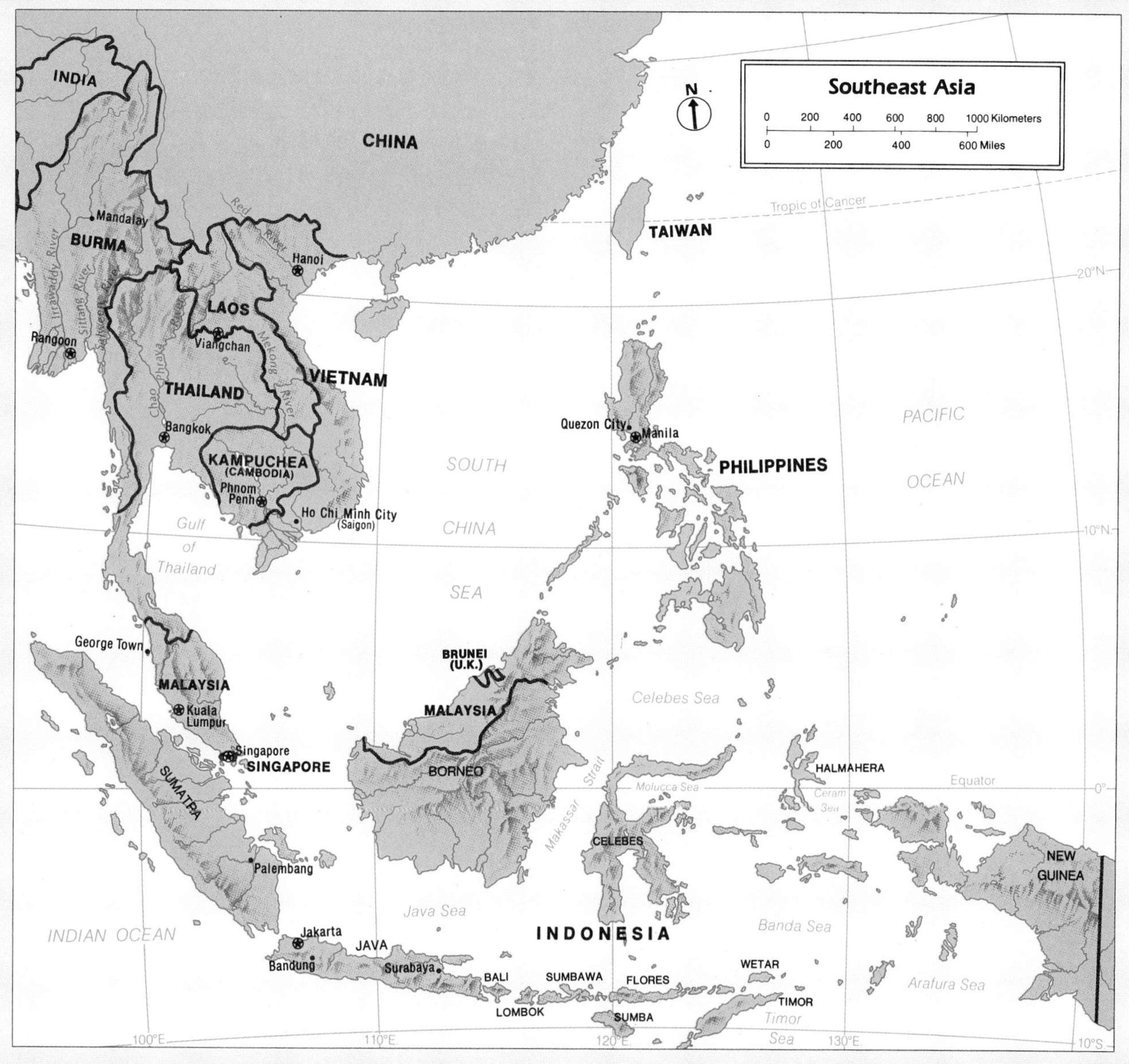

8. What island on the map does the Tropic of Cancer pass through?

9. What is the distance from Kuala Lumpur to Singapore to the nearest hundred miles? To the nearest hundred kilometers?

8. Taiwan
9. 200 miles, 300 kilometers

CONTENT OBJECTIVES

After completing the lesson, students will know:

- how American foreign policy changed toward China
- how the policy of détente eased international tension
- how the Watergate scandal led to President Nixon's resignation

VOCABULARY

détente: a policy aimed at easing tensions between the United States and the major communist powers of the world

ACTIVITY

Objective: To use reference materials

Divide the class into three groups. Have them research various aspects of détente. The first group should find out about the debate in the United Nations that led to expelling the Taiwan government and seating mainland China. This group should concentrate on Taiwan's point of view in the debate. The second group should investigate the details of President Nixon's trip to China and the agreements he reached there. The third should research the Soviet reaction to America's détente with China—as revealed in the UN debate on China, in the official Soviet reaction to Nixon's trip to China, and in any other official Soviet actions of the time. Advise the students that magazine articles on these topics can be found by consulting *Readers' Guide.* Have the three groups report to the class and discuss these various aspects of détente.

27-2 The Nixon Years

As you read, think about these questions:

How did American foreign policy toward China change during the early 1970s?

Why did President Nixon want to improve relations with the Soviet Union?

How did the SALT talks limit the arms race?

How did the Watergate scandal lead to Nixon's resignation from the presidency?

Special Vocabulary détente

During Richard Nixon's years as President, he had to devote much of his time to dealing with the Vietnam War. He also wanted very much to improve American relations with nations around the world. In 1971 Nixon began to carry out a series of bold actions to achieve this goal.

New Relationships

Even before American involvement in Southeast Asia had ended, President Nixon was working on a new international policy. Called *détente,* this policy aimed at easing tensions between the United States and the major communist powers of the world. Nixon wanted to develop new, more positive relationships with China and the Soviet Union and so reduce the risk of future wars.

United States—China Relations. The People's Republic of China was established on the mainland of China in 1949. The United States, however, continued to recognize Nationalist China on thc island of Taiwan as the official government of China. Mainland China was a forbidden land to American travelers and business people.

In 1971 the United States decided it could no longer ignore mainland China, which had a population of more than 700,000,000 people. Until that time, the Nationalist Chinese government had represented China in the United Nations. The United States now proposed that both Chinas

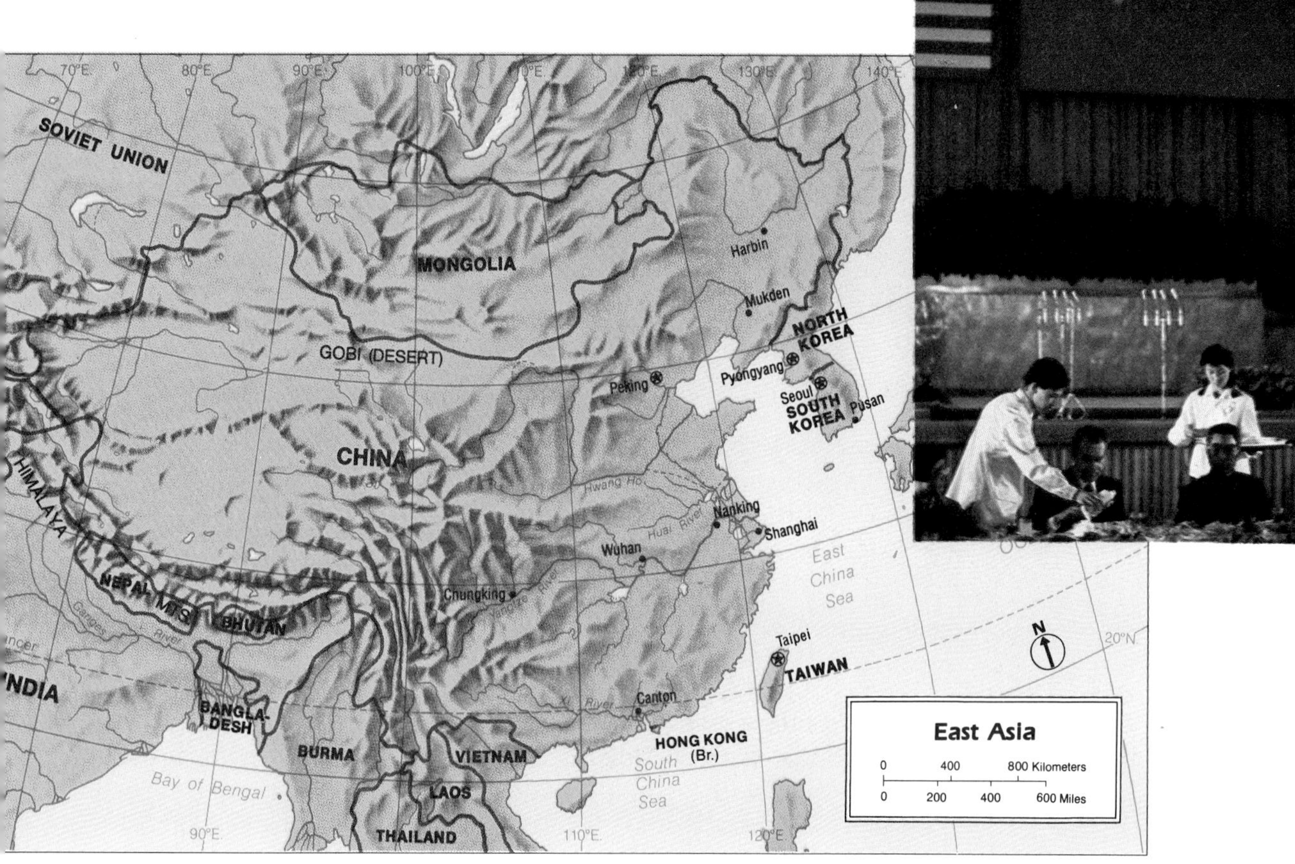

be admitted to the United Nations. The United Nations, however, refused to seat two governments of China. In October the General Assembly of the United Nations suspended the Taiwan government and awarded its seat to the People's Republic of China.

On February 21, 1972, President Nixon arrived in Peking, the capital of the People's Republic of China. Aided by Henry Kissinger, Nixon began moving toward the establishment of diplomatic relations with the People's Republic. After their meetings, the leaders of the two countries issued a formal announcement in which the United States officially recognized the People's Republic. The President's visit also led to a number of important trade agreements and cultural exchanges.

President Nixon attends a state banquet in Peking (upper right). Find Peking on the map of East Asia. This map shows that China is important in world affairs in part because it borders many other nations. With how many nations does it share a border?

ten

Meetings in Moscow. Nixon planned to visit Moscow after his trip to Peking. Despite the fact that the Soviet Union and China both had communist governments, they had become fierce enemies. The United States had to negotiate for better relations with each of them separately.

In signing the SALT treaty, Nixon and Brezhnev hoped to reduce the risk of nuclear war, which continues to endanger the world's population.

In May 1972 President Nixon traveled to Moscow to meet the Soviet chief Leonid Brezhnev. It was the first time that a President had visited the Soviet Union. The two leaders agreed to cooperate on space exploration, health research, and environmental protection. The main goal of their meeting, however, was the signing of agreements reached through the Strategic Arms Limitation Talks (SALT). The United States and the Soviet Union had been carrying on the talks since 1969 in meetings at Helsinki, Finland, and Vienna, Austria. Nixon and Brezhnev signed two agreements providing for a slowdown in the nuclear arms race. Each country would develop only two defensive missile systems. Both countries agreed not to build any more offensive missiles for five years.

The Watergate Scandal

DISCUSSION

Stress to the students that presidential power has increased steadily in the twentieth century, especially since the presidency of Franklin D. Roosevelt. Have the students discuss the reasons for the growth of presidential power. Ask them to what extent this increasing power was attributable to the Great Depression, World War II, the Cold War, the nation's economic problems, and so on. In other words, do they think the growth of power is the natural result of complex events? Or was it the result of a desire for power by an individual or individuals holding the office? Have them explain their answers.

Richard Nixon was a strong leader who sought to expand the powers of the presidency. Some Americans, however, were beginning to wonder if the President was becoming too powerful. Then, in the early 1970s, the debate over presidential power came to a head over a series of events called the Watergate scandal.

Background. In 1972 President Nixon, a Republican, was running for reelection. On June 17 five burglars were caught with wiretapping and photographic equipment in the offices of the Democratic National Committee in Washington, D.C. These offices were located in the Watergate, a large complex of offices and apartments. The Watergate break-in (its purpose was never made clear) was soon linked to Nixon's Committee for the Reelection of the President. John Mitchell, head of the committee, denied any such link.

In November 1972 Nixon defeated his Democratic challenger for the presidency, George S. McGovern of South Dakota, by a huge margin. Most Americans were not overly concerned about the Watergate burglary. A number of news reporters, however, continued to dig into the case.

In early 1973 the Watergate burglars went to trial and two were convicted. John J. Sirica, the presiding judge, said that the full story of their deed had not come out during the trial. White House officials denied any prior knowledge of the crime and said they had not pressured the defendants to remain silent.

The Scandal Unfolds. Throughout most of 1973, a shocked American public followed the unfolding details of the Watergate scandal. In February the Senate set up the Select Committee on Presidential Campaign Activities to hear testimony about the Watergate affair. Senator Sam J. Ervin, Jr., of North Carolina headed the committee. Nixon, on his side, appointed Archibald Cox, a Harvard law professor, as a special prosecutor to investigate Watergate.

The televised hearings held by the Senate Select Committee on Watergate made Senator Sam J. Ervin, Jr., and other committee members well-known throughout the United States.

In May the Senate Select Committee began to hold televised hearings. Millions of Americans watched as John Dean, a former aide to Nixon, charged that the President knew of attempts by his staff to cover up their role in the Watergate burglary. The President, it would seem, had prevented a proper investigation. He was aware that "hush money" was being paid to silence the burglars. He had instructed members of his staff to be uninformative to investigators. In July the hearings revealed that Nixon had tape-recorded all his conversations in the White House. Both Cox and the Senate committee moved to obtain the tapes. Nixon would not hand them over, claiming "executive privilege," or the right of a President to keep certain records confidential.

Judge Sirica ordered Nixon to produce the tapes, but the President refused. He offered instead to provide summaries of the tapes and ordered Cox not to seek other presidential records. Cox rejected this compromise, whereupon Nixon had him fired and replaced by Leon Jaworski, a Texas lawyer. Both the attorney general and an assistant attorney general resigned in protest.

During October Nixon's—and the nation's—troubles grew when Vice President Spiro Agnew resigned because of an unrelated scandal. Agnew pleaded "no contest" in court to charges that he had cheated on his income tax. Nixon

When Gerald Ford became President in 1974, he faced the task of restoring people's confidence in government, which had been badly shaken by the Watergate scandal.

appointed Gerald Ford of Michigan, a member of the House of Representatives, to succeed Agnew. Ford became the first Vice President to take office according to the provisions of the Twenty-fifth Amendment.

Resignation. In July 1974 the Supreme Court voted unanimously that Nixon had to release all the tapes. The Court rejected the "executive privilege" argument, ruling that not even the President is above the law. The same month, the House Judiciary Committee voted to recommend three articles of impeachment. These articles charged Nixon with obstructing justice, failing to carry out his constitutional duties, and unconstitutionally defying Congress.

On August 5, faced with almost certain impeachment, Nixon released transcripts of tapes, which revealed that he had been involved in the cover-up from the beginning. On August 8, Nixon resigned the presidency, the first such resignation in American history. The following day, Gerald Ford was sworn in as President. Ford was the first President to have been appointed, rather than elected.

A Lesson Learned. Ford declared "the long national nightmare is over." On September 8, however, he pardoned former President Nixon of "all offenses against the United States," greatly angering many Americans who believed Nixon should stand trial like any other citizen. Ford explained that he thought it was important for the country to leave Watergate behind and move on to new business.

The Watergate scandal had placed the nation in turmoil. Three members of Nixon's Cabinet were convicted along with several of his key aides. People's faith in government and politicians was badly shaken. Nevertheless, Americans were dramatically reassured that the American constitutional system worked. A free press, Congress, and the Supreme Court had halted an abuse of presidential power. The system of checks and balances had proved itself again.

ANSWER THESE QUESTIONS

1. When did President Nixon visit the People's Republic of China?
2. What were the results of Nixon's visit?
3. What two agreements reached through the Strategic Arms Limitation Talks did Nixon and Brezhnev sign in 1972?
4. Of what crimes did the articles of impeachment accuse Nixon?
5. What lesson did the American people learn from Watergate?

ANSWER THESE QUESTIONS

1. February 1972
2. The United States officially recognized the People's Republic; trade agreements were set up, as were cultural exchanges.
3. The United States and the Soviet Union would build only two defensive missile systems and would build no new offensive missiles for five years.
4. obstructing justice, failing to carry out his constitutional duties, unconstitutionally defying Congress
5. that the Constitution and the system of checks and balances worked

PEOPLE IN AMERICA

Romana Acosta Bañuelos

President Nixon charted a new course not only in foreign policy, but also in his choices for high government office. More than any President before him, he selected highly qualified women and members of minority groups. An outstanding example is Romana Acosta Bañuelos, who served as treasurer of the United States from 1971 to 1974. She became the first Mexican American woman to hold that high government post. Her duties included writing checks for all funds spent by the government and supervising the destruction of worn-out currency. In addition, her signature appeared on all the nation's paper money.

Born in 1925 in Miami, Arizona, Bañuelos grew up in Mexico in the states of Sonora and Chihuahua. In 1949 she bought a tortilla stand in Los Angeles for $400. That was the beginning of Ramona's Mexican Food Products, Inc. The company got that name because everyone kept mispronouncing Romana. By 1970 Bañuelos had built her company into a $6 million business that distributed Mexican food products throughout southern California and several other states. Most of her more than one hundred fifty employees were Mexican Americans.

Not only was Bañuelos successful herself, but she also worked to help other Mexican Americans succeed. In 1964 she founded the Pan American National Bank in East Los Angeles. At that time it was the only bank in the United States owned and operated by Mexican Americans. In 1969 she also organized a college scholarship program to help Mexican American students obtain the education they needed to succeed in American society.

In 1974 Bañuelos resigned as treasurer of the United States and returned to her business and her involvement in banking and community affairs. By 1979 her company had more than four hundred employees, including her two sons, who were both vice presidents.

CONTENT OBJECTIVES

After completing the lesson, students will know:

- about the history of the struggle in the Middle East between the Arabs and the Israelis
- America's difficulties in maintaining good relations with all the countries in the Middle East
- that an oil embargo by the OPEC nations put an end to the era of cheap energy in the United States and other industrial nations

VOCABULARY

mandate: a right to oversee the affairs of a country or territory

27-3 The Middle East

As you read, think about these questions:

Why is the Middle East important to the United States?

Why has the United States tried to maintain a balance of power in the Middle East?

How has OPEC changed America's relationship to Arab nations of the Middle East?

Special Vocabulary mandate

The area known as the Middle East is southwestern Asia and northeastern Africa. The Middle East has always had great importance to the world. First, its location at the crossroads of Africa, Asia, and Europe makes it a gateway to three continents. Second, three of the world's most important religions—Judaism, Christianity, and Islam—were founded there. Furthermore, today the valuable oil reserves of countries such as Iran, Saudi Arabia, Kuwait, Algeria, and Libya make the Middle East vital to the world's economy.

United States—Israeli Relations

Between the Jordan River and the Mediterranean Sea lies the land once known as Palestine. Hebrews first occupied this land four thousand years ago. Later, Arabs moved into the region. Before the twentieth century, two groups shared the region, but with Arabs in control.

A New Nation. In 1923 the League of Nations awarded Great Britain the *mandate* to administer Palestine. A mandate is the right to oversee the affairs of a country or territory. In the years after World War I, Jewish refugees from Europe began arriving in Palestine. By 1940 the number of Jews there had risen to nearly 500,000. The Arabs grew alarmed at the increasing numbers of Jewish immigrants. They did not want a separate Jewish state in Palestine.

In 1947 the United Nations decided to divide Palestine into two independent states, one Jewish and one Arab. The city of Jerusalem, sacred to Jews, Christians, and Arabs,

The flag of Israel—here flying over Palestine for the first time—represented the planting of the democratic system in the Middle East, where it had never before taken root.

would be an international city. On May 14, 1948, the last day of the British mandate, the Jewish section of Palestine became the nation of Israel. The next day, the Arabs of Palestine along with the armies of several Arab nations attacked Israel. The war finally ended on January 7, 1949. By that time, the Israelis had gained territory beyond what the United Nations had originally set aside for them. The plan for an Arab part of Palestine could not be put into effect. As a result, about 700,000 Arabs fled Israel. They became refugees in neighboring Arab countries.

Throughout the early 1950s, tension between Arabs and Israelis remained high. Some Arab groups launched terrorist attacks and blockades against Israel. Israel fought back, determined to survive. France and Great Britain joined Israel in October 1956. Their goal was to reclaim the Suez Canal, which Egypt had taken control of earlier that year. Both the United States and the Soviet Union objected. Strong pressure from the United States halted the invasion on November 6, 1956. A United Nations peace-keeping force was assigned to the area (see page 601).

The Six-Day War. Ten years later relations between the Arabs and Jews were still hostile. On May 23, 1967, Egypt announced that the Gulf of Aqaba would be closed to Israeli shipping. The Gulf was Israel's only outlet to the Red Sea.

At the same time, Egypt's President Gamal Abdel Nasser asked the United Nations to withdraw the peace-keeping force it had placed in Egypt in 1956. The UN obliged Nasser. On June 5, 1967, the Israelis, fearing an Arab attack, sent

ACTIVITY

Objective: To summarize information

Have the students make a time line of Israel's history from 1923 to 1967. Ask two or three students to write their time lines on the chalk board. Then have the class discuss the importance of various events and how one leads to another.

their aircraft against twenty-seven Arab airfields. In their careful assault the Israelis destroyed over four hundred aircraft of the air forces of Jordan, Syria, and Egypt. Lacking air support, Israel's neighbors were defeated in six days. The Israelis seized the Sinai Peninsula and the Gaza Strip from Egypt. From Jordan they took the land west of the Jordan River. They gained the Golan Heights at Syria's expense.

Israeli Prime Minister Golda Meir—shown here meeting with State Department officials—grew up in Milwaukee, Wisconsin, where she later taught school.

Continued United States Support. By the late 1960s, the United States had become the major supplier of arms to Israel. The Soviet Union, on the other hand, supplied arms to many Arab nations. The United States was concerned about maintaining peace in the Middle East. President Nixon was aware that war there might give the Soviets an excuse to come into the region. Nixon aimed to keep a balance of arms between Israel and the Arab nations. He did not want either side to be one-up on the other. For example, he denied Israel's request for more fighter planes in 1970. Six months later, however, he reversed his decision upon learning that the Arabs were building their military power. Israel, with a population of fewer than 4,000,000 as compared with 100,000,000 Arabs, felt heavily dependent on America's support and friendship.

These oil pipes in Kuwait symbolize the power held by oil-rich nations in a world dependent on petroleum.

United States—Arab Relations

The United States also maintained important relations with the Arab nations of the Middle East. The Arab nations provide the United States and other western nations with much of their oil. Good relations became important to protect American oil companies' investments and assure the flow of oil to America.

American ties with Lebanon were created even before its independence in 1943. As an important banking center of the Middle East, Lebanon had many financial dealings with Americans. When communist groups threatened to overthrow the government of Lebanon in 1958, the United States laid down the Eisenhower Doctrine to end the threat (see page 601).

The United States also established close ties with Iran. In 1946 the United States pressured the Soviets to leave northern Iran. In expelling the Soviets, the United States was supporting Iran and its ruler, the Shah. By 1973 Iran was the fourth largest producer and the second largest exporter of oil. Most of its income came from the sale of oil.

Saudi Arabia gained the attention of the United States when oil was discovered there in the 1930s. American and foreign companies and the rulers of the country cooperated closely to develop the oil industry. Saudi Arabia rapidly became the major supplier of oil to the West.

Disagreements with Middle Eastern States. No Arab state in the Middle East was happy with the increasing American economic and military support of Israel. The position of the

United States between Israel and the Arab nations became even more difficult as the Arabs sought to gain control of their oil production. They believed that they should receive most of the profits from the sale of their oil rather than the American and other foreign companies.

In May of 1973, President Anwar el-Sadat of Egypt warned King Faisal of Saudi Arabia that he would soon attempt to retake land lost by Egypt in the Six-Day War. King Faisal warned that the United States must support the Arabs in this effort or else American interests would suffer.

On October 6, 1973—on the Jewish holiday of Yom Kippur—Egypt, Syria, and Iraq attacked Israel. The same day, the Arabs reminded President Nixon of King Faisal's warning. They said they would slow the flow of oil to the United States if America increased aid to Israel. In spite of the warning, President Nixon ordered a \$2.5 billion package of arms aid to Israel. Nixon wanted to offset Soviet aid for Egypt and Syria. At first the Arabs made heavy gains in their surprise attack, but the aid from the United States helped Israel to reduce them. An uneasy truce came on November 7. Henry Kissinger arranged a cease-fire the following May.

OPEC. Meanwhile, on October 19, 1973, Saudi Arabia placed an embargo on shipments of oil to the United States and some other western countries. As a result, the United

Despite the common interests of Arab leaders such as Anwar Sadat (left) and King Faisal of Saudi Arabia, efforts to unite all the Arab forces have failed.

Henry Kissinger meets with Egyptian Minister Fahmy (center) and Saudi Arabian Foreign Minister Sakkaf in 1974 to seek an end to the Arab oil embargo.

States experienced its first oil shortage, in the winter of 1973–1974. Saudi Arabia was joined in the embargo by several other members of the Organization of Petroleum Exporting Countries (OPEC). This organization had been formed by five oil-producing nations in 1960. Other nations joined it as time went on. All these nations wanted to gain control of oil prices, which had been falling. For many years, the great amount of oil on the world market helped keep oil prices low. In December 1973 the Saudis raised the price of a barrel of oil to $22.60. Only four years earlier, Middle Eastern oil had sold for $1.00 to $1.20 per barrel. The oil embargo ended on March 18, 1974. OPEC's message was clear. The OPEC members intended that industrial nations should never again take the supply of oil for granted. At the same time, people in the United States began thinking about ending American dependence on foreign oil.

No less important, the era of cheap energy was over for the United States—and for most of the world. Many people in America came to recognize for the first time how dependent on other parts of the world the nation had become.

DISCUSSION

Have the students discuss how the United States has reacted to the Arab oil embargo of 1973–1974. Specifically, have them talk about what changes in everyday American life began with this event. Also, ask them if this event lead to any changes in most Americans' perceptions of the United States as a world leader. Do the students think that the United States has made adjustments in its foreign policy because of the "oil weapon"? How do the Israelis view the American commitment to defend Israel in the light of the American need for oil?

ANSWER THESE QUESTIONS

1. When did Great Britain receive a mandate to govern Palestine?
2. What upset the United Nations' plan to divide Palestine into two separate nations?
3. Why did Israel attack the Arab air bases at the outbreak of the Six-Day War in 1967?
4. Why did the Arab oil producers want to control oil pricing?
5. What were the results of President Nixon's refusal to stop further aid for Israel in 1973?

ANSWER THESE QUESTIONS

1. 1923
2. Israel had gained territory beyond that originally set for it.
3. Egypt closed the Gulf of Aqaba to Israeli shipping, the UN peacekeeping force was removed from Egypt, and the Israelis feared an Arab attack.
4. They wanted to increase the profits from the sale of oil.
5. OPEC imposed an embargo on shipments of oil to the United States.

THINKING THINGS THROUGH

1. to protect Southeast Asia from armed attack **2.** American leaders believed that if Vietnam fell to the communists, so would its neighbors. **3.** It caused Americans to lose faith in the idea of a quick and easy victory. **4.** The United States officially recognized the People's Republic and concluded trade agreements and cultural exchanges. **5.** by agreeing to cooperative

Chapter 27 SUMMARY

During the 1960s the United States intervened in Vietnam to prevent a communist takeover. Although most Americans supported United States involvement in the war at first, they had reversed their attitude by 1971. In early 1973 the United States signed a peace treaty and American troops left South Vietnam.

In 1972 President Nixon visited China to establish friendlier relations with the People's Republic. He also began a policy of détente with the Soviet Union. In 1972 Nixon and Soviet leaders signed the SALT agreement to slow down the arms race. Nixon's involvement in the Watergate scandal led to his resignation from the presidency in 1974.

Maintaining the balance of power in the Middle East was another foreign policy problem during this period. American friendship with the Arabs suffered because the United States supported Israel in two wars with the Arab states. Also during this time, the Arab nations wanted more independence from western oil companies. They established OPEC and began setting their own oil prices. An Arab oil embargo in 1973 created oil shortages in the United States and western Europe.

Chapter 27 TEST

WORDS TO REMEMBER

Match each of the following words with the correct definition below.

a 1. détente b 3. mandate
d 2. incursion c 4. domino theory

a. a lessening of international tensions
b. the right to oversee a country's affairs
c. the belief that the fall of one country to communism endangers its neighbors
d. a raid

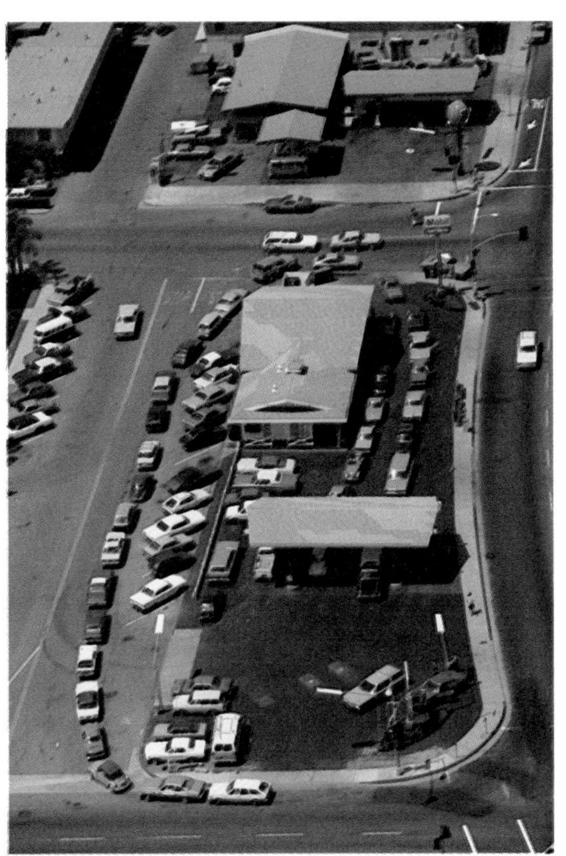

RELATED MATERIALS

Duplicator/Copy Masters: Activities 57, 58, 59; Quiz 56
Workbook pages 83-85

programs with the Soviets and signing the SALT treaty **6.** He was the first Vice President to take office under the Twenty-fifth Amendment. **7.** He took part in a cover-up of the role of the White House staff in the Watergate break-in and lied to the American people about it. **8.** the Sinai Peninsula and the Gaza Strip **9.** the Arab embargo of oil, imposed in response to American support of Israel

WORKING WITH SKILLS

1. 100°E **2.** 1000 kilometers **3.** north **4.** Chao Phraya **5.** Red River **6.** Manila **7.** Bangkok **8.** Singapore **9.** Jakarta

---

THINKING THINGS THROUGH

1. Why was SEATO formed?
2. Why did the United States become involved in the war in Vietnam?
3. How did the Tet offensive affect Americans' attitudes toward the Vietnam War?
4. How did United States relations with China change as a result of Nixon's visit?
5. How did Nixon achieve détente with the USSR?
6. What was the significance of Gerald Ford's appointment as Vice President?
7. Why was President Nixon forced to resign?
8. What territory did Israel win from Egypt in the Six-Day War?
9. What caused the oil shortage in the United States in 1973 and 1974?

WORKING WITH SKILLS

Use the map skills you have learned to collect the following information from the map on page 663.

1. Near what longitude is Bangkok located?
2. What is the distance between Bangkok and Hanoi in kilometers?
3. What direction would you travel to reach Bangkok from Kuala Lumpur?
4. On what river does Bangkok lie?
5. On what river is Hanoi located?
6. Which city is farther north, Bangkok or Manila?
7. Which city is closer to Rangoon, Viangchan or Bangkok?
8. Which capital shown on the map is closest to the equator?
9. Which capital on the map is farthest south?

ON YOUR OWN

1. Twice since 1950 the United States has sent troops to fight in wars in Asia. Make a chart in which you list some ways that the Korean War and the Vietnam War were similar and some ways that they were different. Consider such things as why the United States entered the war, how the war was fought, support for the war in the United States, and the outcome of the war. Use information from your textbook and from encyclopedias or other reference books.
2. Since the oil embargo of 1973 and 1974, Americans have tried to conserve energy in order to reduce dependence on foreign oil sources. List five ways the ordinary person can cut down on the amount of energy he or she uses. Share your list with the class.
3. The picture on page 676 shows a long line of cars at a service station during the 1973 oil embargo. This event showed how dependent America had become on oil for energy. Think about the ways we use oil to satisfy needs and provide comforts. Then make a list of such uses of oil. Be specific. For instance, if you choose to include "transportation," be sure to list specific types such as automobiles and airplanes. If you need help, look up "oil" or "petroleum" in an encyclopedia.

QUESTIONS TO ANSWER

1. separate but equal facilities (segregation) **2.** La Raza Unida **3.** Civil Rights Act **4.** Sun Belt **5.** spin-offs **6.** Robert H. Goddard **7.** Tonkin Gulf **8.** SALT **9.** OPEC

THINKING THINGS THROUGH

1. equal access to public transportation **2.** It called attention to the Indians' demands. **3.** lower construction costs, credit offered to veterans by the government, small down payments on mort-

Unit 9 TEST

WORDS TO REMEMBER

Choose the correct definition for each of the words listed below.

a 1. incursion
   a. a raid
   b. a long trip
   c. the end of a war

c 2. détente
   a. the keeping of the peace by UN forces
   b. a stalemate during war
   c. easing tensions between the United States and communist powers

c 3. stereotype
   a. an unfavorable judgment
   b. a source of misinformation
   c. a false mental picture

a 4. megalopolis
   a. an almost continuous urban sprawl
   b. the space city described by Jules Verne
   c. the area between a city and its suburbs

b 5. Vietnamization
   a. converting the North Vietnamese to democracy
   b. training the South Vietnamese to fight in place of American troops
   c. uniting the country of Vietnam

b 6. *barrio*
   a. a meeting of a Mexican American political party
   b. a Spanish neighborhood
   c. a neighborhood ruined by poverty

a 7. domino theory
   a. If one country goes communist, so will its neighbors.
   b. No international conflict is easy to solve.
   c. If one side in war uses guerrilla tactics, so must the other side.

b 8. mandate
   a. the right to vote for representatives in government
   b. the right to oversee the affairs of a territory
   c. a formal statement by OPEC

QUESTIONS TO ANSWER

1. In the case of *Brown v. Board of Education of Topeka*, the Supreme Court ruled that the principle of ________ was unconstitutional.
2. The political party that helped Puerto Ricans gain a voice in political affairs was called ________.
3. In the 1970s the government began enforcing Title VII of the ________ of 1964, which outlaws discrimination based on race *or* sex.
4. According to the 1980 census, many Americans in the North and Northeast were moving to the region known as the ________.
5. Everyday by-products of space research, such as freeze-dried foods, are called ________.
6. Research by ________ provided the basis of modern rocketry.
7. The ________ Resolution in 1964 gave President Johnson great freedom to send military aid to Southeast Asia.
8. The main goal of President Nixon's trip to the USSR in 1972 was to sign the ________ agreements.
9. To control oil prices, oil-producing nations formed ________ in 1960.

RELATED MATERIAL
Duplicator/Copy Master Tests 57-59

gages, long-term mortgages available, jobs plentiful **4.** Skylab, Soyuz, and Apollo docking in space, and *Voyager 1* and *2* **5.** forced Nixon to give up the tapes by rejecting his "executive privilege" argument **6.** because more American troops were sent in, public opinion turned sharply against continuing in the war **7.** balance of power

PRACTICE YOUR SKILLS

1. a. introduction
body
conclusion
b. conclusion
2. a. southeast; southeast (accept south); northwest
b. Thailand, Kampuchea, and Vietnam
c. Rangoon

THINK THINGS THROUGH

1. What goals did the Freedom Riders seek to accomplish?
2. What was the effect of AIM's occupation of Wounded Knee?
3. Why were more people able to afford their own homes in the 1950s and 1960s than in earlier times?
4. What space projects did NASA undertake in the 1970s?
5. How did the Supreme Court's July 1974 decision on the White House tapes help lead to Nixon's resignation?
6. Why was the Tet offensive considered a victory for North Vietnam?
7. What policy did the United States follow in selling arms to the Middle East during the 1960s and 1970s?

PRACTICE YOUR SKILLS

1. Review the material on simple written reports on page 653. Then answer the following questions.
   a. What are the three main parts of a simple report?
   b. Where in a report would you look for a summary of the information covered?
2. Look at the map of Southeast Asia on page 663 for the answers to these questions.
   a. In what direction would you travel from Celebes to reach Wetar? From George Town to Palembang? From Phnom Penh to Mandalay?
   b. Which countries border the Gulf of Thailand?
   c. What city lies between the Irrawaddy and the Sittang rivers?

Mercury astronauts (from left to right) are Scott Carpenter, Gordon Cooper, John Glenn, Virgil Grissom, Walter Schirra, Alan Shepard, and Donald Slayton.

Unit 10

CHALLENGES OF A NEW AGE

Unit Ten examines the foreign and domestic policies of Presidents Nixon, Carter, and Reagan. The topics discussed in the unit include the following: the importance of conserving natural resources and finding new fuel sources; food shortages in the Third World; worldwide inflation; American foreign policy in the Middle East, Central America, Asia, and Africa; the problems and prospects of American cities; and education and human rights.

Alexander Calder's sculpture "Flamingo"

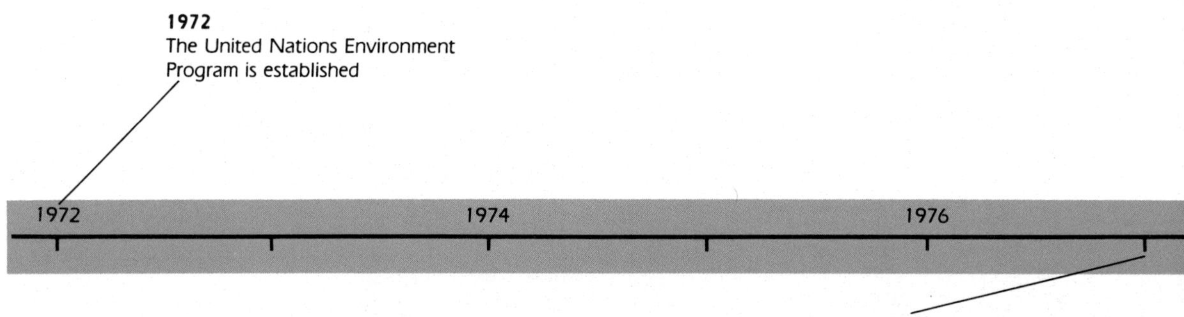

1972
The United Nations Environment Program is established

1977
Egyptian president Sadat visits Israeli prime minister Begin in Jerusalem

The *Columbia* lift-off, Kennedy Space Center, 1982

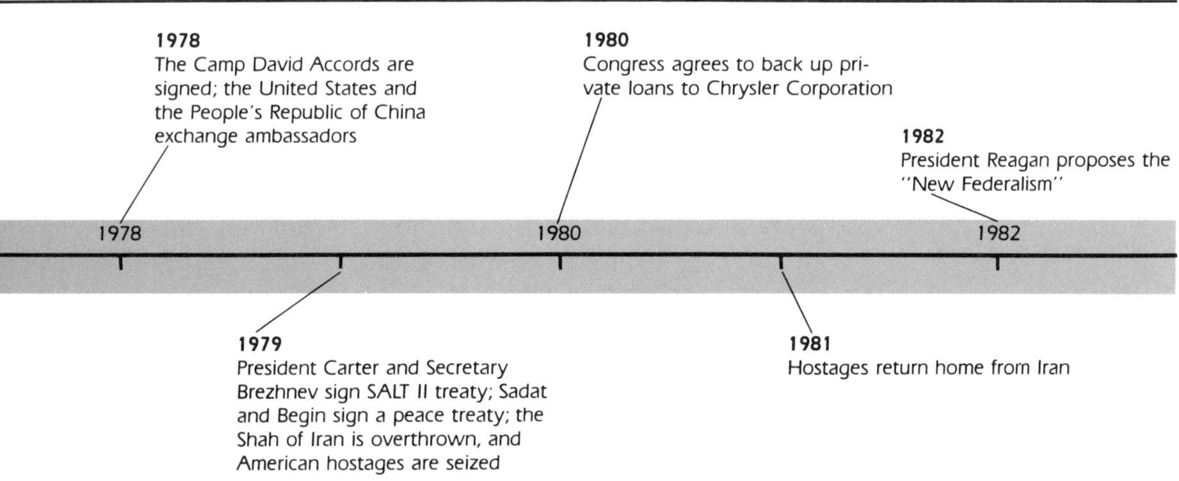

1978
The Camp David Accords are signed; the United States and the People's Republic of China exchange ambassadors
1980
Congress agrees to back up private loans to Chrysler Corporation
1982
President Reagan proposes the "New Federalism"
1978
1980
1982
1979
President Carter and Secretary Brezhnev sign SALT II treaty; Sadat and Begin sign a peace treaty; the Shah of Iran is overthrown, and American hostages are seized
1981
Hostages return home from Iran

Chapter 28 focuses on the world as a global society. Lesson 28-1 discusses the declining availability of many natural resources, suggests some alternative energy sources, and

Chapter 28
PRICES, PRODUCTION, AND SCARCITY

details the problems of feeding the world's vast population. Lesson 28-2 discusses worldwide inflation and its effects, discusses the problem of stagflation in many industrial nations, and explains how world trade has changed in response to changing economic and political conditions.

CONTENT OBJECTIVES

After completing the lesson, students will know:

- the importance of conserving natural resources, especially nonrenewable ones
- about alternatives to traditional energy sources
- that many Third World countries do not have enough food for their people
- about the Green Revolution

VOCABULARY

nonrenewable resources: resources, including oil, coal, and other minerals, that are limited
Third World: the developing countries of Africa, Asia, and Latin America
fossil fuels: coal, oil, and natural gas
nuclear power: energy that is released from atoms
solar power: power from the sun
famine: a serious shortage of food that results in widespread hunger and starvation

28-1 A Global Perspective

As you read, think about these questions:

Why must the countries of the world depend on one another to supply natural resources?

What new sources of energy are being developed for the future?

What are some of the reasons why it is difficult to feed all the world's people?

What was the Green Revolution?

Special Vocabulary	nonrenewable resources	nuclear power
	Third World	solar power
	fossil fuels	famine

An outcome of the age of space travel is that it has enabled people to see the world in a new way. The astronauts who traveled into space were the first human beings actually to see the entire world at a glance. The pictures they made from space have allowed those of us on the earth to share the view they had. The pictures show the earth without any national boundaries, reminding us that all human beings share the same planet with all its resources and problems.

Buckminster Fuller, an American architect and teacher, calls the world "Spaceship Earth." He points out that like a spaceship, the earth is a closed environment containing everything that people need in order to live. Fuller warns, though, that people everywhere must take care of the world which they share. Whatever happens in any one part of the planet can affect people living in all the other parts. In years to come, decisions made today about the world's resources, environment, and economy will be critical for Spaceship Earth.

Natural Resources

The products of nature that can be used by people are called natural resources. Supplies of some resources such as soil, water, and forests can be replaced or renewed by careful use and planning. Other resources, including oil, coal, and other minerals, are *nonrenewable resources.* These resources are limited. They must be used carefully in order to make them last as long as possible. When they run out someday, other resources will have to be found to take their place.

Importing Resources. Natural resources are not equally divided among the nations of the world. Some nations have many more than others. Most of the industrial countries of North America and Western Europe have excellent farmland and plentiful supplies of minerals. Their industries, however, require even greater quantities of minerals. The industrial nations, therefore, import resources from all over the world to use in manufacturing. Efficient means of transportation have made these resources readily available throughout the world.

A country such as Japan, with very few natural resources, was able to become an industrial power because it could import the resources it lacked. The Japanese trade their manufactured goods for food and raw materials.

The United States depends on natural resources from many parts of the world. Although the United States is an important oil producer, it also needs oil from foreign countries to supply its enormous needs. The countries of the Middle East are an important source of oil for American cars and industry. One third of the iron ore for making steel is imported from Canada, Venezuela, and Liberia. To make high-quality steel, American companies must import manganese and chromium from countries in Africa and Asia. Much of the gold, potassium, and zinc for industrial production must be brought to the United States from foreign countries. All these mineral resources are nonrenewable.

The United States imports some of its oil from Europe. The workers on these rigs are bringing up oil from the floor of the North Sea, which has some of the world's richest deposits.

Industrial countries import many resources from what is sometimes called the *Third World.* The Third World is made up of the developing countries of Africa, Asia, and Latin

DISCUSSION

Review for the students the fact that the United States and other industrial countries must import many resources from Third World countries. Tell the students that in recent years many Third World countries have raised prices drastically on their resources in an attempt to improve their economies, knowing that the industrial countries must have what they are selling. Have the students discuss the mutual dependence of industrial countries and countries with resources. Ask them if they think it is fair and reasonable for Third World countries to ask for a share of the profits from the goods that will be made from their resources. Why or why not?

America. The so-called First World is composed of the industrialized countries of North America and Europe as well as Japan. The so-called Second World consists of all communist countries. Many of the Third World countries, including the oil-producing countries of the Middle East, have large supplies of nonrenewable resources. These resources are essential to the industrial economies of the First and Second Worlds.

Environmental Protection. During the 1960s and 1970s, people around the world began to realize more keenly than ever that air and water are valuable resources. Americans watched with concern as bodies of water like the Great Lakes and even the oceans became polluted. Layers of air pollution hung like clouds of poisonous gas over industrial cities throughout the world. More powerful automobiles and new chemicals contributed to this increase in pollution. As the population of the world rapidly grew, almost everywhere there were more wastes of all kinds.

People of many nations demanded new legislation to control pollution. In the United States, federal, state, and local governments passed laws to limit the amount of pollution that cars and industries can put into the environment. International cooperation was also needed. Pollution does

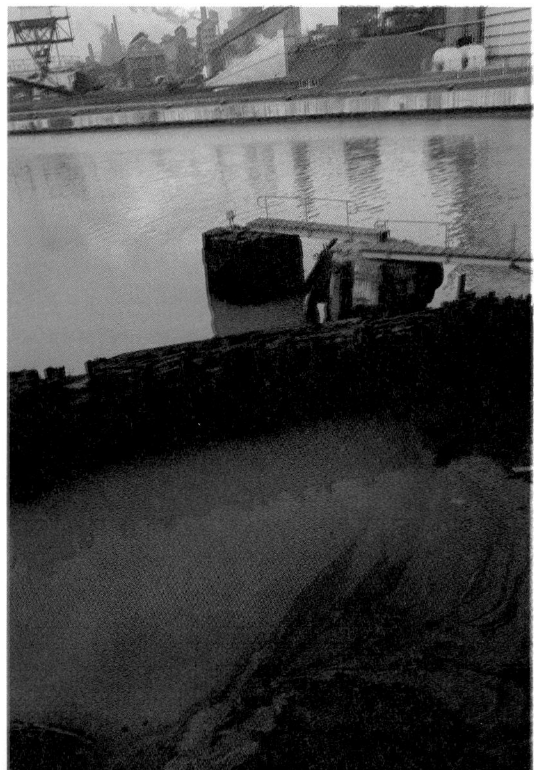

The first federal pollution control law was passed in 1899. It was aimed at keeping waterways clean. Unfortunately, the law was almost never enforced. Today stricter federal, state, and local laws are being passed and enforced.

Special solar collectors absorb sunlight, which is converted to energy. Scientists are searching for better ways to collect and store the sun's heat. Solar energy could then provide economical heating and cooling systems.

Nuclear energy is less expensive and cleaner to use than energy from fossil fuels. Nuclear power plants, however, are extremely expensive to build. Many nations cannot afford to build them. Some people also fear that nuclear power is dangerous. Should something go wrong in a nuclear power plant, radioactivity could be released into the atmosphere. The disposal of radioactive wastes from nuclear reactors is another problem. Because of these difficulties, the future of nuclear power remains uncertain.

Another form of energy that scientists have been exploring is *solar power*, or power from the sun. Large plates or panels collect the heat of the sun to use as energy. Scientists have also developed small batteries called solar cells that produce electricity when sunlight strikes them. Wind and even the heat from the interior of the earth may eventually become sources of energy.

Feeding the World's Population

Some Third World countries do not have enough food for their people. Many of these nations have large populations that are growing steadily. The population of India, for example, has been growing by several million people each

In addition to being a great industrial nation, the United States is also a mighty agricultural nation. Many countries depend upon the United States for a significant part of their grain.

The "Haves" and the "Have Nots." The world seems to be divided into countries that "have" and countries that "have not." Most of the developing countries of the Third World are "have nots." During the 1970s a terrible *famine* took place in Africa. A famine is a serious shortage of food that results in widespread hunger and starvation. There was little rain at that time and few crops could grow. Thousands of people died because they did not have enough food to eat. At that same time in Southeast Asia, many countries had difficulty raising enough food because of wars and revolutions.

In contrast, fertile land and modern agricultural technology enable American farmers to grow more food than the people of the United States need. Farmers in the United States produce eleven percent of the wheat and sixteen percent of the meat in the world. In 1979 the United States produced more than half the corn grown in the world. Most

ACTIVITY

Objective: To use reference materials

Divide the class into three groups to investigate alternative energy sources and food supplies. Advise them that the *Readers' Guide to Periodical Literature* is a likely source for information on their topics, as is the vertical file in the library. Have one group research and report to the class on electric-powered automobiles; the second, houses with solar energy and underground houses; the third, alternative food supplies such as plants harvested from the oceans. In each case, students should try to find out about specific products being developed, results of any scientific testing, and how useful or practical the item is.

of the corn grown in other countries is used to feed people. In the United States corn is fed to the livestock that will become meat products. It is cheaper to feed people on grain products such as corn than on meat. Because the United States is so fortunate, however, Americans can afford to eat meat. The United States exports its surplus of food to countries around the world.

WORLD POPULATION AND FOOD PRODUCTION

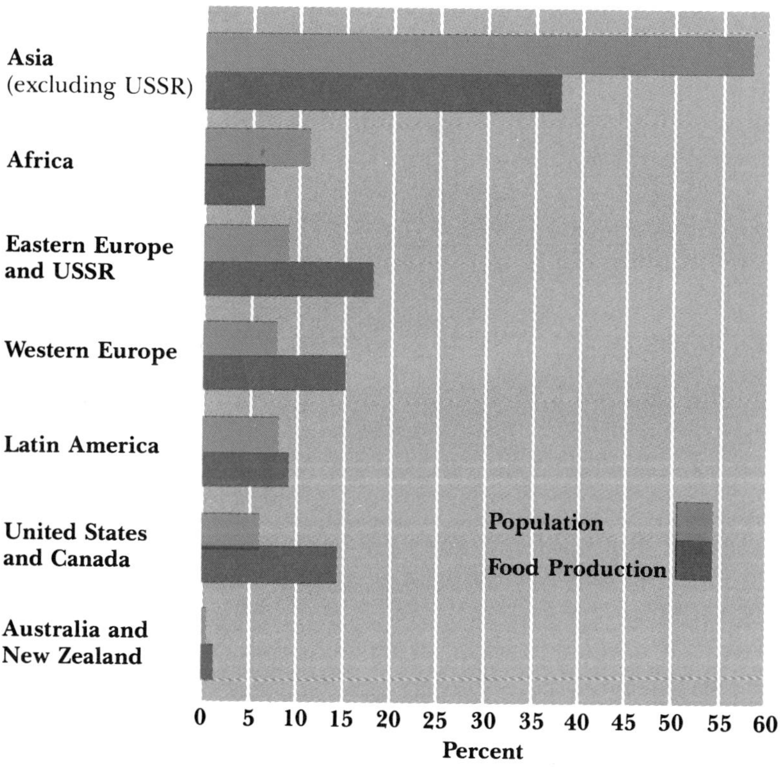

The Green Revolution. Since World War II the United States has made its farm technology available to foreign countries. Government specialists have traveled to Third World countries to advise them on farming methods. They have taught these countries better ways to use their soil. They have shown them how insect sprays, fertilizers,—and, most important, new kinds of crops—can help raise the yield of food.

During the 1960s farmers in several Third World countries greatly increased their production of grains. This remarkable achievement became known as the "Green Revolution." The development of higher-yield varieties of rice and wheat made the Green Revolution possible. These grains can now produce larger supplies of food. New kinds of fertilizers and insect sprays were also developed during the Green Revolution. Agricultural advisers showed farmers how to make the most of their land by planting more than one crop. The Green Revolution came about as a result of experiments by scientists working for the Ford Foundation and the Rockefeller Foundation in the United States.

New kinds of seeds have helped increase the production of grain in many nations. These East Indian farmers are examining grain samples from a research institute in India.

A Third World country that especially benefited from the Green Revolution was India. During the 1950s and 1960s, just after India had gained its independence, the nation suffered from terrible famines. Only by importing food from the United States did India prevent mass starvation. Since the Green Revolution, though, India is now producing a surplus of grain.

ANSWER THESE QUESTIONS

1. What is the Third World?
2. What are some resources that the United States must import?
3. How did the higher cost of oil lead to explorations for new supplies?
4. Why is the United States able to send food to other nations?
5. What was the Green Revolution?

ANSWER THESE QUESTIONS

1. the developing countries of Africa, Asia, and Latin America
2. oil, iron ore, manganese, chromium, gold, potassium, and zinc
3. The costly processes of drilling for oil in the oceans, building oil pipelines, and extracting oil from rock became worthwhile.
4. because fertile land and technology allow the nation to produce more food than it needs
5. a dramatic increase in agricultural production in the Third World, made possible by improved grain crops and agricultural technology

CONTENT OBJECTIVES

After completing the lesson, students will know:

- about the problems caused by worldwide inflation
- what stagflation is
- how the patterns of world trade have changed since the 1960s
- about multinational corporations

VOCABULARY

inflation: a continuing rise in the prices of goods and services
demand-pull inflation: inflation caused by a demand for goods, which causes a rise in prices
cost-push inflation: inflation caused by a push for higher wages resulting in higher prices
fixed income: one that stays the same, such as the income elderly people receive from pensions
recession: a period in which production declines and people have less money to spend
stagflation: a stagnant and inflationary time in the economy
petrodollars: the money that countries and individuals earned from the sale of petroleum

28-2 The World Economy

As you read, think about these questions:

What were some causes of the inflation of the 1970s and early 1980s?

Why is it important to cure inflation?

What changes in world trade occurred during the 1960s and 1970s?

What efforts were made to improve world trade?

Special Vocabulary	inflation	recession
	demand-pull inflation	stagflation
	cost-push inflation	petrodollars
	fixed income	

In 1972 an international group of economists met in Rome to discuss world economic problems. The Club of Rome, as the group called itself, published a report of its discussions. In this report, the Club of Rome said that there are "limits to growth." This meant that as the economies of nations grow, problems develop that make continued growth undesirable or even impossible. For example, the greater the numbers of factories, the greater is the damage to the environment. The Club of Rome declared that the nations of the world must change their policies, which emphasize unlimited economic growth. Unless they do, the Club concluded, the entire world faces a terrible future.

Although not everybody agreed with this gloomy prediction, the report started people thinking about the problems it raised. People could see that supplies of oil were scarce and that the cost was rising. Prices of all kinds of goods were going up at an alarming rate in the industrial nations, and in many countries food was in limited supply. What caused these serious problems? How could countries meet these challenges in the world economy?

Inflation

The 1970s were a period of worldwide *inflation*, or a continuing rise in the prices of goods and services. Prices in the United States more than doubled. This meant that by 1980 it

people receive from pensions. Inflation decreases the buying power of the money that they receive.

Stagflation. Before the 1970s people believed that a little inflation brought prosperity. Moderate rises in prices meant high production and lots of jobs. If inflation began to get out of hand, governments could fight it with such actions as cutting spending and raising taxes. Taking steps like these sometimes had the effect of creating a *recession*, a period in which production declines and people have less money to spend. After the recession slowed the rise in prices, the economy could begin to grow again.

During the 1970s, however, the industrial nations began to encounter a new type of economic condition—inflation combined with a slow-moving economy. Economists called this condition *stagflation*—a stagnant and inflationary time. Although prices were rising, economies seemed unable to grow. This lack of growth brought the loss of jobs, with less money for many individuals to spend.

Faced with both inflation and recession at once, governments are not always certain what to do. Some economists are convinced that a recession is still needed to reduce inflation. Others think that governments should put controls on wages and prices to limit inflation without creating unemployment. Still others suggest that entirely new solutions to economic problems must be found.

DISCUSSION

Have students discuss the problem of unemployment during periods of stagflation. Explain that some economists think that high unemployment is necessary to reduce spending and thereby inflation. Other economists say that the human cost of high unemployment is too great and that, in any case, unemployment does not cure inflation. Some people favor wage and price controls, as the text mentions, to keep down inflation. Have the students offer solutions to the unemployment problem when both inflation and recession are present.

World Trade

For a long time after World War II, the United States had the strongest economy of all the industrial nations. This made the American dollar the strongest currency. Many countries used the dollar as their currency in world trade. Until 1971 the United States allowed foreign countries to exchange their American dollars for gold.

Changing Patterns of Trade. By the 1960s the pattern of the world economy began to change. European countries such as Great Britain, France, West Germany, and Italy had rebuilt their industries. Japan had created a very strong industrial economy. These countries challenged the lead of American industry. As competition in world trade grew during the 1970s, some nations began to consider the use of tariffs and quotas to limit imports. Most countries, however, sought to

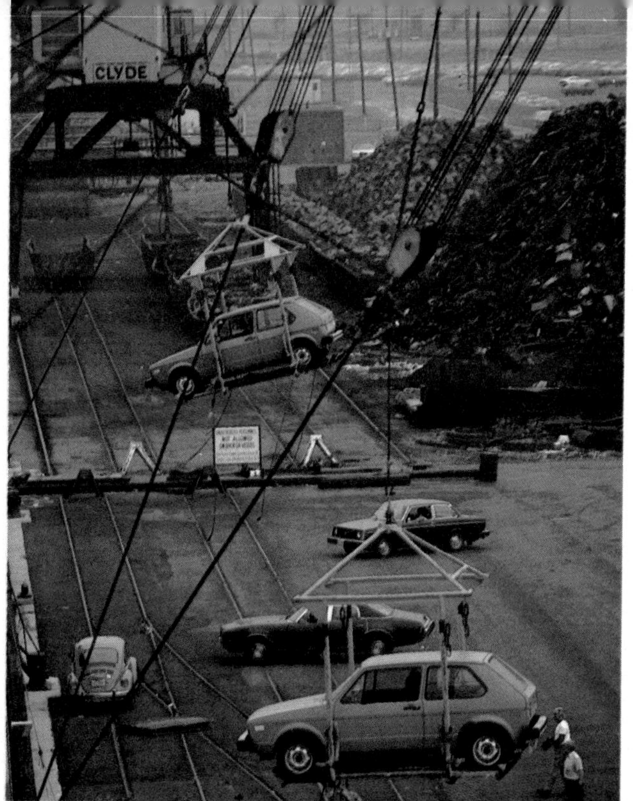

The United States exports and imports more goods than any other country. A worldwide fuel shortage in the 1970s made small foreign cars popular in this country.

cooperate to keep international trade free of restrictions and beneficial for all nations of the world.

During the 1970s some countries, especially in the Middle East, gained large amounts of wealth as a result of their oil exports. Economists made up the word *petrodollars* to refer to the money that countries and individuals earned from the sale of petroleum. Much of this money went toward improvement programs for the people of the oil-producing countries. Some of the petrodollars were used to buy companies and real estate in the United States and other western nations. Many people feared these investments would allow the citizens of oil-producing nations to control the economies of the countries where they invested. Despite these fears, petrodollars seemed to strengthen the economies of the countries in which they were invested.

The rise in oil prices that brought billions of petrodollars to oil producers made trading conditions worse for many Third World countries. As these nations spent more and more of their limited wealth on oil, they had less to spend on food for their people and on machinery needed to build or modernize their industries. Higher prices for oil also helped raise the prices of all the manufactured goods that Third World countries imported. At the same time, prices for the crops and natural resources, which are the main exports of most of the Third World, remained steady or even fell. These nations found they were being driven ever further into poverty.

Trade with Communist Countries. The industrial nations found new opportunities for trade with communist countries during the 1970s. The Soviet Union and its allies needed the technology of western nations. Also the Soviet Union was not always able to raise enough wheat to supply the needs of its people. As a result, it had to buy wheat from grain-producing nations, especially the United States, Canada, and Australia. The People's Republic of China, another communist power, began to buy goods from the United States in the late 1970s.

Trade with communist nations can cause political problems. When the Soviet Union invaded Afghanistan in 1979,

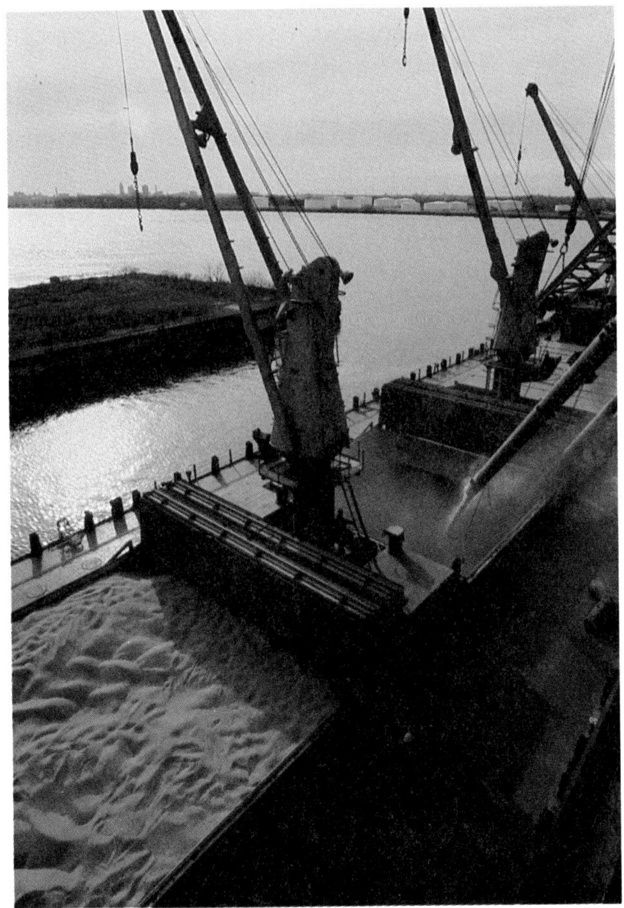

In 1979 the United States government placed restrictions on trade with the Soviet Union. These restrictions prevented the shipment of about 18 million tons (16 million metric tons) of corn, wheat, and soybeans to the USSR.

the United States and other western nations cut back their trade with the Soviets. In 1981 West Germany agreed to buy natural gas from the Soviet Union. Many people feared that the Soviets would use this agreement to try to influence West German politics.

Multinational Corporations. During the 1970s multinational corporations or multinationals, as they are known, began to play a major role in world trade. A multinational is a giant corporation that does business in many countries. There were well over ten thousand multinationals, of which about three thousand were based in the United States. Such corporations had foreign sales that totaled around one trillion dollars. They developed natural resources and manufactured and sold their products in over one hundred countries all over the world. For example, oil drilled in the Middle East could be refined in the United States or western Europe by a multinational and then sold by it in many countries. Having one company organize all the necessary steps helped smooth the process of sale and distribution.

During the 1970s some people became concerned about the growth of multinational corporations. Governments began to worry about the enormous economic power of the multinationals. Some labor groups maintained that American multinationals increased unemployment in the United States by opening factories in other countries. Yet the operations of the multinationals—and the needs they met—showed how interrelated the national economies of the world had become.

ACTIVITY

Objective: To summarize main ideas

Have the students review the "World Trade" section of this lesson. Ask them to write a summary of the main points of the section, under the title "How Trade Has Changed and Why." Give the students the option of using an outline or a list for their summaries. After the papers are completed, have the students discuss why they chose the form they did to capture the main ideas of the material.

Cooperation for the Future. Many international organizations were set up to expand and improve world trade. More than seventy-five nations belonged to the General Agreement on Tariffs and Trade (GATT), which worked to reduce barriers to free trade. The International Monetary Fund (IMF), a special agency of the United Nations, helped about 130 member nations build and maintain healthy economies. The fund provided money to help nations pay their foreign debts. Another UN agency, the United Nations Conference on Trade and Development, mainly tried to solve the trade problems of Third World nations.

During the 1970s many Third World countries began to call for a "new international economic order." That is, they wanted to establish a new system of world trade and foreign

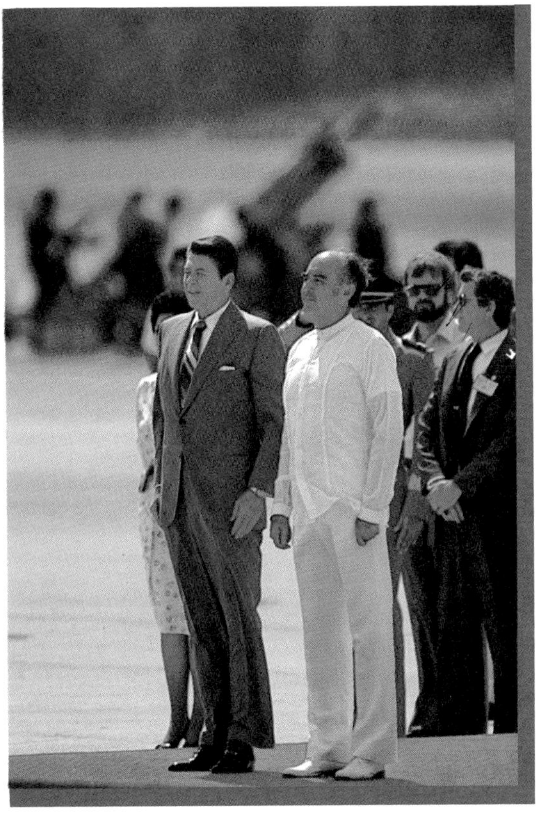

President Reagan and President José López Portillo of Mexico were two of the world leaders who attended the Cancún conference in 1981.

aid that would be more beneficial to their nations. In October 1981 the leaders from the United States, seven other industrialized nations, and fourteen Third World countries met in Cancún, Mexico. Together, these leaders discussed the economic problems facing the Third World and some possible new solutions. The Cancún meeting produced no specific plans for action. Still, it was an important first step in meeting the challenges of a changing world economy.

ANSWER THESE QUESTIONS

1. How does inflation affect people living on fixed incomes?
2. Who benefits from inflation?
3. What is stagflation?
4. How did the rise in the price of oil hurt Third World countries?
5. How did the pattern of the world economy begin to change during the 1960s?

ANSWER THESE QUESTIONS

1. It reduces their buying power.
2. those borrowing money, because they will pay back a loan with dollars that are worth less
3. inflation and recession at the same time
4. They had to pay more for fuel and then had less to spend on food, technology, and other needs; also, their income from crops did not rise.
5. Japan and many nations of Europe rebuilt their economies, became industrial powers, and began to compete with the United States; however, restrictions on trade were kept to a minimum.

Working with Skills

STUDY SKILLS

ACTIVITY

Objective: To write a research paper

Review for the students the essential points of preparing a research paper, including the choosing of a topic, the research, the notetaking, the outline, and the writing. Ask them to consider especially the possibility of including a graph, chart, or map. You may want the students to select a topic from Chapter 28, as an exercise in choosing a topic. Or you may want to assign some of the following topics from the chapter: (1) the growth of Japan as an industrial nation, (2) how the Middle Eastern nations are using their oil income, (3) the controversy over grain sales from the West to Communist nations, or (4) promising proposals from the Cancún meeting.

Research Papers

In a research paper, the writer brings together ideas and information from many sources in order to explore a topic in depth. To prepare and write a research paper, you will need to use many of the study skills that you have learned in earlier units.

The first—and perhaps most important—step in writing a research paper is choosing a topic. The topic must be broad enough to be interesting, but not too broad for a research paper. For example, the topic "Sailing Ships" is probably much too broad for a research paper. However, "Sailing Ships of Columbus's Time" gets the topic down to a more manageable size.

Once you have chosen a topic, you can begin your research. Reference works such as encyclopedias and almanacs may provide some basic information on your subject. For more detailed information, you will want to consult books and magazine articles on your topic. The card catalog and *The Readers' Guide* will be your most helpful tools in finding sources of information. You should also examine the bibliography, or list of sources, in each book you use. The bibliography lists additional books and articles that you may find useful.

As you read your source materials, you should take careful notes. Use a separate file card or cards for each source. Write the source and page number for the material at the top of the card. You may want to refer to page 283 for a review of notetaking. Do not summarize quotations you may want to use in your paper, however. Instead, you should record them word for word.

As you take notes, be sure to record important information about each source used on a separate file card. Such information should include the author, title, publisher, and date of publication of each book. For a magazine article, it should include the author, the title of the article, the name of the magazine, the date or number of the issue, and the page numbers of the article. Keep these cards in a separate file. At the end of the paper, you will list a bibliography of your sources in alphabetical order. Your teacher or librarian can help you with this part of your paper.

RELATED MATERIAL

Duplicator/Copy Master Activity 61

The next step is to organize the ideas and information you have gathered. Just as in writing a simple report, you will need to arrange your ideas in a logical order. An outline will help you organize the large amount of information you have collected. First, arrange your note cards according to topics. Then, plan and write out an outline as you learned to do on page 355.

A well-organized outline will greatly ease the writing of the paper. Simply fill in the points of your outline with details from your notes. Use quotes, if possible, to add interest. Use your best writing skills to produce a paper that is clear and interesting. As you write, consider whether graphs, charts, or other illustrations could help present your information more clearly. Leave space to include them in the final version of your paper.

Below are some suggested topics for a research paper. They are taken from the material in Chapter 28. You may have ideas for some other related topics. Discuss these ideas with your teacher. Then choose a topic and write a research paper.

1. the Green Revolution
2. the work of the International Monetary Fund
3. the need for international cooperation in environmental protection matters
4. the growing importance of alternative energy sources

THINKING THINGS THROUGH

1. Good transportation systems enabled Japan to import the natural resources needed for manufacturing. 2. The demand for goods in short supply causes prices to rise. 3. It was the strongest currency and was used as the currency of world trade because it could be exchanged for gold. 4. Inflation can drive up the cost of goods or natural resources that a country must

Chapter 28 SUMMARY

In the 1970s many countries became concerned about the problem of natural resources. Some countries tried to develop alternate sources of energy, such as nuclear power or solar energy. Attempts were also made to develop new reserves of oil.

A few Third World countries were able to produce large amounts of oil. Most poor nations, however, had trouble paying for the rising cost of fuel. The high cost of oil made it hard for these countries to build strong economies. Oil-producing countries invested their wealth in industrialization and a higher standard of living.

In the 1970s the Third World countries also faced the need to feed growing populations. Often they had to buy food from countries that produced a surplus. The Green Revolution helped some countries to increase their food production.

Inflation was also a problem in many countries. The inflation could be tied to many causes: demand for goods, higher costs of oil, and wages and prices. Rising prices hurt many people with fixed incomes. The inflation of the 1970s was often accompanied by a slow-moving economy—a situation called stagflation.

New patterns of world trade developed in the 1960s and 1970s. Multinational corporations were a growing power. The United States and western Europe increased trade with communist countries. A world economy developed. The problems of energy, environment, and food production overflowed national boundaries.

Chapter 28 TEST

WORDS TO REMEMBER

Match each of the following words with its correct definition below.

i 1. stagflation
c 2. petrodollars
a 3. famine
e 4. Third World
f 5. fossil fuels
d 6. inflation
g 7. solar power
h 8. nuclear power
b 9. recession

a. serious shortage of food
b. a time in which production declines
c. money earned through sale of oil
d. a rise in prices
e. the developing nations of Africa, Asia, and Latin America
f. coal, oil, and other energy sources formed from ancient plants and animals
g. energy from the sun
h. energy from an atom
i. inflation combined with a slow-moving economy

THINKING THINGS THROUGH

1. How could Japan, which has few natural resources, become an industrial nation?
2. How do the market forces of supply and demand sometimes create inflation?
3. Why did the American dollar play such an important part in world trade after World War II?
4. How does a rise in prices in one country help bring inflation in other countries?
5. Why did some people fear the investment of petrodollars in their countries?

RELATED MATERIALS

Duplicator/Copy Masters: Activities 60, 61; Quiz 60
Workbook pages 86-88

buy from other countries. **5.** They were afraid that the oil-producing countries would control the economies of the countries where they made the investments.

WORKING WITH SKILLS

1. The topic must be broad enough to be interesting, but not too broad to be covered in one research paper. **2.** outlining

---

WORKING WITH SKILLS

Reread the lesson on research papers on pages 700-701. Then answer the following questions.

1. Why is choosing the topic such an important step in writing a research paper?
2. What study skill can help you organize your ideas?

ON YOUR OWN

1. The question of nuclear power is an important one for the future. Its benefits must be weighed against its disadvantages. Imagine you are preparing for a debate on nuclear power. Decide whether to make an argument for or against nuclear power. If you argue for nuclear power, write a list of at least five advantages to the use of nuclear power. If you argue against nuclear power, list at least five disadvantages.
2. Find a newspaper or magazine from 1970. Many libraries have these. Your librarian can help you to find them.

   Use the advertisements in this newspaper or magazine to check the prices of five items such as food, cars, clothing, and houses. Now find the prices for the same items in a current newspaper or by going to the store. How much change do you find has taken place? What types of goods have the largest price rises? If this rate continued what would be the cost of those goods ten years from now?
3. The automobile showroom on the left is in Kuwait, an OPEC nation. It is symbolic of the rapid changes oil-rich nations have undergone as a result of their sudden wealth. Choose one of the OPEC nations and use the *Readers' Guide* to find articles on how that nation is using its oil wealth to improve life for its people. For example, improvements might include the construction of hospitals and schools or the development of new industries. Write a brief report describing one such project.

Chapter 29
CURRENT POLITICS

Chapter 29 covers the foreign policy, economy, and domestic problems of the United States in the 1970s and 1980s. Lesson 29-1 discusses America's relationships with the Soviet Union, Middle Eastern nations, and Iran. Lesson 29-2 examines American concern for human rights and explains how it affected America's relations with Central American, Asian, and African nations. Lesson 29-3 discusses problems in the American economy, possible solutions to those problems, and programs for those in need.

CONTENT OBJECTIVES

After completing the lesson, students will know:
- why the Senate never voted on the SALT II treaty
- how the United States acted as peacemaker between Israel and the Arab nations
- the history of the conflict with Iran

VOCABULARY

terrorism: the use of violence to frighten people into accepting certain policies or demands

exile: someone who is forced to live in another country or chooses to do so

hostage: a captive who is held for either money or other demands

29-1 A Precarious Peace

As you read, think about these questions:

What were United States goals in the Middle East during the 1970s?

Why were Anwar el-Sadat's policies toward Israel of historic significance?

Why did Iran turn against America after the fall of the Shah?

Special Vocabulary terrorism exile hostage

During the 1970s the United States faced a world less friendly and less respectful than that of twenty years earlier. Vietnam was now a single country—under communist rule. The Yom Kippur War of 1973 and OPEC had threatened the supply of oil from the Middle East. In spite of détente, the Soviet Union seemed to be growing in military strength. Revolutions in many countries of the Middle East, Africa, and Latin America created new concerns for the United States government.

United States Foreign Policy

Americans needed to be able to guard the security of their country without getting into another Vietnam-like war. Instead of sending soldiers to fight in far-off lands, the United States would have to rely on diplomacy from now on to settle international problems.

SALT II. Disarmament talks had ended in the late 1960s and early 1970s. The United States and the Soviet Union, however, began a new set of meetings called SALT II. SALT I (see page 666) had limited the number of weapons each of the two countries might have. American officials hoped the new meetings would keep the two powers equal in their supplies of nuclear weapons.

In 1979 the two sides finally reached an agreement. President Jimmy Carter and Soviet Secretary Brezhnev met in Vienna and signed a treaty. SALT II, like SALT I, seemed to promise a lessening of tension between the United States and the Soviet Union. Within the United States, however, many Americans worried about the terms of SALT II. Some people believed that the Soviet Union had gained too much by the treaty.

Then in December 1979, Soviet troops marched into Afghanistan. American officials angrily protested this invasion. One of the ways Americans protested was to refuse to bring the SALT II treaty to the Senate for a vote. The United States and the USSR would have to start new talks in order to keep the precarious, or shaky, peace.

The outcome of the SALT II agreement was in doubt even before it was shelved in 1979. Many senators believed that the agreement did not really provide for arms control.

Carter and China. President Nixon's trip to China in 1972 improved relations between the United States and China. President Carter wanted to continue this new friendship. In December 1978, Carter agreed to set up full diplomatic relations with the People's Republic of China and to exchange ambassadors with it. The United States hoped that with China as an American friend, the Soviets might decide to be less aggressive. Chinese officials also hoped for a less threatening Soviet Union. They wanted increased trade with the United States to help make China more modern.

Relations with Neighbors. The United States also sought to improve relations with its close neighbors, Mexico and Canada, during the 1970s. Many Canadians worried that the United States economy and culture were somehow affecting Canada for the worse. For example, United States firms owned many important businesses in Canada. The Canadian Parliament, therefore, passed laws encouraging Canadians to gain control of such companies. American and Canadian leaders met to talk about common concerns, such as air pollution, and to strengthen relations between their two nations. The leaders also sought fresh ways in which Canada and the United States could work together.

President Carter and Canadian Prime Minister Pierre Trudeau met in 1980 to discuss common concerns. Later Congress approved the construction of the Alaskan Highway natural gas pipeline across western Canada.

United States officials held talks with Mexican officials, as well. During the 1970s hundreds of thousands of poor Mexican citizens illegally crossed the border into the United States to look for jobs. Some people in the United States complained that these Mexicans took jobs that American workers might otherwise have had. The governments of the United States and Mexico, therefore, cooperated in seeking ways to limit this illegal immigration. People in the United States and in Mexico hoped that the huge new discoveries of petroleum in Mexico during the 1970s would provide at least a partial answer to the problem. Mexican leaders hoped to use income from the sale of petroleum to other countries to develop their nation's economy and so to create new jobs for Mexican workers.

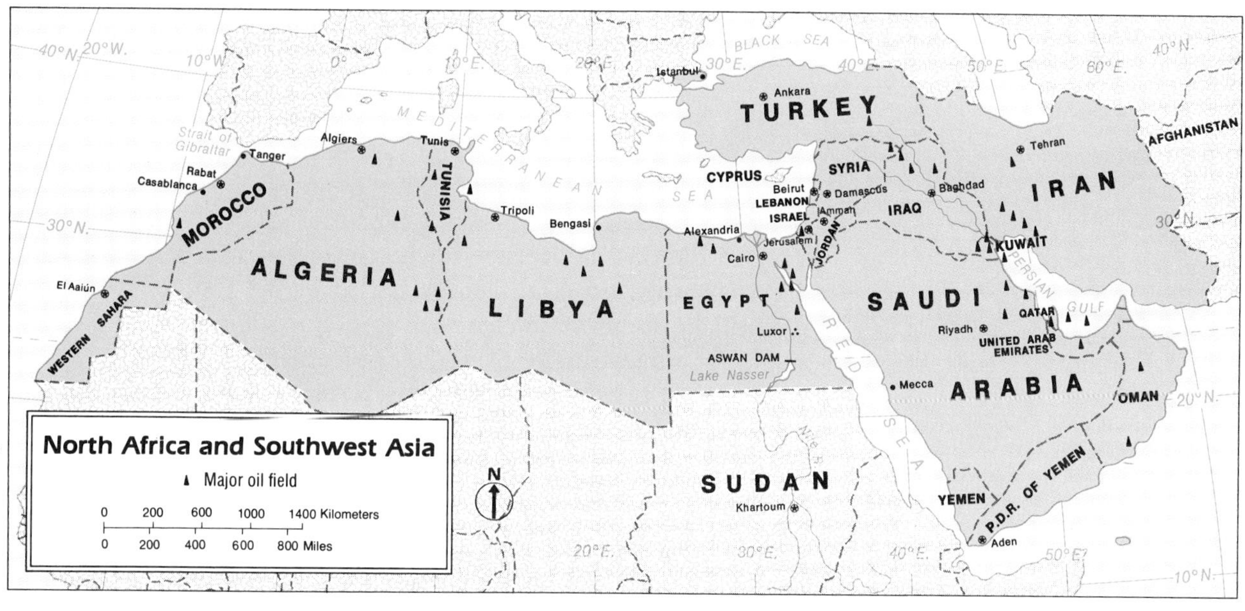

This map shows the major oil fields in the Middle East. In which bodies of water are there offshore oil wells? Off the coasts of which countries are these wells located?

Mediterranean Sea, Persian Gulf; Tunisia, United Arab Emirates, Kuwait

The Way Toward Peace in the Middle East

In the Middle East, the United States continued trying to keep the friendship of both Israel and the Arab countries. The Yom Kippur War in 1973 showed that the Arab countries had more strength than Americans or Israelis had guessed. If another war broke out between Israel and its Arab neighbors, the United States, Israel's best friend, might find itself without enough oil. In addition, the United States had to worry that the Soviet Union might gain support among Middle Eastern countries.

The Camp David Accords represent one of the great mediation efforts in diplomatic history. Bringing about this agreement was one of the triumphs of Jimmy Carter's presidency.

ACTIVITY

Objective: To recognize points of view

Divide the students into three groups to reenact the Middle East negotiations at Camp David, Maryland. One group will represent the Israelis; the second, the Egyptians; and the third, President Carter and his staff. Suggest that the students review Lesson 27-3 as well as the material in this lesson. Also, on a world map, review the locations of Israel, Egypt, and the other Middle Eastern nations. Then have them negotiate specifically the use of the Suez Canal and the return of the land on the Sinai Peninsula to Egypt.

The Camp David Accords. Late in 1977 the prospects for peace in the Middle East took a stunning turn for the better. President Anwar el-Sadat of Egypt announced suddenly that he was willing to visit Israel. Since Israel's birth in 1948, the Arab nations had refused even to recognize the Jewish state. As a result, no Arab leader had ever set foot in Israel nor publicly discussed peace with Israeli leaders.

The government of Israel welcomed Sadat's offer. The Egyptian president arrived in Jerusalem on December 29, 1977, as millions of people in the United States watched on television. The Israeli prime minister, Menachem Begin, welcomed Sadat with full honors. Soon afterward, Begin visited Egypt, and the two leaders began a series of talks to try to settle their differences.

The talks did not go smoothly. Many people in Israel were suspicious of Egypt and opposed returning any of its lands. The issue threatened to end the chance for an agreement. The United States offered to act as a go-between. President Carter invited Sadat and Begin to meet with him at Camp David, Maryland, near Washington. There the two Middle East leaders made an exciting breakthrough. In September 1978 they agreed to what were called the Camp David Accords, a set of principles for peace between Israel and Egypt.

After further talks, Sadat and Begin signed a peace treaty at the White House on March 26, 1979. Israel agreed to withdraw from the Sinai Peninsula in several stages. Egypt recognized Israel for the first time. Soon afterwards, Israeli ships were allowed to go through the Suez Canal.

Continuing Problems. Most Arab countries angrily criticized Sadat for making a separate peace with their common enemy, Israel. They demanded that Israel give up land to create a homeland for Palestinian refugees (see page 671). In turn, Israel charged that a group of Palestinians called the Palestine Liberation Organization (PLO) was engaging in *terrorism* against Israel. Terrorism is the use of violence to frighten people into accepting certain policies or demands.

In October 1981 President Sadat of Egypt was assassinated by certain members of the Egyptian army. The assassins believed that Egypt should base its policies only on Muslim teachings. Sadat was succeeded by vice president Hosni Mubarak, who promised to continue the peace process.

Three former Presidents—Nixon, Ford, and Carter—arrive at President Sadat's funeral. President Reagan, who did not attend, had only recently recovered from an assassination attempt.

Conflict with Iran

America had another close ally in the Middle East in the Shah of Iran, Mohammad Reza Pahlavi. Iran supplied a large part of the oil used in the United States and Western Europe. In addition, the United States monitored the USSR's military strength from bases in Iran. For much of the 1970s, the United States supplied Iran with planes and other weapons.

During the 1960s and early 1970s, the Shah tried hard to make Iran more modern. He broke up some large landholdings and gave the land to small farmers. He also gave women the vote and worked to provide them with greater legal rights and job opportunities.

Revolution. In spite of these actions, the Shah made many enemies inside his own country. The Muslim clergy felt that the Shah's modernization efforts violated important religious principles. They believed that Iran had become too westernized, too much like the United States and countries in Europe. Many Iranians also accused the Shah of allowing his secret police to torture and murder those who opposed him.

In 1978 demonstrations against the Shah broke out in Iran. By the fall, riots had taken place in the capital city, Teheran. Strikers shut down the Iranian oil fields, threatening the country's economy.

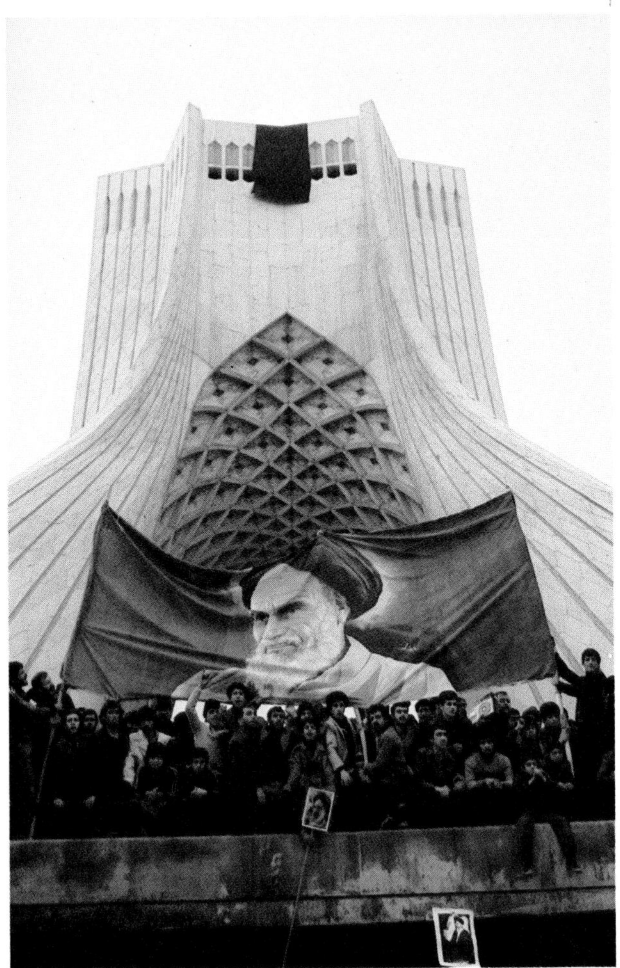

Iranian revolutionaries united under the banner of Ayatollah Ruhollah Khomeini in 1979. After the overthrow of the Shah, Khomeini put into effect many Islamic laws that limited the activities of the Iranian people.

DISCUSSION

Explain to the students that hostages have been taken in many nations, for political and nonpolitical reasons. Some public officials claim that it is wrong for governments to negotiate with terrorists, because even talking to them grants them a kind of authority or respectability. Other public officials think that any government has a responsibility to save the lives of the hostages, who are generally innocent pawns. Have the students discuss the issue of negotiating with terrorists for the lives of innocent people. What kinds of demands can a government agree to?

Opponents of the Shah looked for leadership to the popular religious leader, Ayatollah Ruhollah Khomeini. Khomeini was living as an *exile* in France. An exile is someone who is forced to live in another country, or chooses to do so, because of his or her opposition to the government. Very shortly the Shah's opponents had enough strength to overthrow him.

Like Khomeini before him, the Shah became an exile—on January 16, 1979. Khomeini quickly returned to Iran in triumph. He proclaimed the new Islamic Republic of Iran. Khomeini and the leaders of the Iranian Revolution denounced the United States for having supported the Shah.

The Hostage Crisis. In October 1979 the United States allowed the Shah, who had cancer, to enter the United States for medical treatment. This action angered many anti-Shah Iranians. On November 4, a group of armed Iranians broke

After 444 days as hostages in Iran, fifty-two Americans returned to the United States in January 1981. They were welcomed home with parades, joyous celebrations, and an official ceremony at the White House.

into the American embassy in Teheran. They took as *hostages* over fifty Americans who were working there. Hostages are captives who are held for either money or other demands. The Iranians said that they would release the Americans only if the Shah was returned to Iran to stand trial. The Iranians also wanted the United States to admit guilt for crimes committed by the government of the Shah. President Carter, of course, would not agree to do this.

For months, the United States tried without success to gain release of the hostages. Meanwhile, the Shah had gone to Panama and then to Egypt, where he died in July 1980. Carter's failure to end the hostage crisis became an issue in the 1980 presidential election. Carter lost the election to Ronald Reagan, the Republican candidate. Still, Carter continued to work for release of the hostages. On January 20, 1981, just moments before he left office, American diplomats reached an agreement with the Iranian government. In return for release of the hostages, the United States would free Iranian money and property seized during the crisis.

ANSWER THESE QUESTIONS

1. What was the subject of SALT II?
2. For what reason did the United States recognize the People's Republic of China in 1978?
3. How did Sadat anger other Arab leaders?
4. What were the Camp David Accords?
5. Why was the Shah overthrown by the Iranian people?

ANSWER THESE QUESTIONS

1. equalizing the supplies of nuclear arms maintained by the United States and the USSR
2. The United States thought that Chinese-American friendship would make the Soviets less aggressive and help guarantee peace in Asia.
3. by recognizing Israel and making a separate peace with it
4. a set of principles for peace between Israel and Egypt
5. because his efforts at modernization offended devout Muslims and because of reports that his secret police tortured those who opposed him

Objective: Once the students have completed this page, they will know how to paraphrase a document.

Working with Skills

READING SKILLS

ACTIVITY

Objective: To paraphrase a document

Have the students paraphrase a document or a section of a document such as the following: "Whenever the President transmits to the President pro tempore of the Senate and the Speaker of the House of Representatives his written declaration that he is unable to discharge the powers and duties of his office, and until he transmits to them a written declaration to the contrary, such powers and duties shall be discharged by the Vice President as Acting President." (Section 3, 25th Amendment to the Constitution) Also ask the students questions about the passage, such as: How many people does the President notify?

ANSWER

to achieve peace in the Western Hemisphere, to ensure equal access to the canal for all nations, and to defend the canal

Paraphrasing a Document

You will recall learning about paraphrasing in Chapter 7. Take some time now to review that lesson on pages 167–172.

In 1977 the United States and Panama signed a new treaty concerning the Panama Canal. This treaty said that the canal belonged to Panama and that Panama would take over actual control of the canal in 1999. Some people in both countries bitterly opposed the treaty. However, the United States Senate ratified it in 1978. The people of Panama, in a special election, also approved the treaty.

Both countries were concerned about keeping the Panama Canal open to continued use by all countries. They expressed this concern in a protocol, or a written document added to the treaty. Read Article I of this protocol below.

Whereas the . . . neutrality of the Panama Canal is important not only to the commerce and security of the United States of America and the Republic of Panama, but to the peace and security of the Western Hemisphere and to the interests of world commerce as well:

Whereas the . . . neutrality which the United States of America and the Republic of Panama have agreed to maintain will ensure permanent access to the canal by . . . all nations on the basis of entire equality:

Whereas the said regime of effective neutrality shall constitute the best protection for the canal and shall ensure the absence of any hostile act against it:

The contracting parties to this protocol have agreed upon the following:

The contracting parties hereby acknowledge the regime of permanent neutrality for the canal established in the Treaty Concerning the Permanent Neutrality and Operation of the Panama Canal and associate themselves with its objectives.

The last two paragraphs of this protocol could be paraphrased as follows: The signers of this treaty agree to recognize the policy of neutrality for all time as the basis of the treaty and to work to achieve the aims of neutrality.

Now put into your own words the three reasons for this agreement, which are given in the first three paragraphs.

RELATED MATERIAL

Duplicator/Copy Master Activity 63

29-2 Concern for Human Rights

As you read, think about these questions:

How have governments in Central America responded to revolutionary movements?

How have American Presidents responded to human rights problems in Asia?

What policy did black South Africans protest during the 1970s?

Special Vocabulary human rights apartheid

CONTENT OBJECTIVES

After completing the lesson, students will know:

- that President Carter spoke out in favor of human rights around the world
- that the United States tried to discourage communism but encourage human rights in Central America
- that human rights became a major issue in relations with South Korea
- that blacks in Rhodesia won independence from Great Britain and called their new nation Zimbabwe

VOCABULARY

human rights: the basic rights to life, liberty, and equality of opportunity

apartheid: official segregation of the races

Like earlier Presidents, Jimmy Carter opposed the spread of communism. Carter, however, also stressed that the United States should support *human rights* around the world. Human rights are the basic rights to life, liberty, and equality of opportunity. Carter spoke out against the behavior of the Soviet Union when it violated the human rights of its citizens. He also accused other nations of violating people's human rights.

Central America

In Central America, a small number of families own almost all the land. Most of thc people live in poverty, with little voice in the government. During the 1970s revolutionary movements developed in several Central American countries. In some cases, these movements were supported by the communist government of Cuba. The governments of these nations sometimes used imprisonment and torture to put down the rebels. The United States, therefore, had two problems. First, it had to find ways to limit the spread of communism in Central America. Second, it wanted to let governments that violated human rights know of American displeasure.

Nicaragua. The country of Nicaragua provides an example of the problems in Central America. Nicaragua had been ruled by one family, the Somozas, since 1936. Anastasio Somoza, president since 1967, did little to improve the living conditions of the people. A growing number of Nicaraguans

United States Ambassador Lawrence Pezzullo, fifth from the left, meets with the Nicaraguan *junta,* or council, in August of 1979. The Sandinistas were named for Augusto Sandino, a guerrilla leader whom Somoza had executed in 1934.

criticized the government. In the 1970s a movement of revolutionaries—the Sandinistas—used guerrilla warfare to oppose Somoza. In turn, Somoza made his policies even harsher.

The United States hoped to bring peace to Nicaragua and guard the human rights of the Nicaraguan people. At the same time, President Carter wanted to keep Nicaragua friendly to the United States. He had to walk a tightrope.

In May 1979 the Sandinistas forced President Somoza to flee the country. The rebel leaders took over a country that had been badly hurt by the savage fighting. Thousands of Nicaraguans had lost their lives. American leaders urged the Sandinistas not to adopt communism. The Americans hoped that Nicaragua would not become a source of communist revolutions elsewhere in Central America.

José Napoleón Duarte served on a civilian-military junta that had governed El Salvador since 1979. He was sworn in as president of the country on December 13, 1980.

El Salvador. In 1980 a similar pattern of events seemed to be unfolding in nearby El Salvador. Guerrillas there were waging war against the government of José Napoleón Duarte. After coming to power in 1979, his government had made an effort to break up large plantations and give the land to poor farmers. Government troops, however, grimly went about the job of finding and killing the guerrillas.

In December 1980 people in the United States were shocked by the murder of four American nuns in El Salvador. It appeared that members of El Salvador's armed forces were responsible. In response, President Carter stopped economic and military aid to El Salvador. He restored the aid just one month later, however, when he learned that Cuba and Nicaragua had supplied military aid to the guerrillas. When the Reagan administration took office, American aid to El Salvador continued, as did American concern about human rights in the war-torn nation.

Asia

Respect for human rights also became an issue in American relations with allies in Asia during the 1970s. Park Chung Hee, the president of South Korea, for example, sometimes used oppressive policies to maintain order. Without order, he insisted, South Korea would be inviting invasion by communist forces. The South Korean government sent to jail some newspaper reporters, religious leaders, and other public figures who disagreed with its policies. When large numbers of South Koreans objected to such treatment, the government used police and army troops to crack down on them. In June 1979 President Carter visited South Korea. Park marked the visit by releasing many political prisoners from jail. This gave new hope that human rights would be more respected in South Korea in the future.

In the Philippines, the government of Ferdinand Marcos also used stern measures to force the Filippino people to accept its rule. During the 1970s communist guerillas fought with government troops. Furthermore, Muslims in the southern Philippines called for independence. Marcos responded by declaring martial law, or rule by the military, in 1972. Marcos ended martial law in 1981. Still, dissatisfaction with his government remained widespread.

In Asia as in Central America, the United States balanced its desire for strong, dependable allies with its concern for the human rights of individuals. The administrations of both Jimmy Carter and Ronald Reagan continued close relations with these Asian governments. At the same time they sought to influence them to make their actions toward their own people more democratic and humane.

DISCUSSION

Remind the class that the United States and South Korea have been close allies since the Korean War. Have the students discuss how far the American government can go in pressuring friendly nations to respect human rights. Have them debate whether the United States should cut off diplomatic relations with, and economic aid to, nations that limit freedom of speech, imprison people without trial, and torture prisoners. Point out that some people fear that the United States will be left without allies if relations are broken off with every nondemocratic government. Ask the students what they think about that issue.

Africa

By the mid-1970s, all the former European colonies in Africa had won their independence. In several nations, however, black Africans continued to struggle for their rights against oppressive governments.

Robert Mugabe became prime minister of the new republic of Zimbabwe in April 1980. He surprised his critics by including in his government a number of his black opponents and two white ministers.

Zimbabwe. In 1965 the British settlers in the colony of Rhodesia declared their independence from Great Britain. Great Britain and most other nations, however, refused to recognize the independence of Rhodesia. They did this because white settlers did not allow blacks—who greatly outnumbered whites by twenty-two to one—to have any voice in running the government.

In 1978 the government of Rhodesia finally agreed to allow moderate blacks to form a government. Black guerrilla groups in the nation, nevertheless, refused to recognize the new government. They claimed that whites were still controlling the government from behind the scenes. Battles between the guerrillas and government troops broke out.

In 1979 the British served as a go-between for the government and the rebels. The talks finally led to an agreement. New elections were held in 1980. A black majority gained control of the parliament. Great Britain recognized the independence of Rhodesia, which was renamed Zimbabwe after an ancient African kingdom. The United States, which had worked with Great Britain in bringing about this compromise, was hopeful that the new government would help make southern Africa stable.

ACTIVITY

Objective: To identify issues and questions

Divide the class into four or five groups. Ask each group to choose one country in Central America, Asia, or Africa mentioned in this lesson. Have the groups do some research to find more information about the role the American government has played in the affairs of that country. Have the groups report their findings to the class and compare when and why the United States was involved, for how long, and what the results were.

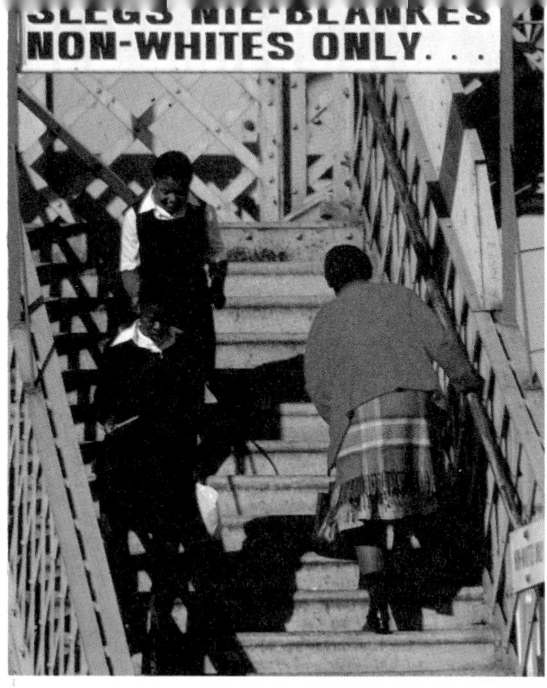

The South African policy of apartheid continues to cause controversy. In 1981 a proposal was made to establish a single department of education for all races, but the government decided to continue its policy of separate schools.

The Republic of South Africa. Since the 1940s the rulers of South Africa had followed a policy known as *apartheid.* Apartheid means official segregation of the races. The white people of South Africa ruled in spite of the fact that eighty-three percent of the people are nonwhite.

In the 1970s many black South Africans protested apartheid. In 1976 hundreds of people were killed in riots at Soweto, near Johannesburg. The United States joined other nations in condemning the government of South Africa. President Carter believed that South Africa should grant basic human rights to blacks, especially the right to vote.

In the United States, the South African policy of apartheid has led to controversy. Some people have called for American businesses in South Africa to leave the country. The businesses, however, have pointed out that they paid the same wages to workers regardless of race. They said that they tried to bring about integration of the races in work areas.

ANSWER THESE QUESTIONS

1. Who were the Sandinistas?
2. What event led President Carter to cut off aid to El Salvador?
3. When did President Marcos declare martial law in the Philippines?
4. Why did guerrillas in Rhodesia oppose the black government established in 1978?
5. Why do some people object to United States corporations doing business in South Africa?

ANSWER THESE QUESTIONS

1. Nicaraguan revolutionaries who overthrew Somoza
2. the murder of four American nuns
3. 1972
4. They claimed whites were still controlling the government.
5. because of South Africa's policy of apartheid

LAW AND THE CITIZEN

A Balance of Rights

Sometimes one of the rights guaranteed in the Constitution comes into conflict with another right. In such cases, the courts must seek a way to balance everyone's rights in the fairest way possible. Working out such a balance may take many years and several decisions. Two recent cases show how this process works. In each, the right to a fair trial appeared to conflict with the right to a public trial.

The first case, *Gannett Co. v. DePasquale*, grew out of a murder trial in New York. The defendant in the murder case asked the judge to keep reporters out of a pretrial hearing, where the court would decide what evidence to accept. The judge granted the defendant's request, saying that newspaper and television stories might influence the jury when the case went to trial. In response, Gannett Newspapers, a nationwide newspaper chain, went to the Supreme Court. The chain argued that barring reporters from the courtroom violated the Sixth Amendment and would make people suspicious about what went on in the court. In 1979 the Supreme Court ruled five to four against Gannett. The Court said that the Sixth Amendment gives only the defendant a right to a public trial. If the defendant gives up that right, the press and public have no right in the courtroom.

Some people thought the decision applied only to hearings. Others believed it also applied to criminal trials. State judges used the decision to close criminal trials to the press and public more than thirty times during 1979 and 1980. After reporters were kept out of a murder trial in Virginia, newspapers protested again. The Richmond Newspapers went before the Supreme Court, arguing that the First Amendment gives the public a right to gather information about government activities.

One year to the day after its 1979 decision, the Supreme Court ruled in the case of *Richmond Newspapers v. Virginia.* This time it agreed with the newspapers. In a seven to one decision, the justices said the public does have a right to observe government operations, including trials. For the first time, gathering information was called a constitutional right. Nearly all criminal trials must now be open to the press and public.

tion, unemployment, and bankruptcies **6.** a plan to shift social programs to state governments in order to cut back federal spending for those programs

WORKING WITH SKILLS

The signers of the treaty agree that the canal will be neutral territory for all time, in war or peace. Each country is responsible for seeing that its ships honor this neutrality.

---

5. Why were many Americans concerned about private industry in the 1970s?
6. What was the "New Federalism" proposed by President Reagan?

WORKING WITH SKILLS

Put the following paragraph, known as Article II of the protocol to the Panama Canal Treaty, into simple words.

The contracting parties agree to observe and respect the regime of permanent neutrality of the canal in time of war as in time of peace and to ensure that vessels of their registry strictly observe the applicable rules.

ON YOUR OWN

1. Use an encyclopedia to research either Nicaragua or El Salvador. Write a short report. Include the country's population, its chief farm products and industries, and a brief chronological list of important events in its history. Then see if you can find any current news on the country. Look in newspapers and recent news magazines. Write a final paragraph in your report to sum up the current situation.
2. Look through a current daily newspaper for news of relations between Israel and its Arab neighbors—Egypt, Syria, Jordan, and Lebanon. Check through the daily papers every day for a week. Make notes on the articles that you find. Compare the current situation with that as described in your textbook. What changes have occurred? Write a short report to present your findings.
3. Bankruptcy signs like the one on this page often indicate a weakening economy. Look up bankruptcy in an encyclopedia or interview the owner of a local business to find out about the process of declaring bankruptcy. Then make a list of reasons why a person or a corporation may be declared bankrupt.

Chapter 30 focuses on some of the basic problems facing the United States as the twentieth century draws to a close. Lesson 30-1 discusses the problems of the cities, redevelopment and "urban homesteading," and the cities' transportation needs. Lesson 30-2 examines the quality of life in the United States, including living conditions for the growing older population and changes in the educational system.

Chapter 30
TOWARD TOMORROW'S AMERICA

CONTENT OBJECTIVES

After completing the lesson, students will know:
- about changes in cities in recent years
- that cities tried attracting new industry and initiating redevelopment projects to help their economies
- about the "new towns" of urban planners
- about the problems of mass transit systems in cities

VOCABULARY

tax base: the amount and value of taxable property
service industry: an industry that does not manufacture products but rather provides services for people
condominium: building in which the apartments or lofts are individually owned
rapid transit: transportation systems such as subways, streetcars, and trains that have land set aside solely for their use
subsidy: grant of money

30-1 Rebuilding America

As you read, think about these questions:
What are some of the problems of America's cities?
How are cities working to solve their problems?
What ideas can urban planners borrow from "new towns"?
How have Americans' transportation habits changed since the early 1970s?

Special Vocabulary	tax base	rapid transit
	service industry	subsidy
	condominium	

As America approaches the twenty-first century, people in many walks of life are working to prepare the nation to meet the requirements of a new age. One important requirement is maintaining American cities as convenient and exciting places to live and work in.

The Cities

Every American city is unique. This is so because the things that make up a city—its history, industry, people, location, climate, and services—are different in every case. The one thing all cities have in common, however, is change. Cities are constantly creating new needs and new problems. Over the past few decades, developments in American society as a whole have greatly affected cities. Many of the effects have not been for the better.

Programs known as "urban homesteading" allowed people to buy old, run-down houses at very small cost. The buyers had to agree to fix up the houses and live in them for a period of time. In cities like Baltimore, urban homesteading renewed neighborhoods that had seemed hopelessly gone only a few years earlier.

Real estate developers also played a role in urban development. By building new complexes or rehabilitating old ones, they brought new life to city neighborhoods. Many cities offered developers incentives like tax breaks, land deals, or help in raising money for the projects. Many rehabilitated apartment or industrial buildings were sold as *condominiums.* Condominiums are buildings in which the apartments or lofts are individually owned. Owners of such units then added to the cities' tax revenues.

Yet such solutions to city decline did not always help the poor and unskilled residents. New industry often offered jobs only to highly educated or skilled workers. Urban redevelopment also meant higher rents. Lower-income and elderly people often could not afford to remain in a neighborhood after it was renewed. In some cases, they benefited from the services provided by the increased tax base. However, they also needed help to find housing and jobs.

It is difficult to believe that this was once a run-down area. Rehabilitation does more than improve the appearance of a neighborhood. It also increases the value of the property.

New Towns. One influence on urban development came from a movement that began during the 1920s and 1930s. Urban planners at that time began to promote a new kind of community called a "new town." These communities would be built from scratch with open spaces in and around them.

The people who lived in them would also work there. New towns were expected to be self-maintaining. That is, they would provide all the varied needs of the residents.

One of the first sizable new towns was Columbia, Maryland. This community was planned for over 100,000 people. The master plan called for a cluster of townhouses and apartments surrounded by acres of recreation land. The plan also included an artificial lake, shopping malls, walkways, and bike paths. A corporation raised $2 billion to create Columbia and began construction in 1965. By 1982 Columbia was a pleasant suburban community of 49,000 people.

Arcosanti was planned as a different type of new town. It is being built near Phoenix, Arizona. Designed by architect Paolo Soleri, Arcosanti will eventually house 5000 people on just 14 acres (5.6 hectares) of land. About 3000 acres (1200 hectares) of surrounding land will be preserved in a natural state. Arcosanti will derive most of its energy from the sun.

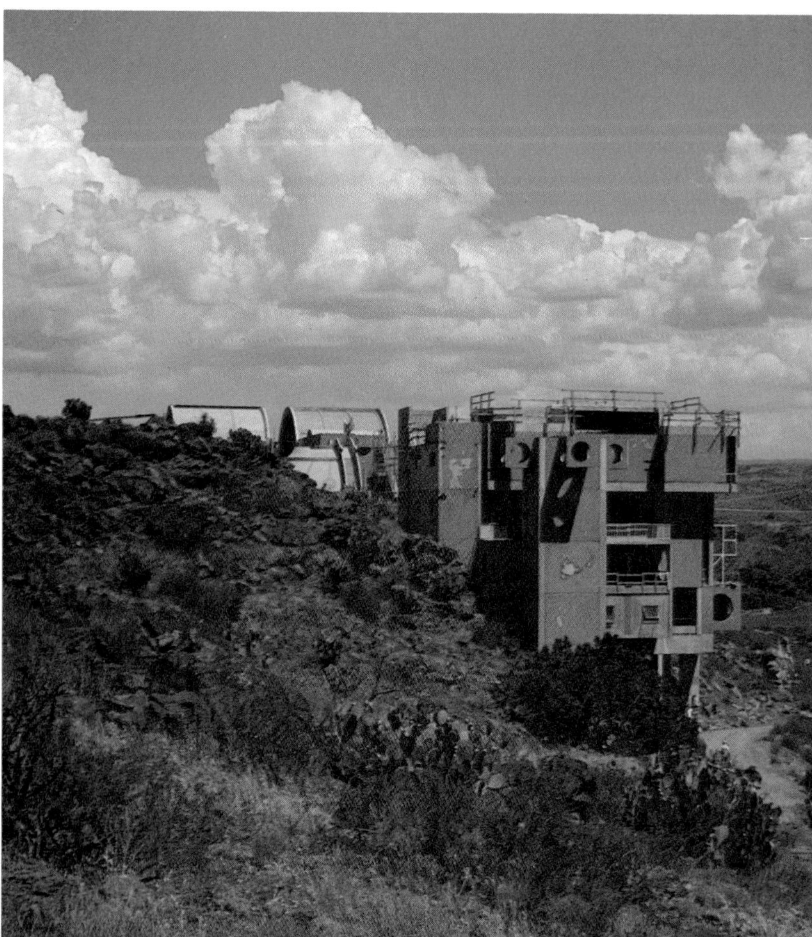

This photograph of Arcosanti shows how the architect's plans were being carried out. Notice that the buildings were being made to fit into the landscape. The hill, for example, was not flattened to make way for the construction work.

Looking Toward the Future. It seems unlikely that new towns will be home to millions of people in the future. The expense of building such new communities is enormous. The new town concept, however, provided ideas that were used in the redevelopment of "old towns." For example, urban planners used clustered housing and carefully designed recreation areas to help make many existing cities much more livable.

In the future, cities will also need to cooperate more fully with their suburbs. In turn, suburban governments will have to see city problems as partly their problems. An entire metropolitan area is economically linked together. Only invisible boundaries separate a city from its suburbs. Many shared problems can only be solved if the entire metropolitan area cooperates.

Transportation

A reliable and efficient system of transportation is required by Americans in rural areas as well as by those living in the cities and suburbs. Since the 1970s, however, the patterns of all transportation in the United States have been changing. Before the Arab oil embargo of 1973, few people gave much thought to fuel conservation or the cost of getting around in their automobiles. After the embargo, Americans began to search for cheaper and more efficient ways of traveling.

Researchers continued to develop alternative fuels, such as the gasohol being pumped into this car. They were also experimenting with engines that would be more efficient than those used in most automobiles in the early 1980s.

Automobiles. Americans used automobiles in ninety percent of all their traveling. No other people depended so heavily on the automobile. The cost of owning and operating an automobile rose steadily after the early 1970s. A barrel of oil that cost two dollars in 1973 cost thirty-four dollars in 1982. As a result, Americans began to conserve fuel. They cut back on unnecessary driving and started to buy smaller cars.

Many of the small energy-efficient cars were foreign imports. American auto makers who produced mostly large automobiles began to lose sales to foreign manufacturers, notably Japanese and German. In response, American auto makers retooled their plants to meet the demand for smaller automobiles. More than anything else, Americans in the 1980s wanted automobiles that gave good gas mileage.

Alternative fuels also helped cut down the use of gasoline. Gasohol, a mixture of gasoline and ethanol, was sold at many service stations. Ethanol is a clean-burning, renewable fuel

DISCUSSION

Have the students discuss the automobile, why people like it, what problems it brings to cities, and what its future might be. Explain to the students that some cities, such as San Francisco, place a tax on cars coming in from the suburbs. Others, like Honolulu, have a "car pool lane" that cars can use only if they carry three or more people. Have students discuss these measures and other ways that other cities can productively regulate cars.

made from plants. Synthetic, or artificial, fuels were also being developed. Much research was needed, however, before synthetic fuels could become widely used.

Researchers were also working to develop electric automobiles. These automobiles used no gasoline. Instead they were powered by several large batteries that would be recharged from time to time. Electric automobiles could not travel long distances, but they could be useful for commuting and other local driving. Besides saving gas, electric automobiles would not pollute the air or make noise.

A new kind of battery may make it possible for electric cars to travel long distances. The battery uses air, water, and aluminum plates. It must be "re-fueled" with water about every 250 miles (400 kilometers).

Americans will probably continue their dependence on the automobile. Efforts, nevertheless, have been underway to reduce automobile use. Advertising programs that preach fuel conservation urged Americans not to be "fuelish." Commuters were asked to travel in car pools. In addition, the national speed limit on highways was set at 55 miles (88 kilometers) per hour. This law helped save lives as well as gasoline.

Mass Transit. The increasing gasoline prices helped persuade many city dwellers to use mass transit. Mass transit is a system of public transportation used to move large numbers of people in a metropolitan area. A city's mass transit

In the early 1980s the Metro, Washington's rapid transit system, had about 33 miles (53 kilometers) of track in the city and nearby suburbs. When it is completed, it will cover about 100 miles (160 kilometers).

network may include a *rapid transit* system. Rapid transit systems have land—rights of way—set aside solely for their use. Rapid transit includes subways, streetcars, and trains. (Because buses share the road with automobiles, they are not considered rapid transit.) New York City, Boston, Chicago, San Francisco, and Washington, D.C., all had rapid transit.

Many cities did not need, or could not afford, rapid transit. In such cities, buses provided good public transportation. Los Angeles, for instance, did not have rapid transit. Instead, the nation's third largest city had a bus system and a large network of automobile freeways.

Many mass transit systems faced financial problems. The cost of running public transportation was on the rise. When cities raised fares, they lost riders. If they kept fares low, they could not meet expenses. In any case, many cities depended on *subsidies*, or grants of money, from federal or state governments. With federal cutbacks in the 1980s, the future of mass transit was uncertain. Still, the demand for mass transit was great—and growing. Federal, state, and local government need to work together to provide Americans with efficient and fairly priced mass transit.

ANSWER THESE QUESTIONS

1. What American industries suffered most from foreign competition?
2. What industries were helping to revitalize American cities?
3. How did urban redevelopment sometimes hurt lower-income people?
4. What is rapid transit?
5. Why did cities try to avoid raising fares on their mass transit systems?

ANSWER THESE QUESTIONS

1. automobiles, shoes, steel, and some electronic goods
2. computer industry, service industries
3. They could not afford to live in a neighborhood once it was rehabilitated and the rents were raised.
4. a transportation system, such as subways, streetcars, or trains, with land set aside solely for its use
5. because higher fares caused them to lose riders.

Working with Skills

MAP SKILLS

ACTIVITY

Objective: To read a relief map

Make available to the students a relief map of Asia. Have them find the elevation for the Himalayas. To help the students understand that a relief map shows only a range of elevations, have them look up in reference sources the elevations of individual peaks in the Himalayas, such as Mount Everest and Annapurna. Then have them compare these figures with the elevation for the Rocky Mountains and for individual peaks such as Pikes Peak.

ANSWERS

1. blue; white
2. Memphis: sea level to 300 meters (sea level to 984 feet); El Paso: 600 to 1500 meters (1969 to 4921 feet); Los Angeles: sea level to 300 meters (sea level to 984 feet)
3. Rocky Mountains
4. southwestern United States, east of the Sierra Nevada
5. Mexico
6. 600 to 1500 meters (1969 to 4921 feet)
7. Wichita

Reading a Relief Map

A relief map is a map that shows the physical features of a region. These features may include mountains, valleys, and plains. To show something "in relief" means to make it stand out from its surroundings, as hills and rock formations do in a landscape.

Relief maps generally use lines, shadings, and colors to show physical features. On the type of relief map on the next page, the mapmaker actually draws in mountains to give a realistic impression of their size and location.

Relief maps divide territory into regions of different elevation. The elevation of an area is its height above sea level, in feet or meters. The mapmaker most often uses different colors to represent different elevations. Here, the map of North America shows six levels of elevation, each in a different color. The legend in the lower left-hand corner tells you how to interpret the colors.

According to the legend, the lowest place on this map is below sea level; the highest is above 9843 feet (3000 meters). Most of the eastern half of the United States is less than 984 feet (300 meters) above sea level. The western half of the country is much higher.

Study the map and its legend to find the answers to these questions.

1. What color represents the lowest elevations? The highest?
2. How high above sea level is Memphis, Tennessee? El Paso, Texas? Los Angeles?
3. What North American mountain range is highest?
4. Where is the lowest spot on the continent located?
5. What North American country lies almost entirely above 1969 feet (600 meters)?
6. At what elevation are the Great Plains?
7. Which city lies at a higher elevation, Chicago or Wichita?

RELATED MATERIAL

Duplicator/Copy Master Activity 66

education that Americans need. Governments, schools, and parents have all worked together to make sure that these needs were met.

The Role of Government. Federal, state, and local governments have spent more money on education than on any other activity except national defense. State and local governments have had the primary responsibility for education. In fact, the Constitution does not list education as one of the concerns of the federal government. Beginning in the 1950s, however, the federal government played an increasingly important role in American education.

The federal government first stepped in to ensure that students of all races would have equal opportunities for education. Federal courts ordered many local school boards to bus children to achieve racial balance in schools. Busing helped to integrate schools in some places, but in other places it became a highly controversial issue. During the 1980s governments at all levels began to look for alternatives to busing.

The federal government acted to guarantee equal education for all people in other ways. It insisted, for example, that students with visual or other handicaps be provided the education they need in public schools. It also supported bilingual education programs for thousands of students who spoke little or no English. The federal government also provided grants to encourage students with special academic or artistic talents. It funded vocational programs to train students for jobs. Federal grants and loans helped needy students obtain a college education.

The largest federal education program, called Title I, provided extra help in reading and mathematics to more than five million students. Eighty-five percent of all school districts in the United States participated in Title I.

During the 1980s the federal government began to reconsider its role in education. President Ronald Reagan and the Congress cut the funds for some education programs. He suggested that the federal government should turn over more of the responsibility for education to state and local governments. Many state and local governments, however, lacked the funds necessary to continue many of these educational programs. All levels of government will need to work together to provide the best possible education for Americans of all ages.

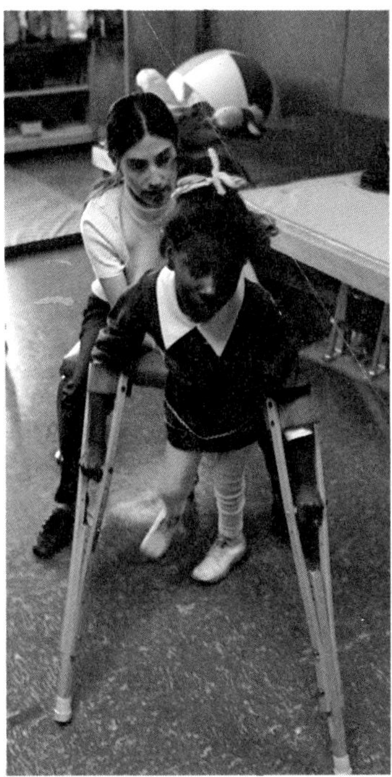

The installation of elevators and wheel chair ramps in schools and other public buildings has made life easier for the handicapped.

DISCUSSION

Have the students discuss how education should be financed. Point out that in recent years various pressure groups have been lobbying for additional educational opportunities—in bilingual education, cultural studies, skills for the handicapped, the arts, and so on. Yet governmental funding for education has been dropping at the same time. What responsibility does the government have for education and for what types of programs? Ask students to discuss what role can be played by business and private groups and by volunteer teachers or coaches—in the performing arts, for example.

Changes Ahead. Developments in technology will change the work world in the years ahead. New technology will eliminate some jobs and create others. In fact, many young people of today will one day work at jobs that do not even exist now. Schools will have to adapt themselves to training students for these changes.

As technology changes our society, workers will no longer be able to depend on having the same type of job during their entire working life. Education and re-education will become more truly a lifelong process. To help, many schools will become community schools operating from early morning until late at night. These schools will serve students of all ages.

Technology will also change the classroom itself. Computers and other electronic tools will become as important as blackboards. Using computers, students will be able to draw upon a mountain of information not even dreamed of a few years ago. Experts already have developed computer-assisted learning systems to help students learn a wide range of skills. In addition to computers, these systems use videodiscs. These discs resemble phonograph albums but store images as well as sound. Using a videodisc player connected to a television set, a student can read pages from a book, view a film, or even study the movements of a ballet dancer in slow motion.

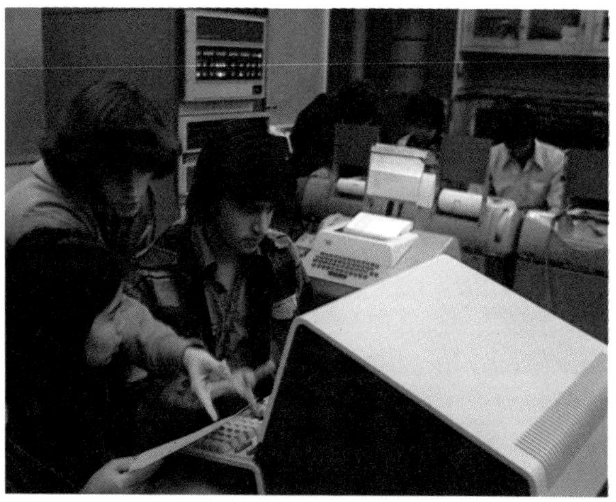

Computers were already appearing in many classrooms by the 1980s. The teacher in this science class helps her students call up the information they want.

Students in the future will need help in dealing with the vast amount of information made available by the new technology. Teachers will assist students in learning to separate important from unimportant information. They will continue to train students to think critically and make judgments, for there is no substitute for the human brain—and there is not going to be one. Above all, schools of tomorrow, like schools of the past, will prepare students to assume their roles as responsible American citizens in a democratic society.

Shortly after taking her place on the Supreme Court, Sandra Day O'Connor posed for this photograph with the other justices—(from left to right) Harry Blackmun, Thurgood Marshall, William Brennan, Jr., Warren Burger, Byron White, Lewis Powell, Jr., William Rehnquist, and John Stevens.

Preserving Our Rights

All citizens would certainly agree that the rights guaranteed by the Constitution are most important to the quality of American life. Protecting these rights in a changing nation and world will remain a top priority for the American people and their government.

Interpreting the Constitution. As wise as the founders of the United States were, they could not predict the America that exists today. The founders, nevertheless, provided us with a Constitution that still works. The Constitution served four million Americans in 1787. It served more than 226 million by the 1980s. As the nation grew and changed, Congress made new laws to deal with new situations. And all the while, the Supreme Court continued to judge and interpret those laws according to the principles set down in the Constitution.

You have learned how the American courts have helped guarantee the rights of minority groups in America. These guarantees will continue to be in force as minority groups grow and as new immigrants come to America. Likewise, you have learned about laws to prevent the misuse of computers in ways that might violate citizens' rights to privacy. In the years ahead, Congress and the courts must continue to make sure that new technology does not endanger anybody's constitutional rights.

The Promise Continues. In one sense, the American Revolution has never ended. Each generation of Americans has held visions of what the American future would be. These visions have not always been shared by all. The American future that Thomas Jefferson envisioned differed greatly from that imagined by Alexander Hamilton. Yet America became both Jefferson's great democratic nation and Hamilton's great industrial nation. The generations to come will also pursue their own visions of America. There will be disagreements, but America's strength has always come from the give and take among its diverse people.

The promise of America has been expressed many times, but never better than in the Declaration of Independence. In timeless words Jefferson told the world what America stands for: "We hold these truths to be self-evident, that all men are created equal, that they are endowed by their creator with certain unalienable Rights, that among these are Life, Liberty and the pursuit of Happiness." This ideal continues alive and flourishing—for all who will create tomorrow's America, the next shining generation of This Great Nation.

ANSWER THESE QUESTIONS

1. It was increasing.
2. senior citizen centers, low-cost housing and transportation, homemaker services, visiting nurses, meals on wheels
3. Increasing benefits were exceeding the taxes paid into the social security fund.
4. by requiring integration and adequate public education for the disabled; by funding many special programs such as vocational education and Title I
5. People of all ages will train for jobs in the new technology; students will use computers, videodiscs, and other technology.

ANSWER THESE QUESTIONS

1. How was the average age of the American population changing?
2. What are some ways in which communities helped the elderly?
3. What problems did social security face?
4. How did the federal government help provide equal education?
5. In what ways will education change in the future?

Sandra Day O'Connor

PEOPLE IN AMERICA

In 1873 the Supreme Court upheld the decision of an Illinois judge that Myra Bradwell, the first woman to apply to practice law, be denied a license to do so. "The . . . destiny of women," wrote Justice Joseph Bradley, "[is to] fulfill the noble . . . offices of wife and mother." Today more than 50,000 American women are lawyers. In 1981 one of those 50,000, Sandra Day O'Connor, became the first woman to serve on the nation's highest court—the Supreme Court.

O'Connor grew up on a ranch in Arizona. By the time she was sixteen, she had finished high school and was ready for college. Five years later she graduated third in her law-school class at Stanford University in California. She soon found out, however, that no law firms were hiring women—except as secretaries.

O'Connor was persistent and soon found a job as deputy county attorney in San Mateo, California. She and her husband, John, also a lawyer, next lived and worked in Germany for three years. In 1959 she opened her own law firm but spent much of the following five years caring for the couple's three sons. By 1965 O'Connor was again ready for a full-time job in law.

After four years as an assistant attorney general in Arizona, O'Connor was appointed to fill a vacancy in the state senate. She was elected to two terms in her own right, beginning in 1970. In 1972 O'Connor was elected majority leader—the first woman majority leader of any state legislature. Despite her success in the state senate, O'Connor longed to return to the practice of law. In 1974 she won a seat as a judge on the Maricopa County Superior Court. Five years later she was appointed to the Arizona Court of Appeals.

As O'Connor sees her job, "the role of the judge is to interpret the law, not make it. I do not believe it is the function of the judiciary to . . . change the law because times . . . or . . . social mores [customs and rules] have changed." O'Connor's nomination to the Supreme Court by Ronald Reagan and her confirmation by the Senate were welcome signs. Times, indeed, had changed since Myra Bradwell was denied a career in law 108 years before.

THINKING THINGS THROUGH

1. It brings new businesses into the city and increases tax revenues without raising tax rates. **2.** advantage: revitalizes run-down neighborhoods; disadvantage: drives out lower-income people **3.** It will house 5000 people on just 14 acres (5.6

Chapter 30 SUMMARY

The United States will continue to face challenges. Industrial problems have hurt the economic health of some cities. Cities have had a hard time keeping up services as population and tax revenues decline.

Cities have worked hard to bring business and people back. Service industries and the computer industry have brought new life to some cities. People came back into older neighborhoods through programs such as urban homesteading.

Americans conserved fuel in the 1980s. Auto makers began producing smaller, fuel-efficient cars. Research continued on nonpetroleum fuels and on electric cars. Urban Americans were riding on mass transit more. Federal cutbacks, however, made the future of mass transit uncertain.

Americans were concerned with providing a decent quality of life for all people. As the American population grew older, providing for the elderly became a major responsibility. The federal government as well as local communities helped senior citizens. At the same time, older Americans contributed richly to American life.

Providing adequate education was another concern of Americans. The federal government funded programs to assure equal education to all Americans. The cooperation of all levels of government would be needed to maintain these programs in the face of federal cutbacks.

New technology will have a major influence on education. Many adults will need to retrain as the kinds of jobs change.

Chapter 30 TEST

WORDS TO REMEMBER

Choose the correct word from the list below to complete each sentence.

a. subsidies
b. rapid transit
c. service industries
d. tax base
e. age pyramid

1. A city may set aside special land for a kind of public transportation known as __b__.
2. An __e__ shows the relative size of different age groups within a population.
3. A city can increase its __d__ by bringing in businesses with taxable property.
4. Cities have many banks, medical centers, restaurants, and other __c__.
5. Federal and state __a__ help cities maintain their services.

THINKING THINGS THROUGH

1. Why is increasing a city's tax base probably the best solution to its financial problems?
2. What are one advantage and one disadvantage of urban redevelopment?
3. What are some unusual characteristics of the new town Arcosanti?
4. How did drivers try to cut down on gasoline use?
5. What forms of mass transit did American cities use?
6. What were some ways in which the American population was changing?
7. What were some needs of the elderly?

RELATED MATERIALS

Duplicator/Copy Masters: Activities 64, 65, 66, 67; Quiz 62
Workbook pages 92-94

hectares) of land; it is solar-powered. **4.** cutting back on unnecessary driving and buying smaller, fuel-efficient cars **5.** buses and rapid transit **6.** The population was growing older; percentage of Hispanics was increasing. **7.** financial aid, medical care, and protection from crime

WORKING WITH SKILLS

1. Appalachian Mountains **2.** Hudson Bay **3.** Greenland **4.** Regina **5.** sea level to 300 meters

---

WORKING WITH SKILLS

Study the relief map on page 735. Then answer the questions.

1. What mountain range in the eastern United States has elevations of 600 meters or higher?
2. What large bay in Canada has low lands on all sides?
3. What large island near North America is almost completely covered by an ice cap?
4. Which Canadian city lies at a higher elevation, Regina or Winnipeg?
5. What is the elevation of most of the eastern part of the United States?

ON YOUR OWN

1. Interview an adult family member or a neighbor who drives. Choose someone who has been driving since at least the early 1970s. Ask the person to compare driving a car today with driving in the early 1970s. Have him or her consider the cost of gasoline, the size and efficiency of cars, the driving habits of Americans, and government regulations such as speed limits and safety requirements. Write your findings in a report to be presented to the class.
2. Construct an age graph for the population of your school. Get the figures you need from the school office. First, decide on a scale for your graph. For example, you might let one inch equal fifty students. Construct the graph, allowing one block for each grade. What does your chart show about your school population? What grade has the largest number of students?
3. The photograph on the left shows a NASA design for a future space colony. The rotating sphere, which provides gravity like that of the earth, is the suggested home for 10,000 members of a space manufacturing work force. Imagine that you are a NASA designer and write a description of the inside of the space colony.

THINK THINGS THROUGH

1. demand-pull inflation: increased demand for goods; cost-push inflation: the wage-price spiral **2.** United Nations Conference on Trade and Development (UNCTAD), International Monetary Fund **3.** The United States monitored Soviet military strength from nearby Iran; also, Iran sold Americans oil. **4.** a tax cut, a cut in government spending, a balanced budget **5.** rapid growth in the Hispanic population **6.** senior citizen centers, low-cost housing and transportation, visiting nurses, homemaker services, meals

UNIT 10 TEST

WORDS TO REMEMBER

Replace the words in italics in each sentence with a word from the following list that has the same meaning.

a. subsidy
b. famine
c. dividends
d. tax base
e. apartheid
f. stagflation
g. fossil fuels
h. terrorism
i. petrodollars

f 1. Economists worried about the *combination of inflation plus a slow-moving economy* in the 1970s.

e 2. Some people have called on American businesses to leave South Africa because of that country's policy of *officially segregating the races.*

b 3. During the 1970s many countries in Africa experienced *serious shortages of food,* leading to widespread starvation.

d 4. As the suburbs grew, the *amount and value of taxable property* in cities declined.

h 5. The Middle East has long been subject to *the use of violence to achieve political ends.*

a 6. Some cities received a *grant of money* from the federal government to help build new housing.

g 7. Among the nonrenewable resources, the ones of most concern today are *coal, oil, and natural gas.*

c 8. When President Nixon froze wages and prices, he also froze *profits companies pay to stockholders.*

i 9. In the 1970s, many Middle East countries earned a great deal of *money from the sale of petroleum.*

QUESTIONS TO ANSWER

Choose the letter of the word or words that correctly answer each question.

d 1. Which of the following is *not* a nonrenewable resource?
a. oil
b. coal
c. natural gas
d. water

b 2. What fraction of the world's population does not get enough to eat?
a. one third
b. one fourth
c. one half
d. two thirds

a 3. The United States cut back trade with the USSR in 1979 in response to the Soviet invasion of what country?
a. Afghanistan
b. Iran
c. Poland
d. West Germany

b 4. What Arab leader first recognized the state of Israel?
a. Anastasio Somoza
b. Anwar el-Sadat
c. Park Chung Hee
d. Hosni Mubarak

c 5. Which former British colony in Africa is now known as Zimbabwe?
a. South Africa
b. Soweto
c. Rhodesia
d. Namibia

RELATED MATERIAL
Duplicator/Copy Master Test 63-65

on wheels **7.** funded vocational education and Title I programs; gave grants and loans to needy students **8.** economic problems facing the Third World **9.** Increasing costs and cutbacks in federal and state subsidies resulted in financial problems.

PRACTICE YOUR SKILLS

1. a. card catalog and the *Readers' Guide* b. a list of sources consulted during research c. author, title, publisher, and date of publication **2.** a. with different colors b. 600 to 1500 meters (1969 to 4921 feet) c. Duluth

---

c 6. Which of the following is *not* a part of "Reaganomics"?
   a. a tax cut
   b. a balanced budget
   c. wage and price controls
   d. reduced government spending

d 7. Which is the fastest growing minority group in America?
   a. blacks
   b. Asian Americans
   c. Polish Americans
   d. Hispanics

a 8. What did Americans want most from their cars in 1980?
   a. good gas mileage
   b. less pollution
   c. noiselessness
   d. small size

b 9. What percentage of American schools participated in the Title I program?
   a. sixty
   b. eighty-five
   c. thirty
   d. fifty

THINK THINGS THROUGH

1. What are the two kinds of inflation and what causes them?
2. What international organizations work to improve world trade?
3. Why was Iran an important ally of the United States?
4. What were the three main parts of Reaganomics?
5. What has been the biggest change in America's ethnic make-up since the 1950s?
6. How have communities tried to meet the needs of senior citizens?
7. What help did the federal government give to education in the 1960s and 1970s?
8. What issues did world leaders discuss at the Cancún conference?
9. What problems did rapid transit systems face in the 1970s and 1980s?

PRACTICE YOUR SKILLS

1. Reread the feature on research papers on pages 700–701. Then answer the following questions.
   a. What library sources should you use in doing research for a paper?
   b. What is a bibliography?
   c. What information should you record on a file card for each book you use?

2. Look again at the relief map of North America on page 735 to answer the following questions.
   a. How are the different regions of elevation indicated?
   b. What elevation is represented by the color orange?
   c. Which of the following cities lies above 984 feet (300 meters)—Havana, Halifax, or Duluth?

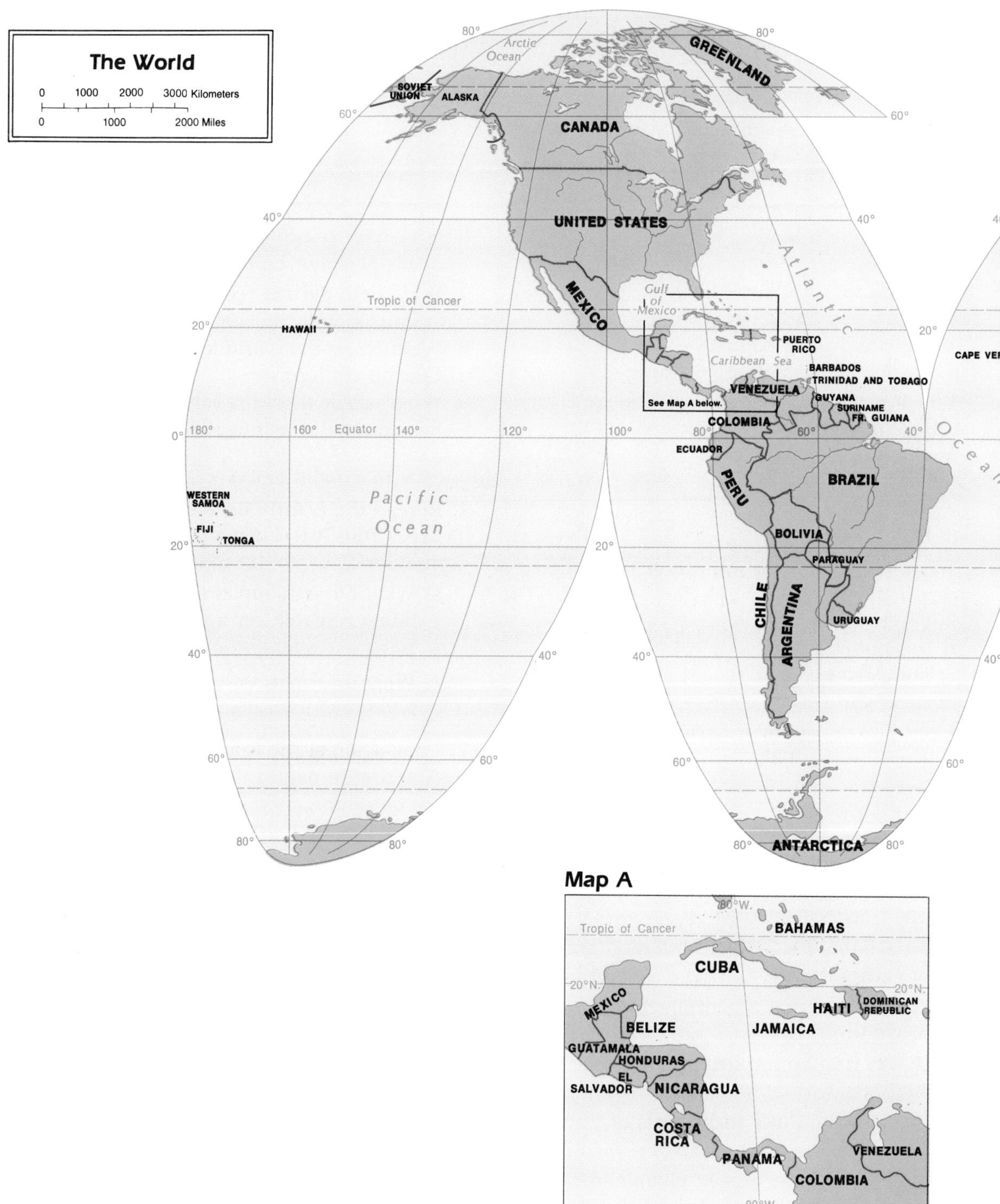

The World
0 1000 2000 3000 Kilometers
0 1000 2000 Miles
Arctic Ocean
GREENLAND
SOVIET UNION
ALASKA
CANADA
UNITED STATES
MEXICO
Gulf of Mexico
Atlantic Ocean
Tropic of Cancer
HAWAII
PUERTO RICO
Caribbean Sea
BARBADOS
TRINIDAD AND TOBAGO
CAPE VERDE
VENEZUELA
GUYANA
SURINAME
FR. GUIANA
See Map A below.
COLOMBIA
Equator
ECUADOR
PERU
BRAZIL
Pacific Ocean
WESTERN SAMOA
FIJI
TONGA
BOLIVIA
PARAGUAY
CHILE
ARGENTINA
URUGUAY
ANTARCTICA
Map A
80°W.
Tropic of Cancer
BAHAMAS
CUBA
20°N.
MEXICO
BELIZE
HAITI
DOMINICAN REPUBLIC
JAMAICA
GUATAMALA
HONDURAS
EL SALVADOR
NICARAGUA
COSTA RICA
PANAMA
VENEZUELA
COLOMBIA

GREENLAND
Arctic Circle
ICELAND
NORWAY
SWEDEN
FINLAND
UNITED KINGDOM
IRELAND
See Map C below.
SOVIET UNION
MONGOLIA
N. KOREA
S. KOREA
JAPAN
CHINA
PORT.
SPAIN
Black Sea
Mediterranean Sea
TURKEY
SYRIA
LEB.
ISRAEL
IRAQ
JORDAN
IRAN
KUWAIT
AFGHANISTAN
PAKISTAN
NEPAL
BHU.
BNGL.
BURMA
TUNISIA
MOROCCO
ALGERIA
LIBYA
EGYPT
SAUDI ARABIA
QATAR
U.A.E.
OMAN
INDIA
LAOS
TAIWAN
NIGER
CHAD
SUDAN
YEMEN
P.D.R. OF YEMEN
DJIBOUTI
Arabian Sea
THAILAND
VIETNAM
PHILIPPINES
Pacific Ocean
NIGERIA
CAMEROON
CENTRAL AFRICAN REPUBLIC
ETHIOPIA
SOMALIA
SRI LANKA
KAMPUCHEA
MALAYSIA
SINGAPORE
MALDIVES
See Map B below.
GABON
CONGO
UGANDA
KENYA
Equator
NAURU
ZAIRE
RWANDA
BURUNDI
PAPUA NEW GUINEA
SOLOMON ISLANDS
Indian Ocean
INDONESIA
TANZANIA
COMOROS
ANGOLA
MALAWI
ZAMBIA
MOZAMBIQUE
ZIMBABWE
MADAGASCAR
MAURITIUS
BOTSWANA
NAMIBIA
VANUATU
FIJI
Tropic of Capricorn
AUSTRALIA
SWAZILAND
LESOTHO
SOUTH AFRICA
NEW ZEALAND
Antarctic Circle
ANTARCTICA
Map B
MAURITANIA
MALI
SENEGAL
GAMBIA
NIGER
UPPER VOLTA
GUINEA-BISSAU
GUINEA
BENIN
TOGO
NIGERIA
SIERRA LEONE
IVORY COAST
GHANA
LIBERIA
Equator
Map C
UNITED KINGDOM
DENMARK
NETHERLANDS
EAST GERMANY
POLAND
SOVIET UNION
BELGIUM
WEST GERMANY
LUX.
CZECHOSLOVAKIA
LIECH.
AUSTRIA
HUNGARY
FRANCE
SWITZ.
ROMANIA
YUGOSLAVIA
SAN MARINO
ANDORRA
ITALY
BULGARIA
ALBANIA
TURKEY
GREECE

PRESIDENTS AND VICE PRESIDENTS

No.	Name	Years in Office	Political Party	State	Vice President
1	George Washington	1789-97	None	Va.	John Adams
2	John Adams	1797-1801	Federalist	Mass.	Thomas Jefferson
3	Thomas Jefferson	1801-9	Republican	Va.	Aaron Burr George Clinton
4	James Madison	1809-17	Republican	Va.	George Clinton Elbridge Gerry
5	James Monroe	1817-25	Republican	Va.	Daniel D. Tompkins
6	John Quincy Adams	1825-29	Republican	Mass.	John C. Calhoun
7	Andrew Jackson	1829-37	Democratic	Tenn.	John C. Calhoun Martin Van Buren
8	Martin Van Buren	1837-41	Democratic	N.Y.	Richard M. Johnson
9	William Henry Harrison	1841	Whig	Ohio	John Tyler
10	John Tyler	1841-45	Whig	Va.	
11	James K. Polk	1845-49	Democratic	Tenn.	George M. Dallas
12	Zachary Taylor	1849-50	Whig	La.	Millard Fillmore
13	Millard Fillmore	1850-53	Whig	N.Y.	
14	Franklin Pierce	1853-57	Democratic	N.H.	William R. King
15	James Buchanan	1857-61	Democratic	Pa.	John C. Breckinridge
16	Abraham Lincoln	1861-65	Republican	Ill.	Hannibal Hamlin Andrew Johnson
17	Andrew Johnson	1865-69	Republican	Tenn.	
18	Ulysses S. Grant	1869-77	Republican	Ill.	Schuyler Colfax Henry Wilson
19	Rutherford B. Hayes	1877-81	Republican	Ohio	William A. Wheeler
20	James A. Garfield	1881	Republican	Ohio	Chester A. Arthur
21	Chester A. Arthur	1881-85	Republican	N.Y..	
22	Grover Cleveland	1885-89	Democratic	N.Y.	Thomas A. Hendricks
23	Benjamin Harrison	1889-93	Republican	Ind.	Levi P. Morton
24	Grover Cleveland	1893-97	Democratic	N.Y.	Adlai E. Stevenson
25	William McKinley	1897-1901	Republican	Ohio	Garret A. Hobart Theodore Roosevelt
26	Theodore Roosevelt	1901-9	Republican	N.Y.	Charles W. Fairbanks
27	William Howard Taft	1909-13	Republican	Ohio	James S. Sherman
28	Woodrow Wilson	1913-21	Democratic	N.J.	Thomas R. Marshall
29	Warren G. Harding	1921-23	Republican	Ohio	Calvin Coolidge

30	Calvin Coolidge	1923-29	Republican	Mass.	
31	Herbert Hoover	1929-33	Republican	Calif.	Charles G. Dawes Charles Curtis
32	Franklin D. Roosevelt	1933-45	Democratic	N.Y.	John N. Garner Henry A. Wallace Harry S Truman
33	Harry S Truman	1945-53	Democratic	Mo.	Alben W. Barkley
34	Dwight D. Eisenhower	1953-61	Republican	N.Y.	Richard M. Nixon
35	John F. Kennedy	1961-63	Democratic	Mass.	Lyndon B. Johnson
36	Lyndon B. Johnson	1963-69	Democratic	Texas	Hubert H. Humphrey
37	Richard M. Nixon	1969-74	Republican	N.Y.	Spiro T. Agnew Gerald R. Ford
38	Gerald R. Ford	1974-77	Republican	Mich.	Nelson A. Rockefeller
39	James E. Carter, Jr.	1977-81	Democratic	Ga.	Walter F. Mondale
40	Ronald Reagan	1981-	Republican	Calif.	George H. Bush

FACTS ABOUT THE STATES

State	Order of Admission to Union	Date of Admission	Capital	Members in House of Representatives*
Alabama	22	1819	Montgomery	7
Alaska	49	1959	Juncau	1
Arizona	48	1912	Phoenix	5 (+1)
Arkansas	25	1836	Little Rock	4
California	31	1850	Sacramento	45 (+2)
Colorado	38	1876	Denver	6 (+1)
Connecticut	5	1788	Hartford	6
Delaware	1	1787	Dover	1
Florida	27	1845	Tallahassee	19 (+4)
Georgia	4	1788	Atlanta	10
Hawaii	50	1959	Honolulu	2
Idaho	43	1890	Boise	2
Illinois	21	1818	Springfield	22 (−2)
Indiana	19	1816	Indianapolis	10 (−1)
Iowa	29	1846	Des Moines	6
Kansas	34	1861	Topeka	5

*Numbers in ( ) indicate changes in the number of representatives based on population shifts determined by the 1980 census.

State	Order of Admission to Union	Date of Admission	Capital	Members in House of Representatives*
Kentucky	15	1792	Frankfort	7
Louisiana	18	1812	Baton Rouge	8
Maine	23	1820	Augusta	2
Maryland	7	1788	Annapolis	8
Massachusetts	6	1788	Boston	11 (−1)
Michigan	26	1837	Lansing	18 (−1)
Minnesota	32	1858	St. Paul	8
Mississippi	20	1817	Jackson	5
Missouri	24	1821	Jefferson City	9 (−1)
Montana	41	1889	Helena	2
Nebraska	37	1867	Lincoln	3
Nevada	36	1864	Carson City	2 (+1)
New Hampshire	9	1788	Concord	2
New Jersey	3	1787	Trenton	14 (−1)
New Mexico	47	1912	Santa Fe	3 (+1)
New York	11	1788	Albany	34 (−5)
North Carolina	12	1789	Raleigh	11
North Dakota	39	1889	Bismarck	1
Ohio	17	1803	Columbus	21 (−2)
Oklahoma	46	1907	Oklahoma City	6
Oregon	33	1859	Salem	5 (+1)
Pennsylvania	2	1787	Harrisburg	23 (−2)
Rhode Island	13	1790	Providence	2
South Carolina	8	1788	Columbia	6
South Dakota	40	1889	Pierre	1 (−1)
Tennessee	16	1796	Nashville	9 (+1)
Texas	28	1845	Austin	27 (+3)
Utah	45	1896	Salt Lake City	3 (+1)
Vermont	14	1791	Montpelier	1
Virginia	10	1788	Richmond	10
Washington	42	1889	Olympia	8 (+1)
West Virginia	35	1863	Charleston	4
Wisconsin	30	1848	Madison	9
Wyoming	44	1890	Cheyenne	1

GLOSSARY

PRONUNCIATION KEY

Consonant Sounds

b	**bib**	r	**roar**
ch	**church**	s	**miss, sauce, see**
d	**deed**	sh	di**sh**, **sh**ip
f	**f**ast, **f**i**f**e, o**ff**, **ph**ase, rou**gh**	t	**tight**
g	**gag**	th	pa**th**, **th**in
h	**h**at	*th*	ba**th**e, **th**is
hw	**wh**ich	v	ca**v**e, **v**al**v**e, **v**ine
j	**j**u**dg**e	w	**w**ith
k	**c**at, **k**i**ck**, pi**qu**e	y	**y**es
l	**l**id, needle	z	ro**s**e, si**z**e, **x**ylophone, **z**ebra
m	a**m**, **m**an, **m**u**m**	zh	gara**g**e, plea**s**ure, vi**s**ion
n	**n**o, sudde**n**		
ng	thi**ng**		
p	**p**o**p**		

Vowel Sounds

ă	p**a**t	oi	b**oy**, n**oi**se, **oi**l
ā	**ai**d, th**ey**, p**ay**	o͝o	b**oo**k
â	**ai**r, c**a**re, w**ea**r	o͞o	b**oo**t, fr**ui**t
ä	f**a**ther	ou	c**ow**, **ou**t
ĕ	p**e**t, pl**ea**sure	ŭ	c**u**t, r**ou**gh
ē	b**e**, b**ee**, **ea**s**y**, l**ei**sure	û	f**i**rm, h**ea**rd, t**e**rm, t**u**rn, w**o**rd
ĭ	p**i**t	yo͞o	ab**u**se, **u**se
ī	b**y**, g**uy**, p**ie**	ə	**a**bout, sil**e**nt, penc**i**l, lem**o**n, circ**u**s
î	d**ea**r, d**ee**r, f**ie**rce, m**e**re	ər	butt**er**
ŏ	p**o**t, h**o**rrible		
ō	g**o**, r**ow**, t**oe**		
ô	**a**lter, c**au**ght, f**o**r, p**aw**		

Stress Marks

Primary Stress' **biology** (bī **ŏl'**ə jē)

Secondary Stress' **biological** (bī'ə **lŏj'**ĭ kəl)

abolitionist (ăb'ə **lish'**ə nĭst) a person who wanted to end slavery

adjourn (ə **jûrn'**) stop meeting

administration (ăd mĭn'ĭ **strā'**shən) the President, Vice President, and their advisers who set the policies of government

affluent (**ăf'**lo͞o ənt) rich

age pyramid (āj **pĭr'**ə mĭd) a graph that shows the relative sizes of various age groups in the population

agriculture (**ăg'**rĭ kŭl'chər) the planting, caring for, and harvesting of crops

alien (**ā'**lē ən) a person living in another country, who has not become a naturalized citizen

alliance (ə **lī'**əns) an agreement between groups to help each other during times of trouble

ally (**ăl'**ī) a friend who helps in times of trouble

amendment (ə **mĕnd'**mənt) addition or change

amnesty (**ăm'**nĭ stē) a pardon for offenses against a government

amphibious force (ăm **fĭb'**ē əs fôrs *or* fōrs) a military force that can travel on land and water

anarchist (**ăn'**ər kĭst) one who is against all forms of government

annexation (ăn'ĭk **sā'**shən) the adding of a new territory to a country

anthropologist (ăn'thrə **pŏl'**ə jĭst) a scientist who studies groups of people

Antifederalist (**ăn'**tē-**fĕd'**ər ə lĭst) a person in early American history who was opposed to the Constitution

anti-imperialist (**ăn'**tē-ĭm **pîr'**ē ə lĭst) a person who opposes imperialism

anti-Semitism (**ăn'**tē-**sĕm'**ĭ tĭz'əm) the hatred or persecution of Jews

apartheid (ə **pärt**′hīt′) official segregation of the races
appeasement (ə **pēz**′mənt) keeping peace by satisfying potential enemies at any cost
apprentice (ə **prĕn**′tĭs) a person who works for a master artisan while being trained to become a skilled worker
appropriation (ə prō′prē **ā**′shən) spending
archaeologist (är′kē **ŏl**′ə jĭst) a scientist who studies the things left behind by people who lived long ago
armistice (**är**′mĭ stĭs) cease-fire
arsenal (**är**′sə nəl) storehouse for weapons and ammunition
artillery (är **tĭl**′ə rē) cannon and other large guns
artisan (**är**′tĭ zən) a person who has been trained in a special skill
assembly line (ə **sĕm**′blē līn) a system in which unfinished products move past workers, each of whom finishes part of the product
assumption (ə **sŭmp**′shən) taking over of debts
astrolabe (**ăs**′trə lāb′) an instrument that shows a ship's position in relation to the sun and other stars
atmosphere (**ăt**′mə sfîr′) the air that surrounds the earth
atrocities (ə **trŏs**′ĭ tēs) extremely cruel actions

bankruptcy (**băngk**′rŭpt′sē) a situation in which a company no longer has enough money to stay in business
barrio (**bä**′rē′ō′) a neighborhood in the United States where Spanish is the main language
bicameral (bī **kăm**′ər əl) made up of two houses
bill (bĭl) a written proposal for a new law
bimetallism (bī **mĕt**′l ĭz′əm) the use of two metals, gold and silver, for money
Blitzkrieg (**blĭts**′krēg′) a quick, destructive form of warfare used by Germans in World War II; it means "lightning war" in German
blockade (blŏ **kād**′) the closing off of an area to prevent people and supplies from going in and out
bond (bŏnd) a paper that promises that the government will repay the money it borrows plus additional money that is called interest
boycott (**boi**′kŏt′) a refusal to buy or use a product
brinkmanship (**brĭngk**′mən shĭp′) pushing a dangerous situation to the limit of safety in order to obtain the greatest advantage

Cabinet (**kăb**′ə nĭt) the official group of advisers to the President
campaign (kăm **pān**′) a series of planned battles
canal (kə **năl**′) a waterway dug across land for ships to sail through
candidate (**kăn**′dĭ dāt′) a person who runs for political office
casualty (**kăzh**′o͞o əl tē) a soldier killed or wounded
cattle baron (**kăt**′l **bâr**′ən) owner of a large ranch
censor (**sĕn**′sər) control what is said or written
census (**sĕn**′səs) the count of the American population taken every ten years
charter (**chär**′tər) license; official document
checks and balances (chĕks, **băl**′ən sĭz) a system in which each branch of the government has some power over the other branches
civilization (sĭv′ə lĭ **zā**′shən) a society in which people build cities and work at jobs other than farming
civil rights (**sĭv**′əl rītz) rights guaranteed by the government to protect persons from unjust acts by government or individuals
civil war (**sĭv**′əl wôr) a war between the citizens of the same country
class rules (klăs ro͞ols) customs that need to be followed by people of various ranks in a group

climate (**klī′**mĭt) usual weather
cold war (kōld wôr) a bitter economic and political rivalry that stops short of a shooting war
collective bargaining (kə **lĕk′**tĭv **bär′**gĭn ĭng) the process through which workers negotiate as a group with employers for better wages, hours, and conditions
colony (**kŏl′**ə nē) one or more settlements
commerce (**kŏm′**ərs) the buying and selling of goods from different places
communism (**kŏm′**yə nĭz′əm) an economic system in which the government owns factories and all other means of production
commuter (kə **myo͞ot′**ər) a person who travels a distance to work
compact (**kŏm′**păkt′) agreement
compass (**kŭm′**pəs) an instrument used in sailing that tells direction
compromise (**kŏm′**prə mīz′) an agreement in which each side gives up something it wants
computer (kəm **pyo͞o′**tər) an electronic device designed to perform mathematical tasks
concentration camp (kŏn sən **trā′**shən kămp) prison camp for political prisoners
concurrent (kən **kûr′**ənt) shared
condemn (kən **dĕm′**) officially express disapproval of behavior
condominium (kŏn′də **mĭn′**ē əm) a building in which the apartments or lofts are individually owned
confederacy (kən **fĕd′**ər ə sē) a number of groups that band together
conquistadores (kŏn **kwĭs′**tə dôrs′) conquerors
conscription (kən **skrĭp′**shən) the drafting of people for military service
conservation (kŏn′sər **vā′**shən) the wise use of natural resources
constitution (kŏn′stĭ **to͞o′**shən) a written plan of government
consumer (kən **so͞o′**mər) a person who uses money to purchase goods or services
containment (kən **tān′**mənt) a policy of preventing Soviet influence from spreading beyond areas already controlled by the Soviet Union
contraband (**kŏn′**trə bănd′) war materials bound for the enemy
convention (kən **vĕn′**shən) formal meeting
convoy (**kŏn′**voi′) cargo ships traveling in groups, escorted by warships
cooperative (kō **ŏp′**ər ə tĭv) a business that workers own together
corollary (**kôr′**ə lĕr′ē) a statement that follows or adds to the meaning of a statement made earlier
corporation (kôr′pə **rā′**shən) an organization that can own property and make contracts as if it were an individual
cosmopolitan (kŏz′mə **pŏl′**ĭ tən) representative of many parts of the world
cost-push inflation (kôst-po͝osh ĭn **flā′**shən) inflation caused by a push for higher wages resulting in higher prices
coureur de bois (kü **rûr′**də bwä′) a hunter and trapper in the woods of New France
credit (**krĕd′**ĭt) a system of buying goods and paying for them later
critical (**krĭt′**ĭ kəl) testing
culture (**kŭl′**chər) the way a group of people lives
culture area (**kŭl′**chər **âr′**ē ə) one in which all the groups of people live in a similar way

defensive (dĭ **fĕn′**sĭv) the protecting of home territory against attack
deficit (**dĕf′**ĭ sĭt) the amount spent by the government each year above what is received in taxes
delegate (**dĕl′**ĭ gət′) a person given power to act for others
demand-pull inflation (dĭ **mănd′**-po͝ol ĭn **flā′**shən) inflation caused by a demand for goods
democratic (dĕm′ə **krăt′** ĭk) a kind of government in which the people, through their representatives, decide what to do in matters that concern everybody
deport (dĭ **pôrt′**) to send out of the country an alien who is thought to be dangerous to the peace and safety of the United States

depression (dĭ **prĕsh'**ən) a reduction or slowing of business activity
desegregation (dē sĕg'rĭ **gā'**shən) ending of segregation
détente (dā **tänt'**) a policy aimed at easing tensions between the United States and the major communist powers of the world
dictator (**dĭk'**tā'tər) a ruler who has complete control of a nation
diplomatic ties (dĭp'lə **măt'**ĭk tīz) formal international relations
direct relief (dĭ **rĕkt'**rĭ **lēf'**) money or a job given to people by the federal government
direct tax (dĭ **rĕkt'**tăks) a charge a customer must pay in addition to the price of the goods
discrimination (dĭ skrĭm' ə **nā'**shən) mistreatment of one group of people by another who regard them as inferior or undesirable
dividend (**dĭv'**ĭ dĕnd') the profit companies pay to stockholders
domino theory (**dŏm'**ə nō' **thē'**ə rē *or* **thîr'**ē) a theory that if one country fell to the communists, its neighbors would also fall
due process (do͞o **prŏs'**ĕs' *or* **prō'**sĕs') the right to a trial in court
duty (**do͞o'**tē *or* **dyo͞o'**tē) charges made by a government on goods people bring in or take out of the country
dynasty (**dī'**nə stē) a group of rulers from the same family or line

economy (ĭ **kŏn'**ə mē) the way people produce, distribute, and use goods and services
elector (ĭ **lek'**tər) a person chosen by state officers for the specific purpose of electing the President and Vice President
emancipation (ĭ măn'sə **pā'**shən) the freeing of those in slavery
encomendero (ĕn kō mən **dĕ'**rō) landowner who was in charge of Indians in the area
enumerate (ĭ **no͞o'**mə rāt') list
environment (ĕn **vī'**rən mənt) a combination of climate, or usual weather; land; water resources; and plant life
epidemic (ĕp'ĭ **dĕm'**ĭk) an outbreak of disease that affects many people at the same time
evidence (**ĕv'**ĭ dəns) facts that seem to prove a theory
exile (**ĕg'**zīl') someone who is forced to live in another country or chooses to do so
expedition (ĕk'spĭ **dĭsh'**ən) an organized group of people making a trip
export (ĭk **spôrt'**) send to other places to be sold

famine (**făm'**ĭn) a serious shortage of food that results in widespread hunger and starvation
favorable balance of trade (**fā'**vər ə bəl **băl'**əns, trād) when one country sells more goods to another country than it buys from it
federal (**fĕd'**ər əl) a system of government that divides the powers of government between the states and central government
Federalist (**fĕd'**ər ə lĭst) a person in early American history who was in favor of the Constitution
federation (fĕd'ə **rā'**shən) an association of groups that have a common goal or a common purpose
fixed income (fĭksd **ĭn'**kŭm') income that stays the same, such as a pension received by an elderly person
foreign policy (**fôr'**ĭn **pŏl'**ĭ sē) the plan of action a nation uses in dealing with other nations
fossil fuels (**fŏs'**əl **fyo͞o'**əlz) coal, oil, and natural gas, all of which were formed from plants and animals that lived millions of years ago
foundry (**foun'**drē) place where metal and ore are melted and molded
free state (frē stāt) one without slaves
frontier (frŭn **tîr'**) the edge of the settled area

geologist (jē **ŏl**'ə jĭst) a scientist who studies the history of the earth and its life, especially as it can be known from rocks

ghetto (**gĕt**'ō) an area in cities of eastern European countries where Jews were forced to live

glacier (**glā**'shər) a huge sheet of ice

gold standard (gōld **stăn**'dərd) the use of only gold by the government to back its money

grievance (**grē**'vəns) a reason for being angry

guerrilla warfare (gə **rĭl**'ə **wôr**'fâr') hit-and-run raids by small armed bands

habitant (**hăb**'ə tənt) a simple farmer in Canada who worked the land and paid rent to a landowner

hacienda (hä'sē **ĕn**'də) large ranch house

homestead (**hōm**'stĕd') settle on government lands

hostage (**hŏs**'tĭj) a captive held for money or other demands

human rights (**hyōō**'mən rītz) basic rights to life, liberty, and equality of opportunity

immigrant (**ĭm**'ĭ grənt) a person who comes to live in one country after leaving his or her home country

imperialism (ĭm **pîr**'ē ə lĭz'əm) the practice of gaining control of other lands and other peoples

import (ĭm **pôrt**') bring in from other places

impressment (ĭm **prĕs**'mənt) forcing individuals to serve in a navy or army

incursion (ĭn **kûr**'zhən) raid

indentured servant (ĭn **dĕn**'chərd **sûr**'vənt) a man, woman, or child who agreed to work for a master for a certain length of time in return for payment of passage

indirect tax (ĭn'də **rĕkt**' tăks) a charge placed on goods before the customer buys them

infantry (**ĭn**'fən trē) foot soldiers

inflation (ĭn **flā**'shən) a continuing rise in the prices of goods and services

initiative (ĭ **nĭsh**'ə tĭv) way for voters to start a new law through a petition

injunction (ĭn **jŭngk**'shən) a court order that prohibits a specific action

integration (ĭn'tĭ **grā**'shən) the mixing of races

intendant (ĭn **tĕn**'dənt) a French official appointed by the king who held the real power in New France

interchangeable parts (ĭnt'ər **chān**'jə bəl pärts) standard parts that fit a manufactured product (as a gun)

intermontane (ĭn tər **män**'tān) between the mountains

interstate (**ĭn**'tər stāt') between the states

intolerable (ĭn **tŏl**'ər ə bəl) unbearable

iron curtain (**ī**'ərn **kûr**'tn) the invisible border between the communist and noncommunist worlds

irrigation (ir'ĭ **gā**'shən) the bringing of water to dry fields from rivers or lakes by means of ditches

isolationism (ī'sə **lā**'shə nĭz'əm) the practice of a country that has little to do with other countries

land company (lănd **kŭm**'pə nē) a business that controls land

land grant (lănd grănt) a gift of land from the government or a king

legend (**lĕj**'ənd) a story handed down from parents to children over a long period of time

legislature (**lĕj**'ĭs lā'chər) a lawmaking body made up of representatives of the people

liberate (**lĭb**'ə rāt') to free

limited liability (**lĭm**'ĭ tĭd lī'ə **bĭl**'ĭ tē) protection for stockholders of a corporation from having to pay its debts if it goes out of business

literacy test (**lĭt′**ər ə sē tĕst) a test that determines whether a person can read and write
loyalist (**loi′**ə lĭst) American faithful to the king in the Revolutionary War

mandate (**măn′**dāt′) a right to oversee the affairs of a country or territory
manifest destiny (**măn′**ə fĕst′ **dĕs′**tə nē) an expectation that people think is guaranteed to come true
manufacturing (măn′yə **făk′**chər ĭng) the making of large amounts of goods by hand or machine
massacre (**măs′**ə kər) the horrible killing of a large number of people
mass culture (măs **kŭl′**chər) a culture in which the vast majority of people share the same values and ways of living
media (**mē′**dē ə) means of modern mass communication
mediator (**mē′**dē ā′tər) one who acts as a go-between to bring arguing parties together to settle their differences
megalopolis (mĕg′ə **lŏp′**ə lĭs) an almost continuous urban area made up of several cities and their suburbs
mercantilism (**mûr′**kən tē lĭz′əm) a theory that the country that has the most wealth has the most power
metropolitan area (mĕt′rə **pŏl′**ə tən **âr′**ē ə) a city and its suburbs
migrate (**mī′**grāt′) move with the seasons
militarism (**mĭl′**ĭ tə rĭz′əm) a strong emphasis on military preparedness
miniaturization (min′ē ə chə rĭ **zā′**shən) the making of parts smaller and smaller
minutemen (**mĭn′**ĭt mĕn′) American volunteer soldiers who had promised to answer without delay any call to fight
mission (**mĭsh′**ən) a community that began as a religious center
mobile (**mō′**bəl *or* bēl′ *or* bīl′) being able to move from one place to another
mobilize (**mō′**bə līz′) assemble armies and make them ready for war
monopoly (mə **nŏp′**ə lē) complete control
mutiny (**myōōt′**n ē) open rebellion

nationalism (**năsh′**ə nə lĭz′əm) strong devotion to one's nation or national group
nativism (**nā′**tĭ vĭzm) a strong opposition to immigration
naturalization (năch′ər ə lĭ **zā′**shən) the granting of citizenship to a person born in another country
navigation (năv′ĭ **gā′**shən) the science of determining a ship's position and course
negotiate (nĭ **gō′**shē āt′) work out terms
neutrality (nōō **trăl′**ĭ tē) not taking either side in a disagreement
nonrenewable resources (nŏn rĭ **nōō′**ə bəl rĭ **sôr′** sĭz) resources that are limited
nuclear power (**nōō′**klē ər **pou′**ər) energy released from atoms
nullify (**nŭl′**ə fī′) legally cancel

oasis (ō **ā′**sĭs) a wet, fertile place in the desert
occupation (ŏk′yə **pā′**shən) job
offensive (ə **fĕn′**sĭv) the entering of enemy territory to fight
omnibus bill (**ŏm′**nĭ bŭs′ bĭl) single proposal made up of several different bills
opinion (ō **pĭn′**yən) a statement of reasons for a decision by judges
opinion poll (ō **pĭn′**yən pōl) survey of public attitudes
ordinance (**ôr′**dn əns) law

pardon (**pär′**dn) to excuse someone from a past offense without punishment
Parliament (**pär′**lə ment) the lawmaking body of England
patent (**păt′**nt) the right of an inventor to use and sell an invention
patriot (**pā′**trē ət) a person who agreed with the colonists' side in the Revolutionary War

patriotism (**pā**'trē ə tĭz' əm) a feeling of keen pride in one's nation
peninsula (pə **nĭn**'sə lə) a piece of land surrounded by water on three sides
petition (pə **tĭsh**'ən) make a formal request
petrodollars (**pĕt**'rō dŏl'ərz) money that countries and individuals earn from the sale of petroleum
Pilgrim (**pĭl**'grĭm) a person going on a journey for religious purposes
plateau (plă **tō**') high, level land
platform (**plăt**'fôrm') a formal statement of political principles
political machine (pə **lĭt**'ĭ kəl mə **shēn**') an organization set up to get and keep political power
political party (pə **lĭt**'ĭ kəl **pär**' tē) a group of people with certain ideas about how government should be run and who tries to get its candidates elected to government office
poll tax (pōl tăks) a tax that a person has to pay in order to vote
polluted (pə **lo͞o**'tĭd) dirty
popular sovereignty (**pŏp**'yə lər **sŏv**'ər ən tē *or* **sŏv**'rən) voters in an area deciding for themselves whether to accept or reject slavery
portage (**pôr**'tĭj) a path between two rivers along which people must carry their boats
potlatch (**pŏt**'lăch') feast at which chiefs and nobles showed off their wealth
preamble (**prē**'ăm'bəl) an introduction
precedent (**prĕs**'ĭ dnt) an example to be followed or referred to later
prejudice (**prĕj**'ə dĭs) the judging of people on the basis of limited and biased information, usually negative
presidio (prĭ **sĭd**'ē ō') military base
prime minister (prīm **mĭn**'ĭ stər) the leader of the British Parliament
productivity (prə'dŭk **tĭv**'ĭ tē) the rate at which workers produce goods and services
prohibition (prō'ə **bĭsh**'ən) the banning of alcoholic beverages
propaganda (prŏp'ə **găn**'də) communications used to make people think a certain way
public domain (**pŭb**'lĭk dō **mān**') an area open for use by anyone
Puritan (**pyo͝or**'ĭ tən) a person who wanted to purify the Church of England

quarter (**kwôr**'tər) give soldiers places to live
quota (**kwō**'tə) a specified share of the total amount

railhead (**rāl**'hĕd) the end of the line on a railroad
rapid transit (**răp**'ĭd **trăn**'sĭt) subways, streetcars, and other transportation systems with land set aside solely for their use
ratify (**răt**'ə fī') approve
rationing (**răsh**'ən ĭng) the limiting of the amount of goods that people can buy
reaper (**rē**'pər) a machine for cutting grain
recall (rĭ **kôl**') a way for the voters to remove a bad official from office before the end of a term
recession (rĭ **sĕsh**'ən) a period in which production declines and people have less money
reconstruction (rē'kən **strŭk**'shən) the setting up of new state governments
referendum (rĕf'ə **rĕn**'dəm) a process in which the voters decide on a bill that has been brought up in the state legislature
regiment (**rĕj**'ə mənt) a military unit organized to act together
region (**rē**'jən) an area characterized by the look of the land, climate, and plant life
regulatory commission (**rĕg**'yə lə tôr'ē kə **mĭsh**'ən) a government body set up to control the actions of certain industries
repeal (rĭ **pēl**') withdraw
reservation (rĕz'ər **vā**'shən) land set aside for a special purpose
resolution (rĕz'ə **lo͞o**'shən) formal expression of opinion
ruling council (**ro͞o**'lĭng **koun**'səl) a group of officers that made the everyday decisions in New France

sacred (**sā**'krĭd) holy
saga (**sä**'gə) a tale of heroic or brave deeds
secede (sĭ **sēd**') withdraw
section (**sĕk**'shən) one square mile (division of township)
sectionalism (**sĕk**'shə nə lĭz'əm) the practice of holding one's own section of the country higher than other sections or than the country as a whole
sedition (sĭ **dĭsh**'ən) the act of causing rebellion against the government in power
segregation (sĕg'rĭ **gā**'shən) the system of forcing a certain group of people to live and conduct their affairs separately from the majority of people
seigneur (sān **yûr**') a French noble
seigneuries (sān yə **rēz**') the land sold to French nobles in America
sentry (**sĕn**'trē) a soldier stationed at a post to keep watch
service industry (**sûr**'vĭs **ĭn**'də strē) an industry which provides services rather than goods to the public, such as health care, insurance, or banking
sharecropping (**shâr**'krŏp' ĭng) a system under which a landowner allowed people to live on and farm a piece of his or her land in return for the largest share of the. crops raised
siege (sēj) the surrounding of a fort or a city by an army to starve it into submission
smuggle (**smŭg**'əl) sell goods to another country illegally
sod (sŏd) the crust of the soil
solar power (**sō**'lər **pou**'ər) power from the sun
specialization of labor (spĕsh'ə lĭ **zā**'shən, **lā**'bər) a system in which each person has his or her own special job to do
sphere of influence (sfĭr, **ĭn**'flo͞o əns) the control of some part of a country by a foreign country
stagflation (stăg **flā**'shən) inflation combined with a slow-moving economy
stalemate (**stāl**'māt') a time when neither side is winning (in a war)
standard of living (**stăn**'dərd, **lĭv**'ĭng) the total amount of goods and services that an individual or group consumes
stereotype (**stĕr**'ē ə tīp') a false mental picture of a whole group based on limited information about just one or very few members of that group
stockade (stŏ **kād**') a wall of tree trunks
stockholder (**stŏk**'hōl'dər) a person who owns shares of a corporation
stock market (stŏk **mär**'kĭt) a place where shares of stock are bought and sold
strait (strāt) a narrow channel
strategic (strə **tē**'jĭk) important for overall military success
subsidy (**sŭb**'sĭ dē) a grant of money from the federal or state government
sue (so͞o) start a lawsuit
summit conference (**sŭm**'ĭt **kŏn**'fər əns *or* frəns) a meeting attended by the heads of government
surplus (**sûr**'pləs) leftover portion
sweatshop (**swĕt**'shŏp') a hot, crowded shop where immigrants worked for very low wages

tariff (**târ**'ĭf) tax on imports
tax base (tăks bās) the amount and value of taxable property
temperance (**tĕm**'pər əns *or* prəns) the refraining from drinking alcoholic beverages
tenement (**tĕn**'ə mənt) a crowded apartment building
terrace (**tĕr**'əs) a huge steplike piece of land with a level surface
terrain (tə **rān**') the physical features of a geographical area
territory (**tĕr**'ĭ tôr'ē) a region with lawmakers and a delegate to Congress
terrorism (**tĕr**'ə rĭz'əm) the use of violence to frighten people into accepting certain policies or demands
theory (**thē**'ə rē) a thoughtful guess by scientists to explain how and why something happens

Third World (thûrd wûrld) developing countries in Africa, Asia, and Latin America
tory (**tôr'ē**) loyalist (to Great Britain) during the Revolutionary War
township (**toun'**shĭp') square part (of the Northwest Territory), 6 miles (9.6 kilometers) on a side
tract (trăkt) a stretch of land
trade union (trād **yōōn'**yən) an organization of workers who work at a single skilled trade
transcontinental (trăns'kŏn tə **nĕn'**təl) crossing a continent
trench warfare (trĕnch **wôr'**fâr') a war in which soldiers fight from long ditches dug in the ground
trust (trŭst) an arrangement through which one company owns or controls a number of other companies
tyrant (**tī'**rənt) unjust ruler

ultimatum (ŭl'tə **mā** təm) a set of severe demands
unconstitutional (ŭn'kŏn stĭ **tōō'**shə nəl) not allowed by the Constitution
unicameral (yōō'nĭ **kăm'**ər əl) consisting of one house
union (**yōōn'**yən) an organization created to promote the interests of workers
unity (**yōō'**nĭ tē) oneness
urbanization (ûr'bən ĭ **zā'**shən) the change from being a largely rural country to one in which many people live in cities

veto (**vē'**tō) the power to refuse a law proposed by the legislative branch
viceroy (**vīs'**roi') person governing in a king's place
Vietnamization (vē ĕt'nə mə **zā'**shən) policy during the Vietnam War to reduce United States troop strength in Vietnam and train the South Vietnamese to take over the fighting themselves
vigilante (vĭj'ə **lăn'**tē) a citizen who maintains order and punishes criminals until law officers arrive
voyageur (vwä yä **zhûr'**) a trader who traveled into the wilderness of New France in search of furs

War Hawks (wôr hôks) legislators who favor war
ward (wôrd) a city voting district
writs of assistance (rĭts, ə **sĭs'**təns) legal papers allowing British soldiers to enter any home or store in search of smuggled goods

yellow journalism (yĕl'ō **jûr'**nə lĭz'əm) a kind of reporting that gets the reader's attention with big headlines and pictures of crimes, accidents, or wars

INDEX

In this index *c* indicates a chart; *g* indicates a graph; *m* indicates a map; and *p* indicates a picture.

ACKNOWLEDGMENTS

These materials were produced with the assistance of Ligature Publishing Services, Inc.

QUOTATION ACKNOWLEDGMENTS

4 adapted from *Southwestern Indian Ceremonies* by Tom Bahti, with permission of KC Publications © 1970. **31** *The Travels of Marco Polo*, edited by Manuel Komroff, © 1926 by Horace Liveright, New York, with permission of the publisher. **94** *The Works of Anne Bradstreet in Prose and Verse*, edited by John H. Ellis. **132** © 1963 American Heritage Publishing Co., Inc., Reprinted by permission from *The American Heritage History of the Thirteen Colonies*. **151** *Life in America*, vol. 1, by Marshall B. Davidson © 1974 by Houghton Mifflin Co. **214** *Readers' Guide to Periodical Literature*, © 1981 by H. W. Wilson Co., Material reproduced by permission of the publisher. **305** quotation from Elias Pym Fordham in *The Annals of America*, vol. 4, 1797–1820 © 1968 by Encyclopaedia Britannica, Inc. **397** adapted from *Life Under the "Peculiar Institution"* by Norman R. Yetman © 1970 by Holt, Rinehart and Winston, Inc. Reprinted by permission of Holt, Rinehart and Winston, CBS College Publishing. **435** *We Were There: The Story of Working Women in America* by Barbara Meyer Wertheimer © 1977 by Pantheon Books, a Division of Random House, Inc. **448** *The Autobiography of Mother Jones* by Mary Harris Jones, 3rd Edition, revised © 1980 by Charles H. Kerr Publishing Co. **459** from *The Speeches of William Jennings Bryan*, Revised and Arranged by Himself, Funk & Wagnalls—By permission of Harper & Row Publishers, Inc. **519** *My Life and Work* by Henry Ford and Samuel Crowther, © 1922 by Doubleday, Page and Co. as quoted in *In Search of America: Community/ National/ Identity/ Democracy*, edited by David H. Fowler, Eugene D. Levy, John W. Blassingame and Jacquelyn S. Haywood. © 1972 by Holt, Rinehart and Winston, Inc. Reprinted by permission of Holt, Rinehart and Winston, CBS College Publishing. **546** *Hard Times* by Studs Terkel © 1970, Pantheon Books, A Division of Random House, Inc. **634** adapted from an address by Melissa A. Thompson, *Congressional Digest*, vol. 56, June–July 1977. **634–635** adapted from a statement by Phyllis Schlafly, *Congressional Digest*, vol. 56, June–July 1977.

ILLUSTRATION ACKNOWLEDGMENTS

The following abbreviations are used for a few sources from which many illustrations were obtained:

BA	The Bettmann Archive	NYPL	New York Public Library
BS	Black Star	SB	Stock Boston
CP	Culver Pictures, Inc.	UPI	United Press International
GC	The Granger Collection	WC	Woodfin Camp and Associates
LC	Library of Congress		
NYHS	New-York Historical Society, NYC		

i Appliqué quilt, 1853, detail, Indianapolis Museum of Art. **iii** "Pinwheel Quilt," reproduced from *America's Quilts and Coverlets* by permission of the publishers, E.P. Dutton, Inc., New York. **v** (Left) Sebastian Cabot, "Mappemonde" 1544, detail, Bibliothèque Nationale, Paris; (Right) NYHS. **vi** Detail, Historical Society of Pennsylvania. **vii** Detail, Kiplinger Collection, U.S. Capitol Historical Society. **viii** Detail, LC. **ix** "American Progress," detail, lithograph by George Crofutt from a painting by John Gast, LC. **x** (Right) "Mural of the Changing West" by Thomas H. Benton, detail, New School for Social Research; (Left) Detail, Franklin D. Roosevelt Library. **xi** Tilt ("Together Protect the Community"), detail, mural by John Weber, Chicago, Ill., photograph by Lee Balterman. **xii** Detail, NASA. **xiv** (see iii). **xviii** (Top) Detail, City Art Gallery, Bristol, England; (Bottom) (see i).

Unit 1

2 Denver Art Museum. **3** Sebastian Cabot, "Mappemonde" 1544, Bibliothèque Nationale, Paris. **4** Museum of the American Indian, N.Y.C. **5** National Museum of Anthropology, Mexico. **6** Denver Museum of Natural History. **7** Helga Teiwes, Arizona State Museum, University of Arizona. **9** National Museum of Anthropology, Mexico. **11** James P. Rowan. **14** James P. Rowan. **17** (Right) Bohdan Hrynewych, SB. (Left) Cary Wozinsky, SB. **20** (Top) Theodore J. Richardson, Alaska State Museum; (Bottom) Los Angeles County Museum of Natural History. **21** (Top) Robert Frerck, Odyssey Productions; (Bottom) Courtesy Field Museum of Natural History, Chicago. **23** George Catlin, "Buffalo Hunt Under Wolfskin," American Museum of Natural History. **24** Rare Book Division, NYPL. **25** American Museum of Natural History. **27** Robert Frerck, Odyssey Productions. **28** Michael Holford, Courtesy National Maritime Museum. **29** (Top) The Mariners Museum, VA.; (Bottom) Bob Amft, Jefferson Field House, Chicago Park District. **30** (Top) British Museum Publications Ltd; (Bottom) British Museum Publications Ltd. **32** Ms. Bodley 264, folio 218 r Marco Polo at Venice, Bodleian Library, Oxford. **33** (Top) National Maritime Museum, London; (Bottom) Istituto Musevo Di Stroia Della Scienza. **35** (Top) Courtesy U.S. Naval Academy Museum. (Bottom) LC. **36** Raccolta di Palazzo Tursi, Genoa, Italy. **37** Metropolitan Museum of Art. **41** Courtesy The Newberry Library, Chicago. **42** NYHS. **43** The Science Museum. **45** Aldus Books. **47** City Art Gallery, Bristol, England. **49** Portugaliae Monumenta Cartographica, Library of Congress. **50** Robert Frerck, Odyssey Productions. **51** Robert Frerck, Odyssey Productions. **52** (Top) Robert Frerck, Odyssey Productions; (Bottom) CP. **53** Biblioteca National, Spain. **54** (Top) Hans Silvester, Photri; (Bottom) History of America of 1886, Vol. II, Houghton Mifflin. **56** Milt and Joan Mann, Cameramann International. **59** Robert Frerck, Odyssey Productions. **60** LC. **61** Robert Frerck, Odyssey Productions. **65** L.R. Batchelor, "Building the Walls of Montreal," Public Archives of Canada. **66** "Landing of Nicolet" by Edwin W. Deming, Wisconsin Historical Society. **67** Chicago Historical Society. **69** Thomas Patten, "An East View of Montreal, Canada," Public Archives of Canada. **71** E.F. Brickdale, "Arrival of the Brides at Quebec," Public Archives of Canada, Ottawa. **72** J.H. De Rinzy, "Frontenac On the Way to Cataraqui," Public Archives of Canada. **75** Robert Frerck, Odyssey Productions. **76** Robert Frerck, Odyssey Productions. **77** Ms. Laud. Misc. 678, folio 2, Bodleian Library, Oxford.

Unit 2

79 NYHS. **80** The Charleston Museum. **81** (Right) NYPL; (Left) National Portrait Gallery, Washington, D.C. **83** Colonial National Historical Park, U.S. Dept. of Interior. **84** (Right) I.N. Phelps Stokes Collection, Art, Prints and Photographs Division, NYPL, Astor, Lenox and Tilden Foundations; (Left) Chicago Historical Society. **86** National Maritime Museum. **89** (Top right) Charles Hoffbauer, "Samoset Bids Pilgrims Welcome," Courtesy New England Mutual Life Insurance Co.; (Top left) Museum of the City of New York; (Bottom) Metropolitan Museum of Art. **90** BA. **91** "Hooker's Party Coming to Hartford" by Church, Wadsworth Atheneum. **93** Michael P. Manheim, Gartman Agency. **94** East Midland's Photographic Service, England, Courtesy St. Botolph's Church. **97** Independence National Historical Park Collection. **100** Independence National Historical Park Collection. **104** Samuel de Champlain, "Les Voyages," 1632, Newberry Library. **107** U.S. Department of the Interior, National Park Service. **108** American Antiquarian Society. **110** Mississippi Historical Society. **113** Cal Sacks, 21 Oak Ridge Park, Westport, CT. **114** Rare Books and Manuscripts Division, NYPL, Astor, Lenox and Tilden Foundations. **115** State Historical Society of Wisconsin. **117** "Britain's Glory or the Reduction of Cape Breton," (Webster Collection #907), Courtesy New Brunswick Museum. **118** Thomas Davies, "A View of Fort La Galet," The National Gallery of Canada, Ottawa. **120** Thomas Davies, "A View of the Lines and Fort Ticonderoga, 1759," NYHS. **126** New York State Historical Association, Cooperstown. **127** Courtesy The Bostonian Society. **128** Michael P. Manheim, Gartman Agency. **129** Fishmongers Company of London. **131** The Huntington Library, San Marino, California. **137** Old Print Shop, 150 Lexington Ave., N.Y.C. **138** "The Stamp Act of 1765," Fourth of July Memento, Courtesy Time, Inc. **139** (Top) Apco; (Bottom) LC. **141** GC. **142** LC. **144** Rhode Island Historical Society. **145** Museum of the City of New York, Harry T. Peters Collection. **149** Atwater Kent Museum, Philadelphia, PA.

Unit 3

152 Guilford Courthouse, National Military Park. **153** Historical Society of Pennsylvania. **154** Lawrence S. Williams, H. Armstrong Roberts. **155** Historical Society of Pennsylvania. **156** GC. **157** (Top) Independence National Historical Park Collection, Dept. of Interior; (Bottom) LC. **158** GC. **161** Chicago Historical Society. **163** LC. **164** (Top) LC; (Bottom) GC. **166** John Trumbull, "The Declaration of Independence," U.S. Capitol Historical Society. **174** CP. **175** John Trumbull, "Capture of the Hessians at Trenton," Yale University Art Gallery. **176** Collection of the Valley Forge Historical Society. **178** Valley Forge Historical Society. **179** Pennsylvania Historical Museum Commission. **181** Collection of Preston Davie, Courtesy Mrs. Preston Davie, 71 E. 71st St., N.Y.C. **182** John Trumbull, "Surrender of Lord Cornwallis," Yale University Art Gallery. **183** Grogan Photography. **185** U.S. Naval Academy Museum. **186** Claudia Cappelle. **187** Courtesy, The Henry Francis Du Pont Winterthur Museum. **189** Lee Balterman. **190** NYPL, Astor, Lenox and Tilden Foundations. **193** National Park Service. **194** NYPL. **196** Burton Historical Collection, Detroit Public Library. **197** Peabody Museum of Salem. **198** Rand McNally. **199** NYPL, Astor, Lenox and Tilden Foundations. **203** I.N. Bartfield Galleries, Inc. **204** Essex Institute. **205** NYHS. **207** (Top) Historical Society of Pennsylvania; (Bottom) Virginia Museum. **209** (Right) GC; (Left) GC. **211** GC. **213** LC. **217** LC. **218** Gartman-Photri Agency. **219** Photri. **220** Photri. **223** GC. **225** GC. **227** Courtesy White House, Washington, D.C. **229** Photri.

Unit 4

262 LC. **263** Kiplinger Collection, U.S. Capitol Historical Society. **264** NYHS. **267** (Top) GC; (Bottom) BA. **268** (Right) Smithsonian Institution;

(Left) Independence National Historical Park Collection, Dept. of Interior. **269** NYPL. **271** BA. **272** GC. **273** (Right) Fogg Museum; (Left) GC. **275** (Right) Jamestown-Yorktown Foundation; (Left) Colonial Williamsburg Photo. **276** "The Old Plantation," Abby Aldrich Rockefeller Folk Art Collection, Williamsburg, Virginia. **277** Hudsons Bay Co. **278** BA. **279** FDR Library, National Archives. **281** Kentucky Historical Society. **282** NYHS. **285** The Metropolitan Museum of Art, Wm. Nelson, Bequestor. **286** Photri-Gartman Agency. **287** White House Historical Association, Photograph by National Geographic Society. **288** (Top) Old Print Shop; (Bottom) Louisiana State Museum. **289** Charles Russell, Amon Carter Museum. **291** Courtesy The Mariners' Museum of Newport News, Va. **292** Courtesy The Essex Institute, Salem, Massachusetts. **295** (Top) The Collection of the Century Association; (Bottom) Yale University. **297** Courtesy U.S. Naval Academy Museum. **298** The Kiplinger Washington Collection. **299** Photri. **301** Pennsylvania Academy of Fine Arts. **302** Samuel F.B. Morse, "The Old House of Representatives," The Corcoran Gallery of Art. **303** BA. **304** Gift of Mrs. Charles Francis Adams, Courtesy Museum of Fine Arts, Boston. **307** The Peale Museum. **308** Wisconsin Historical Society. **309** (Top) Maryland Historical Society; (Bottom) I.N. Phelps Stokes Collection, Art, Prints & Photographs Division, NYPL, Astor, Lenox & Tilden Foundations. **310** Chicago Historical Society. **311** Smithsonian Institution. **313** (Right) BA; (Left) Eyre Crowe, "Slave Market at Richmond Virginia." **314** (Top) LC; (Bottom) BA. **315** "Progress of Cotton" (#9:Reeding or Drawing In), Yale University Art Gallery, Mabel Brady Garvan Collection. **319** (Right) NYHS; (Left) The Corcoran Gallery of Art. **321** Oklahoma Historical Society. **323** LC. **325** Church of Jesus Christ of Latter Day Saints. **327** Chicago Historical Society. **328** California State Library. **329** Levi Strauss & Co. **331** Chessie System. **333** San Jacinto Museum of History, Texas.

Unit 5

335 "Behold Oh America, Your Sons," LC. **336** Brooklyn Museum, Francis G. Mayer Collection. **337** (Right) GC; (Left) GC. **339** LC. **341** The Metropolitan Museum of Art. **342** GC. **343** Anne S.K. Brown, Military Collection, Brown University Library. **344** LC. **346** (Right) GC; (Left) GC. **347** GC. **348** Illinois State Historical Library. **350** Thomas Hovenden, "The Last Moments of John Brown," Metropolitan Museum of Art. **351** LC. **353** (Top) LC; (Bottom) Collection of Frederick H. Meserve, N.Y. **354** LC. **357** LC. **358** Museum of the Confederacy. **359** Kean Archives. **361** GC. **362** (Right) American Antiquarian Society; (Left) Valentine Museum, Richmond, Virginia. **363** LC. **366** The Collection of the Century Association. **367** BA. **368** GC. **370** Baltimore Museum of Art, Garbisch Collection. **371** (Right) Chicago Historical Society; (Left) LC. **372** LC. **374** (Top) National Archives; (Bottom) American Heritage. **375** LC. **378** The Collection of the Century Association. **380** Claudia Cappelle. **381** National Archives. **383** GC. **384** "Harpers Weekly," LC. **385** "Harpers Weekly," BA. **386** LC. **390** Winslow Homer, "Upland Cotton," detail, collection of Weil Brothers-Cotton, Inc. **391** (Top) LC; (Bottom) CP. **393** Rand McNally & Co. **394** GC. **395** GC. **396** Chicago Historical Society. **399** LC.

Unit 6

402 "American Progress," lithograph by George Crofutt from a painting by John Gast, LC. **403** BA. **404** Pennsylvania Historical and Museum Commission. **405** Courtesy The Union Pacific Railroad. **408** The Thomas Gilcrease Institute of American History and Art, Tulsa, Oklahoma. **409** Courtesy U.S. Steel Corporation. **410** GC. **411** BA. **415** Montana Historical Society. **416** The Walters Art Gallery, Baltimore. **417** (Top) LC; (Bottom) The Stackpole Co., Harrisburg, Pennsylvania. **419** Solomon D. Butcher Collection, Nebraska State Historical Society. **421** BA. **422** GC. **423** BA. **424** South Dakota Memorial Art Center. **426** Biggs Photography. **427** BA. **428** NYHS. **429** NYHS. **430** (Top) Chicago Historical Society; (Bottom) Lewis Hines, "Tenements," International Museum of Photography, George Eastman House. **432** Philadelphia Museum of Art. **434** Alfred Stieglitz, "The Steerage," Private Collection. **435** Associated Photographers. **436** University of Illinois, Chicago Circle Campus, Jane Addams Memorial Collection. **437** Jacob A. Riis Collection, Museum of the City of New York. **442** A.T. & T. Co. Photo Service. **443** Coverdale and Colpitts. **444** (Top) BA; (Bottom) BA. **445** BA. **448** GC. **449** (Top) WPA, National Archives; (Bottom) BA. **450** BA. **451** BA. **452** Chicago Historical Society. **453** BA. **455** BA. **456** "The Lost Bet," after a painting by Joseph Klir, 1892, Chicago Historical Society. **458** BA. **461** (Top) GC; (Bottom) BA. **464** Brown Brothers. **465** Chicago Historical Society. **466** UPI. **469** CP.

Unit 7

472 LC. **473** "Mural of the Changing West," by Thomas Hart Benton, New School for Social Research. **474** Photri. **475** Wilhelm Hein, "Narrative of the Expedition of an American Squadron to the China Seas & Japan," U.S. Navy Government Document. **477** (Top) Louis Choris, "Port of Honolulu," 1800; (Bottom) CP. **478** *New York Journal* 1898, LC. **480** Vermont Council of the Arts. **482** Theodore Roosevelt Association. **483** Chicago Historical Society. **485** Photri. **486** Colorado Historical Society. **488** Theodore Roosevelt Association. **489** CP. **490** BA. **491** CP. **493** Courtesy United States Naval Academy Museum. **495** Norfolk Museum of Arts and Sciences. **496** Linda Christenson, Courtesy Smithsonian Institution. **497** UPI. **498** BBC Hulton Picture Library. **499** BA. **501** Courtesy The CUNARD LINE. **502** UPI. **507** (Right) National Archives, U.S. War Dept.; (Left) LC. **508** (Right) National Archives, U.S. War Dept, General Staff; (Left) UPI. **509** Imperial War Museum. **510** GC. **511** National Archives. **513** The Trustees of The Imperial War Museum, London. **514** UPI. **517** GC. **518** GC. **519** Courtesy Ford Motor Co., Dearborn, Michigan. **520** Minnesota Historical Society. **521** (Right) GC; (Left) GC. **522** UPI. **523** (Right) GC; (Left) BA. **524** GC. **525** BA. **527** GC. **529** (Right) GC.; (Left) GC. **531** Courtesy Wards Inc. **532** GC. **533** U.S. Bureau of Engraving. **534** BA. **536** Courtesy Herbert Hoover Presidential Library.

Unit 8

542 UPI. **543** Franklin D. Roosevelt Library. **544** National Archives, National Recovery Administration. **545** Alexander Brook, "Georgia Jungle," Carnegie Institute. **547** (Top) Dorothea Lange, "Bread Line," LC; (Bottom) LC. **549** The Oakland Museum, California. **550** Dorothea Lange, LC. **551** UPI. **554** (Top Right) Franklin D. Roosevelt Library; (Top Left) Herbert Hoover Presidential Library; (Bottom) GC. **556** UPI. **557** Photri. **558** Wide World. **560** (Top) BS.; (Bottom) UPI. **562** e.t. archive. **565** Franklin D. Roosevelt Library. **566** Navy Combat Art Collection. **567** (Right)ACME; (Left) Life Picture Service. **568** Trustees of Imperial War Museum. **570** Illingworth, "The Way of the Stork," *Punch* 29, 1941. **571** Franklin D. Roosevelt Library. **572** National Archives. **573** (Top) UPI; (Bottom) LC. **574** (Top) LC; (Bottom) National Archives. **577** (Top) GC; (Bottom) UPI. **578** LC. **579** U.S. Department of Army. **581** BA. **582** U.S. Department of Army. **583** Courtesy The United Nations. **587** LC. **588** Wide World. **589** GC. **590** Fitzpatrick, *St. Louis Post Dispatch.* **592** (Right) UPI; (Left) UPI. **593** Courtesy Air Force Art Collection. **594** (Right) UPI; (Left) Wide World Photos. **595** Hugh Cabot, "The Corpsmen," Navy Combat Art Collection. **597** UPI. **598** Columbia University. **599** Courtesy Columbia University. **600** Department of State, LC. **601** *New York Times.* **602** UPI. **603** Marc & Evelyne Bernheim, WC. **604** Dan Budnik, WC. **605** UPI Telephoto. **606** UPI. **609** Bill Mauldin & Will-Jo Associates, Inc. **611** Norman Rockwell, "The Four Freedoms," LC.

Unit 9

612 UPI. **613** Tilt ("Together Protect the Community") mural by John Weber, Chicago, Illinois, photograph by Lee Balterman. **614** Verner Wolff, BS. **615** Leonard Freed, Magnum. **616** Danny Lyon, Magnum. **617** UPI. **619** (Top) UPI; (Bottom) Bruce Davidson, Magnum. **620** (Right) Magnum; (Left) UPI. **622** UPI. **623** Goff, Magnum. **625** Lester Sloan, WC. **626** UPI. **627** UPI. **628** Michael Heron, WC. **630** (Right) UPI; (Left) UPI. **632** (Right) UPI; (Left) UPI. **633** (Right) Susan McElhinney, WC; (Left) Werner Wolff, BS. **637** Bob Adelman, Magnum. **638** NASA. **639** Magnum. **641** Atoz Images. **642** Jeffrey J. Foxx, WC. **644** Lee Balterman, Gartman Agency. **646** John Lei, SB. **647** (Right) Courtesy IBM; (Left) Courtesy UNIVAC. **649** NASA. **650** NASA. **651** NASA. **655** Lee Balterman, Gartman Agency. **656** U.S. Department of Army. **657** UPI. **659** (Right) Leif Skoogfors, WC; (Left) Hector Robertin, U.S. Army Special Photo Dept. **660** UPI. **661** UPI. **665** Liason Agency Inc. **666** UPI. **667** J.P. Laffont, Sygma. **668** J.P. Laffont, Sygma. **669** Dept. of Treasury. **671** UPI. **672** UPI. **673** Fred Ward, BS. **674** Henri Bureau, Sygma. **675** UPI. **676** Tony Korody, Sygma. **679** NASA.

Unit 10

680 "Flamingo," stabile by Alexander Calder, Robert Mayer, Atoz Images. **681** NASA. **682** Courtesy The United Nations. **683** WC. **684** John Launois, BS. **686** Chuck O'Rear, WC. **687** Wm. Hubbell, WC. **688** Wendy Watriss, WC. **689** Craig Aurness, WC. **691** Courtesy The United Nations. **694** (Right) Museum of the City of New York; (Left) H. Armstrong Roberts Inc., Stock Photography. **696** Sepp Seitz, WC. **697** Liaison Agency. **699** Dennis Brack, BS. **703** Anthony Howarth, WC. **704** Courtesy The United Nations. **705** Artie Grace, Sygma. **706** Sygma. **708** Sygma. **709** Sygma. **710** Alain Keler, Sygma. **711** D. Goldberg, Sygma. **714** (Top) P. Chauvel, Sygma; (Bottom) Owen Franken, Sygma. **716** Owen Franken, Sygma. **717** W. Campbell, Sygma. **720** Owen Franken, Sygma. **721** Arnold Zann, BS. **722** Mike Maple, WC. **723** Leo Choplin, BS. **725** UPI. **726** WC. **727** Lee Balterman. **728** Courtesy Sloan Kettering Cancer Center. **729** Michael P. Manheim, Gartman Agency. **730** WC. **731** Dennis Brack, BS. **732** Tom Sobol, BS. **733** Dennis Brack, BS. **737** Donald Dietz, SB. **739** (Top) Jeffrey J. Foxx, WC; (Bottom) Peter Simon, SB. **740** Sepp Seitz, WC. **741** Arnold Zann, BS. **742** Robert McElroy, WC. **743** Paris, Sygma. **745** Tom Zimberoff, Sygma. **747** Adler Planetarium, NASA.

ABCDEFGHIJ—RRD— 8765432